CONTENTS

Chapter 6: The Flea Market Scene Today

Part Two: FLEA MARKET PRICES – Categories A to Z

Part Three: REFERENCE SOURCES

PREFACE

Welcome to a somewhat unconventional price guide. It is designed to serve the non-traditionalist independent buyer and collector as well as the person collecting in "established" categories. The approach is informal. When you read the category introductions and carefully scan the listings, you will find a fair amount of humor. Do not be afraid to laugh. This book is about the pure fun and joy of collecting.

The flea market and garage sale markets are huge—far larger than the collector, dealer, and decorator markets to which over ninety percent of the books about antiques and collectibles cater. The more flea markets and garage sales I visit, the more I realize that seventy to eighty percent of the material found at flea markets cannot be researched in a general antiques and collectibles price guide. This title seeks to remedy that situation.

The Official Guide to Flea Market Prices contains dozens of unconventional categories. It offers the opportunity to test the waters by introducing new collecting categories and having a little fun at the same time. Some categories eventually work their way into my *The Official Rinker Price Guide to Collectibles* while others fall by the wayside. Alas, some collecting categories only enjoy a brief moment in the sun. This is why there are dozens of new categories included in this book for the first time and why some categories found in previous editions are missing.

Criteria

Availability and affordability are the primary factors determining what collecting categories do and do not appear in this book. Objects do not have to be 25, 50, or 100 years old to be included. If it is collected and offered for sale in quantity at flea markets, I have tried to include it.

Because many objects appeal to multiple buyers, I urge you to become familiar with the index. The object you are attempting to research may be in this book. You simply are not looking in the correct collecting category.

Discounted contemporary merchandise, manufacturer and store overstock, and holiday remnants are not included. Tube socks, cheap Asian knockoffs, clothing odds and ends, cassette tapes, and handcrafted products, all too common at some flea markets, are not collectible. This book is not a price guide to junk.

This is the third edition of this title to use category advisors. The increasing number of business card and seeker classified advertisements in trade periodicals convinced me that there was a wealth of fun categories and collectors of the somewhat unusual that should be included in this guide. More than thirty-five individuals responded positively to my request for assistance, many for the third time. The name and address of the advisor appears at the end of the introduction of the category to which they contributed.

The information in this book is solid, thorough, and fresh. If objects are repeated, it is because they are extremely common and provide a means for those individuals with an interest in tracking the market.

Ideal Companions

I recommend using *The Official Guide to Flea Market Prices* in conjunction with two other House of Collectibles titles. First, use *The Official Directory to U.S. Flea Markets, 7th ed.* to locate the flea markets near you and in any area you plan to visit. You have to find treasures before you can buy them. Second, information and values for objects in the more traditional collectibles categories seen at flea markets is found in **The Official Rinker Price Guide to Collectibles,** also published by House of Collectibles. Its focus is on objects made after 1920.

Credit Where Credit Is Due

Hopefully, we will never fail to recognize that it is our users to whom we owe the most thanks for this and previous editions of this title. We thank you for your continued support and look forward to continuing to earn your vote of confidence through this and subsequent editions of this title.

House of Collectibles is now part of Crown's Three Rivers imprint. It is an honor and privilege to be part of an imprint that includes Martha Stewart and Ralph and Terry Kovel among its authors.

It is with sadness that we say goodbye to Laura Paczosa, our previous House of Collectibles' editor, and wish her well with her graduate studies. We are delighted to say hello to Dorothy Harris, an old friend. Dorothy's antiques and collectibles commitment, marketing savvy, and dedication are reflected in the changes found in this title.

This book is fun to do, which is why it is a favorite among the Rinker Enterprises staff. Although each staff member worked at one time or another on the full range of tasks involved in preparing this title, each also had specific responsibilities. Kathy Williamson researched and compiled the bulk of the listings. She also was the liaison with the category advisors. Dena George was responsible for photographs and scanning images, compiling listings, and proofreading. Nancy Butt updated the reference information. Dana Morykan did the final page layout and reviewed the listings. The text matter and field research was my responsibility. Virginia Reinbold kept Rinker Enterprises on a secure financial footing and Richard "Cap" Schmeltzle kept the place shipshape. I am proud to be part of this seasoned staff.

Because the list is extensive, we end by offering a general thanks to the advisors, auctioneers and auction companies, collectors, dealers, publishers, flea market owners and managers, mall owners, trade periodical staff members, show promoters, and others in the antiques and collectibles trade who have willingly and generously shared their information and images in the preparation of this title.

Kudos to those individuals associated with the operation of flea markets. We have seen first hand how hard these individuals work. Few in the trade work harder. Keep up the good work.

Ideally, one likes to end on an up note. Not this edition. During 2000, we lost Helen Robinson, founder of the Kane County Flea Market and a legend in the trade. We are richer for having known her. Our deepest sympathies to her extended family and friends.

Let Me Know What You Think

As much as I would like this book to be perfect, it is not. We all make mistakes. If you spot information that you believe is incorrect or have a suggestion to make that you think will improve the next edition, I encourage you to send your comments and/or criticisms to: Harry L. Rinker, Rinker Enterprises, Inc., 5093 Vera Cruz Road, Emmaus, PA 18049.

Harry L. Rinker
Emmaus, PA
March 2001

INTRODUCTION

GOOOOD MORNNNNINGGGG, Flea Marketeers. Welcome to ***The Official Guide to Flea Market Prices.*** Today's specials are the very best goodies, tidbits, and knickknacks found in every flea market throughout the good old U.S. of A. It's all here—neatly printed and organized for your use and reading pleasure.

Sound a bit like a carnival barker? It should. Going to a good flea market will produce as much fun, enjoyment, treasures, and memories as a visit to any carnival. Flea marketeering is a grand adventure. You have an idea of what to expect, but you know there will be a number of surprises. If you are lucky, you will grab a brass ring.

Find It Here First

The Official Guide to Flea Market Prices provides a first look at many potential collecting categories. Collectibility is tested at the flea market level. Dealers are continually offering material not seen previously. The successful sale of new groups of items immediately attracts the attention of other dealers. Their enthusiasm spreads. Before long, a new collecting category enters the established market.

Spotting these new categories before they appear as a regular entry in a general antiques and collectibles price guide is a challenge, one in which we think we excel. Expect to find a new category here first!

Not every hunt is successful. Some categories in this book may be dropped in subsequent editions. Not all efforts to establish a new collecting category succeed. For those that do not make it, may they enjoy their brief moment in the sun.

In an effort to add breadth and diversity to the categories appearing in this book, over 75 specialized collectors were approached to act as category advisors and contribute information about their collecting specialty. More than half responded positively. When an advisor is responsible for the information in a category, his or her full name and address is listed at the end of the category introduction.

What good are price listings if you do not know how to use them? This book combines general information about flea marketeering and specific sources such as collectors clubs, periodicals and reference books with price listings by category—all the tools necessary to enhance your flea marketing experience and further your education in your chosen areas of interest. Although new when you first buy it, this book will quickly become a much consulted friend, one with which you will look forward to spending a great deal of time.

Three Parts

The Official Guide to Flea Market Prices is divided into three principal parts.

PART ONE

The first part is a guide for flea marketeers. It helps you identify a "true" flea market, tells you how to find and evaluate flea markets, provides a list of the top thirty flea markets nationwide, gives tips for surviving the flea market experience and honing your shopping skills, and provides in-depth analysis of the current flea market scene.

Much of the information is duplicated from previous editions. You will find minor changes in the sections dealing with general guides to flea market locations, trade papers, and top thirty flea markets. Chapter 6, "The Flea Market Scene Today," has been totally rewritten to reflect changes within the flea market scene over the past two years.

In talking with individuals who purchased earlier editions of this book, I was surprised to learn how many "experienced" flea marketeers had skipped this first part. They made a mistake. Even the most experienced flea marketeer will find something of value. One of the worst mistakes you can make in the antiques and collectibles field is to assume that you know all you need to know.

PART TWO

The second part of the book is devoted to price listings by category. Previous users are advised to thumb through the categories and not rely on the assumption that they know what the book contains. This edition of *The Official Guide to Flea Market Prices* contains numerous new categories.

You deceive yourself if you assume this book is just another antiques and collectibles price guide. Not true. This book was prepared using the premise that everything imaginable turns up at a flea market—from the finest antiques to good reusable secondhand items. *The Official Guide to Flea Market Prices* contains dozens of categories that are not found in any other antiques and/or collectibles price guide.

In a few categories you will not find specific priced items. Instead you are provided with general information that allows a broad understanding of the category. Occasionally, you are referred to specialized books on the subject.

One of the great joys about working on the categories in this book is that so many are supported with collectors' clubs, newsletters, and periodicals. You will find full addresses for these listed in the appropriate category before the price listing.

The Official Guide to Flea Market Prices provides the Rinker Enterprises, Inc., staff and me an opportunity to let our hair down. If you are comfortable with a formal traditionalist price guide approach this price guide is not for you. Category introductions range from serious to humorous to sublime. If the key to a great flea market is that it evokes these emotions and more within you, why should this book do any less?

PART THREE

Although I am not certain why, the third part of this book, which contains reference material for flea marketeers, including the "Flea Marketeer's Annotated Reference Library" and a list of "Antiques and Collectibles Trade Papers," is often completely overlooked by purchasers of this book. I strongly recommend that you become familiar with this section. The information not only helps you become highly proficient as a flea marketeer but also serves as your introduction to many other wonderful areas within the antiques and collectibles field.

Let's Go!

It is time to honor the cry of the Circus ringmaster: "On with the show." Take a moment and read the program (the first section) before you watch the acts in the center ring (the second section) and then relive the memories (the third section). Most of all, don't forget—the entire purpose of the performance is for you to have fun.

Part One

A
FLEA MARKET
EDUCATION

Chapter 1
WHAT IS A FLEA MARKET?

It is difficult to explain the sense of excitement and anticipation felt by collectors and dealers as they get ready to shop a flea market. They are about to undertake a grand adventure, a journey into the unknown. Flea markets turn the average individual into an explorer in search of buried treasure. The search is not without adversity. Conditions ranging from a hostile climate to intense competition may be encountered. Victory is measured in "steals" and stories that can be shared at the end of the day.

Flea markets provide the opportunity for prospective collectors to get their feet wet in the exciting world of antiques and collectibles and for novice dealers to test their merchandise and selling skills at minimal expense. Many first contacts, some of which last a lifetime, are made between collectors and dealers there. More than any other environment in the antiques and collectibles trade, the flea market is the one forum where everyone is on equal footing.

Before you learn how to find, evaluate, and survive flea markets, it is important that you understand exactly what a flea market is, how it fits into the antiques and collectibles marketplace, and the many variations that exist. This is the first step to identifying the flea markets that are most likely to provide the greatest opportunities for you.

Defining a Flea Market

Few terms in the antiques and collectibles field are as difficult to define as "flea market." If you visit the Rose Bowl Flea Market in Pasadena, California, you will find discontinued and knock-off merchandise, crafts, clothing (from tube socks to dresses), home-care items, plants of all types, and specialty foods as much in evidence as antiques and collectibles. On the other hand, if you visit the Ann Arbor Antiques Market in Michigan, you will find primarily middle and upper-level antiques and collectibles. Both are flea markets, yet they are light-years apart from one another.

The flea market concept is generations old. As it spread around the world, each country changed and adapted the form to meet its own particular needs. Regional differences developed. In New England, the Mid-Atlantic states, and the Midwest, the term generally is used to describe a place where antiques and collectibles are sold. In the South and Southwest, the term is more loosely interpreted to include craft, secondhand, and discounted goods.

It is not hard to see why this confusion exists. *Webster's Ninth New Collegiate Dictionary* (Springfield, MA: Merriam-Webster, Inc., 1984) defines a flea market as "a usually open-air market for secondhand articles and antiques." Individuals involved with antiques and collectibles do not equate secondhand (recycled or reusable) goods with antiques and collectibles. Although the dictionary may lump them together, collectors and dealers clearly differentiate one from the other.

The flea markets described in this book fit a much more narrow definition than the dictionary definition.

Flea market means a regularly scheduled market, held either indoors or outdoors, in which the primary goods offered for sale are those defined by the trade as antiques or collectibles. Occasionally, some handcrafted products and secondhand goods may be found among the offerings, especially in the seasonal and roadside flea markets where professional flea market dealers mix with individuals selling on a one-shot basis.

The problem with defining "flea market" with an antiques and collectibles perspective is that a multiplicity of flea market types exist. There are the seasonal flea markets such as Renninger's Extravaganza (Kutztown, Pennsylvania) and Brimfield's (Brimfield, Massachusetts), the monthlies such as the Metrolina Expo (Charlotte, North Carolina), and numerous weeklies scattered across the country.

One of the best ways to understand what an antiques and collectibles flea market encompasses is to discuss how it differs from three other closely related institutions in the antiques and collectibles trade: the antiques mall, the garage sale, and the antiques show. While the differences may appear subtle, they are significant to collectors and dealers.

Prior to the arrival of the antiques mall, there was a clearly defined ladder of quality within the antiques and collectibles community that progressed from garage sale to flea market to small show to major show or shop. This is how most goods moved through the market, and the route many dealers used to establish themselves in the trade. Two things changed the equation: collectors recognized the role flea markets played as the initial source of goods and actively participated as a means of eliminating the "middleman" and the antiques mall came into existence.

Antiques malls arrived on the scene in the early 1980s. As the decade of the 1990s ends, the trend is toward the Super Mall, a mall with 300 plus dealers that offers a full range of services from direct sales to auctions. Malls developed because flea market sellers wanted a method to do business on a daily basis without the overhead of owning a shop. They also sought an indoor environment free from the vagaries of weather. Additionally, the buying public was delighted to find as many sellers as possible in one location.

Malls differ from flea markets in that they are open for business on a daily basis (a minimum of five and often seven days a week), the display and sales process is often handled by a manager or other mall representative, a more formal business procedure is used, and the quality of material is somewhat higher than that found at flea markets. The main drawbacks are that the buyer generally has no contact with the owner of the merchandise and price negotiation is difficult.

Garage sales are usually one-time events, often conducted by people with no pretensions of being antiques or collectibles dealers. They are merely attempting to get rid of items they no longer find useful. While it is true that some antiques and collectibles enter the market through this source, most individuals conducting garage sales have enough good sense to realize that this is the worst way to sell these items. Emphasis in a garage sale is on secondhand merchandise.

A recent development in the garage sale area is the annual or semiannual community garage sale. A promoter rents a large hall or auditorium and sells space to any individual wishing to set up. Usually there is a rule that no established antiques and collectibles dealers are allowed to take part. However, many dealers sneak in with friends or simply use a different name to rent a space in order to "pick" the merchandise during setup. Although community garage sales fit the dictionary definition of a flea market, the large volume of secondhand merchandise distinguishes them from the flea markets discussed in this book.

An antiques show consists of a number of professional dealers (weekend, full-time, or a combination of both) who meet in a fixed location on a regular basis, usually two to three times each year, to offer quality antiques and collectibles to collectors, interior decorators, and others. Once an antique or collectible reaches the show circuit, it is usually priced close to book value. Flea markets thrive on the concept that merchandise priced for sale is significantly below book value. While this is more myth than reality, it prevails.

Confusion arises because a number of monthly flea markets have dropped the term "flea market" from their titles. They call themselves "shows" or "markets." They do not use "flea" because of a growing list of problems, ranging from unscrupulous dealers to an abundance of unmarked reproductions, that plagued flea markets in the 1990s. Calling yourself something else does not change what you really are. Most monthly markets and shows are nothing more than flea markets in disguise.

Seasonal Flea Markets

Seasonal flea markets are those held a maximum of three times a year. Theoretically, they are held outdoors. However, many sites now provide either indoor or pavilion shelters for participants. Most have clearly established dates. For example, Renninger's Extravaganza is held the last weekend in April, June, and September.

If there is a Mecca in the flea market world, it is Brimfield. The name is magic. You are not an accomplished flea marketeer until you have been there. Actually, Brimfield is not a flea market, it is an event. In early May, July, and September over fifteen separate flea markets open and close. On Fridays the dealer count exceeds 1,500. Area motel rooms are booked over a year in advance. Traffic jams last hours.

For the past several years Renninger's has been promoting seasonal markets during the winter months at its Mount Dora, Florida, location. They are an important stop on the Southern winter circuit. Although there are a few seasonal markets in the Midwest, none are on a par with the Renninger's Extravaganzas and the Brimfield weeks.

Monthly Flea Markets

The monthly flea market's strength rests on a steady dealer clientele supplemented by other dealers passing through the area, a frequency that allows dealers enough time to find new merchandise, and a setting that is usually superior to the seasonal and weekly flea markets. The monthlies range from the upscale Ann Arbor Antiques Market to the mid-range antiques and collectibles show copycat (for example, the Fairgrounds Antiques Market in Phoenix, Arizona) to the something-for-everybody flea market (like the Kane County Flea Market in St. Charles, Illinois).

Most of the monthly flea markets have some outdoor spaces. The Kentucky Flea Market in Louisville, Kentucky, and the Fairgrounds Antiques Market in Phoenix, Arizona, are two exceptions. Flea markets with outdoor space operate only during warm weather months, generally April through November. A few of the larger operations (e.g., the Springfield Antiques Show & Flea Market in Springfield, Ohio) operate year-round. Double-check the schedule for any flea market you plan to visit between November and April, even those located in the South and Southwest.

Another strength of the monthly flea markets rests in the fact that they attract a large number of dealers who appear regularly. Collectors and dealers have time to cultivate good working relationships. A level of buying trust is created because the collector knows that he or she will be able to find the seller again if questions develop.

Courtesy Americana Enterprises, Inc.
Long Beach Outdoor Antique & Collectible Market

Weekly Flea Markets

The weekly flea markets break down into two types: those held on a weekday and those held on a weekend. The weekday markets are primarily for dealers in the trade. Monday flea markets at Perkiomenville, Pennsylvania, and Wednesday flea markets at Shipshewana, Indiana, are legends. These markets begin in the predawn hours. The best buys are found by flashlight as participants check merchandise as it is being unpacked. Most selling ends by 9:00 a.m. These markets appeal primarily to individuals actively involved in the resale of antiques and collectibles. Most collectors prefer something a bit more civilized.

Renninger's in Adamstown, Pennsylvania, shows the staying power of the weekend flea market. Within driving distance of several major population centers, yet far enough in the country to make the day an outing, Renninger's combines an ever-changing outdoor section with an indoor facility featuring primarily permanent dealers. Renninger's is open only on Sundays, except for Extravaganza weekends. Because buyers like to shop on Saturdays as well, Renninger's Promotions created Renninger's in Kutztown, Pennsylvania.

Weekend flea markets are now a fixture across the country and constitute the largest segment of the flea market community. It is common to find several in one location as each tries to capitalize on the success of the other. However, their quality varies tremendously.

The biggest problem with weekend flea markets is merchandise staleness. Many dealers add only a few new items each week. Collectors shop them on a four- to eight-week cycle. The way to avoid missing a shot at a major new piece is to maintain a close working relationship with several dealers. Most weekend flea market dealers shop the market. They can be your eyes when you are not there.

As with the monthly flea markets, you can buy from indoor dealers knowing that you are likely to find them if a problem develops later. Be much more careful when purchasing from the transient outside dealers. Get a valid name, address, and phone number from anyone from whom you make a purchase.

One of the things I like best about large weekend flea markets is that they feature one or more book dealers who specialize in antiques and collectibles books. I always stop at these booths to check on the latest titles. In some cases, I find a book I never saw advertised in the trade papers. Some of the dealers offer search services for out-of-print titles. Spending time getting to know these book dealers is something you will never regret.

Roadside Flea Markets

I have ignored roadside flea markets up to this point because the merchandise they offer is usually of garage sale quality. This is not to say that I have not found some great buys at roadside markets. However, when I consider the amount of time that I spend finding these few precious gems, I realize I can do much better at a traditional flea markets.

Chances are that you collect one or two specific categories. If so, not every type of flea market is right for you. How do you find the best markets? What type of evaluation can you do in advance to avoid the frustration of coming home empty-handed? These questions and more are answered in the next chapter.

Chapter 2
FINDING AND EVALUATING FLEA MARKETS

In order to attend a flea market, you have to locate one. It is not as easy as it sounds. In order to thoroughly research the available markets in any given area, you will have to consult a variety of sources. Even when you have finished, you are still likely to spot a flea market that you missed in your research along the way. I told you there was a strong sense of adventure in flea marketeering.

Flea Market Guides

There are four national guides to United States flea markets. Buy them all.

The Flea Market Shopper's Companion: A Complete Guide for Buyers and Sellers Coast to Coast by James Goodridge (Kensington Publishing, 850 Third Avenue, New York, NY 10022).

Prior to the publication of *The Flea Market Shopper,* James Goodridge edited four regional flea market guides published by Adams Publishing. Goodridge's new title combines the information into a single volume, a concession to the fact that today's flea marketeer is as much a national shopper as a regional shopper. The book lists flea markets alphabetically and provides information about size, trading days, parking, and types of traders. *The Flea Market Shopper* also contains buying and selling tips. This paperback retails for $9.95.

The Original Clark's Flea Market U.S.A.: A National Directory of Flea Markets and Swap Meets (Clark Publications, 5469 Inland Cove Ct., Milton, FL 32583 / (850) 623-0794).

Clark's, issued quarterly, lists over 2,000 flea markets and swap meets. The guide is organized alphabetically by state. The secondary organization is city or town closest to the flea market within the state. You will find information on name, address, days and occasionally hours of operation and telephone number. Information provided about each market varies greatly. Completely missing are directions for hard-to-find markets. I buy an issue every year or two as a safety check against my regular sources. A one-year subscription is $30.00. Single copies are available from the publisher at $8.00, a price that includes postage and handling.

The Official Directory to U.S. Flea Markets, Seventh Edition, edited by Kitty Werner (House of Collectibles, Ballantine Division of Random House, 201 East 50th Street, New York, NY 10022).

The Official Directory under Kitty Werner's direction gets better with each edition. The book covers over 800 flea markets in the United States, Canada, and Europe. Yes, Canada and Europe—it's time someone paid attention to our northern neighbor and our cousins abroad. Each listing contains information about a flea market's dates, hours, admission, location, a very detailed description of the type of merchandise found, dealer rates, and a telephone number and full address for the chief contact person. I especially like the list of "Other Flea Markets" found at the end of most state listings. These are markets that did not respond to the questionnaire. Werner advises users to "please call first" to make certain they are open. You can purchase a copy of this guide in most larger bookstores. It is a bargain at $10.00.

U.S. Flea Market Directory: Guide to the Best Flea Markets in All 50 States, Third Edition, edited by Albert LaFarge (Griffin Trade, St. Martin's Press, 175 5th Avenue, New York, NY 10010).

Designed to compete with *The Official Directory,* it provides detailed information that includes maps and travel directions, days and times, number of dealers, description of goods sold, dealer information, and other useful tidbits for approximately 1,000 flea markets nationwide. As one might expect, LaFarge covers many of the same flea markets that are found in *The Official Directory.* However, there are enough differences to make both books a must buy. *U.S. Flea Market* retails for $6.99 and is available at most bookstores.

Antiques and collectibles flea markets are not unique to the United States. In fact, the modern flea market originated in Paris. Flea markets play a vital role throughout Europe, especially in France, Great Britain, and Germany.

Travel Keys (PO Box 160691, Sacramento, CA 95816) has published a separate flea market guide for France, Great Britain, and Germany, each edited by Peter B. Manston. Although badly in need of revision, the books still have value if you are traveling abroad. First, many of the flea markets are decades old—same time, same place. If possible, double-check before setting out. Once at a market, do not hesitate to ask dealers to recommend other flea market venues. Second, the introductory material is a must read, especially the section on export laws and regulations. This is information you will not find anywhere else.

National and Regional Shop Guides

NATIONAL GUIDES

In the late 1990s a day "antiquing" means visiting a variety of selling markets. A flea market stop is combined with a visit to nearby antiques and collectibles malls. For this reason, I recommend the new 2000 edition of Judy Lloyd's *No-Nonsense Antique Mall Directory.* It covers 5,000 malls throughout the United States. It is available only by mail order. Send a check for $20.75, the price includes fourth class postage, to FDS Antiques, PO Box 188, Higginsport, OH 45131.

Kim and David Leggett's *Leggetts' Antiques Atlas: 2000 East Edition* and *Leggetts' Antiques Atlas: 2000 West Edition* (Three Rivers Press, a division of Crown Publishers, Inc., New York, NY) are also useful. Since they are standard inventory in most bookstores, they are easier to fine than Lloyd's *No-Nonsense Antique Mall Directory.* The vase majority of the listings in the Leggetts' two volumes consist of the name, street address (unfortunately not always complete) and telephone number of an auction, shop, mall or show. Like the Yellow Pages, businesses can purchase a more detailed listing or display advertisement. At $18.00 per edition, they represent a modest investment to ensure you have a comprehensive understanding of the antiques opportunities in an area you are planning to visit.

REGIONAL GUIDES

A number of specialized regional guides for locating antiques and collectibles flea markets, malls, and shops exist. Most are published by trade papers. A few are done privately. None focus solely on the flea market scene.

The *AntiqueWeek Central Antique Shop Guide* and *AntiqueWeek Eastern Antique Shop Guide* (AntiqueWeek, PO Box 90, Knightstown, IN 46148 [800] 876-5133) are typical. Organization is by state, region, and by city and town within a region. Brief listings for each business are supplemented by display advertising. Each edition covers flea markets, malls, shops, shows, and more. The coverage gets better with each edition. The principal problem with these and similar guides is that you have to pay a fee to be listed. As a result, coverage is limited to those willing to pay. However, they are a great starting point and a bargain at $3.50 each.

When planning to visit a new area, contact some of the trade papers that serve the region and ask if they publish a regional guide or know of such a guide. Regional guides are inexpensive, ranging from $5 to $15. Many of the businesses listed in the guide sell it across the counter. I always pick up a copy. The storage pouch located behind the front driver's seat of my car is littered with road maps and regional guides, most of which show signs of heavy use.

Resource Directory

David Maloney Jr.'s *Maloney's Antiques and Collectibles Resource Directory, 5th Edition* (Antique Trader Books, Krause Publications, 700 E. State St., Iola, WI 54990) contains category listings for antiques shops and flea markets. The listings include addresses and telephone numbers. Hopefully, you own a copy of Maloney's book. If you do not, you should. Make a resolution—right now—to buy a copy the next time you visit a bookstore or the stand of an antiques and collectibles book seller at a flea market. The book retails for $29.95. It is the best investment anyone in the trade can make. If you do not think so, I will give you your money back.

Trade Newspapers

The best source of flea market information is advertisements in trade newspapers. Some papers put all the flea market advertisements in one location, while others place them in their appropriate regional section. Most trade papers' events calendars include flea markets with the show listings. Once again, the problem rests with the fact that all advertising is paid advertising.

Not all flea markets advertise in every issue of a trade paper. Some advertise in papers outside their home area because the locals know where and when to find them. Flea markets that operate between April and September usually do not advertise in December and January. The only way to conduct a complete search is to obtain a four- to six-month run of a regional paper and carefully scan each issue. When doing this, keep your eyes open for reports and features about flea markets. As advertisers, flea markets expect to get written up at least once a year.

The following is a list of national and regional trade papers that I recommend you consult for flea market information. You will find their full addresses and phone numbers (when known) in the listing of trade newspapers at the back of this book.

This list is by no means complete. I am certain that I have missed a few regional papers. However, these papers provide a starting point. Do not be foolish and go flea marketeering without consulting them.

NATIONAL TRADE PAPERS

The Antique Trader Weekly, Iola, WI
AntiqueWeek, Knightstown, IN
Antiques & the Arts Weekly, Newtown, CT

Collectors News, Grundy Center, IA
Maine Antique Digest, Waldoboro, ME
Warman's Today's Collector, Iola, WI

REGIONAL TRADE PAPERS

New England

Cape Cod Antiques Monthly, Farmington, NH
The Fine Arts Trader, Randolph, MA
The Journal of Antiques and Collectibles,
    Sturbridge, MA
MassBay Antiques / North Shore Weekly,
    Needham, MA
New England Antiques Journal, Ware, MA
New Hampshire Antiques Monthly,
    Farmington, NH
Treasure Chest, Providence, RI
Unravel the Gavel, Ctr. Belmont, NH
The Vermont Antique Times, Manchester
    Center, VT

Middle Atlantic States

Antiques & Auction News, Mount Joy, PA
Antiques Guide of NJ, So. NY, NYC &
    Eastern PA, Morristown, NJ
Antiques Tattler, Adamstown, PA
The New York Antique Almanac, New York,
    NY
New York City's Antique News, New York,
    NY
New York-Pennsylvania Collector,
    Canandaigua, NY
Northeast Journal of Antiques & Art,
    Hudson, NY
Renninger's Antique Guide, Lafayette Hill, PA

South

Antique Gazette, Iola, WI
The Antique Shoppe, Keystone Heights, FL
The Antique Shoppe of the Carolinas,
    Lancaster, NC
Carolina Antique News, Charlotte, NC
Cotton & Quail Antique Trail, Monticello,
    FL
MidAtlantic Antiques Magazine, Monroe, NC
The Old News Is Good News Antiques
    Gazette, Hammond, LA
Southern Antiques, Decatur, GA
Southeastern Antiquing and Collecting
    Magazine, Acworth, GA
The Vintage Times, Macon, GA

Midwest

The American Antiquities Journal,
    Springfield, OH
The Antique Collector and Auction Guide,
    Salem, OH
Antique Review, Worthington, OH
Auction Action Antique News, Shawano, WI
The Auction Exchange, Plainwell, MI
Auction World, Benson, MN
The Collector, Heyworth, IL
Collectors Journal, Vinton, IA
Discover Mid-America, Kansas City, MO
Great Lakes Trader, Williamstown, MI
Indiana Antique Buyer's News, Silver Lake, IN
Ohio Collectors' Magazine, Piqua, OH
The Old Times, Maple Lake, MN
Yesteryear, Princeton, WI

Southwest

The Antique Register & Country Register,
    Inc., Phoenix, AZ
The Antique Traveler, Mineola, TX
Antiquing Texas, The Woodlands, TX
Arizona Antique News, Phoenix, AZ

West Coast

Antique & Collectables, El Cajon, CA
Antique Journal for California and Nevada,
    Alameda, CA
Antique Journal for the Pacific Northwest,
    Portland, OR
Antiques Plus, Salem, OR
Collector, Pomona, CA
Mountain States Collector, Evergreen, CO
Old Stuff, McMinnville, OR
The Oregon Vintage Times, Eugene, OR
West Coast Peddler, Whittier, CA

NFMA (National Flea Market Association of Owners & Managers)

In 1997 Jerry Stokes founded the National Flea Market Association of Owners & Managers (PO Box 18646, Charlotte, NC 28218). Its Mission Statement reads: "The National Flea Market Association is dedicated to creating and presenting the cleanest, most convenient shopping facilities for you and your family."

The Association issues a newsletter, offers educational programs, and holds conventions. Its Internet website's (www.fleamarkets.org) intent is to exchange ideas, co-advertise, promote, and better the flea market shopping venues for people concerned.

The vast majority of the flea markets that comprise the membership of the NFMA are swap meets, places where you are more likely to find discounted new merchandise, farm produce, crafts, contemporary collectibles (many speculative), and blatant reproductions than antiques and collectibles. There will be an occasional jewel, but discovering it requires a great deal of hunting.

Which Flea Market Is Right for You?

The best flea market is the one at which you find plenty to buy at good to great prices. This means that most flea markets are not right for you. Is it necessary to attend each one to make your determination? I do not think so.

I am a great believer in using the telephone. If long distance rates jump dramatically as a result of the publication of this book, I plan to approach AT&T and ask for a piece of the action. It is a lot cheaper to call than to pay for transportation, lodging, and meals, not to mention the value of your time. Do not hesitate to call promoters and ask them about their flea markets.

What type of information should you request? First, check the number of dealers. If the number falls below one hundred, think twice. Ask for a ratio of local dealers to transient dealers. A good mix is 75% local and 25% transient for monthly and weekly markets. Second, inquire about the type of merchandise being offered for sale. Make a point not to tell the promoter what you collect. If you do, you can be certain that the flea market has a number of dealers who offer the material. Do not forget to ask about the quality of the merchandise. Third, ask about the facilities. The more indoor space available, the higher the level of merchandise is likely to be. What happens if it rains?

Finally, ask yourself this question: Do you trust what the promoter has told you?

When you are done talking to the promoter, call the editor of one of the regional trade papers and ask his or her opinion about the market. If they have published an article or

Courtesy Palmer Wirfs & Associates

review of the market recently, request that a copy be sent to you. If you know someone who has attended, talk to that person. If you still have not made up your mind, try the local daily newspaper or chamber of commerce.

Do not be swayed by the size of a flea market's advertisement in a trade paper. The Kane County advertisement is often less than a sixteenth of a page. A recent full-page advertisement for Brimfield flea markets failed to include J & J Promotions or May's Antique Market, two of the major players on the scene. This points out the strong regional competition between flea markets. Be suspicious of what one promoter tells you about another promoter's market.

Evaluating a Flea Market

After you have attended a flea market, it is time to decide if you will attend it again, and if so, how frequently. Answer the following nineteen questions "yes" or "no." In this test, "no" is the right answer. If more than half the questions are "yes," forget about going back. There are plenty of flea markets from which to choose. If twelve or more are answered "no," give it another chance in a few months. If seventeen or more answers are "no," plan another visit soon.

There are some flea markets that scored well with me, and I would like to share them with you. They are listed in the next chapter.

Flea Market Quick Quiz

1. Was the flea market hard to find? ___ Yes ___ No
2. Did you have a difficult time moving between the flea market and your car in the parking area? ___ Yes ___ No
3. Did you have to pay a parking fee in addition to an admission fee? ___ Yes ___ No
4. Did the manager fail to provide a map of the market? ___ Yes ___ No
5. Was most of the market in an open, outdoor environment? ___ Yes ___ No
6. Were indoor facilities poorly lighted and ventilated? ___ Yes ___ No
7. Was there a problem with the number of toilet facilities or with the facilities' cleanliness? ___ Yes ___ No
8. Was your overall impression of the market one of chaos? ___ Yes ___ No
9. Did collectibles outnumber antiques? ___ Yes ___ No
10. Did secondhand goods and new merchandise outnumber collectibles? ___ Yes ___ No
11. Were reproductions, copycats, fantasy items, and fakes in abundance? (See Chapter 5.) ___ Yes ___ No
12. Was there a large representation of home crafts and/or discontinued merchandise? ___ Yes ___ No
13. Were the vast majority of antiques and collectibles that you saw in fair condition or worse? ___ Yes ___ No
14. Were individuals that you expected to encounter at the market absent? ___ Yes ___ No
15. Did you pass out fewer than five lists of your "wants"? ___ Yes ___ No
16. Did you buy fewer than five new items for your collection? ___ Yes ___ No
17. Were more than half the items that you bought priced near or at book value? ___ Yes ___ No
18. Was there a lack of good restaurants and/or lodging within easy access of the flea market? ___ Yes ___ No
19. Would you tell a friend never to attend the market? ___ Yes ___ No

Chapter 3
TOP U.S. FLEA MARKETS

Deciding which markets will and will not appear on the list is not an easy task. There are thousands of flea markets throughout the United States.

Everyone has regional favorites that failed to make the cut. There simply is not room to list them all. In making my choices, I used the following criteria. I wanted to provide a representative sample from the major flea market groups—seasonal, monthly, and weekly. Since this guide is designed for the national market, I made certain that the selection covered the entire United States. Finally, I selected flea markets that I feel will "turn on" a prospective or novice collector. Nothing is more fun than getting off to a great start.

This list is only a starting point. Almost every flea market has a table containing promotional literature for other flea markets in the area. Follow up on the ones of interest. Continue to check trade paper listings. There are always new flea markets being started.

Finally, not every flea market is able to maintain its past glories. Are there flea markets that you think should be on this list? Have you visited some of the listed flea markets and found them to be unsatisfactory? As each edition of this guide is prepared, this list will be evaluated. Send any thoughts and comments that you may have to: Harry L. Rinker, Rinker Enterprises, Inc., 5093 Vera Cruz Road, Emmaus, PA 18049.

The "Top U.S. Flea Markets" list contains the following information: name of flea market, location, frequency and general admission times, type of goods sold and general comments, number of dealers, indoors or outdoors, special features, current admission fee, and address and phone number (if known) of manager or promoter.

Seasonal Flea Markets

1. **"AMERICA'S LARGEST" ANTIQUE AND COLLECTIBLE SALE**

    Portland Expo Center, Portland, OR. Multnomah County Expo Center, Exit 306B off I-5; Saturday 8 a.m. to 6 p.m. and Sunday 9 a.m. to 5 p.m., early March, mid July, and late October; antiques and collectibles; 1,250+ dealers in March and October, indoors; 1,500+ dealers in July, indoors/outdoors; admission—$5 per person; parking—$5; Palmer/Wirfs & Associates, 4001 N.E. Halsey, Suite 5, Portland, OR 97232, (503) 282-0877, Fax: (503) 282-2953, www.palmerwirfs.com.

    Also check out Palmer/Wirfs & Associates' Cow Palace Shows, San Francisco, CA. exit off Hwy. 101; Saturday and Sunday, for 2001: February and September, usually the end of the month, Saturday 8 a.m. to 6 p.m.; Sunday 9 a.m. to 5 p.m; antiques and collectibles; over 400 dealers; indoors; admission—$5.

2. **BRIMFIELD**

    Rte. 20, Brimfield, MA 01010; six consecutive days in May, July, and September; antiques, collectibles, and secondhand goods; 3,000+ dealers. Indoors/outdoors; includes more than 20 individual antiques shows with staggered opening and closing dates, shows have different promoters; admission—varies according to field, ranging from free admission to $5; average parking fee—$3 to $6; www.brimfield.com.

    Brimfield Acres North, 120 Richards Ave., Paxton, MA 01612, (508) 754-4185 or (413) 245-9471, www.brimfield2000.com.

Central Park Antiques Shows, P.O. Box 224, Brimfield, MA 01010, (413) 596-9257, Fax: (413) 599-0298.

The Dealers' Choice and Faxon's Midway Shows, P.O. Box 714, Fiskdale, MA 01518, (508) 347-3929.

Heart-O-The-Mart, P.O. Box 26, Brimfield, MA 01010, (413) 245-9556, Fax: (413) 245-3542, www.brimfield-hotm.com

J & J Promotions, P.O. Box 385, Rte. 20, Brimfield, MA 01010, (413) 245-3436 or (978) 597-8155, www.jandj-brimfield.com

Jeanne Hertan Antiques Shows, P.O. Box 628, Somers, CT 06071, (860) 763-3760 or (413) 245-9872.

Mahogany Ridge, P.O. Box 129, Brimfield, MA 01010, (413) 245-0381.

May's Antique Show, P.O. Box 416, Rte. 20, Brimfield, MA 01010, (413) 245-9271, Fax: (413) 245-9509, www.maysbrimfield.com.

The Meadows Antique Shows, Inc., P.O. Box 374, Brimfield, MA 01010, (413) 245-9427 or (413) 245-3215, Fax: (413) 736-0362, www.brimfieldantiqueshows.com.

New England Motel Antiques Market, Inc., P.O. Box 186, Sturbridge, MA 01566, (508) 347-2179, Fax: (508) 347-3784, www.antiques-brimfield.com.

Shelton Antiques Shows, P.O. Box 124, Brimfield, MA 01010, (413) 245-3591.

Sturtevant, P.O. Box 468, Brimfield, MA 01010, (413) 245-7458.

You can subscribe to the Brimfield Antique Guide from Brimfield Publications, P.O. Box 442, Brimfield, MA 01010; (413) 245-9329, www.brimfieldguide.com, email: brimfieldp@aol.com. Three issues for $13.95, first class mail.

3. RENNINGER'S EXTRAVAGANZA

Noble Street, Kutztown, PA 19530; Thursday, Friday, and Saturday of last full weekend of April, June, and September, Thursday opens 10:00 a.m. for pre-admission only ($40 per car carrying one to three people), Friday, 7 a.m. to 6 p.m., and Saturday, 7 a.m. to 5 p.m; antiques and collectibles; 1,000+ dealers; indoors/outdoors; admission—$6 on Friday, $4 on Saturday; Renninger's Promotions, 27 Bensinger Dr., Schuylkill Haven, PA 17972; call Monday through Friday (570) 385-0104, Saturday (610) 683-6848, www.renningers.com.

Monthly Flea Markets

4. ALAMEDA POINT ANTIQUES AND COLLECTIBLES FAIRE

Located at the former Naval Air Station, Alameda, CA, exit off Hwy. 880; first Sunday of every month, January through December, 6 a.m. to 3 p.m.; 600+ booths; antiques, collectibles and vintage furnishings—all items must be at least 20 years old; admission—VIP entry (6 a.m.) $10; early buyer (7:30 a.m.) $5; general admission (9 a.m.) $3; parking—free; Antiques By The Bay, Inc., 1000 Central Ave., Alameda, CA 94501, (510) 522-7500, Fax: (510) 864-9198, email: shows@antiquesbythebay.com.

5. ALLEGAN ANTIQUES MARKET

Allegan County Fairgrounds, Allegan, MI 49010; last Sunday of the month, April through September, 7:30 a.m. to 4 p.m; antiques and collectibles; 400+ dealers indoors/outdoors—admission—$3; Larry L. Wood, 2030 Blueberry Dr. N.W., Grand Rapids, MI 49504, (616) 453-8780 for show information or www.alleganantiques.com.

Courtesy Alleghen Antique Market

6. ANN ARBOR ANTIQUES MARKET

5055 Ann Arbor-Saline Rd., Ann Arbor, MI 48103; May through August and October (third Sunday of the month), April and September (Saturday and Sunday, weekend of third Sunday of month); November market usually occurs second Sunday of month; 7 a.m. to 4 p.m; antiques and select collectibles; 350+ dealers; all under cover; admission— $5; Nancy and Woody Straub, Managers, P.O. Box 1260, Panacea, FL 32346, (850) 984-0122.

7. THE FLEA MARKET AT BIRMINGHAM FAIRGROUNDS

Alabama State Fairgrounds, Birmingham, AL 35208; exit 120 off I-20, follow signs for Alabama State Fair Complex; first weekend of every month, year-round, plus second and third weekends in December, Friday, 3 p.m. to 7 p.m., Saturday 9 a.m. to 6 p.m., Sunday, 9 a.m. to 5 p.m; antiques, collectibles, and new merchandise (somewhat swapmeet-like); 100's of dealers; mostly indoors; admission—free; parking—free; The Flea Market at Birmingham Fairgrounds, 27050 E. 14th St., Catoosa, OK 74015, 800-362-7538.

8. BURLINGTON ANTIQUES SHOW

Boone County Fairgrounds, Burlington, KY 41005; third Sunday of the month, April through October, 8 a.m. to 3 p.m.; antiques and collectibles; indoors/outdoors; admission—$3; early buyers 5 a.m. to 8 a.m.—$5; Paul Kohls, Manager, P.O. Box 58367, Cincinnati, OH 45258, (513) 922-5265, Fax: (513) 922-5907.

9. CENTREVILLE ANTIQUES MARKET

The St. Joseph County Grange Fairgrounds, M-86, Centreville, MI 49032; one Sunday per month, May through October, excluding September, 7 a.m. to 3 p.m.; antiques and collectibles, no reproductions; 500+ dealers; admission—$4; Robert C. Lawler Management, 1510 N. Hoyne, Chicago, IL 60622, (773) 227-4464, Fax: (773) 227-6322, www.antiquemarkets.com.

Courtesy Centreville Antiques Market

10. FAIRGROUNDS ANTIQUES MARKET

Arizona State Fairgrounds, 19th Ave. & McDowell, Phoenix, AZ 85009; four times/year, third weekend quarterly, call for dates and times; antiques, collectibles, and crafts. Antique glass and clock repairs; 100 to 200 dealers summer, 400 to 600 dealers winter; indoors; admission—$3; Jack Black Enterprises, P.O. Box 39005, Phoenix, AZ 85069-9005, (800) 678-9987 or (602) 943-1766, www.jackblack.com.

11. FLEA MARKET AT THE NASHVILLE FAIRGROUNDS

Tennessee State Fairgrounds, Wedgewood and Nolensville Rd., Nashville, TN 37204; fourth Saturday and Sunday of every month except December, Saturday 6 a.m. to 6 p.m., Sunday 7 a.m. to 4 p.m.; antiques and collectibles, crafts and some new merchandise, indoors/outdoors; about 2,000 booths; admission—free; parking—$2; Nashville Fairgrounds Flea Market, P.O. Box 40208, Nashville, TN 37204, (615) 862-5016, www.tennesseestatefair.org.

12. GORDYVILLE USA FLEA MARKET & AUCTION

Gifford, IL 61847: Rte. 136, 7.5 miles east of I-57; second full weekend (Friday, Saturday, Sunday) of each month; Friday 4 p.m. to 9 p.m., Saturday 9 a.m. to 6 p.m., and Sunday 9 a.m. to 4 p.m.; 400+ dealers, antiques, collectibles, vintage items, arts, crafts, indoors/outdoors; auctions start Saturday, 10 a.m., and Sunday, 11 a.m.; admission—free; Gordon Hannagan Auction Company, P.O. Box 490, Gifford, IL 61847, (217) 568-7117, Fax: (217) 568-7376.

13. KANE COUNTY FLEA MARKET

Kane County Fairgrounds, Rte. 64 & Randall Road, St. Charles, IL 60174; first Sunday of every month and preceding Saturday afternoon, except New Year's and Easter, year-round; Saturday 12 p.m. to 5 p.m. and Sunday 7 a.m. to 4 p.m.; antiques, collectibles, and some crafts; (a favorite in the Midwest, especially with the Chicago crowd); indoors/outdoors; country breakfast served; admission—$5 (children under 12 free); Kane County Flea Market, Inc., P.O. Box 549, St. Charles, IL 60174, (630) 377-2252; www2.pair.com/kaneflea/.

14. KENTUCKY FLEA MARKET

Kentucky Fair and Exposition Center at junction of I-264 and I-65, Louisville, KY.; three- or four-day show, dates vary, check trade papers; antiques, collectibles, arts and crafts, and new merchandise; about 1,000 booths; indoors, (climate-controlled); admission—free; parking—$3 at facility; Stewart Promotions, 2950 Breckinridge Ln., Suite 4A, Louisville, KY 40220, (502) 456-2244, Fax: (502) 456-2298, www.stewartpromotions.com.

15. LAKEWOOD ANTIQUES MARKET

Lakewood Fairgrounds, I 75/85 to Exit 243 East, Atlanta, GA; second weekend of every month, Friday through Sunday, January through December, Friday and Saturday 9 a.m. to 6 p.m., Sunday 10 a.m. to 5 p.m.; antiques and collectibles, 1,500+ dealers, indoors/outdoors; admission—$3; parking—free; Diane Dominick, Lakewood Antiques Market, P.O. Box 6826, Atlanta, GA 30315, (404) 622-4488, Fax (404) 627-2999.

16. LONG BEACH OUTDOOR ANTIQUE & COLLECTIBLE MARKET

Veterans Stadium, Lakewood Blvd. and Conant St., Long Beach, CA; third Sunday of each month, 8 a.m. to 3 p.m.; antiques and collectibles only (including vintage clothing, pottery, quilts, primitives, and advertising); 800+ dealers; admission—early admission (5:30 a.m. to 6:30 a.m.) $10, general admission $4.50; parking—free; Americana Enterprises, Inc., P.O. Box 69219, Los Angeles, CA 90069, (323) 655-5703, www.longbeachantiquemarket.com.

Courtesy Americana Enterprises, Inc.
Long Beach Outdoor Antique
& Collectible Market

17. METROLINA EXPO

7100 North Statesville Rd., Charlotte, NC; I-77 to Exit 16A; Friday, Saturday, and Sunday of every month based on the first Saturday of each month, year-round; 8 a.m. to 5 p.m. Friday and Saturday, 9 a.m. to 5 p.m. Sunday; antiques and collectibles; indoors/outdoors; about 1,500 to 2,000 dealers. Metrolina hosts three Spectaculars yearly: April, June and November, Thursday through Sunday, 5,000+ dealers; Spectacular admission: Thursday $10; Four-day pass, Thursday through Sunday $15; Friday, Saturday, and Sunday $6/day; call for early buyer's fee and sneak preview fee. Metrolina Expo Center, P.O. Box 26652, Charlotte, NC 28221, (704) 596-4643 or (800) 824-3770, Fax: (704) 598-8786, www.metrolinaexpo.com.

18. PRIDE OF DIXIE ANTIQUES MARKET

North Atlanta Trade Center, Norcross, GA; fourth weekend of every month; Friday, Saturday 9 a.m. to 6 p.m.; Sunday 11 a.m. to 5 p.m.; antiques and collectibles; 300 to 350 dealers, 800 dealer booths; indoors (climate controlled); admission—adults $4, children free; parking—free; North Atlanta Trade Center, 1700 Jeurgens Ct., Norcross, GA 30093, (770) 279-9853, Fax: (770) 279-0019.

19. ROSE BOWL FLEA MARKET

Rose Bowl in Pasadena, CA at 1001 Rose Bowl Dr.; second Sunday of every month; antiques, collectibles, primitives, vintage clothing, jewelry, arts and crafts and new merchandise; about 2,200 vendors; regular admission (9 a.m. to 3 p.m.)—$6, early bird admission (7:30 a.m. to 9 a.m.)—$10; VIP admission (6 a.m. to 7:30 a.m.)—$15; Canning Attractions, P.O. Box 400, Maywood, CA 90270, (323) 560-SHOW (7469); www.rgcshows.com.

20. RUMMAGE-O-RAMA

Wisconsin State Fair Park, Milwaukee, WI, I-94 to Exit 306; held 13 times a year, January through May and September through December, first weekend of the month and sometimes an additional weekend (call for dates), 10 a.m. to 5 p.m.; indoors; antiques, collectibles, arts and crafts, new merchandise; varies between 450 to 750 dealers; admission—$2; parking—free; Rummage-O-Rama, Inc., P.O. Box 510619, New Berlin, WI 53151, (414) 521-2111.

21. SANDWICH ANTIQUES MARKET

The Fairgrounds, State Rte. 34, Sandwich, IL 60548; one Sunday per month, May through October, 8 a.m. to 4 p.m.; antiques and collectibles; 600+ dealers; indoors/outdoors; admission—$5; parking—free; Robert C. Lawler, Sandwich Antiques Market, 1510 N. Hoyne, Chicago, IL 60622, (773) 227-4464, Fax: (773) 227-6322, www.antiquemarkets.com.

22. SCOTT ANTIQUE MARKETS

Ohio Expo Center, Columbus, OH; Saturday 9 a.m. to 6 p.m. and Sunday 10 a.m. to 4 p.m., November through June (weekend dates vary, check Scott advertisements in the trade papers); antiques and collectibles; 1,600+ booths; indoors; admission—$3; parking—free; Scott Antique Markets, P.O. Box 60, Bremen, OH 43107, (740) 569-4112, Fax: (740) 569-7595, www.scottantiquemarket.com. Scott conducts a second monthly flea market—The Scott Antique Market, Atlanta Exposition Centers, adjacent north and south facilities, I-285 to Exit 40 at Jonesboro Rd., three miles east of Atlanta airport—second weekend of every month, about 2,400 booths.

23. SPRINGFIELD ANTIQUES SHOW AND FLEA MARKET

Clark County Fairgrounds, Springfield, OH, exit 59 on I-70; third weekend of the month, year-round, excluding July, Saturday 8 a.m. to 5 p.m. and Sunday 9 a.m. to 4 p.m.; Extravaganzas are held in May, July, and September; more than half the market is antiques and collectibles; 400 dealers indoors/900 dealers outdoors in warm weather; admission—$2; Extravaganza admission—$3; early buyer's fee (Friday morning)—$10; Steven and Barbara Jenkins, P.O. Box 2429, Springfield, OH 45501, (937) 325-0053.

24. SUPER FLEA

Greensboro Coliseum Complex, Greensboro, NC 27416; monthly but weekend of the month may vary (call for dates), Saturday 8 a.m. to 5 p.m., Sunday 10 a.m. to 5 p.m.; antiques, collectibles, arts and crafts, some new merchandise; about 300 dealers; indoors; admission—$2; parking—$3; Super Flea, P.O. Box 16122, Greensboro, NC 27416, (336) 373-8515, www.superflea.com.

Weekly Flea Markets

25. ADAMSTOWN

Rte. 272, Adamstown, PA 17517; Sundays; antiques, collectibles, and secondhand material; admission—free; three major markets:

Renninger's; Sundays, year-round, 7 a.m. to 4 p.m., indoors/outdoors; Renninger's Promotions, 27 Bensinger Dr., Schuylkill Haven, PA 17972; phone on Sunday (717) 336-2177.

Shupp's Grove; April through October, 7 a.m. to 5 p.m., outdoors; Shupp's Grove, P.O. Box 892, Adamstown, PA 19501, (717) 484-4115, www.shuppsgrove.com.

Stoudtburg Antiques Mall, Sundays, year-round, 7:30 a.m. to 4 p.m.; indoors/outdoors; Carl Barto, 2717 Long Farm Ln., Lancaster, PA 17601, (717) 569-3536 or (717) 484-4385.

26. ANNEX ANTIQUES FAIR AND FLEA MARKET

Sixth Ave., between 24th and 26th Sts., New York City, 10116; year-round, Saturday and Sunday, sunrise to sunset; mostly outdoors with an indoor area; variety of merchandise including antiques and collectibles; 700+ dealers; admission—$1 for antique market, flea market is free; Annex Antique Fair, P.O. Box 7010, New York, NY 10116, (212) 243-5343.

27. ANTIQUE WORLD AND MARKETPLACE

10995 Main St., Clarence, NY 14031. (Main St. is Rte. 5); every Sunday, 8 a.m. to 4 p.m.; three buildings; (one devoted to antiques and collectibles, one to flea market material, and one as an exhibition building); 350 dealers in winter/ 650 dealers in summer; indoors/outdoors; admission—free; Antique World, 10995 Main St., Clarence, NY 14031, (716) 759-8483, Fax: (716) 759-6167, www.bodnarchuk.com/antique_world.

28. FIRST MONDAY TRADE DAYS

Canton, TX 75103 (two blocks from downtown square); Friday through Sunday (Friday before the first Monday of each month) 7 a.m. to dusk; antiques, collectibles, new merchandise, crafts (Note: This belongs in the book—not because it is a great source for antiques and collectibles, but because it is the best known swap meet–flea market in the world); 4,000+ booths; antiques and collectibles located on three-acre plot north of Courthouse; admission—free; parking—$3; City of Canton, P.O. Box 245, Canton, TX 75103, (903) 567-6556, Fax: (903) 567-1753, www.firstmondaycanton.com.

29. LAMBERTVILLE ANTIQUES FLEA MARKET

Rte. 29, 1.5 miles south of Lambertville, NJ 08530; Wednesday, Saturday, and Sunday, outdoors 6 a.m. to 4 p.m.; indoors 8 a.m. to 4 p.m.; antiques and collectibles only; 150 dealers; admission and parking—free; Heidi and Tom Cekoric, 1864 River Rd., Lambertville, NJ 08530, (609) 397-0456.

30. RENNINGER'S ANTIQUE CENTER

Hwy. 441, Mount Dora, FL 32757; Saturdays and Sundays, 8 a.m. to 4 p.m.; 500 dealers indoors; 200 to 400 dealers outdoors; admission—free. Extravaganzas on third weekend of November, January, and February. Friday 10 a.m. to 5 p.m., Saturday and Sunday 8 a.m. to 5 p.m.; antiques and collectibles; 1,500+ dealers; indoors/outdoors; Extravaganza admission—three-day pass $15, Friday $10, Saturday $5, and Sunday $3; Florida Twin Markets, Inc., P.O. Box 1699, Mount Dora, FL 32756, (352) 383-8393, www.renningers.com

31. SHIPSHEWANA AUCTION AND FLEA MARKET

On State Rte. 5 near the southern edge of Shipshewana, IN 46565; Tuesday 7 a.m. to 5 p.m., Wednesday 7 a.m. to 3 p.m., May through October, antiques, collectibles, arts and crafts, new merchandise, and produce (you name it, they sell it); can accommodate up to 800 dealers; indoors/outdoors; admission—free; June, July, August parking—$2; Shipshewana Auction, Inc., P.O. Box 185, Shipshewana, IN 46565, (219) 768-4129, Fax (219) 768-7041, www.tradingplaceamerica.com.

Thus far you have learned to identify the various types of flea markets, how to locate them, the keys to evaluating whether or not they are right for you, and my recommendations for getting started. Next you need to develop the skills necessary for flea market survival.

Chapter 4
FLEA MARKET SURVIVAL GUIDE

Your state of exhaustion at the end of the day is the best gauge that I know to judge the value of a flea market—the greater your exhaustion, the better the flea market. A great flea market keeps you on the go from early morning, in some cases 5:00 a.m., to early evening, often 6:00 p.m. The key to survival is to do advance homework, have proper equipment, develop and follow a carefully thought-out shopping strategy, and do your follow-up chores as soon as you return home.

If you are a Type-A personality, your survival plan is essentially a battle plan. Your goal is to cover the flea market as thoroughly as possible and secure the objectives (bargains and hard-to-find objects) ahead of your rivals. You do not stop until total victory is achieved. If you do not have a Type-A personality it does not matter. You still need a survival plan if you want to maximize fun and enjoyment.

Advance Homework

Consult a flea market's advertisement or brochure. Make certain you understand its dates and time. You never know when special circumstances may cause a change in dates and even location. Check the admission policy. It may be possible to buy a ticket in advance to avoid the wait in line at the ticket booth.

Determine if there is an early admission fee and what times are involved. Admitting collectors and others to the flea market through the use of an early admission fee is a growing practice at flea markets. In most cases the fee is the cost of renting a space. The management simply does not insist that you set up. Actually, this practice had been going on for some time before management formalized it. Friends of individuals renting space often tagged along as helpers or assistants. Once inside, the urge to shop superseded their desire to help their friend.

Review the directions. Are they detailed enough to allow you to find the flea market easily? Remember, it still may be dark when you arrive. If you are not certain, call the manager and ask for specific directions.

Make certain of parking provisions, especially when a flea market takes place within a city or town. Local residents who are not enamored with a flea market in their neighborhood take great pleasure in informing police of illegally parked cars and watching the cars get towed away. In some cases, parking may be more of a problem than locating the flea market. Avoid frustration and plan ahead.

Decide if you are going to stay overnight either the evening before the flea market opens or during the days of operation. In many cases local motel accommodations are minimal. It is common for dealers as well as collectors to commute fifty miles each way to attend Brimfield. The general attitude of most flea market managers is that accommodations are your problem, not theirs. If you are lucky, you can get a list of accommodations from a local Chamber of Commerce. The American Automobile Association regional guidebooks provide some help. However, if you attend a flea market expecting to find nearby overnight accommodations without a reservation, you are the world's biggest optimist.

If possible, obtain a map of the flea market grounds. Become familiar with the layout of the spaces. If you know some of your favorite dealers are going to set up, call and ask them for their space numbers. Mark the location of all toilet facilities and refreshment stands. You may not have time for the latter, but sooner or later you are going to need the former.

Finally, try to convince one or more friends, ideally someone whose area of collecting is totally different from yours, to attend the flea market with you. Each becomes a second set of eyes for the other. Meeting at predesignated spots makes exchanging information easy. It never hurts to share the driving and expenses. Best of all, war stories can be told and savored immediately.

Flea Market Checklist

To have an enjoyable and productive day at the flea market, you need the right equipment. What you do not wear can be stored in your car trunk. Make certain that everything is in order the day before your flea market adventure.

CLOTHING

Most flea markets you attend will either be outdoors or have an outdoor section. If you are lucky, the sun will be shining. Beware of sunburn. Select a hat with a wide brim. I prefer a hat with an outside hat band as well. First, it provides a place to stick notes, business cards, and other small pieces of paper I would most likely lose otherwise. Second, it provides a place to stick a feather or some other distinguishing item that allows my friends to spot me in the crowd. Some flea marketeers advertise their collecting wants right on their clothing. Others use the band of their hat as a holder for a card expounding their collecting wants. Make certain that your hat fits snugly. Some flea market sites are quite windy. An experienced flea market attendee's hat looks as though it has been through the wars. It has.

I carry sunglasses, but I confess that I rarely use them. I find that taking them on and off is more trouble than they are worth. Further, they distort colors. However, I have found them valuable at windswept and outdoor markets located in large fields. Since I usually misplace a pair a year, I generally buy inexpensive glasses.

The key to dressing for flea markets is a layered, comfortable approach. The early morning and late evening hours are often cool. A light jacket or sweatshirt is suggested. I found a great light jacket that is loaded with pockets. Properly outfitted, it holds all the material I would normally put in my carrying bag.

You must assume that it is going to rain. I have never been to Brimfield when it was not raining. Rain, especially at an outdoor flea market, is a disaster. What is astonishing is how much activity continues in spite of the rain. I prefer a poncho over a raincoat because it covers my purchases as well as my clothing. Most flea markets offer ponchos for sale when rain starts. They are lightweight and come with a storage bag. Of course, you have to be a genius to fold them small enough to get them back into their original storage bag. One I purchased at Kane County lasted years. Mrs. Robinson, being a shrewd promoter, just happened to have them imprinted with information about her flea market. I had a great time there so I have never objected to being a walking bulletin board on her behalf.

The ideal footwear for a flea market is a well broken-in pair of running or walking shoes. However, in the early morning when the ground is wet with dew, a pair of waterproof work boots is a much better choice. I keep my running shoes in the car trunk and usually change into them by 9:00 a.m. at most flea markets.

Rain at outdoor flea markets equals mud. The only defense is a good pair of galoshes. I have been at Brimfield when the rain was coming down so fiercely that dealers set up in tents were using tools to dig water diversion ditches. Cars, which were packed in the nearby fields, sank into the ground. In several cases, local farmers with tractors handsomely supplemented their income by pulling out the stuck autos.

FIELD GEAR

I always go to a flea market planning to buy something. Since most flea market sellers provide the minimum packaging possible, I carry my own. My preference is a double-handled canvas bag with a flat bottom. It is not as easy an item to find as it sounds. I use one to carry my field gear along with two extra bags that start out folded. I find that I can carry three filled bags comfortably. This avoids the necessity of running back to the car each time a bag is filled.

If you are going to buy something, you have to pay for it. Cash is always preferred by the sellers. I carry my cash in a small white envelope with the amount with which I started marked at the top. I note and deduct each purchase as I go along. If you carry cash, be careful how you display it. Pickpockets and sticky-fingered individuals who cannot resist temptation do attend flea markets.

Since I want a record of my purchases, I pay by check whenever I can. I have tried to control my spending by only taking a few checks. Forget it. I can always borrow money on Monday to cover my weekend purchases. I carry a minimum of ten checks.

Most flea market sellers will accept checks with proper identification. For this reason, I put my driver's license and a major credit card in the front of my checkbook before entering the flea market. This saves me the trouble of taking out my wallet each time I make a purchase.

A surprising number of flea market sellers take credit cards. I am amazed at this practice since the only means they have of checking a card's validity is the canceled card booklet they receive each week. They wait until later to get telephone authorization, a potentially dangerous practice.

I buy as much material through the mail as I do at flea markets. One of the principal reasons I attend flea markets is to make contact with dealers. Since flea markets attract dealers from across the country, I expand my supplier sources at each flea market I attend.

The key is to have a wants list ready to give to any flea market seller that admits to doing business by mail. My wants list fills an 8½ inch by 11 inch sheet of writing paper. In addition to my wants, it includes my name, post office box address, UPS (i.e., street) address, and office and home telephone numbers. I also make it a point to get the full name and address of any dealer to whom I give my list. I believe in follow-up.

Not every dealer is willing to take a full-page wants list. For this reason, I hand out my business card. However, I am smart. The back of my business card contains an abbreviated list of my wants and a blank line for me to add additional information. Do not pass up this opportunity for free advertising by using only one-sided business cards. I have received quotes on a few great items as a result of my efforts.

I carry a simple variety-store ten-power magnifying glass. It is helpful to see marks clearly and to spot cracks in china and glass. Ninety-nine percent of the time I use it merely to confirm something that I saw with the naked eye. Jewelers loupes are overkill unless you are buying jewelry.

Years ago I purchased a good Swiss Army pocket knife, one which contains scissors as part of the blade package. It was one of the smartest investments that I made. No flea market goes by that I do not use the knife for one reason or another. If you do not want to carry a pocket knife, invest in a pair of operating room surgical scissors. They will cut through almost anything.

I am a buyer. Why do I carry a book of sales receipts? Alas, many flea market sellers operate in a nontraditional business manner. They are not interested in paper trails, especially when you pay cash. You need a receipt to protect yourself. More on this subject later.

I keep a roll of toilet paper in the car and enough for two sittings in my carrying bag. Do not laugh; I am serious. Most outdoor flea markets have portable toilets. After a few days, the toilet paper supply is exhausted. Even some indoor facilities run out. If I had five dollars from all the people to whom I supplied toilet paper at flea markets, I would be writing this book in Hawaii instead of Pennsylvania.

I carry a mechanical pencil (a ball-point pen works just as well). When I pick up someone's business card, I note why on the back of the card. Use the pencil to mark dealer locations on the flea market map. I do not always buy something when I first spot it. The map helps me relocate items when I wish to go back for a second look. I have wasted hours at flea markets backtracking to find an item that was not located where I thought it was.

Anyone who tells you they know everything about antiques and collectibles and their prices is a liar. I know the areas in which I collect quite well. But there are many categories where a quick source-check never hurts. Every general price guide is different. Find the one that best serves your needs and use it consistently. You know you have a good command of your price guide when you do not have to use the index to locate the value for the item you are seeking. I scored some major points with dealers and others when I offered to share information with them.

FROM THE CAR TRUNK

My car trunk contains a number of cardboard boxes, several of which are archival file boxes with hand inserts on the side. I have them because I want to see that my purchases make it home safe and sound. One of the boxes is filled with newspaper, diapers, and some bubble wrap. It supplements the field wrapping so that I can stack objects on top of one another. I check the trunk seals on a regular basis. A leaking car trunk once ruined several key purchases I made on an antiquing adventure.

A wide-brim hat may protect the face and neck from the sun, but it leaves the arms exposed. I admire those individuals who can wear a long-sleeved shirt year-round. I am not one of them. In the summer, I wear short-sleeved shirts. For this reason, I keep a bottle of sun block in the trunk.

I also have a first-aid kit that includes aspirin. The most used object is a Band-Aid for unexpected cuts and scratches. The aspirin comes in handy when I have spent eight or more hours in the sun. My first-aid kit also contains packaged cleaning towelettes. I always use one before heading home.

It does not take much for me to get a flea market high. When I do, I can go the entire day without eating. The same does not hold true for liquid intake. Just as toilet paper is a precious commodity at flea markets, so is ice. I carry a small cooler in my trunk with six to a dozen cans of my favorite beverage of the moment. The fastest way to seal a friendship with a flea market dealer is to offer him or her a cold drink at the end of a hot day.

Clothing Checklist

_____ Hat
_____ Sunglasses
_____ Light jacket or sweatshirt
_____ Poncho or raincoat
_____ Waterproof work boots or galoshes

Field Gear Checklist

_____ Canvas bag(s)
_____ Cash, checkbook, and credit cards
_____ Wants lists
_____ Business (Collector) cards
_____ Magnifying glass
_____ Swiss Army pocket knife
_____ Toilet paper
_____ Sales receipts
_____ Mechanical pencil or ballpoint pen
_____ This price guide

Car Trunk Checklist

_____ Three to six cardboard boxes
_____ Newspaper, bubble wrap, diapers, and other appropriate material
_____ Sun block
_____ First-aid kit
_____ Cooler with cold beverages

How to Shop a Flea Market

After having attended flea markets for a number of years, I would like to share some suggestions for bagging the treasures found in the flea market jungle. Much of what I am about to tell you is simply common sense, but we all know that this is probably the most ignored of all the senses.

Most likely you will drive to the flea market. Parking is often a problem. It does not have to be. Most people park as close to the main gate as possible. However, since most flea markets have a number of gates, I usually try to park near a secondary gate. First, this allows me to get closer than I could by trying for the main gate. Second, I have long since learned that whatever gate I use is "my" main gate, and it serves well as home base for my buying operations.

As soon as I arrive at the flea market, I check three things before allowing my buying adrenaline to kick into high gear—the location of the toilets, the location of the refreshment stands, and the relationship between outdoor and indoor facilities. The latter is very important. Dealers who regularly do the flea market are most likely to be indoors. If I miss them this time around, I can catch them the next. Dealers who are just passing through are most likely set up outdoors. If I miss them, I may never see them again.

I spend the first half hour at any flea market doing a quick tour in order to understand how the flea market is organized, spot those dealers that I would like to visit later, and develop a general sense of what is happening. I prefer to start at the point farthest from my car and work my way back, just the opposite of most flea market shoppers. This method makes trips back to the car shorter each time and reduces the amount of purchases that I am carrying over an extended period of time.

Whenever I go to a flea market to buy, I try to have one to four specific categories in mind. If one tries to look at everything, one develops "antiques and collectibles" shock. Collectors' minds short-circuit if they try to absorb too much. They never get past the first aisle. With specific goals, a quick look at a booth will tell me whether or not it is likely to feature merchandise of interest. If not, I pass it by.

Since time is always at a premium, I make it a practice to ask every dealer, "Do you have any...?" If they say "no," I usually go to the next booth. However, I have learned that dealers do not always remember what they have. When I am in a booth that should have the type of merchandise that I am seeking, I take a minute or two to do a quick scan to see if the dealer is right. In about 25% of the cases, I have found at least one example of the type of material for which I am looking.

I eat on the run, if I eat at all. A good breakfast before the market opens carries me until the evening hours when dusk shuts down the market. I am at the flea market to stuff my bag and car trunk, not my face.

When I find a flea market that I like, I try to visit it at least once in the spring and once in the late summer or early fall. In many flea markets the same dealers are located in the same spot each time. This is extremely helpful to a buyer. I note their location on my map of the market.

When I return the next time, I ask these dealers if they have brought anything that fills my needs. If they say "yes," I take a quick look and decide immediately what I do and do not want to buy. I ask them if they mind holding the items I agreed to buy so that I can move on quickly. I make a commitment to stop back and pay in a few hours. Some agree and some do not. Those who have done business with me previously and know my buying pattern are more willing to accede to my wishes than those who do not. I do not abuse the privilege, but I do not hesitate to take advantage of it either.

GUARANTEES

There is an adage among antiques and collectibles collectors that "if you bought something at a flea market, you own it." I do not support this approach. I feel every seller should unconditionally guarantee his merchandise. If I find a piece is misrepresented, I take it back.

I try to get a receipt for every purchase that I make. Since many individuals who sell at outdoor flea markets are part-time dealers, they often are unprepared to give a receipt. No problem. I carry a pad of blank receipts and ask them to fill one out.

In every case, I ask the dealers to include their name, shop name (if any), mailing address, and phone number on the receipt. If I do not think a dealer is telling me the truth, I ask for identification. If they give me any flack, I go to their vehicle (usually located in their booth or just outside their indoor stand) and make note of the license plate number. Flea market dealers, especially the outdoor group, are highly mobile. If a problem is discovered with the merchandise I bought, I want to reach the dealer in order to solve the problem.

Whenever possible, the receipt should contain a full description of the merchandise along with a completeness and condition statement. I also ask the dealer to write "money back guaranteed, no questions asked" on the receipt. This is the only valid guarantee that I know. Phrases such as "guaranteed as represented" and "money back" are open to interpretation and become relatively meaningless if a dispute develops. Many flea market dealers are reluctant to provide this guarantee, afraid that the buyer will switch a damaged item for a good one or swipe a part and return the item as incomplete.

SHOPPING AROUND

I always shop around. At a good flea market, I expect to see the same merchandise in several booths. Prices will vary, often by several hundred if not several thousand percent. I make a purchase immediately only when the price is a bargain, i.e., priced way below current market value. If a piece is near current market value, I inspect it, note its location on my map, and move on. If I do not find another in better good condition, at a cheaper price, or both, I go back and negotiate with the dealer.

I take the time to inspect carefully, in natural sunlight, any piece that I buy. First, I check for defects such as cracks, nicks, scratches, and signs of normal wear. Second, if the object involves parts, I make certain that it is complete. I have been known to take the time to carefully count parts. The last two times that I did not do this, the objects that I bought turned out to be incomplete when I got them home.

I frequently find myself asking a dealer to clean an object for my inspection. Outdoor flea markets are often quite dusty, especially in July and August. The insides of most indoor markets are generally not much better. Dirt can easily hide flaws. It also can discolor objects. Make certain you know exactly what you are buying.

I force myself to slow down and get to know those dealers from whom I hope to make future purchases. Though it may mean that I do not visit the entire flea market, I have found that the long-term benefits from this type of contact far outweigh the short-term gain of seeing every booth.

Flea Market Food

Flea market food is best described as overcooked, greasy, and heartburn-inducing. I think I forgot to mention that my first-aid kit contains a roll of antacid pills. Gourmet eating facilities are usually nonexistent. Is it any wonder that I often go without eating?

Several flea markets take place on sites that also house a farmer's market. When this is the case, I take time to shop the market and purchase my food at one of its counters.

I do make it a point to inquire among the dealers where they go to have their evening meals. They generally opt for good food, plenty of it, and at inexpensive prices. At the end of the day I am hungry. I do not feel like driving home, cleaning up, and then eating. I want to eat where the clientele can stand the appearance and smell of a flea marketeer. I have rarely been disappointed when I followed a flea market dealer's recommendation.

The best survival tactic is probably to bring your own food. I simply find this too much trouble. I get heartburn just thinking about a lunch sitting for several hours inside a car on a hot summer day. No thanks; I buy what I need.

Mailing List/Newsletter

Many flea markets actively recruit names for promotional mailings. Several send monthly, bi-monthly, or quarterly newsletters to their customers. I always take a minute or two to fill out their request card. It is not my nickel paying for the mailing.

Follow-Up

Immediately upon returning home, or at worst the next day, unpack and record your purchases. If you wait, you are likely to forget important details. This is not the fun part of collecting. It is easy to ignore. Discipline yourself. Get in the habit. You know it is the right thing to do, so do it.

Review the business cards that you picked up and notes that you made. If letters are required, write them. If telephone calls are necessary, make them. Never lose sight of the fact that one of your principal reasons for going to the flea market is to establish long-term dealer contacts.

Finally, if your experiences at the flea market were positive or if you saw ways to improve the market, write a letter to the manager. He or she will be delighted in both instances. Competition among flea markets for dealers and customers is increasing. Good managers want to make their markets better than their competitors'. Your comments and suggestions will be welcomed.

Chapter 5

HONING YOUR SHOPPING SKILLS

Earlier I mentioned that most buyers view flea markets as places where bargains and "steals" can be found. I have found plenty. However, the truth is that you have to hunt long and hard to find them, and in some cases, they evolve only after intense bargaining. Shopping a flea market properly requires skills. This chapter will help shape and hone your shopping skills and alert you to some of the pitfalls involved with buying at a flea market.

With What Type of Dealer Are You Dealing?

There are essentially three types of dealers found at flea markets: the professional dealer, the weekend dealer, and the once-and-done dealer. Each brings a different level of expertise and merchandise to the flea market. Each offers pluses and minuses. Knowing which type you are dealing with is advantageous.

PROFESSIONAL DEALER

So many flea markets developed in the 1980s and 1990s that there are now professional flea market dealers who practice their craft full-time. Within any given week, you may find them at three or four different flea markets. They are the modern American gypsies. Their living accommodations and merchandise are usually found within the truck, van, or station wagon in which they are traveling. These individuals survive on shrewdness and hustle. They want to turn over their merchandise as quickly as possible for the best gain possible and are willing to do whatever is necessary to achieve this end.

Buy from professional flea market dealers with a questioning mind; i.e., question everything they tell you about an object from what it is to what they want for it. Their knowledge of the market comes from hands-on experience. It is often not as great as they think. They are so busy setting up, buying, selling, and breaking down that they have little time to do research or read trade literature. More than any other group of dealers in the trade, they are weavers of tales and sellers of dreams.

The professional flea market dealer's circuit can stretch from New England to California, from Michigan to Florida. These "professionals" are constantly on the move. If you have a problem with something one of these dealers sold you, finding him or her can prove difficult. Do not buy anything from a professional dealer unless you are absolutely certain about it.

Judge the credibility and integrity of the professional flea market dealer by the quality of the merchandise he or she displays. You should see middle- and high-quality material in better condition than you normally expect to find. If the offerings are heavily damaged and appear poorly maintained, walk away.

Do not interpret what I have said to imply that all professional flea market dealers are dishonest. The vast majority are fine, upstanding individuals. However, as a whole, this group has the largest share of rotten apples in its barrel—more than any other group of dealers in the flea market field. Since there is no professional organization to police the trade and promoters do not care as long as their space rent is paid, it is up to you to protect yourself.

The antiques and collectibles field works on the principle of *caveat emptor*, "let the buyer beware." It is important to remember that the key is to beware of the seller as well as his merchandise. It pays to know with whom you are doing business.

WEEKEND DEALERS

Weekend flea market dealers are individuals who have a full-time job elsewhere and are dealing on the weekends to supplement their income. In most cases, their weekday job is outside the antiques and collectibles field. However, with the growth of the antiques mall, some of these weekend dealers are really full-time antiques and collectibles dealers. They spend their weekdays shopping and maintaining their mall locations, while selling on the weekend at their traditional flea market location.

In many cases, these dealers specialize, especially if they are in a large flea market environment. As a result, they are usually familiar with the literature relating to their areas of expertise. They also tend to live within a few hours' drive of the flea market in which they set up. This means that they can be found if the need arises.

ONCE-AND-DONE DEALERS

Once-and-done dealers range from an individual who is using the flea market to dispose of some inherited family heirlooms or portions of an estate to collectors who have culled their collection and are offering their duplicates and discards for sale. Bargains can often be found in both cases. In the first instance, bargains result from lack of pricing knowledge. However, unless you are an early arrival, chances are that the table will be picked clean by the regular dealers and pickers long before you show up. Bargains originate from the collectors because they know the price levels in their field. They realize that in order to sell their discards and duplicates, they will have to offer their merchandise at prices that are tempting to dealer and collector alike.

The once-and-done dealers are the least prepared to conduct sales on a business basis. Most likely they will not have a receipt book or a business card featuring their address and phone number. They almost never attempt to collect applicable sales tax. There is little long-term gain in spending time getting to know the individual who is selling off a few family treasures. However, do not leave without asking, "Is there anything else you have at home that you are planning to sell?"

Spend some time with the collector. Strike up a conversation. If you have

Courtesy American Enterprises, Inc.
Long Beach Outdoor Antique & Collectible Market

mutual collecting interests, invite him or her to visit and view your collection. What you are really fishing for is an invitation to view his or her holdings. You will be surprised how often you will receive one when you show genuine interest.

What Is It?

You need to be concerned with two questions when looking at an object: What is it? and How much is it worth? In order to answer the second question, you need a correct answer to the first. Information provided about objects for sale at flea markets is minimal and often incorrect. The only state of mind that protects you is a defensive one.

There are several reasons for the amount of misidentification of objects at flea markets. The foremost is dealer ignorance. Many dealers simply do not take the time to do proper research. I also suspect that they are quite comfortable with the adage that "ignorance is bliss." As long as an object bears a resemblance to something good, it will be touted with the most prestigious label available.

When questioning dealers about an object, beware of phrases such as "I think it is...," "As best as I can tell," "It looks exactly like," and "I trust your judgment." Push the dealers until you pin them down. The more they vacillate, the more suspicious you should become. Insist that the sales receipt carry a full claim about the object.

In many cases misidentification is passed from person to person because the dealer who bought the object trusted what was said by the dealer who sold it to him. I am always amazed how convinced dealers are that they are right. There is little point in arguing with them. The only way to preserve both individuals' sanity is to walk away.

If you do not know what something is, do not buy it. The general price guide and any specific price guides that you have in your bag can point you in the right direction, but they are not the final word. If you simply must find out right that minute and do not have the reference book you need, check with the antiques and collectibles book dealer at the market to see if he has the title you need in stock.

Stories, Stories and More Stories

A flea market is a place where one's creative imagination and ability to believe what is heard are constantly tested. The number of cleverly crafted stories to explain the origin of pieces and why the condition is not exactly what one expects is endless. The problem is that they all sound plausible. Once again, I come back to the concept upon which flea market survival is founded: a questioning mind.

I often ask dealers to explain the circumstances through which they acquired a piece and what they know about the piece. Note what I said; I am not asking the seller to reveal his or her source. No one should be expected to do that. I am testing the openness and believability of the dealer. If the dealer claims there is something special about an object (e.g., it belonged to a famous person or was illustrated in a book), I ask to see proof. Word-of-mouth stories have little credibility in the long run.

Again, there are certain phrases that serve as tip-offs that something may be amiss. "It is the first one I have ever seen," "You will never find another one like it," "I saw one a few aisles over for more money," "One sold at auction a few weeks ago for double what I am asking," and "I am selling it to you for exactly what I paid for it" are just a few examples. If what you are hearing sounds too good to be true, it probably is.

Your best defense is to study and research the area in which you want to collect before going to flea markets. Emphasis should be placed equally on object identification and an understanding of the pricing structure within that collecting category. You will not be a happy person if you find that although an object you bought is what the seller claimed it was, you paid far more for it than it is worth.

Period, Reproduction, Copycat, Fantasy or Fake

The number of reproductions, copycats, and fantasy and fake items at flea markets is larger than in any other segment of the field. Antiques malls run a close second. In fact, it is common to find several dealers at a flea market selling reproductions, copycats, and fantasy items openly. When you recognize them, take time to study their merchandise. Commit the material to memory. In ten years, when the material has begun to age, you will be glad that you did.

Although the above terms are familiar to those who are active in the antiques and collectibles field, they may not be understood by some. A period piece is an example made during the initial period of production or an object licensed during a person's, group's, or show's period of fame or stardom. The commonly used term is "real." However, if you think about it, all objects are real, whether period or not. "Real" is one of those terms that should set your mind to questioning.

A reproduction is an exact copy of a period piece. There may be subtle changes in areas not visible to the naked eye, but essentially it is identical to its period counterpart. A copycat is an object that is similar, but not exactly like the period piece it is emulating. It may vary in size, form, or design elements. In some cases, it is very close to the original. In auction terms, copycats are known as "in the style of." A fantasy item is a form that was not issued during the initial period of production. An object licensed after Elvis's death would be an Elvis fantasy item. A Chippendale-style coffee table, a form which did not exist during the first Chippendale period, is another example.

The thing to remember is that reproductions, copycats, and fantasy items are generally mass-produced and start out life honestly. The wholesalers who sell them to dealers in the trade make it clear exactly what they are. Alas, some of the dealers do not do so when they resell them.

Because reproductions, copycats, and fantasy items are mass-produced, they appear in the market in quantity. When you spot a piece in your collecting area that you have never seen before, quickly check through the rest of the market. If the piece is mint, double-check. Handle the piece. Is it the right weight? Does it have the right color? Is it the quality that you expect? If you answer "no" to any of these questions, put it back.

The vast majority of items sold at any flea market are mass-produced, twentieth-century items. Encountering a

new influx of never-seen-before items does not necessarily mean they are reproductions, copycats, or fantasy items. Someone may have uncovered a hoard. The trade term is "warehouse find." A hoard can seriously affect the value of any antique or collectible. All of a sudden the number of available examples rises dramatically. So usually does the condition level. Unless the owner of a hoard is careful, this sudden release of material can drive prices downward.

A fake is an item deliberately meant to deceive. They are usually one-of-a-kind items, with many originating in shops of revivalist craftspersons. The folk art and furniture market is flooded with them. Do not assume that because an object is inexpensive, it is all right. You would be surprised how cheaply goods can be made in Third World countries.

It is a common assumption that reproductions, copycats, fantasy items, and fakes are of poor quality and can be easily spotted. If you subscribe to this theory, you are a fool. There are some excellent reproductions, copycats, fantasy items, and fakes. You probably have read on more than one occasion how a museum was fooled by an object in its collection. If museum curators can be fooled, so can you.

This is not the place for a lengthy dissertation on how to identify and differentiate period objects from reproductions, copycats, fantasies, or fakes. Read the books suggested in the "Flea Marketeer's Annotated Reference Library" that appears on page 478.

What follows are a few quick tips to put you on the alert:

1. If it looks new, assume it is new.
2. Examine each object carefully, looking for signs of age and repair that should be there.
3. Use all appropriate senses—sight, touch, smell, and hearing—to check an object.
4. Be doubly alert when something appears to be a "steal."
5. Make copies of articles from trade papers or other sources that you find about period, reproduction, copycat, fantasy, and fake items and keep them on file.
6. Finally, handle as many authentic objects as possible. The more genuine items you handle, the easier it will be to identify impostors.

What's a Fair Price?

The best selling scenario at a flea market is a buyer and seller who are both extremely happy with the price paid and a seller who has made sufficient profit to allow him or her to stay in business and return to sell another day. Reality is not quite like this. Abundance of merchandise, competition among dealers, and negotiated prices often result in the seller being less than happy with the final price received. Yet the dealers sell because some money is better than no money.

Price haggling is part of the flea market game. In fact, the next section discusses this very subject in detail. The only real value an object has is what someone is willing to pay for it, not what someone asks for it. There is no fixed price for any antique, collectible, or secondhand object. All value is relative.

These considerations aside, there are a few points relating to price and value that the flea marketeer should be aware of. Try to understand these points. Remember, in the antiques and collectibles field there are frequently two or more sides to every issue and rarely any clear-cut right or wrong answer.

First, dealers have a right to an honest profit. If dealers are attempting to make a full-time living in the trade, they must triple their money in order to cover their inventory costs, pay their overhead expenses, which are not inconsequential, and pay themselves. Buy at thirty cents and sell at one dollar.

The problem is that many flea market dealers set up at flea markets not to make money but simply to have a good time. As a result, they willingly sell at much lower profit margins than those who are trying to make a living. It is not really that hard to tell which group is which. Keep the seller's circumstances in mind when haggling.

Second, selling is labor and capital-intensive. Check a dealer's booth when a flea market opens and again when it closes. Can you spot the missing objects? When a dealer has a "good" flea market, he or she usually sells between fifteen and thirty objects. In most cases, the inventory from which these objects sold consists of hundreds of pieces. Do not think about what the dealer sold, think about what was not sold. What did it cost? How much work is involved in packing, hauling, setting up, and repacking these items until the objects finally sell. Flea market sellers need a high profit margin to stay in business.

Third, learn to use price guide information correctly. Remember the prices are guides, not price absolutes. For their part, sellers must resist the temptation to become greedy and trap themselves in the assumption that they deserve book price or better for every item they sell. Sellers would do better to focus on what they paid for an object (which, in effect, does determine the final price) rather than on what they think they can get for it (it never sells as quickly as they think). They will make more on volume sales than they will trying to get top dollar for all their items.

Price guide prices represent what a "serious" collector in that category will pay provided he or she does not already own the object. An Elvis Presley guitar in its original box may book for over $500, but it has that value only to an Elvis Presley collector who does not already own one. Price guide prices tend to be on the high side.

Fourth, the IRS defines fair-market value as a situation where there is a willing buyer and seller, neither compelled to buy or sell, and both parties equally knowledgeable. While the first and second part of this equation usually apply, the third usually does not. There is no question that knowledge is power in the flea market game and sharing it can cost money. If money were the only issue, I could accept the idea of keeping quiet. However, I like to think that a sale involves transfer of information about the object as well as the object itself. If there were a fuller understanding of the selling situation by both sides, there would be a lot less grousing about prices after the deal is done.

Finally, forget about book value. The only value an object has is what it is worth to you. This is the price that you should pay. The only person who can make this judgment is you. It is a decision of the moment. Never forget that. Do not buy if you think the price is unfair. Do not look back if you find later that you overpaid. At the moment of purchase you thought the price was fair. In buying at a flea market, the buck stops in your heart and wallet.

Flea Market Haggling

Few prices at a flea market are firm prices. No matter what anyone tells you, it is standard practice to haggle. You may not be comfortable doing it, but you might as well learn how. The money you save will be your own.

In my mind there are only three prices: a bargain price, a negotiable price, and a ridiculous price. If the price on an object is already a bargain, I pay it. I do this because I like to see the shocked look on a seller's face when I do not haggle. I also do it because I want that dealer to find similar material for me. Nothing encourages this more than paying the price asked.

If the price is ridiculous, marked several times above what it is worth, I simply walk away. No amount of haggling will ever get the price to where I think it belongs. All that will

happen is that the dealer and I will become frustrated. Who needs it? Let the dealers sit with their pieces. Sooner or later, the message will become clear.

I firmly believe it is the responsibility of the seller to set the asking price. When an object is not marked with a price, I become suspicious that the dealer is going to set the asking price based on what he or she thinks I can pay. I have tested this theory on more than one occasion by sending several individuals to inquire about the value of an unmarked item. In every case, a variety of prices were reported back to me. Since most of the material that I collect is mass-produced, I walk away from all unpriced merchandise. I will find another example somewhere else. This type of dealer does not deserve my business.

I have too much to do at a flea market to waste time haggling. If I find a piece that is close to what I am willing to pay, I make a counter-offer. I am very clear in what I tell the seller. "I am willing to pay 'x' amount. This is my best offer. Will you take it?" Most dealers are accustomed to responding with "Let's halve the difference." Hard though it is at times, I never agree. I tell the dealer that I made my best offer to save time haggling, and I intend to stick by it.

If the flea market that I am attending is a monthly or weekly, I may follow the object for several months. If it has gone unsold at the end of four to five months, I speak with the dealer and call attention to the fact that he has been unsuccessful in selling the object for the amount asked. I make my counter-offer, which sometimes can be as low as half the value marked on the piece. While the dealer may not be totally happy selling the object at that price, the prospect of any sale is often better than keeping the object in inventory for several more months. If the object has been sold before I return, I do not get upset. In fact, I am glad the dealer received his price. He just did not get it from me.

In Summary

If you are gullible, flea markets may not be for you. While not a Darwinian jungle, the flea market has pitfalls and traps which must be avoided in order for you to be successful. The key is to know that these pitfalls and traps exist.

Successful flea marketeering comes from practice. There is no school where you can learn the skills you need. You fly by the seat of your pants, learn as you go. The tuition that you pay are the mistakes you make along the way.

You can lessen your mistakes by doing homework. Research and study what you want to collect before you start buying. Even the most experienced buyers get careless or are fooled. Buying from the heart is much easier than buying from the head.

Never get discouraged. Everyone else you see at the flea market has experienced or is experiencing exactly what is happening to you. When you become a seasoned veteran, you will look back upon the learning period and laugh. In the interim, at least try to smile.

Chapter 6
THE FLEA MARKET SCENE TODAY

Change is occurring; and, it is very noticeable. This is truer today than it was two years ago. In fact, it is accelerating. Fasten your seat belts, the terrain ahead appears rather rough.

Positive Signs, Even Among the Negative

Today's flea market is a happening, not just a place where antiques and collectibles are sold. Flea market promoters and dealers learned during the 1990s that good merchandise alone is not enough to attract buyers. Customers want more.

Traditional business practices that proved adequate for more than half a century are not as effective as they had once been. Merchandise no longer sells itself. Survival is linked to change. Flea market promoters recognize it is essential that they expand their customer base. Flea market sellers have to market more aggressively and rethink their merchandise offerings.

The great news is that flea market promoters and sellers are changing. Promoters are using a variety of methods ranging from discount entrance coupons to staging special events, such as verbal appraisal clinics, to attract new buyers. The Renningers introduced the concept of a specialized mini-show as part of their summer 2000 Kutztown Extravaganza. This is an idea worth pursuing. I am aware of several antiques show promoters who have used it effectively.

The Alameda Point Antiques and Collectibles Faire held at the former Naval Air Station in Alameda, California, has just acquired a large building to offer indoor as well as outdoor booths at its shows. It also has developed an auction facility near the flea market site. Auction previews will be held during the flea market week. The auction will occur the following Friday.

Several promoters, e.g., Jack Black Enterprises (Fairgrounds Antiques Market, Phoenix, AZ) and Metrolina Expo, reduced the frequency of their shows. The result is not negative, but positive. The remaining shows are strong. By concentrating their efforts, these promoters are ensuring that they will continue to serve their customers and the trade.

Yesterday, I received an e-mail from Southern Mecca (7400 Chef Menteur Hwy., #29, New Orleans, LA 70126) announcing the creation of a new "antiques" show in the New Orleans area the third weekend every month between January and October. It is exciting to see a new launch. Rest assured I will follow its progress.

Give the Customers What They Want

Traditional sellers assume that customers will buy what they offer. Successful sellers have learned to put their personal likes and dislikes aside and offer merchandise the customers want.

More than ever before, the flea market scene is trendy. Unfortunately, the trendsetters are more likely to come from outside rather than inside the trade. When a flea market seller asks me what it takes to be successful, my stock answer is: "Sell only merchandise Martha Stewart has written about in the past six months. If six months have passed and it has not sold, get rid of it and replace it with her latest pronouncements." Those who think this advice is ludicrous should talk with those sellers who are following it.

What do buyers want? As in the past, the answer is post-1945 collectibles. The amount of pre-1945 merchandise found at flea markets continues to decrease. Actually, using 1945 as the key date is a very conservative approach. Interest has declined significantly in many collecting categories for objects made between 1945 and 1960s. The Sixties and Seventies are the hot decades at today's flea market.

Buyers want objects they can use immediately. Collectors no longer are the dominant buyers at flea markets. Today's hot buyer is an individual who is seeking objects for decorating purposes, to actually use (recycle), or capture a nostalgic memory from the past. Fix-it-uppers and damaged objects no longer have a place at flea markets.

The sophistication level of flea market buyers continues to increase. Buyers are more knowledgeable about what is available and, more importantly, what the correct price point is. They are comparison shoppers. While not demanding bargain prices for every object they buy, they respond far better to prices that are modest as opposed to greedy.

Flea Market Chic

I shriek every time I hear the phrase, "Flea Market Chic." Junkyard Chic is more like it. The general principal appears to be the more damaged and beat up the object is the better. Another approach is to buy anything, paint it white, add a few decals (floral motifs are a favorite), and display it. What happened to good taste? Even Charlie the Tuna on his worst day did better.

Now that I have told you how I feel personally, I want to reinforce a trend noted earlier. If this is what the buyers want then sell it to them. It is fun to see the 1950s/60s cash from trash movement recycled in a new form.

In my last "Flea Market Scene Today" report, I stated: "The flea market decorating style is in its infancy." It is no longer an infant. It is a young adult. It is almost impossible to pick up an architectural, Country, decorator, living-style, or women's magazine without finding one or more articles devoted to Flea Market Chic.

Flea Market Chic is a major reason why flea market attendance is up. Promoters and buyers hope the trend continues for another decade or longer. So do I.

Courtesy Centreville Antiques Market

Internet

Much has changed on the Internet since I wrote: "Flea markets and auctions are the two principal buying sources for people selling and auctioning material on the Internet." I no longer see the flea market as a primary source for material offered for sale on the Internet. Good, bad, or indifferent, the primary source today appears to be basements, attics, garage sales, and church sales.

What the Internet has done is develop an entirely new group of individuals who love buying antiques and collectibles. While their initial exposure comes from the Internet, they are quickly finding that there are other places to fulfill their cravings. Flea markets are one of them.

More and more flea market promoters are developing their own websites. This is an important promotional effort and needs to continue. It is also critical that promoters link their sites to the heavily trafficked auction and direct sale sites. More and more individuals plan their travels based upon what they find on the Internet. Information that is easy to find is the most effective.

A Final Note

Permit me one final thought. The key to having an enjoyable experience at a flea market does not rest with the manager, the dealers, the physical setting or the merchandise. The key is you. Attend with reasonable expectations in mind. Go to have fun, to make a pleasant day of it. Even if you come home with nothing, savor the contacts that you made and the fact that you spent a few hours or longer among the goodies.

As a smart flea marketeer, you know the value of customers to keep flea markets alive and functioning. When you find a good flea market, do not keep the information to yourself. Write or call the regional trade papers and ask them to do more stories about the market. Share your news with friends and others. Encourage them to attend. There is plenty for everyone.

Happy Hunting from all of us at Rinker Enterprises, Inc.

PRICE NOTES

Flea market prices for antiques and collectibles are not as firmly established as those at malls, shops, and shows. As a result, it is imperative that you treat the prices found in this book as "guides," not "absolutes."

Prices given are based on the national retail price for an object that is complete and in fine condition. These are retail prices. They are what you would expect to pay to purchase the objects. They do not reflect what you might realize if you were selling objects. A "fair" selling price to a dealer or private collector ranges from 20% to 40% of the book price, depending on how commonly found the object is.

Prices quoted are for objects that show a minimum of wear and no major blemishes to the display surface. The vast majority of flea market objects are mass-produced. As such, they survive in quantity. Do not buy damaged or incomplete objects. It also pays to avoid objects that show signs of heavy use.

Regional pricing is a factor within the flea market area, especially when objects are being sold close to their place of manufacture. When faced with higher prices due to strong regional pricing, I offer the price an object would bring in a neighboring state or geographic area. In truth, regional pricing has all but disappeared due to the large number of nationally oriented antiques and collectibles price guides, magazines, newspapers, and collectors' clubs.

Finally, "you" determine price; it is what "you" are willing to pay. Flea market treasures have no fixed prices. What has value to one person may be totally worthless to another. Is it possible to make sense out of this chaos? Yes, but in order to do so, you have to jump in feet first: attend flea markets and buy.

Happy Hunting! May all your purchases turn out to be treasures.

ABBREVIATIONS

# = number
3D = three-dimensional
adv = advertising
C = century
c = circa
circ = circular
cov = cover(ed)
d = diameter, deep
dec = decoration
dj = dust jacket
ed = edition
emb = embossed
expo = exposition
ext = exterior
FH = flat handle
ftd = footed
gal = gallon
ground = background
h = height, high
HH = hollow handle

hp = hand painted
illus = illustrated, illustrator, illustration(s)
imp = impressed
int = interior
j = jewels
K = karat
l = length, long
lb(s) = pound(s)
litho = lithograph(ed)
MBP = mint in bubble pack
mfg = manufactured
MIB = mint in box
MIP = mint in package
MISB = mint in sealed box
mkd = marked
MOC = mint on card
MOP = mother of pearl
orig = original
oz = ounce(s)

pc(s) = piece(s)
pt = pint
pp = page(s)
pkg(s) = package(s)
pr = pair
pt = pint
pub = published, publisher
qt = quart
rect = rectangular
sgd = signed
SP = silver plated
SS = sterling silver
ST = stainless steel
sq = square
unmkd = unmarked
Vol = volume
w = width, wide
yg = yellow gold
yr = year

Part Two

FLEA MARKET

PRICES

Categories A to Z

ABINGDON POTTERY

The Abingdon Sanitary Manufacturing Co. began manufacturing bathroom fixtures in 1908 in Abingdon, Ill. In 1938, they began production of art pottery made with a vitreous body. This line continued until 1970 and included more than 1,000 shapes and pieces. Almost 150 colors were used to decorate these wares. Given these numbers, forget about collecting an example of every form in every color ever made. Find a few forms that you like and concentrate on them. There are some great ones.

Club: Abingdon Pottery Club, 210 Knox Hwy. 5, Abingdon, IL 61410.

Bookends, pr, horse head, black, 7" h . . .34
Bookends, pr, sea gull, #305, 6" h 65
Bowl, Regency, #536, ming white 22
Bowl, Round Bulb, #543, white, pink
    square base, 2.25" h 10
Candleholders, pr, Seashell, #50-3, pink .16
Console Bowl, #512, 14.5 x 9 x 2.5" 10
Console Bowl, #532, sky blue, 14" l 15
Cookie Jar, Hobby Horse, #602 75
Cookie Jar, Humpty Dumpty, #663 130
Cookie Jar, Jack O'Lantern, #674, 8" h . .500
Cookie Jar, Little Bo Peep 100
Cookie Jar, Money Bag, #588, 8" h 50
Cookie Jar, Train, #651 225
Cornucopia, #569, black, 5.5" h 40
Figure, duck, pink, 5" h 15

Vase, Classic, #120, glossy pink glaze, 1947-49, 10" h, $30. —Photo courtesy Ray Morykan Auctions.

Figure, partially nude female, #3904,
    white, 10" h 350
Figure, stork, 5" h 50
Flower Bowl, Round Bulb, #519, blue,
    2.5" h 10
Flower Bowl, Seashell & Scroll, blue-
    gray, 11.5" l 20
Planter, #437, 10" l 7
Planter, Fan & Bow, hp flowers, 8" h 35
Planter, Seashell, 7" h, 5" pedestal
    base 60
Vase, #115, 9.75" h, 6.375" d 15
Vase, #116, pink, 10" h 45
Vase, #149, cream, ribbed panels, blue
    and burgundy flowers, 3" h 8
Vase, #620, 8.75" h 45
Vase, Acanthus, #486, pink, 10.75" h 20
Vase, Bow Knot, #593, 9" h 35
Vase, Double Cornucopia, #482, pink,
    6" h 15
Vase, Fern Leaf, #424, salmon, 6" h 160
Vase, Floral, #176, double handled,
    10" h 35
Vase, Hand, #312, 6" h 10
Vase, Iris, #628, Iris, 8" h 200
Vase, Oyster Shell, #444, gray, 8" h 15
Vase, Quilted, #599, pink, 9" h 5
Vase, Ribbon, #462, 4" h 9
Vase, Star, #463, 7.25" h, 7.375" d 115
Vase, Swirl, #512, pink, 7" h 18
Vase, Swirl, #513, 9" h 15

ACTION FIGURES

Action, action, action! Action is the key to action figures. Action figures show action. You can recognize them because they can be manipulated into an action pose or are molded into an action pose. There is a wealth of supporting accessories for most action figures, ranging from clothing to vehicles, that is as collectible as the figures themselves. A good rule is the more pizzazz, the better the piece.

Emphasis is placed on pieces in mint or near-mint condition. The best way to find them is with their original packaging. Better yet, buy some new and stick them away. Unless noted, prices quoted are for action figures out of their packaging.

Club: Classic Action Figure Collector's Club, P.O. Box 2095, Halesite, NY 11743.

Periodicals: *Lee's Action Figure News & Toy Review,* 556 Monroe Turnpike, Monroe, CT 06468; *Tomart's Action Figure Digest,* 3300 Encrete Ln., Dayton, OH 45439.

FIGURES

Addams Family, Remco, Lurch, 1964,
4" h 125
Addams Family, Remco, Morticia,
1964, 4" h 150
Addams Family, Remco, Uncle Fester,
1964, 4" h 175
Aladdin, Mattel, Aladdin with Abu,
Series 1, 1993, 5" h 7
Aladdin, Mattel, Palace Guard Rasoul,
Series 2, 5" h 5
Alien, Kenner, Alien, 1979, 18" h 275
Alien, Kenner, Apone, Series 1, 1992,
5" h 5
Alien, Kenner, Panther Alien, Series 3,
1994 3
A-Team, Galoob, Amy Allen, 1984, 6" h . .12
Avengers, ToyBiz, Loki, Series 1, 1997,
5" h 5
Avengers, Toy Biz, Scarlet Witch,
Series 1, 1997, 5" h 5
Batman: Dark Knight, Kenner, Bruce
Wayne, Series 1, 1990, 5" h 12
Batman: The Animated Series, Kenner,
Penguin, Series 1, 1992 20
Batman Returns, Kenner, Catwoman,
Series 1, 1992, 5" h 12
Batman Returns, Kenner, Penguin,
Series 1, 1992, 5" h 20
Battle Beasts, Hasbro, Lion, Series 1,
1987, 2" h 4
Battle Beasts, Hasbro, Tiger, Series 1,
1987, 2" h 6
Battlestar Galactica, Mattel, Ovion,
Series 1, 1978, 3.75" h 12
Beetlejuice, Kenner, Shish Kebab,
Series 1, 1989, 5" h 5
Best of the West, Marx, Janice West,
1965, 12" h 30
Best of the West, Marx, Princess Wild
lowers, 1965,12" h 45
Bionic Six, LJN, Bionic Quad Runner,
1986. 3.75" h 10
Bionic Six, LJN, Bunji, 1986, 3.75" h 10
Bionic Woman, Kenner, Fembot, 1976,
12" h 75

Bionic Woman, Kenner, Jamie Sommers,
1976, 12" h 50
Black Hole, Mego, Captain Holland,
Series 1, 1979, 3.75" h 10
Black Hole, Mego, Pizer, Series 1, 1979,
3.75" h 15
Black Star, Galoob, Gargo with Alien
Demon, Series 1, 1984, 5" h 10
Black Star, Galoob, Gargo with Alien
Demon, Series 2 10
Bonanza, American Toys, Ben, 1966,
9" h 75
Bonanza, American Toys, Ben's
Palamino, 1966 45
Bonanza, American Toys, Outlaw, 1966,
9" h 75
Bravestarr, Mattel, Deputy Fuzz, 1986,
6" h 15
Buck Rogers, Mego, Buck Rogers,
12" h 35
Buck Rogers, Mego, Killer Kane, 1979,
3.75" h 12
Butch and Sundance, Kenner, Butch
Cassidy, 1979, 3.75" h 5
Captain Power, Mattel, Major Hawk
Masterson, 1987, 3.75" h 5
Centurians, Kenner, Ace McCloud, 1986,
7.5" h 12
Centurians, Kenner, Dr. Terror, 1986,
7.5" h 10
CHIPS, Mego, Ponch, 1979, 3.75" h 10
Chuck Norris Karate Komandos, Kenner,
Tabe, 1986, 6" h 8
Clash of the Titans, Mattel, Pegasus,
1980, 3.75" h 20
Comic Action Heroes, Mego, Aquaman,
1975, 3" h 30
Comic Action Heroes, Mego, Captain
America, 1975, 3" h 25
Comic Action Heroes, Mego, Sawbones,
6" h 12
Commando, Diamond Toys, Blaster,
1985, 3.75" h 8
C O P S, Hasbro, Berserko, 1988, 6" h 4
C O P S, Hasbro, Taser, 1988, 6" h 5
Defenders of the Earth, Galoob, Flash,
1986, 6" h 10
Defenders of the Earth, Galoob, Ming,
1986, 6" h 4
Doctor Who, Mego, K9, 1976, 8" h 150
Dukes of Hazzard, Mego, Bo, 1981,
3.75" h 8

Dukes of Hazzard, Mego, Cletus, 1981,
  3.75"h 10
Dune, LJN, Baron Harkonnen, 1984, 6" h .15
Dune, LJN, Sardaukar Warrior, 1984,
  6" h 20
Dungeons & Dragons, LJN, Strongheart,
  Series 1, 1983, 5" h 15
Dungeons & Dragons, LJN, Warduke,
  Series 2, 1984, 3.75" h 12
Flash Gordon, Mego, Dale, 1976, 8" h 40
Flash Gordon, Mego, Zarkov, 1976, 8" h . .65
Ghostbusters, Kenner, Bad to the Bone,
  Series 2, 1987 18
Ghostbusters, Kenner, Stay Puft, Series
  1, 1986, 5" h 20
Go-Bots, Tonka, Dozer, 1983, 3.75" h 5
Grizzly Adams, Mattel, Grizzly Adams,
  1978, 8" h 10
Happy Days, Mego, Potsie, 1978, 8" h . . .30
He-Man: Masters of the Universe,
  Mattel, He-Man, Series 1, 1982, 5" h . .18
Indiana Jones: Temple of Doom, LJN,
  Indiana Jones, 1984, 6" h 70
Inspector Gadget, Galoob, Inspector
  Gadget, 1986, 12" h 60
James Bond, Gilbert, James Bond,
  1965, 12" h 125
James Bond, Gilbert, Odd Job, 1965,
  12" h 250
James Bond: Moonraker, Mego, 1979,
  12" h 50

Teenage Mutant Ninja Turtle, Playmates,
Michelangelo, with nunchukus, MOC, $30.

Lion King, Mattel, Mufasa, 1994 3
Lone Ranger, Gabriel, 1982, Lone Ranger,
  1982, 3.75" h 3
Lord of the Rings, Knickerbocker, Frodo,
  1979, 4" h 45
Major Matt Mason, Mattel, Doug Davis,
  1966, 6" h 85
Man From U N C L E, Gilbert, Lilya
  Kuryakin, 1966, 12" h 75
M A S K, Kenner, Gator with Dusty
  Hayes, 1986, 1.5" h 10
Micronauts, Mego, Time Traveler, 1976,
  3.75" h 5
Noble Knights, Marx, Gold Knight, 1968,
  12" h 95
Planet of the Apes, Mego, Burke, 1974,
  8" h 75
Planet of the Apes, Mego, Zira, 1974,
  8" h 40
Police Academy, Kenner, Claw, 1989,
  5" h 3
Rambo, Arco, Black Dragon, 1985,
  2.5" h 1
Robocop, Kenner, Ace Jackson, 1989,
  5" h 3
Six Million Dollar Man, Kenner, Steve
  Austin, 1975, 12" h 25
Starsky and Hutch, Mego, Huggy Bear,
  1976, 7" h 25
Super Powers, Kenner, Aquaman,
  Series 1, 1984, 5" h 15
Teenage Mutant Ninja Turtles, Play-
  mates, April O'Neil, Series 1, 1988,
  5" h 40
Terminator 2, Kenner, Blaster T-1000,
  1992, 5" h 5
Terminator 2, Kenner, Talking Terminator,
  Series 2, 1992, 5" h 7
Thundercats, LJN, Berbil Bill, 1986-87,
  6" h 20
Thundercats, LJN, Cheetara, 1986-87,
  6" h 45
Transformers, Generation 1, Tailbreaker,
  Series 1, 1984 80
Transformers, Generation 1, Wind-
  charger, Series 1, 1984 10
Tron, Tomy, Flynn, 1981, 4" h 40
Universal Monsters, Lincoln Toys,
  Dracula, 1975, 8" h 90
Wizard of Oz, Mego, Cowardly Lion,
  1974, 8" h 15
Wonder Woman, Mego, Steve Trevor,
  1978, 12" h 35

VEHICLES, PLAYSETS & ACCESSORIES

Aladdin, Mattel, Final Battle Playset 4
Aladdin, Mattel, Cave of Wonders 15
Alien, Kenner, Queen Hive Playset 12
A-Team, Galoob, Commander Center . . .50
A-Team, Galoob, Attack Gyro Copter 8
A-Team, Galoob, Interceptor Jet and
 Murdock 20
A-Team, Galoob, Patrol Boat and
 Hannibal 20
Batman: Dark Knight, Kenner, Batcopter,
 1990 60
Batman: Dark Knight, Kenner, Batmobile,
 1990 85
Batman: Dark Knight, Kenner, Batjet,
 1990 35
Batman: Dark Knight, Kenner, Sky Blade,
 1991 18
Batman: The Animated Series, Kenner,
 Aerobat, 1992 6
Batman: The Animated Series, Kenner,
 Batmobile, 1992 12
Batman: The Animated Series, Kenner,
 Turbo Batplane, 1992 40
Batman Returns, Kenner, All-Terrain
 Batskiboat, 1992 30
Batman Returns, Kenner, Bruce Wayne
 Custom Coupe, 1992 12
Battlestar Galactica, Mattel, R C Chlon
 Raider, 1978 65
Beetlejuice, Kenner, Creepy Cruiser 5
Beetlejuice, Kenner, Gross Out Meter 5
Best of the West, Marx, Covered
 Wagon 65
Best of the West, Marx, Pancho Pony . .65
Best of the West, Marx, Thunderbolt
 Horse 30
Black Star, Galoob, Ice Castle 35
Bravestarr, Mattel, Fort Kerium 40
Bravestarr, Mattel, Neutra-Laser 15
Buck Rogers, Mego, Laser Scope
 Fighter, 1979 .30
Buck Rogers, Mego, Star Fighter, 1979 . .38
Butch and Sundance, Kenner, Saloon
 Playset, 1979 .30
Centurians, Kenner, Depth Charger 20
Centurians, Kenner, Wild Weasel 12
Defenders of the Earth, Galoob,
 Mongor's Snake Vehicle 25
Defenders of the Earth, Galoob, Skull
 Copter 10
Dukes of Hazzard, Mego, Boss Hoggs
 Cadillac 45

Dukes of Hazzard, Mego, Daisy's Jeep . .10
Dune, LJN, Sand Worm 25
Dune, LJN, Spice Scout 20
Dungeons & Dragons, Fortress of
 Fangs, 1983 25
Ghostbusters, Kenner, Ecto-1A 15
Go-Bots, Tonka, Commander Center 35
Happy Days, Mego, Fonzie's Jalopy 30
He-Man: Masters of the Universe,
 Attak Trak 8
Man From U N C L E, Jumpsuit Set 65
M A S K, Spectrum Mask 15
Six Million Dollar Man, Kenner, Bionic
 Cycle 5
Super Powers, Kenner, Supermobile,
 1984 85
Terminator 2, Kenner, Bio-Flesh
 Regenerator 10
Terminator 2, Kenner, Heavy Metal
 Cycle 5

ADVERTISING CHARACTERS

Many companies created advertising characters as a means of guaranteeing product recognition by the buying public. Consumers are more apt to purchase an item with which they are familiar and advertising characters were a surefire method of developing familiarity.

The early development of advertising characters also enabled immigrants who could not read to identify products by the colorful figures found on the packaging.

Trademarks and advertising characters are found on product labels, in magazines, as premiums, and on other types of advertising. Character subjects may be based on a real person such as Nancy Green, the original "Aunt Jemima." However, more often than not, they are comical figures, often derived from popular contemporary cartoons. Other advertising characters were designed especially to promote a specific product, like Mr. Peanut and the Campbell Kids.

Clubs: Campbell Collectors International Assoc., 305 East Main St., Ligonier, PA 15658; Campbell Soup Collectors Club, 414 Country Ln. Ct., Wauconda, IL 60084; Sorry Charlie...No Fan Club For You, 7812 N. W. Hampton Rd., Kansas City, MO 64152.

Aunt Jemima, cigarette lighter 150

Aunt Jemima, cookie jar, F & F Mold
and Die 600

Aunt Jemima, mask, paper 500

Aunt Jemima, pancake shaker, plastic,
blue 65

Aunt Jemima, recipe book, *New
Temptilatin' Recipes* 35

Aunt Jemima, salt and pepper shakers,
pr, F & F Mold and Die, 3.5" h 50

Bosco Bear, glass jar, red plastic hat,
7.5" h 12

Campbell Kids, doll, composition, socket
heads, jointed arms, googly eyes,
watermelon mouth, molded painted
clothes, c1916, 9" h 200

Campbell Kids, pinback button, multicolored, boy chef, white lettering,
light blue rim 35

Campbell Kids, tin, 3.75" d 3

Charlie the Tuna, clock, hard clear
acrylic plastic cube with full color
picture paper aplied on inner panels
and inner top surface, electric,
©Star-Kist Foods, 1972, 4" d 50

Chicken Charlie, ashtray, figural, painted
plaster, 1960s, 7" h, 4 x 4.5" base 75

Clark Candy Bar Boy, figure, painted
soft vinyl figure pointing to Clark bar
held in other hand, 1960s, 8.75" h 75

Dutch Boy, hand puppet, 1950s-60s,
8.5 x 15", MIP 25

Elsie and Beauregard, drinking glass,
clear, Dutch theme illus of Elsie and
Beauregard holding tulips to left of
Dutch windmill, c1940s, 4.75" h, 2.5" d .15

Florida Orange Bird, bobbing head, hard
vinyl, spring-mounted head, orange
body with green leaf hair sprig and
arms, yellow accent on beak, tummy,
and paw fronts, matching orange
base with raised yellow "Florida" on
front, "Orange Bird" on reverse,
©Walt Disney Productions, made in
Hong Kong, c1970s, 5.5" h 35

Fresh Up Freddie, figure, soft hollow
vinyl, painted, 3 molded tail feathers,
©1959 7-Up Co, 9" h 175

Fresh Up Freddie, ruler, plastic, transparent, reverse printed on underside
in bright colors, text for bicycling
safety tips, late 1950s, 2 x 6.5" 15

Gerber Baby, doll, cloth body, moving
eyes, 1979, 18" h 10

Little Sprout, Green Giant, doll, plush,
stuffed, felt fabric hair, inset white
plastic eyes, rear of leg stitched
"Exclusively For Green Giant" with
"Animal Toys Plus," original mailing
carton, c1980, 4.25 x 7.5 x 12.5" 15

Mr Zip, pinback button, full color image
on white ground, c1960s 8

Piel Brothers, salt and pepper shakers,
pr, figural, painted composition, front
mkd "Miami," rubber stopper, made
in Japan, c1950s 75

Pillsbury Dough Boy, mixing bowl,
"Poppin Fresh/Home Cooking" with
doughboy logo on front, mkd "Anchor
Ovenware Mixing Bowl 1 qt/Oven &
Microwave Safe" 17

Reddy Kilowatt, alarm clock, electric,
hard plastic case, pedestal base,
"Compliments of Philadelphia Light
and Electric" on dial, c1960s, 5.5" h . . .75

Reddy Kilowatt, ashtray, glass, clear,
applied red and white paint on underside, 3 rests, c1950s, 4.5" d 8

Reddy Kilowatt, hard hat, hard plastic,
yellow, decal of Reddy on front in
yellow head, gloves, and boots, red
body and voltage sprigs, black lettering "Reddy Kilowatt/Your Electric
Servant," int leather and fabric
webbing, 8.5 x 12" 50

*Nipper, sign, porcelain, "His Master's
Voice," 17" h, 23" w, $650.* —Photo cour-
tesy Collectors Auction Services.

Spuds MacKenzie, Anheuser-Busch Bud Light, playing cards, United States Playing Card Co., 1987, $5.

Speedy Alka-Seltzer, bank, soft vinyl, painted, coin slot in top of tablet hat, 1950-60s, 5.5" h 175

Speedy Alka-Seltzer, cup, waxed paper, shades of blue on white ground with Speedy image depicted twice, "Plop Plop-Fizz Fizz-Fast Fast," ©1977 Miles Laboratories, 3.75" h, 2.75" d . . .15

Willie Penguin, figure, plaster, painted, wearing stethoscope and carrying "Dr Kool" medical bag, c1930-40s, 4.75" h, 2.5" d green base 75

Willie Wirehand, hat, diecut cardboard, garrison-style, red, white, and blue design on each side of Willie as Revolutionary War soldier beside "Minutemen For Rural Electrification, and "Stand Your Ground," 2 sides flare open to form tricorn-style cap with red, white, and blue crepe paper lacing in crown, 4 x 12" 35

ADVERTISING ITEMS

Divide advertising items into two groups: items used to merchandise a product and items used to promote a product. Merchandising advertising is a favorite with interior decorators and others who want it for its mood-setting ability. It is often big, splashy and showy. Promotional advertising (giveaways) are primarily collector-driven.

Almost every piece of advertising appeals to more than one collector. As a result, prices for the same piece will often differ significantly, depending on who the seller views as the final purchaser. Most advertising is bought for the purpose of display. As a result, emphasize theme and condition. The vast majority of advertising collectibles are two-dimensional. Place a premium on large three-dimensional objects.

Clubs: Advertising Cup and Mug Collectors of America, P.O. Box 680, Solon, IA 52333; Antique Advertising Assoc. of America, P.O. Box 1121, Morton Grove, IL 60053; Inner Seal Club (Nabisco), 6609 Billtown Rd., Louisville, KY 40299; Porcelain Advertising Collectors Club, P.O. Box 381, Marshfield Hills, MA 02051; The Ephemera Society of America, P.O. Box 95, Cazenovia, NY 13035; Trade Card Collector's Assoc., 3706 S. Acoma St., Englewood, CO 80110; Tin Container Collectors Assoc., P.O. Box 440101, Aurora, CO 80044.

Periodicals: The Paper and Advertising Collector (PAC), P.O. Box 500, Mount Joy, PA 17552; Paper Collectors' Marketplace (PCM), P.O. Box 128, Scandinavia, WI 54977.

Advertising Tear Sheet, Clay Robinson & Co Live Stock Commission, from Christmas 1903 edition of The Breeder's Gazette, depicts farmer feeding pigs in middle of winter, 10.5 x 14.75" 35

Advertising Trade Card, Columbus Stables, Peck & Lines, 157-181 Middle St., Bridgeport, CT, vignette of stable building with "Accommodations for 175 Horses," WE Holah, Bridgeport, CT 5

Advertising Trade Card, Schoenecker Shoes, small girl with many shoes scene, 3.25 x 5.5" 15

Ashtray, Hilton Hotel, glass 2

Ashtray, Little King Sandwich Shop, glass, 4.75" w 15

Ashtray, Steak House Akasika Misono Tokyo Japan/Tel 583-3389-0637-3418, fish motif, metal, gold lettering, 5" d . . .5

Bank, Batavian National Bank, La Crosse, WI, figural rocket, mkd "Astro Mfg USA E. Detroit US Pat. SND 45961 Berzac Creation" 25

Bank, Mr Bubble, hard plastic, pink, ©Gold Seal Co, c1970, 4 x 4 x 9.5" 35

Bill Clip, Morton's Salt, blue, white, and gold canister image on white ground, blue lettering 15

Blotter, Autocrat Coffee, full color image of product canister and home office building in Providence, RI, bound by small oval cello cap with miniature color lady portrait image, early 1900s, 3 x 8" 15

Blotter, Ralph Kiner-The Home Run King, promoting Niagara Deep Massage machine, 1950s 7

Blotter, Sinclair Oil, 1930s. 6.125 x 3.375" ..6

Booklet, Bamby Bread, Norman Bros, Manchester, NH, "1932 Diary," printed blue and white cover, back cover shows bluetone photo of delivery truck, 2.5 x 4.25" 15

Brochure, Schuco Toys, 8 pp, 1955, 5.75 x 8" 20

Brush, Atlantic Gasoline, emb old car with open front seat and covered rear next to building, "Atlantic Gasoline–Puts Pep in Your Motor," 1920s 85

Brush, Live Stock Commission, Omaha, Chicago, gold lettering on wooden handle, 6" l 20

Calendar, 1891, John Hancock, scene of young boy and girl looking at the Declaration of Independence, Hancock portrait upper left corner, Forbes Co, Boston 10

Calendar, 1905, Kihlberg's Karlsbad Mineral Baths, Excelsior Springs, MO, photo of Mr and Mrs Oscar Kihlberg, 4 x 6.5" 20

Calendar, 1974, Remington DuPont, entitled "Our Wildlife Heritage," Tom Beecham illus, Calendar Promotions, Inc. Washington, IA 4

Can, Compass Brand Tomatoes, DE Foote & Co, Baltimore, MD, paper label, 4 x 5" 15

Charm, Calvert Reserve Blended Whiskey, hard plastic, dark brown, figural bottle with paper label, c1940s, 1.75" h 8

Clicker, Tastycake, white lettering on blue ground, Kirchhof 8

Clock, Full-O-Pep Seeds, aluminum back, tin inside, glass front, TW O'Connell & Co, Chicago, IL, 12" d ..125

Corkscrew, "Cloughs Corkscrew Scotts Emulsion Pat. July 22, 1884," folds to 1.5" l............................15

Dexterity Puzzle, Belding, MI, "Puzzled About Insurance? Call Doug Jenks-Belding 803," 2.5" l, .75" w 12

Display Case, Old Fiorita Nuts, hinged top, 1 shelf, glass front, 19.5" l, 14" h, 7" d 45

Doll, Blue Bonnet Sue, cloth, stuffed, 12" h 5

Drinking Glasses, Wilson Tennis Balls, 6.75" h, 2.375" d, price for set of 6 10

Figure, dog, Ken L Ration, ceramic, brass tag on collar reads "35 CDT 1936 Chicago," "Dog register 1936... 35760" on reverse, cylinder attached to collar contains paper which reads "This dog belongs to..." followed by owner's name, address, and phone number, 19" h, 6" w 90

Fishing Knife, Armour Meat Co, "To a good sportsman from Armour and Company" on front, "Ham What Am" on reverse, knife pulls apart to reveal stainless steel blade mkd "Floating Fish Knife-Japan," 10" l 12

Hand Fan, 666 Laxative-Tonic, diecut cardboard, balsa wood handle, full color illus of youngster and birds singing "666 Carol" from sheet music above examples of product boxes, blue and white reverse with text for various uses of 666 liquid or tables, dated Sep 1936, 7 x 7.5" 15

Bank, Phillips 66, glass, "Phill-up With Phillips 66, See What You Save," 4.75 x 4.75", $35. —Photo courtesy Collectors Auction Services.

Box, Goblin Soap, Cudahy Soap Works, cardboard, $10.

Hand Fan, Birely's Palace of Music, diecut cardboard, wood handle, "Crossing the Brook," front design of sepia floral frame around photo of milkmaid daintily stepping over rocky stream, orange tint accent, blue text on reverse for music dealer sponsor with bluetone photo of J N Birely of Frederick, MD, c1920s, 7 x 9" 35

Hand Fan, Richard Hudnut's Cosmetics, Madame DuBerry illus, 7.25 x 13.75" opened size 15

Hanging Recipe Box, Pompeian Olive Oil, metal, complete with 77 recipe cards, painted measuring table for liquid and dry measures 30

Hairpin Holder, Chevrolet, ivory white celluloid, Chevy logo with "The Only Fine Cars Priced So Low," reverse with local dealership name in gold lettering, int holds original unused metal bobby pins, late 1930s 35

Ice Cream Scoop, Hires Ice Cream, plastic, "Only one taste says Hires to you" 15

Key Fob, Success Manure Spreader, diecut brass, depicts spreader on shield symbol beneath trademark lion head, reverse names product again with maker 15

Letter Opener, LH Hamel Leather Co, inscribed "1916 tenth anniversary 1926" on blade, handle mkd "Tannery Haverhill Mass. and Sales Room Boston Mass," 9.125" l 20

Lighter, Doral Cigarettes, Zippo, Welcome! Tobaccoville N.C.," 2.25" h 12

Lighter, Hires Root Beer, metal, chrome luster finish with antique gold luster panels, "Drink Hires" repeated on both sides, 1 side depicts bottle, other side depicts 6-bottle carton, Hadson, made in Japan, c1960s, 1.75 x 2" 35

Match Holder, "JD Hack General Hardware, Tin Roofing, Agricultural & Mill Supplies, Snow Hill Maryland," attached wood shaped barrel holds matches 20

Match Safe, Cadbury Cocoa, litho top, gold lacquered tin, c1920, 2.5 x 1.75" . .32

Match Safe, "Compliments Cardigan Arms Leeds," inscribed "Home Brewed Ales Unequalled" and "Charlton's Blended Whiskey" on both sides 300

Match Safe, Diamond Match Co, tin holder finished in gold flashing luster 15

Megaphone, Winston Cigarettes, "Yell For Your Team," metal mouthpiece, 10 x 4" 5

Mirror, Fisher Sales Co, "Everett and Ronald Oliver/Ferguson/New Idea/Fox Hudson/Willys Cars Joy, Illinois/phone 2311," depicts family at dinner table praying 5

Needle Pack, Personal Finance Co, 708 Market St, Parkersburg, WV, inside opens to reveal pack of Dix and Rands High Grade Sharps needles and sampling of thread, C R E Tucker, 1933 4

Paperweight, Lyons Flour, cast metal with gold paint, 4.5" l 15

Paperweight, Preferred Life Insurance Co, miniature set of dice inside, "Home Office, Montgomery, AL, 4.25 x 2.75" 35

Pen, Popov Vodka, Metro, 1975 2

Pencil, A C Delco Spark Plugs, orange and blue graphics on celluloid cream ground 8

Pencil Sharpener, Bakers Chocolate, cast iron, mkd "Bakers Chocolate Girl...Regus Pat. Off," 2" h 14

Pillow, Campbell's Tomato Soup, stuffed fabric, with original mailer bag, US Pillow Corp, Long Island, NY, c1960s, 11" l, 8.5" d 15

Pinback Button, Buster Brown Bread, multicolored, gray rim, red rim lettering, depicts Buster as sign painter with "Resolved that the Best Bread People Eat Buster Brown Bread" 15

Pinback Button, Chicago Portland Cement Co, black and white photo of cement bridge at Thebus, IL, "Our Cement," white lettering on blue rim, early 1900s 5

Pinback Button, Lester Pianos, black and white, depicts upright model above name of local merchant, early 1900s 15

Pinback Button, Minnesota Paint Co, multicolored image of unopened can of "Minnesota Linseed Oil House Paints," center of can wrapper depicts state seal of Minnesota 15

Pitcher, Welch's, ceramic, 7.5" h 14

Pocketknife, John Deere, white, 2 blades, 3" l closed size 7

Pocket Mirror, "Brice W. Kennedy, Waynesburg, PA, Jeweler and Optometrist" 10

Pocket Mirror, Knights Life Insurance, clear acetate over lime green textured paper, black printing, knight on horseback symbol, c1940s 15

Postcard, Florida Oranges, Hartman Card Co, Portland, ME, and Tampa, FL, unused 12

Postcard, "You Get Cruise-Ability In Every Pembroke Boat...Express Cruiser 26...Powered By Chrysler" ...5

Poster, Moet Champagne, Parisian woman dancing with a man while holding the Moet Champagne bottle, 18 x 24" 40

Radio, Poll-Parrot Shoes, painted composition figure plastic cube base, product name 1 side, "Quality Speaks For Itself" other side, AM, made in Hong Kong, c1970s, 6.5" h figure, 3.75" base 175

Record, Majestic Radio Co, 78 rpm 30

Ruler, Amos Furniture Co, Asheboro, NC, wooden 4

Salt and Pepper Shakers, pr, Heinz Ketchup, plastic, 4" h 3

Salt and Pepper Shakers, pr., Tappan, figural chef, porcelain, made in Japan, 1960s, 4" h........................6

Seed Sack, Reliable JMS Field Seed, JM Schultz Seed Co, Dieterich IL, 1 bushel, 15 x 30" 8

Sign, Amorita Cigar, metal, "Metal Amorita Cigar Your old...Favorite," 6.75" d 3

Sign, Carstairs Harmony Blended Whiskey, cardboard, "There's always Harmony here," depicts 3 customers enjoying highball while 2 harmonize in song, product bottle pictured on bar, c1940s, 16.5 x 21" wooden frame .50

Sign, Corvette Stingray, metal, "Corvette Sting Ray by Chevrolet/From Dream ...To Reality," 10.5" h, 16" w 10

Sign, Hershey's Syrup, metal, "Stepping Stones to Health/Genuine Chocolate Flavor/Hershey's Syrup" depicts 3 children climbing steps of large Hershey's Syrup cans, 16" h, 12" w ...10

Sign, Oilmax Cement, metal, "For Cementing Oil Wells," Donaldson Art Sign Co, 27.5 x 13" 15

Sign, Patriot Shoes, emb tin, red and white on blue ground, "Wear the Patriot Shoe," ©The Meek and Beach Co, 1920s, 7 x 19.5" 36

Pocket Mirror, Mascot Crushed Cut Tobacco, $60.

Watch Fob, Kellogg's Toasted Corn Flakes, metal, red and black lettering, gold ground, 5.25" l, $150. —Photo courtesy Collectors Auction Services.

Sign, Pontiac, metal, "Pontiac GTO-Nothing Outruns a Mean Old Goat," features 3 different Pontiacs, 15 x 13" .15

Spinning Top, Checkers Confection, litho tin, red, white, and blue, depicts product box with "Happy little spinning top. Round the table creeping, Spin away until you drop/Then I'll know you're sleeping," late 1920s 50

Spinning Top, Pure Oil, celluloid, "Be Sure With Pure," Pure emblem on bottom, Parisian Novelty Co, Chicago .50

Stickpin, Kolb's, thin cut brass, figural youthful baker holding large bread loaf under each arm, sponsor name on apron front, .875" h 8

Tape Measure, General Electric Refrigerators, celluloid, depicts coil-top refrigerator on front, "F.P. Lutz Co. Dayton, Ohio" on reverse, Parisian Novelty Co, Chicago, 1930s 35

Tape Measure, S & H Greenstamps, celluloid 25

Thermometer, Gilbey's Gin & Vodka. 9.125" d 25

Thimble, Dodge-Plymouth, plastic, ivory, red lettering, "Dodge Plymouth Open House 1950, A.C. Baker Dial 7184," .75" h 3

Thimble/Thread Holder, "A stitch in time saves nine. Let us repair your heating plant before it is too late. Banzhaf Oil-O-Matic Heating Service. Phone 8150 Marshalltown Fuel Oil Headquarters" .10

Tin, Bowers Mints, Earle S Bowers Co, Philadelphia, 6.5" d 6

Tin, Bremner Wafers, 11 oz, 1924, 6.5" h .14

Tin, National Pretzel Co, Scranton, PA, copper finish, crest with eagle perched on pretzel, "A Pretzel with a Twist, You Can't Resist" 15

Toy Telescope, "Jack & Jill Teenage Shop, 24 Main St. PH 77 Madison, Ohio #71, 5.5" l 10

Towel Holder, The Exchange State Bank, Nortonville, KS, "Your Towel is Safe Here/Your Money is Safe in The Exchange State Bank," 7.5" l 6

Watch Fob, Shawmut Rubber Footwear, blue and white celluloid on black cardboard fob disk, "Shawmut Rubbers Gives Double The Wear Where The Wear Comes," c1920s-30s 35

Whistle, Endicott-Johnson Shoes 6

AIRLINE & AVIATION

Airline mergers and bankruptcies have produced a wealth of obsolete material. There were enormous crowds at Eastern's liquidation sale in spring 1991. I have a bunch of stuff from Piedmont and Peoples, two airlines that flew into the sunset in the 1980s.

The wonderful thing about airline collectibles is that most of them initially were free. I try to make it a point to pick up several items, from bathroom soap to playing cards, each time I fly. Save the things most likely to be thrown out.

Club: Aeronautica & Air Label Collectors Club, P.O. Box 1239, Elgin, IL, 60121; C.A.L./N-X-211 Collectors Society, 727 Youn Kin Pkwy. S., Columbus, OH 43207; World Airline Historical Society, 13739 Picarsa Dr., Jacksonville, FL 32225.

Advertising Tear Sheet, Delta, "The One Stewardess Airline," 6.5 x 10" 3

Bag, Air New Zealand, teal, white trim and piping, metal zipper, 1970s 10

Book, *So You Want to be an Airline Stewardess*, Keith Saunders, 176 pp, 38 photos, 1967 30

Book, *The Crowded Sky*, Hank Searls, hardcover, 274 pp, 8.5" x6", 1960 4

Bowl, Delta Air Lines, Abco Tableware, NY, 4.625" d, price for set of 4 6

Cup and Saucer, US Air, china, Abco
Tableware, NY, 2.375" h cup, 5" d
saucer 10

Flatware, Eastern Airlines, stainless
steel, Abco Tableware, NY, price for
22 pcs 8

Flatware, Pan American Airlines, International Silver, 1970s, price for 4 pcs .15

Hand Fan, BOAC Airlines, "Speedboat
Routes Across The World," depicts
continents 7

Label, Mason Dixon, figural airplane,
black text, "Mason Dixon Linking
North and South," 5.5" l 8

Lighter, Canadian Pacific Airlines,
inscribed "Madison" on 1 side, mkd
"Super Automatic Lighter-Japan" on
bottom 9

Menu, Pan American Airlines, front
depicts Samboin Temple Gardens,
Kyoto, Japan, line for address and
stamp box on back, 6.25 x 8.75" 6

Model, Air Jamaica Airlines Airbus
A310, 1/2000 scale 24

Newspaper, *American Airlines News*,
Mar 1934 10

Patch, TWA, embroidered cloth, tan
and red logo on white ground, 3" w ...4

Pin, diecut thin brass, Lindbergh flight
commemorative, replica *Spirit of St
Louis* aircraft on fuselage between
wing struts, underside of wing mkd
"NX211," rear fuselage mkd "N.Y. To
Paris May 21, 1927" 35

Pinback Button, National Air Races,
Aug 31 to Sep 3, Cleveland, undated ..15

*Postcard,
"'Plucky'
Lindbergh
Ready to 'Hop
Off'," blue
tones, Ex.
Sup. Co.,
Cago, coupon
on divided
back, 3.25 x
5.25", $18.*

*Pennant, Greater Pittsburgh Airport, dark
blue felt, gold strip and streamers, multicolor airport scene, white lettering, 27" l,
$8.*

Postcard, Pennsylvania Central Airlines,
black and white, depicts DC-3 in
flight, c1950s 5

Tankard, BOAC Airlines, Wade Pottery,
1972...........................33

Ticket, Bonanza Air Lines, hand-written
"PHX to SLC," date stamped "27 Apr
68"...........................7

Timetable, Hellenic Airlines, Jan 1951,
3.75 x 8".......................40

Timetable, Mohawk Airlines, 1954 10

Timetable, National Florida Airlines,
Jun 15, 1983 10

Timetable, Northwest Airlines, Apr 30,
1978...........................2

Wings, Western Airline, junior stewardess kiddie wing, gold with red enamel,
2" w 8

AKRO AGATE GLASS

When the Akro Agate Co., was founded
in 1911, its principal product was marbles.
The company was forced to diversify during
the 1930s, developing floral-ware lines and
children's dishes. Some collectors specialize in containers made by Akro Agate for
the cosmetic industry.

Akro Agate merchandised many of its
products as sets. Full sets that retain their
original packaging command a premium
price. Learn what pieces and colors constitute a set. Some dealers will mix and match
pieces into a false set, hoping to get a better price.

Most Akro Agate pieces are marked
"Made in USA" and have a mold number.
Some, but not all, have a small crow flying
through an "A" as a mark.

Club: Akro Agate Collectors Club, 97 Milford St., Clarksburg, WV 26301.

Ashtray, hexagon shaped, cobalt swirl, 4.5" d 30

Ashtray, leaf shaped, #245, marbleized orange 8

Ashtray, seashell shaped, #246, reddish-brown 10

Children's Dishes, creamer, Chiquita, cobalt 9

Children's Dishes, creamer, Interior Panel, opaque blue, large 40

Children's Dishes, cup, opaque green 7

Children's Dishes, cup, Stippled Band, green, large 20

Children's Dishes, cup, transparent cobalt 14

Children's Dishes, cup and saucer, green 50

Children's Dishes, demitasse cup, J Pressman, green 8

Children's Dishes, demitasse cup, J Pressman, pink 25

Children's Dishes, demitasse cup and saucer, J Pressman, green 8

Children's Dishes, dinner plate, opaque green 8

Children's Dishes, plate, Concentric Rib, opaque green 3

Children's Dishes, plate, Interior Panel, opaque green, large 7

Children's Dishes, plate, Interior Panel, opaque green, small 6

Cornucopia Vase, green and white marbleized, mkd "N.Y.C. Vogue Merc. Co., U.S.A.," 3.25" h, $6. —Photo courtesy Ray Morykan Auctions.

Children's Dishes, plate, J Pressman, green 5

Children's Dishes, saucer, opaque yellow 12

Children's Dishes, set, Stacked Disk, 16 pcs 60

Children's Dishes, set, Stippled Band, plate, cup, and saucer, green, small ..30

Children's Dishes, teapot, Interior Panel, opaque green, large 55

Children's Dishes, teapot, marbleized blue, 2.675" h 8

Children's Dishes, teapot lid, opaque green 10

Children's Dishes, tea set, Gypsy, #234, octagonal, original box, 1930s, price for 15 pcs 100

Children's Dishes, tea set, Little American Maid, #360, octagonal, original box, 1930s, price for 15 pcs 160

Children's Dishes, tumbler, Stacked Disk, beige 12

Children's Dishes, water pitcher, Stacked Disk, opaque green, small 10

Cigarette Holder, cobalt blue, 2.75" h 7

Cornucopia Vase, red, white, and blue, #7657 15

Demitasse Cup and Saucer, jadeite green 10

Dresser Jar, Colonial Lady, opaque white 45

Flowerpot, green and white swirl, 2.375" h 10

Flowerpot, marbleized yellow onyx, vertical ribs, 2.25" h, 2.25" d 10

Flowerpot, oxblood and white 40

Flowerpot, yellow-orange, vertical ribbed edge, 2.25" h 15

Jar, brown and white, emb sleeping Mexican and cactus scene, sombrero shaped lid, 4.5" h, 3.5" d 30

Jardiniere, grayish blue, white, and dark blue swirl, #306, scalloped top 275

Lamp, urn shaped, jadeite and caramel .50

Marble, oxblood swirl, .675" d 10

Planter, oval, green, 6" l 12

Planter, oval, orange swirl, 6 x 3.375 x 2.375" 8

Planter, oval, swirled pastel green, orig metal basket with pink painted finish, 6" l 8

Powder Jar, blue 8

Powder Box, Colonial Lady 50

Toothpick Holder, urn shaped, orange
slag, ftd, square base, beaded top,
base emb "NYC-Vogue Merc. Co.-
USA" 5
Vase, marbleized, daffodil dec on both
sides, 4.5" h 8
Vase, yellow and white, Art Deco style,
8.5" h 100

ALADDIN

The Mantle Lamp Co., of America,
founded in 1908 in Chicago, is best known
for its lamps. However, in the late 1950s
through the 1970s, it also was one of the
leading producers of character lunch
boxes.

Aladdin deserves a separate category
because of the large number of lamp collectors who concentrate almost exclusively
on this one company. There is almost as big
a market for parts and accessories as for
the lamps themselves. Collectors are constantly looking for parts to restore lamps in
their possession.

Club: Aladdin Knights of the Mystic Light,
3935 Kelley Rd., Kevil, KY 42053.

Note: All kerosene lamps are priced with
complete burners.

LAMPS

Caboose, Model B, style B-400, galvan-
ized steel font 125
Floor, Model B, style B-286, oxidized
bronze, 1937 175
Hanging, Model 23, aluminum hanger
and font with white paper shade 50
Hanging, Model BH-2400, brass 80
Shelf, Model B-170, aluminum 50
Table, Model 6, satin brass or nickel 75
Table, Model 12, straight or slant side,
bronze 125
Table, Model 23, style B-2301, brass
plated steel, 1974-77 50
Table, Model 23, style D-2301, Majestic 100
Table, Model B-30. Simplicity, white ...100
Table, Model B-75, Tall Lincoln Drape,
Alacite, blue, purple, with black light,
1940-49 150
Table, Model B-80, Beehive, crystal,
1947-48 100

*Table Lamp,
leaded slag
glass shade,
white milk glass
font, cast iron
base, 24" h,
$425.* —Photo
courtesy
Collectors
Auction
Services.

Table, Model B-108, Colonial, green
crystal, 1933 200
Vase, Model 12, style 1243, green
Venetian Art-Craft 200
Wall, Model B, Alacite, plain glass oil
font with burner 125
Wall, Model C, aluminum font 40

PARTS AND ACCESSORIES

Burner, Model A 60
Chimney, Pyrex, green logo 30
Chimney Extension Tube, metal, 4" 25
Flame Spreader, Model 5 75
Gallery, Model 5 25
Mantle, Lox-on 8
Match Holder, Model 6, with book flame
spreader, and cleaner 125
Shade, glass, style 681, Dogwood,
decorated satin white shade 80
Shade, paper, Alpha, plaim, 14" bottom,
9" top 40
Wall Bracket, Practicus 75
Wick, Model 7 25
Wick, Model C 6
Wick Raiser, Model B 8
Wick Trimmer, 3-prong, for early models 30

ALBUMS

Victorian photograph albums enjoyed
an honored place in the parlor. Common
examples had velvet or leather covers.
However, the ones most eagerly sought by
collectors are those featuring a celluloid
cover with motifs ranging from florals to
Spanish American War battleships.

Most albums housed "family" photographs, the vast majority of which are unidentified. If the photographs are head and shoulders or baby shots, chances are they have little value unless the individuals are famous. Photographs of military figures, actors and actresses and other oddities are worth checking out further.

Cardboard albums still have not found favor with collectors. However, check the interior contents. In many cases, they contain postcards, clippings, matchcovers or photographs that are worth far more than the album.

Celluloid, 2 Victorian women surrounded
   by framed portrait cover, brass latch,
   10.25 x 8.25 x 2" 60
Child's, Holly Hobbie, holds 20 photos,
   4.5 x 5" 4
Handmade, music box on frame plays
   Let Me Call You Sweetheart 12
Leather, emb, contains photos c1800s,
   6 x 4.75 x 2" 30
Leather, inscribed "Statue of Liberty
   New York" on cover, contains photos
   c1920s 25
Leatherette, emb lion on cover, swirl
   pattern acetate lining, pages bound
   by ties, 1950s, 5.5 x 7.5" 7
Souvenir, "Survivors of the *S.S. Norge.*
   Norge Scandv'n Amer. Passenger
   Ship 6/28/1905," 56 pp, c1920s 20
Souvenir, Yosemite National Park,
   leather, contains 70 black and white
   photos, 8.5 x 5.5" 50

*Postcard
Album, olive
green emb
cardboard
covers, 7.5 x
13.5", $15.*

Velour, black and beige, Victorian,
   contains 33 photos, 8.5 x 11" 70
Velvet, silver colored metal latches,
   15 pp, holds 5 x 7 and 2 x 3 studio
   photos, complete with cabinet card . . .5

ALUMINUM, HAND-WROUGHT

Most aluminumware was sold on the giftware market as decorative accessories. Do not be confused by the term "hand-wrought." The vast majority of the pieces were mass-produced. The two collecting keys are manufacturer and uniqueness of form.

Club: Hammered Aluminum Collectors Assoc., P.O. Box 1346, Weatherford, TX 76086.

Brilliantone, tray, hammered, #1023, Wild
   Rose pattern, with matching set of
   8 coasters #1001, 18.5 x 12.5" l 35
Buenilum, candlesticks, pr, hammered,
   3" h 20
Buenilum, candy dish, grape bunch dec,
   twisted handle, bottom stamped
   "B.W. Buenilum," 9" d 3
Buenilum, ice bucket, 5.5" h, 6.5" d 15
Continental, dish, mums motif, ham-
   mered 20
Everlast, bookends, pr, horses motif,
   4.5" sq 55
Everlast, candleholders, pr, flower
   shaped, pie crust base, 2.5" h 22
Everlast, crumb tray, hammered floral
   design, with matching brush, 7.5" l,
   5.5" h 22
Hammered, candleholders, pr, emb
   flower petals dec, 4" d 20
Hammered, condiment dish, glass
   bottom, hammered aluminum lid,
   floral and fruit dec, 8.5 x 7" 10
Hammered, necklace and bracelet,
   attached faux turquoise charms 5
Hammered, serving bowl, 2 rings on
   sides for handles, ring on lid, 8" d,
   4" h 2
Hammered, serving tray, emb sunflower
   dec, scalloped edges, 17.5 x 10.5" 6
Hammered, serving tray, raised flowers
   in center, curled handles, 13.5" l 7

Bread Tray, poinsettia-type floral dec, mkd "Farber & Schlein Inc. Hand Wrought, 1718," 12.5" l, 7" w, $25.

Hand Forged, tray, deer running through
    trees dec around edges, scalloped
    and fluted edges, bottom stamped
    "Forged Aluminum, Design E.M.P.C.
    #857," 15" d 9
Lehman, serving tray, hand forged,
    leaves and flowers dec, scroll
    handles, 13.5" d .6
Palmer Smith, dish, hammered, wheat
    dec, 4.5" d 15
Rodney Kent, bowl, tulip and ribbon
    pattern, ftd, tied bows dec on handles,
    12" d 15
Rodney Kent, chafing dish 25
Rodney Kent, lazy susan, tulip and
    ribbon pattern, 18" d 15
Rodney Kent, plate, mkd "Hand Wrought
    Rodney Kent Silver Co,-437," 7.875" d . .4
Rodney Kent, tray, #404, tulip and ribbon
    pattern 15
Rodney Kent, tray, #408, tulip and ribbon
    pattern, back stamped "Hand Wrought
    Creations by Rodney Kent," ribbon
    design handle, 11.5 x 16.625" 10

AMERICAN BISQUE

The American Bisque Company, founded in Williamstown, West Virginia, in 1919, was originally established for the manufacture of china head dolls. Early on the company expanded its product line to include novelties such as cookie jars and ashtrays, serving dishes, and ceramic giftware.

B. E. Allen, founder of the Sterling China Company, invested heavily in the company and eventually purchased the remaining stock. In 1982 the company changed hands, operating briefly under the name American China Company. The plant ceased operations in 1983.

American Bisque items have various markings. The trademark "Sequoia Ware" is often found on items sold in gift shops. The Berkeley trademark was used on pieces sold through chain stores. The most common mark found consists of three stacked baby blocks with the letters A, B, and C.

Bank, Cinderella 1950, 6.75" h 50
Bank, donkey seated on podium, 6.25" h .22
Cache Pot, cat and ball, 6" h 10
Condiment Jar, little girl, 5" h 40
Cookie Jar, boy pig 50
Cookie Jar, carousel 15
Cookie Jar, chef .70
Cookie Jar, clown, 11.5" h 70
Cookie Jar, dog in basket 20
Cookie Jar, Dutch Girl 50
Cookie Jar, Grandma 50
Cookie Jar, kitten and beehive 42
Cookie Jar, lady pig 60
Cookie Jar, soldier 55
Cookie Jar, yarn doll, 12" h 70
Figurine, Indian, #3598BO, 9.5" h 20
Planter, black bear on log 9
Planter, donkey and cart 150
Planter, circus elephant, 5 x 8" 5
Planter, sailfish, 8 x 10" 22
Planter, Smokey Bear 220

Cookie Jar, churn, mkd "USA," $25.

AMUSEMENT PARKS

From the park at the end of the trolley line to today's gigantic theme parks such as Six Flags Great Adventure, amusement parks have served many generations. No trip to an amusement park was complete without a souvenir, many of which are now collectible.

Prices are still modest in this collecting field. When an item is returned to the area where the park was located, it often brings a 20% to 50% premium.

Club: National Amusement Park Historical Assoc., P.O. Box 83, Mount Prospect, IL 60056.

Brochure, Dorney Park, 1969 65
Magnet, Coney Island, "The Swimming's Fine at Coney Island" 2
Menu, Coney Island, Feltmans Arcade Restaurant, Schlitz Beer adv, 1943 ...50
Mug, Disneyland, "Disneyland Hotel/ Stromboli's Ristorante," restaurant logo on front, Disneyland Hotel log with Tinkerbell on back, mkd "Homer Laughlin China," 1980s, 3.5" h 50
Pinback Button, Atlantic City, multi-colored, woman in red bathing suit playfully splashing water towards male swimmer, swimmers and build-ings in background, 1911, 1.25" d 75

Souvenir Program and Guide Book, Steel Pier, Atlantic City, NJ, 16 pp, 1945, 8.5 x 11", $18.

Pinback Button, Atlantic City, "Ye Olde Mill," multicolored, amusemark park ride with people in boats going into and coming out of ride building, early 1900s, 1.25" d 15
Pinback Button, Disneyland, "Walt Disney World 15 Years," red, blue, and yellow on white ground, castle and Epcot Center surrounded by confetti, 3" d 8
Pinback Button, Dorney Park, Alfundo in center "Dorney Park" above, "Alfundo 85th Year/Allentown, PA" below 16
Pinback Button, "Steeplechase Funny Place," celluloid, backpaper mkd "W.F. Miller, New York," early 1900s, .875" d 175
Pitcher, Coney Island, ruby glass, clear base and handle, inscribed "From Jack to Suzie," 1907, 4.5" h 50
Postcard, Asbury Park, "Station and Park," postmarked Aug 24, 1909 3
Postcard, Coney Island, aerial view of the Half Moon Hotel, boardwalk, and beach 7
Postcard, Coney Island, players on stage at Midget City Opera House at Dreamland, used, 1907 20
Postcard, Dorney Park, Swiss Chalet eatery 5
Postcard, Hershey Park, Hershey Beach Park, swimming pool and bath house, postmarked 1938 3
Ribbon, Coney Island, double, metal and celluloid top, red, white, and blue top ribbon with disk depicting profile of firefighter, bottom ribbon inscribed "21st Annual Convention N.Y.S.F. Asso'n Coney Island Aug. 15, 16, 17, & 18, 1893," heavy paper Whitehead & Hoag Co paper label on back, 8.25" l, 2.675" w 50
Souvenir Folder, Asbury Park and Ocean Grove, NJ, 18 color fold-out views, unused, 1938 9
Ticket Book, Dorney Park, dated 1968, printed by National Ticket Co, Shamokin, PA 20
Ticket Roll, Chesapeake Beach, MD, good for ride on carousel or coaster, 11¢ value 25
Token, Asbury Park 1

ANGELS

Angels were flying high in the mid-1990s. Angels and angel collectibles made the cover of Time and were the subject of a primetime network television series. Some saw it as divine provenance. Others argued it was nothing more than a decorating craze.

There will always be a heavenly chorus of angel collectors, albeit somewhat reduced in size at the moment. Christmas-theme angel collectibles sell well.

Clubs: Angels Collectors' Club of America, 12225 S. Potomac St., Phoenix, AZ 85044; National Angel Collectors' Club, P.O. Box 1847, Annapolis, MD 21404.

Figurine, 4 angels, each holding letter
    to spell out "Noel," 3.5" h 50
Figurine, Goebel, Christmas Angels,
    1 in pink playing harp, other in blue
    playing trumpet, 1976, 3" h, price
    for set of 2 18
Figurine, Josef Originals, 1 blowing
    trumpet, other plugging his ears, hp,
    4.5" h 30
Figurine, Napcoware, #X-6964, 1 angel
    holding Christmas wreather, other
    holding bell, sticker mkd "Napcoware
    Import-Japan" with "N" 12
Ornament, Bradford Exchange, Heaven's
    Little Angels, Loving Kindness, Gentle
    Guardian, and Garden Miracle, price
    for set of 3 15

Limited Edition Plate, Goebel/M.I. Hummel, Germany, Heavenly Angel, 1971, $500.

Ornament, felt, yellow and pink, green
    accent stars, c1950-60s, price for
    pair 5
Ornament, plastic, 1950s 3
Ornament, plastic head, lifelike curly
    hair, gold foil wings, gold cardboard
    skirt covered in net with trim, 3.5" h . . .9
Plate, Avon, angels decorating tree,
    1995, MIB 3
Postcard, 4 angels by tree with candles,
    1 angel holding bell, mkd "Geman-
    American Novelty Art Series No. 1056,
    Printed in Germany," postmarked
    Dec 22, 1909 4
Postcard, star above 2 angels, emb,
    gold highlights, Belgium, used, 1908 . . .5
Salt and Pepper Shakers, pr, ceramic,
    stamped "Japan" on bottom, 4" h 20

ANIMAL DISHES, COVERED

Covered animal dishes were a favorite of housewives during the first half of the 20th century. Grandmother Rinker and her sisters had numerous hens on nest scattered throughout their homes. They liked the form. It did not make any difference how old or new they were. Reproductions and copycats abound. You have to be alert for these late examples.

Look for unusual animals and forms. Many early examples were enhanced through hand-painted decorations. Pieces with painting in excellent condition command a premium.

Bunny, picket fence base, chocolate,
    5" h 20
Bunny, picket fence base, marbleized
    green and white, 5" h 20
Camel, malachite, 6" h 30
Bunny, picket fence base, milk glass . . .15
Cat in Hamper, malachite, 5" h 25
Cat, ribbed base, black amethyst, 5" h . . .15
Cat, ribbed base, carnival glass,
    tangerine, 5" h .18
Hen on Nest, carnival glass, Bermuda
    blue, 3" h 14
Hen on Nest, carnival glass, golden
    honey 13
Hen on Nest, carnival glass, green
    opalescent 13
Hen on Nest, carnival glass, tangerine . .15

Hen on Nest, white milk glass, 6.875" l, $50.

Hen on Nest, champagne opalescent . . .12
Hen on Nest, chocolate, 3" h 15
Hen on Nest, marbleized cobalt blue
   and white 13
Hen on Nest, custard 12
Hen on Nest, golden honey 13
Hen on Nest, green opalescent 12
Hen on Nest, jade 14
Hen on Nest, jade, hp dec 17
Hen on Nest, red .15
Lion, ribbed base, chocolate, 5" h 20
Open Neck Swan, woven nest, marble-
   ized green and white, 5" h 20
Pintail Duck, woven nest, marbleized
   red-orange and white, 5" h 20
Pintail Duck, woven nest, vaseline, 5" h .20
Pony, ribbed base, carnival glass, mala-
   chite, 5" h 25
Rooster, ribbed base, carnival glass,
   cranberry ice, 5" h 15
Rooster, standing, carnival glass,
   golden honey, 5" h 20
Rooster, standing, cobalt blue, white
   head 30
Rooster, standing, cranberry ice 15
Rooster, standing, vaseline 20

ANIMAL FIGURES

Animal collectors are a breed apart. Collecting is a love affair. As long as their favorite animal is pictured or modeled, they are more than willing to buy the item. In many cases, they own real life counterparts to go with their objects. My son's menagerie includes a cat, dog, tarantula, lovebird, two rabbits, a Golden Ball python, and three tanks of tropical fish.

Note: See Breyer Horses and Cat, Cow, Dog, Elephant, Frog, Horse, Owl, and Pig Collectibles for additional listings.

Baby Bear, sun colored, New Martins-
   ville 35
Baby Chicks, New Martinsville 45
Bear, Aldon, 1973, 4" h 3
Bird, orange, Viking Glass, 10" h 45
Bunny, opalescent, hp dec, Fenton, 3" h . .5
Duckling, opalescent, hp dec, Fenton,
   3.5" h 5
Fighting Rooster, L E Smith, 9" h 20
Gazelle, Heisey 1,500
Goose, Duncan Miller 175
Goose, wings half up, Heisey 80
Goose, wings up, Heisey 125
Hen, New Martinsville 75
Lamb, Ceramic Arts Studio, 4.25" h,
   3.5" l 24
Mama Bear, New Martinsville 225
Owl, glass eyes, dark blue frosted,
   Westmoreland 35
Owl, KPM, 3.75" h 6
Pheasant, #6042, head down, 12" h,
   16" l 450
Pheasant, head turned, blue, 12" l 175
Piglet, standing, Heisey 150
Plug Horse, Heisey 115
Pony, standing, Heisey 100
Pouter Pigeon, crystal, Westmoreland,
   2.5" h 25
Rhino, Aldon, 1974, 3.5" h, 7" l 3
Robin on Stump, crystal, Haley Glass . . .25
Squirrel, hp face, hands, feet, and
   jacket, 2" h 22
Squirrel, New Martinsville 45
Swan, crystal, Duncan Miller, 7" h 10

Bird, Royal Dux, Czechoslovakian, 8.5" h, 17" l, $225.

Armadillo, ceramic, gray, unmkd, 7" l, $6.

Swan, crystal, Duncan Miller, 10" h 40
Swordfish, Duncan Miller 250
Thrush, crystal, Haley Glass 20
Thrush, crystal frosted, Haley Glass 30
Thrush, robin's-egg blue frosted, Haley
  Glass 40
Wolfhound, New Martinsville 85

APPLIANCES, ELECTRICAL

Nothing illustrates our ability to take a relatively simple task—e.g. toast a piece of bread—and create a wealth of different methods for achieving it quite like a toaster. Electrical appliances are viewed as one of the best documents of stylistic design in utilitarian form.

Collectors tend to concentrate on one form. Toasters are the most commonly collected, largely because several books have been written about them. Electric fans have a strong following. Waffle irons are pressing toasters for popularity. Modernistic collectors seek bar drink blenders from the 1930s through the 1950s.

Clubs: Old Appliance Club, P.O. Box 65, Ventura, CA 93002; Porcelier Collectors Club, 21 Tamarac Swamp Rd., Wallingford, CT 06492; Upper Crust: The Toaster Collectors Assoc., P.O. Box 529, Temecula, CA 92593.

Blender, Eskimo Whiz Mix, 1940-50s . . .100
Blender, Oster, Model 10, beehive base,
  glass canister 12
Blender, Oster, Model 403 17
Blender, Ronson Cook and Blend, push-
  button, 1960s .75
Blender, Waring, Model 702 60
Blender, Westinghouse, plastic,
  1950-60s 50

Waffle Iron, General Electric, #119W4, chrome plated ext, Bakelite handles, cast aluminum int, 12" w, $35.

Coffee Maker, Westbend, anodized
  aluminum, 1950s 10
Egg Cooker, Hankscraft, chrome lid,
  1940-50s 20
Egg Cooker, Manning Bowman, chrome-
  plated 15
Toaster, Sunbeam, chrome, Bakelite
  base and handles 15
Toaster, Sunbeam, Model 0's Sunbeam
Toaster Model T-20B , black Bakelite
  base, feet, and handles, Art Deco
  design on front and back 10
Toaster, Toastmaster, Model 1-A-1,
  1-slice, serial #370622 20
Toaster, Toast-O-Lator, Long Island City,
  NY, chrome, Bakelite handles. 9.5" h,
  12" l, 4.75" w 60
Toaster, Universal Side Swing, Landers,
  Frary & Clark, Model E9471920 25

Toaster, Protos, chrome plated, 7.25" w, 6.875" h, $35.

ASHTRAYS

Most price guides include ashtrays under advertising. The problem is that there are a number of terrific ashtrays in shapes that have absolutely nothing to do with advertising. Ashtrays get a separate category from me.

With the nonsmoking movement in high gear, the ashtray is an endangered species. The time to collect them is now.

Advertising, Coca-Cola, tin or aluminum tray, litho brown wood grain finish, white rim inscription, 4.5" d 15

Advertising, Cutty Sark, glass, 2.25 x 2.375", MIB 1

Advertising, Del Webb Hotels, glass, amber, 4.5" d 2

Advertising, Pennsylvania Tires, hard rubber, figural tire centered by transparent green glass tray with logo and inscription "Pennsylvania Tires," 1920-30s, 6.25" d 30

Advertising, Pontiac, ceramic, "Pontiac Fine Car," cartoon-style Pontiac chieftain depicted in robe seated against tree stump, underside incised "Pontiac Fleet Sales," 1960s, 5.5" h, 4.5 x 7" base 75

Advertising, Viceroy, ceramic, 2 rests, blue inscription "Smoke Viceroy for that Real Tobacco Taste" with red underline, red and gold star logo symbol, mkd "Salem Pottery #56Z," 5.25" d, .75" h 8

Advertising, Bottle Gas Co., clear glass, center decal, 4.5" w, $4.

Anchor Hocking, green, 4.75" sq 2

Ceramic, boomerang, red speckled, small boomerang center design, c1950s, 12.5" l 15

Chalkware, genies, seated male and female, painted black, pink, and gold, circular depression between legs holds glass insert, 1940s, price for pair 40

Chintz, stacking, set of 4 in holder, 4.5" w 15

Commemorative, Apollo XVII, ceramic, center full color image of emblem for lunar landing Dec 7-19, 1972, 5.5" d ...10

Delft Porcelain, dutch shoes, orig box, 1950s, 2" h, 5.25" l, 2.25" w, price for pair 5

Holt-Howard, Christmas tree 2

Made in Japan, collie, 5.5" d 3

Made in Japan, donkey and cart, 4.5" h ..4

Oakland Raiders, ceramic, white, silver and black helmet in center, gold trim, 4.5" d 8

Occupied Japan, porcelain, emb floral dec, mkd, 2.75" d 2

Occupied Japan, stacking, set of 4, elephant motif, 3 x 2.25" 20

Pressed Glass, scottie dog, emb, frosted, 2.5" d 3

Royal Copley, ducks, Royal Windsor smoking set, 4.5 x 2.5" 8

Royal Haeger, greenish-blue spatter, mkd "R1719 USA," 12" l, 7" w 5

Souvenir, glass, "Duluth Minnesota," boat and lake scene, felt bottom, orig box, 3" d, price for set of 4 5

AUTOGRAPHS

Collecting autographs is a centuries' old hobby. A good rule to follow is the more recognizable the person, the more likely the autograph is to have value. Content is a big factor in valuing autograph material. A clipped signature is worth far less than a lengthy handwritten document by the same person.

Before spending big money for an autograph, have it authenticated. Many movie and sports stars have secretaries and other individuals sign their material, especially photographs. An "autopen" is a machine that can sign up to a dozen documents at one time. The best proof that a signature is authentic is to get it from the person who stood and watched the celebrity sign it.

Clubs: The Manuscript Society, 350 N. Niagara St., Burbank, CA 95105; Universal Autograph Collectors Club, P.O. Box 6181, Washington, DC 20044.

Newsletter: *The Autograph Review,* 305 Carlton Rd, Syracuse, NY 13207.

Periodicals: *Autograph Collector,* 510-A S. Corona Mall, Corona, CA 92879; *Autograph Times,* 1125 W. Baseline Rd. #2-153-M, Mesa, AZ 85210.

Agnew, Spiro, inauguration invitation, inked signature, with envelope, 1969 150
Bush, George, cocktail napkin, ball-point pen signature, imprinted "Aboard the Presidential aircraft" beneath print of Presidential seal 550
Carmichael, Hoagy, photo, casual pose, 8 x 10" 250
Crabbe, Buster, photo, smiling portrait pose in business suit, black and white, 8 x 10" 65
Crichton, Michael, postcard photo from Jurassic Park, color, 7 x 5" 60
Durante, Jimmy, photo, smiling portrait pose, "To Bernard/my best always/ your pal Jimmy Durante," 5 x 7" 125
Eisenhower, Julie and David, photo, black and white, dated 1991, 8 x 10" . .75

Larry Siple, plastic car with NFL decal and Dolphins' helmet, signed on helmet, mkd "Sportstoy by Orange Prod., Chatham, NJ," 3.5" l, 3" h, $25.

Eisenhower, Mamie, photo, smiling portrait pose, ink signature, 8 x 10" . .100
Garcia, Jerry, album, Go to Heaven 350
Greco, Joe, photo, full action, sepia publicity pose, 8 x 10" 75
Grey, Zane, bank check, 1931 200
Hellman, Lillian, program cover, Forrest Theatre, black ink signature 50
Howard, Ron, window card, for Huckleberry Finn, Howard seated on barrel, fishing, signature on lower blank, 10 x 15" 100
Kelly, Grace, card, imprinted "La Princesse de Monaco," inscribed "Many thanks for a wonderful evening and the beautiful red roses, Affectionately Grace," orig hand-written envelope, 5 x 4" 500
Ketchum, Hank, orig green ink sketch of smiling Dennis the Menace and snarling Donald Duck, inscribed "for Frank," 5 x 3" 150
Lee, Gypsy Rose, program, Biography, blue ink signature above image 200
Lord, Jack, letter, both sides of Regency Hotel stationery, 1985 90
Mead, Margaret, newsphoto, article signed under her image 55
Merrill, Dick, First Day Cover honoring Amelia Earhart, 1936 60
Neiman, LeRoy, photo, casual portrait pose, black and white, 8 x 10" 75
Parks, Rosa, card, ink signature, 5 x 3" . .75
Penner, Joe, album page, "You Wanna Buy a Duck," 6 x 4" 30
Porter, Cole, album page, ink signature .225
Ringling, John, ticket/pass, imprinted at top "Ringling Bros. and Barnum & Bailey combined show/Pass... Season 1924," black ink signature . .550
Ruth, Babe, photo, Ruth and wife on Yankees Opening Day, Apr 20, 1939, inscribed "To June/Babe Ruth," black and white, 9 x 7" 750
Sinatra, Frank, album page, blue fountain pen signature 375
Walker, Alice, bookplate, *The Temple of My Familiar,* green ink signature . . .55
Wood, Natalie, photo, smiling, full pose in checked playsuit, black and white, 8 x 10" 550
Young, Brigham, paper, ink signature, 5 x 2" 650

AUTOMOBILE COLLECTIBLES

An automobile swap meet is 25% cars and 75% car parts. Restoration and rebuilding of virtually all car models is a never-ending process. The key is to find the exact part needed. Too often, auto parts at flea markets are not priced. The seller is going to judge how badly he thinks you want the part before setting the price. You have to keep your cool.

Two areas that are attracting outside collector interest are promotional toy models and hood ornaments. The former have been caught up in the craze for 1950s and 1960s Japanese tin. The latter have been discovered by the art community, who view them as wonderful examples of modern streamlined design.

Clubs: Hubcap Collectors Club, P.O. Box 54, Buckley, MI 49620; Spark Plug Collectors of America, 9 Heritage Ln., Simsbury, CT 96070.

Periodicals: *Car Toys,* 7950 Deering Ave., Canoga Park, CA 91304; *Hemmings Motor News,* P.O. Box 100, Rt. 9 W. Bennington, VT 05201; *PL8S: The License Plate Collector's Hobby Magazine,* P.O. Box 222, East Texas, PA 18046.

Note: See Road Maps for additional listings.

Battery Charger, GE Tungar, metal, orig
   paper litho box with instructions,
   8" h, 6" w, 6" d .120
Booklet, New Chevrolet Six, sepiatone
   centerfold photo of 4-door sedan,
   16 pp, c1930s, 6.75 x 9" 15
Bulb Kit, Packard, tin, 6 assorted bulbs,
   4" l, 3.5" w 300
Can, Red Indian Motor Oil, tin, McColl-
   Frontenac Oil Co Limited, 6.5" h, 4" d . .70
Catalog, Buick, Story of the Greatest
   Buick Ever Built," illus, 64 pp, 1926,
   7.5 x 10" 15
Catalog, La Salle, illus, 24 pp, 1927,
   9.5 x 12" 50
Floor Creeper, wood, cobra decal on top,
   Craftsman, Sears and Roebuck, 1960s,
   36" l, 16" w 28
Gas Globe, Marathon Super M, glass
   body, 1 lens, 13.5" d 100

Gas Globe, Skelly Supreme, plastic
   body, 2 lenses, 13.5" d 165
Key Ring Fob, oval, silvered brass,
   depicts early taxi , reverse incised
   "1756," with "Detroit Taxicar &
   Transfer Co," early 1920s 35
Lens Set, Golden Rule, fired on lettering
   and design, 13.5" d 250
License Plate, Iowa, 1930-60s 5
License Plate, Maine, solid brass,
   polished, missing paint, 1948 10
License Plate Attachment, cast metal,
   "Bradenton Fla/The Friendly City,"
   silver luster with blue accent and
   green palm tree, c1940s, 4.5 x 12" 15
Map, Nevada, 1946 15
Map Rack, metal, plastic fronts, 43" h,
   22.5" w, 12" d 110
Mileage Tag, Shell Motor Oil, diecut
   stiff paper, red and orange emblem
   beneath key chain loop, 1930s 8
Pocket Mirror, Socony Motor Gasoline,
   celluloid over metal, Standard Oil Co,
   NY, 3.5" d 70
Seat Belt, Phillips 66, blue, orig box
   with instructions 20
Sign, tin, Ford, "Motorcraft Batteries,"
   red and black on white enamel,
   unused, c1960s, 18 x 24" 15
Spark Plug, Lodge HNLP, 14mm 5
Spark Plug, Tru-Fire 8
Thermometer, Motorcraft Shock
   Absorber, diecut plastic, tan shock
   absorber within white margin,1970s,
   3.75 x 14.5" 8
Tire Rack, tin, wire rack, Atlas Supply
   Co, 8.5" h, 13" w, 10" d 55

Hood Ornament, chrome Art Deco nude with yellow plastic wings, mkd "511" on base, 9" h, 7.5" l, $75.

AUTO RACING

Man's quest for speed is as old as time. Automobile racing dates before the turn of the century. Many of the earliest races took place in Europe. By the first decade of the 20th century, automobile racing was part of the American scene.

The Indianapolis 500 began in 1911 and was interrupted only by World War II. In addition to Formula 1 racing, the NASCAR circuit has achieved tremendous popularity with American racing fans. Cult heroes such as Richard Petty have become house-hold names.

Although interest in Indy 500 collectibles remains strong, the current market is dominated by NASCAR collectibles. Beware of paying premium prices for items made within the last 20 years. In addition, copycat, fantasy and contemporary limited edition items are being introduced into the market as quickly as they can be absorbed. A shake-out appears to be years in the future. In the interim, check your engine and gear up for fast action.

Clubs: St. Petersburg, FL 33733; National Indy 500 Collectors Club, 10505 N. Delaware St, Indianapolis, IN 46280; The National Racing Club, 615 Hwy. A1A North, Ste. 105, Ponte Vedra Beach, FL 32082.

Newsletter: *Quarter Milestones,* 53 Milligan Ln., Abbeville, MS 38601.

Periodical: *RACE Magazine,* P.O. Box 716, Kannapolis, NC 28082.

Advertising Trade Card, Lyos Maid Tea, Stirling Moss, Famous People Tea Card series, J Lyons & Co Ltd, l#25 4
Ashtray, ceramic, Indianapolis Motor Speedway, speedway logo and illus, "Marmon Wasp, 1911 Winner/A. J. Foyt, Jr. 4 Time Winner," sticker mkd "Made In Japan," 4 x 10 x .75" 18
Book, *1969 Auto Racing Guide,* records, schedules, and track diagrams, dealer sample, 96 pp 10
Book, *AAA Contest Board Activity and Press Reference Book,* track records, Indy, Sprintcar, Midget, and Stockcar results, Sam Hanks on cover, 86 pp . .20

Book, *Auto Racing USA 1986 Year in Review* 3
Decanter, clear, "Penske Racing" on front, lists Indianapolis winners from 1977-88 on back 3
Game, Speedway Motor Race, Smith Kline & French Co, Philadelphia, 1930s 50
Lobby Card, Born to Speed, 1946 25
Lobby Card, High Gear, 11 x 14" 20
Magazine, *Auto Racing,* Jun 1967 8
Magazine, *Cavalcade of Auto Racing,* May 1969, 47 pp 3
Pennant, Michael Waltrip, 12 x 30" 6
Photograph, Nutmeg State Special, race car and driver, sepia tone, 1920s 40
Photograph, Peter Kreis and Aaron Vance at Indianapolis Motor Speed-way, black and white, 8 x 10" 5
Postcard, Indianapolis 500, "The start-500 mile sweepstakes, Indianapolis, Ind," 1934 15
Program, Indy 500, Al Unser United States Auto Club, Duquoin State Fair, #13, 1969 15
Program, White Sox Speedway, Los Angeles, midget races, 6 pp, 7.75 x 11" 40
Sign, "Indy 500/Sterling Beer," card-board, emb silver border centered by "Sterling Pure Beer" at bottom, "1974 Johnny Rutherford Av. Spd. 158.589 MPH," center full color photo of Rutherford posed by racing car, 14.5" d 15

Poster, Miller High Life Racing, facsimile signatures of Bobby Allison and Bobby Hillin Jr., biographies and driver and car specifications on back, Miller Brewing Co., 8 x 10", $5.

Yearbook, *Official USAC Auto Racing Yearbook*, 1972 .3

AUTUMN LEAF

The Hall China Co. developed Autumn Leaf china as a dinnerware premium for the Jewel Tea Co. in 1933. The giveaway was extremely successful. The "Autumn Leaf" name did not originate until 1960. Previously, the pattern was simply known as "Jewel" or "Autumn." Autumn Leaf remained in production until 1978.

Pieces were added and dropped from the line over the years. Limited production pieces are most desirable. Look for matching accessories in glass, metal and plastic made by other companies. Jewel Tea toy trucks were also made.

Club: National Autumn Leaf Collector's Club, P.O. Box 162961, Fort Worth, TX 76161.

Baker, fluted .13
Berry Bowl 3
Bread and Butter Plate, 6" d 3
Cake Tin 45
Casserole, cov, 2 qt, 5.5" h 15
Cereal Bowl, 8.25" d 6
Clock, 9.125" d .45
Coasters, set of 4 5
Coffeepot, stamped "Kitchenware,"
  13" h 35
Creamer, Rayed, 4.5" h 20
Cup and Saucer .10

Ball Jug, $35. —Photo courtesy Ray Morykan Auctions.

Custard Dish, 3.5" d 5
Dessert Bowl 6
Dinner Plate, 8" d 12
Fruit Bowl, 5.5" d 5
Gravy Boat 25
Grease Jar, cov, 3" h 16
Luncheon Plate, 9" d 5
Marmalade Bowl, with underplate 12
Mixing Bowl, 6" d 8
Mixing Bowl, 8.75" d, 4.75" h 16
Milk Pitcher, 5.75" h 16
Pie Plate, 9.5" d .5
Pitcher, 6" h 12
Plate, 7.25" d 7
Plate, 10" d 10
Platter, 11.5" l .25
Pot Holders, pr .8
Ramekin, 2" h, 4" d 15
Range Salt and Pepper Shakers, pr, 4" h .15
Salt and Pepper Shakers, pr, Ruffled,
  2.5" h 22
Soup Bowl, 8.25" d 12
Stacking Bowl, 6.5" d, 3.5" h 6
Sugar, cov 16
Teapot, Aladdin, gold dec, 6" h 50
Thermos, 12" h, 8" d 75
Vegetable Bowl, oval, 10.5" l 15

AVON

Avon products, with the exception of California Perfume Co. material, are not found often at flea markets any longer. The 1970s were the golden age of Avon collectibles. There are still a large number of dedicated collectors, but the legion that fueled the pricing fires of the 1970s has been hard hit by desertions. Avon material today is more likely to be found at garage sales than at flea markets.

Club: National Assoc. of Avon Collectors, Inc., P.O. Box 7006, Kansas City, MO 64113.

Periodical: *Avon Times,* P.O. Box 9868, Kansas City, MO 64134.

Cape Cod, cake plate, 10.75" d, 3.25" h . . .42
Cape Cod, cake server 15
Cape Cod, champagne glass, price for
  pair 20
Cape Cod, creamer and sugar, MIB 10
Cape Cod, dessert plate, 7.25" d 12
Cape Cod, dinner plate, 10.75" d 12

Owl, bottle, frosted white glass, gold foil eyes, $5.

Cape Cod, hostess bell, MIB 6
Cape Cod, pie plate server, 10.875" l 22
Cape Cod, vase, orig box, 7.75" h 15
Cape Cod, water pitcher 30
Cape Cod, wine goblet, price for set of 4 .6
Cookbook, *A Celebration of American Cooking*, Jul 4, 1978, 96 pp, 8.5 x 11" . . .3
Corvette Stingray, Wild Country After Shave, green glass, orig box, 1965 5
Figurine, Summer Fun, Jessie Willcox Smith Collection, 1986, 3.75" h, MIB . .12
Frog, sachet holder, 1982 5
Gaylord Gator Soapdish, 1967 3
Great Catch Charlie Brown, soap holder with soap, orig box 5
Hippo Decanter, 1970s 1
Little Miss Lollipop Double Dip Sundae, 1968 3
Mr Presto Change-O 3
Mug, milk glass, Charlie Brown, 1969, 3.5" h 4
Owl, American Wildlife Bronze Collection, 1985, 3" h 10
Parakeet, Moonwind Cologne, 5" h 3
Piano, Tai Winds After Shave, orig box, 1972 1
Rapture Talcum Powder, 5.5" h 6
Small World Gigi Perfume Doll, 1970s, 5" h 6
Sniffy Pin Pal, 1970s 20
Snowman Perfume Pin, 1974 5
Stein, Great American Baseball, 1984 . . .18
Strawberry Bath Gelee, ruby colored glass, 4" h, 2.75" w 4
Turtle, Perfume Glacé, goldtone, rhinestone eyes, orig box, 1971 10
Viking Horn, dark amber glass, gold colored cap and dec, 7 oz, empty, 1966 3
Water Goblet, blue, George Washington medallion on front, 1976 4

BADGES

Have you ever tried to save a name tag or badge that attaches directly to your clothing or fits into a plastic holder? We are victims of a throwaway society. This is one case in which progress has not been a boon for collectors.

Fortunately, our grandparents and great-grandparents loved to save the membership, convention, parade and other badges that they acquired. The badges' colorful silk and cotton fabric often contained elaborate calligraphic lettering and lithographed scenes in combination with celluloid and/or metal pinbacks and pins. They were badges of honor. They had an almost military quality about them.

Look for badges with attached three-dimensional miniatures. Regional value is a factor. I found a great Emmaus, PA, badge priced at $2 at a flea market in Florida: back home, its value is more than $20.

Balloon Aviators Reunion, brass hanger bar with insert typewritten paper slip name of participant, attached ribbon holding celluloid pin for 5th annual reunion in Cleveland of "ABCV" with hot air balloon, 1936 40
Chauffeur, silvered brass, "Illinois Licensed Chauffeur, state seal under "Licensed Chauffeur" designation above engraved serial number "27953," bottom tip mkd "Illinois 1920" 8
Coolidge Nominating Convention, brass bar pin, attached medal for "Usher" at Republican National Convention, 1924, 1.5 x 5" 15
Employee, Coca-Cola, celluloid, "Ask Me," ice chest cooler and case holding bottles, 1930-40, 2.5" d 35
Employee, Indian Refining Co, silvered brass, red accent porcelain enamel image of running Indian, silvered lettering, Whitehead & Hoag, 1930s, 1.5 x 2" 75
Employee, Liberty Aircraft, dark luster metal, clear Plexiglas over black and white photo within orange oval paper rim, identification beneath photo mkd "Aten Co," 1930s 10

Employee, Pep Boys, diecut stiff plastic,
raised relief fleshtone image of
Manny, Moe, and Jack, red and blue
on ivory, 1960s 15
Hat, "Sunoco Dealer," diecut brass,
blue enamel inscriptions and border
accent, Balfour, 1930s 175
Indiana Democratic State Convention,
Indianapolis, Jun 25, 1946, silvered
brass hanger and medallion depicts
FDR with name above "Carry On" 35
Junior Stewardess Nurse/Vista-Dome
North Coast Limited, diecut yellow
plastic, center logo and "Vista Dome,"
1950s 20
Junior World's Fair Fireman, diecut
brass shield, blue and orange enamel
accents, center image of Trylon and
Perisphere, 1939 35
Prohibition National Convention,
celluloid bar hanger with "Delegate,"
2-sided with female angel and 2 city
buildings in Indianapolis, color
Indiana state logo on reverse,
attached red, white, and blue fabric
ribbon, 2 x 6" overall size 20
Taxi Driver, brass, octagonal,
"Middletown Taxi Driver," 1951 8
Veteran Firemen's, silvered brass,
center image of primitive pumper,
inscribed "Veteran Firemen's
Association" 20
Vigilant Fire Co, brass, engraved
"Vigilant" on hanger bar, pendant
depicts firefighting symbols with
inscription for company #2 of
Columbia, PA 15

*Pittsburgh Police, silvered brass, copper
"612," 3.125" h, $15. —Photo courtesy
Collectors Auction Services.*

BAKELITE

This is a great example of a collecting
category gone price-mad. Bakelite is a
trademark used for a variety of synthetic
resins and plastics used to manufacture
colorful, inexpensive, ulitarian objects. The
key word is inexpensive. That can also be
interpreted as cheap. There is nothing
cheap about Bakelite collectibles in today's
market. Collectors, especially those from
large metropolitan areas who consider
themselves design-conscious, want
Bakelite in whatever form they can find.

Buy a Bakelite piece because you love
it. The market has already started to collapse for commonly found material. Can the
high-end pieces be far behind?

Alarm Clock, Westclox, blue case, brass
trim, 4.75" h, 5.125" w 20
Bracelet, black, applied silver, crystal,
and black dec, open back cuff style,
1940s 20
Bracelet, orange marmalade, 3" d 5
Brooch, red, 6 cherries hanging from
piece of wood, 2.875" h, 2.5" w 55
Button, brown, figural horse, carved
main and tail 2
Child's Spoon, green Bakelite handle,
5" l 30
Cigarette Case, black, clear lucite,
5 x 4" 25
Cigarette Holder, multicolored, 4.75" l 5
Clip Pin, carved flower, dark olive, black,
and gold, 2" l, 1.5" w 35
Clock, marbled red, ivory dot inlay,
New Haven, 2.75" sq 500
Dress Clip, caramel, carved, black
beads inserted at top, 2.5" w, 2" l 10
Flatware, 16 pcs, butterscotch 40
Hatpin, marbleized green with rhine-
stone dec, 4" l 10
Humidor, 6" h, 4.25" w 7
Napkin Ring, bird, red, green beak, 3" h .75
Necklace, red, black, green, and yellow
beads, divided by celluloid rings,
12" l 225
Pin, heart shaped, applied wire "Mother"
across front, 1.5 x 1.5" 5
Pin, heart shaped, cream, painted floral
dec, couple kissing in center, mkd
"Occupied Japan" 8

Flashlights, Steward R. Brown, 1940, price each, $30.

Radio, Motorola, model 58G1, 6.625" h,
    10.25" l, 5.5" w .25
Radio, Truetone, model D2102A, white . . .8
Radio, Zenith, model G725, 1950 20
Razor, Schick, Bakelite handle, butter-
    scotch 8
Salt and Pepper Shakers, pr, marbleized
    butterscotch, 1.5" h 50
Smoking Set, pipe, cigar holder, and
    cigarette holder, orange and brown,
    Art Deco style, orig hinged 4 x 7"
    presentation case 30
Thermometer, First National Bank of
    Berwick 10

BANDANNAS

Women associate bandannas with keeping their hair in place. Men visualize stage coach holdups or rags used to wipe the sweat from their brows. Neither approach recognizes the colorful and decorative role played by the bandanna.

Some of the earliest bandannas are political. By the turn of the century, bandannas joined pillow cases as the leading souvenir textile found at sites, ranging from beaches to museums. Hillary Weiss's *The American Bandanna: Culture on Cloth from George Washington to Elvis* (Chronicle Books, 1990), provides a visual feast for this highly neglected collecting area.

The bandanna played an important role in the Scouting movement, serving as a neckerchief for both Boy Scouts and Girl Scouts. Many special neckerchiefs were issued. There is also a close correlation between scarves and bandannas. Bandanna collectors tend to collect both.

1964-65, New York World's Fair, sheer
    fabric, blue border, central Unisphere
    with Pool of Industry, Helaport,
    Monorail, General Electric Exhibition,
    Swiss Sky Ride, Spanish Pavillion,
    and New York City skyline, 28 x 28" . . .15
Atomic Bomb Proving Grounds, mush-
    room cloud rising from test detonation
    near Las Vegas, NV, 1940s, 27 x 27" . . .50
Autry, Gene, sheer fabric, 1940s, 5 x 5.5"
    folded size 75
Boy Scout, Camperee, light gray fabric,
    inked inscription "Mason and Dixon,"
    diecut leather slide fastener, 29 x
    29 x 36 15
California, sheer fabric, state of
    California and tourist attractions,
    state flag, Hollywood scene, Rose
    Bowl, and symbol for Golden Gate
    International Exposition, 19.5 x 20" . . .35
Dempsey, Jack, silk, center blue image
    and border designs, 1930s, 16.5 x
    16.5" 35
Disneyland, white silk-type fabric,
    center outline of California with illus
    of attractions and landmarks with
    text, c1950s, 17.5 x 28" 20
Harrison, Benjamin, silk, inscription
    "Protection To American Labor and
    American Industries," red, white,
    and blue, 20 x 20" 75

Calgary Alberta, multicolored scenes of Central Park, rodeo, Calgary Zoo, and Brahma bull riding, 30.5" h, 31" w, $600.
—Photo courtesy Collectors Auction Services.

Hopalong Cassidy and Topper, dark
green fabric, 1950s, 36" l 35

Howdy Doody, linen, white, inked red,
yellow, blue, and fleshtone, western
scene depicts Dilly Dally and Flub-A-
Dub as fence rail spectators to
Howdy's bronc ride, ©Bob Smith,
1948-51, 9 x 9" .15

Korean War, silk, sheer white, colorful
inked "Thanks To U. N. Forces," flags
of United Nations, Korea, US, and
Great Britain, lower left dated 1951,
11 x 13" 35

Korean War, silk, sheer white, printed
colorful insignia for 11th Airborne,
jet fighter plane, fleshtone image of
nude flying female with spinning
propeller blade on each breast,
inscription "Sappro Hokkaido Japan,"
woven small floral pattern in corner,
early 1950s, 11.5 x 12" 15

Paris Expo, linen, light brown, stitched
image of USA building in white, brown,
green, red, and blue, stitched red
inscription "Exposition Internationale
Paris 1937," 8.5 x 8.5" 15

Straight Arrow, red fabric, Nabisco
premium, red, white, and blue images
of Straight Arrow, Steve Adams,
Packy, and Fury, with gold-plated
slide, and orig mailing envelope with
coupon for additional bandanna,
1949 75

Truman, Harry S, donkeys in white ovals
on brown ground, white edge trim,
12.75 x 12.75" .15

"V" For Victory, linen, red, white, and
blue, orig gold foil tag mkd "Kimball,"
12 x 12" 40

BANKS, STILL

Banks are classified into two types—
mechanical (action) and still (non-action).
Most mechanical banks found at flea markets today are reproductions. If you find
one that you think is real, check it out in one
of the mechanical bank books before buying it.

The still or non-action bank dominates
the flea market scene. There is no limit to
the methods for collecting still banks. Some
favor type (advertising), others composition

(cast iron, tin, plastic, etc.), figural (shaped
like something) or theme (Western).

Beware of still-bank reproductions.
Most banks were used, so look for wear in
places you would expect to find it. Save
your money and do not buy if you are uncer-
tain of a bank's authenticity.

Club: Still Bank Collectors Club of America,
4175 Millersville Rd, Indianapolis, IN 46205.

Newsletter: *Glass Bank Collector,* P.O. Box
155, Poland, NY 13431.

Advertising, Big Boy, soft vinyl, dark
brown molded hair, fleshtone body,
white shirt, black lettering, mkd
"A product of Big Boy Restaurants
of America," ©1973 Marriott Corp,
8.5" h 15

Advertising, Chicken Delight, hard vinyl,
yellow, orange and brown accents,
1960s, 6" h 75

Advertising, Chip's Hamburgers, ceramic,
figural restaurant, coin slot in rear of
pitched roof, c1950-60s, 2.5 x 4 x 2.5" .75

Advertising, Colonel Dixie, painted
composition, gray hair, red mouth
opening, blue eyes, blue hat with
maroon hatband, black jacket over
maroon vest, white trousers, red
base mkd "at your service, Suh,"
7" h 75

*Cast Iron, Indian chief bust, American,
c1978, 7.875" h, $40.* —Photo courtesy
Gene Harris Antique Auction Center, Inc.

Litho Tin, clown, missing trap, Chein, 5.125" h, $35. —Photo courtesy Collectors Auction Services.

Advertising, Electrolux Refrigerator, cast iron, 4" h, 2" w, 1.5" d 325

Advertising, Icee Bear, soft vinyl, seated, red sweater, light blue cup with raised "Icee," c1970s, 7.5" h 35

Advertising, Pepsi-Cola, figural truck, plastic, 3 plastic carriers on litho tin box, wood wheels, decals on doors and back, 3" h, 7.5" l 250

Advertising, Peter's Weatherbird Shoes, cardboard body, gold colored tin top and bottom, 1 side with bird character and images of boys riding scooter, flying kite, and playing ball, other side depicts girl bird character with girls playing jacks, 1930s, 1.25 x 1.75 x 2" 35

Advertising, Wonder Bread, hard plastic, figural bread loaf, 1.75 x 1.75 x 4.25" . .75

Bicentennial, Uncle Sam Money Bank, hard plastic, figural, wearing red, white, and blue outfit, holding banner with text "200 Years," ©1975 All State Management Corp, 3 x 3 x 10.25" 15

Cast Iron, black policeman, hand on hip, holding night stick in hand, 1930s, 2 x 3 x 5.5" 75

Cast Iron, clown, 4" h 5

Cast Iron, elephant, 3.5" h, 4" l 5

Cast Iron, sailor, saluting, painted bright silver, blue and fleshtone accents, 1900s, 2 x 3 x 5.5" 75

Ceramic, money chest, dark green, raised letters "BSB" on top, "Replica, First Money Chest, 1834/Bowery Savings Bank" on underside, 1950s, 4 x 6 x 3" 15

Ceramic, Uncle Sam, "Uncle Sam Bank" decal on front, 1950s, 3 x 4.5 x 6" 35

Character, Bambi, ceramic, Leeds China Co, c1949, 3 x 4 x 7.25" 50

Character, Daffy Duck, metal, leaning against brown tree, name on base, c1946 150

Character, Klondike Mike, ceramic, white hat and shirt, red vest, blue trousers, name in maroon lettering on hat brim, base front mkd "Edmonton Canada," c1960s, 6.25" h 25

Character, Peppermint Patty, composition, figural, smiling full figure, wearing red and black baseball cap, orange shirt, black shorts and sandals, holding orange bat, gold foil sticker mkd "Korea" on underside, ©1977 United Features Syndicate Inc, Determined Productions Inc, 7" h 15

Character, Smokey Bear, ceramic, full figure, holding hat, bear cub standing next to right leg, other bear cub holding hand of shovel next to left leg, gold accent glitter, c1960, 7" h 75

Character, The Three Bears, hard plastic, yellow images on red base, mkd "Made in U.S.A.," 1950s, 3 x 4.5 x 4" . .20

Commemorative, Remember Pearl Harbor, litho tin, figural drum, Ohio Art Co, 3" d, 2" h 50

Metal, Randolph Trust Co, silver luster, blue and white front celluloid insert centered by black and white photo of bank building in Randolph, MA, circular opening at right end for insertion of rolled currency bills, c1920-30s, 2" h, 3.25" w 35

Political, cardboard and metal canister, paper label with repeated "McGovern Shriver" and slogan "Small Change For Big Changes," 1972, 5" h, 3" d 15

BARBED WIRE

Barbed wire is a farm, Western or military collectible. It is usually collected in 18-inch lengths and mounted on boards for display. While there are a few rare examples that sell in the hundreds of dollars for a piece, the majority of strands are common types that sell between $2 and $5 per sample.

Club: American Barbed Wire Collectors Society, 1023 Baldwin Rd., Bakersfield, CA 93304.

BARBERSHOP & BEAUTY PARLOR

Let's not discriminate. This is the age of the unisex hair salon. This category has been male-oriented for far too long. Haven't you wondered where a woman had her hair done in the 19th century? Don't forget drug store products. Not everyone had the funds or luxury to spend time each day at the barbershop or beauty salon.

Club: National Shaving Mug Collectors Assoc., 320 S. Glenwood St., Allentown, PA 18104.

Barber Pole, wood, metal cap, wooden
  pedestal, 50" h, 5" d 275
Blade Bank, brass plaque, used in
  Pullman car on Lehigh Valley Railroad
  1855-1976, 3.5" l, 1.5" w 35
Blade Bank, ceramic, barber chair,
  5" h 100
Blade Bank, ceramic, barbershop
  quartet, "The Gay Blades!," 4.5" h,
  5" w 100
Blade Bank, ceramic, "Razor Bum,"
  8" h 85
Blade Bank, ceramic, shaving brush,
  mkd "Gustin Company, Van Nuys,
  Calif," 5" h 45
Blade Bank, metal, sloped front, 3" h,
  2" w, 1" d 35
Blade Bank, Palmolive Handy Box, 2" h .35

*Shaving Mug, occupational, architect,
gold trim, $125.*

Blade Bank, wood, "The Old Blade,"
  bottom unscrews to remove blades,
  ©1950 Woodcroftlry Shops Inc,
  5.25" h 65
Bookmark, Mennen Products, celluloid,
  single violet on green leaf and stem,
  centered by miniature black and
  white portrait of A G Mennen, black
  lettering, "Use Mennen's Violet Talcum
  Toilet Powder/Admitted To Be The
  Best," early 1900s, 2.5" l 35
Bottle, Ayer's Hair Vigor, J C Ayer's Co,
  cobalt blue, emb, 7.75 x 2.375 x 1.875" .45
Bottle, Blondex Shampoo, Swedish
  Shampoo Laboratories, NY, orig box,
  price for full box 3
Bottle, Dr Ellis Curlast Wave Set, clear
  glass, silver metal lid, 4.75 oz, 5 x
  2.25 x 1" 10
Bottle, Greasy Kid Stuff, Kid Stuff
  Products Inc, plastic, 4 oz, 5.25 x
  1.875 x 1" 10
Bottle, Huntsman Afterglow Shaving
  Lotion, Magitex Co Inc, clear glass,
  black plastic lid, 6 oz, 4.75 x 3 x 1.5" . . .8
Bottle, West Point Hair Trainer, clear
  glass, red metal lid, 1 pt, 9.25 x 2.5" . . .10
Box, Vicky Victory Hairpin Kit, Smith
  Victory Corp, NY, green, blue, and
  white, blue and white lettering,
  1.75 x 2.25 x .5" 3
Clock, Oster Electric Scalp Massage,
  plastic, metal hands, 16" sq 90
Display, Gillette Razor Blades, diecut
  tin, 1-sided, "Besoin De Lames...?,"
  mkd "G. De Andreis S. A. Marseille
  2657," foreign, 7" h, 5.75" l, 4.5" d 55
Flange Sign, diecut porcelain, 2-sided,
  "Gibb's Barber Shop," Belgium, 24" h,
  16" w 325
Flange Sign, porcelain, "Barber Shop,"
  12" h, 24.125" w 175
Hair Curlers Goody Magnetic Rollers,
  MIP 10
Hair Curlers, Tip-Top Curlers, orig box,
  price for 6 10
Hair Cutter, Playtex, Precision Products,
  International Latex Corp, Dover DE,
  brown clear plastic container contains
  stainless steel cutter, double-edge
  blade, and cleaner brush, orig box . . .15
Hair Net, Cupid Fine Mesh Net, Glemby
  Co, orig 6.5 x 5" envelope 5

Shaving Brush, Ever-Ready, black celluloid handle, dark bristles, orig box, $15.

Barbie is collectible, from the doll to her clothing to her play accessories. Although collectors place the greatest emphasis on Barbie material from the 1950s and 1960s, there is some great stuff from the 1970s and 1980s that should not be overlooked. Whenever possible, try to get original packaging. This is especially important for Barbie material from the 1980s forward.

Club: Barbie Doll Collectors Club International, P.O. Box 586, White Plains, NY 10603.

Periodicals: *Barbie Bazaar,* 5617 6th Ave., Kenosha, WI 53140; *Miller's Barbie Collector,* West One Sumner, #1, Spokane, WA 99204.

Hairpin, Vassar Beautifying Butterflies,
   price for 2 4
Jar, Cru Butch Hair Wax, Lucky Tiger
   Mfg Co, clear glass, white metal lid,
   3.5 oz, 2.875 x 2" 10
Jar, Mr Groom Hair Controller, Rexall
   Drug Co, 3/5 oz, 2.75 x 2.25" 8
Razor, Keen Kutter, metal, green plastic
   handle, 4 x 1.625 x .625" 15
Razor Blade, Ever-Ready Radio Steel
   Safety Razor Blade, American Safety
   Razor Corp, wrapped in blue and
   white paper, depicts man shaving,
   blue and white lettering, 1.5 x .875" 5
Razor Blade, Utility Blade, wrapped in
   orange, blue, and gold paper, gold
   lettering, 1.875 x 1" 5
Sign, porcelain, curved, "Look Better/
   Feel Better," barber pole style, red,
   white, and blue, 24" h, 17" w 175
Tin, Reel Man After Shave Talc, Jolind
   Distributor, NY, 3 x 4.75 x 1" 200
Tray, Sav-Ur-Clip Tray, plastic, yellow,
   orig box 15
Whistle, aluminum, Ellis Barber Shop,
   thimble shaped, red enameled
   inscription band with address for
   sponsoring shop, 1930s 8

BARBIE DOLL COLLECTIBLES

As a doll, Barbie is unique. She burst upon the scene in the late 1950s and has remained a major factor in the doll market for more than 40 years. No other doll has enjoyed this longevity. Every aspect of

CLOTHING AND ACCESSORIES

After Five, #934 70
Ballerina, #989 65
Busy Morning, #956 85
Career Girl, #954 150
Dinner at Eight, #946 85
Fancy Free, #943 .30
Flintstones Funwear Gift Set, 1994 10
Floral Petticoat, #921 30
Garden Party, #931 55
Graduation, #945 45
Ice Breaker, #942 60
Mood For Music, #940 90
Nighty Negligee, #965 60
Rain Coat, #949 .40
Singing in the Shower, #988 75
Registered Nurse, #991 100
Solo in the Spotlight, #982 200
Sorority Meeting, #937 70
Sweet Dreams, #973 45
Winter Holiday, #975 80

DOLLS

Australian Barbie, Dolls of the World
   Series, #3626, 1992 40
Ballerina Cara, #9528, 1975 75
Barbie and the All Stars Midge, #9360 . .40
Busy Francie, #3313, 1971 250
Busy Talking Barbie, #1195, 1971 250
Chris, #3570, 1966 250
Egyptian Queen, Great Eras Series,
   #11397, 1994 .70
Fashion Queen Barbie, #870, 1962 500
Free Moving Barbie, #7270, 1974 65

Ken Doll, #1020, bendable legs, 1965, MIB, $450. Wearing #1401 Special Date outfit, 1964-65, MIB, $150.

Gold Medal Olympic Barbie, #7233, 1974 65
Hawaiian Barbie, #7470, 1975 100
Living Skipper, #1117, 1970 150
Now Look Ken, #9342, 1975 80
Quick Curl Skipper, #4223, 1972 125
Rocker Derek, #2428, 1985 35
Scott, #1019, 1979 65
Skooter, #1040, 1965 125
Standard Barbie, #1190, 1969 300
Stars & Stripes Air Force Barbie, #3360, 1990 45
Sun Valley Barbie, #7806, 1973 125
Sun Valley Ken, #7809, 1973 100
Super Teen Skipper, #2756, 1978 50
Talking Barbie, #1115, 1967 300
Talking P J, #1113, 1969 200
Tiff Pose 'N Play, #1199, 1971 175
Todd, #3590, 1965 175
Twist & Turn Christie, #1119, 1969 250
Walk Lively Steffie, #1183, 1971 165
Wet 'N Wild Steven, #4137, 1989 10

OTHER

Arabian Stallion Prancer 55
Barbie and Skipper School 200
Bubbling Spa 45
Check Up & Play Center, 1996 15
Country Camper 70
Keys to Fame Game, 1963 85
Lunch Box, The World of Barbie, King Seeley Thermos, 1971 70
Midnight Black Stallion 40
Pool Party, 1973 .60

BARWARE

During the late 1960s and early 1970s it became fashionable for homeowners to convert basements into family rec rooms, often equipped with bars. Most were well stocked with both utilitarian items (shot glasses and ice crushers) and decorative accessories. Objects with advertising are usually more valuable than their generic counterparts.

Bar Set, wood, barbershop motif, contains bottle opener, corkscrew and stopper, 1940s 10
Cocktail Shaker, chrome, grape and leaf etching, complete with 8 glasses, 1940s 45
Cocktail Shaker, figural fire extinguisher, windup, plays How Dry I Am, made in Japan, 11" h 20
Cocktail Shaker, glass, chrome lid, recipes and barware dec, 8.25" h 10
Cocktail Set, Hazel Atlas, hunting scene, contains mixer with chrome cover, 8 glasses 15
Cocktail Set, Mr Bartender Regal Bar Set, contains stainless steel stirrer/ spoon with red plastic tip, 6" glass shakers, shot glass, stainless steel strainer and tongs, 7" h stainless steel shaker, and 2 chrome whiskey bottle pourer spouts, orig box 8
Cocktail Shaker, chrome, black trim, Chase, 11.5" h .50
Cocktail Shaker, silver-plated, bottom stamped "Christophe/2829540," 8.75" h 40

Cocktail Shaker, clear glass with yellow, black, and red dec, mkd "Bloomfield Industries, U.S.A.," 7.625" h, $45.

Dispenser, glass, chrome top, "Bourbon"
   painted on front in white lettering,
   holds 32 oz, 11" h, 3.5" sq 5
Glass, "Don Ho Polynesian Palace,
   Wakiki Hawaii Cinerama Reef Towers
   Hotel," clear, red lettering 5
Ice Bucket, pressed glass, 5.5" h 3
Ice Tongs, Bakelite handles 12
Jigger/Opener, mkd "Cavalier," National
   Silver Co, holds 2 oz, 5.75 x 2.5" 15
Measure, Mr Woodpecker The Barkeep
   Martini Measure, #515, jiggers for
   vermouth and gin, 12" l, orig box 10
Pitcher, Ambassador Scotch, bottom
   mkd "Blended Scotch Whiskey/86
   Proof/The Jos. Garneau Bros, New
   York," 5.5" h 4
Recipe Book, *Burke's Complete Cocktail
   and Tastybite Recipes,* 125 pp, 1936 . . .7
Spritzer Bottle, red, c1950s 5
Stemware, cocktail, Baccarat, Orion
   pattern, 4" h, price for set of 4 35
Swizzle Stick, glass, strawberry, 7" l 2
Vermouth Dispenser, syringe shaped,
   sterling silver, Gorham 75

BASEBALL CARDS

Baseball cards date from the late 19th century. The earliest series are tobacco company issues dating between 1909 and 1915. During the 1920s American Caramel, National Caramel, and York Caramel issued cards.

Goudey Gum Co. (1933 to 1941) and Gum, Inc. (1939), carried on the tradition in the 1930s. When World War II ended, Bowman Gum of Philadelphia, the successor to Gum, Inc., became the baseball giant. Topps, Inc., of Brooklyn, NY, followed. Topps purchased Bowman in 1956 and enjoyed almost a monopoly in card production until 1981 when Fleer of Philadelphia and Donruss of Memphis challenged its leadership.

In addition to sets produced by these major companies, there are hundreds of other sets issued by a variety of sources, ranging from product manufacturers such as Sunbeam Bread to Minor League teams. There are so many secondary sets now issued annually that it is virtually impossible for a collector to keep up with them at all.

The field is plagued with reissued sets and cards, as well as outright forgeries. The color photocopier has been used to great advantage by unscrupulous dealers.

The listing below is simply designed to give you an idea of baseball card prices in good to very good condition and to show you how they change, depending on the age of the cards that you wish to collect. For detailed information about card prices, consult the following price guides: James Beckett, *Beckett Baseball Card Price Guide No. 22,* Beckett Publications, 2000; Bob Lemke, ed., *Standard Catalog of Baseball Cards, 9th Edition,* Krause Publications, 1999; and *Sports Collectors Digest Baseball Card Price Guide, 14th Edition,* Krause Publications, 2000. Although Beckett is the name most often mentioned in connection with price guides, I have found the Krause guides to be more helpful.

Periodicals: *Beckett Baseball Card Monthly,* 15850 Dallas Pkwy., Dallas, TX 75248; *Card Trade,* 700 E. State St., Iola, WI 54990.

Bazooka, 1959, #8, Del Crandall 6.00
Bazooka, 1960, #4, Hank Aaron 12.50
Bazooka, 1961, #36, Bill Tuttle 1.50
Bazooka, 1962, #7, Orlando Cepeda . . 2.50
Bazooka, 1963, #13, Camilo Pascual . . 1.00
Bazooka, 1964, #32, Sandy Koufax 9.50
Bazooka, 1965, #35, Ken Boyer 1.00
Bazooka, 1966, #4, Richie Allen 1.00
Bazooka, 1967, #19, Jim Fregosi 1.00
Bowman, 1948, #33, Bill Johnson 3.00
Bowman, 1949, #2, Whitey Lockman . . 2.50

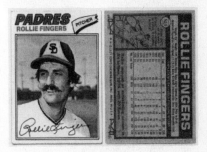

Topps, 1977, #523, Rollie Fingers, $2.
—Photo courtesy Ray Morykan Auctions.

Bowman, 1950, #56, Del Crandall 7.50
Bowman, 1951, #1, Whitey Ford 65.00
Bowman, 1952, #1, Yogi Berra 40.00
Bowman, 1953, #16, Stu Miller 15.00
Bowman, 1954, #62, Enos Slaughter . . 5.00
Bowman, 1955, #10, Phil Rizzuto 8.00
Donruss, 1981, #2, Rollie Fingers 05
Donruss, 1982, #3, Steve Garvey 05
Donruss, 1983, #90, Rod Carew 10
Donruss, 1984, #40, Mike Fuentes 03
Donruss, 1985, #52, Fernando Valenzuela .03
Donruss, 1986, #15, Tony Perez 05
Donruss, 1987, #106, Orel Hershiser . . .04
Donruss, 1988, #171, Cal Ripken 10
Donruss, 1989, #91, Jose Canseco 02
Donruss, 1990, #4, Ken Griffey Jr 10
Donruss, 1991, #118, Alan Trammell . . .02
Fleer, 1960, #79, Ralph Kiner 1.25
Fleer, 1961, #26, Wes Farrell 35
Fleer, 1963, #27, Tom Cheney 1.85
Fleer, 1970, #59, 1962 Yankees/Giants,
  World Series 12
Fleer, 1971, #38, 1940 Reds/Tigers,
  World Series 12
Fleer, 1972, #11, Cy Young, Famous Feats
  Series 20
Fleer, 1973, #3, Jim Thorpe, Wildest Days
  and Plays Series 25
Fleer, 1974, #2, Spring Training, Baseball
  Firsts Series .03
Fleer, 1975, #19, Cy Young, Pioneers
  Series 12
Fleer, 1981, #20, Nino Espinosa 01
Fleer, 1982, #82, Tom Seaver 10
Leaf, 1948-49, #127, Enos Slaughter . .75.00
Leaf, 1960, #32, Bill Tuttle 35

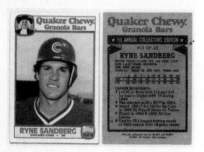

*Topps, 1986, #13, Ryne Sandberg, Quaker
Chewy Granola Bars premium, 75¢.*
—Photo courtesy Ray Morykan Auctions.

O-Pee-Chee, 1965, #207, Pete Rose . . .22.00
O-Pee-Chee, 1966, #6, Chuck Schilling . . .35
O-Pee-Chee, 1967, #5, Whitey Ford . . . 3.00
O-Pee-Chee, 1968, #21, Ron Davis 35
O-Pee-Chee, 1969, #56, Rich Reese 30
O-Pee-Chee, 1970, #45, Dave Johnson .30
Topps, 1951, #9, Washington Senators . .25.00
Topps, 1952, #190, Don Johnson 4.00
Topps, 1953, #86, Billy Martin 15.00
Topps, 1954, #248, Al Smith 2.50
Topps, 1956, #70, Jim Rivera 1.25
Topps, 1957, #30, Pee Wee Reese 8.00
Topps, 1958, #104, Jim Pendleton 1.50
Upper Deck, 1989, #35, Ricky Jordan . .03
Upper Deck., 1990, #13, Deion Sanders .05
Upper Deck, 1991, #157, Matt Williams .02
Upper Deck, 1992, #134, Barry Bonds . .03

BASEBALL MEMORABILIA

What a feast for the collector! Flea
market vendors often display caps, bats,
gloves, autographed balls and photos of
your favorite all-stars, baseball statues,
regular and world series game programs
and team manuals or rosters. Do not overlook secondary material such as magazine
covers with a baseball theme. Condition
and personal preference should always
guide the eye.

Be careful of autograph forgeries. The
general feeling among collectors is that
more than 50 percent of the autographed
baseballs being offered for sale have fake
signatures. But do not let this spoil your fun.
There is plenty of good stuff out there.

Clubs: Society for American Baseball
Research, 812 Huron Rd. E. #719, Cleveland,
OH 44115; The Glove Collector Club, 14057
Rolling Hills Ln., Dallas, TX 75240.

Periodicals: *Sports Collectors Digest,* 700 E.
State St, Iola, WI 54990; *Tuff Stuff,* 700 E.
State St, Iola, WI 54990.

Bagatelle Game, Brinkman Baseball
  Game, litho tin, Brinkman Engineering
  Co, 1930s 50
Bank, glass, figural baseball, Detroit
  Tigers head image on front, Mobil Oil
  flying red horse symbol on reverse,
  1930s, 3" d, 2.5" d black metal base . . .60

Pennant, felt, American League All Stars, Philadelphia, Pa, 1976, $15.

Bobbing Head, Cincinnati Reds, composition, spring mounted head, gold round base, Sports Specialties, made in Japan, c1967, 6.5" h 150

Booklet, American League schedule, Spalding premium, 1955, 2.25 x 4" 15

Drinking Glass, Baltimore Orioles "World Champions 1966," 4.5" h, 3.5" d 10

Glove, brown leather, fielder's, #A2212, silver inscription "Ted Williams," Wilson, 1950-60s 40

Greeting Card, "A Baseball Game For You," full color illus, black and red inscription, game instructions on inside front, Hallmark, 1940-50s, 4.75 x 5.75" closed size 20

Mask, Mike Schmidt, plastic, burgundy center "P," stamped "Halloween Night At The Vet," 1985, 7 x 10.5" 10

Mug, Phillies, white, red inscription, 1970-80, 3.25" h, 3" d 8

Pass, brown leather folder wallet, gold-lettered "Compliments of American League," reverse side pocket holds 1966 "Annual Pass To All Grounds," "William M. Dickey and Party" written in cursive script, American League President Joseph E Cronin facsimile signature, 3 x 4.75" 190

Pennant, white felt, New York Yankees "World Champions," blue and red lettering, stapled 6.5 x 7" team photo, c1960s, 11.5 x 28.5" 20

Pennant, yellow-gold felt, 1974 All Star Game, image of Three Rivers Stadium accented by green playing field and outer circle landscaping, pirate symbol above stadium with "Pittsburgh," 12 x 30" 10

Pinback Button, Boston Red Sox, "1946 World Champions," red and white ...20

Pinback Button, Brooklyn Dodgers, black and white Ebbets Field illus on blue ground, black inscription "National League Champions," 1940s 45

Pinback Button, "N. Y. Black Yankees," 1940s 15

Pinback Button, New York Yankees, "American League Champions," 1940s 20

Press Pin, brass, figural baseball, issued for 1941 World Series 450

Yearbook, *1967 Los Angeles Dodgers*, 8.25 x 10.75" 15

Yearbook, *1968 Famous Slugger*, 68 pp, Hillerich & Bradsby Co, 4.5 x 6.5" 10

Yearbook, *1966 New York Mets*, 52 pp, 8.5 x 11" 20

BASKETBALL MEMORABILIA

As the price of baseball cards and baseball memorabilia continues to rise, collectors are turning to other sports categories based on the affordability of their material. Basketball and football are "hot" sport collecting fields.

Collecting generally centers around one team, as it does in most other sport collecting categories. Items have greater value in their "hometown" than they do "on the road." You know a category is gaining strength when its secondary material starts to bring consistently strong prices.

Periodicals: *Beckett Basketball Card Magazine,* 15850 Dallas Pkwy., Dallas, TX 75248; *Sports Cards Magazine,* 700 E. State St, Iola, WI 54990; *Tuff Stuff,* 700 E. State St, Iola, WI 54990.

Basketball, miniature, Indiana Hoosiers ..4

Basketball, sgd by Alonzo Mourning, Spalding 50

Bobbing Head, Portland Trailblazers, composition, spring mounted head, round gold base with decal, mkd "Made in Korea/NBA Approved American Sports Sales Ltd," 1970s, 7" h 30

Book, *Basketball For the Player, the Fan, and the Coach,* illus, 1953 15

Pinback Button, Kutztown Normal School "State Champions," 1916-17, $15.

Drinking Glass, clear, Ohio State, front depicts head coach Fred Taylor, Ohio State Buckeye basketballer and list of team members on reverse, 1961-62, 6.5" h 10

Figure, Starting Lineup, Kevin McHale ..10

Media Guide, 1986 NCAA Basketbal Guide, 500 pp, 1985 season 10

Photograph, Wilt Chamberlain playing San Francisco Warriors in NBA finals, 1967, 12.5 x 9" 25

Poster, Bill Bradley, Sports Illustrated, 1970 10

Program, University of Wyoming at University of Washington, Hec Edmundson Pavillion, Seattle, Feb 9-19, 1951, 8 pp 15

Program, University of Redlands 15th Annual International Basketball Tournament, 1961, 7.5 x 10.25" 4

Trading Card, Hoops, 1989-90, #21, Michael Jordan 20

Trading Card, SkyBox, 1994, #67, Shaquille O'Neal 12

Trading Card, Topps, 1969-70, #1, Wilt Chamberlain 18

Trading Card, Upper Deck, 1991-92, #45, Magic Johnson 10

Travel Clock, Baltimore Bullets, leatherette case, dial face mkd "1969 copyright by NBA Properties," 2.25" sq 25

Yearbook, *Converse,* 64 pp, photos and statistics, 1970 10

Yearbook, *Syracuse University,* 84 pp, 1990-91 3

BASKETS

A tisket, a tasket, who's got the basket? Baskets, ranging from old timers to contemporary craft and "collectible" types, are readily found at flea markets.

Note: See Longaberger Baskets for additional listings.

Berry, split wood, crisscross bands, 5.75" h, 7" d 45

Burden, woven splint, square bottom, round rim, old patina, 16" h, 14" sq 45

Buttocks, woven splint, bentwood handle, 20 ribs, old patina, 15 x 14", 9" h plus handle 65

Cheese, round, hexagon weave, woven splint, openwork X's below wrapped rim, 9.25" d 125

Drying, woven splint, open weave wire bottom, branded bentwood handle, 15 x 14.5" 70

Egg, wire, orange paint 15

Field, woven splint, round, bentwood rim handles, 12.75' h, 18" d 85

Gathering, woven splint, rect, boat-shaped, shallow, high handle, 12 x 18.5" 55

Hanging, metal, painted white, 8.5" h, 3.5" d 15

Laundry, woven splint, rim handles, dark finish, 16" h, 26" d 50

Easter Basket, multicolored woven splint, green straw handle, red woven trim, $35.

Native American, Hopi, coil, tri-color
check design in rust, black, and
natural, rim and outer body stitches
missing, 5.625" h, 9.5" d 80
Native American, Papago Indian, pine
needle 12
Native American, Pima Indian, hand-
woven horsehair 10
Potato, ash splint, round 35
Storage, woven splint, rect, dark stain
with red-orange and blue strips
woven in, cov, 19.5" l 70
Tobacco, splint, open weave, shallow,
38" l 75
Utility, wicker, nesting set of 3, duck-
shaped 5
Utility, woven splint, bentwood handle,
round, faded green and purple paint,
12.5 x 13.5", 10" h plus handle 45
Vegetable, woven splint, bentwood
handle, rect, red, blue, and natural,
17 x 10.5", 10" h plus handle 75

BATMAN

"Galloping globs of bat guano, Caped
Crusader!" and similar cries may be heard
as the Dark Knight and his sidekick are
summoned to restore peace to Gotham City.

The saga of the search for Batman and
Robin-related items began with Batman's
appearance in 1939 in issue #27 of
Detective Comics. Today, Boy Wonder and
Caped Crusader collectibles are found in
almost every medium imaginable. Local flea
markets offer a large variety of batgoodies
capable of making any bat collector go
batty!

Club: Batman TV Series Fan Club, P.O. Box
107, Venice, CA 90294.

Action Figure, Batman "Wall Scaler,"
Batman: Dark Knight, Kenner, 1990,
5" h, MIP 25
Action Figure, Robin, Batman Returns,
Kenner, 1992, 5" h, MIP 20
Action Figure, Joker, Batman: Legends
of, Kenner, 1994, 5" h, MIP 15
Action Figure Accessory, Laser Blade
Cycle, Batman Returns, Kenner, 1992,
MIB 25

Brush, Batman Styling Brush, hard
plastic, Avon, ©1976 DC Comics,
2.75 x 8.5 x 2" box 15
Colorforms, ©1066 National Periodicals
Publications, 8 x 12.25 x 1", MIB 15
Coloring Book, Batman Saves the Town,
Holloway candy premium, 16 pp,
Western Printing Co, ©1966 National
Periodical Publications, 4.25 x 4.75" . .50
Doll, Bat Troll, hard vinyl, mkd "By Sheri/
Made In Brooklyn, New York," c1966,
9" h, MOC 20
Figure, Batman, rubber, paint accents,
mkd "Hong Kong," c1966, 5.5" h 35
Flicker Watch, white vinyl straps and
case, c1966, 6.25" l 20
Frame Tray Puzzle, The Villains, wood,
scene of Joker, Riddler, and Penguin
in front of money chest with Batman
in background, Playskool, 11.5 x
13.5 x 14" 15
Game, Batman Card Game, Ideal, ©1966
NPP Inc, 6.5 x 10.5 x 1.5" 20
License Plate, aluminum, silk screen
design of Batman and Robin descend-
ing, Groff Signs Inc, ©1966 National
Periodical Publications, 6 x 12" 15
Lunch Box, plastic, blue, full color sticker
on front, Batman and Joker scene,
Canadian Thermos Products Ltd,
©1982 DC Comics, 8 x 9.5 x 5" 40
Mask, soft plastic, cowl shaped, diecut
eye and mouth openings, blue, black
accent over face, raised black and
gold bat symbol at bottom center,
Ideal Toy Corp, ©1966 NPP Inc,
9 x 10 x 11.5" 70

Comic Book,
Detective
Comics, #367,
$15.

Model, Batmobile, assembled, Aurora,
c1966, 2.5 x 6.5 x 1.75" 45
Mug, china, white, color image of
Batman and Robin running on front
and back with name below, mkd
"Salem," ©1966 National Periodical
Publications, 3" h 15
Mug, hard plastic, white, decal on front
with logo and Batman and Robin
portraits above "Batman with Robin
the Boy Wonder," Arrow Plastics Mfg
Co, ©1966 NPP Inc, 4" h 25
Photograph, black and white, Adam
West and Burt Ward in full costume,
blue facsimile signatures, "Batman
and Robin Appear in Every Exciting
Issue of Batman, Detective and
World's Finest Comics" text at bot-
tom with DC logo, 8.5 x 11" 35
Sign, Batman and Robin All Star Ice
Cream, stiff paper, "Vanilla Ice Cream
With Banana Marshmallow," ©1966
National Periodical Publications Inc,
24 x 44" 150
Toothbrush, hard plastic, battery oper-
ated, 3-D figures of Batman and Robin
atop rectangular base, "Brush Each
Day/Zing/Pow," Janex Corp, ©1077
DC Comics 50
Toy, Batman and Robin Wrist Light, hard
plastic, battery operated, attached
yellow vinyl wrist strap, Bantamlite,
©1966 NPP, 2.25" d 50
Toy, Batman's Batmaker-Pak, missing
accessories, Mattel, ©1966 NPP Inc .15
Toy, Batman Mobil Rat Lab, hard plastic,
black and yellow, red int, orig box,
Mego, ©1975 National Periodical
Publications, 8 x 14 x 7" 75
Toy, Batmobile, hard plastic, battery
operated, orig box, Ahi/Azrak-Hamway
International Inc, ©1978 DC Comics,
4 x 10 x 3.25" .175
View-Master, Good Guys Gift Pack,
complete with hard plastic viewer,
8 reels featuring Batman and Robin,
Superman, Aquaman, Wonder Woman,
and Shazam, GAF, ©1975 National
Periodical Publications, MIP 15
Wallet, vinyl, snap closure strap at top,
inside plastic picture pages, snap
closure compartment, coin holder,
and magic slate compartment with

wood stylus, complete with card
mkd "The Penguin Batman's Droll
Opponent," Standard Plastic Products
Inc, ©1966 National Periodical
Publications, 3.5 x 4.5" 35
Yo-Yo, hard plastic, color decal on each
side, with clear plastic display case,
Duncan, ©1978 DC Comics 8

BAUER POTTERY

J. A. Bauer established the Bauer
Pottery in Los Angeles in 1909. Flowerpots
were among the first items manufactured,
followed by utilitarian items. Dinnerware
was introduced in 1930. Artware came a
decade later. The firm closed in 1962.

Periodical: *Bauer Quarterly,* P.O. Box 2524,
Berkeley, CA 94702.

DINNERWARE

La Linda, creamer, light blue, 2.25" h,
5.25" l 15
La Linda, cup 10
La Linda, custard 6
La Linda, gravy boat, turquoise 20
La Linda, platter, 10" l 12
La Linda, ramekin 6
La Linda, teapot, 6 cup 30
Monterey, bread and butter plate, 6" d . . .8
Monterey, creamer 10
Monterey, fruit bowl, ftd, 9" d 40
Monterey, soup bowl 25
Ring, carafe, burgundy, 7" h 35
Ring, cereal bowl, 5" d 25

*Ring, mixing bowls, nesting set of four,
$175.* —Photo courtesy Ray Morykan
Auctions.

Ring, coffee server, copper handle ..... .50
Ring, cup and saucer, yellow .... .45
Ring, mixing bowl, green, 5.75" d ...... .40
Ring, mixing bowl, yellow, 8.5" d, 4.75" h .50
Ring, mug, copper and wood handle,
   3.75" h .... .12
Ring, pie plate, yellow, 9.5" d .... .35
Ring, pitcher, 5.75" h .... .40
Ring, plate, red, 8" d .... .20
Ring, platter, yellow, 12.25" l, 9" w ...... .60
Ring, salt and pepper shakers .... .20

OTHER

Cereal Canister, strawberry pattern,
   6.5" h, 6.25" w .... .100
Cocoa Canister, strawberry pattern,
   4.5" h, 4.25" w .... .75
Cookie Jar, "Snack Bar," strawberry
   pattern, 8" h .... .100
Cracker Crumb Canister, strawberry
   pattern, 4" h, 5" d .... .55
Flour Canister, strawberry pattern,
   8.5" h .... .95
Jardiniere, green speckled glaze, 6.5" h,
   8.5" l .... .15
Planter, turquoise, mkd "USA 4," 4" h,
   4.875" d 8
Planter, figural swan, matte glaze,
   11 x 4.5 x 6.25" .... .40
Rice Canister, apple pattern, 6.5" h,
   4.5" w .... .65
Rice Canister, strawberry pattern,
   6.5" h .... .100
Rose Bowl, green speckled glaze,
   5.5" w .... .25
Shaker, fish shaped, turquoise 7
Vase, #214, 7.5" h .... .60

BEANIE BABIES

While there is still an active secondary resale market for Ty's Beanie Babies, the market collapse is at hand. A year from now, sellers will thank their lucky stars if they can get these prices.

The items are priced each. Beanie Babies without tags have little or no value.

Periodicals: *Beans & Bears Magazine*, P.O. Box 1050, Dubuque, IA 52004; *Mary Beth's Bean Bag World Montly*, 2121 Waukegan Rd, Suite 120, Bannockburn, IL 60015.

Ally the Alligator, #4032, retired 10/97,
   1st generation tag .... .350
Baldy the Eagle, #4074, retired 5/98,
   3rd or 4th generation tag .... .17
Batty the Bat, #4035, retired 3/99, 4th
   or 5th generation tag 8
Bernie the St Bernard, #4109, retired
   9/98, 4th or 5th generation tag .... .10
Bessie the Cow, #4009, retired 9/98,
   4th generation tag .... .55
Blackie the Bear, #4011, retired 9/98,
   1st generation tag .... .350
Blizzard the Snow Tiger, #4163, retired
   5/98, 1st generation tag .... .350
Bones the Brown Dog, #4001, retired
   9/98, 1st generation tag .... .350
Bongo the Brown Monkey, #4067,
   retired 12/98, brown tail .... .125
Bruno the Terrier, #4183, retired 9/98 8
Bubbles the Fish, #4078, retired 1997,
   3rd generation tag .... .150
Bucky the Beaver #4016, retired 1/98,
   3rd generation tag .... .80
Bumble the Bee, #4045, retired 1996,
   3rd generation tag .... .450
Butch the Dog 8
Cheeks the Baboon .... .12
Chip the Calico Cat, #4121, retired
   3/31/99, 4th generation tag 8
Chocolate the Moose, #4015, retired
   12/98, 1st generation tag .... .425
Chops the Lamb, #4019, retired 1997,
   3rd generation tag .... .200
Claude the Crab, #4083, retired 12/98,
   4th generation tag 8

Fleece the Lamb, new tag, $5.

Coral the Tie Dyed Fish, #4079, retired
1996, 3rd generation tag 200
Cubbie the Bear, #4010, retired 1/98,
1st generation tag 450
Curly the Bear, #4052, retired 12/98, 4th
generation tag 15
Daisy the Cow, #4006, retired 9/98, 1st
generation tag 275
Derby the Brown Horse, #4008, 3rd
generation tag 150
Digger the Crab, #4027, retired 1995,
1st generation tag 750
Doby the Doberman, #4110, retired
12/98, 5th generation tag 10
Doodle the Rooster, #4174, retired 35
Dotty the Dalmatian, #4100, retired
12/98, 5th generation tag 10
Echo the Dolphin, #4180, retired 5/98,
5th generation tag 14
Erin the St Patrick's Bear, #4186 12
Flash the Dolphin, #4021, retired 1997,
4th generation tag 90
Glory the Bear, #4188, retired 12/98 25
Gobbles the Turkey, #4034, retired
3/31/99, 4th generation tag 8
Jolly the Walrus, #4082, retired 5/98,
5th generation tag 12
Lizzy the Lizard, #4033, retired 1/98, 3rd
generation tag 200
Quackers the Duck, #4024, retired 5/98,
3rd generation tag 75

BEATLES

Ahhh! look, it's the Fab Four! The collector will never need Help to find Beatle
memorabilia at a flea market—placemats,
dishes, records, posters and much more.
The list is a Magical Mystery Tour. John,
Paul, George and Ringo can be found in a
multitude of shapes and sizes. Examine
them carefully. They are likely to be heavily
played with, so conditions will vary from
poor to good.

Clubs: Beatles Connection, P.O. Box 1066,
Miami, FL 33780; Working Class Hero
Beatles Club, 3311 Niagara St., Pittsburgh,
PA 15123.

Periodicals: *Beatlefan,* P.O. Box 33515,
Decatur, GA 30033; *Good Day Sunshine,* P.O.
Box 1008, Los Angeles, CA 90066;

Strawberry Fields Forever, P.O. Box 880981,
San Diego, CA 92168.

Book, *We Love You Beatles,* Margaret
Sutton, Doubleday & Co, 1st ed, 48 pp,
1971, 8.25 x 10.75" 15
Brooch, metal, guitar shaped, gold
luster, inset celluloid covered black
and white photo disk, Randall, ©Nems
Enterprises Ltd, 1964, 1.5 x 4" 50
Charm Bracelet, goldtone metal, disk
charm with "The Beatles" on 1 side
and individual band member names
on other side in dark brass finish, and
2" d leather disk with name printed in
black on 1 side and band image on
other , c1964, 7" l 50
Costume, Blue Meanie, thin molded
mask, 1 pc rayon outfit, Collegeville,
©1968 King Features, orig 8.5 x 11 x
3" box 75
Magazine, *Beatles on Broadway,*
Whitman Publishing Co, 1964 10
Notebook, lined stiff paper, front cover
features color group photo with
facsimile signatures, Westab, ©Nems
Ltd, London, c1964, 8.5 x 10.5" 35
Paint Set, The Beatles Yellow Submarine
Water Color Set, unused, Craftmaster,
©1968 King Features Syndicate, 6.25
x 9.25 x .75x" box 50

Sheet Music, Roll Over, Beethoven,
recorded by The Beatles, words and
music by Chuck Berry, pub by Jewel
Music Pty, Ltd., Australia, c1956, $30.

Soaky Bottle, Paul McCartney, Colgate-Palmolive, 1965, $60.

Pillow, stuffed, closeup image of band with facsimile signatures along bottom, blue backing, Nordic House, c1964, 12 x 12 x 2.5" 100

Poster, "The Beatles In Concert," black and white, for films shown Dec 1-3, 1977 at Changes in Soho, NY, 13 x 17.5" 50

Radio, battery operated, 8" h movable John Lennon figure attached to black hard plastic base with raised text "John Lennon," orig box 50

Record, *Beatles Fan Club Christmas Record*, 33 1/3 rpm, blurry abstract photo design on sleeve front, crude people illus on reverse with "The Official Beatles Fan Club of Great Britain Presents The Beatles' Seventh Christmas Record/Happy Christmas 1969" 45

Record, *Paperback Writer/Rain*, 45 rpm, yellow and orange swirl label, sleeve features color photos on front and back, Capitol, 1966 35

Record, *Yellow Submarine/Eleanor Rigby*, 45 rpm, browntone photos on sleeve, Capitol, 1966 85

Record Case, plastic, "The Beatles Disk-Go-Case," blue, depicts Beatles portraits with facsimile signatures, Charter Industries, ©1966 Nems Enterprises Ltd, 8.5" h, 7.5" d 175

Stationery, 20 sheets of paper, matching envelopes, yellow submarine against waves scene, orig box, Unicorn Creations Inc, 1968, 8.5 x 11" 50

Suitcase, vinyl, zippered front, Air Flite, ©Nems Enterprises Ltd, c1964, 12 x 13 x 5" 375

Ticket, diecut stiff paper, black and yellow, for 1964 movie *A Hard's Day's Night*, printed "Embasy Theater" and "930," unused, 3.5 x 9" 40

BEATNIK MEMORABILIA

After World War II, a variety of disaffected people—returning G.I.'s, jazz musicians, liberal writers, and other nonconformists— began to coalesce in Greenwich Village in New York City and the North Beach area of San Francisco. They were dissatisfied with the conventional values of society. They were interested in seeing the world in terms of creativity rather than commerce. They were provocative in appearance and attitude.

In the 1950s, a number of authors, including Allen Ginsberg, Jack Kerouac, and William Burroughs received mainstream exposure. They, and those who believed as they did in an alternative view of society, became known as "Beats" or "Beatniks." Books, records, posters, pamphlets, leaflets, and other items associated with the era are highly collectible. Although widely ridiculed in their day, the contributions they made to art, literature, and music are recognized for their importance and significance in American culture. The "Beats" continued the tradition of Bohemian nonconformity and produced thousands of very desirable items for collectors from 1947-1962.

Advisor: Richard M. Synchef, 208 Summit Dr., Corte Madera, CA 94925, (415) 927-8844.

Note: Prices listed for items in excellent to near mint condition. All books are first editions with dust jackets in near fine or better condition.

Book, *Tales of Beatnik Glory,* Ed Sanders, NY, Stonehill Publishing Co, 1975, by the Fugs founder turned activist 120

Book, *The Adept,* Michael McClure, NY, Delacorte, 1971, award winning author's second novel 120

Book, *The Essential,* Lenny Bruce, John Cohen, eds, NY, Doublas, 1970 150

Book, *The Frisco Kid,* Jerry Kamstra, NY, Harper & Row, 1975, tales of San Francisco North Beach Bohemian area 100

Booklet, Poor Richard's Guide to Non-Tourist San Francisco, Unicorn Publishing Co, 1958, "Visit Beat Generation Bohemia" 150

Booklet, Prospectus for *Naked Lunch,* William Burroughs, NY, Grove Press, 1962, 16 pp 250

Cigarette Holder, black plastic, cardboard display backing, c1950s 50

Magazine, *City Lights Journal, #3,* San Francisco, City Lights Books, 1953 . .250

Magazine, *Evergreen Review, #2,* "The San Francisco Scene," NY, Grove Press, Inc, 1959 150

Magazine, *Life,* Sep 21, 1969, "Squaresville vs Beatsville" 60

Magazine, *Playboy,* "The Beat Issue," Jul 1, 1959 75

Paperback Book, *Beat, Beat,* William Brown, NY, Signet, 1959 50

Paperback Book, *Beatville, USA,* George Mandel, NY, Avon, 1961 60

Paperback Book, *How to Talk Dirty and Influence People,* Lenny Bruce, Chicago, Playboy Press, 1966, autobiography 75

Paperback Book, *Nova Express,* William Burroughs, Grove Press, Inc, 1965 . .125

Comic Book, "Conspiracy Capers," The Conspiracy, Kathleen Cleaver and Susan Sontag, Chicago, IL, 1969, $250.

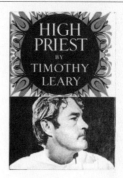

Book, High Priest, *by Timothy Leary, Cleveland, OH, New American Library, Inc., 1st ed, 1968, $175.*

Paperback Book, *The Beat Generation & the Angry Young Men,* Gene Feldman, NY, Dell, 1959 80

Record, *Kaddish,* Allen Ginsberg, monaural LP, Atlantic Verbun Series #4001, 1965 225

Record, *Poetry for the Beat Generation,* Jack Kerouac, monaural LP, Hanover Records 550

Record, *San Francisco Poets,* monaural LP, Hanover Records, 1959 250

BEER CANS

Beer can collecting was very popular in the 1970s. Times have changed. The field is now dominated by the serious collector and most trading and selling goes on at specialized beer can-ventions.

The list below contains a number of highly sought-after cans. Do not assume these prices are typical. Most cans fall in the 25-cent to 50-cent range. Do not pay more unless you are certain of the resale market.

There is no extra value to be gained by having a full beer can. In fact, selling a full can of beer without a license, even if only to a collector, violates the liquor laws in a large number of states. Most collectors punch a hole in the bottom of the can and drain out the beer.

Club: Beer Can Collectors of America, 747 Merus Ct., Fenton, MO 63026.

Ballantine Beer, 100th Anniversary, Ballantine Brewing, Newark, NJ, 1940s 50

Stoney's Pilsener Beer, Jones Brewing Co., Smithton, PA, cone top, $50.

Black Label Beer, Brewing Corp of America, Cleveland, OH, cone top, 1940s 40

Bub's Beer, Peter Bub Brewing, Winona, MN, pull top, 1960s 3

Burgermeister Pale Beer, San Francisco Brewing, San Francisco, CA, flat top, 1940s 50

Canadian Ace Beer, Canadian Ace Brewing, Chicago, IL, cone top, 1950s 35

Country Club Beer, Goetz Brewing, St Joseph, MO, cone top, 1950s 55

Denver Beer, Tivoli Brewing, Denver, CO, pull top, 1960s 13

Dis-Go Near Beer, Eastern Brewing, Hammonton, NJ, 1970s 25

E & B Special Beer, Ekhardt & Becker, Detroit, MI, cone top, 1940s 75

General Pulaski, Pulaski Brewing, Hammonton, NJ, cone top, 1970s 15

Gettelman Beer, Gettelman Brewing, Milwaukee, WI, flat top, 1950s 30

Golden Grain Beer, Maier Brewing, Los Angeles, CA, pull top, 1960s 10

Heidelberg Beer, Carling Brewing, Baltimore, MD, pull top, 1960s 5

Iroquois Draft Ale, Iroquois Brewing, Buffalo, NY, pull top, 1970s 20

Krueger Cream Ale, Krueger Brewing, Newark, NJ, flat top, 1940s 160

Old Tavern Beer, Warsaw Brewing, Warsaw, IL, pull top, 1960s 10

Pabst Blue Ribbon, Pabst Brewing, Milwaukee, WI, flat top, 1950s 25

Pfeiffer Beer, Pfeiffer Brewing, Detroit, MI, flat top, 1950s 25

Rainier Bold Malt Liquor, Rainier Brewing, Seattle, WA, 1970s 12

Rheingold Scotch Ale, Liebmann Brewing, New York, NY, 1950s 35

Sheridan Beer, Walter Brewing, Pueblo, CO, pull top, 1970s 8

Stag Beer, Griesedieck Western, Belleville, IL, 1950s 6

Sterling Draft Beer, Sterling Brewing, Evansville, IN, pull top, 1960s 3

Whales White Ace, National Brewing, Baltimore, MD, pull top, 1960s 10

BELLS

Bell collectors are fanatics. They tend to want every bell they can find. Admittedly, most confine themselves to bells that will fit on a shelf, but there are those who derive great pleasure from an old school bell sitting on their front lawn.

Be alert for wine glasses that have been converted into bells. They are worth much less than bells that began life as bells. Also, collect Limited Edition bells only if you like them, not with the hope they will rise in value. Many Limited Edition bells do not ring true on the resale market.

Club: American Bell Assoc. International, Inc, P.O. Box 19443, Indianapolis, IN 46219.

Call, double-chiming, Ezra Cone, Gong Bell Mfg Co, East Hampton, CT, 1860s, 10.5" l 75

Ceramic, rose motif, heart shaped handle, 4.5" h 10

Cow, sheet copper, 6" h 30

Glass, millefiori dec, red bird finial, 3.25" h 30

Ceramic, purple violets and green leaves on light blue ground, gold trim, 4.5" h, $12.

Glass, milk glass, ruffled, Daisy and
Button pattern, Fenton, 6" h 15
Lawn Ornament, bell and yoke, cast
iron, painted black 75
Limited Edition, commemorating the
Investiture of The Prince of Wales,
Jul 1969, 8" h 150
School, #7, turned wood handle 40
Sleigh, set of 50 stamped steel bells,
riveted to leather strap 75
Tap, pewter and brass, 4" h 50
Tea, glass and silver, removable silver
filigree overlay, 4.75" h 100
Tea, silver-plated, teardrop shaped,
Gorham, 3.75" h 35

BIBLES

The general rule to follow is that any
Bible less than 200 years old has little or no
value in the collectibles market. Many people have trouble accepting this argument.
They see a large late 19th century family
Bible filled with engravings of religious
scenes and several pages containing information about the family. It is old and
impressive. It has to be worth money. Alas,
it was mass produced. The most valuable
thing about it is the family data and this can
be saved with the aid of a photocopier.

An average price for a large family
Bible from the turn of the century is
between $35 and $75, although there are
Bibles that sell for a lot more.

The Pronouncing Edition of the Holy Bible,
*pub by A. J. Holman & Co., Philadelphia,
PA, c1900, 10 x 12.75", $50.* —Photo
courtesy Ray Morykan Auctions.

BICENTENNIAL

America's 200th birthday in 1976 was
PARTY TIME for the nation. Everyone and
everything in the country had something
stamped, painted, printed, molded, cast and
pressed with the commemorative dates
1776-1976. The American spirit of "overdo"
and "outdo" always puts our nation in a
great mood. We certainly overdid it during
the Bicentennial.

The average flea market will have a
wide variety of Bicentennial goodies.
Remember the Bicentennial was only a
quarter century ago. This is one category
where you only want to buy items in fine or
better condition.

Ashtray, metal, hexagon shaped, emb
Liberty Bell in center surrounded by
"American Revolution Bicentennial
1776-1976," 7 x 9" 5
Bell, carnival glass, figural Liberty Bell,
"1776" on 1 side, "1976" on reverse,
2.75" h 15
Bell, glass, iridescent blue, 4 medallions
in relief of George Washington,
Thomas Jefferson, John Adams,
and Benjamin Franklin, eagle finial,
Fenton 6.5' h 50
Belt Buckle, brass, antique finish,
"Spirit of '76," flag with fife and
drum players in relief 10
Book, *Full-Color Bicentennial Needle-
point Designs,* Carol Belanger Grafton .2
Bottle, Log Cabin Syrup, Liberty Bell
with "1776-1976" 5
License Plate, cast metal, Pennsylvania,
state symbol with "1776/1976" 10
Magazine, *Saturday Evening Post,*
10 pp pull-out portfolio of Norman
Rockwell Covers, Bicentennial issue
Jul/Aug 1976 5
Paperweight, iridescent blue, Paul
Revere on front, paper label mkd
"Bicentennial 1776-1976/Handmade
Holly City Bottle, Millville, NJ, United
States of America" 10
Plate, glass, clear, "United States of
America" across top, "1776 Bicen-
tennial 1976" across lower rim, emb
13 stars, eagle with shield, arrows
and olive branches, Avon, 9 x 6.5" 5

Calendar Plate, "200th Anniversary Year 1776-1976," gold rim, $15.

Playing Cards, Kem Plastic Playing
    Cards, authorized by US Bicentennial
    Society, MIB .15
Thermometer/Wall Plaque, early Ameri-
    can motif with "1776-1976," Model
    M23, Miller Studio Inc, orig box 5
Train, complete with 24 pc track, engine,
    and American Bicentennial caboose,
    George Washington box car, Abraham
    Lincoln box car, Liberty Bell box car,
    Declaration of Independence box car,
    and power pack, Bachman 150

BICYCLES

    Bicycles are divided into two groups—
antique and classic. Chances of finding an
antique bicycle, such as a high wheeler, at
a flea market are slim. Chances of spotting
a great balloon tire classic are much
greater.

    Do not pay much for a bicycle that is
incomplete, rusted, or repaired with non-
original parts. Replacement of parts that
deteriorate, e.g., leather seats, is acceptable. It is not uncommon to heavily restore
a bicycle, i.e., to make it look like new. If the
amount of original parts is less than half,
question an extremely high price.

    There is a great market in secondary
material from accessories to paper
ephemera in bicycle collectibles. Since
most bicycle fanatics haunt the automobile

flea markets, you might just get lucky and
find a great bicycle item at a low cost at an
antiques and collectibles flea market.

Clubs: Classic Bicycle & Whizzer Club of
America, 35769 Simon Dr., Clinton
Township, MI 48035; International Veteran
Cycle Assoc., 248 Highland Dr., Findlay, OH
45840; Vintage Bicycle Club of America, 325
West Hornbeam Dr, Longwood, FL 32779;
The Wheelmen, 63 Stonebridge Rd., Allen
Park, NY 07042..

Newsletters: *Bicycle Trader,* 858 Stanyan
St., San Francisco, CA 94117; *Classic Bike
News,* 5046 E. Wilson Rd., Clio, MI 48420.

BICYCLES

Colson Clipper, 1949 1,200
High Wheel, Standard Columbia, Pope
    Mfg Co, leather snaps on wheels,
    saddlebag behind molded leather
    seat, hand brake, rubber tires, paint
    chips, overall wear, 59" h, 66" w . . .2,400
Murray, ladies, restored, 1959 350
Schwinn Fleet, restored, 1960s 1,000
Schwinn Heavy Duty, restored, 1961 . . .500
Schwinn, men's, missing fender light
    and horn button, repainted, 1940 400
Sears, ladies, 3 speed, 1970s 100
Tricycle, wooden seat, metal pedals
    and handles, hard rubber tires, 19" h,
    12.5" w, 31" l .100
Texas Ranger, orig condition, 1960s 125
Wards Duralium, 1937 700
Western Flyer, orig parts, repainted,
    1960 150

Huffy, lady's Westpoint, 3-speed, 26", $30.
—Photo courtesy Ray Morykan Auctions.

BICYCLE RELATED

Advertising Tear Sheet, Junior Trikes and Bikes, 1954, 5.5 x 13.5" 6

Advertising Tear Sheet, New Departure Bicycles, man and woman on bike near river, 1941, 5.5 x 13.5" 5

Advertising Tear Sheet, Oveman Wheel Co, Chicopee Falls, Victor Bicycles, The Finest Product of the Century, 12 x 8.25" 5

Badge, aluminum pendant depicting official seal for state of MA, rim inscription "Mass. Division League of American Wheelmen," reverse mkd "11th Annual Meet. Boston. May 30th 93," attached fabric ribbon 35

Book, *50 Years of Schwinn-Built Bicycles–The Story of the Bicycle and Its Contributions to Our Way of Life 1895-1945,* ©1945 Arnold, Schwinn & Company, Chciago 50

Book, *Bicycles,* Alan Dahnsen, photos and illus, hardcover, 48 pp, 1978, 8.375 x 6.875" 3

Charm, Schwinn Bicycles, maroon plastic, different world globe image on each side, inscription "Ride The World Cycles," rim inscription "Arnold Schwinn & Co., Chicago,"1930s 8

Pin, metal, faced by porcelain disk with "Union" over patriotic shield, O'Hara Dial Co, Waltham, MA 35

Shelby Traveler, new spring seat, tires, and pedals, professionally restored, $375.
—Photo courtesy Collectors Auction Services.

Pinback Button, "Columbia Bicycles," miniature replica nameplate inscribed "You See Them Everywhere," inscription for dealership in Scranton, PA 8

Pinback Button, "Big 4 Line," black lettering on orange ground 8

Pinback Button, "New Brunswick Tires," golden warrior goddess holding pink streamer inscribed "New Brunswick Tires Are Up To Date," bicycle wheel with blue wheel in background 8

Pinback Button, "Old Hickory," black lettering on horizontal brown and tan bands, Tonk Mfg Co, Chicago 8

Postcard, real photo, 3 Edwardian ladies and 2 bicycles 5

Seat, leather, padded, chrome springs front and rear, chrome rail, Persons-Majestic, new old stock 50

Sign, metal, "Schwinn Quality Chicago-Schwinn Built Bicycles," 16" h, 12" w .10

Stud, brown horse head on black and white bike wheel with red "G.R.A.H.C." 12

Stud, multicolored illus of cyclist on tandem bicycle, red inscription "Cycling Pleasure Increased By High Admiral Cigarettes" 15

Tray, metal, litho illus of man riding vintage bicycle, "Howe Bicycles Tricycles," 10.75 x 13.25" 5

Watch Fob, Columbia Bicycles, ivory, mounted celluloid disk and miniature compass, inscribed "Compliments of Pope Mfg Co Boston," 1892 20

BIG LITTLE BOOKS

The first Big Little Book was published by Whitman Publishing Co., in 1933. As with any successful endeavor, copycats soon appeared. Saalfield Publishing Co. was first with the introduction of its line of Little Big Books. Lesser known and less successful imitators include Engel-Van Wiseman, Lynn Publishing Co., Goldsmith Publishing Co., and Dell Publishing Co.

Condition and story content are the keys to determining value. Prices listed are for books in fine condition.

Club: Big Little Book Collectors Club of America, P.O. Box 1242, Danville, CA 94526.

Hal Hardy in the Lost Land of Giants,
#1413, $25.

Andy Panda and Tiny Tom, #1425 10
Apple Mary and Dennis Foil the
    Swindlers, #1130 10
Arizona Kid, The, #1192 5
Buck Jones, the Rough Riders, #1486 ...10
Calling W1XYZ Jimmy Kean Radio Spys,
    #1412 5
Charlie Chan, #1478 15
Dick Tracy and the Man with No Face,
    #1491 10
Donald Duck Is Here Again, #1484 20
Freckles and the Lost Diamond Mine,
    #1164 10
G-Men on the Job, #1168 5
Ghost Avenger, #1462 15
Hall of Fame of the Air, #1159 5
Harold Teen Swinging at the Sugar
    Bowl, #1418 5
Houdini's Magic, #715 15
In the Name of the Law, #1124 10
Junior G-Men, #1442 10
Mandrake the Magician and the Mid-
    night Monster, #1431 15
Maximo the Amazing Superman, #1436 ..15
Peggy Brown in the Big Haunted House,
    #1491 10
Pluto the Pup, #1467 20
Punch Davis of the Aircraft Carrier,
    #1440 10
Ray Land of the Tank Corps, #1447 5
Red Death on the Range, #1449 10
Terry Lee Flight Officer USA, #1492 10
Tom Beatty Ace of the Service, #1420 ...15
Uncle Sam's Sky Defenders, #1461 10

BISQUE

Every time I look at bisque figures, I think of grandmothers. I keep wondering why I never see a flea market table labeled "Only things a grandmother would love."

Bisque is pottery ware that has been fired once and not glazed. It is a technique that is centuries old and is still being practiced today. Unfortunately, some of today's figures are exact copies of those made hundreds of years ago. Be especially aware of bisque piano babies.

Collectors differentiate between Continental (mostly German) and Japanese bisque with premiums generally paid for Continental pieces. However, the Japanese made some great bisque. Do not confuse the cheap five-and-dime "Occupied Japan" bisque with the better pieces.

Dollhouse Doll, bride and bridegroom,
    cloth stuffed bodies, bisque limbs
    and shoulder heads, 4.125" h 50
Figurine, bathing beauty, relaxing at
    seaside, blonde hair, yellow swimsuit,
    2.5" h 38
Figurine, girl with dove, pastel colors,
    9.75" h, 3.75" base 50
Figurine, pig, head stuck in fence post,
    German, 3" h, 4.5" w 50
Figurine, unicorn, 6" h 5

Figurine, mallard, mkd "Special Edition,
Birds in Flight Collection, Limited Series,
Flight of the Mallard, Taiwan," 9" h, $15.

Music Box, nurse carrying tray to
   patient, plays "You Light Up My Life" . .5
Nodder, man and woman, back of dress
   mkd "5898," 2.5" h 35
Pincushion, figural doll, blonde hair,
   pink dress, 2 x 2.5" 35
Spill Vase, young boy feeding peacock
   out of large open basket 50
Teapot, oval concentric ribbing on sides,
   gold speckled highlights, mkd "Made
   in England," c1920s 50
Wall Plaque, mermaid, blonde hair,
   holding big bubble in hands, mkd
   "Norcrest, Japan," 4.5" h, 3" w 35

BIZARRE ART

There is some really great stuff made by
senior citizen groups and community organizations that can be found at local bazaars,
church rummage sales and so on. Of
course, after a few years, these items often
turn up at flea markets.

Some bazaar craftspeople also create
unique decorative accessories that may
hold some resale value. Other stuff is just
"stuff" and can be had for pennies on the
dollar. Perhaps some day this tacky stuff
will catch a decorator's eye and skyrocket
in value!

Bread Basket, swan, made from plastic
   milk jug 50
Dish Towel, crocheted hanger, button
   attached 2.00
Door Knob Hanger, needlepoint on
   plastic mesh, Christmas greetings . 2.00
Honey Do List Holder, wood, figural
   hammer, hp, clip to hold list of
   things to do 3.00
Lamp Shade, plastic bottle with colorful
   beads and cutout work 2.00
Ornament, cross, needlepoint on plastic
   mesh 2.00
Ornament, Rudolph head, brass bell
   head, pipe cleaner antlers, glued-on
   facial features 50
Plant Hanger, macramé 50
Potholder, cloth, patchwork design
   with stitched-on daisies 1.00
Tissue Box Holder, needlepoint on
   plastic mesh, colorful design 3.00

BLACK MEMORABILIA

The Black memorabilia category is
viewed quite broadly, ranging from slavery-
era items to objects showing ethnic stereo-
types. Prices range all over the place. It
pays to shop around.

Because Black memorabilia embodies
a wide variety of forms, the Black memorabilia collector is constantly competing with
collectors from other areas, e.g., cookie jar,
kitchen and salt and pepper collectors.
Surprisingly enough, it is the collectors of
Black memorabilia who realize the extent of
the material available and tend to resist
high prices.

Reproductions, from advertising signs
(Bull Durham Tobacco) to mechanical
banks (Jolly Nigger), are an increasing
problem. Remember—if it looks new,
chances are it is new.

Club: Black Memorabilia Collector's Assoc.,
2482 Devoe Ter., Bronx, NY 10468.

Newsletter: *Blackin',* 559 22nd Ave, Rock
Island, IL 61201.

Advertising Trade Card, Clark's ONT
   Spool Cotton, black boy fishing,
   4.5 x 3" 5
Advertising Trade Card, Rising Sun
   Stove Polish, black woman with out-
   stretched arms 3

*Child's Handkerchief, printed cotton,
children in various poses, mkd
"Marguerite Hillgren."* —Photo courtesy
Alderfer Auction Company.

Rattle, celluloid, made in Japan, 8" h, $45.
—Photo courtesy Collectors Auction Services.

Ashtray, ceramic, black saxaphone
  player, mkd "Made in Japan," c1930s,
  4.25" figure on 4.5 x 5.5" base 175
Bank, painted composition, spring
  mounted bobber head, black body,
  black and white eyes with blue
  accents, pink lips, brown eyebrows,
  gold ring and pearl earring inserted
  in each ear, mkd "Kenmar/Japan,"
  1960s, 6.5" h 35
Decanter, black clown, Japan, 8.5" h 20
Figurine, hollow bisque, seated black
  boy eating watermelon slice, c1900s,
  1.5 x 2.5 x 3" 75
Pencil Holder, celluloid, alligator eating
  black boy, souvenir from Atlantic City,
  1930s, 7.5" l 45
Postcard, 3 black children, "Ah's about
  as mad as ah can be. Yo' all cain't go
  an' two-time me," unused, Genuine
  Curteich-Chicago C T Art-Colortone ..10
Postcard, black mammy talking to 3
  well-dressed women, "The Love
  Drop," 1906 5
Postcard, linen, color, C T Chocolate
  Drops Comics, "Yo' all ah new in dis
  neighborhood–An don' kno an one...,"
  Quality Graphics, c1939 45
Recipe Box, plastic, red, front has
  plastic raised relief mammy head,
  Fosta Products, 1950s, 3 x 3.5" 35
Salt and Pepper Shakers, pr, black chef
  and cook, ceramic, white, gold
  accents, gold spoon in hand, made
  in Japan, 1930s, 4.5" h 35
Sheet Music, *Darktown Patrol*, Howard
  A Burr, 7 pp, ©1892 John F Ellis Co,
  Washington, DC, printed black and
  white cov 7

Sheet Music, *The Cotton Pickers,* Chas
  S Tarbox, McKinley Music Co, 1898 ..20
Shot Glass, 2 native adults and 2 native
  children by tree, "Here's Looking at
  You," 2.5" h 4
Toy, wood and string, mechanical,
  jointed, two 8.25" vertical rods suspending 4" figure of black boy wearing red skirt, yellow eyes with black
  dots, white mouth area dotted in red,
  mkd "Japan," c1935 35
Valentine, black girl carrying flowers,
  sgd "To Virginia E. from Donald T.
  1932," Germany, 6 x 3.5" 3
Valentine, black girl wearing yellow
  dress with pink polka dots, blue hair
  ribbon, flirty eyes, 4.5 x 2.5" 10
Whisk Broom, wooden, smiling black
  face, painted features, 9" h 65

BLAIR CERAMICS

After a stint at Purinton Pottery where
he was instrumental in designing several
Purinton patterns, including Apple, William
Blair moved to Ozark, Missouri, and opened
his own pottery there in 1946. Reacting neg-
atively to the traditional round dinnerware
shape, Blair produced square, rectangular,
and other geometric-shaped wares. Gay
Plaid, with its horizontal forest green stripes
and brown and chartreuse vertical stripes,
is the most highly sought after pattern.

At its peak, Blair Pottery employed thirty workers, produced as many as 3,500
pieces per week, and shipped to all forty-
eight states, Canada, Cuba, and Hawaii.
Neiman-Marcus and Marshall Field were
among the department stores that carried
Blair ceramics.

Bowl, 9" d 15
Bread and Butter Plate, 6" d 1
Casserole 20
Coffee Server 35
Coffee Server, individual 30
Cream Soup Cup, closed handle 12
Cream Soup Saucer 6
Creamer 4
Cup, open handle 4
Dish, 4" d 2
Gravy Boat, stick handle 12
Jug, ice lip 15

Jug, small 12
Mug 12
Plate, 7" d 4
Plate, 10" d 10
Platter, lug, 14" l 12
Relish Dish, 3-part .12
Soup Bowl, cov onion with stick handle . .8
Tumbler 18
Vegetable Bowl, divided 12
Vegetable Bowl, handled, 10" d 12

BLUE RIDGE

Southern Potteries of Erwin, Tenn., produced Blue Ridge dinnerware from the late
1930s until 1956. Four hundred patterns
graced eight basic shapes.

Club: Blue Ridge Collectors Club, 208 Harris
St., Erwin, TN 37650.

Newsletter: *National Blue Ridge
Newsletter,* 144 Highland Dr., Blountville,
TN 37617.

Periodical: *Blue Ridge Beacon Magazine,*
P.O. Box 629, Mountain City, GA 30562.

Becky, platter, 14 x 11.25" 10
Bluebell Bouquet, bread and butter
   plate, 6" d 10
Cherries, dinner plate, 10.5" d 5
Chicken and Rooster, plate, 9.25" d 28
Christmas Tree, plate, 10.25" d 40
Cock O' the Walk, saucer 10
Crab Apple, bread and butter plate, 6" d . .3
Crab Apple, creamer 10
Crab Apple, dinner plate, 9.25" d 25
Crab Apple, fruit bowl, 5.25" d 7
Crab Apple, platter, 14 x 11" 20
Crab Apple, serving bowl, 9.25" d 100
Crab Apple, sugar, cov 8
French Peasant, bread and butter plate,
   6" d 40
French Peasant, plate, 7.75" d 85
Fruit, salt and pepper shakers, pr, 2.5" h .10
Fruit, trivet, 6" sq 85
Green Briar, dinner plate, 9.5" d 10
Green Briar, gravy boat, 8" l, 2.5" h 10
Gumdrop Tree, child's creamer and
   sugar 70
Gypsy Fruit, plate, 10" d 12
Leafy Fruit Ring, bread and butter plate,
   6" d 8

Lovely Linda, dinner plate, 8.375" d 8
Lyonnaise, cup and saucer 70
Lyonnaise, salad bowl, Candlewick
   shape 130
Mardi Gras, creamer, Colonial style 3
Nocturne, dinner plate, 10.25" d 14
Peony, dinner plate, 8.75" d 25
Plantation Ivy, casserole, cov 50
Verona, plate, 10.5" d 20
Weathervane, cup and saucer 7
Weathervane, dinner plate, 10.5" d 14
Wrinkled Rose, creamer and sugar 20
Wrinkled Rose, cup and saucer 10
Wrinkled Rose, platter, 11.5 x 9" 9
Wrinkled Rose, soup bowl 7

BOOKENDS

Prices listed below are for pairs. Woe
to the dealer who splits pairs apart!

Club: Bookend Collector Club, 4510 NW 17th
Pl., Gainesville, FL 32605.

Aluminum, flying mallard, mkd "Bruce
   Fox," 7" h, 5.5" w 25
Brass, dachshund, 4.5" l, 4.75" h 70
Brass, Dante bust, Bradley & Hubbard,
   6" h, 4" w 80
Brass, duck heads, 5.5" h 6
Brass, elephant, mkd "1975 S.C.C." 10
Brass, little girl kneeling, Art Nouveau
   style, 4.5" h 35
Brass, University of Richmond, 5.5" h,
   5" w 10
Bronze, Abraham Lincoln, 5" h 15
Bronze, dolphins, 4.5 x 2.75 x 6.25" 20

Cast Iron, Amish couple, 5" h, $35. —Photo
courtesy Collectors Auction Services.

Bronze, elephant, 4" l, 3.5" h 50
Bronze, woman's face, Gromley, 7.75" h,
 5" w 150
Cast Iron, fly fisherman, 6" h 40
Cast Iron, Shakespeare's Home in
 Stratford-on-Avon, ©1925 Aronson
 Made in USA, 3.5" h, 4.5" w 18
Cast Iron, The Thinker 12
Ceramic, black poodle, Japan, 6 x 3" 10
Ceramic, Garfield and Odie, Enesco 15
Chalkware, Victorian ladies sewing,
 c1930s 25
Copper, cardinals, mkd "Cardinal Copr
 1928," 3.5" h 20
Glass, elephants, Blenko, 6 x 6" 25
Glass, horse head, Federal Glass,
 5.5 x 4.5" 10
Metal, American eagle 10
Metal, scottie dogs, white, 4.5" h, 3.5" l . .15
Metal, terrier pups, 6 x 4 x 3.5" 25
Wood, elf, seated on tree stump reading
 book, stamped "Made in Western
 Germany," 6.5" h 40

BOOKMARKS

Don't you just hate it when you lose your place in that book you've been reading? Bookmarks can help keep your sanity and they're easy to find, easy to display and fun to own.

Bookmark collecting dates back to the early 19th century. Bookmarks have been made from a wide variety of materials, including celluloid, cloth, cross-stitched needlepoint in punched paper, paper, sterling silver, wood and woven silk. Heavily embossed leather markers were popular between 1800 and 1860. Advertising markers appeared after 1860.

Woven silk markers are a favorite among collectors. T. Stevens of Coventry, England, manufacturer of Stevensgraphs, is among the most famous makers. Important U. S. companies that made woven silk bookmarks include John Best & Co., Phoenix Silk Manufacturing Co., J. J. Mannion, and Tilt & Son.

The best place to search for bookmarks is specialized paper shows. Be sure to check all related categories. Most dealers file them under subject headings, e.g.,

Insurance, Ocean Liners, World's Fair and so on.

Club: Antique Bookmark Collector's Assoc., 2224 Cherokee, St., Louis, MO 63118.

Newsletter: *Bookmark Collector,* 1002 W 25th St, Erie, PA 16502.

Armour's Extract of Beef, celluloid,
 diecut, black and white adv text on
 reverse, Armour & Co, Chicago,
 1.75 x 3.5" 35
Celery Stalks, celluloid, green, banded
 by 2 thin red lines, black lettering,
 "Chas. H. Kuehne Commission Co.
 Kansas City" .35
Cunningham Pianos, celluloid, purple
 and white floral bouquet, white
 lettering, "Matchless Cunningham
 Upright, Grand And Player Pianos"
 with Philadelphia address 8
Ericsson Line, celluloid, orange and
 blended gray fish, black and white
 reverse, "It Takes A Live Fish To Go
 Up Stream, Any Dead One Can Float
 Down," 3.25" l .15
Floral Bouquet, celluloid, blue, "God is
 our Refuge and Strength" 15
Lucas Tinted Gloss Paint, celluloid, diecut, color image of hand emerging
 from white shirt cuff, black text on
 palm of hand, black and white text
 on reverse, John Lucas & Co, 2.5 x
 5.25" 35
Meadow Gold Butter, yellow flowers on
 green leaves above product package,
 reverse lists branch offices in US
 cities, Fox River Butter Co 35
S Hamilton Company, celluloid, blue
 floral motif, black lettering, "We Sell
 Everything Musical," with "And Only
 The Best Of Everything" 8

A Century of Progress, Chicago-1934, diecut copper with blue enameled scenes, 4.5" l, $10.

The Union Press, celluloid, holly berries and leaves, black lettering, "Reading maketh a full man, conference a ready man, and writing an exact man," sponsor name on underside blade ...15

The Witching Hour, celluloid, diecut, image of mahogany standing clock trimmed in brass, souvenir for stage play at Hackett Theatre, black and white text on reverse, early 1900s, 1.5 x 5" 35

Utopian Chocolates, celluloid, figural gray owl, black lettering for Dow & Boston Co, Pulver Co, Rochester 35

BOOKS

There are millions of books out there. Some are worth a fortune. Most are hardly worth the paper they were printed on. Listing specific titles serves little purpose in a price guide such as this. By following these 10 guidelines, you can quickly determine if the books that you have uncovered have value potential.

1. Check your book titles in *American Book Prices Current,* which is published annually by Bancroft-Parkman, Inc., and is available at most libraries, as well as *Huxford's Old Book Value Guide,* published by Collector Books. When listing your books in preparation for doing research, include the full name of the author, expanded title, name of publisher, copyright date and edition and/or printing number.
2. Examine the bindings. Decorators buy handsomely bound books by the foot at prices ranging from $40 to $75 per foot.
3. Carefully research any children's book. Illustration quality is an important value key. Little Golden Books are one of the hottest book areas in the market today. In the late 1970s and early 1980s, Big Little Books were hot.
4. Buy all hardcover books about antiques and collectibles that you find that are less than $5. There is a growing demand for out-of-print antiques and collectibles books.

5. Check the edition number. Value, in most cases, rests with the first edition. However, not every first edition is valuable. Consult *Black's Bibliography of American Literature* or *Tannen's How to Identify and Collect American First Editions.*
6. Look at the multi-faceted aspects of the book and the subject that it covers. Books tend to be collected by type, e.g., mysteries, westerns, etc. Many collectors buy books as supplements to their main collection. A Hopalong Cassidy collector, although focusing primarily on the objects licensed by Bill Boyd, will want to own the Mulford novels in which Hopalong Cassidy originated.
7. Local histories and atlases always have a good market, particularly those printed between 1880 and 1930. Add to this centennial and other celebration volumes.
8. Check to see if the book was signed by the author. Generally an author's signature increases the value of the book. However, it was a common practice to put engraved signatures of authors in front of books during the last part of the 19th century. The Grant signature in the first volume of his two-volume memoir set is not original, but printed.
9. Book-club editions have little or no value with the exception of books done by George and Helen Macy's Limited Editions Club.
10. Accept the fact that the value of most books falls in the 50¢ to $2 range and that after all your research is done, this is probably what you'll get.

Club: Antiquarian Booksellers Assoc. of America, 20 W. 44th St., 4th Flr., New York, NY, 10036.

Newsletter: *Rare Book Bulletin,* P.O. Box 201, Peoria, IL 61650.

Periodicals: *Biblio Magazine,* 845 Wilamette St., Eugene, OR 97401; *Book Source Monthly,* 2007 Syossett Dr., P.O. Box 567, Cazenovia, NY 13035; *Firsts: The Book Collector's Magazine,* P.O. Box 65166, Tucson, AZ 85728.

BOOTJACKS

Unless you are into horseback riding, a bootjack is one of the most useless devices that you can have around the house. Why do so many individuals own one? The answer in our area is "just for nice." Actually, they are seen as a major accessory in trying to capture the country look. Cast iron reproductions are a major problem, especially for "Naughty Nellie" and "Beetle" designs.

Cast Iron, beetle, painted black, 9.25" l . .40
Cast Iron, cut-out scroll design, Downs
    & Co, 13.5" l 200
Cast Iron, cut-out wheel in center,
    late 19th C, 10.75" l 650
Cast Iron, figural devil, painted white
    horns and arms, cut-out circular eyes
    and stomach, painted red mouth,
    c1880-90, 10.5" l 300
Cast Iron, figural mermaid, outstretched
    arms, lying atop green seaweed, orig
    paint, c1900, 11" l 500
Cast Iron, heart and keyhole cut-outs,
    forked end, gold and white paint,
    9.375" l 175
Cast Iron, open heart and circle,
    scalloped sides, 13" l 225
Cast Iron, pair of pheasants, 19" l 225
Cast Iron, triangles in center, early
    20th C, 13.5" l 150
Cast Iron, V-shaped, ornate 45
Wood, hand carved pistol, folding-type,
    brass hinges and pins, c1860-70,
    10" l 350

Aluminum, "101 Ranch," figural steer head, 11.5" h, $82. —Photo courtesy Collectors Auction Services.

Wood, heart shaped loop, 25.5" l 125
Wood, Levi's adv, black emblem, 11.5 x
    3.5" 20
Wood, walnut, lady's legs with pointed
    toes, folding type, brass hinges and
    pins, c1860-70, 10" l 350

BOTTLE OPENERS, FIGURAL

Although this listing focuses on cast iron figural bottle openers, the most sought-after type of bottle openers, do not forget the tin advertising openers. Also known to some as church keys, the bulk still sell for between $2 and $10, a very affordable price range.

Clubs: Figural Bottle Opener Collectors Club, 9697 Gwynn Park Dr., Ellicott City, MD 21042; Just For Openers, P.O. Box 64, Chapel Hill, NC 27514.

Note: Listings are for cast iron bottle openers unless noted.

Alligator with Boy, black boy being bitten
    by alligator, 3" h 75
Bear, aluminum, holding cap in hand,
    wearing red top, blue pants, 3" h 150
Bear Head, wall mount, 3" h 150
Bottle, Deppen's Queen Quality Beer,
    1910s 25
Bulldog, 4" h 75
Cowboy, pot metal, clutching cactus,
    4.625" h 250
Dachshund, Wilton Flats 75
Dog, aluminum, barking brown dog
    and white dog sitting at base of
    crescent moon, 2" h 75
Dragon, open mouth, arched back,
    curled tail, 5" h 350
Elephant, open mouth, raised trunk,
    4.25" h 250
Four-Eyed Man with Moustache, wall
    mount, 32" h 75
Golf Bag and Caddie 50
Heart in Hand, upturned hand with cut-
    out heart in palm, 4.25" h 350
Lobster, flat back 35
Lobster, souvenir of Crustys North
    Kingstown, RI 3
Man and Woman, sitting on park bench,
    wood, 6 x 4 x 2" 15
Mother Goose, aluminum, 3.75" h 50

Parrot on Perch, painted yellow, blue, green, and red, 5" h, $60.
—Photo courtesy Collectors Auction Services.

Native American, wood 3
Pretzel, 3.375" h 250
Rooster, 3.125" h 50
Teeth, brass, mkd "Bottle Chops,"
    3.25" h 75

BOTTLES

Bottle collecting is such a broad topic that the only way one can hope to survive is by specialization. It is for this reason that several bottle subcategories are found elsewhere in this book. Bottles have a bad habit of multiplying. Do not start collecting them until you have plenty of room. I know one person whose entire basement is filled with Coca-Cola bottles bearing the imprint of different cities.

There are many bottle categories that are still relatively inexpensive to collect. In many cases, you can find a free source of supply in old dumps. Before getting too deeply involved, it pays to talk with other bottle collectors and to visit one or more specialized bottle collector shows.

Club: Federation of Historical Bottle Collectors, P.O. Box 1558, Southampton, PA 18966.

Periodical: *Antique Bottle and Glass Collector,* P.O. Box 180, East Greenville, PA 18041.

Note: Consult Maloney's Antiques & Collectibles Resource Directory, by David J. Maloney, Jr., at your local library for additional information on regional bottle clubs.

Adirondack Springs Mineral Water,
    White Hall, NY, emerald green, 1 pt ..45
Angostora Bitters, Prussian blue, smooth
    base, c1890, 4.375" h 60

Back Bar, clear, silver overlay cockfight
    scene, smooth base, tooled mouth,
    c1890-1910, 11" h 110
Castor Oil, aqua, pontil scarred base,
    rolled lip, c1835-50, 5.125" h 70
Cologne, opalescent turquoise blue,
    12-sided, smooth base, flared lip,
    3" h 100
Congress & Empire Spring Co, Hotchkiss'
    Sons, Saratoga, NY, Congress Water,
    American, emerald green, smooth
    base, applied double collar mouth,
    c1865-75, 1 pt 100
Crafts Distemper & Cough Remedy,
    amber, 6.5" h......................8
Dr D Jaynes Tonic Vermifuce, aqua,
    5.5" h 3
Dr Miles Restorative Nervine, aqua, 8" h .2
Dr Wilson's Hair Restorer, amber, smooth
    base, tooled lip, c1880-90, 7.75" h ...110
E I Barnett Magic Cure Liniment, Easton,
    PA, aqua, 6.25" h 10
Eversweet Milk, American Pure Milk
    Co, Philadelphia, clear glass, smooth
    base, applied mouth, "Pure Sterile,"
    1 qt 165
Highrock Congress Spring, C & W,
    Saratoga, NY, teal blue, smooth
    base, applied double collar mouth,
    c1865-75 200
Hoods Sarsaparilla, aqua, 8.5" h 3
Idaho Ginger Beer, Fish and Drug bot-
    tling Co., Pocatello, ID 125
IDAHO GINGER BEER Idaho's only one,
    by The Fish Drug and Bottling Co.,
    Pocatello, ID 125
Log Cabin Cough and Consumption
    Remedy, amber, smooth base, tooled
    lip, c1885-95, 7" h 130
Peppersauce, cathedral, green, open
    pontil, applied double collar mouth,
    c1850-60, 8.625" h 200
Poison, cobalt, Tinct Iodine, Curtis Bay
    Pharmacy, Baltimore, MD, ABM label,
    skull & crossbones, 1 oz 15
Poison, green, orange and white pyro
    lettering "Lin. Belladon. Poison,"
    polished pontil, tooled lip, c1880-1900,
    8" h 90
Rohrer's Expectoral Wild Cherry Tonic,
    Lancaster, PA, golden amber, iron
    pontin, applied sloping double collar
    mouth, c1855-70, 10.5" h 450

Mobiloil, baked-on logo, 1 pt, 1950s, 10.75" h, $120. — Photo courtesy Collectors Auction Services.

San Remo Toilet Water, Dr J B Lynas & Son, Logansport, 5.5" h 12

Saratoga Seltzer Water, teal blue, smooth base, applied mouth, c1870-80, 1/2 pt 125

Scent, clear, figural seahorse, 26 ribbed spiral pattern swirled to right, applied clear glass rigaree, c1830-50, 3.375" h 110

The Great Dr Kilmers Swamp Root Kidney, Liver & Bladder Remedy, aqua, 8" h 10

Warners Safe Kidney & Liver Cure, Rochester, NY, amber, 9.25" h 25

White House Brand Vinegar, clear, 1 pt 20

Youatts Gargling Oil, Comstock & Bros, NY, aqua, 9" h .40

BOXES

We have reached the point with some 20th century collectibles where the original box may be more valuable than the object it held. If the box is colorful and contains a picture of the product, it has value.

Boxes have always been a favorite among advertising collectors. They are three-dimensional and often fairly large in size. The artwork reflects changing period tastes. Decorators like the pizzazz that boxes offer. The wood box with a lithographed label is a fixture in the country household.

Advertising, American Biscuit & Mfg Co, wood, litho paper label, parrot, 10.5" l 75

Advertising, Bromo Seltzer, wood, stenciled labels, 9.5" l 175

Advertising, Delco Light Batteries, wood, 4 compartments, "Don't Spill Liquid/Delco Light Batteries/Dayton, Ohio," 43.5" l, 22" h, 10.5" d 30

Advertising, Foley's Honey and Tar Compound, wood, dovetailed, stenciled labels, 24.25" l 65

Advertising, Kow-Kure, wood, dovetailed, litho paper label, 12.25" h 60

Advertising, Magnolia Brand Condensed Milk, wood, stenciled letters, 13" h . . .35

Advertising, Peters Cartridge, wood, debossed lettering, text on 4 sides, "Steel Where Steel Belongs/Small Arms Ammunition/The Peters Cartridge Co. Cincinnati O. U.S.A.," 14.5" l, 9.5" w, 9.125" d 70

Advertising, Robinson Bros Crackers and Fine Cakes, wood, litho paper labels on front and 1 side, factory and eagle vignettes, 23.5" l 175

Advertising, Winan Bros Indian Cure, wood, stenciled labels, 12.25" l 65

Advertising, Winchester Repeater Shells, cardboard, paper label on 3 sides and bottom, 12-25 gauge shells, Winchester Repeting Arms Co, New Haven, CT, 4.5" l 4.25" w, 2.5" h 30

Band, floral, wallpaper, brown and green, off-white ground, bentwood, 13.75" l 175

Hat, cov, bent laminated wood, leather strap handle, black painted label, int paper label, 16.25" h, 12" d 70

Advertising, Peters Target Paper Shot Shells, paper litho over cardboard, Peters Cartridge Co., 4.25" h, 4.25" w, 2.5" d, $75. —Photo courtesy Collectors Auction Services.

Toothpick Holder, gypsy pot, dark brown slag, $8.

Advertising, Rush Park Seed Co., wood, paper decal on front and inside lid, 5.5" h, 28" w, 13.5" l, $175. —Photo courtesy Collectors Auction Services.

Knife, bentwood, cutouts and wooden
  knob fasteners on laminate sides,
  old varnish finish, 11.75" l 45
Writing, olive wood veneer, mahogany
  bands, fitted int, brass lock and key,
  inlaid medallion on lid replaced,16" l .225

BOYD CRYSTAL ART GLASS

The Boyds, Bernard and his son, purchased the Degenhart Glass Factory in 1978. Since that time, they have reissued a number of the Degenhart forms. Their productions can be distinguished by the color of the glass and the "D" in a diamond mark. The Boyd family continues to make contemporary collectible glass at its factory in Cambridge, Ohio.

Newsletters: *Boyd's Crystal Art Glass,* 1203 Morton Ave, P.O. Box 127, Cambridge, OH 43725; *Jody & Darrell's Glass Collectibles Newsletter,* P.O. Box 180833, Arlington, TX 76096.

Chick Salt, cobalt 10
Figurine, Artie, penguin, mirage 8
Figurine, Bingo, deer, milk white 14
Figurine, Brian, bunny, bamboo 12
Figurine, Chuckles, clown, blue 12
Figurine, Eli and Sarah, Amish couple,
  milk chocolate 20
Figurine, Freddie, hobo clown, cashmere
  pink 8
Figurine, Fuzzy, teddy bear, black 12

Figurine, Jeremy, frog, alpine blue 8
Figurine, kewpie, vaseline 12
Figurine, Mabel, cow, vaseline 12
Figurine, Panda, white 15
Figurine, Patrick, balloon bear, nile green .8
Figurine, Pooche, dog, pale orchid 14
Figurine, Rex, dinosaur, vaseline 16
Figurine, Sammy, squirrel, mirage 13
Figurine, Teddy, tugboat, cashmere pink .12
Figurine, Virgil, clown, red 12
Figurine, Willie, mouse, pink 9
Slipper, bow, tangy lime 9
Slipper, cat, nutmeg 10
Toothpick Holder, black 15
Toothpick Holder, Indian Head, vaseline . .8

BOYD'S BEARS & FRIENDS

Gary and Tina Lowenthal of McSherrytown, Pennsylvania, began the Boyd plush toy line in 1979. The Boyd name came from Boyd, Maryland, the location of the Lowenthal's antiques business.

An active secondary market, especially on the Internet, has developed for discontinued Boyd plush toys and cast resin collectibles. Prices should be viewed as highly speculative. Like many collectibles of this type, their primary appeal is to the buyer's heart, not head. Boyd does not release production numbers. Scarcity is more related to speculative hoarding than actual lack of product.

Newsletter: *Lions, Tigers & Boyds, Oh My!,* P.O. Box 1393, Easton, MA 02334.

Bearstone, Angelica, The Guardian,
  #2266 85
Bearstone, Bailey, Poor Ole Bear 70
Bearstone, Bailey & Becky, The Diary,
  #228304 55

Bearstone, Bailey, The Cheerleader, #2268 .... .50

Bearstone, Bessie, The Santa Cow, #2239 .... .80

Bearstone, Cookie Catberg, #2250 ...... .60

Bearstone, Edmond, The Graduate ..... .50

Bearstone, Elliott, The Hero, #2280 ..... .75

Bearstone, Flash McBear, photographer .65

Bearstone, Hop-along Deputy .... .65

Bearstone, Manheim, The Eco-Moose, #2243 .... .75

Bearstone, Neville, The Compubear .... .55

Dollstone, Anne, The Masterpiece, #3599 .... .40

Dollstone, Caitlin, Diapering Baby, #3525 .60

Dollstone, Karen, Mother's Present, #3501-01 .... .50

Dollstone, Natalie and Joy, #3519 ...... .50

Dollstone, Whitney with Wilson, #3524 . .45

Folkstone, Abigail, Peaceable Kingdom, #2829 .... .40

Folkstone, Beatrice, The Giftgiver, #2836 .45

Folkstone, Buster Goes a Courtin', #2844 .55

Folkstone, Ernest Hemmingmoose, The Hunter, #2835 .... .45

Folkstone, Nanny, The Snowman, #2817 .50

Folkstone, Pearl, The Knitter, #36501 .... .25

Folkstone, Ziggy, The Duffer, #2838 ..... .45

Plush, Allie Fuzzbucket .... .10

Plush, Barkley McFarkle 7

Plush, Harvey Hoppleby 8

Plush, Millie LaMoose .... .10

Plush, Paddy McDoodle Bear 8

BOY SCOUTS

Collecting Boy Scout memorabilia is a mature field with well-established subcategories. Books have been published detailing at least seventeen of these subs.

Most collectors focus mainly on cloth patches. There are many kinds and each has devotees. Merit badges, Cub Scout insignia, High Adventure patches, Jamboree patches, Council patches, and Order of the Arrow are just a sampling.

Because OA (Order of the Arrow) patches were issued locally in small quantity and collectors all over the country are seeking them, prices on scarce issues have been driven up to thousands of dollars. Prices for old insignia and handbooks and pre-1940 uniforms have also risen.

Boy Scout collectors buy, sell and trade at Trade-O-Rees. Most are held annually under the management of local collectors and attract from 50 to 200 collectors. These events are great learning opportunities as experienced collectors willingly help out those with less knowledge.

Advisor: Cal Holden, Box 264, Doylestown, OH 44230, (330) 658-2793.

Clubs: American Scouting Traders Assoc., P.O. Box 210013, San Francisco, CA 94121; International Badgers Club, 2903 W. Woodbine Dr., Maryville, TN 37803; National Scouting Collectors Society, 806 E. Scott St., Tuscola, IL 61953.

Periodicals: *Fleur-de-Lis,* 5 Dawes Ct., Novato, CA 94947; *Scout Memorabilia,* (Lawrence L. Lee Scout Museum and Max I. Silver Scouting Library), P.O. Box 1121, Manchester, NH 03105.

Book, *Winter Camping*, proof copy in wraps, slight wear, 1927 .... .25

Diary, Boy Scout, cov scuffed, 1941 ..... .20

Equipment Catalog, 1917 .... .25

Handbook, *Boy Scout Handbook*, soft cov, 1910 .... .700

Handbook, *Boy Scout Handbook*, 1st ed, 10th printing, spine stripped, edge worn .... .100

Handbook, *Boy Scout Handbook*, 3rd ed, 1st printing, slight wear .... .40

Belt, "National Scout Jamboree, Virginia, 1981" on buckle, George Washington profile and scout, brown leather belt with emb scrolls and scouting emblem, mkd "Toolcraft, Top Grain Cowhide," 32" l, $20.

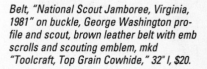

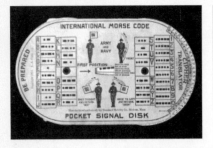

Pocket Signal Disc, International Morse Code, ©1914 L. A. Clapp, Standard Novelty Co., Melrose, MA, 5.75 x 3.25", $45.

Handbook, *Scout Master Handbook*,
    3rd ed, 2 vol, 1937 30
Hat Pin, Den Mother's, "Cub Scouts
    BSA," painted .4
Medal, Eagle, Robbins 3, ribbon slightly
    faded, 1940 80
Merit Badge, First Aid, square, 1920s 3
Merit Badge, Music, narrow, tan,
    1936-46 5
Merit Badge, Plumbing, square, 1920s . .25
Neckerchief, square, red, NJ, 1937 110
Patch, Order of the Arrow, Lodge 62,
    Sioux, first jacket patch, fully
    embroidered 1,000
Patch, Order of the Arrow, Lodge 151,
    first fully embroidered flap 8
Patch, Order of the Arrow, Lodge 542,
    Kiminschi, first and only flap, not
    fully embroidered 2,100
Patch, Region 1, type R2, felt, 77 mm d . .90
Patch, Region 10, type 3B 20
Patch, Sea Scout Skipper, gauze back . . .5
Patch, Star, type 3, fat star, no knot,
    early 1920s 200
Patch, Tenderfoot, type 7, embroidered
    cut edge, gauze back 3
Pennant, felt, blue, white inscription,
    c1940, 30" l 20
Pin, Tenderfoot, silver plated, horizontal
    slogan, safety pin clasp 100
Pin, Wolf, Cubs BSA, first type, square . .50
Pinback Button, "Do A Good Turn Daily,"
    multicolored portrait, dark blue
    ground, 1920s 15

BRASS

Brass is a durable, malleable and ductile metal alloy, consisting mainly of copper and zinc. It appears in this guide because of the wide variety of objects made from it.

Bookends, pr, praying hands, 3 x 2.25 x
    7.25" 30
Cigarette Case, engraved pagoda scene
    on 1 side, flowers and bird in flight on
    other side, 3.25 x 3.125" 10
Corkscrew, turned hardwood handle,
    5" l 35
Figure, bulldog, mkd "Made in India,"
    4.5" l 12
Letter Opener, emb floral garland and
    trailing vines on handle, 9.5" l 10
Lumber Gauge, Fringeli Rule Co,
    Cleveland, OH 20
Microscope, C Reichert Wien, #18565,
    14" h, 4.25 x 6" base 200
Mortar and Pestle, unmkd, 3.5" h 25
Motor Car Lamp, S F Edge Ltd, London,
    12 x 5.5" 35
Pillbox, enameled dec, blue forget-me-
    not on white ground, dark blue and
    gold enamel trim, 1.75" w, 1.375" d,
    .875" h 10
Pipe Holder, figural dog, 4" l, 3.5" h 6
Skater's Lantern, 7.25" h 60

Kettle, riveted handle, $80.

Towel Holder, lion head 45
Trivet, cat surrounded by horseshoe
   with "Good Luck," England, c1930   . . .30
Wall Hanging, bird in flight, mkd
   "Lunenburg N.S.," 12" wingspan 5
Watering Can Nozzle, 4.125" w 18
Zippo Lighter, emb race car on front,
   bottom stamped "F&X" 5

BREWERIANA

Beer is a liquid bread, or so I was told growing up in Pennsylvania German country. It is hard to deny German linkage with the brewing industry when your home community contained the Horlacher, Neuweiler and Uhl breweries.

Brewery signs and trays, especially from the late 19th and early 20th centuries, contain some of the finest advertising lithography of the period. Three-dimensional advertising figures from the 1930s through the 1970s are no slouches, either. Brewery advertising has become expensive. Never fear. You can build a great breweriana collection concentrating on barroom accessories such as foam scrapers, coasters and tap knobs.

Clubs: American Breweriana Assoc., Inc., P.O. Box 11157, Pueblo, CO 81001; East Coast Breweriana Assoc., P.O. Box 64, Chapel Hill, NC 27514; National Assoc. of Breweriana Advertising, 2343 Met-To-Wee Ln., Wauwatosa, WI 53226.

Ashtray, Grain Belt Beer, glass, red
   print, 1950s 3
Back Bar Statue, Blatz Beer, metal,
   banjo player and bottle, 1950s 95
Bank, Metz Beer, ceramic, 1950s, 6.5" h .28
Bank, Yankee Beer, figural 16 oz can,
   1950s 100
Bottle Display, Stag Stout, cardboard,
   unused, 9 x 14" .8
Bottle Opener, Esslinger's Beer, bottle
   shaped, 1940s 25
Bottle Opener, Krueger Beer and Ale,
   1940s 5
Box Cutter, Walter's Beer, 1950s 15
Brochure, Coors, "Time in a Bottle," 8 pp,
   history of Coors Brewery up to 1984 . .10
Can, E & B Special, cone top, 1940s 75

Can, Hamms Beer, flat top, 1940s 18
Coaster, Schaefer Beer, 100th Anniver-
   sary, 1940s, 4.25" d 8
Coin, Clipper Ale, "Your Good Health
   Brewed By Harvard," 1930s 16
Coin, Old Dutch Beer, 1950s 10
Cookbook, *Walter's Beer Chinese Cook-
   book*, 64 pp, 1950s 40
Drinking Glass, Pacific Beer, etched,
   gold rim, 1900s 80
Greeting Card, Pabst Brewing, "Season's
   Greetings," 1950s, 6 x 8" 20
Key Chain Fob, Harvard Brewing, 1930s .14
Letterhead, Lebanon Valley Brewing,
   1945 10
License Plate, Sunny Beer, metal, 1960s,
   11 x 5.75" 6
Light, Burger Beer, reverse glass, tin
   frame, 1950s, 10 x 10" 100
Lighter, Falstaff Beer, 1950s 14
Match Safe, Union Brewing, Newark,
   NJ, metal and leather, 1900s 28
Menu Sheet, Piels Beer, 1950s, 6.5 x
   10.5" 5
Pinback Button, Olympia Beer, 1970s 4
Playing Cards, Peoples Beer, used,
   1950s 18
Pocket Mirror, Old German Beer, gold
   dog, 1950s 70
Postcard, Maier & Zobelin's Brewery,
   used, 1891 5
Postcard, Terre Haute Brewing, color,
   1909 8
Record, *Ballantine Beer, Sing Along
   with Mitch Miller*, 33 1/3 rpm, 1950s . . .3

Sign, Kaier's Beer, diecut cardboard, 16.5" h, 19.5" w, $100. —Photo courtesy Collectors Auction Services.

Tray, Hornung Beer, Jacob Hornung Brewing, Philadelphia, PA, 12" d, $65.

Salt and Pepper Shakers, pr, West
   Virginia Special Export, painted labels,
   1940s 70
Scraper, Schmidt's Beer, Bakelite,
   2-sided, 1940s .15
Sign, Ballantine's On Tap, reverse glass,
   1940s, 17.5 x 15" 65
Sign, Eigenbrot Brewery, "Schiller Beer,"
   Baltimore, MD, tin over cardboard,
   1910s, 13.25 x 9.25" 60
Sign, Great Falls Select Beer, molded
   plastic, 1970s, 18 x 11.5" 24
Sign, Kaiers In Bottles And Cans, foil
   covered composition, 1940s, 10 x 9" . .25
Sign, Knickerbocker Draft, emb tin,
   1950s, 9.5" d 15
Stock Certificate, Fehrs Brewing,
   Louisville, KY, 1940s, 12.25 x 9.5" 16
Tap Knob, Columbia Beer, Bakelite,
   printed aluminum insert, 1940s 75
Thermometer, Horlacher Beer,
   Allentown, PA, "It's a case of Flavor,"
   1950s, 9 x 36" .100
Tray, Iroquois Beer & Ale, 1940s, 13" d . .30
Tray, Palisades Beer, oval, 1910s,
   16.5 x 13.5" 100

BREYER HORSES

    The Breyer line of plastic model horses
has been on the market since the 1950s.
During the past five decades the company
has not only produced a line of horses but
also dogs, wildlife and farm animals. In 1984
Breyer Molding Company was sold to
Reeves International and moved from
Chicago to New Jersey. The Breyer company is still in business today.

    Breyer consists of four lines that are
differentiated by height. *Traditional* (horses
and animals in separate categories), which
average around nine inches; *Classic,* which
average six inches; *Little Bit,* which stand
around four inches; and *Stablemates,*
which average three inches.

Advisor: Antina Richards-Pennock, c/o
Warhawk Hobbies, 3206 S. Alpine Rd.,
Rockford, IL 61109, e-mail:warhk98@aol.com.

Newsletter: *The Model Horse Trader,* 34428
Yucaipa Blvd, #E119, Yucaipa, CA 92399.

Periodicals: *Hobby Horse News,* 2053
Dyrehaven Dr., Tallahassee, FL 32311, *Just
About Horses,* (company-sponsored), 14
Industrial Rd., Pequannock, NJ 07440.

TRADITIONAL SERIES

Brahma Bull, #70, gray and white 45
Elephant, #91, gray 25
Family Arabian Foal, #9, alabaster 25
Family Arabian Mare, #8, alabaster 30
Fighting Stallion "Ponakah-Eemetah,"
   #897, buckskin .50
Five Gaiter "Project Universe," #117,
   pinto 50
Foundation Stallion, #64, black, MIB 45
Halla, #63, bay 50
Icelandic Porcelain, #79192, brown and
   white 200
Jumping Horse, #300, bay 55
Morganglanz, #59, chestnut 40
Mustang, #87, buckskin 50

Five Gaiter Palomino, #53, glossy, $100.

Oxydol, #917, alabaster 45
Proud Arabian Mare, #849, mare 35
Running Foal, #849, pinto, MIB 35
Saint Bernard, #321 35
Secretariat "Decorator," gold charm . . .50
Sea Star, #16, chestnut 35
Silver Comet Polo Pony, #700594, dapple .40
Touch of Class, #420, bay 55
Westen Pony, with saddle, #41, pinto . . .30

OTHER SERIES

Classic Black Beauty, #3040, 4 horses,
　MIB 85
Classic "Terrang," #605, bay 25
Little Bit Quarter Horse, #9015, bay 11
Stablemate Draft Horse, #5055,
　chestnut 10
Stablemate Morgan Mare, #5038, bay . . .10
Stablemate Native Dancer, #5023, gray . .9

BRITISH ROYALTY COLLECTIBLES

　　This is one of those categories where you can get in on the ground floor. Every king and queen, potential king and queen and their spouses is collectible. Buy commemorative items when they are new. I have a few Prince Harry items. We may not have royal blood in common, but...

　　Most individuals collect by monarch, prince, or princess. Take a different approach—collect by form, e.g., mugs, playing cards, etc. British royalty commemoratives were made at all quality levels. Stick to high-quality examples.

　　As in any modern collectible category, prices are speculative. This is especially true for limited edition Princess Di commemoratives. It is common to find recent issues at flea markets selling for much less than their original price.

Club: Commemorative Collector's Society, Lumless House, Gainsborough Rd., Winthrope, Near Newark, Nottingham NG24 2NR, U.K.

Badge, Queen Victoria Jubilee, fabric
　and metal, inscription on reverse of
　pendant "Jubilee year 1887," red,
　white, and blue striped fabric ribbon
　mounted over thin brass rods 50

Calendar/Thermometer, 1943, Queen
　Elizabeth and King George, 7.25 x 7" . .10
Carte de Visite, Prince Edward and
　Alexandra of Denmark, c1863, 2.5 x
　4.25" 40
Cup and Saucer, Princess Margaret,
　Aynsley, 1958 .50
Handkerchief, King George and Queen
　Mary, "Jubilee, 1910-1935" 30
Magazine, *Royalty Monthly*, #1, Jul 1981 .15
Pinback Button, King George VI and
　Queen Elizabeth Coronation, domed,
　celluloid portrait, inscribed "Long
　May They Reign/Coronation 1937,"
　rear fastener pin holds miniature light
　bulb and metal wire which illuminates
　button when pressed, orig box,
　Litbadge, 1.5" d 15
Pinback Button, King George VI and
　Queen Elizabeth Coronation, red,
　white, and blue, bluetone photos,
　depicts world globe with countries
　of British Empire, crossed British
　and Empire flags, rim inscription
　"Coronation of Their Majesties King
　George VI and Queen Elizabeth,"
　dated 1937 8
Pinback Button, Royal Tour Souvenir,
　red, white, and blue, center red heart
　symbol holding black and white profile
　photos above inscription "Always In
　Our Hearts," outer inscription "Royal
　Tour Souvenir 1954/Australia" 15
Plate, Queen Alexandra and King Edward
　VII, 5" d 18

Plate, Edward VIII, mkd "Wedgwood England," numbered, 8.375" sq, $50.

Souvenir Book, Queen Elizabeth II, "A Queen Is Crowned," 24 pp, black and white illus, $5.

Playing Cards, Queen Mother and King George VI, double deck, Anderson's, Edinburgh, MIP 75
Pocket Mirror, Queen Elizabeth, celluloid, tinted photo, c1936-37, 2 x 2.75" ..15
Postcard, Edward VII Coronation, postmarked Jun 1902 8
Program, King George and Queen Elizabeth Coronation, 32 pp, May 12, 1937, includes centerfold procession route map and genealogical table of royal family, 8.5 x 11" 15
Tin, Queen Elizabeth II, litho tin, color portrait in royal military uniform, repeated royalty symbols around perimeter, mkd "Made In England By Edward Sharp & Sons Ltd. of Maidstone, Kent," c1953, 4 x 5.5 x 1.5" 8
Tobacco Card, King George at Wimbledon, #18, Our King & Queen series, W D & H O Wills Ltd, 1937, 14 x 2.5" ...3
Vase, King George VI and Queen Elizabeth, profiles 1 side, eagle on other side, Wm H Plummer & Co, NY .600
Wristwatch, Charles and Diana, clear crystal over dial face features portraits with first name, marriage year, and royalty symbol, 1981 50

BURMA SHAVE

The famous Burma Shave jingle ad campaign was the brainstorm of Allan Odell, son of Burma-Vita's founder, Clinton M. Odell. The first sets, six signs placed 100 feet apart, appeared in 1926 on a stretch of road from Minneapolis to Albert Lea. Success was instantaneous and the Burma Shave name was fixed in the minds of drivers across the country. If You...Don't Know...Whose Signs These Are...You Haven't Driven...Very Far...Burma Shave.

Advisor: Steve Soelberg, 29126 Laro Dr., Agoura Hills, CA, 91301, (818) 889-9909.

Aerosol Can 100
After Shave, full 75
Blades 20
Gift Set, complete 200
Jar, cov, empty 20
Jar, open, empty 15
Letterhead 50
Lotion Bottle, empty 15
Lotion Bottle, full 50
Printer's Blocks 50
Shaving Cream Tube 25
Sign, roadside, individual 200
Sign, roadside, set of six 1,500
Talc 50
Toy Truck, metal 50
Trolley Ad 200

BUSTER BROWN

R. F. Outcault could have rested on his Yellow Kid laurels. Fortunately, he did not and created a second great cartoon character—Buster Brown. The strip first appeared in the Sunday, May 4, 1902, *New York Herald*. Buster's fame was closely linked to Tige, his toothily grinning evil-looking bulldog.

Most of us remember Buster Brown and Tige because of Buster Brown Shoes. The shoe advertisements were popular on radio and television shows of the 1950s. "Look for me in there too."

Club: R. F. Outcault Society, 103 Doubloon Dr., Slidell, LA 70461.

Advertising Tear Sheet, *Ladies Home Journal,* Sep 1924, "Buster Brown Shoes/Save Childrens Feet Needless Suffering," 3 children putting skates on over their shoes, 10 x 14" 20
Bank, Buster and Tige, cast iron, 5" h ...10
Blotter, "Brownbilt Shoes for Men—for Women, Buster Brown Shoes for Boys—for Girls, Buster Brown Tread Straight Shoes/Enjoy Glorious Foot Health in Shoes Correctly Styled," 6.25 x 3.5" 10

Child's Feeding Dish, ceramic, Bavarian, 6" d, $35. —Photo courtesy Gene Harris Antique Auction Center, Inc.

Book, *My Resolutions*, R F Outcault, 1906 40
Candy Container, papier-mâché 175
Clock, light-up, "Buster Brown America's Favorite Children's Shoes," Pam Clock Co, Rochelle, NY 250
Creamer, hp, transfer of Buster Brown pouring tea into teacup for Tige, 3.75" h, 2.5" d .45
Figurine, Buster, holding Tige, #5655, made in Japan, 3.5" h 10
Game, Buster Brown at the Circus, complete, Selchow & Righter, NY . . .250
Kite, Buster and Tige, "Buster Brown Shoes For Boys," 1940s 10
Pencil Sharpener, plastic 3
Pinback Button, celluloid, "Resolved– That if it busted, it wasn't Buster Brown Hose Supporter" 10
Pinback Button, "Member Buster Brown Gang," 1950s .10
Pinback Button, Buster in brimmed hat bearing his name, back paper text "Look for Buster's Picture on the Sole of Every Shoe Manufactured by Brown Shoe Co, St Louis" 75
Pocketknife, light brown jigged bone handle, oval "Brown Shoes Company, St. Louis," and "Buster Brown Shoes," 4 blades, 1930s, 3.625" l 70
Pocket Mirror, "Buster Brown Vacation Days Carnival," 2.125" 5
Postcard, valentine, "I've Gone Without Long Enough, I'm Going to John A. Roberts and Co., Utica, NY," 1906 10

Watch Fob, Buster and Tige with 2 children on front, reverse inscription "Buster Brown Blue Ribbon Shoes for Boys, for Girls, White House Shoes for men, for women/Brown's 5 Mark means Quality" 125
Whistle, litho tin, light yellow, colorful Buster and Tige, "Tread Straight Shoes" on perimeter of barrel, "Buster Brown Shoes" on 1 end, "Brownbilt Shoes" on other, mkd "Made in Germany," 1930s 50

CALCULATORS

The Texas Instruments TI-2500 Datamath entered the market in the early 1970s. This electronic calculator, the marvel of its era, performed four functions—addition, subtraction, multiplication, and division. This is all it did. It retailed for over $100. Within less than a decade, calculators selling for less than $20 were capable of doing five times as many functions.

Early electronic calculators are dinosaurs. They deserve to be preserved. When collecting them, make certain to buy examples that retain their power transformer, instruction booklet, and original box. Make certain any calculator that you buy works. There are few around who know how to repair one.

It is a little too early for a category on home computers. But a few smart collectors are starting to stash away the early Texas Instrument and Commodore models.

Casio FX-2500, scientific 3
Commodore 899A 15

Casio FX-451, $5.

Hewlett Packard 45, scientific 50
Novelty, Dukes of Hazzard, black plas-
    tic, black vinyl case 3
Novelty, Inspector Gadget, Disney, 4 x
    2.5" 5
Novelty, pool table 15
Portland Cement Assoc Soil-Cement
    Calculator, slide-type, ©1964 Perry
    Graf Corp 7
Power Speed Calculator, Rite Autronics
    Corp 5
Texas Instruments 1200, LTA0776 5
Texas Instruments Little Professor, 1978 .10
Texas Instruments Spirit of '76, orig box .20
Texas Instruments SR-50 50

CALENDAR PLATES

Calendar plates are one of the traditional, affordable collecting categories. A few
years ago, they sold in the $10 to $20 range;
now that figure has jumped to $35 to $50.

Value rests with the decorative motif
and the place for which it was issued. A fun
collection would be to collect the same
plate and see how many different merchants and other advertisers utilized it.

Newsletter: *The Calendar,* 710 N. Lake
Shore Dr., Tower Lakes, IL 60010.

1910, Cupid in center 30
1911, bird dogs center 35
1912, biplane, Cincinnati, OH grocery
    adv 65

*1911, "Should auld acquaintance be for-
got, Compliments of G. E. Wakefield," $55.*

1913, Quebec country scene center 30
1914, Washington's tomb, artist sgd
    "A. Smith" 32
1915, boy and girl carrying large wicker
    basket of apples, W H May, Lexington,
    KY adv 35
1916, pair of birds center, The Family
    Liquor Store, Old Cove, F E Smith,
    Steelton, PA adv, sgd "Edwin
    Magargee" 37
1918, violets and 21 clocks from cities
    around the world 28
1919, ship scene center 25
1920, American Eagle and Victory, Great
    World War 32
1921, dove and 5 allied flags 37
1922, dog flushing out birds center 45
1924, flowers, holly berries and leaves
    around calendar 30
1928, deer in field center, Williamsville,
    IL adv 50
1930, Dutch boy and dog, Saunemin, IL
    adv 55
1954, Fiesta ware, ivory 35
1962, Merry Christmas, Gately's 15
1969, God Bless Our House, Meakin 8

CALENDARS

The primary reason calendars are collected is for the calendar art. Prices hinge
on quality of printing and the pizazz of the
subject. A strong advertising aspect adds to
the value.

A highly overlooked calendar collecting
area is the modern art and photographic
calendar. For whatever reason, there is little interest in calendars dating after 1940.
Collectors are making a major mistake.
There are some great calendars from this
later time period selling for less than $2.

"Gentlemen's" calendars did not grace
the kitchen wall, but they are very collectible. Illustrations range from the pinup
beauties of Elvgren and Moran and the
Esquire Vargas ladies in the 1930s to the
Playboy Playmates of the 1960s. Early
Playboy calendars sell in the $50 plus
range.

But, what's the fun of having something
you cannot display openly? The following
list will clear corporate censors with no
problems.

Club: Calendar Collector Society, 18222 Flower Hill Way #299, Gaithersburg, MD 20879.

1876, Centennial/Home Insurance Co, historical scenes 225

1888, Hood's Sarsaparilla 40

1889, Aetna Insurance Co, litho early steam fire engine pulled by 2 racing horses, 6.25 x 9.5" 375

1889, Success Horse Collars 375

1890, Dubuque Fire & Marine Insurance .75

1892, Metropolitan Life Insurance Co, diamond-shaped litho of girl 55

1893, Adams Pepsin Tutti Fruitti Gum 35

1893, Clay & Robinson Livestock, children and flowers 30

1893, Hires Root Beer 175

1893, Prudential Insurance Co 80

1894, Hood's Sarsaparilla, chromolithograph of little girls 50

1897, Boston Rubber Shoe Co 30

1900, United States Fidelity & Guaranty Co 450

1901, American Cereal Co, frolic fortune telling 40

1901, Fairbanks Fairy Soap 65

1901, Houghton Co Brewers, head portrait of game dog holding game bird in mouth 75

1902, John Hancock Mutual Life Insurance Co, young girl asleep next to St Bernard dog 200

1903, Hanan Shoe Co, elves and Indians .175

1904, DeLaval, children in field 250

1938, Gilmore Gasoline, paper, Elvgren pin-up illus, 15.25" h, $30. —Photo courtesy Collectors Auction Services.

1904, Singer, Indian on diecut animal skin, 20 x 16" .150

1904, Sleepy Eye Milling Co, 4.5 x 5.25" .275

1905, Christian Herald, 4 panel diecut, Victorian girls and birds 100

1906, Fleischmann's Yeast, horse-drawn wagon 110

1908, Bemis Brothers Bag Co, first 12 Presidents 90

1911, Pratt's Veterinary Remedies, lady and horse 225

1911, Springfield Breweries, lady in black 400

CALIFORNIA POTTERIES

California pottery collectors divide into three distinct groups—art pottery, dinnerware, and figurine collectors. California art pottery is trendy and expensive. Dinnerware prices are stable. Figurine prices are cooling following a major price run in the mid- and late 1990s.

California pottery collectors focus on firm, pattern, or period within their adopted specialty. Over a dozen checklist books dealing with a specific manufacturer have been published in the last ten years. Each was followed by a short speculative period in the company's product.

Brastoff, Sascha, ashtray, aztec jumping horse, C21, 8" w 45

Brastoff, Sascha, plate, Pagodas, curled lip, 12" d 85

Brastoff, Sascha, vase, Rooftops, F20, 6" h 45

Brayton Laguna, figurine, pelican, mkd "Brayton Laguna 41-43," 7.5" h 25

Brayton Laguna, planter, woman standing with 2 Irish wolfhounds, 10.75" h . .25

Brayton Laguna, vase, woman carrying 2 baskets, 7.75" h 25

DeBow, dresser lamp, woman holding basket, mkd "DeBow of California Original by Suzanne," 9.5" h, price for pair 35

DeForrest, onion dish, hp dec, 4.5" h, 4.25" w 25

DeRosa, nightlight, figural comical train, rose, green, blue, and brown on off-white ground, 5.5" l, 4.5" w 10

Freeman-McFarlin, ashtray, mottled
green, 7.5 x 4.5" 5
Garden City, vase, red-orange, 7.5" h . . .125
Gilner, planter, elf sitting on tree stump,
1950 10
Keeler, Brad, salt and pepper shakers,
pr, figural bass, paper label, 4" h 40
Lerner, Claire, box, 4 padded feet, 1950s .10
Manker, console bowl, airbrushed peach,
rose, and seafoam to white on rim,
10" d, 2.5" h 50
Manker, vase, square, green-yellow,
7" h, 3.5" w 10
McColloch, Steward B, figurine, bird of
paradise, mkd "Steward B McColloch
Calif," 12" h 25
Miramar of California, planter, greenish-
yellow, crimped edges, metal holder,
1950s, 7.5" l, 3.5" h 12
Moreno, Frank, vase, red and green drip
glaze on brown ground, mkd "705
Frank Moreno, Calif. USA," 6" h, 7" d . . .8
Rumph, mug, bird sitting on hollow tree,
1970s, 7" h 15
Schoop, Hedi, figurine, woman walking
poodle, gray and pink, 11" h 50
Schoop, Hedi, planter, girl holding book,
floral motif, lilac, purple, green, brown,
pink, mustard, and flesh tones, 9" h . . .20
Schoop, Hedi, wall pocket, angel girl,
mauve hair ribbon, 8" h 50
Twin Winton, spoon rest, Dutch girl,
mkd "Twin Winton Capistrano
California" 15
Wallace China, cup and saucer, Little
Buckaroo, Westward Ho, 2.5" h cup,
4.875" d saucer 50

*Miramar of California, cov casserole, #644,
metal stand, 8.625" d casserole, 1956, $18.*

Wallace China, plate, Chuck Wagon,
6.5" d 20
Weil Ware, vase, hp floral design, 7.5" h .20

CALIFORNIA RAISINS

California Raisins are those adorable
claymation raisins seen on television commercials sponsored by the California Raisin
Advisory Board. The American viewing
public fell in love with the Raisins' conga
line performance of Marvin Gaye's hit single "I Heard It Through the Grapevine." The
exploitation of these wrinkled raisins soon
followed, much to the delight of the
Advisory Board. California Raisins were
soon found dancing their way across a myriad of merchandise from address books to
welcome mats.

Activity Book, The California Raisins
Animated Sticker Album, Applause,
©1988 Calrab, Diamond Publishing,
8.5 x 11" 5
Belt, elastic, metal clasp 6
Book, *Raisin' The Roof*, ©1988 Calrab . . .10
Cross Stitch Kit, Justin X Grape, 5 x 5" . .10
Doll, stuffed, wearing sunglasses and
sneakers 4
Figure, Ben Indasun, Hardee's premium,
1987, 2" h 3
Flicker Card, Beebop, 1988, 2.75 x 2" 2
Key chain, metal, "Ooohoo" singers 5
Pennant, felt, on wooden stick, Ice
Capades souvenir, 21.5" l 10
Pinback Button, jogger 3
Poster, "I Heard It Through The Grape-
vine," 22 x 28" 8
Potholder, 7.75" x 7.75" 2
Puzzle, The California Raisins, 500 pcs,
American Publishing, 14 x 14" box,
MIB 10
Radio, battery operated, AM/FM, Nasta,
8" h, orig 11 x 7.5" box 75
Ramp Walker, Tiny Goodbite, 1988, 3.5" h .10
Record, *Claymation Christmas Celebra-
tion, Rudolph the Red-Nosed Reindeer*,
45 rpm, 1987 .5
Record, *Meet the Raisins*, LP 8
Record, *The California Raisins Sing The
Hit Songs*, LP, 1987 8
Sunglasses, red plastic, 2 applied raisin
figures on each side 8

Trading Card, Captain Toonz, MIP 5
Tumbler, ribbed base, Indiana Glass Co,
   5.25" h 8
Umbrella, vinyl, yellow, 22" l 15
Wastebasket, plastic, 10.25" h 20
Wristwatch, conga dancer attached to
   white band, Nelsonic, ©1988 Calrab,
   Applause, 7.5" l, MIP 35

CAMARK POTTERY

Camark pottery derives its name from
its location in Camden, Arkansas. The company was organized in 1926 and produced
decorative and utilitarian items in hundreds
of shapes, colors, and forms. The pottery
closed in 1986.

Club: National Society of Arkansas Pottery
Collectors, 2006 Beckenham Cove, Little
Rock, AR 72212.

Cabinet Vase, light blue, 2 handled, 3" h . .7
Console Bowl, Iris 35
Creamer and Sugar, burgundy, mkd
   "USA 830, 5.25 x 3.25" 10
Ewer, Iris, pink 90
Figurine, climbing black cat, painted
   green eyes, mkd "USA 058L," 15" l . . .50
Flower Frog, Pansy, seafoam green,
   USA 095, orig sticker mkd "Camark
   Deluxe Artware," 2.75" h, 4.5" w 10
Pillow Vase, Morning Glory, ftd, oval,
   7.5" h, 9" w 70

*Planter, swans, white with gold trim, #521,
late 1930s, 7.25" h, $35. —Photo courtesy
Ray Morykan Auctions.*

Pitcher, blue swirl, 3.125" h, 2.5" d 10
Pitcher, cat handle, green, 7.5" h 100
Pitcher, emb leaf, dark green, N 98, 6" h . .20
Pitcher, fig leaves cluster and figs each
   side, dark green, USA 224, 5.625" h 8
Planter, double swan, black, mkd
   "Camark S21," 7.5" h 10
Relish Dish, indented ear of corn inside
   bowl, yellow, USA 507, 9.25" l 15
Salt and Pepper Shakers, pr, "S" and
   "P" shaped, azurite blue, 2.75" h 15
Soap Dish, bathtub shaped, green, mkd
   "Hot Springs National Park, Ark,"
   3.5 x 2" 5
Vase, matte white, 2 handled, 3" h, 5" w .15
Vase, seashell, glossy green, USA 121,
   6" h, 10" w 15

CAMBRIDGE GLASS

The Cambridge Glass Company of
Cambridge, Ohio, began operation in 1901.
Its first products were clear tableware.
Later color, etched, and engraved pieces
were added to the line. Production continued until 1954. The Imperial Glass Company
of Bellaire, Ohio, bought some of the
Cambridge molds and continued production
of these pieces.

Club: National Cambridge Collectors, Inc.,
P.O. 416, Cambridge, OH 43725.

Periodical: *The Daze,* P.O. Box 58, Clio, MI
48420.

Apple Blossom, bowl, low, ftd, yellow,
   gold trim, #3400/3, 11" d 125
Apple Blossom, cranberry dish, yellow .125
Apple Blossom, nut dish, yellow 100
Buzzsaw, punch bowl, with stand, ladle,
   and 10 cups, milk glass 400
Caprice, ashtray, moonlight blue, #206 . .10
Caprice, bowl, 4 ftd, crimped, #66, blue,
   13" 150
Caprice, candleholders, pr, #647, blue . .150
Caprice, champagne, moonlight blue . . .25
Caprice, cup and saucer, crystal 15
Caprice, jug, 32 oz, #179, blue 500
Caprice, juice tumbler, #300, crystal 15
Caprice, relish, 3 part, #122, 8" 50
Caprice, rose bowl, #235, blue 450
Caprice, salt and pepper shakers, pr,
   moonlight blue 125

Caprice, creamer and open sugar, blue, $35.

Caprice, tumbler, 10 oz, ftd, #300, crystal .15
Caprice, tumbler, 12 oz, flat, #310, blue .150
Caprice, epergne, #1358, crystal 375
Caprice, vase, smooth top, #344, amber .100
Caprice, water goblet, #300, blue 60
Caprice, wine, #300, crystal 25
Chantilly, pitcher, crystal 325
Cleo, butter base, amber 10
Cleo, sugar sifter, glass lid, blue 1,500
Crown Tuscan, lamp, #3500/42, 12" h ...650
Diane, vase, #3400/17, crystal, 11" h 950
Everglades, bowl, with swans, frosted,
  14" 125
Lynbrook, cocktail 10
Lynbrook, sherbet, low 10
Lynbrook, tea tumbler, ftd, 12 oz 15
Nudes, ivy bowl, cobalt, 9.5" 900
Pristine, cocktail shaker, crystal 80
Rondo, sherbet 10
Rondo, wine 15
Rose Point, cake plate, crystal 65
Rose Point, goblet, 3 oz, #3121 30
Rose Point, ice bucket, #3400/851 200
Rose Point, marmalade, with liner, #147 .225
Rose Point, oil, ftd, #3400/161 275
Rose Point, plate, #3900/24, 10.5" d ...225
Rose Point, relish, 3 part, #3900/69, gold
  encrusted, 6.5" 85
Rose Point, sherbet, 6 oz, #3121, crystal .25
Rose Point, sugar, #3900/41, crystal 25
Rose Point, torte, rolled edge, #3900/166,
  crystal 75
Rose Point, vase, #1233 175
Rose Point, vase, #6004, 12" h 275
Wildflower, butter, #3400/52, crystal, 5" .150
Wildflower, plate, 2 handled, #3400/118,
  6" d 25
Wildflower, relish, 3 part, #3500/69, 6.5" ..25
Wildflower, vase, #1430, crystal, 8" h ...175

CAMEOS

Cameos are a form of jewelry that has never lost its popularity. Cameos have been made basically the same way for centuries. Most are dated by their settings, although this is risky, since historic settings can be duplicated very easily.

Normally, one thinks of a cameo as carved from a piece of conch shell. However, the term cameo means a gem that is carved in relief. You can find cameos carved from gemstones and lava. Lava cameos are especially desirable.

Beware of plastic and other forms of copycat and fake cameos. Look carefully at the side. If you spot layers, shy away. A real cameo is carved from a single piece. Your best defense when buying a cameo is to buy from a dealer that you can find later and then have the authenticity of the cameo checked by a local retail jeweler.

Bracelet, 8 oval coral, shell, mother-of-
  pearl and onyx cameos, 14K yellow
  gold wiretwist mounts spaced by
  textured roundels 925
Bracelet, lava, various color panels,
  Victorian 14K yg mounting 1,300
Brooch, agate, Victorian, bust of woman
  with flowers in hair, gold knife-edge
  and beadwork frame, 19K yg setting . .800
Brooch, carved shell, lilies in the valley,
  gold frame, 1.75" h 150
Brooch, carved shell, young woman
  profile, in vermeil frame 35
Button, pearl, bust and Lily of the Valley
  dec 10
Compact, onyx, marcasite ring, yellow
  guilloche enamel 400
Ear Pendants, tortoise shell and cameo,
  oval tops suspending an openwork
  scrolled tortoise shell frame centered
  by oval shell cameo 300
Pendant, shell, gold frame 100
Pendant/Bracelet, carved white coral,
  gold frames, c1860, 1.75" h, 8" l 300
Pendant/Brooch, carved shell, chariot
  and dancers, 10K gold frame, 2.75 x
  2" 225
Pendant/Brooch, Victorian shell, 3
  Graces, engraved frame, retractable
  bail, 10K yellow gold 325

Pin, carved shell, young woman, 1.5" h . .85
Ring, gentleman's, agate, black and
   white classic warrior profile, 14K
   white gold 100
Stickpin, opal, carved, gold frame, ruby
   and diamond highlights, 14K yg setting, mkd "Tiffany & Co" 650

*Boy Scout
Kodak,
folding
single lens,
olive green,
$60.*

CAMERAS

    Just because a camera is old does not
mean it is valuable. Rather, assume that the
more examples of a camera that were
made the less likely it is to be of any value.
Collectors seek unusual cameras or examples from companies that failed quickly.
    A portion of a camera's value rests on
whether it works. Check bellows cameras
by shining a strong light over the outside
surface while looking at the inside. Also
check the seating on removable lenses.
    Collectors have begun to focus on
35mm cameras. A collection can be built of
early models at a modest cost per camera.
There is also a growing market in camera
accessories and ephemera.

Clubs: American Photographic Historical
Society, Inc., 1150 Avenue of the Americas,
New York, NY 10036; American Society of
Camera Collectors, 7952 Genesta Ave., Van
Nuys, CA 91406; National Stereoscopic
Assoc., P.O. Box 14801, Columbus, OH
43214; Photographic Historical Society, Inc.,
P.O. Box 39563, Rochester, NY 14604.

CAMERA

Adam & Co, Deluxe Hand Reflex Plate
   Camera, Kodak Aero-Ektar lens,
   1900-10, 4" w 350
Asahi, Pentax Auto 110, interchangeable
   lens, automatic shutter, f2.8 lens,
   18mm wide angle, 24mm normal,
   50mm tele lenses, flash, winder,
   and cases, 1979-83 50
Eastman Kodak, Brownie Cresta III,
   black plastic body, sculpted gray
   plastic top housing, 1960s 10
France, Physiographe Stereo Camera,
   1896-1920, 7" h 2,000
Honeywell, Electric Eye 35, 35 mm,
   c1962 20

Houghton, Ticka, 1905-14, 2.5" d 300
Leica, #271255, 1938, 5.5" w 350
Minolta, Electro Shot, 35 mm, 1965 30
Moonflex, rack focusing, c1957 75
Newman and Guardia, Box Plate
   Camera, c1910-30, 5" w 400
Olympic Junior, Bakelite half-frame,
   127 film, c1934 75
Polaroid, Model 95, cast aluminum body,
   folding bed style, brown leatherette
   covering, 1948-53 25
Salex, Tropical Reflex Camera, teak
   and brass, Taylor Hobson Cooke
   lens, tan leather bellows, 1910-20,
   6" h 500
Sanderson Tropical Camera, teak and
   brass plate, 1910-20, 5.5" h 650
Thornton Pickard, Triple Extension Half
   Plate Field Camera, mahogany and
   brass, 1905-10, 8.5" h 250

CAMERA RELATED

Catalog, Korona, 52 pp, 1926 25
Clock, light-up, plastic, "Kodak/America's
   Storyteller," Dualite Inc, Williamsburg,
   OH, 19" d 50
Display, diecut cardboard, stand-up,
   woman wearing bathing suit holding
   film and camera, "Stop here for...
   Kodak Verichrome Film," 54" h, 21" w .115
Exposure Meter, auxiliary cdS, Canon,
   1965-67 15
Manual, Leica Reflex Housing, 9 pp, 1956 .5
Manual, Sound Kodascope, FS-10-N,
   service and parts, large format, 55 pp,
   c1947 8
Range Finder, Nikon, Varifocal 150

CAMERAS, NOVELTY

Plastic cameras depicting cartoon characters Mickey Mouse, Bugs Bunny, Punky Brewster, Holly Hobbie, Teenage Mutant Ninja Turtles, etc., are a fun collecting area that can really brighten up a shelf. The most striking are the "face" cameras resembling some of these characters, clowns, bears, or Santa Claus, and even a full-figure Charlie Tuna.

Early 1930s Kodak box and folding cameras can be found in red, blue, brown, green, pink, and some even more exotic colors. The challenge exists in finding an example of each model in each color.

The Art Deco crowd will want both sizes of the Beau Brownies and the diamond, lightning bolt, and step patterns of the folding Petites.

Collecting cardboard covered disposable cameras is the new craze. Rewrapped and reloaded models advertising products such as Winchester bullets, Playboy, Budweiser, college sports teams, cereals, etc., are the most desirable.

Note: Prices listed are for cameras in excellent condition.

Bear's Head, 110 film, removable nose
    is lens cap, made in Taiwan 30
Bino/Cam 7800, combination 7 x 20
    binoculars and 110 film, Tele-Tasco
    112mm f5.6 lens, single speed 1/125
    shutter, c1977-81 150
Brenda Starr Cub Reporter, black
    Bakelite, 127 film 100
Bugs Bunny, plastic, figural, green,
    high relief figure of reclining Bugs
    Bunny, Helm Toy Co, ©1976 Warner
    Bros, 2.25 x 4.75 x 4.25" 15
Cabbage Patch Kids, plastic, 110 film,
    green decal on front, flip-flash, Play-
    time Products, c1984 10
Cat Holding Fish, Micro 110, c1988 25
Cinnamon Toast Crunch, disposable 8
Clown Face, 110 film, removable nose
    is lens cap, clown's hat is shutter
    release, made in Taiwan 35
Davy Crockett, black plastic, Crockett
    and rifles on metal faceplate, Herbert
    George Co 35

Dick Tracy, plastic, Laurie Import, Hong
    Kong, c1974 8
G I Joe, plastic, 126 film, olive drab,
    compass on top, Nasta Industries,
    1984 8
Hulk Hogan, 110 film, Remco, 1991 8
Incredible Hulk, 126 film 30
J C Whitney, disposable, "Everything
    Automatic" 12
Kodak Beau Brownie, box, Art Deco
    front, sizes 2 and 2A, pink 175
Kodak Petite, folding, orig colored
    bellows 150
Kodak Pocket Jr, folding, No 1 and 1A . .50
Kodak Rainbow Hawkeye, box, various
    colors, sizes 2 and 2A 30
Marlboro Cigarettes, plastic, 110 film,
    figural cigarette pack, c1989 35
Mickey Mouse, figural Mickey head
    with red bow tie, 110 film, c1985,
    Helm Toy Co 15
Punky Brewster, red plastic, 110 film,
    applied decals, with carrying case,
    c1984, Helm Toy Co 8
Reese's Peanut Butter Cup, plastic,
    110 film, Nasta Industries, 1991 5
Roy Rogers Jr, black plastic, 127 film . . .40
Sonic & Knuckles, disposable 15
Teenage Mutant Ninja Turtles Talking
    Camera, Remco, 1991 15
Transistomatic Radio Camera, combina-
    tion G E transistor radio and Kodak
    Instamatic 100 camera, c1964 100
Yogi Bear, figural head, lens in mouth . .30

Pepsi and Coca-Cola Cans, Eiko, price each, $35.

CANDLEWICK

Imperial Glass Corporation issued its No. 400 pattern, Candlewick, in 1936 and continued to produce it until 1982. In 1985 the Candlewick molds were dispersed to a number of sources, e.g., Boyd Crystal Art Glass, through sale.

Over 650 items and sets are known. Shapes include round, oval, oblong, heart, and square. The largest assortment of pieces and sets were made during the late 1940s and early 1950s. Watch for reproductions!

Club: The National Candlewick Collector's Club, 6534 South Ave., Holland, OH 43528.

Bowl, 400/74B 100
Bowl, 400/106B, floral cut 125
Bowl, 400/125, divided, 11" l 550
Candleholders, pr, 400/80 35
Candleholders, pr, 400/86 85
Candleholders, pr, 400/207, 3 toed 250
Candleholders, pr, 400/405, square 200
Candy Dish, 400/140 375
Candy Dish, 400/206 225
Champagne, 400/190 15
Cheese and Cracker Set, 400/88 65
Compote, 400/45 .25
Compote, 400/66B 30
Creamer and Sugar, 400/122, floral cut . .25
Decanter with Stopper, 400/163 650
Deviled Egg Tray, 400/154 175
Fork and Spoon, 400/75 30
Goblet, 400/3400, 9 oz 20
Juice Tumbler, 400/19 15
Marmalade, 400/19 50
Mayonnaise, 400/84, 3 pc, divided 60
Pickle, 400/57, 7" 35
Pitcher, 400/18, 80 oz 325
Pitcher, 400/19, 40 oz 275
Pitcher, 400/24, 80 oz 200
Plate, 400/10D, 10" d 45
Plate, 400/1D, 6" d 9
Plate, 400/5D, 8" d 9
Plate, 400/7D, 9" d 15
Platter, 400/131D, 16" l 275
Relish, 400/55, floral cut 50
Relish, 400/102, 5 part, 13" 75
Relish, 400/213, 3 part, 10" 90
Relish, 400/268, 2 part, 8" 30
Salad Bowl, 400/75B, 10" d 50

Jelly Dish, 400/52, divided, handled, 6", $20.

Sherbet, 400/190 .20
Tumbler, 400/19, 12 oz 15
Tumbler, 400/19, 14 oz 30
Vase, 400/21, 8.5" h 450
Vase, 400/87C 50
Vase, 400/87F, floral cut 70
Vase, 400/87F, graduated bead 35
Water Goblet, 400/3800 125
Water Tumbler, 400/19 15
Wine Goblet, 400/3400 30

CANDY COLLECTIBLES

Who doesn't love candy? Forget the chocoholics. I'm a Juicy Fruit man. Once you start looking for candy related material, you are quickly overwhelmed by how much is available. Do not forget the boxes. They are usually discarded. Ask your local drugstore to save the more decorative ones for you. Today's garbage is tomorrow's gold.

Club: Candy Container Collectors Club of America, P.O. Box 352, Chelmsford, MA 01824.

Box, Segars Chocolate Candy, litho
    paper over cardboard, matching lid,
    repeated brown diamond logo for
    "Heide's Confectionary Chocolates
    & Bon Bons," label for "Heide's
    Marshmallow Chocolate Segars,"
    on side panel, c1920s, 9 x 9 x 4" 15
Container, Franklin Caro Co, glass, emb
    lettering on lid, "Franklin Caro Co.
    Richmond VA" emb on lower front
    panel, 11.75" h, 5" w 75

Container, Rowntree's Gums, glass, emb tin lid, 7" h, 5.5" w 85

Dispenser, Mints and Chewing Gum, National Self Service, metal and glass, plate mkd "Chicago Gum and Candy Co. Chicago, Ill," 15" h, 8" w, 5.5" d 150

Display, Life Savers, metal, glass dividers with decal, 5.25 h, 6.25" w . . .30

Display, Wrigley's Spearmint Gum, cardboard, figural pack of gum, 10" h, 35.75" w, 8.125" l 200

Figurine, Sebastian Miniature, candy salesman offering product to druggist holding sample in hand, foreground of druggist counter with small bucket of "Necco Sweets," red lettering on end of counter for "Fine Candies Since 1847 By Necco," "A Call From the Candy Man In 1880" on base, ©1949 P W Baston, 1950s, 3" h 75

Pinback Button, "Join Us In Our Work To Remove 20% Sales Tax On Candy, Gum, Nuts," c1930s, 1" d 8

Sign, porcelain, "Hollingsworth's Unusual Candies/For Those Who Love Fine Things," 1940s, 12 x 29" 250

Sign, porcelain, "Whitman's Choclates & Confections," 1930-40s, 13 x 40" . . .350

Snow Globe, M&M's Secret Santa, 4" h, 2.5" w 25

Stickpin, brass, diecut celluloid, flat, "A I T Chocolates," reverse with logo and "H D Foss & Co, Quality Chocolate/ Boston, Mass," early 1900s 15

Pinback Button, Schutter's Old Gold Candy, litho tin, Andy Gump image, Parisian Novelty Co., 1" d, $10.

CAP GUNS

Classic collectors collect the one-shot, cast iron pistols manufactured during the first third of the 20th century. Kids of the 1950s collect roll-cap pistols. Children of the 1990s do not know what they are missing. Prices for roll-cap pistols are skyrocketing. Buy them in working order only. Ideally, acquire them with their original accessories, e.g., holsters, fake bullets, etc.

Club: Toy Gun Collectors of America, 3009 Oleander Ave., San Marcos, CA 92069.

Andes, The Big Noise, nickel-plated cast iron, 5.5" l .75

Dent, Buddy, nickel-plated cast iron, single shot, 1930, 4.5" l 40

Hamilton, Cheyenne Shooter, nickel finish diecast white metal, ivory plastic grips with gold "CS" symbol, 1955-60, 9.75" l, orig box 50

Hubley, Colt .45, nickel silver finish metal, gold luster cylinder, ivory plastic grips, 1960s, 13.5" l 50

Hubley, Teddy, cast iron, single shot, 5.625" l 40

Hubley, Texan, nickel-plated cast iron, red star on grip, 9.25" l 150

Kenton, Bandit, nickel-plated cast iron, single shot, 1940s, 7.25" l 40

Kenton, Biff Jr, cast iron, 4.125" l 40

Kenton, Gene Autry, silvered cast iron, marbled ivory plastic grips, c1940, 6.5" l, orig box .175

Kenton, Law Maker, cast iron, ivory plastic grips with raised image of cowboy hat, spur, and star, c1950-51, 8.5" l 125

Kenton, Pony, cast iron, single shot, 5.125" l 30

Kenton, Western, cast iron, 7" l 30

Kilgore, Big Bill, nickel-plated cast iron, 1936, 4.875" l 40

Kilgore, Eagle, silver nickel finish white metal, ivory plastic grips with soaring eagle in relief, c1950s, 8" l 40

Mattel, Fanner-50, chrome luster finish diecast white metal, wood-grained ivory plastic grips, 8 metal bullets on sealed blister card, 10.75" l, orig box 75

Hubley, Atomic Disintegrator, silvered cast white metal, red plastic grips, 7.5" l, $300. —Photo courtesy Gene Harris Antique Auction Center, Inc.

National, Wild West, nickel-plated cast iron, single shot, 6.5" l 60

Roy Rogers, gold luster finish white metal, scrolled designs with "RR" on each grip, 1950s, 2.75" l 35

Schmidt, Alan Ladd, chrome-plated diecast finish, 10.5" l 125

Schmidt, Lasso 'em Bill, diecast metal, 10.5" l 40

Schmidt, Range Rider, silver nickel finish metal, checkered dark copper luster plastic grip inserts, "Range Rider" on each side, c1950-55, 10" l . .50

Stevens, Cowboy King, nickel finish cast iron, black handles with inset red glass jewels, relief image on 1 side of cowboy with 2 guns drawn, Indian on other side with tom-tom and shield, scroll work on barrel and gun, 1940, 9" l 175

Stevens, Pet, cast iron, single shot, 4.125" l 30

CARNIVAL CHALKWARE

Carnival chalkware is my candidate for the kitsch collectible of the 1980s. No one uses quality to describe these inexpensive prizes given out by games of chance at carnivals, amusement parks, and ocean boardwalks.

The best pieces are those depicting a specific individual or character. Since most were bootlegged (made without permission), they often appear with a fictitious name, e.g., "Smile Doll" is really supposed to be Shirley Temple. The other strong collecting subcategory is the animal figure. As long as the object comes close to capturing the appearance of a pet, animal collectors will buy it.

Newsletter: *Chalk Talk,* 720 Mission St., South Pasadena, CA 91030.

Ashtray, girl with dog, 11.5" h 50

Ashtray, Popeye, standing on tray, 2 rests, 11" h 125

Bank, cat, black and white, 12" h 8

Bank, elephant, 9" h 10

Bank, elephant, standing on drum, 3.5 x 5 x12" 30

Bank, lion, 8.5" h .25

Bank, pig, seated, ear down 10

Bank, squirrel eating acorn, 8.5" h, 9.5" w .20

Figure, basket of flowers, 9.5" h 20

Figure, Betty Boop, 6" h 55

Figure, black panther, open mouth, green eyes 10

Figure, boxer dog, 6" h 10

Figure, Donald Duck, 15" h 35

Figure, French girl, blue hat and coat, 15" h 10

Figure, horse, white, black mane and tail, 9" h, 11" l 8

Figure, Indian on horse, 10.5" h, 9.5" l 30

Figure, Jumbo the elephant, 9" h 10

Figure, Kewpie, wings on back, dark eyes, auburn hair, red hands, belly button, and mouth, rosy cheeks 50

Figure, Lone Ranger, 15" h 15

Figure, Apache Babe, ©B.G. 1936, 14" h, $70.

Figure, owl, multicolored, 10" h, 4.5" d,
   8.5" w at base 20
Figure, Pinocchio, 15" h 65
Figure, Porky Pig, red vest, cap, black
   tie, 10.25" h 50
Figure, Rin Tin Tin, 14" h, 8.5" w 20
Figure, sailor girl, 15" h 25
Figure, singing cowboy 20
Figure, Snow White, 15" h 15

CARTOON COLLECTIBLES

This is a category with something for
each generation. The characters represented here enjoyed a life in comic books
and newspaper pages or had a career on
movie screens and television.

Every collector has a favorite. Buy
examples that bring back pleasant memories. "That's All Folks."

Note: For information on collector clubs/fan
clubs for individual cartoon characters,
refer to Maloney's Antiques & Collectibles
Resource Directory by David J. Maloney,
Jr., published by Antique Trader Books.

Andy Panda, mug, ceramic, white,
   black, blue, and dark red accents,
   smiling Andy with arm as handle in
   saluting position, black and white
   decal name on back, ©1954 Walter
   Lantz, underside stamped "Made in
   Japan," 3.5" h .55

*Popeye Pipe Toss Game, ©1935 King
Features Syndicate, $75.* —Photo courtesy
Collectors Auction Services.

*Mister Magoo,
soaky bottle,
Colgate-
Palmolive, 1960s,
$35.*

Barney Google, game, Barney Google
   An' Snuffy Smith Times A Wastin!,
   Milton Bradley, ©1963 King Features
   Syndicate, 8.375 x 16.5 x .25" box 15
Barney Google, sheet music, cover
   shows Barney riding along on Spark
   Plug, race track tower in background,
   ©1923 Jerome Remick, 9.125 x 12.25" .20
Betty Boop, figure, bisque, wearing
   green outfit, red shoes, holding black
   accordion with gold accent,
   ©Fleischer Studios, stamped "Japan"
   on reverse, 1930s, 3.25" h 75
Blondie and Dagwood, greeting card,
   "A Christmas Message To My Wife,"
   Hallmark, ©1944 King Features
   Syndicate, 4.75 x 5.75" 15
Bugs Bunny, wall plaque, composition
   wood, smiling Bugs Bunny in center
   wearing yellow gloves, white ground,
   "Bugs Bunny This Funny Little Rabbit
   Is Called Bugs Bunny" text at bottom,
   c1940, 4.5 x 5.5 x .25" 60
Dennis the Menace, hand puppet, soft
   vinyl head, cloth body, 5.5 x 9.5" 15
Dudley Do-Right, dinnerware set, Dining
   With Dudley Do-Right, plastic, 3 pcs,
   6.75" d plate, 4.75" d bowl, and 3.5" h
   blue opaque tumbler, Libbey, ©1980
   Pat Ward 40
Felix the Cat, box, Felix the Cat Candies
   and Toy, punch-out card on front of
   Felix sawing log and humming while
   mouse holds his ears in window,
   reverse shows daily comic strip of
   dog winning first prize and Felix showing him to his doghouse, Otto Messmer
   art, ©1952 King Features Syndicate,
   .875 x 2.5 x 3.75" 30

Felix the Cat, figure, celluloid, smiling, walking pose with hands behind back, made in Japan, 1920s, 3.5" h . . .75

Happy Hooligan, figure, bisque, dark orange cap and vest, black scarf, black pants, green base, Germany, #8232, c1910, 8.5" h, 2.5" d 35

Linus the Lionhearted, thermos, metal, red plastic cup, colorful image of Linus golfing, Aladdin Industries, ©1965 General Foods, 6.5" h 100

Little Lulu, crayons, box shows Lulu on front writing her name on easel, back shows 3 of 8 crayons inside, each with different images of Lulu and friends, Milton Bradley, ©1948 Marjory H Buell, 2.75 x 3.75" 15

Little Lulu, doll, stuffed, smiling full figure, yarn hair, label mkd "Hand-made By Hazel," 1940s, 17" h 75

Little Nemo, postcard, color image of Nemo, The Princess, Flip and friends greeting Dr Pill at palace steps, ©1907 New York Herald Co, Tuck, 3.5 x 5.5" 35

Magilla Gorilla, comic book, #2, cover shows Magilla surfing and holding umbrella over his head, repeated image on back, Gold Key, 1964 15

Mister Magoo, sign, white textured fabric, red and black art depicting Mr Magoo holding up light bulb, "Mister Magoo Says It's Easy To See The Best Bulb Value Is G-E," 1980s, 14.75 x 25" .35

Nancy and Sluggo, paper dolls, Whitman, #1979, 16 pp, ©1974 United Features Syndicate, 10 x 12.875" 15

Pogo, greeting card, Pogo and Albert in Christmas outfits, Pogo holding box of ornaments as raccoon wraps cord around Albert, "Season's Greetings From Simon and Schuster," ©1975 Selby Kekky Executrix, 4 x 5.25" 15

Pogo, poster, "Vote Pogo for President," shows Albert wearing derby and smoking cigar while dragging Pogo forward, ©1979 Estate of Walt Kelly, 14 x 22" 15

Porky Pig, mug, glass, smiling Porky image on front waving hat, name at bottom in black, name on reverse in white, ©1975 Warner Bros, 5.5" h, 2.75" d 8

Raphael, Teenage Mutant Ninja Turtles, baseball glove, Remco, Major League Model, green and yellow, $20.

Rocky and Bullwinkle, puzzle, Rocky and His Friends, 63 pcs, Whitman, ©1960 Pat Ward, 6.875 x 9.25 x 1.75" box 15

Schmoo, pin, plaster, figural, unmkd, 1940s, 1 x 1.875 x .5" 75

Schmoo, planter, figural, white ceramic, opening in back, late 1940s, 4.75" h, 3.25" d 45

Spark Plug, candy container, figural, glass, depicts Spark Plug wearing patched blanket with his name on it, ©1923 King Features Syndicate, 1.5 x 4 x 3" 80

Spark Plug, doll, plush, wearing yellow felt blanket with name in black letters, stamped "DeBeck" on underside of right foot, ©1923 and 1924 King Features Syndicate, 2.25 x 8.5 x 6.25" .35

Underdog, wristwatch, white face on chrome accent case, full figure Underdog image, red second hand, black vinyl simulated alligator skin band, A & M, ©1984 Pat Ward 50

Woody Woodpecker, coloring book, #1252, full color front and back cover showing Woody sitting on moon painting stars pink, 64 pp, Whitman, ©1954 Walter Lantz Productions, 8.375 x 10.75" .18

Woody Woodpecker, kazoo, plastic, figural, Kellogg's Cereals premium, 1960s, 6.5" h 25

Yellow Kid, ice cream mold, full figure, hinged, 4.75" h 175

CASH REGISTERS

If you want a cash register be prepared to put plenty of money in the till. Most are bought for decorative purposes. Serious collectors would go broke in a big hurry if they had to pay the prices listed below for every machine they buy.

Beware of modern reproductions. Cash registers were meant to be used. Signs of use should be present. Many machines have been restored through replating and rebuilding. Well and good. But when all is said and done, how do you distinguish a modern reproduction from a refurbished machine? When you cannot, it is hard to sustain long-term value.

Club: Cash Register Collectors Club of America, P.O. Box 20534, Dayton, OH 45420.

Improved Sun, #10, oak, transparent
　celluloid keys, change drawer with
　6 coin and 3 bill compartments 300
National, brass, marble shelf, emb front
　lift top panel, orig "Gilbertson & Son"
　marquee, 16 x 23 x 19.5" 225
National, candy store model, brass,
　marble, glass and wood, 20.5" h . . .1,400
National, nickel finish, emb case, "The
　Amount of Your Purchase" marquee,
　restored, c1893, 18 x 8.5 x 15" 1,000
National, oak elaborate filigree design,
　4 drawers, 33 x 30 x 21" 4,000
National, #7, candy store model, detail
　adder 325
National, #52.25, emb brass, ornate
　ledge on 3 sides, side casing holds
　tape, 17" h 800
National, #313, emb brass, marble ledge,
　17" h 850
National, #317, emb brass, marble ledge,
　side casing holds tape, "Amount
　Purchased" marquee, 17" h 550
National, #452-2, oak, 2 drawer, crank .850
National, #1040, patent date 8-30-1913 .300
NCR, #3, wood, light color, carved wild-
　flower dec on drawer 725
Western, Verdic-Corbin Co, Detroit,
　barbershop, plated cast iron, heavily
　emb, 5 cents to $1, restored, castings
　replated, marquee and number tabs
　replaced, 21 x 9 x 15" 750

CASSETTE TAPES

Flea markets thrive on two types of goods—those that are collectible and those that serve a secondhand function. Cassette tapes fall into the latter group. Buy them for the purpose of playing them.

The exception is when the promotional pamphlet covering the tape shows a famous singer or group. In this case, you may be paying for the paper ephemera rather than the tape, but you might as well have the whole shooting match.

Several times within recent years there have been a number of articles in the trade papers about collecting eight-tracks. When was the last time you saw an eight-track machine? They are going to be as popular in thirty years as the wire tape recorder is today. Interesting idea—too bad it bombed.

Average price $1 to $2.

CAST IRON

This is a category where you should be suspicious that virtually everything you see is a reproduction or copycat. Even cast iron frying pans are being reproduced.

One key to spotting newer material is the rust. If it is orange in color and consists of small pinpoint flakes, forget it. Also check paint patina. It should have a mellow tone from years of exposure to air. Bright paint should be suspect.

Note: See Banks, Bookends, Bottle Openers, Doorstops and Griswold for additional listings.

Ashtray, flip top lid mkd "Richmond"
　in raised lettering, inside lid mkd
　"The Richmond Foundary Mfg Co,
　Richmond, Virginia," 4" d, " h 10
Ashtray, drunk hanging on lightpost 5
Bank, base mkd "Billiken, back mkd
　"Good Luck," 4.25" h 25
Bank, cat on tub, painted gray 100
Bank, Indian, Hubley, 9.5" h 50
Bank, Pluto, Walt Disney, 9" l, 8.75" h 85
Bank, Woolworth building, 5.75" h,
　2.75" w, 2.25" d 65

Frying Pan, unmkd, $35.

Bootjack, longhorn steer, 9.25 x 4" 5
Bookends, pr, Amish man and woman
    seated on bench, 4.75" h, 4" l 35
Bookends, pr, English Setter, 9" l, 5" h,
    3" d 30
Broom Holder, black man, mkd "Patd
    Jan 9 1894," 4.5" h 400
Coffee Grinder, red, removable chrome
    hopper, 10" h, 6" d wheel 35
Corn Sheller, 7.5" l 85
Dinner Bell, 11.5 x 11" 50
Doorstop, crying baby kneeling on
    pillow, fists clenched at shoulders,
    8.75" h 85
Fan, non-oscillating, Eskimo, 8" blade,
    11" h 12
Figure, horse, 2.5" h, 3.5" l 10
Figure, swan, painted black highlights,
    2.5" h, 3" l 8
Figure, skunk, standing on log, "Souvenir
    of Plymouth Mass," wheat penny
    dated 1939 at end of log, 2.5 x 3.25" . . .10
Floor Grate, Victorian, ornate pattern,
    12 x 10" 30
Food Mold, alphabet letters, John Wright,
    10 x 14" 5
Letter Opener, owl, 8.5" l, 1.5" w 200
Match Holder, figural duck, mkd "Fire
    King Gas Ranges," 4.5" l, 2.25" h,
    2.5" w 150
Notary Seal Press, mkd "Patent Oct 9,
    1883, 11" h, 6.75" l base 50
Nutcracker, racehorse, wooden base,
    8 x 5" 6
Pencil Holder, penguin 70
Rope Pulley, Myers, 10" h, 6" d 10
Salt and Pepper Shakers, pr, Amish
    man and woman on rocking chairs 4
Weather Vane, horse and buggy, 3-point
    leaf base, 16" h, 5.5" w base 6

CATALOGS

Catalogs are used as excellent research sources. The complete manufacturing line of a given item is often described, along with prices, styles, colors, etc. Old catalogs provide a good way to date objects.

Many old catalogs are reprinted for use by collectors as an aid to identification of their specialities, such as Imperial and The Cambridge Glass Co.

Collecting Hint: The price of an old catalog is affected by condition, data, type of material advertised, and location of advertiser.

Ball & Ball, Whitford, PA, #47, cabinet
    hardware, 1947, 24 pp, 8.5 x 11" 35
Bausch & Lomb Optical Co, Rochester,
    NY, microscopes and accessories,
    12 pp, 1921, 6.5 x 9.5" 20
Berger Bros Co, Philadelphia, PA, #10,
    tinplate, metal, and roofing supplies,
    209 pp, 1924, 6 x 9" 32
Bryant Electric Co, Bridgeport, CT,
    electrical supplies, 206 pp, 1924,
    7.5 x 10.75" 28
F C Taylor Fur Co, St Louis, MO, fishing
    supplies, 32 pp, 1947, 8.25 x 10.25" 37
Federal Telephone Mfg Co, Buffalo, NY,
    instructions for installation and
    operation of federal amplyfying trans-
    formers, 12 pp, 1924, 5.25 x 8" 25
George Murphy Inc, New York, NY,
    photography supplies, 272 pp, 1940,
    6 x 9" 28

The West Branch Cedar Chests, West Branch Novelty Co, Milton, PA, 15 pp, Spring 1928, 12 x 9", $30.

Jasper Cabinet Co, Jasper, IN, furniture,
56 pp, 1965, 8.5 x 11" 25

Karlan & Bleicher Inc, New York, NY,
jewelry, 78 pp, 1948, 9 x 12" 33

McKinley Music Co, Chicago, IL, sheet
music and music books, 48 pp, c1900,
8 x 10.25" 15

Montgomery Ward Co, Chicago, IL, #95,
Fall and Winter, 1921, 890 pp, 9.25 x
13.25" 75

Pitts Auto Equipment Co, Pittsburgh,
PA, Spring and Summer, 32 pp, 1932,
8.5 x 11" 34

Spiegel Inc, Chicago, IL, Diamond Jubilee
issue, 590 pp, 1940, 9.25 x 13.5" 40

Taylor Instrument, Rochester, NY,
weather instruments, 164 pp, 1912,
5.25 x 7.5" 25

The Astrup Co, Cleveland, OH, #20,
awning and tent supplies, 170 pp,
1929, 3.75 x 7" .32

Thomas G Plant Co, Boston, MA,
autumn and winter styles of ladies'
shoes, 32 pp, 4.25 x 6" 20

W & H Walker, Pittsburgh, PA, Fall,
104 pp, c1936, 5.25 x 7.75" 15

W Atlee Burpee Co, Philadelphia, PA,
seeds, 160 pp, 6 x 8.75" 9

CAT COLLECTIBLES

It is hard to think of a collecting category that does not have one or more cat-related items in it. Chessie the Cat is railroad oriented; Felix is a cartoon, comic, and toy collectible. There rests the problem. The poor cat collector is always competing with an outside collector for a favorite cat item.

Cat collectors are not nearly as finicky as their pets. I have never seen a small cat collectibles collection. In addition, unlike most dog collectibles collectors, cat collectors are more willing to collect objects portraying breeds of cats other than the one that they own.

Club: Cat Collectors, P.O. Box 150784, Nashville, TN 37215.

Book, *What Happened To Tommy*,
Stecher Lithographic Co. New York,
drawings and verses by Frances
Brundage, 1921, 10.5 x 7.5" 20

Postcard, cat wearing dress, digging in open purse, artist sgd "A Thiele," $15.

Bookends, pr, black and white cats,
looking up, cast iron, hp, 5.5" h, 5.5" l,
3.125"w 20

Cameo, seated cat, blue agate, .625" h . .35

Creamer, black cat, Fitz & Floyd 20

Doorstop, cast iron, worn paint, 9" h . . .100

Figure, arched back cat, iridescent
green, Celleni, 11.5" h 150

Figure, black cat with arched back on
base, chalkware, 2.75" h 15

Figure, cat on basket, cobalt, Mosser
Glass 12

Figure, hand carved wood, c1970, 6" h . .10

Figure, Mitzi the cat, white, green eyes,
3" h, 2.75" w 15

Figure, pink floral dec, Fenton, 3.75" h . . .50

Figure, reclining cat, gray and white,
Lefton, 3.5" l 8

Figure, white, gray, and black, green
eyes, unmkd, 6 h 5

Matchcover, Frenchy's Black Cat
Restaurant, San Antonio, TX 5

Match Holder, folk art style, black,
painted black highlights, 11.75" h 15

Napkin Holder, ceramic, 3 kittens in
basket 15

Nodder, Siamese cats in wicker basket,
1940s 35

Planter, cat on ball of yarn, Royal Copley,
7" h, 5" w 10

Postcard, little girl with black cat and
devil, Halloween scene, postmarked
1909 15

Salt and Pepper Shakers, pr, cat with
fish bowl, 3.5" h 5

Sign, Black Cat Cigarettes, "They Taste
Better!," emb tin, 23.25" h, 23.25" w . .700

String Holders, cat with ball of yarn,
Fitz and Floyd 70

Stuffed Animal, gray, longhaired, Dakin,
 1983, 10" h 10
Windup, Figaro, litho tin, Marx, 2.5" h,
 4.5" l 45

CAVES & CAVERNS

 An amazing variety of antique items are available on American (and foreign) caves and caverns. Collectibles on caves and caverns can be broken down into two categories: paper items and non-paper items.

 Paper collectibles include books, pamphlets, brochures, postcards, photos, stereo views, posters, sheet music, postage stamps, and even stock certificates from cave corporations. Books and pamphlets on United States caves date from the early 1800s with tourist brochures and postcards dating from the turn of the century. Photos and stereoviews of caves started with the Waldack views of Mammoth Cave in the 1860s. Early cave posters (mainly of French and Belgium caves) date to the late 1800s with more recent posters from caves throughout the world. Cave postage stamps have never been produced in the United States, but are available from many other countries.

 Non-paper collectibles include souvenir items such as plates, spoons, pennants, paperweights, glasses, hats, nodders, ashtrays, and patches.

 China souvenirs made in Germany and Austria were imported by Wheelock, JonRoth, and others from the early 1900s through about 1934. After 1934 Staffordshire English china was imported by Mammoth Cave, Howe Caverns, Luray Caverns, and Carlsbad Caverns. Most recent souvenirs are made in Japan and China.

 Items pertaining to Floyd Collins, the famous cave explorer who died in Sand Cave in 1925, are also considered cave collectibles.

 It should be noted that items removed from caves such as stalagtites or archaeological pieces (arrowheads, etc) are not considered cave collectibles. In most states removing anything from a cave is illegal and can result in a fine or jail time, as happened in a recent Kentucky case.

Advisors: Gordon and Judy Smith, P.O. Box 217, Marento, IN 47140, (812) 945-5721, e-mail: glstis@aol.com.

Book, *Adventure Is Underground,*
 Halliday, dj, 1959 25
Book, *Caves of Missouri,* Bretz, dj,
 1956 100
Book, *Caverns of Virginia,* McGill, 1933 . .60
Book, *The Caves Beyond,* Brucker and
 Lawrence, dj, 1955 30
Brochure, Luray Caverns, 1950s 1
Brochure, Blue Grottoes of Virginia,
 1935 5
Brochure, Mammoth Cave, 1880 35
Matchbook Cover, Crystal Cave, WI,
 1940 3
Nodder, Mammoth Onyx Cave, KY 40
Paperweight, Luray Caverns, 1910 40
Paperweight, Meramec Caverns, 1950 . .15
Patch, Bluespring Caverns, 1990 5
Pennant, Carlsbad Caverns, 1950s 5
Pennant, Floyd Collins Crystal Cave,
 1940s 40
Photograph, Cave of the Winds, CO,
 Jackson, 1910 50
Photograph, group entering Mammoth
 Cave, 1935 30
Plate, Dixie Caverns Turkey Wing,
 Japan, 1950 15
Plate, Mark Twain Cave, MO, Wheelock,
 Germany, 1910 75
Plate, Howe Caverns, Staffordshire,
 1940s 25

Plate, Pillared Palace, Merengo Cave, Indiana, c1960, $20.

Book, Tragedy of Sand Cave, *by Howard W. Hartley, Standard Press, 1925, $75.*

Postcard, Carlsbad Caverns, linen, 1920-50 15
Postcard, Daussa's Cave, Put-In-Bay, OH 25
Postcard, Wind Cave Stereo Postcard, Butcher 100
Postcard, Wonderland Cave, Bermuda, 1920 10
Poster, Carlsbad Caverns, Santa Fe Railroad, 1940 75
Poster, Grottes deHan, Belgium, 1910 . .500
Souvenir Spoon, Carlsbad Caverns National Park, 1940 25
Souvenir Spoon, Mammoth Cave, enameled handle, 1910 100
Toothpick Holder, Horse Cave, KY, made in Germany, 1933 75
Record, *The Ballad of Floyd Collins*, 1925 25
Stereoview, Mammoth Cave, Hains, 1896 75
Stereoview, Wind Cave, SD, Hook 55

CELLULOID

Celluloid is the trade name for a thin, tough, flammable material made of cellulose nitrate and camphor. Originally used for toilet articles, it quickly found a use as inexpensive jewelry, figurines, vases, and household items. In the 1920s and 1930s, it was used heavily by the toy industry.

Examine ivory or tortoise shell pieces before buying. Both were well imitated by quality celluloid.

Club: Victorian Era Celluloid Collectors Assoc., P.O. Box 470, Alpharetta, GA 30239.

Bank, red, "Season's Greetings, The Tresler Oil Company, Phone Mt. Orab 100, Save with Comet," 2.25" h, 4.25" l 5
Bookmark, Wisner Pianos, diecut, pink to red carnation on green stem, black inscriptions, white ground, early 1900s .7
Bridge Game Counter, figural female bather in tinted pink swimsuit, 2 arms jointed to turn and serve as pointers to 4 card suit symbols, 1920-30s, 2.5" h, 1 x 2.25" black base 35
Brooch, figural pipe, black, glittering crystal rhinestones dec 40
Dresser Box, 3 Brownies holding Victorian hand fan dec, orig lining, decorated brass clasp, 15" l, 3.375" h, 4.25" d 40
Fan Box, "Fans" in ornate nouveau style across top, raised floral and leaf motif along rim and base, 12.5 x 4 x 2.75" 30
Figure, pelican, 3.5" h 10
Figure, reindeer, Occupied Japan, 5" h, 5.5" l 10
Hair Comb, faux tortoise shell, cattail design, 4 x 3.25" 20
Hair Receiver and Powder Box, amber, pearlized pink top 10
Handkerchief Box, ivory, light pink satin lining, metal latch, 5.5" sq 20
Pencil Sharpener, figural pelican, 3" h . . .35
Pin, dachshund, wearing mountain climbing outfit and smoking pipe, Japan, 2.75 x 1.5" 20
Pinback Button, N Y State Horticultural Society, red apple image, 1.25" d 3

Pocket Mirror, celluloid back, vacuum cleaner adv, black and white photo image, 2.25" h, $45.

Pocket Mirror, "Compliments of Harry Bond., Hartford, Conn.," Whitehead & Hoag 10

Powder Puff, marbleized pink and white, ribbed handle with hole for hanging, top has cream twist off knob to insert powder, 11" l 10

Rattle, googly eyed doll, cloth body, 7" l .20

Razor, blade mkd "Joseph Helliot's Celebrated Razor," 6" l 10

Ring Box, Art Deco style, gold scrolling leaf dec, mkd "Dennison" 10

Roly Poly, owl, orange, black highlights, mkd "VCO/USA," 4" h 200

Shoe Horn, horse head, brass ring through nose, 7.5" l 4

Straight Razor, carved art nouveau woman on handle, blade mkd "The Barbers Delight" 35

Tape Measure, sailing ship, cloth tape, 2.5 x 2.5" 50

Travel Clock, fold-out, pearlescent pink laminated amber, New Haven Clock Co, 4.25" h open size 20

Windup, doll on swing 60

CEREAL BOXES

There is no better example of a collectible category gone mad than cereal boxes. Cereal boxes from the first half of the twentieth century sell in the $15 to $50 range. Cereal boxes from the 1950s through the 1970s can sell for $50 and up. Where's the sense?

The answer rests in the fact that the post–World War II cereal box market is being manipulated by a shrewd speculator who is drawing upon his past experience with the lunch box market. Eventually, the bubble will burst. Don't get involved unless you have money to burn.

Club: Sugar-Charged Cereal Collectors, 5400 Cheshire Meadows Way, Fairfax, VA 22032.

Corn Fetti, Post, Captain Jolly, 1953, 9.5" h 75

Corn Flakes, Kellogg's, flying Superman offer, 1955, 9.5" h 350

Corn Kix, General Mills, Disneyland light-up offer, 1950s, 8.5" h 150

Grape Nuts, Post, plastic century boats offer, 1955, 6.5" h 100

Grape Nuts, Post, Roy Rogers, 1950s, 10" h 150

Krinkles, Post, 1951, 7.5" h 65

Muffets Shredded Wheat, Quaker, Sgt Preston's trail kit offer, 1956, 8" h 125

Pep, Kellogg's, Tom Corbett space goggles offer, 1952, 8.5" h 350

Puffed Wheat, Quaker, Gabby Hayes gun collection offer, 1951, 9" h 200

Quisp, Quaker, space trivia game on back, 1985 25

Raisin Bran, Post, Captain Video spaceman toy inside, 1953, 8" h 250

Raisin Bran, Post, Roy Rogers western ring offer, 1953, 8" h 350

Rice Krispies, Kellogg's, Annie Oakley doll offer, 1955, 10.25" h 100

Sugar Pops, Kellogg's, Superman flying rocket offer, 1956, 9.5" h 300

Sugar Smacks, Kellogg's, Admiral portable TV offer, 1957, 10" h 150

Sugar Smacks, Kellogg's, Ringling Bros Lou Jacobs, Armed Forces shoulder patch inside, 1953, 9.5" h 200

Sugar Smiles, General Mills, 1953, 9.5" h 100

Toasties, Post, Li'l Abner pop-out picture, 1957, 12" h 75

Toasties, Post, Roy Rogers pop out card inside, 1950s, 11.5" h 300

Trix, General Mills, Trix plush rabbit offer, 1985 10

Wheat Chex, Ralston Purina, space binoculars offer, 1953, 9" h 350

Wheaties, General Mills, Lone Ranger hike-o-meter offer, 1957, 10.25" h 300

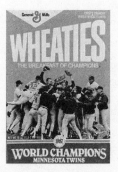

Wheaties, General Mills, 1987 World Champions Minnesota Twins, 18 oz, $10.

CEREAL PREMIUMS

Forget cereal boxes. The fun rests with the non-edible goodies found in the box. Premiums have changed a great deal over the past decade. No self-respecting manufacturer in the 1950s would have offered a tube of toothpaste as a premium. Yuck!

Collectors draw a distinction between premiums that came with the box and those for which you had to send away. The latter group is more valuable because the items are often more elaborate and better made.

Club: Sugar-Charged Cereal Collectors, 5400 Cheshire Meadows Way, Fairfax, VA 22032.

10 Shooter Tank, General Mills, hard
    plastic, orig mailing box, c1956,
    3 x 5 x 3.5" 60
Andy Pafko Scorekeeper Baseball Ring,
    Muffets Shredded Wheat, Quaker,
    brass, mechanical, with instructions
    and orig mailing box, 1949 150
Captain Jolly Comic Book, Post, 1954 ...25
Cereal Bowl, Post, plastic, 1950s, 5.5" d .15
Figure, Robin Hood characters, Sugar
    Smacks, Kellogg's, set of 5, c1968 90
Figure, dinosaur, Wheat Honeys,
    Nabisco, soft plastic, 1950s 5
Figure, elephant, Sugar Pops, Kellogg's,
    plastic, 1956 5
Figure, Sky King character, Rice Honeys,
    Nabisco, plastic, 1956, 2.5" h 10
Fugure, Jolly the Circus Horse, Toasties
    Corn Flakes, Post, paper punch-out,
    1956, 5" h 10
Gabby Hayes Western Wagon, Quaker
    Oats, balsa and cardboard, 1952 35
Hop Harrigan Para-Plane, Grape Nut
    Flakes, Kellogg's, 4 stiff paper punch-
    out sheets, 9" l launching stick, and
    red rayon fabric sheet, orig 5.5 x 14"
    mailing envelope, 1955 300
Howie Wing Rubber Band Pilot's Pistol,
    Kellogg's, cardboard punch-out,
    c1938, 4.5 x 8" 70
Lone Ranger Mask, Wheaties, General
    Mills, cardboard cut-out, 1954 15
Looney Tunes Notch-Em Toy, Raisin
    Bran, Post, diecut cardboard punch-
    out, 1956, 6" h 15

Spoon, Kellogg's Frosted Flakes, Tony the Tiger on handle, Old Company Plate, 1965, $18.

Paul Jung and Lou Jacobs Shuttle-
    Action Toy, Sugar Smacks, Kellogg's,
    diecut cardboard, 1953, 10" l 45
Rocket to the Moon Ring, Kix, brass,
    adjustable, red plastic launcher 75
Seadog Spy Kit, Cap'n Crunch, Quaker
    Oats, blue plastic, complete with orig
    instruction folder, 1974 20
Space Patrol Hydrogen Ray Gun Ring,
    Ralston Purina, metal and plastic,
    1954, 1.5" l 150
Strato Helmet, Betty Crocket Pick-A-
    Pack, General Mills, cardboard cut-
    out, 1956, 8" h 45
Superman Satellite Launcher, Corn
    Flakes, Kellogg's, plastic, 1956, 4" l ...35
Tie Tack, Count Chocula, brass luster
    white metal, 1.125" h 15

CHARACTER BANKS

These lovable creatures just beg for your money. Although pre-1940 bisque, cast iron, and tin character banks exist, this form reached its zenith in the age of injection molded vinyl plastic. Post-war examples are bright, colorful, and usually large in size. They make a great display collection.

Watch out for contemporary banks, especially ceramic models. Any bank less than ten years old should be considered garage sale fodder—worth $1 to $2 at most.

Addams Family "Thing," battery operat-
    ed, plastic, orig box, Poynter Products
    Inc, ©1964 Filmways TV Productions
    Inc, 3.5 x 4.5 x 3.5" 75

Snoopy, clear glass, 6" h, $25.

Buster Brown and Tige, cast iron, horseshoe over horse with bust image of Buster atop horse's back and image of Tige at bottom of horseshoe, c1910, 4.25" h, 4.75" w 175

Donald Duck, painted composition, full figure Donald resting head against raised arm, 1960s, 3.5 x 3.5 x 5.75" 15

Humpty Dumpty, ceramic, Humpty Dumpty sitting on wall, back of head incised "Alice in Philcoland," c1949, 3.5 x 3.5 x 6" 50

Mickey Mouse, brass, book form with cream-colored emb oilcloth fabric, Mickey and "Mickey Mouse Bank" on front, slot on top of bank with "Coins and Bills," orig key, Zell Products Co, 1930s, 3 x 4.25 x 1" 150

Philadelphia Eagles, ceramic, figural football, simulated gold lacing, green and silver eagle's helmet decal, c1960s, 7" l, 4" d 15

Popeye, metal, "Popeye Bank" on base front, mkd "1929 King Features Syndicate," 6.5" h, 2.5" d base 175

Porky Pig, metal, Porky standing next to barrel, Warner Bros copyright, c1940s, 3.75" h, 2.5" d 175

Scooby Doo, plastic, gumball, Hasbro, 1968, 4.25 x 4.5 x 3" 20

Superman, dime register, litho tin, image of Superman breaking chains on top, logo on 3 sides, ©1940s D C Comics, 2.5 x 2.5 x .75" 75

Uncle Don's Ernest Saver Club, tin top and bottom, cardboard body with paper label cover, front photo of Uncle Don shaking hands with Mr Ernest Saver, address for NY bank on right, 1920s, 1.5 x 3 x 2.25" 15

CHASE CHROME & BRASS CO.

The Chase Chrome and Brass Company was founded in the late 1870s by Augustus S. Chase and some partners. Through numerous mergers and acquisitions, the company grew and grew. The mergers helped to expand the product line into chrome, copper, brass, and other metals. Several name changes occurred until the company was sold as a subsidiary of Kennecott Corp in its merger with Standard Oil in 1981.

Most items are marked.

Club: Chase Collectors Society, 2149 West Jibsail Loop, Mesa, AZ 85202.

Candlesticks, pr, Bubble, copper and orange Catalin, 1935 110

Candy Dish, chrome and glass, ribbed handle, divided glass insert, 5.625" d, 4.75" h 25

Cocktail Shaker, chrome, black bands, black Bakelite knob, black Bakelite ring around bottom, 11.5" h, 3.75" d . . .25

Coffee Server, Continental, chrome and Bakelite, Walter Von Nessen, 1936 . .100

Coffee Server, Diplomat, chrome, Bakelite handle, Walter Von Nessen, 1932 .275

Creamer and Sugar with Tray, Savoy, chrome, 1936 80

Crumber and Brush, chrome, Bakelite handle 35

Dinner Bell, Manchu, chrome, Catalin handle, 1936 60

Bookends, pr, Art Deco cats, brass, mkd "Chase," 7.5" h, 4 x 2.5" base, $350.

Ice Bowl and Tongs, chrome, Russel
　Wright, 1934 90
Nut Dish, chrome, 2 bowls joined by
　center loop handle, 4.5" d, 4.5" h 5
Powder Puff Holder, brass base, chromed
　top, yellow Bakelite handle, frosted
　glass insert, 4.5" h, 4.5" d 10
Salt and Pepper Shakers, pr, chrome,
　Skyway, white base 25
Sauce Bowl Set, chrome, gravy server,
　spoon, and tray, Walter Von Nessen,
　1936 75
Smoking Stand, brass, Stratosphere,
　Walter Von Nessen, 1934 325
Table Lighter, Fireball, chrome, 1936 45
Tea Service, Comet, chrome and Bake-
　lite, Walter Von Nessen, 1934 350
Vase, chrome, flared rim, 6.5" h, 4.5" d . . .10
Watering Can, copper and brass, 1934 .100

CHILDREN'S BOOK SERIES

　　Most of these children's books, often
referred to as young adult books, are collected by series. Not surprisingly, books
whose main character is male are generally collected by men; those with a heroine
are collected by women. Obtaining a complete run of a particular series is possible
and would make for an interesting collection. Happy hunting!

Club: The Society of Phantom Friends, P.O.
Box 1437, North Highlands, CA 95660.

Periodicals: *Mystery & Adventure Series
Review,* P.O. Box 3488, Tucson, AZ 85722;
Yellowback Library, P.O. Box 36172, Des
Moines, IA 50315.

BONNIE AND DEBBIE by Rebecca Caudill

Happy Little Family, 1947 25
Schoolhouse in the Woods, 1949 20
Tree of Freedom, 1949 30
Up & Down the River, 1951 20

CHIP HILTON by Clair Bee

Chip Hilton: Backcourt Ace, #19, 1961 . . .45
Chip Hilton: Blackboard Fever, #10, 1953 .15
Chip Hilton: Dugout Jinx, #8, 1952 12
Chip Hilton: Fourth Down Showdown,
　#15, 1956 20

Chip Hilton: No Hitter, #17, 1959 35

GREAT BRAIN by John D. Fitzgerald

Great Brain, 1967 25
More Adventures of Great Brain, 1969 . .20

HAPPY LION by Louise Fatio

Happy Lion, 1954 50
Happy Lion & the Bear, 1964 25

EDITH THE LONELY DOLL by Dare Wright

Edith & Midnight, 1978 85
Holiday for Edith & the Bears, 1958 65
Lonely Doll Learns a Lesson, 1961 45

FAMOUS HORSE STORIES by Rutherford Montgomery

Capture of the Golden Stallion 10
Golden Stallion and the Wolf Dog 15
Golden Stallion's Revenge 12
Golden Stalliion to the Rescue, 1954 35
High Country, 1938 25

KEN HOLT MYSTERY STORIES by Bruce Campbell

Clue of the Marked Claw 10
Mystery of the Plumed Serpent, 1962 . .100
Mystery of the Sultan's Scimitar, #18,
　last title in series, 1963 350

LITTLE LEAGUE by Curtis Kent Bishop

Little League Amigo, 1964 18
Little League Little Brother, 1968 12
Little League Victory, 1967 10

*Bobbsey Twins,
by Laura Lee
Hope, The
Bobbsey Twins
at Cherry
Corners, 1927,
$15.*

NODDY by Enid Blyton

Do Look Out Noddy, 1957 20
Hurray for Little Noddy, 1950 20
Noddy and His Car, 1951 20
Noddy and the Bumpy Dog, 1957 20
Noddy Gets Into Trouble, 1954 20

TOM CORBETT SPACE CADET by Carey Rockwell

Danger in Deep Space 15
Sabotage in Space 15
Stand By for Mars, 1952 5
Treachery in Outer Space, #6, 1954 15

CHILDREN'S COLLECTIBLES

Mothers of the world unite. This category is for you. The children who used it hardly remember it. It's the kind of stuff that keeps your children forever young in your mind.

There is virtually nothing written about this collecting category so what to collect is wide open. One collector I know has hundreds of baby planters. To each her own.

Club: Treasures for Little Children, 8201 Pleasant Ave. S., Bloomington, MN 55420.

ABC Plate, Sunbonnet Babies, 6.25" d . . .25
Baby Bottle, clear glass, 3 Bears theme, 6.25" h 10
Baby Bottle Sterilizer, Capson Mfg Co, Chicago, model E, aluminum sterlizer rack, pan, funnel, with nipple jar and cap, 6 bottle capacity, orig box 20
Baby Carriage, wicker, cloth cushioned int, metal and wood handle, metal carriage with locking mechanism for handle, front adjusts downward, hood flips backwards, metal wheels with rubber tires, mkd "Gendrom Made in Toledo, Ohio, U.S.A.," 42" h, 54" w . . .275
Baby Shoes, pr, black leather, ankle strap 35
Bib, linen, white embroidery 30
Bottle, Dr Drakes Glesso Children's Coughs, paper label 30
Cap, boy's, wool, c1930 20
Bottle, Mennen Baby Oil, clear glass, emb rose, light blue, red, and dark blue label and letters, full 10

Chair, arrow back, dec, polychrome fruit and flowers, brown repaint, 10" w seat, 23.75" h overall 165
Christening Gown, cotton, long sleeves, embroidered hem and yoke, lace trim and tucking, c1900 85
Dish Set, Circus theme, Edwin M Knowles China Co, service for 4 80
Doll, Amish, white cotton and navy blue wool body, green cotton dress, early 20th C, 13.25" l 150
Dollhouse, Rich, Colonial style, gypsum and hardboard, steel reinforced edges, steel int stairs, 6 rooms, 1930s, 25" h, 35" w, 14" d 300
Dress, girl's, calico, blue, 2 pc, matching bonnet, c1900 160
High Chair, hickory, 4 spindle back, rect food tray on hinged arms, woven splint seat, splayed base, shaped footrest, box stretchers, State of Indiana Farm Industries, Putnamville, IN, 1930s, 13" w seat, 14" d, 40" h 300
Pedal Car, jeep, metal body, rubber tires, painted star on hood, plastic headlights and front bumper, orig condition, 15" h, 21" w, 39" l 225
Plate, divided, Circus scene, Hazel Atlas .10
Pull Toy, horse, wooden, painted dec, 7.75" h, 10.5" l 50
Quilt, pieced, baby blocks, crib size, blue, outline quilting of blocks, 36 x 45" . . .125
Rattle, celluloid, teething ring, silhouette pictures, dated 1916 85
Reamer, crystal frosted, chicks dec 60
Rocking Horse, carved wood, carved detail mane and tail, leather ears, 23.5" h, 11.5" w, 32" l 300

Jolly-Tune the Clown, Mattel, cardboard box, tin lid, hard plastic head, fabric-covered spring body, 5.675" w, $18.

Toy, Suzy-Q Automatic Ironer, GW, Japan, battery operated, mangler type iron, tin, pink and blue, orig box, 12.25" w, 7" h, $150.

Sled, metal and wood, gooseneck front
  for holding ropes, painted dec, 18" h,
  17" w, 41" l 400
Toy, organ, litho tin, crank handle to play
  music, #130, 9.5" h, 7.25" w, 4.75" d 70
Wagon, Aircruiser, metal body, metal
  steering bar and puller, metal wheels
  with hard rubber tires, front wheel
  steering, orig paint, 13" h, 17" w, 44" l .500
Warming Dish, divided, Hankscraft, 9" d .15

CHINTZ CHINA

Chintz China—or "All-Over-Floral" as it is known in England and Australia—is best described as flowered wallpaper applied to ceramics. Introduced in the early 1800s and made in various forms until well into the 1960s, chintz became a hot collectible in 1996 and continues to grow in popularity.

Czechoslovakian, Dutch, German, and Japanese chintz is less expensive than earthenware chintz made in Staffordshire, England. English bone china—especially Shelley—has become more collectible in the last year but 1930-1960 earthenware chintz still commands the highest prices. The best known of the factories are Grimwades (Royal Winton) James Kent, A. G. Richardson (Crown Ducal), Elijah Cotton (Lord Nelson) and Midwinter. Royal Winton has always been considered the most desirable, but Crown Ducal has increased in price since Winton, Kent, and Cotton have been reproduced.

Chintz ware was exported to North America, particularly Canada, in vast quantities from the 1920s until the 1960s. Grimwades alone produced more than seventy chintz patterns. Prices vary widely depending on pattern, shape, and condition. Most Royal Winton, James Kent, and Lord Nelson pieces have the pattern name incorporated into the backstamp, making identification easier. Read the *Charlton Standard Catalogue of Chintz, 3rd Edition,* to familiarize yourself with different patterns and shapes.

Now that Royal Winton and James Kent are reproducing chintz in their original patterns and shapes it is important to study the backstamps. New Winton has the date 1995 incorporated into the backstamp; this is when the company was bought and does not refer to the date of production. Check the website www.chintznet.com for examples of old and new backstamps. Several altered backstamps have turned up so do your homework.

For more information on chintz china visit www.chintznet.com/susan.

Advisor: Susan Scott, 882 Queen Street West, Toronto, Ontario M6J 1G3, (416) 538-8536, fax (416) 534-4814, e-mail: susanscottca@aol.com.

Clubs: Chintz World International, P.O. Box 50888, Pasadena, CA 91115; Royal Winton Collectors' Club, 2 Kareela Rd., Baulkham Hills NSW2153, Australia; R.W.I.C.C., Dancer's End, Northall, Bedfordshire LU6 2EU, England.

Grimwades' Royal Winton, cup and saucer, Julia, $200.

A. G. RICHARDSON

Bowl, Peony, scalloped, 5" d 150
Cup and Saucer, Blue Chintz 125
Plate, Spring Blossom, 6" sq 125
Vase, Marigold, 8" h 300

ELIJAH COTTON, LORD NELSON

Bud Vase, Rosetime 125
Cake Plate and Server, Green Tulip,
   white border 300
Cup and Saucer, Royal Brocade 50
Plate, Green Tulip, 8.5" sq 175
Stacking Teapot, Marina, all-patterned .600

GRIMWADES' ROYAL WINTON

Basket, Shrewsbury, Rowsley shape . .475
Butter Dish, Estelle, Ascot shape 225
Butter Pat, Royalty, 3.25" 75
Candy Box, cov, ftd, Kew 325
Candy Dish, Evesham, open handles,
   7 x 4" 275
Cup and Saucer, Joyce-Lynn 100
Eggcup, double, Summertime 175
Jampot, White Crocus, ceramic lid and
   liner 300
Plate, Victorian Rose, Ascot shape, 7" . .150
Toast Rack, Florence, Queen shape,
   4 bar 350

JAMES KENT

Candy Dish, Florita, frilled edge, 5.5" . . .125
Creamer and Sugar, Du Barry 200
Cup and Saucer, Rosalynde, Diamond
   shape 125
Eggcups, Marigold, 4 cups with tray . . .350
Nut Dish, Du Barry 65

*Grimwades' Royal Winton, salt and pepper
shaker set, Evesham, $300.*

*Elijah Cotton,
Lord Nelson,
bud vase,
Heather, $100.*

Plate, Apple Blossom, octagonal, 9" . . .175
Tray, Hydrangea, 10 x 5" 125

MIDWINTER

Bowl, Brama, 5" d 45
Cake Stand, Lorna Doone, 2-tier with
   metal handles 50
Relish Dish, silverplate handle, Lorna
   Doone spoon 100

SHELLEY

Creamer and Sugar, Summer Glory 200
Pin Dish, Marguerite, 4.75" d 100
Plate, Rock Garden, 6" d 90
Set, cup and saucer with 6" plate,
   Pansy 325
Teapot, Melody, 3 cup 400

CHRISTMAS

Of all the holiday collectibles,
Christmas is the most popular. It has grown
so large as a category that many collectors
specialize in only one area, e.g., Santa
Claus figures or tree ornaments.

Anything Victorian is "hot." The
Victorians popularized Christmas. Many
collectors love to recapture that spirit.
However, prices for Victorian items, from
feather trees to ornaments, are escalating.

Learn to distinguish turn-of-the-century
ornaments from modern examples.
Moderately priced boxes of old ornaments
can still be found. Happy hunting, Ho! Ho!
Ho!

Club: Golden Glow of Christmas Past, 6401
Winsdale St., Minneapolis, MN 55427.

Book, *A Christmas Carol,* Charles Dickens, Julian Brazelton illus, New York Pocket Book, 1940 4

Book, *Christmas Everyday and Other Stories Told for Children,* William Dean Howells, ©1892 W D H, Harper, NY ...15

Book, *The Night Before Christmas,* Clement Clarke Moore, Grosset and Dunlap, 9.5 x 12" 5

Candy Container, painted glass, Santa on rocking horse 50

Candy Container, plastic, Santa on skis, 5" h 10

Catalog, Christmas Ideas Vol 11, #6, Dec 1954 4

Catalog, Sears Christmas Wish Book, 1950s 40

Creamer, holly leaves and candles dec, mkd "Watt Pottery Company, Christmas 1957," 4.5" h 150

Creche, set, 20 pcs, ceramic, painted, Infant Jesus separate from crib, 1950s, 5" h 45

Dinnerware, Noritake, Home for Christmas, plate, cup, and saucer 30

Figure, Beagle dog, wearing Santa hat, holding candy cane in mouth, Lefton ..5

Figure, elf, hp face, felt clothes, Japan, 9.75" h 4

Figure, Santa, composition face, felt clothes, cardboard legs, cotton beard, on mica-covered cardboard disk, mkd "Japan," 1950s, 5" h 25

Handkerchief, Santa and Mrs Claus dropping toys to waiting children, candle and cookies hanging from boughs on each corner, 12.75" sq ...150

Puzzle, Santa Claus Puzzle Box, Milton Bradley, set of 3 in orig box, c1925, $250.

Stereograph, "The Christmas Tree and Toys," #P11 P-2205, Keystone View Co, description of Billy and Betty's Christmas on back, $25.

Magazine, *Better Homes & Gardens,* "Christmas Ideas For 1959" 3

Magazine, *Woman's Day,* Dec 1960, Christmas recipes 4

Motion Lamp, Merrie-Merrie Christmas Tree, Econolite, 1951 125

Music Box, figural Christmas tree, holly berry dec, plays Jingle Bells, paper label mkd "Lefton #1365," 8" h 10

Ornament, glass, child's face 45

Ornament, glass, "Christmas Cross," Reed & Barton, orig red felt case, 1974 25

Ornament, glass, "Home for Christmas," Betsey Clark, Hallmark, orig box, 1986 .10

Ornament, spun glass, angel, 3.5" h 4

Pinback Button, "Santa Claus Wants To See You At Gately & Britton's," Santa wearing green holly crown with red berries, black lettering 50

Plate, Christmas tree, Holt-Howard, 1959, 9.75" l 10

Plate, "Good Will Towards Men," Frankoma, 1965 150

Postcard, dog holding "Merry Christmas" greeting in mouth and American flag in paw, 3-cornered hat on head, sprig of holly below, mkd "Xmas Dogs/series No. 1," c1900s 2

Postcard, woman wearing hat, "A Merry Christmas," postmarked 1909, used 4

Record, *Beatles Fan Club Happy Christmas Record,* 1968 50

Record, *Snoopy's Merry Christmas Album,* 1978 20

Salt and Pepper Shakers, pr, Fitz & Floyd, 6" h 30

Star, 5-point, heavy gauge wire, red,
orig paint, lighted, c1930s, 18" d 20
Tree, plastic coated cardboard needles,
Japan, 9" h 40

CHRISTMAS & EASTER SEALS

Collecting Christmas and Easter Seals is one of the most inexpensive "stamp" hobbies. Sheets usually sell for between 50¢ and $1. Most collectors do not buy single stamps, except for the very earliest Christmas seals.

Club: Christmas Seal and Charity Stamp Society, P.O. Box 18615, Rochester, NY 14618.

CIGARETTE & CIGAR

Cigarette products contain a warning that they might be hazardous to your health. Cigarette and cigar collectibles should also contain a warning that they may be hazardous to your pocketbook. With each passing year, the price for cigarette and cigar-related material goes higher and higher. If it ever stabilizes and then drops, a number of collectors are going to see their collections go up in smoke.

The vast majority of cigarette and cigar material is two-dimensional, from advertising trade cards to posters. Seek out three-dimensional pieces. There are some great tins out there.

Clubs: Cigar Label Collectors International, P.O. Box 66, Sharon Center, OH 44274; Cigarette Pack Collectors Assoc., 61 Searle St., Georgetown, MA 01833; International Seal, Label & Cigar Band Society, 8915 E. Bellevue St, Tucson, AZ 85715.

Cigar Box, Sandow, wood, litho paper
overlay depicting strongman, repeated name on outer lid edges with repeated image of forearms chained at wrists, ©1894, 3 x 5 x 6.5" 35
Cigar Box Opener, cast iron, silver paint
finish, 1.75" h diecut image of George Washington on 3" l handle, c1889 15
Cigarette Dispenser, metal, "Cigarettes/ 30¢," center turn knob, 26" h, 18" w . .175

Display, Whiz Bakelite Cigar Holders,
litho cardboard, contains 12 cigar holders, Whiz Mfg Co, Division of Eastern Briar Pipe Co, Brooklyn, NY, 10.25" h, 9" w .70
Fan, Florence Walton Cigar, diecut cardboard, Art Nouveau design of lady portrait framed in gold emb floral motif, adv tex on reverse for Irwin Horst, Schaefferstown, PA, c1920s, 7 x 8.5" 35
Flange Sign, "Colonial Club 5¢ Cigars,"
painted metal, 8.75" h, 18.5" w 600
Match Safe, silver luster brass, celluloid
wrapper with "Union-Made Cigars/It Represents Living Waves and Not Child Labor," reverse panel shows miniature envelope cover with "Smoke Union-Made Cigars," top panel with "Blue Label Cigars Are Not made By the Trust" 75
Pinback Button, "Join the Army of
Recruit Little Cigar Smokers," multicolored, military cadet in dress uniform on red ground, white lettering, 1920s . .8
Pinback Button, "Welcome Back Johnny,"
Philip Morris, bellhop image, red rim, white lettering, 1940s 65
Poster, Camel Cigarettes, paper, "Don't
Get Your Wind!," full color image of woman holding lighted cigarette between fingertips, open Camel pack image, ©1935 R J Reynolds Tobacco Co, 10 x 21" 45

Pinback Button, Maquoketa Cuban Hand Made Cigars, celluloid over metal, 1.75" d, $82. —Photo courtesy Collectors Auction Services.

Poster, Lucky Strike Cigarettes, cardboard, easel back, "Luckies–A Light Smoke Of Rich, Ripe-Bodied Tobacco/ It's Toasted," image of woman holding cigarette and smiling at man, open pack of cigarettes in foreground, 36" h, 27.5" w 175

Sign, tin, "Phillies/America's No 1 Cigar," emb lettering, rolled edge, 13" h, 20.25" l.........................70

Thermometer, Chesterfield King Cigarettes, litho tin, raised relief cigarette pack image against golden yellow tobacco leaves with blue border, c1940s, 6 x 13" 25

Thermometer, Fatima Cigarettes, metal, porcelain enamel, cigarette package image, 1930s, 7 x 27 x 1" 65

Tin, Louis Dobbelmann's Golden Leaf Navy Cut Tobacco, floral motifs, Dutch harbor scene, nationlity flags, lady trumpeter seated on broad eagle wings above ocean waters, 2.25 x 3.25 x .75" 50

CIGARETTE LIGHTERS

Cigarette lighters come in all shapes and sizes. Collections could be assembled focusing on several different categories, i.e., flat advertising lighters, figural lighters, or even figural advertising lighters. The possibilities are endless. Buy lighters in good condition only. Scratches and/or missing parts greatly detract from a lighter's value. Remember, cigarette lighters were mass-produced and are therefore plentiful.

Clubs: International Lighter Collectors, P.O. Box 536, Quitman, TX 75783; Pocket Lighter Preservation Guild & Historical Society, Inc., 380 Brooks Dr., Suite 209A, Hazelwood, MO 63042.

Advertising, Kroehler Furniture, Zippo, brushed finish, black and green enameled "Kroehler World's Largest Furniture Manufacturer" 1 side, list of furniture other side, 1956 .20

Dunhill, Rollalite, table, polished finish, engine-turned line designs, green felt on base, 2.5" h 55

Advertising, Dodge Pickup Truck, chrome body, cloisonné dec, 2.375" h, $35. —Photo courtesy Collectors Auction Services.

Evans, table, Mobilgas winged Pegasus logo, clear acrylic base, antique brass colored Evans insert, red Pegasus horse inside base, 3.25" h ...60

Figural, pistol, Occupied Japan, chrome finish metal, black plastic grip panel on each side, orig box, 1950s, 4" l 20

Marathon, Klix, burnished brass tone, engraved Art Nouveau panels, flat ...20

Parker, Flaminaire, plain brushed finish .10

Regens, stainless steel, vertical line pattern, squeeze lever action, orig box with instructions 25

Regens, US Air Force, stainless steel, blue enameled USAF emblem on both sides, squeeze lever action, orig box with instructions 20

Ronson, Dureum, combination lighter/ compact, gilt and black enamel finish, engraved panel with color enamel flowers, 1940s, 2.5 x 4.25" 30

Ronson, Realite, polished finish, pin-up girls depicted on multicolored side panels, Japan 25

Ronson, Varaflame, table, metal and wood, cork case, orig box, 3.5 x 2 x 2" .20

Ronson, Venus, table, antique frosted brass, silver line designs on sides, cork at base, 3" h, 2" d 35

Royal, combination cigarette case/lighter, brushed finish, engraved line design on both sides, orig box, 4.5 x 3 x 5" ...25

Souvenir, Zippo, polished finish, affixed white metal seahorse, clam, shells, starfish, and "Ocean City, MD" on side, slim 1974 30

Thorens, table, white marble base, 3.5" h .35

CIRCUS

Traveling tent circuses were an exciting event in rural towns across the country—evidence the large amount of memorabilia left behind.

Every circus collector should make it a point to see the great annual circus parade held in Milwaukee. It features equipment from the Circus World Museum in Baraboo, Wisconsin.

Clubs: Circus Fans Assoc. of America, P.O. Box 59710, Potomac, MD 20859; Circus Historical Society, 4102 Idaho Ave., Nashville, TN 37209.

Pinback Button, "A Happy New Year/ Charmion," sepia photo of vaudevile strong lady, early 1900s, 1.25" d 15

Pinback Button, "Cygnet Circus R U Going," multicolored, center clown image, black lettering, white ground, c1910, 1.25" d 15

Pinback Button, "Just Tell Him That You Saw Us/Long and Short Man," image of giant bending over and poking Keystone Cop in chest, c1910 15

Pinback Button, P T Barnum image with name above, ...15

Poster, Cole Bros Circus, "World's Largest Chimpanzee/Johnstown, Friday, June 3," 50" h, 28" w 20

Program, Cole Bros. Circus with Ken Maynard Wild West Show, 8 pp, 22.75" h, 17" w, $165. —Photo courtesy Collectors Auction Services.

Poster, Mills Bros Three Ring Circus/ 27th Annual Tour, Triangle Poster Co, Pittsburgh, PA, 41" h, 14" w 20

Poster, Ringling Bros and Barnum & Bailey Circus, paper litho, center leopards head, 43.5" h, 29" w 120

CLICKERS

If you need a clicker, you would probably spend hours trying to locate a modern one. I am certain that they exist. You can find a clicker at a flea market in a matter of minutes. As an experiment, I tried looking up the word in a dictionary. It was not there. Times change.

Although most clickers were produced as advertising promotions, I believe their principal purpose was to drive parents crazy.

Blue Ribbon Bananas, celluloid, cluster of ripe yellow bananas held by blue string and tag at upper stalk stem, black lettering, white ground 8

Craddock Shoes, black, white, and red, red bell symbol, "Long Wear Shoes/ Craddock-Terry Co," Kirchhof 15

Green Duck Novelty Co, green and white, duck symbol with "100% Union Made," and "Buttons/Badges/Emblems That Click," 1930s 35

Halloween Witch, orange, black, and white, Kirchhof 15

Little Sergeant Shoes, orange, black, and white sentry soldier on light gray ground, black lettering, Kirchhof 8

Nolde's Bread, light blue, red lettering outlined in white, 1940s 15

Peters Weatherbird Shoes, full color image of bird in school clothing on lime green ground 15

Poll-Parrot Shoes, multicolored image of green and red parrot on yellow ground, red lettering, Rand & Co 15

Purity Ice Cream, red, white, and blue celluloid disk on tin flange clicker, Parisienne Novelty Co, 1930s 15

Purity Salt, yellow and blue, black and white logo name, depicts 2 salt shakers emptying contents above product image, "Guaranteed Free-Running In Any Climate," Kirchhof . . .15

Left: Advertising, Buster Brown Shoes, $15. Right: political, "'Click with Dick' Nixon for President," blue on silver, 2" h, $5.
—Photo courtesy Ray Morykan Auctions.

RCA, brown, black logo, T Cohn, 1930s . . .35
Red Goose Shoes, red goose symbol
  on yellow ground, Kirchhof 15
Sealtest, red and white, logo with "The
  Sealtest System of Laboratory Pro-
  tection," Kirchhof, 1930s 15
Snapper Mowers, blue and orange,
  dapper turtle figure above "Click
  Broncos," 1960s 8
Sundial Shoes, red, depicts clown,
  Kirchhof, 1930s 15
State Auto Insurance, red and blue on
  gray, Kirchhof, 1930s 15
Tastycake, white lettering on blue
  ground, Kirchhof 8
Zig Zag, product name in blue lettering,
  "The Food Confection" in red letter-
  ing on olive green ground, Germany,
  1930s 50

CLOCKS

Look for clocks that are fun (have motion actions) or that are terrific in a decorating scheme (a school house clock in a country setting). Clocks are bought to be seen and used.

Avoid buying any clock that does not work. You do not know whether it is going to cost $5, $50, or $500 to repair. Are you prepared to risk the higher numbers? Likewise, avoid clocks with extensively damaged cases. There are plenty of clocks in fine condition awaiting purchase.

Club: National Assoc. of Watch and Clock Collectors, Inc., 514 Poplar St., Columbia, PA 17512.

Advertising, Admiral/Radios/Refrigera-
  tors, neon, c1940s, 20" d 175
Advertising, Amalie Motor Oil, light-up,
  metal body, glass face and cover,
  15" d 225
Advertising, American Express, "Money
  Orders Since 1882," light-up, 1960s,
  13 x 26" 200
Advertising, Calumet Baking Powder,
  regulator, calendar, oak case, "Time
  To Buy Calumet Baking Powder/Best
  by Test," Sessions, 38.5" h, 16" w 450
Advertising, Cities Service, light-up,
  green, white, and red, Telechron,
  1950s 375
Advertising, Clicquot Club Beverages,
  light-up, c1959, 15" sq 175
Advertising, Elgin Watches, metal hous-
  ing, tin clock face, reverse painted
  glass cover, neon, 22" d, 5.5" d 275
Advertising, Exide Batteries, light-up,
  Pam Clock Co, 1950s 225
Advertising, Marshall-Wells Paints,
  center image of man with can and
  brush and "Good Paint Costs Less,"
  Telechron, 1950s 200
Advertising, Mercury Outboard Motors,
  light-up, metal body, glass face and
  cover, center decal, 15" d 200
Advertising, Skelly, woodgrain type
  background with center logo, metal
  rim, diamond shaped, 15.5" d 275

Advertising, Lucky Strike Tobacco, round oak case, 15" dial, $450. —Photo courtesy Gene Harris Antique Auction Center, Inc.

Alarm, Luxor IV, wind-up, cardboard face, man's head as hour hand, glass front, metal case, ©Burke & James, Inc, Chicago, 4.5" h, $220. —Photo courtesy Collectors Auction Services.

Advertising, St Joseph Aspirin, blue
  and white, 1950s 200
Advertising, "Teper's Jewelers/370
  Franklin Ave," metal rim and housing,
  glass face, plastic sides, Gruen, 17" d,
  4.5" d 60
Advertising, Tetley, "Tea Time," light-up,
  metal body, 1940s, 14" sq 400
Advertising, Texaco, alarm, metal body,
  cardboard face, glass cover, Westclox,
  5.25" h 325
Advertising, Westinghouse Radio,
  "Listen…And You'll Buy A Westing-
  house Radio," light-up, red, black,
  and white, Telechron, 1950s 350
Character, Mickey Mouse, alarm, metal,
  Walt Disney Productions, made in
  Germany, 6.25" h, 5" w 75
Character, Roy Rogers and Trigger,
  enameled metal case, clear crystal
  over dial face, name below alarm
  dial, Ingraham, 1950s, 5 x 5 x 2" 175
Character, Snoopy, alarm, metal, red,
  yellow face with image of dancing
  Snoopy, brass accent bells on top,
  Blessing, ©United Features Syndicate
  Inc, 1970, 5.25" h, 3.625" d 45
Character, Star Wars, battery operated,
  hard plastic, R2-D2 and C-3PO images
  attached to base, orig box, Bradley,
  ©1982 Lucasfilm Ltd, 3 x 7 x 8.5" 50
Figural, football, "Touchdown," electric,
  desk, hard plastic, on circular base,
  orig box, c1960, Sessions 35

Mantel, carved marble, H Z Rhoads,
  Lancaster, PA, 13.5" h, 18" w, 7" d 225
Mantel, wood, tin clock face, cathedral
  style, reverse painted glass door,
  lion and horse logo, with key and
  pendulum, Welch Mfg Co, 18.5" h,
  10" w, 4" d 120

CLOTHES SPRINKLERS

Before steam irons, clothes requiring ironing had to be manually dampened with water. Some housewives used soda pop bottles or other common bottles, with sprinkler caps attached, while others owned more decorative figural bottles made especially for this purpose. These are the bottles that are now sought after by collectors willing to pay $20 and up for the more common examples and as much as several hundred dollars for the extremely rare bottles. It is estimated that close to 100 different sprinkle bottles were manufactured.

Bottle, plastic, adv 40
Bottle, plastic, plain, various styles 20
Cat, black, 7.5" 150
Cat, Siamese, various shades of cream
  and tan, Cardinal 200
Cat, stray 100
Cat, various colors, marble eyes,
  Cardinal 300
Chinaman, Emperor 100
Chinaman, Sprinkle Plenty, common,
  yellow and green 45
Chinaman, Sprinkle Plenty, head is
  sprinkler 125

Elephant, ceramic, happy face, trunk forms handle, $275.

Chinaman, white, blue trim, Cleminson . .55
Clothespin, various colors 225
Dachshund, green coat, red bow tie,
　very rare 500
Dearie is Weary, yellow dress, holding
　iron, head is sprinkler, rare 350
Dutch Boy 250
Dutch Girl, plastic 75
Dutch Girl, wetter-downer 250
Elephant, trunk up, gray and pink,
　common 100
Elephant, trunk up, shamrock on tummy,
　white and pink 150
Fireman, holding hose with sprinkler,
　cap in front, rare 600
Kitchen Prayer Lady, Enesco, rare 500
Mammy, white dress with red trim　. . . .300
Mary Poppins, clear glass, holding
　umbrella and purse 90
Mary Poppins, wearing hat and dress
　with striped skirt, Cleminson 300
Merry Maid, glass, various colors, new .100
Myrtle, white dress with polka-dot top,
　sprinkler in back of head, Pfaltzgraff .300
Poodle, standing on hind legs, pink or
　gray 300
Rooster, long neck, plastic cap, 10" h . .175
Sadiron, ceramic, blue flowers 100
Sadiron, ceramic, ivy 85
Sadiron, ceramic, souvenir, theme park
　adv 90
Sadiron, ceramic, woman ironing 95
Sadiron, plastic, green 30

CLOTHING & ACCESSORIES

　Decide from the outset whether you are buying clothing and accessories for use or display. If you are buying for use, apply very strict standards with respect to condition and long-term survival prospects. If you only want the items for display, you can be a little less fussy about condition.

Club: The Costume Society of America, P.O. Box 73, Earleville, MD 21919.

Newsletters: *Adornment,* 1333A North Ave., Box 103, New Rochelle, NY 10804; *Lill's Vintage Clothing Newsletter,* 19 Jamestown Dr., Cincinnati, OH 45241; *The Vintage Connection,* 904 N. 65th St., Springfield, OR, 97478.

Afternoon Dress, 2-pc, ivory silk, lace
　appliqué and ruching on bodice, c1900 .50
Bathing Blouse, black cotton, fuchsia
　piping trim, matching bloomers,
　fuchsia stockings, c1890 75
Bodice, black silk satin, sequins and
　beads dec, c1890 35
Bonnet, black ruched velvet, insect dec
　in sequins and velvet, with feathers and
　net, black silk lining, label mkd "L. E.
　Gallagher, Philadelphia," c1870 90
Chemise, ivory silk lace, floral pattern
　on net, ivory satin trim, c1910 50
Child's Robe, white chenille, blue Scottie
　dog and trim .40
Dress, girl's, red cotton, blue, yellow,
　green, and white rick-rack dec, mkd
　"Fluffy Ruffle, Arlington, TX," 1940s　. .20
Gentleman's Vest, rose on ivory silk
　brocade, ivory polished cotton lining,
　c1870 20
Girdle, Real-Form Girdle of Grace, Ski-Hi,
　orig box, 1950s 20
Hat, derby, black ribbon and bow,
　Dranna, 5th Ave, NY, 1930-40s 30
Hat, gray wool, black woven bank and
　visor trim, black cord chin strap with
　black side buttons, 1950s 30
Jacket, girl's, ivory crepe with ruching
　on bodice, silk bows on sleeves and
　front, muslin lining, linen fringe trim,
　c1880 20
Poncho, felt, turquoise, hand embroi-
　dered gold floral design on front and
　back, gold fringe 20

Afternoon Dress, 2-pc, beige open-weave with silk ribbon piping and trim, labeled "Rouff, 13 BD Haussmann, Paris," c1870, $275. —Photo courtesy Alderfer Auction Company.

Fan, black lace with sequins, celluloid sticks, 8.5" l, $40.

Robe, mens, burgundy rayon, c1940 15
Shirt, boys, flannel, pink, green, and
    brown plaid, 1940s 20
Shirt, child's, western style, gaberdine,
    cream and black, white plastic but-
    tons, white cord trim at front and back
    of yoke, white and black chain stitched
    designs on front yoke 50
Suspenders, woven silk, gold-green
    and pink, c1805, 1.125 x 39" 100
Sweater, acrylic/mohair, red, white,
    and blue stripes on front and sleeves,
    knit cuffs and waist band, mother-of-
    pearl type buttons, 1960s 30
Vest, brown leather, red, blue, and black
    wool plaid lining, 4 patch pockets,
    button front, buckle style adjusters
    at sides, 1950s 50

COCA-COLA

John Pemberton, a pharmacist from
Atlanta, Georgia, is credited with creating
the formula for Coca-Cola. Less than two
years later, he sold out to Asa G. Candler.
Candler improved the formula and began
advertising. By the 1890s America was
Coca-Cola conscious.

Coke, a term first used in 1941, is now
recognized worldwide. American collectors still focus primarily on Coca-Cola material designed for the American market.
Although it would take a little effort to
obtain, a collection of foreign Coke advertising would make a terrific display. What a
perfect excuse to fly to the Orient.

Club: The Coca-Cola Collectors Club, P.O.
Box 49166, Atlanta, GA 30359; The Cola
Club, P.O. Box 392, York, PA 17405.

Advertising Tear Sheet, Edgar Bergen
    holding bottle by microphone, Charlie
    McCarthy looking into cooler, radio
    promo, 10.5 x 13" 7
Ashtray, Bakelite, "Drink Coca-Cola In
    Bottles," 1940s 50
Ashtray, glass, "Coke adds life to...
    everything nice" 3
Bag Rack, tin, "Take Home A Carton of
    Coca-Cola," 6-pack in cardboard
    carrier inside yellow circle, 1930s,
    16 x 36" 650
Bottle Carrier, emb tin, 6" h, 8.25" w,
    5" d 35
Bottle Carrier, plastic, "Drink Coca-Cola
    In Bottles," 1950-60s 18
Bottle Opener, bottle shaped, c1950 ...200
Bottle Opener, stainless steel, ribbed,
    Dow, c1940 45
Brochure, Westinghouse Select-o-Matic
    vending machine, 3.5 x 9" 25
Calendar, 1937, Jul pad only, 26" h,
    13.5" w 55
Calendar, 1950, 2 month sheets, pretty
    women and coke bottle illus, 1950,
    22" h, 13" w 45
Cash Register Topper, wood, chrome
    bottom, "Drink Coca-Cola," 1950,
    11.5 x 6" 275
Chalkboard, hardboard, "Drink Coca-
    Cola/Have A Coke, It's Refreshing,"
    30" h, 18" w 65
Clock, electric, red circle with "Drink
    Coca-Cola," silhouette girl below,
    1939 825
Clock, light-up, hp roman numerals,
    red paint trim, c1958 450
Coaster, foil, hand holding bottle, 1950s ..5

Cooler, metal, bottle opener on side, restored, 35" h, 25" w, 17.5" d, $825. —Photo courtesy Collectors Auction Services.

Cooler Bag, vinyl, 1970s 35
Counter Sign, wood and glass, "Coca
Cola/Please Pay When Served,"
1948, 18 x 8.5" 375
Display, figural bottle, painted red and
white, 1950s, 40" h 415
Door Bar, wrought iron, attached rails,
adjustable, 1 930s 475
Drinking Glass, bell shaped, 1940s 15
Fan, "Drink Coca-Cola in Bottles,"
wicker 65
Hatpin, cloisonne dec, "Drink Coca-
Cola," c1930s, 1.5 x 2" 350
Kick Plate, emb tin, "Drink Coca-Cola,
bottle on left, c1930s, 11.5 x 35" 1,200
Letterhead, Western Coca-Cola Bottling
Co, Chicago, IL, 1909 20
Menu Board, emb tin, "Drink Coca-Cola/
Delicious and Refreshing," girl silhou-
ette at bottom right, 1940, 20 x 28" . . .450
Needle Holder, dated 1924, 3 x 2" 20
Pen and Pencil Set, figural baseball
bats, Coca-Cola and Detroit Tigers
adv, engraved "batter up" on fountain
pen tip, orig box, c1930s 80
Pencil Box, cardboard, "Drink Coca-
Cola/Delicious Refreshing" on lid, "A
Pure Drink of Natural Flavors" on
back, contains 2 pencils, pen holder,
pen point, eraser, ruler, and 2 blotters .35
Pinback Button, "Have a Good Day,"
1980s 2
Pinback Button, "Member of Coca-Cola
Bottle Club," hand holding bottle,
1930s 65

*Limited Edition Plate, Coca-Cola Santa
Claus Heritage Collection, "Good Boys and
Girls," Cavanagh, 1995, $45.*

Toy Truck, Buddy L, 1950s, $200.

Pocketknife, celluloid, 2 blades, "Drink
Coca-Cola in Bottles," Remington,
c1935 125
Serving Tray, metal, woman in ice skat-
ing outfit with bottle in hand, mkd
"Copyright The Coca-Cola Co 1941/
The American Art Works, Inc,
Coshocton, Ohio/Made in USA,"
10.625" w, 13.375" l, 1.25" d 250
Sheet Music, *I'd Like to Buy the World
a Coke,*1970 20
Sign, cardboard, "Entertain Your Thirst/
Drink Coca-Cola/Delicious and Re-
freshing," woman at microphone
holding bottle, 1941 825
Sign, cardboard, "Grilled Cheese Sand-
wich and Coca-Cola In Bottles/35¢,"
©1952 The Coc-Cola Co, 16" h, 11" w .200
Sign, cardboard, "Have a Coke," bottle
on iceberg, 1944, 20 x 36" 550
Sign, cardboard, "Hello Refreshment,"
girl exiting pool, 1942 775
Sign, diecut cardboard, easel back,
"Drink Coca-Cola For Sparkling
Holidays/Bring Home The Coke,"
1956 355
Sign, diecut tin, emb bottle, 1933,
12 x 39" 775
Sign, porcelain, "Drink Coca-Cola,"
bottle on right, mkd "made in
England," 1950s, 16 x 22" 650
Syrup Barrel, wood, varnished, paper
decal on top, label mkd "The Coca-
Cola Company, Kearny, Los Angeles,
New Orleans, St Louis, Atlanta,
Baltimore, Chicago, Dallas," 10 gal,
21" h, 13.5" w 125
Thermometer, tin, "Drink Coca-Cola/
Sign of Good Taste," 1950s, 30" h 375
Thimble, aluminum, pebbled surface,
red band around bottom with emb
"Drink Coca-Cola in Bottles" 25

Tip Tray, woman holding soda glass,
"Drink Coca-Cola/Relieves Fatigue
5¢," 1907 .... .375
Yearbook, service dept, Coca-Cola
Bottling Co, Atlanta, GA, 1923 ...... .20

COINS, AMERICAN

Just because a coin is old does not
mean that it is valuable. Value often
depends more on condition than on age.
This being the case, the first step in deciding if any of your coins are valuable is to
grade them. Coins are graded on a scale of
70 with 70 being the best and 4 being good.

Start your research by acquiring Marc
and Tom Hudgeons' *The Official Blackbook
Price Guide to United States Coins* (House
of Collectibles). Resist the temptation to
look up your coins immediately. Read the
hundred-page introduction, over half of
which deals with the question of grading.

Do not overlook the melt (weight) value
of silver content coins. In many cases,
weight value will be far greater than collectible value.

Club: American Numismatic Assoc., 818 N.
Cascade Ave., Colorado Springs, CO 80903.

Periodical: Krause Publications has several
coin-related magazines. Contact the company at 700 E. State St., Iola, WI 54990.

COINS, FOREIGN

The foreign coins that you are most
likely to find at a flea market are the leftover
change that someone brought back from
their travels. Since the coins were in circulation, they are common and of a low grade.
In some countries, they have been with-
drawn from circulation and cannot even be
redeemed for face value.

If you are a dreamer and think you have
uncovered hidden wealth, use Chester L.
Krause and Clifford Mishler's *Standard
Catalog of World Coins* (Krause Publications).
This book covers world coinage from 1701
to the present.

Avoid ancient coinage. There are
excellent fakes on the market. You need to
be an expert to tell the good from the bad.

Coins are one of those categories where it
pays to walk away when the deal is too
good. Honest coin dealers work on very
small margins. They cannot afford to give
away anything of value.

COLLEGE COLLECTIBLES

Rah, rah, rah, sis-boom-bah! A college
education respectable again. Alumni tout
their old alma mater and usually have a
souvenir of their college days in their office
at home or work.

You will not find a Harvard graduate
with a room full of Yale memorabilia and
vice versa. These items have value only to
someone who attended the school. The
exception is sport-related college memorabilia. This has a much broader appeal,
either to a conference collector or a general sports collector.

Advertising Tear Sheet, Notre Dame
College for Women, MD, college
building scene, 1897 8
Badge, Middlebury College Fire Dept ...45
Book, *Tales of Bowdoin College Maine,*
Minot & Snow, illus, 378 pp, 1901 30
Booklet, From Cabin to College and
Back Home Again, Berea College,
Berea, KY .... .10
Cup and Saucer, Bates College, "1846-
1946," red transfer, mkd "Wedgwood
of Etruria & Barleston, Made in
England" .... .15

*Postcard, photo of Lehigh University
Library, Bethlehem, PA, black and white,
1905, 5.5 x 3.5", $12.*

Cup and Saucer, Rutgers University,
"Collegii Rutgersensis In Nova
Caesarea Sigillium," and "Sol Lustitiae
et Occidentem" on gold emblem 12

Dance Card, Alpha Tau Omega fraternity,
Colby College, 8 pp, 2.5 x 4" 7

Dart Board Cover, Trenton State College,
1970s 10

Magazine, *Conley's Football Guide*,
Conley Sports Publications, UCLA's
Gary Beben on cover, 1967 3

Newspaper, *Our College Times*,
Elizabethtown, Lancaster, PA, Jun 10,
1930, 8 pp 6

Pennant, felt, Indian River Community
College, 1960, 26" l, 8.5" h 5

Photograph, Becker College basketball
team, 1928, 13.5 x 11.5" 10

Pinback Button, Southwestern College
Inter High School Music Festival,
April 29-30, 1938, 1.5" d 3

Postcard, Northrop and Gillett Houses,
Smith College, Northampton, MA,
used, 1916 4

Postcard, South Campus, Mount Holyoke
College, South Hadley, MA, used, 1910 .4

Program, Army vs Boston College,
Nov 11, 1989 5

Program, May Day, Earlham College,
Richmond, IN, May 18, 1957, 44 pp,
8 x 11" 10

Token, Soulé College, encased penny,
"The South's Greatest School of
Business" 18

Yearbook, Centenary College, LA, 1937 . .10

Yearbook, Michigan State College, 1948 . .5

Yearbook, Western State Teacher's
College, Kalamazoo, MI, 400 pp, c1929 .6

COLLEGE PLATES

A college, university, institute, academy, private or prep school plate can be a
truly unique gift for anyone that has been to
that school. There are even plates that celebrate high schools. I have found over the
years that I have never sold a plate that
was not appreciated...due to sentimental
value. After all, if you went to that school,
you have a vested interest. How the eyes of
a very old grad will light up when he or she
receives this "one-of-a-kind" gift that trig-
gers a flood of nostalgic memories of days

gone by. This is almost matched by the
smiles and grins of more recent grads as
they look back on recent history. Plates are
a truly memorable gift and are always
appreciated.

Plates were made by a variety of makers from Rowland and Marcellus (turn of
the century) to Wheelock in Gemany (early
teens) to Balfour, who may still make them.
Among the most popular makers were
Wedgwood, Spode, Lenox, and Lamberton
Scammell. Others not quite so popular were
Vernon Kilns, Syracuse China, and
Staffordshire. The tenacious and lucky flea
market seeker can still find a few plates at
the very low price of $5, but most plates
now are going in the $15 and up range.
Some that are on the internet are going for
outrageous prices as several people get in
a bidding war for that particular college, but
that is an abberation greatly enjoyed by the
seller only.

Advisor: Pat Klein, P.O. Box 262, East Berlin,
CT, 06023, (860) 680-3973, e-mail:
pklein262@yahoo.com

Amherst College, Wedgwood 14
Boston University, Wedgwood 37
Cornell University, Wedgwood 33
Duke University, Wedgwood 14
Harvard University, Wedgwood 11
Russell Sage College, Wedgwood 25
Rutgers University, Homer Laughlin 5
Smith College, Wedgwood 37
Syracuse University, Syracuse China 8
Tufts College, Wedgwood 40

*Sweetbriar College, Virginia, blue and
white, Royal Cauldon, $36.*

University of Chicago, Ida Noyes Hall, mkd "Copeland Spode, England," 1931, 10.5" d, $30.

University of Georgia, Royal Cauldon . . .19
University of Missouri, Staffordshire 23
University of Pennsylvania, Wedgwood .40
Wesleyan, Connecticut 12
William & Mary, Staffordshire 25
Yale University, Rowland and Marcellus .58

COLORING BOOKS

The key is to find these gems uncolored. Some collectors will accept a few pages colored, but the coloring had better be neat. If it is scribbled, forget it.

Most of the value rests on the outside cover. The closer the image is to the actual character or personality featured, the higher the value. The inside pages of most coloring books consist of cheap newsprint. It yellows and becomes brittle over time. However, resist buying only the cover. Collectors prefer to have the entire book.

Alf, Checkerboard Press, 1987 2
All About Indians, Whitman, 1958 12
Andy Griffith Show, Saalfield, 1963 35
Animal Alphabet to Color, Merrill Publishing Co, 1935 .4
Bedknobs and Broomsticks, Whitman, 1971 10
Beetle Bailey, Lowe, 1961 20
Beverly Hillbillies, Watkins-Strathmore, 1964 30
Bewitched Fun and Activity Book, Treasure Books, 1965 15
Bonanza, Saalfield, 1970 15

Boots and her Buddies, Saalfield, 1941 . .35
Car 54, Where Are You?, Whitman, 1962 . .30
Chiquita Banana, American Publishing Co, 1970 4
Cisco Kid, Saalfield, 1954 15
Dick Van Dyke, Saalfield, 1963 20
Diff'rent Strokes, Playmore Publishing, 1983 10
Dudley Do-Right Comes to the Rescue, Saalfield, 1969 5
Elizabeth Taylor, Whitman, 1954 40
Emergency, Saalfield, 1976 10
Finian's Rainbow, Artcraft, 1970s 12
Flintstones, Artcraft, 1964 20
Gabby Hayes, Abbott Publishing, 1954 . .25
Gumby and Pokey, Whitman, 1967 20
Incredible Hulk, Whitman, 1977 10
Julia, Saalfield, 1968 15
Journey to the Center of the Earth, Whitman, 1968 .10
Land of the Giants, Whitman, 1969 10
Lassie, Watkins/Strathmore, 1961 40
Laurel and Hardy, Saalfield, 1972 10
My Favorite Martian, Whitman, 1960s . . .20
Patience and Prudence, Lowe, 1957 35
Peanuts, Artcraft, 1971 22
Peanuts Funtime Coloring Book 3
Planet of the Apes, Saalfield, 1974 10
Play School, Merrill, 1961 25
Pluto, Whitman, 1971 12
Real Western, Lowe, 1960s 20
Round about America...A Coloring Book of the United States, Whitman, 1938 . . .4
Rowan & Martin's Laugh-In, Saalfield, 1968 10
Tales of the Vikings, Saalfield, 1960 32
That Girl, Saalfield, 1960s 25

The Tiger in the Tank, Humble Oil and Refining Co, 32 pp, early 1960s, 8.5 x 7.5", $15.

Lone Ranger, Whitman, 1974, unused, $15.

The Amazing Spider-Man, "The Oyster
 Mystery," Marvel Comics, Whitman,
 #1061, 60 pp, 1976 4
The Beatles, Saalfield, 1962 90
The Sunshine Family, Whitman,1975 5
Thundercats, "Mandora and the Pirates,"
 48 pp, unused, 1986 3
Tippee-Toes, Whitman, 1969 10
Tonto, Whitman, 1957 25
Tubsy, Whitman, 1968 10

COMBS

 A comb's value rests in its design and
the material from which it is made. The
more elaborate the comb—the higher the
price.

 An interesting collection can be built
inexpensively by collecting giveaway
combs. It is amazing how many individuals
and businesses, from politicians to funeral
parlors, use this advertising media.

Club: Antique Comb Collectors Club
International, 90 Highland Ave., #1204,
Tarpon Springs, FL 34689.

Aluminum, diecut, Denver House adv,
 handsaw shape, pocket size 28
Brass, purse, folding, enamelled, rhinestone champagne glass motif 50
Celluloid, amber, side comb 6
Celluloid, black, curved, wavy teeth,
 applied ivory strip with glittery red
 and green checkerboard design,
 3.75 x 1.5 x 4" 35

Celluloid, cream, intertwined flowers
 and vines forming heart motif, 5 x 4" ..40
Celluloid, faux tortoise shell, cattail
 design, 4 x 3.25" 25
Celluloid, faux tortoise shell, emb dec,
 graduated prongs, Art Nouveau molding, 4 x 3.25" 25
Celluloid, faux tortoise shell, hp floral
 motif, mkd "Modele Depossé France,"
 3" l, 2" w 15
Celluloid, tuck comb, faux tortoise shell,
 amethyst colored rhinestones 75
Celluloid, faux tortoise shell, lace and
 plume motif, 6 x 3.75" 35
Mother-of-Pearl, purse comb, folding,
 Wiesner of Miami 50
Plastic, enamelled roses, daisies, and
 lilies, 2.5" h, 2" w 10
Plastic, faux tortoise shell, eagle design,
 brilliant rhinestones set in brass
 frame, 4" l, 5.5" w 45
Plastic, side comb, floral spray design,
 ornate, green and blue rhinestones,
 1960s 20
Plastic, "Vote Muskie, Comb Nixon Out
 of Your Hair," blue, inscriptions on
 both sides, 7" l 15
Tortoise Shell, tuck comb, domed top,
 etched leaf design, 9 rhinestones,
 1920s 28

COMEDIAN COLLECTIBLES

 Laughter is said to be the best medicine. If this is true, why does it hurt so much
when Abbot & Costello meet the Mummy?

 Comedian collectibles span the known
mediums of radio, vaudeville, television,
standup, and cinema. The plight of Charlie
Chaplin echoes in the antics of Whoopie
Goldberg. Comedian collectibles also
reflect the diversity of those mediums. Feel
free to laugh out loud the next time you find
a Groucho Marx eyeglass and mustache
mask—I do.

Clubs: Abbott & Costello Fan Club, P.O. Box
2084, North Hollywood, CA 91610;
International Jack Benny Fan Club, 9461
Skyline Blvd., Piedmont, CA 94611; Three
Stooges Fan Club, P.O. Box 747, Gwynedd
Valley, PA 19437.

Abbott & Costello, folder, announcing comedy mystery "Bud Abbott & Lou Costello Meet the Killer, Boris Karloff," Eros Theatre, Jan, 27, 1950, sepiatone photo of Abbott & Costello fleeing under the hands of Karloff, 5.75 x 8.5" .15

Abbott & Costello, poster, "Abbott & Costello Love... Popsicle," full color photo image, polka dot border, "For Swell Gifts Save Coupons From Polka Dot Bags," ©1954 Popsicle, 11 x 15" . .50

Benny, Jack, figure, plaster, painted features, brown jacket and tie, white shirt, tan trousers, black shoes, unmkd, 1970s, 16.5" h, 5.5 x 6.5" brown base 35

Benny, Jack, postcard, cartoon western cattle roundup scene of Benny riding lizard, "Jack 'Buck' Benny Just Rolling Along," unused 10

Berle, Milton, signed photograph, black and white, smiling Berle lighting cigar, "Best Wishes Milton Berle," 8 x 10" . .10

Burns, George, signed photograph, black and white, 8 x 10" 10

Chaplin, Charlie, ashtray, figural, ceramic, black derby over molded hair, Lego, Japan, c1970s, 6.5" h 35

Chaplin, Charlie, figure, hard plastic, red jacket, movable arm on inner elastic stringing, black molded hair and facial markings, lower torso of flexible oilcloth-like tube over inner stringing, made in Italy, 1960s, 7" h . . .50

Chaplin, Charlie, movie program, *The Great Dictator,* United Artists, 1940, 9 x 12" 60

Three Stooges, comic book, Gold Key #10005-509, No. 25, Sep 1965, $15.

Laurel and Hardy, *Big Little Book Type,* Saalfield, #1086, 1934, 4.5 x 5", $40.

Chaplin, Charlie, movie still, black and white, Chaplin and 2 others on snowy mountain, "Mount Lincoln/Elevation 8300 Feet," c1924, 8 x 10" 15

Durante, Jimmy, pinback button, "Gimme Jimmy! The Candidate," c1948, 1.25" d .8

Gleason, Jackie, window card, Papa's Delicate Condition, 1962, 14 x 22" 35

Hackett, Buddy, autograph, PS, black and white, black ink signature, 8 x 10" .8

Harpo Marx, record, 45 rpm, *Harp by Harpo,* 1950s 35

Hope, Bob, decanter, Jim Beam Bourbon Whiskey, commemorating Bob Hope 14th Annual Desert Classic, 1973, 3.25 x 6.25 x 10" 15

Hope, Bob, program, 20 pp, black and white photos, movie scenes, photos and text for performance for State Dept in Moscow, c1959, 9 x 12" 20

Hope, Bob, record, 33 1/3 rpm, *Hope in Russia and One Other Place,* Decca . .20

Laurel and Hardy, jack-in-the-box, cardboard enclosure box with full color art on side panels, fabric ribbon loop extending outward from center beside printed "Pull My Tie," Lakeside, made in Japan, 1960s, 3.5 x 3.5 x 4.5" .35

Lewis, Jerry, record, LP, *Just Sings,* Decca 5

Lewis, Jerry, window card, *The Ladies Man,* color scene of Lewis clinging to ceiling rafter with 8 admiring young starlets, 1961, 14 x 22" 35

Little Rascals, comic book, Dell, #1297, Mar-May, 1962 15

Marx Brothers, program, "The Cocoanuts," Lyric Theatre, 42nd Street near Broadway, New York City, announcing performances beginning Mon, Jun 7, 1926, 4.5 x 10.5" 175

Marx Brothers, sheet music, *Sailin'
  Away on The Henry Clay,* 1917,
  10.5 x 13.5" 140
Murphy, Eddie, record, *Eddie Murphy:
  Comedian,* LP, Columbia Records,
  FC39005, 1983 6
Skelton, Red, photo, black and white,
  8 x 10" 3
Three Stooges, mask, Moe, molded
  hard thin shell plastic, molded hair,
  1970s, 9" h, 7" w 75
Three Stooges, record, *The Nonsense
  Song Book,* 33 1/3 rpm, Coral, 1950s ..40

*Joe Palooka Lost
in the Jungle,
Harvey Comics,
Vol 1, #115,
Jun 1960, $10.*

COMIC BOOKS

Comic books come in all shapes and
sizes. The number that have survived is
almost endless. Although there were
reprint books of cartoon strips in the 1910s,
1920s, and 1930s, the modern comic book
originated in June 1938 when DC issued
Action Comics No. 1, marking the appearance of Superman.

Comics are divided into Golden Age,
Silver Age, and Contemporary titles. Before
you begin buying, read John Hegenberger's
Collector's Guide to Comic Books (Wallace-
Homestead, 1990) and D. W. Howard's
Investing in Comics (The World of
Yesterday, 1988). The dominant price guide
for comics is Robert Overstreet's *The
Overstreet Comic Book Price Guide.*

Most comics, due to condition, are not
worth more than 50¢ to a couple of dollars.
Very strict grading standards are applied to
comics less than 10 years old. The following
list shows the potential in the market. You
need to check each comic book separately.

Periodicals: *Comic Buyer's Guide,* 700 E.
State St, Iola, WI 54990; *Overstreet's Comic
Book Marketplace,* Gemstone Publishing
(West), P.O. Box 180900, Coronado, CA
92178.

Note: Prices listed are for comic books in
good condition.

Advanced Dungeons and Dragons, DC,
  #1, Dec 1988 ....2.00
Adventures of Superman, DC, #424, Jan
  1987 50
All-Star Western, DC, #1, Sep 1970 ...2.00

Animal Man, DC, #2, Oct 1988 80
Aquaman, DC, #10, Aug 1963 ....18.00
Battlestar Galactica, Marvel, #2, Apr
  1979 80
Binky's Buddies, DC, #3, May 1969 ...50
Blackhawk, DC, #166, Nov 1961 ......8.00
Black Panther, Marvel, #1, Jan 1977 ..2.50
Captain America, Marvel, #122, Feb
  1970 ....2.00
Captain Storm, DC, #5, Feb 1965 .....3.00
Conan the Barbarian, Marvel, #2, Dec
  1970 ....20.00
Daredevil, Marvel, #4, Oct 1964 ......60.00
Defenders, Marvel, #2, Oct 1972 .....5.00
Dennis the Menace, Marvel, #5, Mar
  1982 30
Dennis the Menace and His Friends,
  Fawcett, #7, Aug 1970 ....1.00
Detective Comics, DC, #266, Apr 1959 .20.00
Dynamo, Tower, #1, Aug 1966 ....12.00
Freedom Fighters, DC, #3, Aug 1976 ..30
From Beyond the Unknown, DC, #6,
  Sep 1970 40
Get Smart, Dell, #1, Jun 1966 ....10.00
Ghost Rider, Marvel, #1, Aug 1973 ....8.00
Godzilla, Marvel, #2, Sep 1977 ....1.00
Green Lantern, DC, #5, Apr 1961 .....60.00
Hawkman, DC, #11, Jan 1966 ....10.00
House of Mystery, DC, #180, Jun 1969 .1.00
Howard the Duck, Marvel, #5, Sep
  1976 50
Incredible Hulk, Marvel, #150, Apr 1972 1.00
I Spy, Gold Key, #1, Aug 1966 ....1.00
Johnny Quest, Comico, #6 ....2.00
Karate Kid, DC, #1, Apr 1976 50
Logan's Run, Marvel, #3, Mar 1977 ...50
Nanny and the Professor, Dell, #1, Aug
  1970 ....3.00
Spider-Woman, Marvel, #18, Sep 1979 .20

Nancy and Sluggo, Dell, #184, Oct 1961, $9.

Star Trek, Gold Key, #51, Mar 1978 ... 5.00
Swamp Thing, DC, #1, Nov 1972 ..... 15.00
The Atom, DC, #5, Mar 1963 .... 25.00
The Demon, DC, #2, Oct 1972 .... 3.00
The Hulk, Marvel, #2, Apr 1977 ...... 2.00
The Jetsons, Charlton, #2, Jan 1971 .. 4.00
The Six Million Dollar Man, Charlton,
   #2, Aug 1976 .... .70
Transformers, Marvel, #1, Sep 1984 .. .80

COMMEMORATIVE MEDALS

From the late nineteenth century through the 1930s, commemorative medals were highly prized possessions. The U.S. Mint and other mints still carry on the tradition today, but to a far lesser degree.

Distinguish between medals issued in mass and those struck for a limited purpose, in some cases in issues of one for presentation. An old medal should have a surface patina that has developed over the years causing it to have a very mellow appearance. Never, never clean a medal. Collectors like the patina.

In most medals, the metal content has little value. However, medals were struck in both silver and gold. If you are not certain, have the metal tested.

Club: Token and Medal Society, Inc., P.O. Box 366, Bryantown, MD 20617.

American Kennel Club Award, silver,
   engraved "Ebony Girl," round ...... .40
Battle of Leipzig, bronze, eagles fighting
   on obverse, patriotic society's memorial building on reverse, round ..... .25

Belgian Aero Club, bronze, obverse
   shows winged nude male in ocean
   looking up at biplane, 3 goddesses
   and globe on reverse, club name
   below, round 100
Bordeaux Pharmacy Society Centenary,
   bronze, Georges Deniges bust, lab
   equipment, rect, 1934 .... .30
California State Floral Society, silver,
   roses on obverse, reverse engraved
   to "Mrs Townsend for Vase Bouquet,"
   round .... .45
College of Pharmacology & Science,
   Philadelphia, white metal, mouse and
   microscope on obverse, inscription
   on reverse, round .... .15
Duke & Duchess of Connaught, silver,
   conjoined busts on obverse, soldiers
   and arms on reverse, round .... .70
Edinburgh School of Medicine, silver,
   column with serpent on obverse,
   open wreath on reverse, engraved
   inscription to recipient, round ...... .65
Gerhard Friederich, Lutheran Pastor in
   Frankfurt, silver, bust with inscription
   "SC. C. Zollman," round, 1858 125
Gorgas Essay Contest, bronze, bust of
   Gorgas on obverse, inscription on
   reverse, suspended from purple
   ribbon pin, 1929, round .... .40
Halley's Comet, silver, sun and allegor-
   ical scene, round 350
Hebrew Union College, bronze, bust of
   founder on obverse, building on
   reverse, 1945, round .... .28
King of Romania, bronze, bust of Carol
   I on obverse, reverse shows goddess
   with laurel wreath in center, scenes
   of battle, parade, and homecoming,
   S C Kullrich, round 120

Third National Shooting Festival, San Francisco, 1901, gold, 2.25" w, $150.

Kronstadt Rifle Club, bronze, building
on obverse, inscription on reverse,
1886, round 25
Mara Theresa's Recover From Small
Pox, silver, bust on obverse, kneeling
figure on reverse, round 100
Martin Luther King, bronze, bust,
Courbier, round 225
The Dreyfus Affair, bronze, General
Mercier bust, round, 1906 130
Union League, silver, shield and banner
on obverse, blank reverse 70

COMPACTS

Compacts are small portable cosmetic
makeup boxes that contain powder, mirror,
and puff. The vanity case is the more elaborate compact. It contains multiple compartments for powder, rouge, and/or lipstick. Compacts that were used up until the
1960s, when women opted for the "au
naturel" look, are considered vintage.

Vintage compacts were made in a variety of shapes, sizes, combinations, and in
almost every conceivable natural or man-
made material. Many are also multipur-
pose, such as the compact/watch, com-
pact/purse, and compact/lighter and
appeal to both compact collectors and collectors of the secondary accessory.

Club: Compact Collectors, P.O. Box 40,
Lynbrook, NY 11563 (516) 593-8746, fax: (516)
593-0610.

*Gwenda (UK), enameled white metal,
loose powder, lid with blue foil ground and
plastic cov, transfer scene, "New York
World's Fair" enameled in black on
reverse, sgd, $180.*

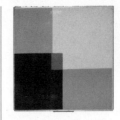

*Pilcher, brass,
enameled cov,
black, gray,
white, and red,
2.875" sq, $35.*

Astor-Pak, round compact, bone colored
plastic, silvertone Scottie dog centered on top of ivorene lid, reverse side
black, 3.5" d 100
Ciner, mini compact, square, goldtone,
with matching lipstick, compact lid
and lipstick tube cov in brown alligator leather, int mirror and powder
well, goldtone alligator applied to top
of lipstick tube and centered on compact lid, brown corduroy fitted case,
powder lid sgd, 2" sq 175
Coty, "Memo," goldtone compact, with
matching lipstick/perfume combination, book shape, emb basketweave
design on lid, cartouche on polished
goldtone spine, lipstick/perfume
combination designed to resemble
pencil, 1 side of tube contains creamy
lipstick, other side contains small
bottle of Chypre perfume, 3.5 x 2.25"
lipstick, 3.5" 175
E A M, black enamel and silvertone
tango chain vanity, silvertone
cartouche centered on lid, int reveals
mirror, powder and rouge compartments, lipstick attached by enamel
link chain, 2.5 x 3.5" 150
Elgin, square compact, hammered gold-
tone, American, rhinestone Christmas
bell center lid dec, red crystal move-
able clapper, 2.75" sq 80
Karess, round compact, woman's pro-
file, rose, and star on goldtone top
lid dec, on dark blue and black background framed with goldtone bars,
silvertone bottom lid, 1.75" d 125
Le Rage, compact/bracelet, goldtone,
wrist watch shape, hours on lid of
compact set with green and clear
stones, moveable hands, bubble link
chain, int reveals mirror and puff,
England, 1.5" d 350

Raquel, gold emb green leather vanity, book shape, int reveals metal framed mirror, powder and rouge compartments, 2 x 3" 100

Rex, round brushed silver tango chain compact, polished goldtone floral lid dec, lipstick attached by chain to compact, 3.5" d 175

Stratton, Wedgwood, Jasperware, convertible goldtone compact, lid inset with cameo of "Three Graces" Aglair, Euprosyne and Thalia, blue label on int beveled mirror reads "The cameo on this STRATTON PRODUCT is made by "Josiah Wedgwood & Sons, Ltd," 3.25" d 75

Unknown Manufacturer, oblong vanity, Bakelite, clear and green colored rhinestone ext dec, int reveals mirror, removable cov powder and rouge containers and lipstick compartment, carrying cord, tassel, 2.25 x 4" 375

Unknown Manufacturer, red faux leather compact, hat box shape, snaps open and shut, faux zipper, int reveals mirror and puff, carrying handle, 3 x 2.25" 100

Unknown Manufacturer, round silver-tone compact, plastic discs on sides depicting musician in relief playing instruments, 2.25" d 65

Unknown Manufacturer, U.S. Navy hat, plastic 80

Volupte, square compact, goldtone, lid resembles gift package, raised gift card and bow lid dec, 3" sq 50

CONDOM TINS

Condom tins have finally come "out of the closet"! Referred to by Playboy as "Sin Tins," there was a time when people were too embarassed to collect them or admit they owned one. Now it's agreed these tins are little works of art!

The earliest tins (1920s) are round and made of aluminum, all embossed with no color. Later tins (1940s) with colorful lithography are more collectible. Condoms were also marketed in paper and cardboard containers, from the early 1920s to the present. These are also collectible, but not nearly as desirable as the tins.

The five most common condom tins are the aluminum 3 Merry Widows and lithographed Ultrex Platinum, Ramses, Sheik, and Dean's Peacocks. In fact the Dean's Peacocks (pretty as it is) has been named "The 'Prince Albert' of condom tins!" (And the Ultrex Platinum, is the "Edgeworth.")

Note: The following tins are rectangular unless noted otherwise. Prices are for tins in pristine condition.

Apris, Killian Mfg Co, Akron, OH, leaping gazelle 150

Caravan, Tiger Skin Rubber Co, New York, NY, desert scene 150

Chariots, Goodwear Rubber Co, New York, NY, horse race 200

Derbies, Jay Dee Drug Co, Chicago, IL, jockey's cap and 2 riding crops 100

Double-Tip, Department Sales Co, New York, NY, girl and her reflection in river 300

Gold Dollar, Allied Latex Sales Co, New York, NY, gold coins 250

Le Transparent Trojan, Youngs Rubber Corp, Inc, New York, NY, Eiffel Tower .175

Patrol, Wilson-Robinson Co, Inc, Boston, MA, war planes 700

Rainbow, Dean Rubber Mfg Co, beautiful rainbow 550

Shadows, Young Rubber Corp, New York, NY, "As Thin as a Shadow— Strong as an Ox!" 125

Sheik, Julius Schmid, Inc, New York, NY, arab on horseback 25

Silver Knight, L J McFaddin Co, Cedar Rapids, IA, knight head 250

Texide, L E Shunk Latex Products, Inc, Akron, OH, native rubber plantation workers 50

Akron Tourist Tubes, Akron Rubber Supply Co., Akron, OH, $500.

Golden Pheasant, WH Reed & Co, $100.
—Photo courtesy Past Tyme Pleasures.

Three Pirates, Akron Rubber Supply Co,
    Akron, OH, girls on ship dressed in
    pirate costumes 400
Trianon, Gotham Rubber Co, Chicago,
    IL, Disney-like castle 350

CONSTRUCTION SETS

Children love to build things. Building block sets originated in the nineteenth century. They exist in modern form as Legos and Lego imitators.

The Erector Set was popular with aspiring engineers. Alfred Carlton Gilbert, Jr., began his business by producing magic sets as the Mysto Manufacturing Company. With the help of his father, he bought out his partner and created the A. C. Gilbert Company located on Erector Square in New Haven, Connecticut.

Clubs: A. C. Gilbert Heritage Society, 1440 Whalley, Ste. 252, New Haven, CT 06515; Anchor Block Foundation, 1670 Hawkwood Ct., Charlottesville, VA 22901; Girder and Panel Collectors Club, P.O. Box 494, Bolton, MA 01470.

A C Gilbert, Erector Set, #6.5, with case,
    c1948 45
A C Gilbert, Erector Set, # 8.5, with case .200
A C Gilbert, Erector Set, #10051, with
    case 38
A C Gilbert, Erector Set, #10053, with
    case 25
A C Gilbert, Erector Set, #10601, Road
    Building Equipment, orig box 32
A C Gilbert, Erector Set, Science-Career
    Series Electric Engine, 1959 30

American Model Builder Set, complete
    with instructions, and painted wood
    oak box, c1913 25
Bayko Building Set, England, complete
    with 34 pp instruction booklet, 1940s .80
Bilt E-Z Architectural Outfit Set, Scott
    Mfg Co, Chicago, 518 pcs 190
Gabriel, 70 pcs, yellow carrying case . . .10
Halsam, American Logs Add On Set,
    46 pcs 15
Halsam, American Plastic Bricks, #745,
    585 pcs 70
Meccano, Erector Set, #2, Evolution Set,
    207 pcs 20
Meccano, Erector Set, #10 40
Meccano, Erector Set, #301, 190 pcs 5
Mysto Co, Erector Set, #4, wood, 1912 . .40
Playskool, Lincoln Logs, 187 pcs 15
Playskool, Lincoln Logs, #884, 72 pcs 5
Playskool, Lincoln Logs, #887 20
Playskool, Lincoln Logs, #893, 210 pcs . . .9
Techmaster, Erector Set, #50, 110 pcs . . .15

COOKBOOKS

Eighteenth and nineteenth century cookbooks are expensive, very expensive. The cookbooks that you are most likely to find date from the twentieth century. Most were promotional giveaways. A fair number came with appliances. Some were associated with famous authors. A few years ago, you could buy them in the 50¢ to $1 range and had a large selection from which to choose. No longer. These later cookbooks have been discovered. Prices now range from $5 to $20 for most of them.

Cover art affects price. Many cookbooks are bought for display purposes. Seek out the ones that feature a recognizable personality.

Clubs: Cook Book Collector's Club, 4756 Terrace Dr., San Diego, CA 92116; Cookbook Collectors Club of America, Inc, P.O. Box 56, St James, MO 65559.

Periodical: *Cookbook Collectors' Exchange,* P.O. Box 32369, San Jose, CA 95152.

650 Cookery Recipes, Hildagonda
    Duckitt, Cape Town, 1891 30
1001 Sandwiches, Florence Cowles,
    Boston, 288 pp, 1937 20

Aunt Jenny's 12 Pies Husbands Like Best Recipe Book, *Spry, 1952, $12.*

Adventures in Good Cooking, Duncan Hines, 1939 30

A Year's Dinners, May Little, 436 pp, 1937 25

Art of Cooking & Serving, Sarah Splint, Proctor & Gamble, 252 pp, 1931 10

Aunt Priscilla in the Kitchen, Eleanor Purcell, 176 pp, 1929 30

Belgian Cookbook, Mrs Brian Luck, 151 pp, 1915 35

Book of Famous New Orleans Recipes, spiral bound, illus, 57 pp, c1930 12

Bread Facts, Ward Baking Co, 112 pp, 1920 20

Child Life Cookbook, Clare Judson, Rand McNally, 1926 45

Complete Vegetarian Recipe Book, Ivan Baker, 168 pp, 1969 10

English Inn, Past & Present, Harold, Eberlein, 308 pp, 1926 80

Farm Journal's Complete Pie Cookbook, 308 pp, 1965 12

Fish Cookery, Charles J Davis, 226 pp, 1967 10

Gourmet's Dinners, G S Fougner, 358 pp, 1941 35

Greenwich Village Cookbook, Vivian Kramer, 510 pp, 1969 20

Health in the Household, Susanna Dodds, 602 pp, 1886 .75

Medal of Gold, History of Gold Medal Flour, Wm C Edgar, 373 pp, 1925 55

My Candy Secrets, Mary Elizabeth, 146 pp, 1919 75

New England Cookbook, Eleanor Early, 1954 20

Pennsylvania Dutch Cookery, J G Frederick, 275 pp, 1935 25

Rene Black Cookbook, 205 pp, 1955 20

Taste of Country Cooking, Edna Lewis, 260 pp, 1977 25

To the Queen's Taste, Helen Hilles, 306 pp, 1937 40

COOKIE CUTTERS

When most individuals think of cookie cutters, they envision the metal cutters, often mass produced, that were popular during the nineteenth century and first third of the twentieth century. This is too narrow a view. Do not overlook the plastic cutters of recent years. Not only are they detailed and colorful, they also come in a variety of shapes quite different from their metal counterparts.

If you want to build a great specialized collection, look for cutters that were giveaway premiums by flour and baking related businesses. Most of these cutters are priced in the $10 to $40 range.

Club: Cookie Cutter Collectors Club, 1167 Teal Rd. SW, Dellroy, OH 44620.

Newsletter: *Cookies,* 9610 Greenview Ln., Manassas, VA 20109.

Advertising, Davis Baking Powder, tin, rabbit, dog, duck, and cat 25

Advertising, Garland Stoves and Ranges, flame shape 22

Advertising, Swans Down Cake Flour, aluminum 22

Aluminum, horse, rabbit, lion, and camel, 1960s 3

Metal, duck, Depression glass eye, handmade in Nazareth, PA 125

Metal, heart, diamond, and spade, S J Co, Germany .10

Tin, rabbit, strap handle, early 20th C, $25.

Metal, Trick or Treat Cooky Cutters,
orig box 12
Plastic, 12 Days of Christmas 8
Plastic, arrow, hot pink, Wilton 1
Plastic, Holly Hobbie, American Greet-
ings Corp, price for 7 pcs 25
Plastic, leprechaun, green and tan,
Hallmark, 1979 2
Plastic, Penn State University lion,
white and blue, Monogram Plastics . . .3
Plastic, Snoopy, Charlie Brown, Linus,
and Lucy, United Features Syndicate .30
Plastic, Super Mario Bros, Nintendo,
1989, 4" h, price for set of 4, MIP 7
Plastic, "Love" and heart, red, 1970s 2
Plastic, orange, Tupperware, price for
5 pcs 3
Plastic, question mark, white, Wilton 50
Plastic, star, red, orig card, Southwest
Indian Foundation 5
Tin, bird, spread wings, 4.5" l 15
Tin, dog, 4.5" l 20
Tin, Dutchman, 5.25" h 115
Tin, man, handcrafted, hat and coat,
handle removed, 3 x 5.5" 85
Tin, spade, heart, clubs, and diamond . . .10

COOKIE JARS

    Talk about categories that have gone
nuts over the years. Thanks to the Andy
Warhol sale, cookie jars became the talk of
the town. Unfortunately, the prices reported
for the Warhol cookie jars were so far
removed from reality that many individuals
were deceived into believing their cookie
jars were far more valuable than they really were.

    The market seems to be having trouble
finding the right pricing structure. A recent
cookie jar price guide lowballed a large
number of jar prices. Big city dealers are
trying to sell cookie jars as high ticket art
objects rather than the kitsch they really
are. You be the judge. Remember, all you
are buying is a place to store your cookies.

Club: American Cookie Jar Assoc., 1600
Navajo Rd., Norman, OK 73026.

Newsletter: *Cookie Jarrin',* 1501 Maple
Ridge Rd., Walterboro, SC 29488.

Apples in Barrel, Metlox 50

Basket of Potatoes, McCoy 40
Bear with Beehive, McCoy 100
Brown Bear, Brush 65
Bulldog Cafe, Treasure Craft 60
Bunny Bonnett, Fitz & Floyd 100
Camel, Doranne of California 75
Cat Head, Lefton 75
Cat on Coal Bucket, McCoy 250
Cinderella, Napco 250
Clown, Lane 200
Cookie Cabin, McCoy 60
Cookie Kettle, American Bisque 45
Daisy Bouquet, Metlox 75
Drummer Boy, Enesco 30
Dutch Girl, Red Wing 75
Flowerpot, Metlox 75
Fortune Cookies, McCoy 50
Hi Diddle Diddle, Robinson-Ransbottom .400
Humpty Dumpty, Japan 50
Kermit the Frog, Treasure Craft 50
Kliban Cat on Stool, Sigma 125
Little Red Riding Hood, Napco 250
Monk, Cumberland Ware 50
Monkey with Sailor Cap, DeForrest of
California 150
Nutcracker Rocking Horse, Fitz & Floyd .75
Old Lady in Shoe, Japan 45
Owl, Shawnee .100
Pelican, California Originals 35
Pineapple, Metlox 125
Preacher, Robinson-Ransbottom 100
Raggedy Ann, Twin Winton 40
Rocking Horse, DeForrest of California .100
Santa in Rocker, Lefton 40
Scarecrow, Japan 40
Train Engine, Pfaltzgraff 150
Turkey, Morton Pottery 150
Watermelon, Metlox 350
Winnie the Pooh, Treasure Craft 35

*Winnie Pig,
Shawnee,
blue, $250.*
—Photo
courtesy Gene
Harris Antique
Auction
Center, Inc.

COPPER PAINTINGS

Copper paintings, actually pictures stamped out of copper or copper foil, deserve a prize as one of the finest "ticky-tacky" collectibles ever created. I remember getting a four-picture set from a bank as a premium in the late 1950s or early 1960s. It is one of the few things that I have no regrets about throwing out.

However, to each his own—somewhere out there are individuals who like this unique form of mass-produced art. Their treasures generally cost them in the $15 to $50 range depending on subject.

COSTUMES

Remember how much fun it was to play dress-up as a kid? Seems silly to only do it once a year at Halloween. Down South and in Europe, Mardis Gras provides an excuse.

Collectors are beginning to discover children's Halloween costumes. While you may be staggered by some of the prices listed below, I see costumes traded at these prices all the time.

There doesn't seem to be much market in adult costumes, those used in the theater and for theme parties. Costume rental shops are used to picking them up for a few dollars each.

Cabbage Patch Kids, Tiny Tot 20
Casper the Friendly Ghost, Ben Cooper,
    1961 50
Creature From the Black Lagoon,
    Collegeville, molded plastic mask,
    green vinyl outfit with design on chest,
    rayon legs, ©1980 Universal City
    Studios, Inc, orig 8.5 x 11 x 3" box 40
Donny Osmond, Collegeville, 1977 35
First Man on the Moon, Collegeville,
    molded plastic mask, 1969 60
Fonzie, Ben Cooper, 1964 30
Girl From U.N.C.L.E., MGM, 1967 275
Hee Haw, 1976 20
I Dream of Jeannie, Ben Cooper, plastic
    mask, vinyl top, red vinyl bottom,
    orig box, ©1974 Hanna-Barbera
    Productions Inc 50
Indiana Jones, Ben Cooper, 1982 35

Jet Man, Ben Cooper, 1950s 45
Little Audrey, Collegeville, 1959 75
Mr Peanut, plastic top, cloth bottom,
    1974 25
Planet of the Apes, Warrior, Ben Cooper,
    plastic mask, 1-pc vinyl rayon outfit,
    orig box, ©1974 20th Century Fox Film
    Corp 50
Roger Rabbit, Ben Cooper, 1980s 40
Rusty from Rin-Tin-Tin, Ben Cooper,
    plastic mask, blue fabric neckerchief,
    3.5 x 8.5 x 11" box 50
Six Million Dollar Man, Ben Cooper, 1978 .35
Smurfs, Ben Cooper 25
Star Trek, Klingon, Ben Cooper, 1975 15
Superman, Ben Cooper, 4 pcs, red, yel-
    low, and blue fabric shirt, pants, and
    cape, yellow vinyl belt with goldtone
    metal buckle, large "S" emblem on
    front of shirt, yellow illus of Superman
    and young boy with text "Remember
    This Suit Won't Make You Fly. Only
    Superman Can Fly" along bottom
    margin, orig box, ©1958 Superman
    Inc 200
The Mummy, 1-pc, flannel/rayon, mummy
    image, snake, and bats on chest,
    black arms and legs, no mask, ©1963
    Universal Pictures Inc 20
The Shadow, Collegeville, plastic mask,
    attached red rayon fabric panel,
    black rayon cape with silkscreen
    design, 1973, 8.5 x 11 x 3" box 75
Tom & Jerry, Halco, 1952 40
Woody Woodpecker, Collegeville, 1950 . .50

ET, Collegeville, 1982, $15.

COUNTRY STORE

There is something special about country stores. My favorite is Bergstresser's in Wassergass, Pennsylvania. There is probably one near you that you feel as strongly about. Perhaps the appeal is that they continue to deny the present. I am always amazed at what a country store owner can dig out of the backroom, basement, or barn.

Country store collectibles focus heavily on front counter and back counter material from the last quarter of the nineteenth century and first quarter of the twentieth century. The look is tied in closely with Country. It also has a strong rural small town emphasis.

Drop in and prop your feet up on the potbelly stove. Don't visit a country store if you are in a hurry.

Bin, Butter Cup Popcorn, nursery rhymes scene, paper label, snap top, 10 x 8" . .30
Bin, Jambo Coffee, slant top, man with large white beard on horse, "The World's Best," W J Gould & Co, c1800s, 13 x 10 x 16" 1,100
Cabinet, Humphreys' Remedies, countertop, tin front lists remedies inside cabinet, 27.75 x 20 x 10.25" 400
Cash Register, National, #313, emb brass, marble ledge, missing marquee, 17" h 750
Display, Boston Garter, diecut tin, man examining garter on his leg as he reads instructions from back of box, complete with 5 orig boxes, 9 x 4" ...425

Display Stand, Kellogg's Cereals, metal with cardboard back, 26" h, $385.
—Photo courtesy Collectors Auction Services.

Display Case, National Biscuit Co, countertop, German silver cathedral shaped, etched lettering on front, 1 shelf, 37.5" h 1,500
Display Case, West Hair Nets, litho tin, 3-tier, flapper woman in touring car inside lid, 5 x 6 x 5" closed size 60
Display Stand, oak, tapered, multi-tiered, 2-sided marquee with trademark promotes Beech-Nut products, 41" h ..1,500
Gumball Machine, Chic-Mint, sheet metal body, cast iron base plate and collar, c1915, 12" h 600
Jar, Gardner Salted Peanuts, glass, "Always in Good Taste Gardner Salted Peanuts 5¢," red painted letters, 7.75" h, 7" d 50
Scale, cast iron, orig paint and stenciling, 14" h 200
Sign, Reid's Ice Cream, tin, top depicts woman holding vintage soda fountain glass, lists different flavors available, c1915, 25 x 11" 2,000
Sign, Star Brand Shoes, tin, bust of woman with flowing auburn hair, "Star Brand Shoes Are Better/ Women's Mayflower Shoe $2.50," self-framed, Meek Co, 26 x 18" 300
Spice Bin, 12 compartments, names of different spices on top of compartments, beveled mirrored front, 32 x 10.75" top, 32 x 16.5" bottom 800
Time Clock, oak, Internation Time Recording Co, NY, 43.5" h 550

COUNTRY WESTERN

You don't have to be a "rhinestone cowboy" to enjoy Country Western music and you don't have to travel to Nashville to find its memorabilia. With a large assortment of items available such as sheet music, signed photographs, and record albums, Country Western collectibles won't bring ya' back home empty handed. So go ahead and enjoy yourselves, and "Ya'll come back now, ya' hear?"

Newsletter: *Disc Collector,* P.O. Box 315, Cheswold, DE 19936.

Periodical: *American Cowboy,* P.O. Box 6630, Sheridan, WY 82801.

Sheet Music, Mona Lisa, Conway Twitty, c1959, $8.

Autograph, Patsy Montana & Pancho, PS, black and white glossy, smiling Patsy on horseback, black ink signature "The Best of the West to Larry Bears, Patsy Montana & Pancho," 1950s, 8 x 10" 18

Calendar Card, Asher Sizemore, Little Jimmie, and Patsy Montana, 1943, black and white glossy, photos of various country music performers, Pe-Ru-Na Tonic adv bottem left corner, 4 x 9" 18

Folder, Roy Acuff, browntone photo of smiling Acuff on front cover, text promoting Roy Acuff's Dunbar Cave and Recreation Park at Clarksville, TN, contains 6 x 36" foldout with 9 detachable paper photos of Acuff with family and friends on front, back has words and music to songs, 1940s, 4.5 x 6.5" 25

Magazine, *National Hillbilly News,* Nov-Dec 1947, Vol 3 #2, cover photo of The Plainsmen, back cover with adv for Bing Crosby and Bob Hope promoting US Savings Bonds, 22 pps, 7.5 x 10.75" 18

Postcard, Carter family with The Mariners, used, 1941 14

Record, *Don't Take Your Guns to Town,* Johnny Cash, 45 rpm 45

Record, *Peace in the Valley,* Red Foley, 45 rpm, Decca 10

Record, *Same Train, A Different Time,* Merle Haggard, Capitol 25

Sheet Music, *Stars and Stripes on Iwo Jima,* Bob Wills and His Texas Plow Boys, front cover shows American flag on mountaintop, inset bluetone photo of smiling Wills, 2 pp, 1945, 9 x 12" 10

Sheet Music, *You Two-Timed Me One Time Too Often,* Tex Ritter, cover shows browntone photo of smiling Ritter playing guitar, 4 pp, ©1945 Jenny Lou Carson 12

Song Folio, *Al Clauser and His Oklahoma Outlaws,* cover shows photo of Clauser and his band inset against western theme, purple accent, 48 pp, 1937, 9.125 x 12" 15

Song Folio, *Hit Parade of Cowboy Songs,* inset browntone photos of various performers including Sons of the Pioneers, Red Foley, Bill Boyd, Red River Dave, Deuce Spriggens, 48 pp, ©1946 Chart Music Publishing House, 8.875 x 11.75" 35

COWAN POTTERY

R. Guy Cowan founded the Cowan Pottery in 1913 in Cleveland, Ohio. It remained in almost continuous operation until financial difficulties forced it to close in 1931. Initially, utilitarian redware was produced. Cowan began experimenting with glazes, resulting in a unique luster-ware glaze.

Club: American Art Pottery Assoc., P.O. Box 834, Westport, MA 02790.

Periodical: Cowan Pottery Journal (Cowan Pottery Museum), 1600 Hampton Rd., Rocky River, OH 44116.

Bowl, flaring, blue lustered glaze, 8" d .50
Bowl, flaring, fluted, floral handles, blue luster glaze, 12" d 10
Bowl, lavender int, cream ext, shape #730, 4.5" h, 17" l, 10.5" d 20
Bowl, low, blue luster glaze, 4.5" d 20
Candy Dish, seahorse base, 3.25" h, 6" d .28
Compote, classically styled base, mint green int, ivory ext, 3.25 x 6" 55
Console Set, 4-sided footed bowl, green int, ivory ext, 2 low green candlesticks, stamped mark, 3.25 x 11.25" 55
Console Set, 4-sided low bowl, green int, ivory ext, pair of low ivory candle-sticks, 12.5 x 2.25" bowl 75
Console Set, scalloped ftd bowl, 2 Art Deco low candlesticks, green int, ivory ext, stamped mark, 13d " bowl .100

*Bud Vase, blue
iridescent , 7" h,
$35.*

Flower Frog, Duet, ivory glaze, 7.75 x
6.25" 300
Vase, blue and green swirl, 12" h 75
Vessel, flaring, bright green mottled
matte int, mottled pink ext, stamped
mark, 4 x 6" 350

COWBOY HEROES

The cowboy heroes in this category rode the range in movies and on television. In a way, they were larger than their real life counterparts, shaping the image of how the west was won in the minds of several generations. The contemporary westerns may be historically correct, but they do not measure up in sense of rightness.

The movie and television cowboy heroes were pioneers in merchandise licensing. If you were a child in the 1949 to 1951 period and did not own a Hopalong Cassidy item, you were deprived.

Club: Westerns & Serials Fan Club, 527 S. Front St., Mankato, MN 56001.

Newsletter: *The Cowboy Collector Newsletter,* P.O. Box 7486, Long Beach, CA 90807.

Periodical: *Spur,* (Autry Museum of Western Heritage) 4700 Western Heritage Way, Los Angeles, CA 90027.

Note: For information on fan clubs for individual cowboy heroes, refer to *Maloney's Antiques & Collectibles Resource Directory* by David J. Maloney, Jr., published by Antique Trader Books.

Buffalo Bill, Jr, Little Golden Book, #254, *Buffalo Bill Jr,* cov shows Bill and Calamity on horseback with Indian behind them on horse, 1956 18
Davy Crockett, belt, brown, attached cast metal copper luster high relief buckle with "Davy Crockett Old Betsy," rifle in center, 1950s 30
Davy Crockett, cap, simulated coonskin, dark brown soft vinyl top, gold accent image of Davy holding rifle with his name, Style-A-Head Master Craft, size medium, 1950s, 6 x 8" 40
Davy Crockett, cereal bowl, milk glass, blue image of Crockett crawling toward bear with knife drawn, 4.75" d . .25
Davy Crockett, handkerchief, red, young boys dressed as cowboy, soldier, frontiersman with young girl Indian on horseback and teepees in background, 1950s, 10.75 x 11.5" 40
Davy Crockett, mug, ceramic, beige, brown accents image of Crockett, figural rifle handle, 1950s, 3.25 x 4.5 x 4.75" 25
Gabby Hayes, fan card, sepiatone image of Hayes holding hat, name in white text at bottom, 1940s, 3.25 x 5.25" 25
Gene Autry, autograph, PS, black and white, smiling Autry waving from back of rearing Champion, black facsimile signature at bottom, 1940s, 8 x 10" ...15
Gene Autry, lobby card, Gene Autry in Red River Valley, color photo of Autry fighting with outlaw on top of locomotive, Republic Pictures, 11 x 14" 20
Gene Autry, pop gun, diecut cardboard, text on side promotion "The Gene Autry Show," c1954, 4.625 x 8.75" 35
Gene Autry, record, *The Original Gene Autry Sings Rudolph the Red-Nosed Reindeer & Other Christmas Favorites,* LP, c1960 18
Gene Autry, sheet music, *Thirty-Two Feet and Eight Little Tails,* inset photo of smiling Autry against green ground, images of Santa and reindeer, 6 pp, ©1951 Miller Music Corp, 9 x 12" 14
Hopalong Cassidy, Big Little Book, *Hopalong Cassidy and the Stagecoach,* 48 pp, Samuel Lowe, #511-5, ©1950 Doubleday & Co, 5 x 5" 20

Hopalong Cassidy, greeting card, guns and western motif, front text "Hopalong Cassidy Is Here To Stay," inside text "Howdy! Merry Christmas Pardner!," Buzza Cardozo, c1950, 4.5 x 5.5" 35

Hopalong Cassidy, View-Master reel, "Hopalong Cassidy in the Cattle Rustler," #956, ©1960 Sawyers 15

Ken Maynard, cigar band, "Ken Maynard Western Star First Nat'l," gold foil with red and black accents, center black and white photo of Maynard with white text, unused, 1930s, .875" d 20

John Wayne, Dixie lid, "John Wayne King of the Pecos," purple accent photo of smiling Wayne wearing cowboy hat, 1930s, 2.25" d 15

John Wayne, paper dolls, cover shows Wayne as Green Beret, Navy officer, and rugged cowboy, ©1981 Dover Publications, 9.25 x 12.25" 20

Lone Ranger, badge, white metal, "Lone Ranger Deputy" in black painted relief, 1950s, 2 x 2.25" 30

Lone Ranger, fan card, Silvercup Bread premium, full color image of smiling Lone Ranger twirling lasso on back of rearing Silver, Tonto in background against deep blue sky, facsimile signature "Sincerely The Lone Ranger" at bottom right, ©1938 The Lone Ranger Inc, 4 x 6.5" 25

Tom Mix, comic book, Tom Mix Western, Fawcett, Vol 2, No 9, Sep 1948, $50.

Lone Ranger, horn, litho tin, image of Lone Ranger on Silver against red and yellow ground, teepees accent around bottom, Ichi, Japan, 1960s, 4.75" h, 1.25" d 35

Lone Ranger, magazine, *Radio Guide Magazine*, Vol 7, #48, Sep 17, 1938, black and white cover photo of Lone Ranger on Silver racing across desert, 10.5 x 13.75" 24

Lone Ranger, Official Lone Ranger Pedometer, Cheerios premium, aluminum, enamel center with diecut slots, orig white cloth textured wrist strap, 1948, 2.5" d 35

Roy Rogers, harmonica, metal and plastic, "Roy Rogers Riders," image of smiling Rogers in good luck horseshoe on both sides, 1950s, 1.125 x 4.125" 40

Sunset Carson, tablet, full color portrait of Carson wearing blue outfit next to horse, black facsimile signature at lower left, c1950, 7.875 x 10" 15

Tim McCoy, press book, "Tim McCoy in the Outlaw Deputy," front image of McCoy with inset photo of him interrupting poker game, scene of McCoy holding gun in lower left corner, back cover shows various posters and lobby cards available, 1940s, 4 pp, 11 x 17" 35

Tom Mix, cigar box label, color litho, image of smiling Mix against dark blue ground surrounded by gold accent color, name in relief in red at top, 1933, 10.5 x 12" 35

Gene Autry, jigsaw puzzle, 22 pcs, 5 x 7", $30.

Tom Mix, postcard, full color view of
Mix mansion in Beverly Hills, "Home
of Tom Mix," Pacific Novelty Co,
1920s, used, 3.5 x 5.5" 25

Tom Mix, song folio, *Tom Mix Western
Songs*, cover shows inset photo of
Mix on bucking horse, 64 pp, ©1935
M M Cole Publishing Co, Chicago,
9 x 11.75" 30

Wild Bill Elliott, comic book, #2, front
cover shows Elliott on horseback
wearing red shirt, back cover shows
color photo of him wearing plaid
shirt leaning on saddle, 1950 25

Wild Bill Hickok, book, *Wild Bill Hickok
and Deputy Marshal Joey*, Rand
McNally Golden Elf Book #496, 1950s,
6.75 x 8" 25

Wyatt Earp, record, *The Legend of Wyatt
Earp*, 45 rpm, RCA Victor, 1950s 14

COW COLLECTIBLES

Holy cow! This is a moovelous category, as entrenched collectors already know.

Club: Cow Observers Worldwide, 240 Wahl
Ave., Evans City, PA 16033.

Blotter, Cow Brand Baking Soda, cardboard, blue and white, c1920 10

Butter Print, round, cow, tree, and flower,
scrubbed white, 1 pc turned handle,
5.25" d 150

*Salt and Pepper Shakers, pr, Borden's
Elmer and Elsie, ceramic, 4" h, $100.
—Photo courtesy Collectors Auction
Services.*

*Lamp, Bossy Brand Cigars, glass, White &
Son, 7.5" h, $880. —Photo courtesy
Collectors Auction Services.*

Charm, Elsie the Borden cow, plastic,
gold finish, inscribed "Borden's
Second Hundred Years 1957," image
of founder on reverse, rim mkd "Gail
Borden-Father of the Modern Dairy
Industry–1857" 7

Cookie Jar, Elsie the cow barrel, ceramic,
12.5" h, 8" d 20

Cow Bell, sheet copper, 6" h 30

Creamer, brown, mkd "Germany 10293" .30

Creamer, cow and maid, earthenware,
stylized cow with manganese-sponged
body, Staffordshire, early 19th C 300

Drinking Glass, Elsie the cow portrait,
brown and yellow, 5.5" h 35

Figure, Hagen Renaker, paper label, 2" h .15

Label, Clover Farm Evaporated Milk,
black and white cow standing in field
illus, 8.25 x 2" 8

Magazine, *The Country Gentleman*,
1912, 13.5 x 10.5" 5

Pinback Button, Michigan Milk Products
Assoc, litho tin, red and yellow, state
of Michigan design with dairy cow,
red and white lettering, 1930s 7

Poster, Evaporated Milk–Pure Cow's
Milk, black and white cows illus,
green ground 15

Ramp Walker, plastic, brown and white,
made in Hong Kong, 1950s, 3.5" l, MIP .25

Salt and Pepper Shakers, pr, black and
white, attached shiny gold bell,
unmkd, 3.75" h 3

Salt and Pepper Shakers, pr, ceramic, hp, gold trim, cork bottoms, stamped "24/215," made in Japan, 3" h 10

Sheet Music, *Cow Cow Boogie,* 1942 ...10

Stereoview Card, woman milking cow, 1904 1

Sugar Bowl, Elmer, figural, china, 1930-40 40

Thermometer, Socony Vacuum Sanilac Cattle Spray, wood, 1920s, 19" h 100

CRACKER JACK

You can still buy Cracker Jack with a prize in every box. The only problem is that when you compare today's prizes with those from decades ago, you feel cheated. Modern prizes simply do not measure up. For this reason, collectors tend to focus on prizes put in the box prior to 1960.

Most Cracker Jack prizes were not marked. As a result, many dealers have Cracker Jack prizes without even knowing it. This allows an experienced collector to get some terrific bargains at flea markets. Alex Jaramillo's *Cracker Jack Prizes* (Abbeville Press, 1989) provides a wonderful survey of what prizes were available.

Club: Cracker Jack Collectors Assoc., P.O. Box 16033, Philadelphia, PA 19114.

Advertising Flyer, red and white, "Cracker-Jack, 100 pkgs in case, Trimble, Sides & Co., Phila.," both sides, small center fold, 3.25 x 5.75" .165

Badge, metal, dark charcoal luster finish, "Cracker Jack Police," 1930s 10

Toy Top, litho tin, 1930s, $18.

Booklet, Uncle Sam's Famous National Songs, Jackie & Jack on back cov, 1918, 2.5 x 3.5" 45

Bottle Opener/Corkscrew, metal, "Cracker Jack" 1 side, Angelus Marshmallows other side, 3" l 100

Clicker, litho tin, red painted finish, stamped "Cracker Jack" 15

Coin, Mystery Club, emb aluminum, presidential profile, "Join Cracker Jack Mystery Club, Save This Coin" on reverse, 1930s, 1" d 18

Pinback Button, lady portrait, back paper with red lettering "Cracker Jack Candied Popcorn & Roasted Peanuts," and 5¢ purchase price, 1900s 65

Lapel Stud, Air Corps wings, silvered white metal, center inscription "Cracker Jack Air Corps," 1930s 20

Charm, diecut litho tin, sundial, raised pointer dial, gold rimmed dial face, green roman numerals, 1930s 17

Drawing Book, blue and white cov, nursery rhyme characters on each side, tracing sheets between each page, 4 pp, unused, 1920s, 1.25 x 2.5" .30

Fire Truck, litho tin, red, orange, and black accent, hood mkd "FD," 1930s .50

Medal, gold luster finish, standing goddess figure holding long feather in upraised hand and flaming torch in other hand, inscription "Cracker Jack Salesman 1939 Award," 1.25" d .65

Ring, plastic, figural football, snap-together, 1960s 8

Sailboat, diecut litho tin, red, white, and blue, 1930s 15

Sled, litho tin, emb "Cracker Jack," 2" l .35

Spinner Top, diecut litho tin, red, white, and blue 35

Stand-up, God Bless America, diecut litho tin, red, white, and blue, Pledge of Allegiance text on base, 1940s 20

Stand-up, Harold Teen, multicolor, 2" h ..90

Stand-up, Officer USA, diecut litho tin, golden brown military uniform holding upright sword, 2.125" h 15

Vehicle, Police Patrol, litho tin, 1930s ...50

Vehicle, "The More You Eat–The More You Want" on top, litho tin, 1.75" l 60

Whistle, litho tin, rec, 2-tube 15

CRACKLE GLASS

If crackle glass catches your fancy, beware! It is still being produced by Blenko Glass Company and in foreign countries such as Taiwan and China. Examine prospective purchases carefully. Cracks are often hard to distinguish from the decorative "crackles."

Club: Collectors of Crackle Glass, P.O. Box 1186, N. Massapequa, NY 11758.

Apple, ruby, Blenko, 3.5" h 50
Candy Dish, amberina, Kanawha, 3" h . . .40
Creamer, emerald green, drop over
    handle, Pilgrim, 3.75" h 30
Creamer and Sugar, blue, drop over
    handle, Pilgrim, 3.5" h 50
Cruet, sea green, Pilgrim, 6" h 40
Decanter, charcoal, Blenko, 11.75" h 75
Decanter, topaz, Rainbow, 8.5" h 75
Double-Neck Vase, olive green, Blenko,
    4" h 50
Drinking Glass, sea green, Blenko, 6" h . .50
Hat, blue, Pilgrim, 5" h 40
Jug, amberina, gold drop over handle,
    8.25" h 75
Miniature Jug, blue, drop over handle,
    Pilgrim, 4" h 30
Miniature Pinched Vase, amethyst,
    Pilgrim, 4" h 60
Miniature Pitcher, amethyst, drop over
    handle, Pilgrim, 3.25" h 35
Miniature Pitcher, tangerine, drop over
    handle, Pilgrim, 3.25" h 40
Miniature Pitcher, topaz, pulled back
    handle, Pilgrim, 4.75" h 25
Pinched Vase, lemon lime, Pilgrim, 5" h . .35
Syrup Pitcher, amethyst, pulled back
    handle, Kanawha, 6" h 60

Liqueur Glass, orange, clear applied drop-over handle, Pilgrim , 1949-69, 4" h, $45. —Photo courtesy Ray Morykan Auctions.

Vase, amberina, Hamon, 8" h 75
Vase, olive green, Blenko, 11.25" h 75
Vase, tangerine, Rainbow, 5.25" h 60
Vase, topaz, figural fish, Hamon, 9" h 75

CRECHE COLLECTIBLES

Once primarily a religious holiday decoration, creches have increasingly become a year-round collectible, with many collectors keeping their sets on display in the non-holiday months.

The practice of displaying the Christmas Nativity figures is an ancient one, popularized by St. Francis of Assisi in thirteenth century Italy. By the eighteenth century, the development of the creche figures in Naples had become a fine art.

Creche collectors look for all forms of the Nativity display, from the three-dimensional figures to paper cutouts. Pre–World War II European-made figures are especially desirable, although examples of well-known brand names such as Hummel or Anri in excellent condition will command a good price.

Advisor: Rita B. Bocher, 117 Crosshill Rd., Wynnewood, PA 19096-3511, (610) 649-7520, Fax (610) 649-5782, e-mail: crecher@op.net, Internet: www.op.net/~bocassoc/

Newsletter: *Creche Herald,* 117 Crosshill Rd., Wynnewood, PA 19096.

Decoupage on Wood, 8.5 x 11" 2
Figures, set of 4, composition, cardboard
    stable, Italy, late 1940s, 2-4" h 28
Figures, set of 8, wax, dark brown with
    gold antiquing, 1990s, 1.5-8" h 3

Composition stable, 8 plaster figures, $15.

Figures, set of 11, plastic, home poured
  and painted, 1950s, 2.5-9" 38
Figures, set of 24, wood, 1990s 12
Holy Family, pewter, 4" h 3
Holy Family, porcelain, set of 3 pcs, 1.5" h .4
Holy Family, wood, set of 8 pcs, 5" h 10
Holy Family in Shell, Peru 3
Nativity, hp, on wreath shaped wood,
  El Salvador, 10 x 7.5" 15
Nativity, painted plastic on wooden
  block, Italy, 6 x 4" 10
Nativity, plastic, multicolored silver glitter
  on stable roof, Hong Kong, 3 x 4 x 1" . .21
Nativity Wreath, made from ice cream
  bar sticks and wooden beads, c1982,
  15 x 10.5" 2
Plaque, bronze, Wendell August Forge,
  6 x 4" 7
Plaque, ceramic, gold painted 12
Nightlight, with star and holy family, 6" h .4
Tapestry, cotton, nativity scene, 27 x 20" . .6

CUFF LINKS

Many people consider cuff links to be the ideal collectible. They have been around for centuries and have always reflected the styles, economics, and technologies of their era. Cuff link collecting can be profitable. Rare or unusual finds can be worth substantial dollars. Most serious collectors have had the thrill of buying a pair for "pennies" that turned out to be worth a great deal.

Many cuff link collectors specialize. Areas of specialization include size, shape, and closure type. Other collectors specialize by subject. Examples of this are cuff links that show animals, sports, advertising logos, cars, boats, etc.

Club: National Cuff Link Society, P.O. Box 5700, Vernon Hills, IL 60061.

Brass, lady, emb, Art Nouveau 50
Celluloid, black circle with stamped yellow metal center in white metal frame,
  on card mkd "Jem Snap Links," .5" d .40
Celluloid, green octagonal plaque in
  octagonal white metal frame, mother-
  of-pearl disk in central white metal
  frame, on card mkd "Jem Snap Links,"
  .5" d 40

Sterling silver and enamel with geometric orange and yellow design, David Andersen, 1" l, $250. —Photo courtesy David Rago Auctions, Inc.

Celluloid, triangular geometric pattern,
  purple and black in square white
  metal frame, 4 pcs on orig card mkd
  "50¢/Kum-A-Part," c1914, .5" d 60
Coral, oval, pearl center, Hawaii, c1950 .75
Gold Filled, flower, engraved, square . . .55
Gold Filled, leaf 55
Gold Filled, vine, emb, oval 50
Gold Plated, horse, c1945 65
Milk Glass, flower motif, gold filled,
  c1880 65
Silver, irregular circular disks, die-
  stamped dragonfly, cattails, and water,
  mkd "TR" on front, hinged cuff bottom
  mkd "Pat'd Aug 24, 1880," 1" d 175
Silver, concave polished ovals, crown
  mark for Antonio Pineda and "Hecho
  En Mexico 970," 1.125 x .75" 150
Souvenir, State of Texas, star center 20

CUPIDS

Be suspicious of naked infants bearing bows and arrows. It is not clear if their arrows are tipped with passion or poison.

Club: Cupid Collectors Club, 2116 Lincoln St., Cedar Falls, IA 50613.

Advertising Tear Sheet, *Harper's Bazaar*,
  Chantilly by Houbigant, 1947, 8.75 x
  12.25" 5
Advertising Trade Card, "The Aim of this
  Cherub is to make all the Boys Love
  Oak Hall," chromo litho, cupid in
  wreath, Wanamaker & Brown Clothing
  for Boys, Philadelphia, PA, plain
  back, 1876, L Prang, Boston, 2.75 x
  4.375" 8

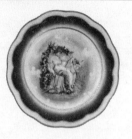

Plate, woman being shot by Cupid's arrow, mkd with crown, shield, and "Bavaria," 8.25" d, $35.

Card Holder, celluloid, embellished gold
Dresdens, c1880-1900, 2 x 4" 65
Decoration, honeycomb and paper, folding, pop-up, cupids around large vase
of heart-shaped flowers, Beistle Co,
c1925, 8" h, 9" w 30
Fabric, silk, cupids, doves, roses, man-
dolins, and tambourines, yellow and
golden yellow, 51" w 100
Limited Edition Plate, Cupids Reflection,
Bessie P Gutman, 10" d 20
Postcard, "To My Valentine," cupids
playing tennis, 1909 7
Puzzle, To My Valentine, hand cut, ply-
wood, cardboard box, 30 pcs, c1909,
3.5 x 5.5" 14
Sheet Music, *You'll Always be the Same
Sweet Girl,* Andrew B Sterling and
Harry VonTilzer, woman wearing hat
in center, 2 cupids at bottom, 1915 7
Tablecloth, paper, stenciled cupids and
hearts dec, 1920 25
Tie, silk, hp cupid with heart, 1930 35
Valentine, "Be My Valentine," 2 cupids
with basket surrounded by roses,
c1912 8

CUSPIDORS

After examining the interiors of some of the cuspidors for sale at flea markets, I am glad I have never been in a bar where people "spit." Most collectors are enamored by the brass cuspidor. The form came in many other varieties as well. You could build a marvelous collection focusing on pottery cuspidors.

Within the past year a large number of fake cuspidors have entered the market. I have seen them at flea markets across the United States. Double-check any cuspidor with a railroad marking and totally discount any with a Wells Fargo marking.

Brass, mkd "Made in England," 4.5" h,
6.25" d 8
Brass, 8" h, 9" d .50
Cast Iron, hat, old black repaint, 7.25" h .225
Cast Iron, porcelanized, light gray, white
int, mkd "Valley RR" 100
Ceramic, grapes and leaves dec, McCoy,
5.25" h, 7.5" d .13
Ceramic, creamy white and light green
shading, pansy decal, 5.25" h, 7.25" d .10
Graniteware, white, 3.25" h, 7" d 12
Graniteware, turquoise blue and white,
white int, black trim, 4" h, 7" w 35
Pewter, with handle, unmkd, 4.75" h 80
Porcelain, green, 8.25" h, 5.125" w 20
Rockingham, brown, sgraffito inscription
"L. J. Underwood, Barberton, Ohio,
July 24, '09," bottom incised "L. J. U.,
7-24-1909," 4.5" d 90
Rockingham, reddish brown to dark
brown drip glaze, 5.25" h, 7.5" d 50
Salt Glazed, green and cream, hanging
leaves and flowers at top and bottom,
scrolling design through center,
4.75" h, 7" d 65
Silver, engraved leaf design, French,
3" h, 5.5" d 90
Stoneware, emb sponged blue earth-
worm pattern .120
Yellow Ware, green, 7" h, 4.5" w 40

Rockingham, emb bows and flower petals on top and around sides, 4.5" h, 9.75" d, $100.

CUT GLASS

Collectors have placed so much emphasis on American Brilliant Cut Glass (1880 to 1917) that they completely overlook some of the finer cut glass of the post–World War I period. Admittedly, much cut glass in this later period was mass produced and rather ordinary. But, if you look hard enough, you will find some great pieces.

The big news in the cut glass market at the end of the 1980s was the revelation that many of the rare pieces that had been uncovered in the 1980s were of recent origin. Reproductions, copycats, and fakes abound. This is one category where you had better read a great deal and look at hundreds of pieces before you start buying.

Condition is also critical. Do not pay high prices for damaged pieces. Look for chips, dings, fractures, and knife marks. Sometimes these defects can be removed, but consider the cost of the repair when purchasing a damaged piece. Of course signed pieces command a higher dollar value.

Club: American Cut Glass Assoc., P.O. Box 482, Ramona, CA 92065.

Atomizer, Harvard pattern, gold-washed
    top, 4" h, 2.5" sq 125
Bowl, low, Thistle pattern, Hawkes 400
Bowl, oval, geometric design, 12.5" l ...375
Celery Tray, hobstars, cross hatch and
    notched prisms on figured blank,
    1.5" l, 5" w 60
Compote, floral pattern, hobstar foot,
    teardrop stem, 9.5" h 400
Compote, Pineapple, paneled cut, scal-
    loped border, paneled pedestal base,
    8" h, 12.5" d 225
Ewer, geometric cut design with circles,
    with stopper, 7.5" h, 6" d base 275
Fernery, hobstar and fan, 3 ftd, 8" d 80
Knife Rest, dumbbell shape, all over
    cutting, Brilliant Period, 3.5" l 25
Napkin Ring, hobstars and bow tie fans .85
Plate, Thistle, 9" d 125
Relish, hobstars, 8" l, 3.5" w 35
Salt and Pepper Shakers, pr, sterling
    silver tops, Hawkes, 6.75" h 450

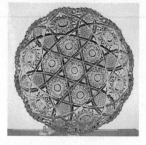

Bowl, scalloped sawtooth edge, American Brilliant period, 3.25" h, 9" d, $150. —Photo courtesy Ray Morykan Auctions.

Scent Bottle, crystal and silver, mkd
    "London 1913-14," 3" h 40
Vase, baluster form, floral design with
    diamond cut band, Monumental,
    18" h 1,100

CZECHOSLOVAKIAN

Czechoslovakia was created at the end of World War I out of the area of Bohemia, Moravia, and Austrian Silesia. Although best known for glass products, Czechoslovakia also produced a large number of pottery and porcelain wares for export.

Czechoslovakia objects do not enjoy a great reputation for quality, but I think they deserve a second look. They certainly reflect what was found in the average American's home from the 1920s through the 1950s.

Club: Czechoslovakian Collectors Guild International, P.O. Box 901395, Kansas City, MO 64190.

Bank, ceramic, black Scottie dog, white
    accents, 4.625" h 50
Barber Bottle, clear, red and silver
    applied design, 5.5" h 40
Basket, white opalescent, raised braid
    design, black trim, 4.5" h 30
Bud Vase, blue, enamel dec, 8.25" h 90
Candleholder, ceramic, angel kneeling,
    3.5" h 50

Decanter, ruby cut to clear, vintage dec, 14" h, $100.

Cow Creamer, seated, brown spots on
    white ground, black handle, 4.75" h . . .35
Earrings, pr, emerald cut crystal center
    surrounded by light green crystals,
    gold filigree setting, .75" l 25
Necklace, black glass and white swirl
    beads with alternating black beads,
    metal flower design closure 50
Necklace, red and clear glass beads,
    red stone set in metal clasp closure,
    14" l 35
Paperweight, pink and white striped
    flowers on clear stems in crystal ball
    in multicolored base, 3" h 150
Pin, plastic, hp, boy and girl in native
    costume, 1.5" h 25
Pitcher, figural bird, red and black
    accents on cream ground, Erphila
    Art Pottery, 5.75" h 85
Pitcher, mottled yellow body, multi-
    colored floral circle, black rim and
    handle, 6.5" h 45
Pocketknife, celluloid, tortoise shell
    case, 1 blade, snuff spoon, ivory
    toothpick, 2.25" l closed 25
Purse, black beads, zip top, black hand
    strap, 4.375 x 6.625" 40
Salt and Pepper Shakers, pr, figural
    ducks, crystal body, porcelain head
    tops, 2" h 40
Vase, leaf and vine dec, pink satin,
    8.25" h 140
Vase, light green, crystal, cane and red
    dec, 5" h 170
Vase, orange to cream to light and dark
    purple sawtooth design, black rim
    edge, 7.25" h .50
Vase, yellow, applied green dec, 9" h . . .70

DAIRY COLLECTIBLES

For decades, the dairy industry has
been doing a good job of encouraging us to
drink our milk and eat only real butter. The
objects used to get this message across, as
well as the packaging for dairy products,
have long been favorites with collectors.

Concentrate on the material associated
with a single dairy, region, or national firm.
If you try to collect one example of every
milk bottle used, you simply will not succeed. The amount of dairy collectibles is
staggering.

Clubs: Diary & Creamers Assoc., Rt. 3, P.O.
Box 189, Arcadia, WI 54612; National Assoc.
of Milk Bottle Collectors Inc., 4 Ox Bow Rd.,
Westport, CT 06800.

Newsletter: *Creamers,* P.O. Box 11, Lake
Villa, IL 60046.

Ashtray, glass, Holland Dairy Foods 3
Book, *When I Grow Up,* Edith E Maddox,
    pub by National Dairy Council, cover
    shows 2 children with Scottie dog,
    illus, 24 pp, 1956, 6 x 8" 8
Bottle Opener, Shoemaker Farms, Greene
    Country, OH, "Purity Protected and
    DagroSealed Milk" 4
Clock, light-up, Sanitary Ice Cream and
    Milk, metal body, glass face and
    cover, 15" d 140
Cookbook, *300 Tasty, Healthful Dairy
    Dishes,* Culinary Arts Institute, Con-
    solidated Book Publishers, Inc,
    Chicago, paperback, 48 pp, 1940 5

Milk Bottle, Haberfield's Pasteurized Cream, emb "Imperial Half Pint," red and black pyroglazed label, Australian, 5.875" h, $12.

Thermometer, waxed cardboard, Muller's Pinehurst Grade A Milk, Rockford, IL, red and white, 6.125" h, $15.

DAKIN FIGURES

The term "Dakin" refers to a type of hollow, vinyl figure produced by the R. Dakin Company. These figures are found with a number of variations—molded or cloth costumed, jointed or nonjointed and range in height from 5" to 10".

As with any popular and profitable product, Dakin figures were copied. There are a number of Dakin-like figures found on the market. Produced by Sutton & Son Inc., Knickerbocker Toy Company, and a production company for Hanna-Barbera, these figures are also collectible and are often mistaken for the original Dakin products. Be careful when purchasing.

DEARLY DEPARTED

I know this category is a little morbid, but the stuff is collected. Several museums have staged special exhibitions devoted to mourning art and jewelry. Funeral parlors need to advertise for business.

I did not put one in the listing, but do you know what makes a great coffee table? A coffin carrier or coffin stand. Just put a piece of glass over the top. It's the right size, has leg room underneath, and makes one heck of a conversation piece.

Ashtray, Scott-Harris Funeral Home,
  Navasota, TX, glass, 5.25" d 5
Box, metal, Boydstun Funeral Home,
  Comanche, OK 5
Brochure, Cadillad Funeral Coach, full
  color illus, 11 pp, 1967 50
Embalmer Eye Caps, plastic 3
Flag, white cross with "Funeral" on pur-
  ple ground, metal pole, 17" h 10
Fly Swatter, Schwenkville Marble &
  Granite Works, "Mark Every Grave,"
  wood handle 4
Hand Fan, Edwards and Cummings
  Funeral Directors, Pasadena, CA 5
Hand Fan, Roberts-Blue Barnett Funeral
  Home, Emporia, KS 12
Hand Fan, W M Thompson Funeral
  Home, "Home Memories," adv text
  on back, 10.75" l 9
Mechanical Pencil, Globe Casket Mfg,
  Denver, CO, "Good Caskets Since
  1860" 3
Paperweight, 1904 World's Fair, Mound
  Coffin Co adv, depicts factory with
  train and rail yard, 2.75 x 4.25" 150
Parlor Chair, oak, padded seat, "White"
  stenciled on back, seat bottom mkd
  "White Funeral Home," 32" h, 13.5" w . .10
Photograph, mother and father looking
  down on young woman in casket,
  black and white, black cardboard
  frame with "Cundiff...Antell, Kansas,"
  8 x 10" 30
Pocket Mirror, Jacob Ewald & Son,
  Funeral Directors, Chicago, IL,
  "Limousine Service/Modern Chapels,"
  1940s 5
Postcard, horse-drawn hearse, real
  photo, c1880 5

Advertising Brush, Rabenold's Funeral Home, Allentown, PA, gold lettering on black-painted wood, 6" l, $8.

Receipt, William Cook Funeral Home,
  Baltimore, MD, funeral expenses 5
Thermometer, Nicholas V Guerro Funer-
  al Home, Pen Argyl, PA, calendar on
  back, 5 x 4" 9
Thermometer, Wilson Funeral Home,
  Clay, WV, metal 12

DEEDS & DOCUMENTS

A document is any printed paper that shows evidence or proof of something. Subject matter ranges from baptismal certificates to stocks and bonds. Flea markets are loaded with old documents. Though they generally have minimal value and are usually copies of the original forms, it makes good sense to check before discarding. It may be of value to its original owner or to a paper-ephemera collector.

Many eighteenth and early nineteenth century deeds are on parchment. In most cases, value is minimal, ranging from a few dollars to a high of $10. First, check to see if the deed is the original document. Most deeds on the market are copies; the actual document is often on file in the courthouse. Second, check the signatures. Benjamin Franklin signed a number of Pennsylvania deeds. These are worth a great deal more than $10. Third, check the location of the deed. If it is a city deed, the current property owner may like to acquire it. If it is for a country farm, forget it.

Finally, a number of early deeds have an elaborate wax seal at the bottom. When framed, these make wonderful display pieces in attorneys' offices.

Club: International Bond & Share Society, 15 Dyatt Place, P.O. Box 430, Hackensack, NJ 07602.

Bill of Sale, Schooner Mariah Meresa, transferring title to 1/16th of the schooner to new owner, 1848, 10.5 x 17 45

Check, vignette of ship, 2¢ tax stamp affixed, canceled, 1867 5

Debt Certificate, Canton, Maine, promising to repay $50 in 10 years, 10.5 x 5.5" 7

Deed, Massachusetts, land in Ashburnham–transfered to Ivers Adams by Asa and Peggy Woods, 1830 20

Deed, Philadelphia, property on Northeast corner of Pratt St and Pine St, Sep 28, 1835 22

Deed, Vermont, land in Windsor County, Sally Banister to Samuel Worcester, dated Dec 26, 1842 6

Document, shipping, sailing ship at upper left, cargo destined for Philadelphia from New York, pre-Civil War dated 6

Marriage Certificate, William Young and Alvina Snyder, NY, Dec 4, 1870, 15 x 17.25" frame size 50

Receipt, Adams Express Co, from Philadelphia to Columbia, PA, 1868 3

Receipt, Gilbert Clock Co, 6 buzz alarm clocks for $3.60, dated Nov 30, 1906, 5.5 x 8" 15

Receipt, Portland & Rumford Falls Railway, for items shipped, 1890s, 8.5 x 3.25" 6

Warrant, Boston, appointing a constable, imprinted city seal with Boston Harbor, 1885 15

DEGENHART GLASS

Degenhart pressed glass novelties are collected by mold, by individual color, or by group of colors. Hundreds of colors, some are nearly identical and were produced between 1947 and 1978. Prior to 1972 most pieces were unmarked. After that date a "D" or "D" in a heart was used.

Do not confuse Kanawha's bird salt and bow slipper or L. G. Wright's mini-slipper, daisy and button salt, and 5" robin-covered dish with Degenhart pieces. They are similar, but there are differences. See Gene Florence's *Degenhart Glass and Paperweights: A Collector's Guide to Colors*

and Values (Degenhart Paperweight and Glass Museum: 1982) for a detailed list of Degenhart patterns.

Club: Friends of Degenhart (Degenhart Paperweight and Glass Museum, Inc,) 65323 Highland Hills Rd., P.O. Box 186, Cambridge, OH 43725.

Animal Dish, cov, robin, custard slag . . .15

Basket, blue, 2.25" h 15

Bell, amber 12

Bicentennial Bell, crystal 8

Bookends, pr, horseheads, 5.5" h 40

Boot, Daisy and Button 25

Candy Dish, Wildflower, opalescent pink, 5.5" h 18

Chick, Vaseline 18

Cup Plate, Heart and Lyre, gold 9

Dog, light pink 20

Hand, sapphire 6

Hat, Daisy and Button, amethyst 8

Jewelry Box, heart, fawn 18

Owl, amethyst, 3.5" h 15

Owl, bluebell 35

Owl, charcoal 40

Owl, pink 25

Paperweight, flowerpot 85

Pooch, ivory slag 20

Priscilla, blue and white 30

Rose Bowl, clear, green and white iridescent, 3.25" h 30

Salt, bird, light green, 1.75" h 10

Salt, Star and Dew Drop, forest green . .12

Salt and Pepper Shakers, pr, crystal 10

Slipper, Kat, sapphire 15

Toothpick Holder, Daisy and Button, blue slag 30

Toothpick Holder, Forget-Me-Not, custard 15

Toothpick Holder, Daisy and Button, light blue milk glass, $12.

DEPRESSION GLASS

Depression Era Glass refers to glassware made between the 1920s and 1940s. It was mass-produced by a number of different companies. It was sold cheaply and often given away as a purchasing premium.

Specialize in one pattern or color. Once again, there is no way that you can own every piece made. Also, because Depression glass was produced in vast quantities, buy only pieces in excellent or better condition.

A number of patterns have been reproduced. See Gene Florence's *The Collector's Encyclopedia of Depression Glass* (Collector Books, revised annually) for a complete list of reproductions.

Clubs: Canadian Depression Glass Assoc., 119 Wexford Rd., Brampton, Ontario, L6Z 2T5 Canada; The National Depression Glass Assoc., P.O. Box 8264, Wichita, KS 67208; 20-30-40's Society, Inc., P.O. Box 856, La Grange, IL 60525.

Newspaper: *The Daze,* P.O. Box 58, Clio, MI 48420.

ADAM, JEANNETTE

Ashtray, 4.5" w, green 23
Ashtray, 4.5" w, pink 30
Berry Bowl, 4.75" d, green 22
Berry Bowl, 4.75" d, pink 23
Butter Dish, cov, pink 125
Cake Plate, ftd, 10" d, green 26
Cake Plate, ftd, 10" d, pink 30
Candy Jar, cov, 2.5" d, pink 120

Adam, vegetable bowl, open, 9" d, pink, $40.
—Photo courtesy Ray Morykan Auctions.

Cereal Bowl, 5.75" d, pink 65
Creamer and Sugar, cov, pink 70
Creamer, green .29
Cup and Saucer, green 32
Cup and Saucer, pink 36
Dinner Plate, square, 9" w, green 28
Dinner Plate, square, 9" w, pink 37
Grill Plate, 9" d, green 26
Pitcher, 32 oz, square base, 8" h, pink . . .45
Platter, oval, 11.75" l, green 36
Platter, oval, 11.75" l, pink 32
Relish, divided, 8" l, green 25
Relish, divided, 8" l, pink 21
Salad Plate, square, 7.75" w, green 17
Salad Plate, square, 7.75" w, pink 19
Salt and Pepper Shakers, pr, 4" h, pink .100
Saucer, square, green 6
Sherbet, 3" h, green 6
Sherbet, 3" h, pink 33
Sugar, covered, green 75
Tumbler, 4.5" h, green 30
Tumbler, 4.5" h, pink 37
Tumbler, iced tea, 5.5" h, green 60
Vase, 7.5" h, green 85
Vase, 7.5" h, pink 450
Vegetable Bowl, cov, round, 9" d, pink . .75
Vegetable Bowl, oval, 10" l, pink 36

AMERICAN SWEETHEART, MACBETH-EVANS

Bowl, oval, monax 85
Bowl, oval, pink .75
Cereal Bowl, pink 18
Cream Soup Bowl, 4.5" d, monax 130
Cup and Saucer, monax 13
Dinner Plate, 9.5" d, monax 28
Lazy Susan, 15.5" d, monax 325
Plate, 8" d, red 125
Plate, 12" d, monax 23
Plate, 12" d, pink 25
Platter, pink 60
Sherbet, ftd, monax 23
Sherbet, ftd, pink 24
Soup Bowl, flat, monax 115
Soup Bowl, flat, pink 75
Tumbler, 5 oz, 3.5" h, monax 100
Tumbler, 10 oz, 4.75" h, monax 175

CHERRY BLOSSOM, JEANNETTE

Berry Bowl, 4.75", green 22
Berry Bowl, 4.75", pink 24
Berry Bowl, 8.75", green 55

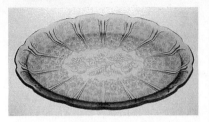

Cherry Blossom, platter, oval, 13" l, pink, $65. —Photo courtesy Ray Morykan Auctions.

Berry Bowl, 8.75", pink 50
Bowl, 2-Handled, 9", pink 60
Butter Dish, cov, pink 125
Cake Plate, 3-leg, 10.75", pink 45
Cereal Bowl, 5.75", green 50
Child's Junior Dinnerware Set, 14 pcs,
　delphite, with box 375
Child's Junior Dinnerware Set, 14 pcs,
　pink, with box .450
Coaster, green 13
Creamer, pink 20
Cup and Saucer, green 30
Cup and Saucer, pink 28
Dinner Plate, 9", delphite 25
Dinner Plate, 9", green 27
Dinner Plate, 9", pink 28
Flat Soup Bowl, 7.75", pink 100
Fruit Bowl, 3-leg, 10.5", green 100
Fruit Bowl, 3-leg, 10.75", pink 110
Grill Plate, 9", pink 40
Oval Bowl, 9", green 50
Oval Bowl, 9", pink 60
Pitcher, 36 oz, AOP, footed, 6.75", pink . . .75
Pitcher, 36 oz, PAT, footed, 8", pink 90
Pitcher, 42 oz, PAT, flat, 8", green 70
Pitcher, 42 oz, PAT, flat, 8", pink 55
Platter, oval, 11", green 50
Platter, oval, 11", pink 50
Platter, oval, 13", divided, pink 85
Salad Plate, 7", pink 26
Sherbet, green 22
Sherbet, pink 22
Sugar, cov, green .45
Sugar, cov, pink 38
Tumbler, 4 oz, AOP, footed, 3.75", green . .22
Tumbler, 4 oz, AOP, footed, 3.75", pink . . .22
Tumbler, 8 oz, AOP, scalloped foot, 4.5",
　pink 40

Florentine No. 2, comport, ruffled, 3.5" h, pink, $15. —Photo courtesy Ray Morykan Auctions.

Tumbler, 9 oz, AOP, round foot, 4.5", pink .45
Tumbler, 9 oz, AOP, round foot, 4.5",
　delphite 25
Tumbler, 9 oz, PAT, flat, 4.25", pink 25
Tumbler, 12 oz, PAT, flat, 5", pink 90

FLORENTINE NO. 2, HAZEL ATLAS

Berry Bowl, 8" d, yellow 34
Berry Bowl, individual, 4.5" d, yellow 22
Butter Dish, cov, crystal 110
Butter Dish, cov, yellow 140
Candlesticks, pr, 2.75" h, yellow 55
Candy Dish, cov, crystal 120
Candy Dish, cov, green 130
Candy Dish, cov, pink 150
Cereal Bowl, 6" d, yellow 30
Cream Soup Bowl, 4.75" d, crystal 16
Cup and Saucer, yellow 13
Cup, crystal 9
Cup, yellow 3
Custard Cup, yellow 125
Dinner Plate, 10" d, green 11
Dinner Plate, 10" d, pink 35
Dinner Plate, 10" d, yellow 12
Gravy Boat and underplate, yellow 90
Gravy Boat, yellow 36
Parfait, 6" h, crystal 35
Parfait, 6" h, yellow 60
Pitcher, 28 oz, cone-ftd, 7.25" h, yellow . .22
Pitcher, 48 oz, flat, ice lip, 7.5" h, pink . .135
Pitcher, 48 oz, flat, no ice lip, 7.5" h,
　green 125
Pitcher, 76 oz, flat, 8.25" h, crystal 120
Pitcher, 76 oz, flat, 8.25" h, green 225
Platter, oval, 11" l, yellow 14
Salad Plate, 8.25" d 7
Salt and Pepper Shakers, pr, green 21
Salt and Pepper Shakers, pr, yellow 55

Saucer, yellow 4
Sherbet, ftd, crystal 4
Sherbet, ftd, pink .10
Sherbet, ftd, yellow 4
Sherbet Plate, 6" d, green 3
Sherbet Plate, 6" d, pink 13
Sherbet Plate, 6" d, yellow 4
Tumbler, 9 oz, ftd, 4.5" h, green 28
Tumbler, 9 oz, ftd, 4.5" h, yellow 35

PETALWARE, MACBETH-EVANS

Berry Bowl, 9" d, cremax with gold trim . .18
Berry Bowl, 9" d, monax 20
Berry Bowl, 9" d, pink 20
Cereal Bowl, 5.75" d, monax 9
Cereal Bowl, 5.75" d, monax florette 13
Cereal Bowl, 5.75" d, monax with gold
  trim 8
Cereal Bowl, 5.75" d, pink 13
Cream Soup Bowl, 4.5" d, cremax 12
Cream Soup Bowl, 4.5" d, cremax with
  gold trim 12
Cream Soup Bowl, 4.5" d, monax with
  gold trim 12
Cream Soup Bowl, 4.5" d, pink 15
Creamer and Sugar, cremax 15
Creamer and Sugar, monax 12
Creamer, monax florette 11
Creamer, pink 15
Cup and Saucer, cremax 6
Salad Plate, 8" d, cremax 5
Salad Plate, 8" d, cremax with gold trim . . .7
Salad Plate, 8" d, monax florette 10
Salad Plate, 8" d, pink 13
Salver, 11" d, cremax 10

*Petalware, salad plate, 8" d, monax with
fruit dec and gold trim, $10. —Photo cour-
tesy Ray Morykan Auctions.*

Salver, 11" d, monax 17
Salver, 11" d, pink 17
Salver, 12" d, monax florette 18
Saucer, cremax with gold trim 1
Saucer, monax 2
Saucer, monax florette 3
Saucer, pink 4
Sherbet, 4" h, monax 20
Sherbet, 4.5" h, cremax with gold trim . . .12
Sherbet, 4.5" h, monax 8
Sherbet, ftd, 4.5" h, red trim floral 45
Sherbet Plate, 6" d, cremax with gold
  trim 2
Sherbet Plate, 6" d, monax 3
Sherbet Plate, 6" d, monax florette 6
Sugar, monax 7
Sugar, open, cremax with gold trim 11
Sugar, open, monax florette 11
Tidbit, center handle, monax 18

SHARON "CABBAGE ROSE," FEDERAL

Bowl, 5" d, amber .8
Bowl, 6" d, pink 32
Bowl, 6.5" d, green 40
Bowl, oval, amber 18
Butter Dish, cov, amber 45
Cake Plate, ftd, 11.5" d, amber 27
Candy Dish, cov, amber 40
Creamer, amber 15
Cream Soup Bowl, pink 50
Cup and Saucer, amber 16
Pitcher, ice lip, amber 125
Platter, pink 32
Soup Bowl, flat, amber 55
Tumbler, 9 oz, thick, 4.125" h, pink 48
Tumbler, 9 oz, thin, 4.125" h, pink 45
Vegetable Bowl, oval, 10", pink 34

SWIRL, JEANNETTE

Berry Bowl, 4.875" d, ultramarine 27
Butter Bottom, pink 32
Butter Dish, cov, pink 200
Butter Dish, cov, ultramarine 325
Candleholders, pr, two-light, ultrama-
  rine 50
Candy Dish, cov, pink 110
Candy Dish, cov, ultramarine 160
Candy Dish, open, 3 legs, pink 14
Candy Dish, open, 3 legs, ultramarine . . .30
Cereal Bowl, 5.25" d, ultramarine 16
Coaster, pink 13
Creamer, ultramarine 16

Swirl, bowl, ftd, 10" d, ultramarine, $40.

Cup and Saucer, ultramarine 17
Cup, pink 9
Cup, ultramarine 14
Dinner Plate, 9.25" d, ultramarine 20
Luncheon Plate, 7.25" d, pink 10
Luncheon Plate, 7.25" d, ultramarine 18
Salad Bowl, 9" d, ultramarine 30
Salad Plate, 8" d, ultramarine 25
Salt and Pepper Shakers, pr, ultrama-
    rine 48
Sandwich Plate, 12.5" d, ultramarine 32
Saucer, ultramarine 3
Sherbet, pink 20
Sherbet, ultramarine 22
Sherbet Plate, 6.5" d, ultramarine 9
Soup Bowl, lug handles, ultramarine 52
Sugar, ultramarine 15
Tumbler, 9 oz, 4" h, pink 25
Tumbler, 9 oz, 4.625" h, pink 26
Tumbler, 13 oz, 5.125" h, ultramarine . . .175

DINNERWARE

There is a growing appreciation for the thousands of dinnerware patterns that graced the tables of low-, middle-, and some upper-income families during the first three-quarters of the twentieth century. Some of America's leading industrial designers were responsible for forms and decorative motifs.

Collectors fall into three groups: those who collect the wares of a specific factory or factories, often with a strong regional emphasis; individuals who are reassembling the set they grew up with; and those who are fascinated by certain forms and motifs. The bulk of the books on the subject appeared in the early 1980s.

Several of the companies have become established collecting categories in their own right. This is why you will find companies such as Blue Ridge and Hall elsewhere in this book.

Club: Haviland Collectors International Foundation, P.O. Box 804262, Santa Clarita, CA 91380.

Periodical: *The Daze,* P.O. Box 57, Otisville, MI 48463.

CASTLETON CHINA, CAPRICE

Bread and Butter plate, 6.25" d 14
Cup and Saucer, ftd, 2.125" 37
Fruit Bowl, 5.5" d 24
Salad Plate, 8.375" d 18
Soup Bowl, flat, 8" d 27

CASTLETON CHINA, DEVON

Cream Soup and Saucer 47
Cup and Saucer, ftd, 2.25" 34
Dinner Plate, 10.75" d 30
Fruit Bowl, 5.5" d 20
Salad Plate, 8.375" d 18
Soup Bowl, flat, 7.875" d 27
Sugar, cov 60
Vegetable Bowl, cov, round 200

CASTLETON CHINA, MA LIN

Bread and Butter Plate, 6.375" d 18
Cream Soup Bowl 50
Demitasse Cup and Saucer 34
Fruit Bowl, 5.5" d 27
Luncheon Plate, 9.125" d 30
Platter, oval, 13.375" 120

Castleton China, Ma Lin, dinner plate, $37.

Haviland, Delaware, dinner plate, $30.

HAVILAND, APPLEBLOSSOM

Bread and Butter Plate, 6.5" d 20
Demitasse Cup and Saucer 34
Dinner Plate, 10.75" d 37
Fruit Bowl, 5" d .24
Salad Plate, 7.5" d 24
Soup Bowl, flat, 7.875" d 34
Sugar, cov 75

HAVILAND, DELAWARE

Bread and Butter Plate, 6.375" d 14
Cream Soup and Saucer 47
Demitasse Cup and Saucer 30
Fruit Bowl, 5.125" d 18
Luncheon Plate, 8.75" d 24
Salad Plate, 7.5" d 20

MINTON, ANCESTRAL

Bread and Butter Plate, 6.125" d 20
Cake Plate, handled, 9.875" sq 100
Demitasse Cup and Saucer, flat 40
Dinner Plate 47
Luncheon Plate, 9" d 45

MINTON, HENLEY #1793

Bread and Butter Plate, 6.5" d 27
Cup and Saucer, ftd, 3" 50
Dinner Plate, 10.75" d 54
Salad Plate, 8" d 34

ROYAL DOULTON, BURGUNDY

Bread and Butter Plate, 6.625" d 10
Cup and Saucer, flat, 2.5" 22
Dinner Plate, 10.625" d 24
Salad Plate, 8" d 14

Soup Bowl, flat, 8" 24

ROYAL DOULTON, CORNWALL

Bread and Butter Plate 14
Cup and Saucer, flat, 2.875" 20
Dinner Plate 27
Salad Plate 20
Sugar, cov, 3.375" h 40

ROYAL WORCESTER, ASTLEY

Bread and Butter Plate 10
Cup and Saucer, flat, 2.5" 27
Dinner Plate 27
Fruit Bowl, 5.5" d 18
Salad Bowl, individual 27

ROYAL WORCESTER, EVESHAM GOLD

Bread and Butter Plate, 6.5" d 5
Cereal Bowl, 6.75" d 14
Luncheon Plate, 9.125" d 10
Salad Bowl, 5.375" d 18
Salt and Pepper Shakers, pr, 4.75" h 27

SYRACUSE CHINA, BRIARCLIFF

Bread and Butter Plate, 6.5" d 10
Dinner Plate, 10" d 24
Fruit Bowl, 5.125" d 18
Luncheon Plate, 9" d 18
Soup Bowl, flat, 8" d 22

SYRACUSE CHINA, SUZANNE

Bread and Butter Plate, 6.5" d 10
Dinner Plate, 10" d 24
Fruit Bowl, 5" d .18
Salad Plate, 8" d 15

Royal Worcester, Evesham Gold, dinner plate, $12.

DIONNE QUINTUPLETS

On May 28, 1934, on a small farm in Callander, Ontario, Canada, five baby girls weighing a total of ten pounds, one and one quarter ounces were delivered into this world with the help of Dr. DaFoe and two midwives.

Due to their parents' poor financial circumstances and the public's curiosity, the quintuplets were put on display. For a small fee, the world was invited to come and see the quints at play in their custom-built home or to buy a souvenir to mark their birth.

The field of collectibles for Dionne Quintuplets memorabilia is a very fertile one!

Club: Dionne Quint Collectors, P.O. Box 2527, Woburn, MA 01888.

Advertising Tear Sheet, Karo Syrup, 8 x
10" 6
Advertising Tear Sheet, Palmolive Soap,
1937 6
Calendar, 1942, "Springtime," Holsum
Bread adv .... .10
Calendar, 1944, "Maytime," F L J Brey-
mam Dry Goods and Ready-to-Wear
Dept, Carlinville, IL adv .... .15
Calendar, 1948, "First Dates" 6
Cereal Bowl and Mug, white china, color
image of Quint in high chair, unmkd,
c1934-35, 5.5" d bowl, 2.75" h mug ...175
Dexterity Puzzle, metal frame, glass top,
3.5 x 5" .... .50
Hand Fan, "Sweethearts of the World,"
adv on back for Refrigerator and
Radio Pioneer, Hanover, PA .... .20
Magazine, *Click*, Jun 1, 1940, "For the
First Time Color Picture Diary of The
Dionne Quints" ....
Paperback Book, *Three Years Old*, 32 pp,
black and white photos, 9.5 x 10" .... .10
Paper Doll Book Set, Let's Play House,
set of 5, ©1940 Merrill Publishing Co,
9.5 x 10.5" .... .600
Platter, white china, color image of Quints
in high chairs, "Dionne Quintuplets
Born May 28, 1934 Callander, Ontario,
Canada/Niagara Falls," maple leaf in
upper center, ©N.E.A., 11.5" d ...... .300

Advertisement, Quaker Mother's Oats, paper, framed, ©1935, 17.75" h, 35" w, $100. —Photo courtesy Collectors Auction Services.

Road Map, Eastern Canada, Imperial
Oil premium, map of Ontario, Quebec,
and Maritime Provinces, denotes
Quints home in North Bay, 1938 5
Sign, diecut cardboard, "Just Name
This Picture of Dr. Dafoe and the
Dionne Quints," sponsored by Quaker
Oats, mkd "Photo World Copyright,
1936, N.E.A.," 10.5 x 13" .... .90
Teacup, "Birthplace of Canada's Famous
Five, Callander, Canada," mkd "Royal
Winton Grimwade/Made in England,"
2.75" h .... .35

DISNEYANA

"Steamboat Willie" introduced Mickey Mouse to the world in 1928. Walt and Roy Disney, brothers, worked together to create an entertainment empire filled with a myriad of memorable characters ranging from Donald Duck to Zorro.

Early Disney items are getting very expensive. No problem. Disney continues to license material. In thirty years the stuff marketed in the 1960s and 1970s will be scarce and eagerly sought. Now is the time to buy it.

Clubs: National Fantasy Fan Club for Disneyana Collectors & Enthusiasts, P.O. Box 19212, Irvine, CA 92713; The Mouse Club, 2056 Cirone Way, San Jose, CA 95124.

Periodical: *Tomart's Disneyana Digest,* 3300 Encrete Ln., Dayton, OH 45439.

Book, Walt Disney Presents Pluto's Play-Time, *Juvenile Productions Ltd., London, 94 pp, 7.625 x 10.25", $35.*

Ashtray, Mickey Mouse, white china, gold trim, color image of Mickey turning his head backwards, small Mickey illus on reverse with Mickey and Disney names, mkd "Made in Bavaria," 1930s, 3 x 3 x .75" 75

Autograph, Funicello, Annette, PS, black and white, purple felt tip pen signature, 8 x 10" 40

Bank/Telephone, Mickey Mouse, pressed steel, diecut cardboard Mickey figure with paper label on front, complete with attached string phone cord and felt covering on underside, N N Hill Brass Co, 1934, 4 x 7.5 x 4.5" 175

Blotter, Donald Duck, Sunoco adv, color image of Donald parked in front of gas pump, 1946, 4 x 6.75" 35

Book, *Disneyland Pictorial Souvenir Book,* 32 pp, 1965, 10.5 x 10.5" 20

Book, *Dumbo, The Story of the Flying Elephant,* 20 pp, Whitman, 1942, 10.25 x 11" 35

Box, Mickey Mouse Cookies, cardboard, fabric handle cord, National Biscuit Co, 1937, 2 x 5 x 2.75" 325

Coloring Book, Walt Disney's Coloring Book, Whitman, 80 pp, 1970s, 8 x 10.75" 15

Cookie Jar, Donald Duck, ceramic, Leeds China, 1947, 7 x 8 x 12" 175

Doll, Ferdinand, composition, jointed, movable head, stenciled bee design with name above leg, Ideal Novelty & Toy Co, 1938, 5.5 x 9 x 8.5" 175

Doll, Mary Poppins, soft plastic body, vinyl arms and head, life-like hair and eyelashes, orig outfit, Horsman, 1964, 6 x 11 x 35" 350

Doll, Peter Pan, hard plastic, movable arms and head, sleep eyes, red outfit with green belt, felt hat, silver metal sword, Duchess Doll Corp, 1950s, 6" h .30

Drinking Glass, Pluto and Goofy, brown and yellow, 1960s, 5" h 40

Eggcup, Donald Duck, figural, china, mkd "Made in Japan," 1930s, 2.25" h, 1.75" d 200

Figure, Bambi, porcelain, Wade, 1970s, 1.5" h 35

Figure, Dumbo, Hagen Renaker, 1950s, 1.5 x 2 x 1.5" 90

Figure, Figaro, ceramic, Shaw, c1946, 2 x 4.5 x 3.75" 175

Figure, Pinocchio, bisque, mkd "Japan," 1940, 4" h 40

Figure, Snow White, soft plastic, Marx, 1972, 5.5" h 12

Flashlight, Pluto, figural, hard plastic, 1950s, 1 x 5 x 1" 45

Greeting Card, Mickey Mouse, "Father's Day? Well It's a Cinch That I'll Let Things Drop" on front, inside text "And Hustle Off a Little Card to Say I Love You Pop," ©1936 Hallmark, 4.25 x 5.25" 60

Greeting Card, Three Little Pigs, Fiddler Pig and Fifer Pig crying on front, inside shows Practical Pig lying sick in bed made of bricks, get well text, orig envelope, White & Wyckoff, 1938, 4.75 x 5" 15

Hair Brush, Donald Duck, dark brown wood, aluminum top panel, painted design, 1938, Hughes-Autograph Brush Co, 2 x 3.75 x 1.5" 35

Record, Walt Disney's Little Toot, *Capitol Records Children's Series, #45-CK 030, distributed in Australia, 45 rpm, $15.*

Horn, Mickey and Minnie, stiff cardboard, images of Mickey and Minnie holding horn, Marks Brothers Co, 1930s, 6.25" h 45

Key Chain/Flashlight, Disneyland, hard plastic, glow-in-the-dark button on side, castle illus on blue ground, 1950s, .5 x .75 x 3" 20

Key Chain/Flashlight, Zorro, hard plastic, glow-in-the dark button on side, hat flips up to reveal Zorro's face, 1958, .5 x 1 x 3.25" 45

Lamp, Doc, painted plaster, 3D Doc figure atop circular base, Lamode Studios, 1938, 9.5" h, 4" d base 125

Lunch Box, Disneyland, emb metal, plastic thermos, full color Magic Kingdom illus, Aladdin Industries, Inc, 1979, 7 x 8 x 4" 12

Lunch Box, Snow White and the Seven Dwarfs, vinyl, Aladdin Industries, 1975, 7 x 9 x 3.5" 90

Map, Disneyland, full color detailed overhead park view with character illus along top margin, 1968, 30 x 45" . .35

Mug, Disneyland, ceramic, front depicts girl in Bavarian outfit, holding flute-type instrument surrounded by green hills, small castle in background, underside mkd "It's A Small World," 3.75" h 20

Paint Box, Mickey Mouse, litho tin, cov depicts Mickey and Donald in outer space painting rocketship, ©1952 Transogram, 4.5 x 5.75 x .5" 20

Pinback Button, gasoline premium, Kay Kamen back paper picturing small image of running Mickey, 1942, 1.25" d, $45.
—Photo courtesy Gene Harris Antique Auction Center, Inc.

Toy Train, Donald Duck Railroad, windup, litho tin, blue engine, red coal car, blue gondola, red caboose, Marx, USA, $400.

Paper Dolls, Mary Poppins, Whitman, 1963, 7.25 x 15.75" 18

Paper Dolls, Snow White and the Seven Dwarfs, Whitman, 1938 40

Pin, Cinderella, figural, metal, Cinderella at bottom of mountain with castle and birds, c1950, 3.25 x 3.75", MOC ...45

Plate, Disneyland, white china, gold trim, castle in center surrounded by scenes of each of the 5 main park areas, 1950s, 9.5" d 25

Puzzle, 20,000 Leagues Under the Sea, Jaymar, 1954, 7 x 10 x 1.75" 30

Puzzle, Davy Crockett, frame tray, Davy and frontiersmen engated in battle with Indians, Jaymar, 1955, 11 x 14" ..15

Record, *The Official Mickey Mouse Club Songs,* 45 rpm, #DBR50, ©1955 Am-Par Record Corp 20

Sheet Music, *Davy Crockett, Farewell,* "As Sung by Fess Parker on the Disneyland Television Show 'Davy Crockett at the Alamo'," 1954, 9 x 12" .20

Sheet Music, *Snow White and the Seven Dwarfs, Someday My Prince Will Come,* 4 pp, ©1937 Irving Berlin Inc, 9 x 12" 15

Sheet Music, *The Three Caballeros, You Belong To My Heart,* 9 x 12" 15

Soaky Bottle, Mickey Mouse, band leader outfit, red, gold accents, 1960s, 9.5" h 30

Toothbrush, Mickey Mouse, hard plastic, transparent green, 3D Mickey head at top of handle, Dupont, 1950s, MOC 10

Watch, Bambi, chromed metal case, Bambi dial illus, hands designed as Bambi's ears, orig green vinyl over leather straps, from US Time series celebrating Mickey's 20th birthday, 1948 90

Watch Fob, Mickey Mouse, silvered brass, incised Mickey image on front, leather strap, Ingersoll, 1.375" d 75

DOG COLLECTIBLES

The easiest way to curb your collection is to concentrate on the representations of a single breed. Many collectors focus only on three-dimensional figures. Whatever approach you take, buy pieces because you love them. Try to develop some restraint and taste and not buy every piece you see. Easy to say, hard to do!

Clubs: Canine Collectors Club, 10290 Hill Rd., Erie, IL 61250; Wee Scots, P.O. Box 450, Danielson, CT 06239.

Newsletter: *COLLIEctively Speaking!,* 331 Regal Dr., Abingdon, MD 21009.

Note: See Poodle Collectibles for additional listings.

Advertising Tear Sheet, winter scene with horse and dog, Mobilgas, "Horsepower sure needs a winter friend," 1944, 10 x 14" 4

Advertising Trade Card, young girl trying to take sign out of dog's mouth, Edwin C Burt Fine Shoes, calendar on reverse, 1879 5

License Tag, Washington, DC, 1938-39, $3.

Planter, ceramic, white with gray spots, black eyes and nose, and pink tongue, 6.75" h, 6" w, $15.

Ashtray, scottie, brass, Dunhill, 5 x 5" . . .25
Bank, Rival Dog Food, metal 3
Book, *The Playful Little Dog,* Jean Horton Berg, Wonder Book, 1951 5
Bookends, pr, greyhounds, Art Deco style, 7.5" h 250
Bookends, pr, scotties, metal, 4.5" h, 4.25" w 35
Bootjack, cocker spaniel, cast iron, 10.5" l, 3" h 5
Dish, ceramic, "To Man's Best Friend His Dog," McCoy, 7.25" d. 2.25" h 55
Doorstop, airedale, molded hard rubber, 10.75" h, 13.5" l 110
Figure, carnival chalkware, German shepherd, 8.5" h, 5" l base 10
Figure, scottie, porcelain, black, gold painted eyes, 3.25" h, 4.25" l 10
Nutcracker, cast iron, 13" l, 6" h 35
Pin, scottie in shoe, wood, hp, 2.75 x 1.5" 15
Planter, hound dog, ceramic, brown and black, 8" l 3
Postcard, Fox Terrier seated, real photo, German, 3.5 x 5.5" 5
Powder Jar, frosted green glass, terrier dog finial, 4.25" h, 4.25" w 100
Ring Holder, dachshund, cast metal, painted pink, pink rhinestone eyes, Revere Mfg, 3 x 4.5" 15
Stickpin, bulldog, 2.75 x .5" 20
Toothpick Holder, dog in doghouse, Vaseline, Summit Glass, 2.5" h 15
Vase, Hush Puppy, brown ears, black paws and nose, hp eyes, 9.5"h, 6" w, 4.5" d 10

DOLL HOUSES & FURNISHINGS

Doll houses and doll house furnishings have undergone a current craze and are highly collectible. Many artists and craftsmen devote hours to making scale furniture and accessories. This type of artist-oriented doll house furnishing affects the market by offering the buyer a choice of an old piece versus a present-day handmade piece.

Petite Princess, Plastic Art Toy Corporation, Tootsietoy, and Renwal are just four of hundreds of major manufacturers of machine-made doll house furniture. Materials range from wood to injection molded plastic. This furniture was meant to be used, and most surviving examples were. The period packaging is its supporting literature and can double the value of a set.

Club: Dollhouse & Miniature Collectors, P.O. Box 16, Bellaire, MI 49615.

Periodicals: *Doll Castle News,* P.O. Box 247, Washington, NJ 07882; *Miniature Collector,* 30595 Eight Mile, Livonia, MI 48152.

DOLL HOUSE

Bliss, paper-on-wood, chromolitho, opening door, front porch with hinged columns, blue-gray roof with dormer windows, overhanging roof with lattice work balcony, 2 rooms, printed carpeting and wallpaper, celluloid windows with lace curtains, electric lights, 2 scratch-built chairs, 16.5" h 1,700
Cohn, ranch house, litho tin, 1950s 75
Horsman, colonial, #6024-4, 1993, MIB . .10
Keystone, 2-story, litho masonite, 6 rooms, fireplace, stairs, and closet . .175
Marx, 2-story, litho tin, removable center chimney, 1964, 22" h 100
Marx, colonial mansion, Florida room . .175
Marx, miniature, 5.25" h, 8.25" l, 3" d 50
Meritoy, Cape Cod, 2-story 150
Ohio Art, Miniature Dollhouse, #95, litho tin, complete with 28 pcs of plastic furnishings, 3 x 8.5 x 5.25" 75
Playsteel, colonial, red roof 150
Rich, 2-story, litho fiberboard, 4 rooms, front stoop with benches 100

Schoenhut, bungalow, painted wood, blue, cream and orange trim, red roof, 11" h, 12.25" w, 12.75" d 275
T Cohn, Spanish style, double patio 125
Wolverine, 2-story, litho tin, 16" h, 21" l, 12" d 10
Wolverine, Country Cottage, #800, 1980s .40

DOLL HOUSE FURNISHINGS

Baby Carriage, Acme Plastics 7
Bathtub, Renwal .10
Bed, Young Decorator, Ideal 15
Bench, Little Hostess, Marx 15
Bird Cage, Commonwealth Plastics 30
Club Chair, Plasco 7
Coffee Table, Marx 5
Coffee Table, Plasco 5
Dresser, opening drawer, Renwal 12
Hamper, Renwal 5
High Chair, Young Decorator, Ideal 25
Lawn Bench, Ideal 20
Lawn Mower, Commonwealth Plastics . .15
Medicine Cabinet, Marx 25
Night Stand, Plasco 5
Night Stand, Renwal 5
Patio Umbrella, Ideal 20
Piano and Bench, Horsman, 2.5" h 10
Ping Pong Table, Marx 25
Playpen, Young Decorator, Ideal 15
Settee, Arcade, cast iron 80
Side Chair, Petite Princess, Ideal, red satin, MIB 20
Swimming Pool, T Cohn 50
Television, Plasco 30
Toilet, Renwal 10
Tricycle, Renwal 15
Triple Swing, Acme Plastics 50

Royal Grand Piano #4425-5 400, Petite Princess Fantasy Furniture, Ideal, $50.

DOLLS

People buy dolls primarily on the basis of sentiment and condition. Most begin by buying back the dolls they remember playing with as a child.

Speculating in dolls is risky business. The doll market is subject to crazes. The doll that is in today may be out tomorrow.

Place great emphasis on originality. Make certain that every doll you buy has the complete original costume. Ideally, the box or packaging also should be present. Remember, you are not buying these dolls to play with. You are buying them for display.

Clubs: Chatty Cathy Collector's Club, P.O. Box 4426, Seminole, FL 33775; Ideal Toy Co. Collector's Club, P.O. Box 623, Lexington, MA 02173; Liddle Kiddles Klub, 3639 Fourth Ave., La Crescenta, CA 91214; Madame Alexander Doll Club, PO Box 330, Mundelein, IL 60060; United Federation of Doll Clubs, 10920 N. Ambassador Dr., Std. 130, Kansas City, MO 64153.

Newsletters: *Betsy's* (McCall) *Fan Club Newsletter,* P.O. Box 946, Quincy, CA 95971; *Doll-E-Gram* (Black Dolls), P.O. Box 1212, Bellevue, WA 98009; *Rags* (Raggedy Ann and Andy), P.O. Box 823, Atlanta, GA 30301; *Toni Dolls Newsletter,* 7431-A LeMunyan Rd., Addison, NY 14801.

Periodicals: *Doll Reader,* 6405 Flank Dr., Harrisburg, PA 17112; *The Cloth Doll Magazine,* P.O. Box 2167, Lake Oswego, OR 97035.

Note: The dolls listed date from the 1930s through the present. For information about antique dolls, see Jan Foulke's *14th Blue Book Dolls and Values* (Hobby House Press: 1999) and Dawn Herlocher's, *200 Years of Dolls,* (Antique Trader Books: 1996).

Advertising, 7-Up Fresh Up Freddie, stuffed, flannel felt fabric body, painted vinyl head, c1958-59, 16" h ..175
Advertising, Cresota Flour, cloth, stuffed, 1972 25
Advertising, Green Giant, cloth, stuffed, orig unopened mailer bag, 1960s, 15" h 15

Theodor Recknagel, German, bisque head, jointed composition body, real hair wig, glass sleep eyes, painted long lashes, open mouth, mkd on back of head "21 Germany R7/A," 12" h, $325.

Advertising, Jack Frost Sugar, cloth, stuffed, blue snow suit with diamond, blue and white stocking cap, 1970s, 18" h 25
Advertising, Pillsbury Poppin' Fresh, soft knitted velour over foam core, white fabric scarf and baker's hat, molded mouth and nose, applied plastic eyes, 1972, 10" h.........................12
American Character, Sweet Sue, hard plastic, vinyl arms, walker, orig bridesmaid outfit, 30" h 400
Arranbee, Miss Coty, vinyl, rooted hair, sleep eyes, high heel feet, orig outfit, 1957, 10" h 125
Arranbee, Nancy Lee, composition, human hair wig, sleep eyes, orig outfit, c1939, 14" h 275
Cameo, Miss Peep, vinyl, pin-jointed arms and legs, 1960s, 18" h 45
Cosmopolitan, Little Miss Ginger, vinyl, jointed waist, rooted hair, sleep eyes, high heel feet, orig outfit, 1957, 10.5" h 100
Effanbee, Heartbeat Baby, composition and cloth, clockwork mechanism, 1942, 17" h 150
Effanbee, Patsy Lou, composition, mohair wig, sleep eyes, metal heart bracelet, orig outfit, c1931, 22" h 550
Horsman, Tiny Tears, vinyl body, hard plastic head, orig outfit, 1950s, 11" h .175
Horsman, Baby Dimples, composition and cloth, blue steel sleep eyes, open mouth with teeth and tongue, early 1930s, 22" h 125

Horsman, Baby Precious, vinyl, rooted
hair, sleep eys, orig outfit, 1950s 40
Horsman, Poor Pitiful Pearl, vinyl, rooted saran hair, orig outfit, c1963, 18" h . .60
Ideal, Deanna Durbin, composition body,
jointed, blue-green sleep eyes, open
smiling mouth, dark brown human
hair wig, orig pink and lavender flowered print dress, hoop petticoat,
socks, and shoes, c1938, 15" h 200
Ideal, Crissy, vinyl body, swivel waist,
growing hair, orig outfit and box,
c1969, 18" h 50
Ideal, Little Miss Revlon, vinyl, black
rooted hair, jointed waist, high heel
feet, orig red and white polka dot
dress, 10.5" h 100
Ideal, Snoozie, cloth body, vinyl arms
and legs, blonde rooted saran hair,
sleep eyes, c1964, 20" h 55
Kathe Kruse, boy, brown hair and eyes,
cotton and felt Bavarian outfit,
black leather shoes, c1949, 14" h . .2,300
Kathe Kruse, girl, cloth body, hard
plastic head, painted eyes, closed
mouth, blonde mohair wig, jointed
shoulders and hips, period cotton
outfit, leather sandals, partial tag,
1950s, 20" h 748
Kathe Kruse, girl, light brown painted
hair and eyes, narrow hips, rayon
dress hat and underwear, 1930s,
17" h 1,800

*Sun Rubber, 1-pc body, molded head with
painted hair and open nurser mouth,
molded diaper, shoes, and socks, mkd
"9A/TOD-L-TOT, ©The Sun Rubber Co
Barberton, O. U.S.A.," 10.5" h, $30.*

Lenci, girl, felt body, brown painted eyes
facing left, blonde mohair wig, felt
coral and gray dress, cape, and hat,
1930s, 12" h 80
Madame Alexander, Scarlet O'Hara,
composition body, jointed at neck,
shoulders, and hips, green sleep
eyes, closed mouth, black mohair
wig, orig costume, cloth label, 1937,
17.5" h 500
Mattel, Baby Skates, vinyl, painted fea-
tures, 1983, 16" h 40
Mattel, Sister Belle, cloth body, yarn
hair, pull-string talker, c1960s, 16" h .175
Natural, Bluette, stuffed vinyl body with
limbs, vinyl head, sleep eyes, rooted
hair, orig outfit, 1955, 20" h 35
Uneeda, I Love You Dolly, vinyl, cloth
body, inset eyes with lashes, 1980,
14" h 15
Vogue, Brikette, vinyl, ball-jointed swiv-
el waist, orange hair, green flirty
sleep eyes, c1959, 22" h 65
Vogue, Ginny, hard plastic, painted
lashes, walker, orig outfit and box,
1950s, 7.5" h .350
Vogue, Jill, hard plastic, sleep eyes,
orig record hop yellow felt skirt,
black jersey top, c1958, 10.5" h 175

DOORSTOPS

Cast-iron doorstops have gone through
a number of collecting crazes over the past
twenty years. The last craze occurred just a
few years ago, raising the prices to such a
level that doorstops are more likely to be
found at antiques shows than at flea markets.

Reproductions abound. A few helpful
clues are: check size (many reproductions
are slightly smaller than the period piece);
check detail (the less detail, the more suspicious you need to be); and check rust
(bright orange rust indicates a new piece).

Club: Doorstop Collectors of America, 2413
Madison Ave., Vineland, NJ 08630

Note: Doorstops listed are cast iron unless
otherwise noted.

Aunt Jemima, single wedge, 7.5 x 3.75" .350
Black Cat, full figure, 7 x 3.75" 130

Rabbit, cast iron, tan body, green grass, Bradley & Hubbard, sgd "B&H 7800," 15.25" h, $400.

Bulldog, Hubley, full figure, 4.625 x 8.5" .325
Cocker Spaniel, mkd "VA Metalcrafters, Waynesboro VA Dream Boy 18-7 1949," wedge back, 9 x 7" 175
Colonial Woman with Muff, mkd "27," 11.5 x 6.5" 275
Conestoga Wagon, 8 x 11" 100
Cottage in the Woods, National Foundry, 4.625 x 10" 325
Daisy Bowl, Hubley, 7.5 x 5.75" 150
Duck, Hubley, wedged back, 5 x 3.75" ..450
Dutch Girl, Judd Co, mkd "1255," 7.125 x 5.75" 225
Fireplace, Eastern Specialty Co, 6.25 x 8" 275
Flower Basket, Bradley & Hubbard, mkd "B&H," 8.625 x 5" 450
Flower Basket, Hubley, mkd "475," 7.25 x 7" 350
Fox Terrier, full figure, 8.5 x 8.75" 100
Gnome, full figure, 13.25 x 6.5" 225
High Heel Shoe 75
Irish Setter, Hubley, full figure, 8.5 x 15.5" 325
Little Red Riding Hood with Wolf, National Foundry, 7.25 x 5.375" 450
Minuet Girl, Judd Co, mkd "1278," 8.5 x 5" 250
Old Ironsides, Kleistone Rubber Specialties, mkd "Old Ironsides," 11 x 8" 175
Parrot on Perch, 11.5 x 4.75" 90
Pied Piper, 7.25 x 5" 375
Poppies and Snapdragons, Hubley, mkd "484," 7.5 x 5" 325
Rabbit by Fence, Albany Foundry, mkd "59," 6.875 x 8.125" 450
Tulip Pot, National Foundry, 8.25 x 7" ...250
Welsh Corgi, Bradley & Hubbard, 8.25 x 5.875" 300
Whippet, Creation Co, 8 x 8.5" 250

DRINKING GLASSES

It is time to start dealing seriously with promotional drinking glasses given away by fast-food restaurants, garages, and other merchants. This category also includes drinking glasses that start out life as product containers.

Most glasses are issued in a series. If you collect one, you better plan on keeping at it until you have the complete series. Also, many of the promotions are regional. A collector in Denver is not likely to find a Philadelphia Eagles glass at his favorite restaurant.

Just a few washings in a dishwasher can cause a major change in the color on promotional drinking glasses. Collectors insist on unused, unwashed glasses whenever possible. Get the glass, and drink your drink out of a paper cup.

Newsletter: *Collector Glass News,* P.O. Box 308, Slippery Rock, PA 16057.

Arby's, Bicentennial, General Bullwinkle Crosses the Delaware, 6" h 3
Aunt Fanny's Cabin's Mint Julip, black Americana theme 3
Batman, "Zok, Whack, Craack," gray and blue, 1960s, 5" h 12
Burger Chef, Endangered Species series, eagle 7
Burger Chef, Friendly Monsters series, Burgerini's rabbit hops away, 1977 ...30
California Raisins, "Dancing Raisins," Indiana Glass Co, 5.25" h 9

Endangered Species, World Wildlife Fund, #2 Black Rhino, 1985, 4" h, $2.

Space Mouse, Walter Lantz, Pepsi, $375. —Photo courtesy *Collector Glass News.*

Centennial Belles 1866-1966, Milleville, NJ, blue with Victorian lady on front . .3
Chicago Daily Tribune, "Great Sea Victory for America," 5.5" h 3
Daytona Beach, ruby glass, 5" h 8
Dr Pepper, Star Trek, Dr McCoy, 1976 . . .15
Faygo Soda, 50th Anniversary, gold logos, 4.375" h 4
Keebler, 135th Anniversary 3
Klondike 75th Anniversary, Steinberger's Beverages, 1873-1948, blue and white, 3.5" h .6
Magic Mountain, Porky and Petunia with cotton candy, 1989 24
Margo Bonded Root Beer, red with syrup line, 4.375" h 16
Montreal Expos, red, white, and blue logo, 4.75" h .3
National Bohemian Beer, red, man's face, 4.375" h 5
National Flag Foundation, Pedestal Series III: British Union 8
Oregon State Fair 100th Anniversary, Governor Mark Hatfield, 1965 8
Pizza Hut, Popples, Puffball Popple 3
Popeye's Fried Chicken, 1978 Sports Series: Popeye 14
Pure Oil, Historic Auto Series, 1914 Rambler 4
Remember Pearl Harbor, Dec 7, 1941, red, white, and blue, 4.75" h 7
Six Flags, Tweety, Sylvester, Bugs, and Taz on palm tree beach, Warner Bros, 1987, 5.75" h .15
Starkist, Charlie the Tuna, smoke glass ftd tumbler, 4.75" h 3
Swartz Peanut Butter, WWF's Jake the Snake 7
Welch's, Flintstones, Fred in sports car, orange, 1962 .8

White Castle, 70th Anniversary, 1921-1991, etched logo 10

DRUGSTORE COLLECTIBLES

Corner drugstores, especially those with a soda fountain, were major hangouts in almost every small town in the United States. Almost all of them dispensed much more than medically related products. They were the 7-11's of their era.

This category documents the wide variety of material that you could acquire in a drugstore. It barely scratches the surface. This is a new collecting approach that has real promise.

Bottle, J W Evans Prescription Druggist, Clinton, IA 7
Cabinet, metal, for storage of corn and bunion plasters, Johnson & Johnson Co, 12.75" h, 13" w 200
Calendar, 1901, Hood's Sarsaparilla, "Patience," full pad, ©1900 C I Hood & Co, Lowell, MA, 6.75" h, 9.75" w . . .100
Calendar, 1902, Frank H Burlin, Druggist, Tomah, WI 10
Display, Floress Lipstick and Nail Lacquers, diecut litho cardboard, 30" h, 40" w 30
Display, Pepto-Bismol, "For Upset Stomach," diecut cardboard, boy seated with dog, product image in lower left, Norwich Parmacal Co Ltd, Toronto, Canada, 31.5" h, 31" w 125
Display, Unguentine For Burns, litho cardboard, "A Norwich Product," woman rubbing product on sunburn, 35" h, 22.5" w 100

Bottle, Toneco Stomach Bitters, emb glass, paper label, with contents, 9.5" h, 2.75" w, $100. —Photo courtesy Collectors Auction Services.

Thermometer, Squirt Soda adv, emb tin, self-framed, 13.5" h, 5.75" w, $160. —Photo courtesy Collectors Auction Services.

Display, Victory Hair Pins, cardboard, complete with 12 boxes mkd "10 cents," 9 x 7 x 8" 45

Flange Sign, Black-Draught, "A Good Laxative," metal, 6.5" h, 12" w 100

Jar, Aspirin, porcelain, scroll work with snake sumbols surrounding "Aspirin," gold accents 15

Jar, Dent's Toothache Gum, tapered form, etched, ribbed pressed glass lid, 12"h 550

Jar, Dr. Miles Anti Pain Pills Cure Headaches, beveled corners, ground lip with swirl design, 16.5" h 650

Jar, Orris Tooth Powder, cylindrical, paper label, faceted ball knob on lid, 12" h 50

Mortar and Pestle, ceramic, gold knob at top, gold "RX," Gilman Bros Inc, Boston, MA, 15" h, 12.5" d 450

Mortar and Pestle, pewter, 3.75" h, 2.75" d 15

Mug, Liggett's Drugstore, white china, blue pinstripe and logo 12

Pill Box, Oak Park Drugstore, 1931 5

Pill Machine, wood and brass construction, grooved, c1870, 15.5" top, 7.5 x 15" base 225

Postcard, "World's Most Unusual Drug Store, Webb's City, St Petersburg, FL, unused, 1940 5

Sign, Chamberlain's Cough Remedy, cardboard, 3-sided, hanging, package depicted on sides, 10" 125

Sign, Drugs and Soda, trapezoidal, crinkled ground, orig copper frame, 29 x 10.5" 725

Sign, Morses' Duchess Filled Candies, cardboard, ©1924 Niagara Litho Co, 34 x 24" 550

Sign, Prescriptions, leaded glass, milk glass and amber colored glass, arched frame, 15.5" h, 63.5" w 250

Sign, Rogers Drugs, lightup, leaded glass, metal housing in center, 27" h, 63" w, 8" d 650

Tip Tray, "Jesse L Ross & Co, Druggists, Waynesburg, PA" imp on bottom, full color illus, mkd "H. D. Beach Co., Coshocton, Ohio No. 1," 16.75" l, 13.75" w, .75" d 250

Tip Tray, Resinol Soap and Ointment, woman with flowing hair, 4.25" d 200

EASTER COLLECTIBLES

Now that Christmas and Halloween collectibles have been collected to death, holiday collectors are finally turning their attentions to Easter. The old Easter bonnet still hangs in the Clothing Collectibles closet, but chicken and rabbit collectors now have to contend with Easter enthusiasts for their favorite animal collectible.

Advertising Tear Sheet, Quaker State Motor Oil, bunny and egg beside can, "Finest Easter gift you can give your car," 10 x 13" 5

Basket, wood, painted flowers, "Made in Germany" paper label on base, 6" d, 10" h with handle 20

Brochure, Paas Dye Company, fold-out, full color illus of Easter egg color kits and price list, 1950s, 11" h 4

Basket, litho tin, nursery rhyme motif, Chein, late 1950s, 7.75" d, $45. —Photo courtesy Ray Morykan Auctions.

*Child's Book,
Peter Rabbit
Story Book,
#507, 45 pp, $8.*

Cake Pan, egg shaped, Wilton, 1983,
  8.5 x 12" 4
Candy Container, paperboard, egg, full
  color illus, 8" l .18
Candy Container, papier-mâché, rabbit
  standing next to basket with flowers,
  yellow and white paint, c1930-40s,
  8" h, 5.5" w 30
Chocolate Mold, standing rabbit, tin,
  2-part mold with separate 2-part molds
  for ears and forelegs, mkd "Anton
  Reiche, Dresden, Germany," 18.5" h .225
Figure, egg, Goebel, #8 "The Lily," made
  in Germany 4
Figure, rabbit, Annalee, 1968, 21" h 10
Greeting Card, "Happy Easter," Minnie
  Mouse, Hallmark, 5.25" h 18
Hat, pink velvet and sheer fabric flowers,
  pink pearl accents, pink velvet ribbon
  forming flat bow at front, pink netting . .9
Magazine, *Golden Magazine*, Apr 1966,
  Jumping Jackrabbit cut-out, Heidi's
  Hairdo's by Neva Schultz, and Easter
  egg decorations with Betty Crocker . . .5
Magazine, *Ideals*, Easter edition, 1955-61,
  7 issues 5
Mask, rabbit, heavy papier-mâché,
  11" h 20
Pez Dispenser, lamb, no feet 7
Planter, chick and bunny in Easter egg,
  Inarco, 1962, 5.25" h 6
Postcard, "A Happy Easter," daisies,
  2 chicks, emb, used, 1914 4
Postcard, chick atop flower covered
  egg, 1910 5
Postcard, rabbits and hatbox, ©S Berg-
  man, postmarked 1918 4
Pull Toy, plastic, rooster on 4 wheels,
  yellow and red, red base with green
  wheels, 6 x 4" .28

Record, 78 rpm, *The Easter Bunny Party/
  Having Fun at the Easter Bunny Party*,
  Voco, 1948 7
Sheet Music, *Easter Parade,* Irving
  Berlin 4
Sign, "Chick-Chick Easter Egg Dye,"
  litho paper, 7.5 x 14.25" 65
Windup, rabbit, fur covered, hops, mkd
  "Japan," 5" h 60

EGGBEATERS

America has borne a grudge against
eggs for decades—evidence the innumerable gadgets invented for beating them.
There were well over 1,000 patents issued
for eggbeaters since 1856. Any collector
should be able to assemble a large collection of eggbeaters without any duplication.

A & J, metal, Big Bingo, 11.75" h 15
A & J, metal, butterscotch Bakelite
  handle, 12.5" h 12
A & J, metal, metal, wood handle,
  13.5" h 15
Alexander & Littlefield Co, Biltrite, 1917,
  9.75" h 45
Androck, stainless steel, red Bakelite
  handle, 12.5" h .6
Androck, Turbine Egg Beatery, 10" h 25
Archimedes Type, New England Egg
  Beater and Mixer, 9.75" h 125
Archimedes Type, Up To Date Egg
  Cream Whip, 1906, 11.5" h 300
Aurelius, Master Egg Beater, 11.5" h . . .450
Belmont Egg Beater, 9.5" h 1,500
Blisscraft of Hollywood, plastic, 12" h . . .75
Chico, Wonder, adjustable D-handle,
  12.25" h 30
Dover, Boston Egg Beater, metal, 10" h . .85
Dunlap, Sanitary Cream & Egg Whip,
  1906, 12.5" h 75

*Archimedes-type wavy dasher, mkd
"Horlick's," adv promotion, c1910, 9.5" l,
$30.*

Dover, steel handle, slotted dashers,
10.5" h 125
Ekco, Maid of Honor, with box, 11.5" h . . .35
Holy-Lyon, egg beater and cream whip,
flanged handle for funnel, 10.5" h 55
Instant Whip, aluminum, 10.5" h 35
Keystone, wall mount, glass jar, 1 qt,
7.25" h 150
Krasberg, Atom Whip, 11.75" h 30
Monroe Bros, Star Egg Beater, 1859,
10.75" h 900
National, Clipper, 1887, 13" h 375
Standard, cast iron, 1880, 9.75" h 350
Taplin, Light Running, metal, table
mount, wood platform, 16.5" h 150
United Royalty, stainless steel, #7, 1921 .10
White and Hallock, Presto Whip, 11.75" h .30
White and Hallock, Whippit, 13.5" h 20

EGGCUPS

Where modern Americans would be hard-pressed to recognize, let alone know how to use, an eggcup, their European counterparts still utilize the form as an everyday breakfast utensil. Their greatest period of popularity in America was between 1875 and 1950—long before cholesterol became a four-letter word.

Collectors place a premium on character eggcups. You can make a great collection consisting of eggcups from breakfast services of hotels, railroads, steamships, or restaurants. As tourists, many of our ancestors had a bad case of sticky fingers.

Club: Eggcup Collectors' Club, 67 Stevens Ave., Old Bridge, NJ 08857.

Blown Glass, clear optic, honeycomb
pattern, blue foot, 1890-1910 90
Blown Glass, yellow opalescent, applied
blue threading, c1790-1800 250
Character, Little Miss Muffet, ceramic,
white, gold rim 8
Character, Mother Goose, ceramic,
yellow 15
Czechoslovakian, black and white geo-
metric design on blue and white
ground, with integral saucer, 1930s . .25
Figural, elephant, kneeling, ceramic,
white, beige, orange, and green,
made in Japan 15

*Homer Laughlin,
Virginia Rose, $8.*

Figural, fish, ceramic, black and white . .12
Figural, rocking horse, ceramic, white,
orange, and black 12
Figural, soldier, wood, red jacket, black
busby, collar, and pants, white belt
and base 5
Figural, squirrel, beside cup, ceramic,
green, white, and brown 8
Goebel, chicken in basket, 1950s 55
Japan, hp, boat crossing water, white,
red, green, and pink, 2.25" h 12
Johnson Bros, Old Britain Castles,
white, brown and yellow highlights . . .6
McKee, double, blue chalaine 30
Noritake, white, gold rim, pink roses,
green foliage 12
Opalescent, double, oval silhouette of
courting Colonial couple, flared base . .12
Pattern Glass, Flat Diamond and Panel,
blue opaque 450
Pattern Glass, Frosted Leaf 100
Pattern Glass, Morning Glory 125
Pattern Glass, Thousand Eye, 3-knob,
blue 70
Plastic, chicken and open egg, 1940s 5
Royal Winton, double, chintz, Old Cot-
tage pattern, 1930s 125

ELEPHANT COLLECTIBLES

Public television's unending series of documentaries on African wildlife has destroyed the fascination with wild animals. By the time parents take their children to the zoo or circus, elephants are old hat, blase. Boo, hiss to public television—those pompous pachyderms. We want the mystery and excitement of wildlife returned to us.

Things were different for the pre-television generations. The elephant held a fascination that is difficult for us to comprehend. When Barnum brought Jumbo from England to America, English children (and a fair number of adults) wept.

There are a few elephant-related political collectibles listed. It is hard to escape the G.O.P. standard bearer. However, real elephant collectors focus on the magnificent beasts themselves or cartoon representations ranging from Dumbo to Colonel Hathi.

Club: The National Elephant Collector's Society, 380 Medford St., Somerville, MA 02145.

Newsletter: *Jumbo Jargon,* 1002 W. 25th St., Erie, PA 16502.

Advertising Tear Sheet, Top Value
　stamps, elephant walking in snow,
　10 x 13" 5
Ashtray, yellow paint 20
Bank, cast iron, 4 x 3" 30
Bank, chalkware, pink, 6.25" h, 3.75"
　base 8
Bell, leaded glass, elephant handle 3
Book, *Jerry Bob and the Bob-Tailed
　Elephant,* Leo Edwards, 1929 5
Bottle, figural, emb "Old Sol," 8.5" h,
　3" w 30
Bottle Opener, cast iron, elephant laugh-
　ing, 3" h, 2" w .30
Cookie Jar, elephant standing, red and
　black highlights on white ground,
　Shawnee 40
Cookie Jar, elephant wearing sailor hat,
　Twin Winton, 8.5" h 20

Bank, cast iron, Arcade, 1910–32, 2.75" h, 4.625" l, $85. —Photo courtesy Gene Harris Antique Auction Center, Inc.

Creamer, porcelain, 5"h 3
Creamer, upraised head and nose, Red
　Wing, 5 x 3 x 2.5" 130
Figure, ceramic, 1934 World's Fair,
　Royal Haeger, 3" h, 5" l 20
Figure, glass, Mosser, 2" h 10
Figure, wood, hand carved, 6" h 5
Game, Feed the Elephant, Cadaco, 1952 . .10
Napkin Ring, plastic, imp "DP," 2" h,
　3.5" l 45
Pie Bird, mkd "Nutbrown Pie Funnel/
　Made in England," 1949, 3.25" h 100
Planter, ceramic, green ears and hind
　legs, white tusks, brown trunk and
　toenails, black and white eyes, some
　brown speckling, 5" h, 6" l 4
Planter, ceramic, elephant standing
　next to bush with Indian rider, Royal
　Haeger, 10" h, 12" w 22
Planter, ceramic, Napco, #36760, 6.75" h . . .6
Snuff Bottle, porcelain, 2.25" h 20
Stuffed Toy, plush, Dakin, 1971, 12" h 15
Toothpick Holder, vaseline glass, Boyd,
　2.5" h, 4" w 10

ELONGATED COINS

Although the elongation of coinage first began in 1893 at the Columbian Exposition in Chicago as souvenirs of that event, the revival of producing and collecting elongated coins began in earnest in the early 1960s. Initially available to the hobbyists and souvenir collectors from a few private roller/producers, the elongation of coins advanced by way of commercial enterprises beginning in 1976 during the Bicentennial celebration. Automated vending rolling machines producing souvenirs are all over the United States and abroad, from historical sites to national parks and amusement areas.

Elongated coins are now on the Internet. Most of the coins are trading and since so many are being produced, there is little value in them. The more serious collectors still deal with "Classic" specimens and of the older productions.

The values for older antique specimens, such as the Lord's Prayer and Masonic emblem, range from $50 upwards to $350. Both are over 125 years old.

For further information on elongated coins, old and modern, contact the advisor listed below.

Advisor: Angelo A. Rosato, 70 Grove St., New Milford, CT, 06776, e-mail: angrospub@aol.com

ELVIS

Elvis Presley was hot, is hot, and promises to be hot well into the future. Elvis collectibles are bought from the heart, not the head. A great deal of totally tacky material has been forgiven by his devoted fans.

Elvis material breaks down into two groups: (1) items licensed while Elvis was alive and (2) items licensed after his death. The latter are known as "fantasy" items. Fantasy Elvis is collectible but real value lies in the material licensed during his lifetime.

Beware of any limited edition Elvis items. They were manufactured in such large numbers that the long-term prospects for appreciation in value are very poor. If you love an item, fine. If you expect it to pay for your retirement, forget it.

Club: Elvis Forever TCB Fan Club, P.O. Box 1066, Pinellas Park, FL 33281.

Comb, hard plastic, clear viny panel on top left with opening for stiff glossy picture of Elvis, facsimile signature, Dupont, 1950s, 1.5 x 5.5" 50
Fan Club Membership Card, inset black and white photo, typed name or orig recipient with facsimile signature, mailing address on reverse, c1956, 2.25 x 3.75" 35
Flicker Key Chain, plastic, full figure images of Elvis singing holding guitar and microphone, c1956, 2 x 2.75" 45
Floater Pen, plastic, "Loving You/Elvis Presley Fan Club" and yellow music notes on gray ground, Graceland illus with Elvis image, 1960s, 8" l 50
Hat, cloth, black top and brim, white center with color illus of Elvis, hound dog, records, and song titles, orig tag mkd "Magnet Hat and Cap Corp," ©1956 Elvis Presley Enterprises 100

Magazine, *Photoplay*, Mar 1960, Vol 57, #3, features Welcome Home Elvis contest, 8.5 x 10.75" 20
Magazine, *Private Lives*, Dec 1956, Vol 1, #11, 5 pp article "Elvis Presley: Music to Sin By," black and white photos, 8 x 10.5" 50
Photograph, Elvis singing and playing guitar, facsimile signature, c1956, 2.5 x 3.5" 28
Pinback Button, full color photo of Elvis wearing green shirt, blue facsimile signature, ©1956 Elvis Presley Enterprises, 3" d 35
Poster, Blue Hawaii, bathing suit-clad women wearing leis and playing ukeleles, 1961, 14 x 22" 50
Poster, Kissin' Cousins, Elvis with hillbilly girls, 1964, 27 x 41" 75
Record, *Blue Suede Shoes/ Tutti Fruitti/ I Got A Woman/Just Because*, 45 rpm, EPA-747, black and white photos on both sides of sleeve, pink and green front text, ©1956 RCA Victor 50
Record, *Don't Be Cruel/Hound Dog*, 45 rpm, front and back photos with facsimile signature, 1956 35
Sheet Music, *Hard Headed Woman*, ©1958 Gladys Music Inc, 9 x 12" 10
Sign, "Elvis Concert Tickets/On Sale Now," paper, red, white, and blue, 1970s, 8 x 22" .50

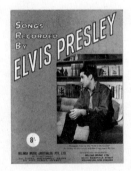

Sheet Music Book, Songs Recorded by Elvis Presley, *Belinda Music Pty, Ltd, Australia*, ©1962, 32 pp, 10 songs, movie photos, $25.

ENESCO

Enesco's product line includes more than 12,000 gift, collectible, and home accent items including the Precious Moments and Cherished Teddies collection. It also markets licensed gifts and collectibles such as Lilliput Lane and David Winter Cottages.

Enesco became a wholly-owned subsidiary of Westfield, Massachusetts-based Stanhome, Inc., a multinational corporation, in 1983. In 1997 The Bradford Group entered into a long-term licensing agreement to market the product lines of Stanhome's subsidiary, Enesco Giftware Group. In 1998 Stanhome, Inc., changed its name to Enesco Group, Inc. Today, Enesco products are distributed in more than thirty countries including Japan, Mexico, and Germany.

Note: Enesco sponsors collector clubs for Cherished Teddies, Christmas ornaments, David Winter Cottages, Memories of Yesterday, and Precious Moments.

Head Vase, 6" h, $75. —Photo courtesy Gene Harris Antique Auction Center, Inc.

Bookends, pr, frogs and flies, 16" h, 4.5" w .20
Candlesticks, pr, swans 25
Cardholder, granny 25
Coffee Cup, butterfly and flowers, mkd
 "Nature Garden Society," 1975, 4" h . . .3
Cookie Jar, Betsy Ross 225
Cookie Jar, space shuttle, 16.5" l, 9.5" w .40
Cutting Board, Dutch boy and girl,
 "Kissin' Don't Last, Cookin' Do" 45
Earring Tree, purple, white lace edge,
 1967, 9" h 10
Figurine, Terrier, 3" h, 5" l 75
Napkin Holder, George Washington
 holding scroll "We the people of the
 United States," 5.75" h 18
Napkin Holder, Snow White 200
Pincushion, Betsy Ross, 4.5" h 65
Pitcher, pink cherry blossoms with pea-
 green tree in relief, 7.5" h 6
Planter, tree house, 5 x 5" 5
Recipe Holder, George Washington 65
Salt and Pepper Shakers, pr, Dutch boy
 and girl, #R-5816, blue and white 6
Salt and Pepper Shakers, pr, egg-shaped,
 violets on white ground, gold trim 15
Salt and Pepper Shakers, pr, Washington
 holding scrolled Bill of Rights, 4.5" h . .20
Salt and Pepper Shakers, pr, Snappy
 the Snail 15
Salt and Pepper Shakers, pr, white
 ducks, 1988, 2.75" h 6
Spoon Holder, Betsy Ross, 5.75" h 20
Spoon Rest, granny, 6.75" h 18
Spoon Rest, Snappy the Snail 12
Tea Bag Holder, snail 6
Teapot, Creamer, and Sugar, Dutch boy
 and girl 125
Toothpick Holder, Dutch boy and girl 30
Toothpick Holder, George Washington,
 4.5" h 35
Trinket Box, figural pineapple, gold trim,
 2.25" h, 3" l 4
Trinket Box, figural rabbit, 1996 10

ERTL BANKS

This is another of those highly speculative areas that are addressed as the need arises. The 1980s and 1990s saw a surge in the number of cast-iron banks produced by several companies, Ertl being the most dominant. These banks were often made to commemorate special events or used as promotions or fundraising efforts for local charities.

Most of the Ertl banks were recently manufactured in Hong Kong. They should only be purchased if in fine condition or better and only if the originally packaging is included. All of the banks are marked and numbered. Avoid any that are not marked. The serial numbers and series numbers are important in cataloging and pricing these items.

Club: Ertl Collectors Club, P.O. Box 500, Dyersville, IA 52040.

A&W Rootbeer #3, 1918 Ford Barrel,
#2975, 1992 65
Abbott Laboratories, 1912 Ford, #2775,
1992 25
Ace Hardware #4, 1913 Ford, #9409,
1992 50
Alex Cooper Auctioneers, 1913 Ford,
#9201, 1984 28
American Red Cross #5, 1905 Ford,
#9685, 1989 35
Amoco 100th Anniversary, 1917 Ford,
#9745, 1989 35
Arm & Hammer, 1913 Ford, #9486, 1987 ..75
Armorall, 1905 Ford, #9783, 1991 32
Asheville Office Supply, 1932 Ford,
#1355, 1992 28
Aunt Millie's 95th Anniversary, 1931
Hawkeye, #H170, 1996 25
Baltimore Gas & Electric, 1918 Ford,
#9870, 1988 34
Barq's Rootbeer #1, 1913 Ford, #9826,
1988 75
C R Friendly Stores, 1917 Ford, #9699,
1989 25
Campbells Pork and Beans, 1918 Ford,
#9184, 1987 50
Campbells Soup, 1951 GMC, #F015,
1995 45
Carl's Chicken Barbeque, Step Van,
#9089, 1989 32
Carnation, 1913 Ford, #9178, 1987 30
Central Hawkeye Gas Engine, 1905 Ford,
#9196, 1987 22
Chambersburg Fire Museum #2, 1913
Ford, #3628 35
Charlter Oak Centennial, 1918 Ford,
#9031, 1989 22
Chemical Bank, 1905 Ford, #1662, 1990 ..22

Allied Van Lines, 1917 Model T Van, $20.

Chicago Tribune, 1917 Ford, #9102, 1988 ..45
Churchill Trucking Company, 1926 Mack,
#9474, 1991 30
Coast To Coast Hardware, 1905 Ford,
#9742, 1988 20
Connecticut State Police, 1931 Hawkeye/
Wrecker, #3768, 1993 55
Cretors Popcorn, 1923 Chevy, #B224,
1994 45
Cumberland Val Tractor Pull, 1960 Ford
Pickup, #B288, 1994 22
Cushman Motor Scooter Club #2, 1938
Chevy, #B076, 1994 25
Dallas Police, 1951 GMC, #B608, 1994 ...35
Dearborn Inn, 1913 Ford, #9684, 1991 15
Detroit News, 1913 Ford, #1667, 1983 65
Deutz-Allis, 1905 Ford, #2217, 1989 15
Domtar Gypsum, 1913 Ford, #9824, 1989 ..15
Dr. Pepper, 1905 Ford, #9739, 1988 65
Dreyers Ice Cream, 1905 Ford, #9671,
1989 65
Dubuque Iowa, 1905 Ford, #9503, 1986 ..18
East Buchanan Iowa, 1913 Ford, #9360,
1985 15
Edys Ice Cream, 1905 Ford, #9644, 1989 ..55
Ertl Toys, 1925 Kenworth, #B069, 1995 ...20
Graves Truck Line, 1931 Hawkeye, #9750,
1992 30
Greene Township Lions Club, PA, 1912
Ford, #7557, 1992 22
Gulf Oil, 1925 KW/Tanker, #9241, 1993 ...34
Harper Charity Cruise, 1959 Chevy
Sedan Delivery, #19620, 1999 26
Hill's Ford #5, 1951 Ford Pickup, #B862,
1997 25
IGA, Volkswagen Conv, #19627, 1999 24
J F Good Company, 1926 Mack, #9332,
1989 20
Jewel Tea Company, 1931 Ford Panel,
#2584, 1994 75
Mopar, Dodge Brothers #3, 1925 KW/
Wrecker, #B510, 1994 40
Napa Auto Parts, 1952 Chevy Pickup,
#23054, 1999 35
Oil Can Henry #1, 1931 Hawkeye/Tanker,
#9897, 1991 65
Penn State Nittany Lions, 1949 Mercury
Custom, #21013, 1999 24
Pepsi-Cola, 1964 Dodge Van, #91501,
1999 27
Popsicle, 1916 Studebaker Panel, #25049,
1999 27

FANS, ELECTRIC

Many people think they have a gold mine when they come across a brass bladed fan. This is most often not the case. Plenty of common mass-produced brass bladed fans are still available. Condition determines price. If, the paint is very good and the brass is polished, the price may jump up to 50% compared to a similar fan in tarnished/rusty condition.

The most desirable fans are older and rarer models with features such as Art Deco design, exposed coils, a light bulb mounted on top of the motor, and use of an alternate power source.

Club: American Fan Collectors Assoc., P.O. Box 5473, Sarasota, FL 34277.
Note: Fans listed in good condition.

EMERSON

444A, Northwind, 2-speed, pot metal cast base, black finish, gold painted blades, 1926, 8" blades 30
1010, ornate motor attached to base by trunnion, formed brass wire guard with large open center ring, brass scalloped Parker blades attached to cast iron hub, 1902-05, 12" blades . . .300
1120, 1903-1904, 16" blades 750
14644, non-oscillator, 3-speed, trunnion motor, brass scalloped Parker blades, 1911-12, 8" blades 175

Barber/Coleman (Barcol), Bakelite base and motor housing, aluminum guard and airplane-style blade, off-center motor, 1920-30s, $30.

1510, open ring S guard, ornate ribbed base, 1906-09, 12" blades 200
1820, ornate motor, S-ring design guard, 1908-1909, 16" blades 450
19646, steel guard, stamped steel hub, brass blades, 1914-18, 12" blades . . .150
27666, 3-speed, oscillator, cast iron base and motor housing, 1919-22, 16" blades 150
29645, 3-speed, oscillator, brass blades, formed steel guard, 1922-25, 9" blades 65
5110, Trojan, ornate ribbed base with cast iron trunnion, brass guard, 1904-05, 12" blades 350
PI 241, 1899-1900, 12" blades 350
Junior, 1925-29, 9" blades 45

GENERAL ELECTRIC

34017, non-oscillating, cast iron base, c1922, 12" blades 75
181327, AK-Ford D, S-wire guard attached to cast iron pancake motor, 1903, 12" blades 250
19X263, oscillator, 2-speed slide switch, c1928, 10" blades 25
236327, Whiz, non-oscillating, polished brass blades, 1-speed toggle switch at base, hunter green, c1924, 9" blades 35
265731, sheet brass blades, pancake motor, 1906, 12" blades 175
861916, kidney oscillator, heavy sheet brass blades with polished brass finish, c1913, 12" blades 250
905585, 1909, 12" blades 125

WESTINGHOUSE

1648641, 3-speed, oscillator, stamped steel motor housing and base, steel open S wire guard, c1923, 12" blades .75
457680, 3-speed, oscillator, stamped steel blades, motor housing and base, 1924, 10" blades 25
W134110, 3-speed slide switch, gun blue brass finish, thin brass wire guard, sheet brass blades, 1912, 8" blades 150
Tank Motor, painted badge with makers name, 1912, 12" blades 100
Vane Oscillator, oscillator, cast iron base, 1911, 12" blades 550

Singer, Ribbonaire, cloth blades, Bakelite housing, 1920s-30s, $55.

Whirlwind, cast iron base, universal
    motor, c1922, 9" blades 25
Whirlwind, stamped steel blades, c1919,
    9" blades 25

OTHER

Berstead Mfg, Eskimo, 45-K, 3-speed,
    oscillator, cast iron base, c1946, 12"
    blades 20
Century/Hunter, 601, c1939, 10" blades . .25
Gilbert, Art Deco, cast iron base, chrome-
    plated guard, blades, and motor hous-
    ing, c1936, 12" blades 75
Ideal, 2-speed, non-oscillator, universal
    motor, c1921, 10" blades 45
Peerless, 240520, 3-speed, oscillator,
    cast iron motor housing and base,
    polished sheet brass blades, c1916,
    10" blades 45
R & M, 1401, cast iron motor, trunnion,
    and base, brass blades and guard,
    1910, 12" blades 150

FARM COLLECTIBLES

The agrarian myth of the rugged individual pitting his or her mental and physical
talents against the elements remains a
strong part of the American character in
the 1990s. There is something pure about
returning to the soil.

The Country look heavily utilizes the
objects of rural life, from cast-iron seats to
wooden rakes. This is one collectible area
in which collectors want an aged, i.e., well-
worn, appearance. Although most of the
items were factory-made, they have a
handcrafted look. The key is to find objects
that have character—a look that gives
them a sense of individuality.

Clubs: Antique Engine, Tractor & Toy Club,
5731 Paradise Rd., Slatington, PA 18080;
Cast Iron Seat Collectors Assoc., P.O. Box
14, Ionia, MO 65335.

Periodicals: Farm Antique News, P.O. Box
812, Tarkio, MO 64491; Farm Collector, 1503
SW 42nd St., Topeka, KS 66609.

Advertising Trade Card, McCormick
    Farm Machinery, fold-out 22
Book, *Handy Farm Devices and How to
    Make Them*, 288 pp, 1913 10
Book, *John Deere Handy Farm Account
    Book*, 40 pp, 8 x 10" 10
Book, *National Farm Tractor and Imple-
    ment Blue Book*, 1963 2
Calendar, 1934, E Finch & Son, Denver,
    NY, Oliver Farm Machinery adv 65
Catalog, Carter Tru-Scale Machine Co,
    Rockford, IL, 13 pp, fold-out 40
Catalog, Jim Brown Farm Catalog, Dec
    1950, 32 pp, 9 x 13" 20
Magazine, *Farm Journal*, Nov 1968 5
Manual, International Harvester, McCor-
    mick Deering #61 Harvester-Thresher,
    1941 10
Manual, John Deere, Operation, Care
    and Repair of Farm Machinery, 15th
    ed, 1940s 30
Needle Book, front text "A stitch in
    time can save livestock too/We've
    got the best in feeds for you...,
    Lab-Mix Formulated Feed/Complete

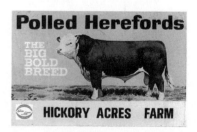

*Sign, Polled Herefords, Hickory Acres
Farm, litho tin, self-framed, 46" h, 70" w,
$130.* —Photo courtesy Collectors Auction
Services.

Spring Scale, Chatillion Improved, NY, pat. Dec 10, 1867, brass, $35.

needle assortment for bags, leather, clothing, darning," reverse shows calf in front of fence with text "Calf Manna, Suckle, and our Lab-Mix Formulated Feed makes livestock farming a pleasure," West Germany . . .4

Pinback Button, "Don't Worry! Conkey Will Cure Me," ailing bird on white ground, black lettering, red rim, 1920-30s 10

Pinback Button, Flint & Walling Farm Products, red and blue star symbol on white ground, gold rim 20

Pinback Button, Peoria Corn Carnival, multicolored, yellow corn ear in green husk on tan ground, dated Oct 12-14, 1903 5

Postcard, Auietam Duck Farm, Franklin County, PA, black and white, 1905 4

Postcard, boy and girl on farm, emb, "Thanksgiving, My wish is that Thanksgiving brings not just what you require but that it also gives to you that which you most desire," 1920s 2

Stereoview, young girl between bull and sheep, "A Little Child Shall Lead Them," Underwood & Underwood, 1901, 7 x 3.5" 10

Tool, asparagus buncher, metal on wood, c1800-1900s 35

Tool, cider press, top grinder with wood slate sides, c1900, 4" h 100

Tool, fence wire stretcher, wooden handle, metal jaws and hook, c1850s 20

Tool, grain scoop, wooden, c1800s, 40" l, 12" w 25

Toy, seeder, cast iron, Arcade, 4" l, 3.5" w .35

Yardstick, wood, "Mowery's Farm Equipment, Massey-Ferguson Tractors & Implements, Prospect, PA/New Holland Farm Equipment/Ontario Grain Drills" 5

FARM TOYS

The average age of those who play with farm toys is probably well over thirty. Farm toys are adult toys. Collectors number in the tens of thousands. The annual farm toy show in Dyersville, Ohio, draws a crowd in excess of 15,000.

Beware of recent "limited" and "special edition" farm toys. The number of each toy being produced hardly qualifies them as limited. If you buy them other than for enjoyment, you are speculating. No strong resale market has been established. Collectors who are not careful are going to be plowed under.

Club: Ertl Collectors' Club, P.O. Box 500, Dyersville, IA 52040.

Newsletter: *Spec-Tacular News,* P.O. Box 368, Dyersville, IA 52040.

Periodicals: *The Toy Tractor Times,* P.O. Box 156, Osage, IA 50461; *Toy Farmer,* 7496 106th Ave. SE, LaMoure, ND 58458; *Tractor Classics CTM,* P.O. Box 489, Rocanville, Saskatchewan SOA 3LO Canada.

1950 Pickup Truck, Auburn Rubber, 4.5" l 20

Arden Milk Truck, Smith-Miller, #204-A, 14" l 300

Avery Tractor, Arcade, hood, no stack, 4.5" l 150

Borden's Golden Crest Dairy Cart, Rich Toys, wood, 18" l 250

Caterpillar Tractor, Arcade, #266X, 1931, 3" l 50

Puzzle, Old Dobbin Picture Puzzles, Parker Bros, diecut cardboard, 1920s, set of 2, $20.

Cattle Farms Truck, Structo, pressed
steel, metallic green cab, silvery gold
trailer, 1950s, 5 x 21 x 7.25" 75

Cattle Trailer, Structo, #708 75

Claas Combine Harvester, Matchbox,
#65, 1968 10

Corn Harvester, Arcade, #4180, 1939,
5" l 100

Corn Planter, Arcade, 1939, 4.5" l 50

Dump Truck, Tonka, pressed steel, 1978,
6.5 x 16.5 x 6.5" 20

Farm Cart, Kenton, mule and black
driver, 10.5" l .400

Farm Set, Fisher-Price, 1960s, 9" h, 11" w . .5

Farm Set, Hubley, diecast, tractor, plow
wagon, spreader, and cultipacker,
orig box, 7 x 18" 220

Farm Wagon, Arcade, with 2 horses
and driver, 10.75" l 500

Farm Wagon, Kenton, cast iron, 2 horses
and figure, 14.5" l 500

Ford Tractor, Tootsietoy, cast metal,
clear plastic cover, orig box, 4.5" l 35

Freeman's Dairy Truck, Dent Toys, slid-
ing doors, 6" l 400

Fun on the Farm Econoline Truck,
Nylint, #7100, 11.25" l 85

International Dump Truck, Arcade,
#1670, 1940, 11.625" l 500

John Deere 6600 Combine, Ertl 75

John Deere Farm Tractor, Auburn Rub-
ber, 5"l 25

John Deere Tilt Bed, Ertl 100

Livestock Truck, Tonka, 1955 150

McCormick-Deering Manure Spreader,
Arcade, with team of horses, 14" l 400

McCormick-Deering Plow, Arcade . . .175

Milk Cart, Hubley, cast iron, 12.5" l 450

Milk Wagon, Kenton, horse and driver,
12.5" l 300

Oliver Plow, Arcade, #4230X, 1941,
6.25" l 175

Shovel Truck, Nylint, pressed steel,
"Michigan" decals with "Clark
Equipment/Model T-24," 1950s, 6 x
17.5 x 27" 75

Stake Pick-up Truck and Horse Trailer,
Tonka, pressed steel, #625, dark metallic greenish-blue, 6 removable white
stake panels, 9" l, 5.25 x 14 x 5.5" 75

Toytown Dairy, Marx, litho tin, windup,
white wheels, red hubs, black horse,
1930s, 3.5 x 10 x 4.5" 200

Tractor, Hubley, diecast, emb "Hubley
Jr," orange, rubber traction tires,
orig box, 7" l .165

Tractor, Hubley, diecast, red, steerable
wheel and spring action seat, rubber tires with spoke wheels, orig
box, 9" l 225

Tractor Loader, Hubley, diecast, orange,
silvered scoop, rubber traction tires,
orig box, 12" l 165

Truck and Tractor, Hubley, diecast truck,
green plastic tractor, orig box, 10" l . .275

FAST-FOOD COLLECTIBLES

If you haunt fast-food restaurants for
the food, you are a true fast- food junkie.
Most collectors haunt them for the giveaways. If you stop and think about it, fast-
food collectibles are the radio and cereal
premiums of the second half of the twentieth century. Look at what you have to eat to
get them.

Whenever possible, try to preserve the
original packaging of the premiums. Also,
save those things which are most likely to
be thrown out. I see a great many Happy
Meals toys and few Happy Meals boxes.

Club: McDonald's Collectors Club, 1153 S.
Lee St., Suite 200, Des Plaines, IL 60016.

Newsletter: *Collecting Tips Newsletter,* P.O.
Box 633, Joplin, MO 64802.

Arby's, bucket, Halloween scene, 1993,
6.5" d 2

Arby's, license plate, Babar's World
Tour, 1990 2

Arby's, mug, Yogi & Friends, plastic,
1994 3

*Tractor and Manure Spreader, Slik Toy,
Lansing Foundry Co. (later Lee Foundry),
$45.*

Burger King, record, The Many Faces of Alf, *33 1/3 rpm, cardboard, Burger King premium offer on back, 1987, 3.75" d, $3.*

McDonald's, bop toy, soft vinyl, inflatable, Ronald McDonald image on front and back, c1970s, 13" h, 4.5" base 15

McDonald's, necktie, 1994 4

McDonald's, radio, hard plastic, battery operated, figural french fries in single red serving cup, golden arch symbol accent with white "McDonald's," fabric carrying strap, ©1977 McDonald's, 2.5 x 4.5 x 6" 20

McDonald's, Star Trek secret compartment ring, Captain Kirk, 1979 5

McDonald's, wristwatch, chromed metal, crystal dial, seated Ronald McDonald, black leather straps, mkd "Japan Quartz," Welby 35

Pizza Hut, box, Dinosaurs series, 1993 ...2

Pizza Hut, Color Your World poster with crayons, 1993 3

Pizza Hut, Eureeka's Castle hand puppet, 1990 2

Pizza Hut, Ferngully terrarium cup with seed packet, 1992 1

Pizza Hut, Land Before Time hand puppet, 1988 5

Pizza Hut, sunglasses, Back to the Future, 1989 3

Roy Rogers, cup critter, 1884, 1.5" h 1

Roy Rogers, cup, pictures of the sea, 1993 .2

Roy Rogers, eraser ring, 1986 4

Roy Rogers, finger puppet, lion crayon finger puppet, 1993 1

Subway, hackeysack ball, 1993, 2" d 1

Taco Bell, box, Taco Bell, Bullwinkle inflatable ball, 1993 5

Little Caesars, doll, Meatsa Meatsa Man, cloth, 1990, 5" h, $8.

Taco Bell, coloring book, Zobilee Zoo, 1984 4

Taco Bell, doll, plush, Hugga Bunch, 1984, 6" h 8

Taco Bell, sand mold, star, Sand City series, 1993 1

Wendy's, book, *Aladdin & His Lamp*, Alf Tales, 1990 2

Wendy's, box, Yogi Bear & Friends series, 1990 2

Wendy's, Bristle Blocks, 1987 4

Wendy's, cup hanger, animals, 1987 2

Wendy's, drinking glass, 1982 World's Fair, Knoxville, TN, 5.625" h 5

Wendy's, drinking straw, plastic, neon, 1993 1

Wendy's, figure, Potato Head Kids, 1987 ..3

Wendy's, Frosty Flyer racer, 1990 2

Wendy's, Glow Friends finger puppet, 3" h 2

Wendy's, mini puzzle, Endangered Animal series, 1993 1

Wendy's, Rocket Writers, 1992 3

Wendy's, stencil ruler, 1986 3

White Castle, bowl, winter scene with Castle friends, 1989, 4.5" d 3

White Castle, Camp White Castle water bottle, 1990 2

White Castle, circus train, 4 pcs 3

White Castle, Silly Putty mold, 1993 1

White Castle, soap dish and soap, Real Ghostbusters Visit Castleland, 1991 ...3

FENTON GLASS

Frank L. Fenton founded the Fenton Art Glass Company in Martins Ferry, Ohio, in 1905. Production began in 1907 and has been continuing ever since.

Early production included carnival, chocolate, custard, pressed, and opalescent glass. In the 1920s stretch glass, Fenton dolphins, and art glass were added. Hobnail, opalescent, and two-color overlay pieces were popular in the 1940s. In the 1950s Fenton began reproducing Burmese and other early glass types.

Throughout its production period, Fenton has made reproductions and copycats of famous glass types and patterns. Today these reproductions and copycats are collectible in their own right.

Clubs: Fenton Art Glass Collectors of America, Inc, P.O. Box 384, Williamstown, WV 26187; National Fenton Glass Society, P.O. Box 4008, Marietta, OH 45750.

Newsletter: *Butterfly Net,* 302 Pheasant Run, Kaukauna, WI 54130.

Block and Star, candlesticks, pr, white milk glass, square 18
Coin Dot, sugar, blue opalescent, large .50
Coin Dot, decanter, cranberry, #894 700
Coin Dot, pitcher, cranberry, #1353 375
Coin Dot, tumbler, cranberry, 10 oz, #1353 60
Coin Dot, pitcher, Hobnail, cranberry, 80 oz 335
Cranberry, tumbler 60
Crystal Frosted, figurine, praying boy and girl 35
Diamond Optic, basket, metal handle, #1502, green 20
Diamond Optic, bonbon, metal handle, #1502, green, 5.5" h 40
Diamond Optic, dresser set, 4 pcs, green 150
Diamond Optic, mayonnaise with ladle, rose 25
Dragon and Lotus, bowl, #1656, green, 9" d 150
French Opalescent, candleholders, pr, cornucopia, #3874 18
French Opalescent, creamer and sugar, iridescent, #3900 12
Hobnail, banana stand, yellow opalescent 235
Hobnail, basket, French opalescent, 4.5" h 30
Hobnail, basket, plum opalescent, oval, 12" 525
Hobnail, basket, topaz opalescent, sgd, 8" h 75
Hobnail, bonbon, blue opalescent, handled, 7" h 30
Hobnail, bowl, plum opalescent, ruffled, 9" d 175
Hobnail, candy box, cov, blue marble . . .30
Hobnail, planter, black, 10" l 10
Hobnail, relish, amber 8
Hobnail, sugar, French opalescent, #3901 . .5
Hobnail, toothpick holder, Colonial amber . .6
Hobnail, vanity set, blue opalescent, 3 pcs 115
Hobnail, vase, French opalescent, 4" h . . .6

Blue Burmese, bell, Lily of the Valley pattern, $75.

Hobnail, vase, French opalescent, #389, 4" h 7
Jacqueline, vase, 5" h 50
Peach Crest, basket, 7" h 40
Peach Crest, basket, 10" h 120
Polka Dot, salt and pepper shakers, pr, cranberry 130
Rose Overlay, basket, #7235, 5" h 50
Rose Overlay, basket, 10" h 110
Silver Crest, banana stand, high 75
Silver Crest, basket, #7336, 6.5" h 30
Silver Crest, bonbon, 5" d 10
Silver Crest, candlesticks, pr, 6" h 75
Silver Crest, compote 10
Silver Crest, lazy susan, 3 tier 45
Silver Crest, vase, 6.25" h 20
Spanish Lace, compote, pink 75
Teardrop, candy box, turquoise 40
Teardrop, condiment set, turquoise 100
Teardrop, sandwich tray, white milk glass 25
Tulip, bowl, cobalt, 9" d 25
Vasa Murrhina, vase, 9" h 150

FIESTA WARE

Fiesta was the Melmac of the mid-1930s. The Homer Laughlin China Company introduced Fiesta dinnerware in January 1936 at the Pottery and Glass Show in Pittsburgh, Pennsylvania. It was a huge success.

The original five colors were red, dark blue, light green (with a trace of blue), yellow, and ivory. Other colors were added later. Fiesta was redesigned in 1960, discontinued about 1972, and reintroduced in 1986. It appears destined to go on forever.

Values rest in form and color. Forget the rumors about the uranium content of early red-colored Fiesta. No one died of radiation poisoning from using Fiesta. However, rumor has it that they glowed in the dark when they went to bed at night.

Clubs: Fiesta Club of America, P.O. Box 15383, Machesney Park, IL 61115; Fiesta Collectors Club, P.O. Box 471, Valley City, OH 44280.

Chartreuse, after dinner cup and
   saucer 525
Chartreuse, coffeepot 485
Chartreuse, cream soup 100
Chartreuse, dessert bowl, 6" d 50
Chartreuse, mug 90
Cobalt, carafe 500
Cobalt, coffeepot 350
Cobalt, fruit bowl, 11.75" d 425
Cobalt, juice tumbler 50
Cobalt, mixing bowl, #1 375
Cobalt, mixing bowl, #2 200
Cobalt, mug 85
Cobalt, mustard 325
Cobalt, pitcher, 2 pint 120
Cobalt, teapot lid 125
Cobalt, water tumbler 100
Green, after dinner cup and saucer 85
Green, bud vase 85
Green, carafe 300
Green, juice tumbler 40
Green, mixing bowl, #1 225
Green, mixing bowl, #3 225
Green, mixing bowl, #4 200
Green, mixing bowl, #5 225

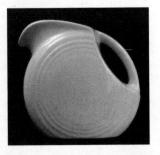

Yellow, disc pitcher, ice lip, 5.625" h, $45.
—Photo courtesy Ray Morykan Auctions.

Green, mixing bowl, #7 475
Green, mustard 250
Green, onion soup, cov 850
Green, plate, 10" d 30
Green, relish 50
Green, salad bowl, ftd 475
Green, teapot, medium 185
Green, water tumbler 65
Green, mixing bowl, #1 365
Ivory, carafe 600
Ivory, coffeepot 390
Ivory, juice tumbler 50
Ivory, mixing bowl, #3 165
Ivory, mug 110
Ivory, onion soup, cov 950
Ivory, plate, 9" d 150
Ivory, teapot, medium 250
Ivory, water tumbler 100
Looney Tunes, creamer and sugar 65
Red, after dinner coffeepot 725
Red, after dinner cup and saucer 125
Red, carafe 475
Red, creamer, individual 370
Red, creamer, stick handle 85
Red, juice pitcher 750
Red, mixing bowl, #1 275
Red, mug 110
Red, mustard base 125
Red, plate, 10" d 50
Red, salad bowl, ftd 650
Red, syrup 675
Red, teapot 265
Turquoise, after dinner cup and saucer .115
Turquoise, carafe 375
Turquoise, casserole, cov 135
Turquoise, coffeepot 250
Turquoise, comport 125
Turquoise, creamer, stick handle 115
Turquoise, juice tumbler 55
Turquoise, mixing bowl, #1 385
Turquoise, mixing bowl, #6 350
Turquoise, mug .55
Turquoise, mustard 275
Turquoise, sugar, cov 40
Turquoise, teapot, medium 150
Turquoise, vase, 8" h 975
Turquoise, water tumbler 85
Yellow, after dinner cup and saucer . . .100
Yellow, comport 100
Yellow, creamer, individual 75
Yellow, juice pitcher 40
Yellow, juice tumbler 40
Yellow, marmalade 350

Yellow, mixing bowl, #1 325
Yellow, mixing bowl, #2 140
Yellow, mixing bowl, #4 145
Yellow, mustard .350
Yellow, plate, 10" d 25
Yellow, sugar, cov, individual 135

FIGURINES

Looking for a "small" with character? Try collecting figurines. Collecting interest in the colorful figurines produced by firms such as Ceramic Arts Studio, Florence Ceramics, Vernon Kilns, and others has grown considerably during the past ten years. Pieces are starting to become pricey. However, there are still bargains to be found. A surprising number of these figurines are found at garage sales and flea markets at prices below $10.

Club: Ceramic Arts Studio Collectors Assoc., P.O. Box 46, Madison, WI 53701.

Newsletter: *Vernon Views*, P.O. Box 945, Scottsdale, AZ 85252.

Note: See specific manufacturers for additional listings.

Abingdon Pottery, goose, #98, 5" h 40
Beswick, calf, 4 x 4" 150
Beswick, Siamese cat, #1559, 4.5 x 7" . . .20
Co-Operative Flint, elephant, crystal,
   large 400
Co-Operative Flint, elephant, green,
   plain back 125
Fenton, bird, iridized glass, hp details,
   2.75" h 20

Spaghetti Art, poodle, unmkd, 4.5" l, $10.
—Photo courtesy Ray Morykan Auctions.

European, bisque, angel, 12.5" h, $75.

Florence Ceramics, Rhett, 9.25" h 85
Fostoria, goldfish, crystal, 4" h 85
Haley, ringneck pheasant, crystal, 11.5" h .20
Imperial, duck, caramel slag, 4.5" h 40
L E Smith, rooster, frosted satin, 2.25" h .10
Lefton, July Angel Girl, #7200 10
Lenox, blue jay, porcelain, 4.25 x 4.5" 30
Maddux, chicken, 8.5" h 15
Modglin's, bunny, 6.75" h 35
New Martinsville, German shepherd 55
New Martinsville, horse, head up 85
New Martinsville, pelican 65
New Martinsville, rooster 60
New Martinsville, squirrel 45
New Martinsville, wolfhound 65
Norcrest, Japan, Shih Tzu, red bow,
   7" h, 8.5" l, 4" w 25
Occupied Japan, black boy eating
   watermelon, bisque, 5" h 45
Occupied Japan, Victorian couple, 4.5
   x 3.25" 10
Paden City, bird, blue, 5" h 165
Paden City, chanticleer 175
Paden City, dragon swan, blue 750
Paden City, goose, light blue, 5" h 100
Paden City, rooster, black 550
Paden City, rooster, head down, blue . .225
Royal Copenhagen, polar bear, #321,
   6.5" l 100
Royal Copley, cat, brown, pink bow,
   8" h 35
Royal Doulton, Rose, rose colored ruf-
   fled dress, blonde ringlets, 4.75" h 45
Royal Haeger, leopard, chartreuse,
   7.75" h 50
Tiffin, cat, frosted black 250
Tiffin, cat, glossy black 400
Vernon Kilns, Dumbo, #41, 5.25" h 5
Wade, lion 5

FINCH, KAY

After over a decade of ceramic studies, Kay Finch, assisted by her husband, Braden, opened her commercial studio in 1939. A whimsical series of pig figurines and hand-decorated banks were the company's first successful products.

An expanded studio and showroom located on the Pacific Coast Highway in Corona de Mar opened on December 7, 1941. The business soon had forty employees as it produced a wide variety of novelty items. A line of dog figurines and themed items were introduced in the 1940s. Christmas plates were made from 1950 until 1962.

When Braden died in 1963, Kay Finch ceased operations. Freeman Mc-Farlin Potteries purchased the molds in mid-1970s and commissioned Finch to model a new series of dog figurines. Production of these continued throught the late 1970s.

*Figurine,
Airedale, red
and black,
#4832, $200.*

Ashtray, swan, 3.5 x 3.5" 40
Bowl, 13.5 x 9" 20
Box, green, square, 4 x 2" 4
Figurine, cat, lavender, turquoise high-
  lights, 3.25 x 3.25" 30
Figurine, Godey man, 9" h 50
Figurine, hippopotamus, open mouth,
  blue ribbon around neck, white
  spots 275
Figurine, Jocko the Monkey, green
  jacket and hat, 4" h 130
Figurine, kitten, purple bow, 3.75" l 25
Figurine, lamb, kneeling, #136 25
Figurine, oriental sage and maiden,
  chocolate brown, gold trim, 5.5" h,
  3 x 2.25" base 25
Figurine, owl, lavender, turquoise high-
  lights, 3.75" h 15
Figurine, Peanuts the elephant, #191,
  8.75" h 150
Figurine, peasant girl, 6.5" h 15
Figurine, Pee Wee Penguin, green and
  yellow, 3.25" h 75
Figurine, pig, 8.25" l 65
Figurine, rabbit, #152, 4 x 2.5" 25
Figurine, squirrel, 3.375" h 35
Lamp, prancing lamb, 10.5" h 150
Mug, light blue, white squirrel seated
  on handle, black highlights 100

Planter, bear, pink, 8" h 5
Planter, cocker spaniel, 10.5" h 20
Planter, leaf, 13" l, 9" w 50

FIRECRACKER PACKS, LABELS & RELATED

This hobby includes, but is not limited to, the collection of Chinese artwork as found on the colorful and often artistic labels found on old packages of firecrackers. These depict a great variety of animals, mythical and comic characters, and patriotic and sporting themes. There are perhaps a thousand different brands that were sold in the United States since about the middle of the 19th century. Since firecrackers originally sold for as little as one cent per thousand and still can be purchased for about one cent each, their labels represent true popular art. The labels range in size from that of a postage stamp to those nearly as large as a newspaper page. A large label was usually pasted on a parcel or "brick" of 20 to 250 packages, and each package also had a label. Some brands had their name or the object named by the brand on a label wrapped around each individual firecracker. Common brands such as Camel, Zebra, and Black Cat were continuously marketed for decades. Other brands of firecrackers are still sold in retail fireworks stands across the country. Perhaps a dozen new brands appear annually. Catalogues, posters, postcards, and advertising depicting firecrackers or fireworks are also collected.

Older firecracker labels do not bear the markings "I.C.C.," "D.O.T.," or "U.N.O." These are acronyms for government agencies first used in the 1950s by regulatory agencies. Prices generally rise for larger labels and those with special artistic appeal. However, some collectors prefer to collect packs or labels from the smallest sizes, called "penny packs" or individual firecrackers with "logo" shellwraps.

Others in the hobby collect fireworks-related items used to celebrate Independence Day, and in the South, Christmas. These items include domestically produced salutes, torpedoes, caps, sparklers, snakes, smokes, whistles, rockets, and many other devices. Yet others collect documents and photographs related to the many fireworks companies that once flourished in the United States. Those interested in capbombs, capcanes, capguns, capstrikes, firecracker mortars, cannon, and pistols, and other hardware items usually are considered toy collectors.

Collectible fireworks-related items are displayed, traded, and sold at the annual conventions of the Pyrotechnics Guild International, Inc.

Advisor: Hal Kantrud, Rte. 7, Jamestown, ND 58401, (701) 252-5639, e-mail: halk995@daktel.com, Internet: www.pgi.org

Newsletter: *The Phoenix,* Rte. 7 Box 52, Jamestown, ND 58401.

Note: Prices listed are for labels. Full packs usually bring 25 to 50% more.

Air Thunder	.25
Buck-A-Roo	.50.00
Chang	.20.00
Devil	5.00
Evergreen	200.00
Four Horsemen	.10.00
Giraffe	.10.00
Hale Bomb	1.00
Ibex	.75.00
Jing Loong Fatshan	.50.00
Kookaburra	.75.00
Link Triad	.25
Merry-Go-Round	.90.00
Nitrate Lightning	3.00
Ozark Buster	100.00
Panther	125.00
Round One	.75.00
Skull	1.00
Tally Ho	100.00

Firecracker Labels. Left: Buddha, Yau Yue, $100. Right: Minute Man Brand, China Fireworks, $50.

Uzi Cracker	.50
Volcano	.25.00
Wotsyboy	500.00
Xmas Crackers	5.00
Yuen Shing Extra	300.00
Zoo	.15.00

FIREHOUSE MEMORABILIA

Firehouse collectors are everywhere. They are doctors, lawyers, businessmen, housewives, as well as firefighters, and they live in every city across America.

Helmets, fire alarm equipment, speaking trumpets, and fire truck equipment are only a few categories of many Firehouse collectibles. Many of the items are over 100 years old, and as with other collectibles, condition is of the utmost importance.

Badges are another area of collecting. They are very popular because they are plentiful and relatively inexpensive.

Clubs: Fire Collectors Club, P.O. Box 992, Milwaukee, WI 53201; The Fire Mark Circle of the Americas, 2859 Marlin Dr., Chamblee, GA 30341.

Badge, "Assistant Chief, Fire Dept., Sprd.," raised center with 3 crossed horns, late 19th C, 2" h	.45
Badge, "Jr. Fireman, Center Twp., V.F.D., PA," 2.5" h	.15
Belt, brown leather, brass lettering "2nd Assistant," 48" l	.40

Badge, 1.875" h, $15.—Photo courtesy Collectors Auction Services.

Belt, leather, brass lettering "Old Town," 1 side painted white, buckle stamped "Dirigo No. 1," 32" l 125

Fire Bucket, leather, red lettering "F.F.D. 16," iron ring handles, 12.5" h, 9.5" d .150

Fire Grenade, glass, aqua, acanthus leaf and lion head pattern, smooth base, ground lip, 1 qt, 1875-95, 6.375" h 120

Fire Grenade, glass, medium cobalt blue, teardrop-shaped, emb "Rockford Kalamazoo Automatic and Hand Fire Extinguisher, Patent Applied For," smooth base, tooled mouth, 1890-1910, 11" h 350

Fireman's Horn, brass, plain, 17" h 300

Fire Mark, cast iron, "Baltimore Equitable Society, Baltimore, Maryland, 1794," clasped hands, salmon-colored paint, 10" l 500

Helmet, metal with hard leather rim, metal figural eagle's head projecting from top, 9.5" h, 15 x 10" 275

Shot Glass, fire bucket shaped, silver-plated, "Little Giant Engine Company 1871, Chicago Fire Department," blue lettering with white badge, Gorham, 2.75" h 125

FIRE-KING

Remember those great coffee mugs you used to find at diners? Those nice big warm cups filled to the brim by a smiling waitress, not the Styrofoam of this decade. Chances are they were Fire-King mugs. Fire-King dinnerware and ovenware was sold in sets from the 1940s through the 1970s. The company guaranteed to replace broken pieces and their colorful wares were quite popular with housewives. While Fire-King has been around for many years, collectors are now discovering quantities at flea markets and many are enjoying this new collecting area.

Club: Fire-King Collectors Club, 1406 E. 14th St., Des Moines, IA 50316.

Azurite Swirl, cereal bowl, 5.875" d 24
Azurite Swirl, cup and saucer 10
Black Dot, pepper shaker 50
Blue Mosaic, creamer and sugar 14
Blue Mosaic, cup and saucer 5
Blue Mosaic, dessert bowl, 4.625" d 7
Blue Mosaic, dinner plate 8
Blue Mosaic, platter, 12" l 20
Blue Mosaic, salad plate, 7.375" d 5
Blue Mosaic, snack tray with cup 6
Copper-Tint Lustre, bowl, oval, divided, 11.75" 5
Golden Shell, berry bowl, 5" d 3
Golden Shell, cereal bowl, 6" d 10
Golden Shell, dinner plate 5
Golden Shell, soup bowl, 8" d 10
Jadeite, bowl, 7.625" d 60
Jadeite, butter, clear lid 115
Jadeite, butter, clear lid, jadeite base ..135
Jadeite, eggcup 45
Jadeite, dessert bowl 12
Jadeite, grease jar, metal screw top lid ..60
Jadeite, grease jar, tulip screw lid 85
Jadeite, loaf pan, handled, 5 x 9" 75
Jadeite, milk pitcher, 20 oz 100
Jadeite, refrigerator dish, clear lid, 4.25 x 4.25" 55
Jadeite, salt and pepper shakers, pr 50
Jadeite, salt and pepper shakers, pr, tulip screw lids 95
Jane Ray, bowl, 4.5" d 20
Jane Ray, cereal bowl, 6" d 24
Jane Ray, mug, 6 oz 25

Oven Glass, deep loaf pan, sapphire blue, 9.125" l, $20.

Jane Ray, platter, oval, 12" l 50
Jane Ray, salad bowl 35
Jane Ray, soup bowl 25
Jane Ray, cup 5
Ovenware, baker, cov, 1 pint, 5.5" d 20
Ovenware, cereal bowl, 5.5" d 20
Ovenware, custard, 5 oz 2
Ovenware nurser, 4 oz 12
Primrose, custard, 6 oz 2
Philbe, casserole, individual, sapphire
   blue 25
Philbe, leftover, 4.5 x 5" 40
Philbe, mug, sapphire blue 30
Philbe, pie plate, sapphire blue, 8.375" d .15
Philbe, refrigerator dish, cov 65
Swedish Modern, mixing bowl, turquoise
   blue, 5" d 35
Swirl Orange Lustre, demitasse cup
   and saucer 15
Tulips, grease jar, cov, cream ground . . .75
Turquoise, cereal bowl, 4.5" d 15

FISHBOWL ORNAMENTS

Long after the goldfish and guppies
have been flushed down the toilet, aquarium owners find they still may have the
ceramic castle, lighthouse, mermaid,
pagoda, shipwreck, or other furniture that
once graced the bottom of their tank.

Aquarium furniture manufactured in
Germany, Japan, and the United States
between 1870 and 1970 is the most collectible. Most examples were originally
sold at neighborhood five and dime stores.

Looking for an interesting subcollec-
tion? Consider fish food containers.

Bathing Beauty, ceramic, reclining on
   shell, green suit, yellow shell, Japan,
   2.25" h 30
Bathing Beauty, ceramic, seated on
   shell, black suit with yellow accents,
   white shell, Japan, 4.75" h 45
Boy on Dolphin, ceramic, multicolored,
   Japan, 3.75" h .20
Castle, ceramic, blue and brown, Japan,
   6" h 20
Diver, ceramic, orange, 3.25" h 12
Diver, ceramic, seated on coral, orange
   and black, Japan, 3.5" h 12
Dragon, ceramic, 3 parts, Japan 2
Mermaid on Snail, ceramic, multicolored,

Japan, 4" h 30
Mermaid, ceramic, reclining, bisque,
   Japan, 4.75" l 25
Mermaid, ceramic, recling on shell,
   multicolored, Japan, 3.5" h 5
Sunken Ship, plastic, bubble stone 3

FISHER-PRICE TOYS

In 1930 Herman Guy Fisher, Helen
Schelle, and Irving R. Price founded the
Fisher-Price Toy Company in Birmingham,
New York. From that year forward, Fisher-
Price toys were built with a five-point
creed: intrinsic play value, ingenuity, strong
construction, good value for the money, and
action. With these principles and manufacturing contributions, the Fisher-Price Toy
Company has successfully maintained
quality and creativity in the toy market.

The collectibility of Fisher-Price toys is
a direct reflection upon their desirability
due to their unique characteristics and subject matter.

Club: Fisher-Price Collectors Club, 1442 N.
Ogden, Mesa, AZ 85205.

Note: Listings for toys in good condition.

Big Performing Circus, #250, 1932 450
Boom Boom Popeye, #491, 1937 550
Bouncy Racer, #8, 1950 40
Buddy Bronc, #430, 1938 200
Bunny Basket Cart, #303, 1960 30
Bunny Drummer, #505, 1946 150
Butch the Pup, #333, 1951 45
Cash Register, #972, 1960 35
Chubby Chief, #110, 1932 450
Dinkey Engine, #642, 1959 60

Pony Express, #733, 1941-44, $225.
—Photo courtesy Gene Harris Antique
Auction Center, Inc.

Donald Duck Drummer, #454, 1949 175
Farmer in the Dell TV Radio, #166, 1963 . .25
Golden Gulch Express, #191, 1961 65
Huffy Puffy Train, #999, 1958 55
Jolly Jumper, #793, 1963 25
Katy Kackler, #140, 1954 45
Looky Chug-Chug, #161, 1949 75
Mickey Mouse Choo-Choo, #432, 1938 .450
Molly Moo Moo, #190, 1956 65
Musical Push Chime, #722, 1950 35
Patch Pony, #616, 1963 25
Peter Pig, #479, 1959 35
Playful Puppy, #625, 1961 35
Puffy Engine, #444, 1951 35
Quacko Duck, #300, 1939 135
Rattle Ball, #682, 1959 20
Rolling Bunny Basket, #310, 1961 35
Scotty Dog, #710, 1933 350
Snoopy Sniffer, #180, 1938 65
Sonny Duck Cart, #410, 1941 75
Suzie Seal, #460, 1961 25
Tawny Tiger, #654, 1962 30
Teddy Bear Xylophone, #777, 1950 35
Timber Toter, #810, 1957 50
Tuggy Turtle, #139, 1959 45
Uncle Timmy Turtle, #125, 1956 50
Whistling Engine, #617, 1957 40
Ziggy Zilo, #737, 1958 50

FISHING COLLECTIBLES

A lot has been written recently about the increasing value of fishing tackle of all types. What has not been said is that high-ticket items are limited in number. Most sell for less than $5.

Fishing collectors emphasize condition. If a rod, reel, lure, or accessory shows heavy use, chances are its value is minimal. Original packaging is also important, often doubling value.

Collectors seek wooden plugs made before 1920 (most that survive were made long after that date), split bamboo fly rods made by master craftsmen (not much value for commercial rods), and reels constructed of German silver with special details and unique mechanical action. Advertising and other paper ephemera round out a collection. Find a pile of this material and you will have made a good catch.

Clubs: American Fish Decoy Assoc., 624 Merritt St., Fife Lake, MI 49633; National Fishing Lure Collectors Club, H.C.#33, Box 4012, Reeds Spring, MO 65737; Old Reel Collectors Assoc., 160 Shoreline Walk, Alpharetta, GA 30022.

Periodical: *Fishing Collectibles Magazine*, P.O. Box 2797, 2 Oak St., Kennebunkport, ME 04046.

Book, *Tying American Trout Lures*,
    Cross, Reuben R, Dodd, Mead, NY,
    1936, first ed, 55 pp 115
Catalog, Edward Vom Hofe, 171 pp,
    1931 300
Catalog, Hardy's Anglers Guide, 419 pp,
    rods, reels, flies, and accessories, 20
    color plates of flies and lures, 1937 . . .55
Catalog, Pflueger, #145, 116 pp, contains
    lures, reels, lines, and accessories,
    1925 85
Creel, reversed birch, brown painted
    rabbits and ducks on side, painted
    fish on lid, lid attached with leather
    laces, leather shoulder strap attached
    to sides 525
Creel, split willow, orig leather hinges,
    metal trimmed leather lid latch, 7.5
    x 11.5" 80
Creel, willow, full length leather hinge
    and strap and buckle lid latch, off
    center hole 140
Fly Box, Hardy Neroda, pipe cleaner
    clips, contains 5 dozen trout flies,
    4 x 6" 165

Creel, wicker and wood, painted red, 15" h, 13" w, 7.5" deep, $135. —Photo courtesy Collectors Auction Services.

License, pinback button, WV, hunting/
fishing, dark green and black, 1940 . . .70
Lure, crab wiggler, Heddon #1800, glass
eyes U-shaped collar, L-rig hardware,
green scale finish, 4" l 30
Lure, minnow, Pepper, 5 hook, glass
eyes, twisted wire hook hangers,
straight rounded props finished with
green back and white belly, 3 hp gill-
marks, c1905 .55
Minnow Bucket, galvanized, torpedo
shaped, sliding lid, iron rings on ends
to attach rope, orig dark green paint,
5 x 28" 145
Poster, Ninth Canadian Fly Fishing Forum,
Toronto, Apr 7-8, 1984, depicts large
feather, lists workshops, exhibits,
and prizes, metal frame, 12 x 28" 30
Reel, bait casting, J W Young, Redditch
Gildex, folding foot, drag lever, click
lever, front and back screw adjusting
shaft tension .40
Reel, fly, Paul H Young, 8.5 ft, 2 pc, 2 tip,
5.82 oz, handwritten tip on label
"Herb & Walt Stream King," and
"boat rod," screw down-locking over
cork reel seat, long cork handle and
red winds, with bag and tube 225
Reel, salmon, STH Reels-IM Cassette,
transparent spool and panels, adjust-
able drag, 4" d, 1" w 55
Reel, trout, Heddon Imperial 125, adjustable drag, 3.25" d, .75" w 50
Reel, trout, Julius Vom Hofe, NY, metal,
wide spool, raised pillar with click
switch, 2" d, 1" w 110
Rod, trout, Cortland 444 Ltd-Impregnated,
made in England, 6.5 ft, 2 pc, 1 tip, 2
slide band over cork reel seat, walnut ferrule plug, with orig bag and
labeled tube .190
Tab, Johnson Reels, diecut litho tin,
1950s 5
Tackle Box, cedar, tongue and groove
strips, shallow lift-out tray, brass
nails, molded folding handle, brass
plated hasp, stamped "Mfg. by
George C. Brown & Co. Greensboro,
N.C.," 7 x 16 x 7.5" 140
Tackle Box, mahogany, 2 lift-out divid-
ed wood trays, brass nails, folding
metal handle, metal hasp for lock,
8 x 16 x 8" 140

FLAGS & FLAG COLLECTIBLES

A basic rule of collecting—the more
made, the lower the value—holds true for
flags as well, ask anyone who owns a 48-
star flag.

Old flags are fragile and can be difficult
to display. Hanging them often leads to
deterioration. If you own flags, you should
be aware of flag etiquette as outlined in
Public Law 829, 7th Congress, approved
December 22, 1942.

Many collectors do not collect flags
themselves but items that display the flag
as a decorative motif. A flag-related sheet
music collection is one example.

Club: North American Vexillological Assoc.,
1977 N. Olden Ave, PMB 225, Trenton, NJ
08618.

Ashtray, Confederate soldier's hat shaped,
center Confederate flag decal, 3.5 x
4.5" 10
Embroidered Panel, eagle and American
flag, brown, white, black, red, and
blue, stained background, 25.25" sq .200
Figurine, angel with flag, Lefton 8
Flag, 38 stars, silk-screened paint on
gauze, framed, c1885, 32.75 x 49" 475
Game, Game of Flags, Cincinnati Game
Co, #1111, ©1896 Fireside Game Co . .45
Game, The Flag Game, McLoughlin
Bros, lid shows George Washington
surrounded by flags, complete with
flag cards and tickets, 1887 50

*Flag, 48 stars, cloth, mkd "U.S.Ens.6," 102" h,
204" w, $150. —Photo courtesy Collectors
Auction Services.*

Hair Bow, fabric, red, white, and blue flag with center star image with detailed Shirley Temple head and neck image on brass clip hair barrette, 1930s, 2 x 4" 75

Lapel Stud, enamel, red, white, and blue flag on white ground, blue ribbon design with brass "R.L.U.S.," c1888 ..15

Pin, diecut brass, mechanical, red, white, and blue flag opens to printed insert paper "To Hell With Spain! Remember The *Maine*," 1898 45

Pinback Button, "Stay Out," center red, white, and blue flag, c1930s 18

Stickpin, brass bug on shell, red, white, and blue, fabric accent flag bow, 2" l ..30

FLAMINGOS

Flamingos offer a wide range of collectibles, from lovely art glass vases to pink plastic yard birds. The most popular flamingos are the graceful ceramic figurines produced en masse in the late 1940s and early 1950s. These were usually sold in pairs with one standing upright and the mate standing in a head-down position. Measurements for pairs always refers to the upright flamingo.

Raised wing or in-flight flamingos, TV lamps and planters are more difficult to find. White flamingos were produced, but they hold little interest to collectors. Also highly prized are mirror-framed air-brushed prints produced by Turner and copycats from that period.

Figure, California Pottery, 18" h, price for pair 350
Figure, chalkware, 6" h 12
Figure, Kelvin, bone china, raised wing, 2.5" h 15
Figure, Lefton China, elegant, 5.5" h, price for pair 45
Figure, Maddux, plain, 8.5" h 20
Figure, unmkd, bone china, raised wing, 1.5" h 4
Figure, unmkd, cold-painted, 13" h 30
Figure, unmkd, large body, leaf base, 11" h 65
Figure, unmkd, raised wing, high relief, 10.5" h 75
Figure, unmkd, mother with 2 babies, raised wing, 9" h 50

Figure, unmkd, papier-mâché, 36" h 75
Figure, Victorian, pot metal, 6" h 35
Mirror, 22 x 34" 125
Planter, Maddux, 10" h 45
Plate, Harker, 2 birds and palms, white ground, 8.25" d 25
Print, Turner, 2 flamingos, orig frame, 22 x 28" 150
Television Lamp, Lane 14" h 150

FLASHLIGHTS

Old flashlights have surged ahead in collectibility. This still new collectible has been gathering a following. The Fourth Annual Flashlight Collector's Convention will be held in Reading, Pennsylvania, in April, 2001. A recent eBay sale saw an early Eveready glove catch flashlight sell for $1,125, yet most sell for very modest prices. Flashlights began to be made in the late 1890s. The American Electrical Novelty & Mfg Co started about 1898 and soon began calling their lights "Ever Ready." Other leaders in the field of portable lighting were: Franco, Kwik-Lite, Bright Star, Burgess, Niagara, USA-Lite, Micro-Lite, Bond, and Winchester.

Many flashlight collectors use their old lights. Flashlights can be found in sterling silver, 14kt gold, hand enameled finishes and with lithographed designs. Collectors look for flashlights with comic characters like Mickey Mouse, Donald Duck, and Popeye and personalities such as Zorro, Roy Rogers, and Dick Tracy. Most people think of flashlights as tube shaped, but the variety of shapes is enormous. There are a whole subcategory of flashlights that are in the shape of products such as beer, brandy, and ketchup bottles, Life Saver's candy and Crayola Crayons. Many collectors also collect early flashlight company catalogs, signs, displays, and even old batteries. A 1936 Mickey Mouse battery alone recently sold for over $400.

Advisor: Stuart L. Schneider, P.O. Box 64, Teaneck, NJ 07666, (201) 599-4250, Fax (201) 599-4251, e-mail: stuart@wordcraft.net, Internet: www.wordcraft.net

Club: Flashlight Collectors of America, P.O. Box 4095, Tustin, CA 92681.

Note: Stuart L. Schneider is the author of *Collecting Flashlights,* Schiffer Publishing. Prices listed are for flashlights in excellent working condition.

Advertising, Lite Savers or Life Savers candy 20
Advertising, Schlitz Beer bottle 15
Bantam-Lite, metal Davy Crockett light, 1959 65
Collins or Campbell No Battery Dynamo Light, 1928 75
Eveready, black and chrome Masterlight, bottom twists open, 1936 125
Eveready, black tubular, glove catch switch, 1909 350
Eveready, silverplated vest pocket light, 1912 patent date 50
Eveready, wall or closet light, hangs on wall, 1931 45
Flippo, plastic Davy Crockett light, 1963 . .30
Franco, early fiber tubular model with Franco switch 45
Kwik-Lite, metal tubular model, opens in middle 75
May Mfg, glass bulbous lens, tubular metal light, 1928 55
Micro-Lite, Cowboy Jim 1955 pull lapel light 30
Ohio Electric Pocket Light, rect, leatherette cover, 1897 1,500
Ray-O-Vac, French Flasher, metal tubular light, 1915 75
Ray-O-Vac, Ray-O-Lite, metal tubular light, 1920 65

Burgess Snaplite. Left: painted Art Deco design, 1930s, $100. Right: light brown leatherette cover with dog design, $25.

Stewart Browne, tubular light, "Mine Approved," 1945 40

FLATWARE

Flatware refers to forks, knives, serving pieces, and spoons, There are four basic types of flatware: (1) sterling silver, (2) silver plated, (3) stainless, (4) Dirilyte.

Sterling silver flatware has a silver content of 925 parts silver per thousand. Knives have a steel or stainless steel blade. Silver plating refers to the elctroplating of a thin coating of pure silver, 1,000 parts silver per thousand, on a base metal such as brass, copper, or nickel silver. While steel only requires the addition of 13% of chromium to be classified stainless, most stainless steel flatware is made from an 18/8 formula, i.e., 18% chromium for strength and stain resistance and 8% nickel for a high luster and long-lasting finish. Dirilyte is an extremely hard, solid bronze alloy developed in Sweden in the early 1900s. Although gold in color, it has no gold in it.

Most flatware is purchased by individuals seeking to replace a damaged piece or to expand an existing pattern. Prices vary widely. The listings represent what a replacement service quotes a customer.

Abbreviations:

FH = Flat Handle   SS = Sterling Silver
HH = Hollow Handle   ST = Stainless Steel
SP = Silver Plated

DIRILYTE, REGAL

Butter Serving Knife, FH, 7.25" l 16
Fish Fork, 7.25" l 16
Gravy Ladle, 6.75" l 38
Iced Tea Spoon, 8.375" l 14
Salad Fork, 6.25" l 14
Tablespoon, 8.375" l 24
Youth Fork, 6.625" l 16

GORHAM, GORHAM SHELL, ST

Butter Serving Knife, HH, 7" l 8
Fork, 7.875" l 7
Salad Fork, 7" l 6
Tablespoon, 8.625" l 10
Teaspoon, 6.125" l 4

GORHAM, HACIENDA, ST

Butter Serving Knife, 7.125" l 16
Cocktail Fork, 5.875" l 16
Iced Teaspoon, 7.75" l 16
Knife, HH, modern blade, 8.5" l 20
Tablespoon, 8.75" l 25
Teaspoon, 6.125" l 15

INTERNATIONAL, NORSE, ST

Butter Spreader, FH, 6.75" l 16
Fork 17
Knife 16
Teaspoon, 6.25" l 14

INTERNATIONAL, TODAY, ST

Butter Serving Knife, FH, 7" l 20
Butter Spreader, FH, 6.125" l 20
Dessert Spoon, 6.875" l 16
Fork 16
Knife 20
Teaspoon 16

ONEIDA, TENNYSON, ST

Butter Serving Knife, HH, 6.5" l 10
Cocktail Fork, 6" l .8
Fork, 7.125" l 10
Fruit Spoon, 5.875" l 4
Tablespoon, 8.375" l 14
Teaspoon, 6" l 8

Tiffany & Co, English King, SS, comprising 10 dinner knives, 8 butter spreaders, 14 dinner forks, 8 luncheon forks, 11 tablespoons, 6 teaspoons, 7 bouillon spoons, and 9 serving pcs, approx. 143 oz, $4,313.
—Photo courtesy William Doyle Galleries.

Reed & Barton, Country French, ST, price for 5-pc place setting, $70.

ONEIDA, WILL 'O' WISP, ST

Butter Serving Knife, HH, 6.75" l 14
Fork, 7.5" l 15
Iced Tea Spoon, 7.5" l 14
Knife, HH, modern blade, 9.25" l 15
Tablespoon, 8.5" l 20
Teaspoon, 6.125" l 14

REED & BARTON, MODERN PROVINCIAL, ST

Butter Serving Knife, FH, 7.25" l 20
Knife 15
Salad Fork 14
Teaspoon 15

FLORENCE CERAMICS

Florence Ward of Pasadena, California, began making ceramic objects as a form of therapy in dealing with the loss of a young son. The products she produced and sold from her garage workshop provided pin money during the Second World War.

Florence Ceramics is best known for its figural pieces, often costumed in Colonial and Godey fashions. The company also produced birds, busts, candleholders, lamps, smoking sets, and wall pockets. Betty Davenport Ford joined the company in 1956, designing a line of bisque animal figures. Production ended after two years.

Scripto Corporation bought Florence Ceramics in 1964. Production was shifted to advertising specialty ware. Operations ceased in 1977.

Club: Florence Collector's Club, P.O. Box 122, Richland, WA 99352.

Julie, 7.25" h, $165.

Pudding, white ceramic base, tin lid, 1890s, $175.

Dalia, 8" h	.25
Elaine and Jim, 6" h	.30
Her Majesty, purple	.100
Jim, 6" h	.35
Lillian, 7.75" h	.45
Linda Lou, 8.25" h	.100
Marilyn, pink gown, gold lace trim	.100
Martha, light blue gown, 22K gold leaf design, hp flowers, lace trim	.350
Matilda, 8.5" h	.100
Molly, 6.5" h	.45
Prima Donna, 10.25" h	.30
Rhett Butler, 9" h	.50
Rosalie, 9.5" h	.230
Sarah	.55
Sue Ellen, 8" h	.50
Vivian, holding umbrella, 7.5" h	.75
Wynkin' and Blynkin', 5.5" h	.215

FOOD MOLDS

Commercial ice cream and chocolate molds appear to be the collectors' favorites. Buying them is now a bit risky because of the large number of reproductions. Beware of all Santa and rabbit molds.

Country collectors have long touted the vast array of kitchen food molds, ranging from butter prints to Turk's head cake molds. Look for molds with signs of use and patina.

Do not forget Jell-O molds. If you grew up in the 1950s or 1960s, you ate Jell-O and plenty of it. Aluminum Jell-O molds came in a tremendous variety of shapes and sizes. Most sell for between 10¢ and $1, cheap by any standard.

Butter, rose, rect, old varnish finish, 5 x 8"	.75
Butter, roses and cherries, rect, old patina, age cracks, 4 x 7"	.100
Cake, lamb, cast iron, 2 pcs, 13" l	.125
Chocolate, Santa, tin, 4 cavities, Germany	.235
Chocolate, standing rabbit, 2-part tin mold with separate 2-part molds for ears and forelegs, mkd "Anton Reiche, Dresden, Germany," 18.5" h	.225
Chocolate, witch, 4 cavities, Germany, early 20th C	.150
Ice Cream, basket, pewter, #598, 3-part, early 20th C	.40
Ice Cream, entwined hearts and "Love," pewter, early 20th C	.30
Ice Cream, witch, pewter, 5.5" h	.150
Pudding, ironstone transfer, floral spray design in bottom, vertical fluting around sides, oval gallery type foot, imp "10," 6.375 x 5 x 2.75"	.20
Pudding, melon shaped, copper, 2 pc, oval hinged handles on top and bottom, mkd "50," 7.5 x 5.75", 3.5" h	.25
Turk's Head, redware, clear glaze, brown flecks, 6" d	.35
Turk's Head, redware, Rockingham glaze	.65

FOOTBALL CARDS

Football cards are hot. Baseball card prices have reached the point where even some of the common cards are outside the price range of the average collector. If you cannot afford baseball, why not try football?

Football card collecting is not as sophisticated as baseball card collecting. However, it will be. Smart collectors who see a similarity between the two collecting areas are beginning to stress Pro-Bowlers and NFL All-Stars. Stay away from World

Football material. The league is a loser among collectors, just as it was in real life.

Periodicals: *Beckett Football Card Magazine,* 15850 Dallas Pkwy., Dallas, TX 75248; *Sports Cards,* 700 E. State St., Iola, WI 54990; *Tuff Stuff,* 700 E. State St., Iola, WI 54990.

Note: The prices listed below are for cards in good condition.

Bowman, 1950, #2, John Greene 20.00
Bowman, 1951, #14, Bob Williams 18.00
Bowman, 1952, #74, Joe Campanella .35.00
Bowman, 1953, #51, John Karras 20.00
Bowman, 1954, #55, Frank Gifford . . .100.00
Bowman, 1955, #158, Chuck Bednarik .25.00
Donruss, 1995, #30, Andre Reed 2.00
Donruss, 1996, #33, Herschel Walker . .05
Fleer, 1961, #30, John Unitas 70.00
Fleer, 1962, #62, Bill Mathis 6.00
Fleer, 1963, #29, Ken Rice 8.00
Fleer, 1974, Hall of Fame, complete
    set (50) 50.00
Fleer, 1975, Hall of Fame, complete
    set (84) 30.00
Fleer, 1978, Team Action, complete
    set (68) 50.00
Leaf, 1948, #45, Jim White 20.00
Leaf, 1949, #150, Bulldog Turner 150.00
Pacific, 1991, complete set (660) 20.00
Pacific, 1992, #33, Wendell Davis 05
Pacific, 1994, complete set (450) 28.00
Philadelphia Gum, 1964, #79, Bart
    Starr 40.00
Philadelphia Gum, 1965, #50, Don
    Meredith 25.00
Philadelphia Gum, 1966, #32, Mike
    Ditka 25.00
Philadelphia Gum, 1967, #169, San
    Francisco 49ers 1.50
Pinnacle, 1991, complete set (415) . . .35.00
Pinnacle, 1992, #1, Reggie White 10
Pinnacle, 1994, #22, Steve Young 1.50
Pinnacle, 1996, #1, Emmitt Smith 2.50
Score, 1989, #92, Reggie White 2.00
Score, 1990, #40, Boomer Esiason 20
Score, 1992, #104, Keith Jackson 05
Score, 1995, complete set (275) 15.00
Topps, 1957, #49, Chuck Bednarik 15.00
Topps, 1958, #9, Cleveland Browns . . . 6.00
Topps, 1959, #26, Walt Michaels 2.00
Topps, 1960, #2, Alan Ameche 5.00

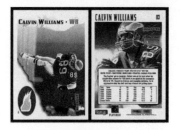

Score, 1995, #83, Calvin Williams, 5¢.
—Photo courtesy Ray Morykan Auctions.

Topps, 1961, #16, Bill George 4.00
Topps, 1962, #4, Joe Perry 9.00
Topps, 1963, #8, Gino Marchetti 5.00
Topps, 1964, #43, Buffalo Bills 4.00
Topps, 1965, #45, Odell Barry 6.00
Topps, 1966, #43, Mickey Slaughter . . . 4.00
Topps, 1992, complete set (45) 25.00
Topps, 1994, #63, Marcus Allen 3.00
Topps, 1995, #39, Ricky Watters 1.00
Topps, 1996, #67, Dan Marino 30.00

FOOTBALL MEMORABILIA

At the moment, this category is heavily weighted toward professional football. Do not overlook some great college memorabilia. Local pride dominates most collecting. Taking an item back to its hometown often doubles its value. Because of their limited production and the tendency of most individuals to discard them within a short time, some of the hardest things to find are game promotional giveaways. Also check the breweriana collectors. A surprising number of beer companies sponsor football broadcasts. Go Bud Light!

Autograph, O J Simpson, sgd *Rolling
    Stone* magazine cover, Sep 8, 1977,
    blue ink signature, 11 x 13.5" 25
Book, *All-American*, John R Tunis, hard-
    cover, 245 pp, 1942 2
Book, *Rosey Grier's Needlepoint For
    Men*, hardcover, 160 pp, ©1973
    Walker & Co, 9 x 11" 15
Cereal Box, Wheaties, full color panel
    photo of Chicago Bears' Walter
    Payton, c1980-90, 2 x 6.75 x 9.5" 15

Tip Tray, 2 boys in football gear, "Wheeling Steel Corporation–Yorkville Works, Home of Ductillite," 6.75 x 4.625", $25.

Drinking Glass, National Football Clinic, clear, front depicts white, maroon, and yellow football passer above "March 23-26, 1970/Dr Harry G. Scott, Executive Director,"and "Kenneth McFarland, banquet speaker," reverse lists clinic staff coaches, 6.25" h, 3" d 15

Game, NBC Pro Playoff Football Game, Hasbro, 1969 15

Game, Sports Illustrated College Football Game, 1972 5

Greeting Card, Baltimore Colts, textured white paper folder card, cartoon cover illus, printed red greeting "Happy Holiday Season From All The Colts," c1960s, 4.5 x 6" 20

Magazine, *Sports Illustrated*, Nov 13, 1978, "Penn State Rolls On" 4

Magazine, *Sports Review Football Illustrated*, 1951, 10.5 x 13.5" 25

Media Pin, CBS Sports College Football ..4

Pinback Button, "No Freedom–No Football," center Liberty Bell image, blue lettering for National Football League Players' Assoc, c1982 15

Pinback Button, "White Owl Football Game of the Week/NBC-TV," figural orange football, black and white owl perched on goal posts, c1950s 10

Planter, shoe kicking football, McCoy ...65

Program, Baltimore Colts "The Huddle," Sep 29, 1969, 68 pp, 8.5 x 11" 5

Wastebasket, litho tin, "Players of the New York Jets," gridiron design around perimeter with oval photos of players, ©1971 National Football League Players Assoc," 16" h, 8.25" d .30

FOSTORIA GLASS

The Fostoria Glass Company was founded in Fostoria, Ohio, in 1887 and moved to Moundsville, West Virginia, in 1891. In 1983 Lancaster Colony purchased the company but produced glass under the Fostoria trademark.

Fostoria is collected by pattern, with the American pattern the most common and sought after. Other patterns include Baroque, Georgian, Holly, Midnight Rose, Navarre, Rhapsody, and Wister. Hazel Weatherman's *Fostoria, Its First Fifty Years*, published by the author about 1972, helps identify patterns.

Clubs: Fostoria Glass Collectors, P.O. Box 1625, Orange, CA 92856; Fostoria Glass Society of America, P.O. Box 826, Moundsville, WV 26041.

American, ashtray, crystal, square 8

American, bread and butter plate, crystal, 6" d 8

American, butter cov, crystal, .25 lb 14

American, candlesticks, pr, ftd, crystal, 8.5" h 35

American, cheese compote, crystal 24

American, creamer and sugar with tray, crystal 40

American, water goblet, crystal, 10 oz ..14

American, old fashioned, crystal, 6 oz ...12

American, rose bowl, 5" d 35

American, salad plate, crystal, 7.5" d 10

American, tumbler, ftd, 9 oz, crystal, 4.25" h 12

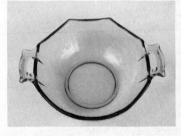

Fairfax, whipped cream bowl, 2-handled, green, 5.5" d, $25.

Beverly, centerpiece bowl, amber, 11" d .45
Beverly, salad bowl, amber, 10" d 35
Fairfax, creamer, azure 25
Fairfax, sugar, azure 25
Figurine, chanticleer, crystal, 10.75" h ..275
Figurine, squirrel, tail up, crystal 45
Hermitage, sherbet ftd 5
Jamestown, champagne, blue 18
Jamestown, juice tumbler, ftd, brown 8
Jamestown, water goblet, amber 6
Jamestown, water goblet, blue 20
Jamestown, water goblet, crystal 12
Jamestown, wine goblet, amber 6
Navarre, candlesticks, pr, #2496, crystal,
    4" h 45
Navarre, salad plate, crystal, 7.5" d 18
Navarre, sherbet, crystal, low 25
Romance, candlesticks, pr, #6023,
    crystal 40
Romance, cocktail, crystal 18
Romance, water goblet, crystal 30
Romance, wine, crystal 35
Vernon, bread and butter plate, azure,
    6" d 6
Vernon, cream soup, azure 35
Vernon, finger bowl, azure 20
Vernon, salad plate, 7.5" d 10
Versailles, cup and saucer, azure 30

FRANCISCAN

Charles Gladding, Peter McBean, and George Chambers organized the Gladding, McBean and Company pottery in 1875. Located in California, the firm's early products included sewer pipes and architectural items. In 1934 the company began producing dinnerware under the Franciscan trademark. The earliest forms consisted of plain shapes and bright colors. Later, the company developed molded, underglaze patterns such as Desert Rose, Apple, and Ivy.

Franciscan ware can be found with a great variety of marks—over 80 were used. Many of the marks include the pattern name and patent dates and numbers.

Club: Franciscan Pottery Collectors Society, 8412 5th Ave. NE, Seattle, WA 98115.

Apple, ashtray, square 275
Apple, child's plate, 3 part 200

El Patio, cup and saucer, turquoise, $20.

Apple, coupe steak plate 200
Apple, milk pitcher 95
Apple, pitcher, 2 1/2 qt 150
Apple, relish, 3 part 85
Cafe Royal, ginger jar 300
Cafe Royal, hurricane lamp with globe .300
Cafe Royal, tea canister 200
Desert Rose, bullion, cov 400
Desert Rose, box, heart shaped 165
Desert Rose, casserole, cov, 2 1/2 qt ...650
Desert Rose, compote, large 75
Desert Rose, grill plate 125
Desert Rose, milk pitcher 100
Desert Rose, relish, 10" d 400
Desert Rose, salt and pepper mill 275
Desert Rose, syrup pitcher 75
Desert Rose, tidbit, 2-tier 200
Desert Rose, turkey platter, 19" l 300
El Patio, cereal bowl 15
El Patio, dinner plate 20
El Patio, platter 30
Forget-Me-Not, cereal bowl 15
Forget-Me-Not, dessert plate 15
Forget-Me-Not, dinner plate 25
Forget-Me-Not, platter, 14" l 35
Heritage, bread and butter plate, 6.25" d ..4
Heritage, butter, cov 15
Heritage, gravy boat 20
Heritage, platter, 14.5" l 20
Ivy, casserole, cov 225
Ivy, teapot 300
Ivy, turkey platter 400
Meadow Rose, baking dish, rect 275
Meadow Rose, teapot 200
Small Fruit, chop plate, 12" d 300
Small Fruit, chop plate, 14" d 400
Small Fruit, water tumbler 125
Wildflower, casserole, cov 900
Wildflower, relish 400
Wildflower, water tumbler 175

FRANKART

Every time there is an Art Deco revival, Frankart gets rediscovered. Frankart was founded in the mid-1920s by Arthur Von Frankenberg, a sculptor and artist.

Frankart figures were mass produced and are identified through form and style, not specific features. While nudes are the most collectible, do not overlook other human figures and animals.

Almost every piece is marked with the company name followed by a patent number or "pat. appl. for." Avoid unmarked pieces. Frankenberg's wares were frequently copied during the late 1920s and early 1930s.

Ashtray, cowboy, 8 x 7" 160
Ashtray, deer, removable black glass
    tray, 6.5" h, 8.5 x 4.5" base 40
Ashtray, nude woman supporting ash-
    tray, 10" h, 6.5" w 25
Bookends, pr, cocker spaniel 65
Bookends, pr, Dutch children, 5.25" h . . .50
Bookends, pr, rearing horse, Art Deco,
    5.75" h 40
Bookends, pr, sailor boy 20
Bookends, pr, Scottie dogs, 4" h, 5.5" l,
    3.5" d 80
Bookends, pr, stylized deer, white metal,
    bronze finish, 5.5" h, 3.75" l 35
Doorstop, horse, monochrome turquoise,
    c1927 90
Figure, standing nude, hands raised
    above head holding attached bowl,
    mkd "Pat. DES. 80059," 24.5" h 225

Bookends, pr, nudes, 8.5 x 5.5", $200.

FRANKOMA

In 1933 John N. Frank, a ceramic art instructor at Oklahoma University, founded Frankoma, Oklahoma's first commercial pottery. Originally located in Norman, it eventually moved to Sapulpa, Oklahoma, in 1938. A series of disastrous fires, the last in 1983, struck the plant.

Look for pieces bearing a pacing leopard mark. These were produced earlier than items marked "FRANKOMA."

Club: Frankoma Family Collectors Assoc, P.O. Box 32571, Oklahoma City, OK 73123.

Ada Clay, coffee mug, #5C, prairie
    green 18
Ada Clay, creamer, #5DA, prairie green,
    3" 9
Ada Clay, creamer and sugar, #23A,
    cherokee red, 3" h 400
Ada Clay, demitasse cup and saucer,
    prairie green .12
Ada Clay, figure, circus horse, black,
    4.5" h 175
Ada Clay, figure, elephant, #160 black,
    3.125" h 250
Ada Clay, figure, English setter, #163,
    prairie green, 3" h 150
Ada Clay, figure, flower girl, prairie
    green, 5.5" h .125
Ada Clay, figure, seated puma, sorghum
    brown, 3" h 200
Ada Clay, figure, swan, #168, 3" h 200
Ada Clay, gravy boat, #5S, prairie green .12
Ada Clay, Thunderbird canteen, red
    bud, 6.5" h 125
Ada Clay, vase, #28, silver sage, 6.5" h .200
Ada Clay, vase, #501, old gold, 2.75" h ..175
Ashtray, #223, clover, desert gold 8
Ashtray, #452, free form, desert gold, 7" d .15
Ashtray, #457, Broadmoor, prairie green .35
Bowl, #201, woodland moss, 9" d 15
Butter, cov, #7K, prairie green 30
Candleholders, pr, #305, prairie green ...20
Centerpiece Bowl, @219, black 50
Figure, bucking bronco, #121, orange
    brown 400
Honey Jug with Bee, #803, desert gold,
    prairie green .13
Lazybones, creamer and covered sugar,
    #4, prairie green 15

Mug, Republican elephant, gray, $28.

Oriental Bowl, #205, brown satin 10
Plainsman, salt and pepper shakers, pr,
    #5HS, prairie green 10
Planter, #14, desert gold 8
Planter, #45, prairie green, 12" h 25
Sapulpa Clay, coffee mug, #5C, prairie
    green 12
Spoon Rest, #4Y, autumn yellow 6
Teapot, #6J, 2 cup, prairie green 12
Toby Mug, cowboy, flame 20
Toby Mug, golfer, desert gold 15
Vase, #65, prairie green, 7" h 20

FRATERNAL ORDER ITEMS

Today, few people understand the dominant societal role played by fraternal orders and benevolent societies between 1850 and 1950. Because many had membership qualifications that were prejudicial, these "secret" societies often were targets for the social activists of the 1960s.

Many fraternal and benevolent organizations have disbanded. A surprising amount of their material has worked its way into the market. Some of the convention souvenir objects are downright funky. Costumes are great for dress-up. Do not pay big money for them. Same goes for ornamental swords.

Fraternal Order of Beavers, medal, enamel,
    red, white, and blue, Lancaster Lodge
    #166, 1.375" d .35
Fraternal Order of Eagle, belt buckle,
    gold-plated, center eagle emblem,
    3.5 x 2.375" 10

Fraternal Order of Eagles, decanter,
    brown, FOE symbol in middle with
    gold eagle, 1897-1973, mkd "OMB
    No 26, 1973 Royal Halburton China" . .10
Fraternal Order of Police, bread and
    butter plate, eagle symbol with banner on rim, double green ring rim,
    Syracuse China, 6" d 10
Knights of Templar, badge, Cross of
    Honor, enamel 20
Knights of Templar, book, *Order of the
    Red Cross,* gilded edges, 200 pp,
    Allen Publishing Co, 1921 10
Masonic, book, *History of the Eastern
    Star Lodge 1823-1923, No.186-F.&A.M.,*
    blue cloth, gold lettering, inscribed
    "Presented to Warren Lodge No. 310
    F.&A.M. with the compliments of
    Bro. James Monagham of Eastern
    Star Lodge, No. 186 F.&A.M., Guest
    of the Masonic Home of Pennsylvania,
    Collegeville PA, April 10th 1923," illus,
    list of members, history, genealogy,
    11 x 8" 10
Masonic, cup and saucer, hp center
    Eastern star surrounded by small
    gold stars, gold band around rim,
    Lefton 8
Masonic, plate, center Masonic emblem,
    floral rim, mkd "Dreseen Hotel China
    Warranted," 9" d 10
Masonic, token, aluminum, front mkd
    "Aladdin Temple Columbus Ohio,"
    Masonic symbol on reverse 4

*Elks, shaving mug, "B.P.O.E." above
12-point elk, "Elite France" stamped on
base, 4" h, $100.* —Photo courtesy
Collectors Auction Services.

Masonic, token, brass, front mkd "115th
Imperial Council Session 1989 Toronto
Canada," Masonic symbol with
"Edward G. McMullan C.D. Imperial
Potentate" 3
Order of Odd Fellows, book, *Gems of
Odd Fellowship in Prose and Poetry*,
Edward P Nowell, 288 pp, 5 x 7.5" 10
Order of Odd Fellows, medal, celluloid
medal and ribbon tie bar, mkd "White-
head & Hoag Co," 1890-1910 12
Shriner, stick pin, brass, Shriner's head
with hp red fez, clutch mkd "Modern
Clutch," 2.5" l 18

FROG COLLECTIBLES

A frog collector I know keeps her collection in the guest bathroom. All the bathroom fixtures are green also. How long do
you think it took me to find the toilet? Thank
goodness I have good bladder control.

In fairy tales frogs usually received
good press. Not true for their cousin, the
toad. Television introduced us to Kermit the
Frog, thus putting to rest the villainous frog
image of Froggy the Gremlin. I am willing to
bet Froggy's "magic twanger" would not
get past today's TV censors.

Club: The Frog Pond, P.O. Box 193, Beech
Grove, IN 46107.

Candleholder, green, Indiana Glass, 5" l,
4" w 3
Cane Handle, figural, silvered white
metal, inset glass eyes, early 1900s,
5.5" h 50
Cookie Jar, mkd "906 USA" 20
Doorstop, cast iron, 5.5" l 12
Figurine, frog holding mushroom, made
in Japan, 5" h 4
Figurine, papa and baby frog, 1" Hagen
Renaker, and .5" l, price for pair 5
Game, Game of Jumping Frog, J H
Singer, c1890 20
Game, The Frog Who Would A–Wooing
Go, The United Games Co, lid depicts
frog in colonial dress with high socks
and lacy cuffs holding hand to head ..60
Key Chain, metal, frog riding bicycle,
c1940, 1" d 8

*Snow Globe,
figural frog with
globe in belly,
plastic, made in
Hong Kong,
1980s, 5" h, $15.*

Match Striker, frog seated on seashell
playing mandolin, mkd "Bassano/
Made in Italy, CP.35" 125
Mug, ceramic, white, small green frog
sitting in bottom, c1972 5
Mustard Jar, plastic spoon, dark green
and brown, made in Japan 6
Salt and Pepper Shakers, pr, Vietri, 4" l ...5
Tin, frogs playing leapfrog illus, emb
alphabet border, 8" d 125
Windup, litho tin, plastic feet, made in
Japan 5

FRUIT JARS

Most fruit jars are worth less than $1.
Their value rests in reuse for canning rather
than in the collectors' market. Do not be
fooled by patent dates that appear on the
jar. Over 50 different types of jars bear a
patent date of 1858 and many were made as
long as 50 years later.

However, there are some expensive
fruit jars. A good price guide is Douglas M.
Leybourne, Jr.'s *The Collector's Guide to
Old Fruit Jars: Red Book No. 8,* published
privately by the author in 1997.

Clubs: Ball Collectors Club, 497 Fox Dr.,
Monroe, MI 48161; Federation of Historical
Bottle Collectors, Inc., P.O. Box 1558,
Southampton, PA 18966; Midwest Antique
Fruit Jar & Bottle Club, P.O. Box 38, Flat
Rock, IN 47234.

Anderson Preserving Co, Camden, NJ,
clear, smooth lip, Mason beaded
neck seal, 1 qt 2

Ball Ideal, clear, glass lid, wire bail, emb lettering, $2.

Ball Ideal, clear, smooth lip, lightning dimple neck seal, concentric circles base, c1933-41,1 pt 2

Ball Improved, blue, smooth lip, glass lid and screw band, 1 pt 20

Ball Mason, aqua, smooth lip, c1900-10, 1 pt 5

Ball Perfect Mason, clear, smooth lip, Mason beaded neck seal, c1923-33, 1 qt 4

Bristol Farm, clear, smoothlip, plastic lid, 1 pt 1

Electrolux, clear, smooth lip, Mason beaded neck seal, 1 pt 1

French's Medford Prepared Mustard, clear, smooth lip Mason beaded neck seal, metal screw cap, 15 oz 8

Genuine Mason, aqua, smooth lip, Mason shoulder seal, 1 pt 6

Hartford Fruit Jar Co, clear, ground lip, glass lid and screw band, 1 pt 45

Improved Crown, clear, smooth lip, glass insert and screw band, 1 pt 2

Kerr Self Sealing, clear, smooth lip, Mason beaded neck seal, 2-pc metal lid, pat Aug 31, 1915, 1 qt 2

Ohio Quality Mason, clear, smooth lip, Mason beaded neck seal, 1 qt 12

Our Pure Food Products, clear, smooth lip, glass insert and screw band, 1 qt . .3

Pearl Fruit Jar, clear, smooth lip,1 pt 8

Reliable Home Canning Mason, clear, smooth lip, Mason beaded neck seal, 1 qt 2

Rylands Barnsley, aqua, smooth lip, Mason shoulder seal, metal screw cap, 3/4 pt 4

Samco Super Mason, clear, smooth lip, Mason beaded neck seal, qt 3

Windsor Coconut, aqua, ground lip, metal screw cap, 1 pt 15

FURNITURE

Much of the furniture found at flea markets is of the secondhand variety.

Arm Chair, Heywood-Wakefield, champagne oak finish, green upholstered dog bone back, shaped tapered arms, bentwood seat frame, slightly bowed seat rail, green upholstered slip seat, elliptical tapered legs, color, maker's mark, and date of August 23, 1953" stamped on underside of seat, period fabric and finish, 18" w, 10.5" d, 33.75" h, seat height 18" 175

Bar Seat, painted metal, foliate back, hide seat 75

Cedar Chest, Lane, waterfall veneer, 1930 175

Chifforobe, herringbone design waterfall veneer, arched center mirror, dropped center section, 4 deep drawers flanked by tall cupboard doors, shaped apron,1935 200

Crock Stand, pine, 3 tier, graduated half round shelves, 3 part stepped scalloped frame, dark finish, 38.75" h, 34.5" w 300

Curio Cabinet, oak, hanging, flat molded cornice, single glazed cabinet door, 6 shelf interior, shaped apron, 18" w, 5.5" d, 38.25" h 150

Occasional Table, Colonial Revival, William and Mary style, Umphrey Mfg Co, Crawfordsville, IN, walnut veneer, 1929, $135.

Dressing Table, pine, scrolled crest, dovetailed drawer, turned legs, tapering feet, red and black graining, yellow striping, gilt stenciled compote of fruit and flowers on crest, emb brass pulls, 23" w, 15.5" d, 34" h .... .400

Drying Rack, pine, 3 square mortised bars on square posts, shoe feet, old green-gray paint, 29.5" w, 49" h 175

End Table, step shelf on square tapered pedestal sides, rect top base, canted incised apron, flat tapered legs, simulated blond oak Formica on shelf and top base, speckled painted sides, 15.75" w, 29.75" d, 22" h, price for pair 100

Filing Cabinet, oak, table top, dovetailed case, 4 drawers hold index cards, brass label holder pulls, 13" w, 16" d, 9" h 150

Footstool, cherry, shaped aprons, bootjack ends, primitive village landscape on top, sponging, old repainting, 13.5" w.......................225

Kneeling Bench, Windsor, splayed base, reeded edge top, bamboo turned legs, gray over olive green and red paint, 36.75" l, 6.75" d, 6" h 325

Night Stand, walnut, waterfall veneer, open shelf above single cupboard door, 1935 200

Rocker, ladder back, turned elongated acorn finials on back posts, 4 serpentine shaped arched slats, paper rush seat, ring and bulbous turned front stretchers, box stretchers, cheese cutter runners, old green repaint over earlier red, replaced seat, 39" h 175

Side Chair, walnut, black satin, shaped back, scrolled side rails, upholstered seat, 1940 350

Side Chair, wicker, square back, diamond and X-shaped designs in tightly woven back, wrapped hip brackets, trapezoidal seat with upholstered seat cushion and braided edge, tightly woven skirt, wrapped legs joined by X-form stretcher, white, 37" h 175

Stool, pine, joined, rect top, splayed base, chamfered corners on square legs joined by stretchers, traces of old red paint, stretchers worn thin, 1 foot replaced, 18" l, 13" w, 16" h 200

Table, cast iron, Vintage pattern, circ top, old worn blue repaint, wooden replacement top, 24" d, 16" h 175

Telephone Table, alder, rect top, rounded end above case with open shelves, cutout support and small drawer, 1937 200

Vanity, walnut, large round mirror, flanked by 2 three drawer sections, dropped center well, 1935 250

Writing Chair, shaped crest rail, vasiform splat, shaped writing surface, turned posts, plank seat, turned front legs and stretcher, splayed base, stenciled foliage on crest and splat, striping, black ground, repaired split on arm, old repaint, 34" h 100

GAMBLING COLLECTIBLES

Gaming devices, gaming accessories, and souvenirs from gambling establishments—from hotels to riverboats—are all collectible.

Gambling collectors compete with Western collectors for the same material. Sometimes the gunfight gets bloody. With the price of old, i.e., late nineteenth- and early twentieth-century, gambling material skyrocketing, many new collectors are focusing on more modern material dating from the speakeasies of the 1920s and the glitz of Las Vegas in the 1950s and 1960s.

Club: Casino Chip & Gaming Tokens Collectors Club, P.O. Box 340345, Columbus, OH 43234.

License Plate Attachment, diecut metal, painted, 7.5" h, 10.5" w, $150. —Photo courtesy Collectors Auction Services.

Slot Machine (trade stimulator), Reel Poker, Western Products, Inc, Chicago, IL, 9.25" h, 9.25" w, $550. —Photo courtesy Collectors Auction Services.

Ashtray, Wilbur Clark's Desert Inn, pot
   metal, Japan, 1950s, 4.75 x 4.75" ..... .45
Book, *Vegas Kard Games*, Edward J
   Pullman, 24 pp, 1961, 5 x 7.125" ...... .15
Book, *Woman's Guide to Gambling*,
   175 pp, 1960s 2
Booklet, Amazingly Different/Herolds
   Club-For-Fun/Reno, Nevada Press,
   shows layouts for roulette, craps,
   blackjack, keno, and slots, center
   photo page of club, 1958, 6.5 x 4" ..... .10
Card and Chip Holder, wood, Bakelite
   knob on top, cardboard cover, com-
   plete with chips, 2" h, 6.5" l, 2.75" w ... .50
Catalog, Crooked Gambling Supply
   Catalog, K C Card Co, #560, c1960s ... .25
Cuff Links, pr, Bakelite, figural dice, 1930s .25
Dice, Sands Casino, Atlantic City, NJ 1
Magazine, *Life,* Jun 19, 1950, "Gambling
   in the USA" 5
Poker Chip, clay, Dixie Inn 5
Poker Chip, mkd "Stedes Bains De Mer
   Mona Co," 1.25" d 5
Postcard, Reno, NV, gambling and craps .. .2
Postcard, "The Gambler," 2 black boys
   gambling, c1900s 8
Slot Machine, Bally, Clover Bell, 1949 .. .800
Slot Machine, Fields, 4 Jacks, 1930 .... .650
Slot Machine, Mills, Bell-O-Matic
   Model M, 25¢, 1968 .... .850
Souvenir, fob-style seashell, stamped
   brass, for Monte Carlo gambling
   resort, depicts casino and palm trees,
   red, white, and blue ribbon attached
   to top loop, 1.125" l .... .18

Spinner Cage, aluminum, mkd "Allied
   Metal Ind. 656 SLA St., Los Angeles,"
   11.5" h, 5.5" w 8
Spinning Wheel, wood, steel spokes
   and center hub, 120 number spots,
   mkd "J. Lobdell, Michigan," 1930s,
   32" d .... .100
Thimble, porcelain, Las Vegas, playing
   cards, slot machine, and dice, price
   for set of 3 4
Token, Harrah's, plastic, brass inserts,
   1.5" d 2

GAMES

Avoid common games, e.g., "Go to the Head of the Class," "Monopoly," and "Rook." They were produced in such vast quantities that they hold little attraction for collectors.

Most boxed board games found are in heavily used condition. Box lids have excessive wear, tears, and are warped. Pieces are missing. In this condition, most games fall in the $2 to $10 range. However, the minute a game is in fine condition or better, value jumps considerably.

Clubs: Assoc. of Game and Puzzle Collectors, PMB 321, 197M Boston Post Rd. West, Marlborough, MA 01752; Gamers Alliance, P.O. Box 197, East Meadow, NY 11554.

Periodicals: *Toy Shop,* 700 E. State St., Iola, WI 54990; *Toy Trader,* P.O. Box 1050, Dubuque, IA 52004.

Across the Continent, Parker Brothers,
   1960 .... .20

Get the Message, Milton Bradley, 1964, $12.

Jungle Hunt, Rosebud Art Co, c1940s, $15.

Truth or Consequences, Gabriel, 1955, $40.

Animal Talk Game, Mattel, 1963 25
Authors, E E Fairchild, c1945 15
Bamboozle, Milton Bradley, 1962 35
Bash!, Milton Bradley 1965 15
Battleship Game, Whitman, 1940 15
Beat the Clock Game, Milton Bradley,
 1969 15
Big Blast, Transogram, 1967 25
Big Business, Transogram, 1954 15
Bionic Woman, The, Parker Brothers,
 1976 18
Blox-O, Lubbers & Bell Mfg Co, 1923 20
Break the Bank, Bettye-B, 1955 45
Car Travel Game, Milton Bradley, 1958 . .20
Cat and Mouse, Game of, Parker
 Brothers, 1964 .15
Cherry Ames' Nursing Game, Parker
 Brothers, 1959 .50
Chop Suey Game, Ideal, 1967 15
Countdown, E S Lowe, 1967 60
Cuckoo, J H Singer, 1891 35
Doc Holliday Wild West Game,
 Transogram, 1960 45
Dream House TV Home Game, Milton
 Bradley, 1968 20
Egg Race Game, Ideal, 1968 18
Exports and Transportation, Game of,
 Mills Games Mfg Co, 1936 12
Fame and Fortune, Whitman, 1962 18
Fan-Tel, O Schoenhut Inc, 1937 18
Foil, 3M, 1969 12
Go For Broke, Selchow & Righter, 1965 . .12
Great Escape, Ideal, 1967 18
Haunted House, Ideal, 1962 60
Have-U "It?," Selchow & Righter, 1924 . .22
How to Succeed in Business Without
 Really Trying, Milton Bradley, 1963 . . .12
Image, 3M, 1972 10

Intrigue, Milton Bradley, 1955 35
Journey to the Unknown Game, Remco,
 1968 100
Junior Executive, The Money Game of,
 Whitman, 1963 .12
Kimbo, Parker Brothers, 1960 15
Lassie Game, Game Gems, 1965 25
Lie, Cheat & Steal, Reiss, 1976 12
Little Red Bushy-Tail, Parker Brothers,
 1921 50
Lot the Calf, Brown Games Inc, 1964 20
Mail Run, Quality Games, 1960 40
Mask, Parker Brothers, 1985 5
Mexican Pete, Parker Brothers, 1940s . .30
Moneypower, Sherman Games, 1980 . . .10
Name That Tune, Milton Bradley, 1959 . .15
No Time For Sergeants, Ideal, 1964 35
Ouija, William Fuld, 1920 15
Park and Shop, Milton Bradley, 1950s . . .40
Parcheesi, Selchow & Righter, 1950s . . .10
Patty Duke Game, Milton Bradley, 1964 .30
Post Office, Hasbro, 1968 20
Raggedy Ann, Milton Bradley, 1954 25
Seven-Up Game, Transogram, 1961 15
Surfside 6, Lowell, 1962 45
Tammy Game, The, Ideal, 1963 18
Track & Trap, Whitman, 1969 15
Uncle Wiggly Game, Milton Bradley,
 1954 20
Underdog, Milton Bradley, 1964 25
Voyage to the Bottom of the Sea Game,
 Milton Bradley, 1964 20
Why, Milton Bradley, 1961 15
Wipe Off Target Game, Milton Bradley,
 1959 12
Wordy, Pressman Toy Corp, 1938 25
You Don't Say Game, Milton Bradley,
 1964-69 10

GARDEN RELATED ITEMS

Are there valuable collectibles in your garden shed or basement? Chances are the answer is yes. Garden-related collectibles are hot. They are featured regularly in illustrations in Country and decorating magazines.

Cast iron garden furniture and cast statuary led the parade a decade ago. Now, watch out for lawn sprinklers, watering cans, and even lawn mowers. Collectors currently prefer pre-1940 examples, but expect this to change.

Is there any hope for old garden hoses? Absolutely not! Send them to the landfill.

Basket, potato, woven, U-shaped wooden handle, Maine 50
Bench, bark cov cedar, straight rails, geometric and random twig design back, twig braces, wide armrests with spindle supports, 14 board seat, c1920 275
Boot Scraper, cast iron, with brush, c1845-65 150
Chair, cast iron, vintage design, white repaint, 14" h seat, 27.25" h, price for set of 4 200
Fencing, cast iron, single panel, 3 posts, extra finials and hardware 225
Garden Stake, black boy fishing, wood cutout, painted, c1950, 28" h 65
Garden Stake, turtle, wood cutout, painted, standing upright, wearing top hat, modern steel base, 25.5" h ...85
Gate, wood, picket, painted gray, New England, 19th C, 49" h, 35.25" w 200

Frog Figure, Weller, Coppertone, 6.5" l, $925. —Photo courtesy Gene Harris Antique Auction Center, Inc.

Water Sprinkler, painted metal, black man holding rubber hose, 36" h, $370. —Photo courtesy Collectors Auction Services.

Picking Ladder, wood, tripod shape, evenly spaced rungs, c1910-30, French, 88" h, 33" w 150
Pitchfork, 3-tined 15
Plant Stand, twig construction, painted white 20
Salesman's Sample, jockey lawn ornament, cast metal, black man on pedestal, red pants, green vest, white shirt, 12.5" h, 4.5" w 375
Seed Packet, California Poppy, Tucker's Seed House, Carthage, MO, #2103, 2.75 x 4.5" 20
Seed Packet, tomato, Burt's, ©Stecher-Traung, Rochester, NY, 5 x 3.25" 5
Sign, "Chief/Authorized Sales & Service/Garden Tractors & Implements," painted metal flange, 2-sided, depicts Indian chief holding arrow, mkd "Scioto Sign Kenton 0," 13.5" h, 17.625" w 100
Sign, "Masterpiece Fertilizers/Geo. W. Fuhr-Azusa.," emb tin, 1-sided, 13.5" h, 20" w 35
Spigot, brass, figural turtle, c1910-30 ...15
Sundial, lead, 9.25 x 9.25" 100
Tool, potato fork 20
Wagon Wheel, wood, metal hub, painted white 50
Water Pump, cast iron, painted black ...50
Watering Can, galvanized, ribbed sides ..30
Watering Can, metal, embellished copper rose and spout, c1885-1900, 24" h 100
Wheelbarrow, cast iron and sheet metal, 1910-30, 25" h, 20" w 85
Wheelbarrow, wood and iron, tapered handles, iron wheel, orig blue paint, 26" h, 28" w, 48" l 450

GAS STATION COLLECTIBLES

Approach this from two perspectives—items associated with gas stations and gasoline company giveaways. Competition for this material is fierce. Advertising collectors want the advertising; automobile collectors want material to supplement their collections.

Beware of reproductions ranging from advertising signs to pump globes. Do not accept too much restoration and repair. There were hundreds of thousands of gasoline stations across America. Not all their back rooms have been exhausted.

Periodicals: *Check the Oil!,* 30 W. Olentangy St., Powell, OH 43065; *Petroleum Collectibles Monthly,* 411 Forest St., P.O. Box 556, LaGrange, OH 44050.

Ashtray, Esso, ceramic, white, center red and blue Esso logo with red and white silhouette of service station employee, "You're Under the Magic Sign!," 1950-60s, 6.75" d 18

Bank, still, Amoco, plastic, white, figural gas pump, paper decal, c1950-60s, 1.25 x 2.5 x 4.25" 90

Bank, still, Fire Chief Gasoline, metal, figural gas pump, paper decal, 5.75" h .300

Banner, Texaco, cloth, "New Texaco Motor Oil!/Lasts Longer–Crack Proof!," Crinnell Litho Co, Inc, NY, 36" h, 80" w 90

Photograph, White Eagle Service Station, litho cardboard in wood frame, 46" h, 66" w, $130. —Photo courtesy Collectors Auction Services.

Fan, Hudson Gasoline, cardboard, 2-sided, 13.5" h, $175. —Photo courtesy Collectors Auction Services.

Calendar, Esso, 1947, paper, full pad, "P. P. Cassetty Difficult, Tennessee," wood frame, 16" h, 9.75" w 35

Cane, Gulf Refining Co, wood, rubber base, 39" l 30

Pencil Clip, Conoco Gasoline, celluloid, oval, silvered tin clip, c1920s 35

Plate, Esso, ceramic, center cartoon illus of dog with small Esso logo by front paws, 8" d 25

Pump, Bennett Good Gulf, porcelain, slug plate mkd "Model 748 dated 5-67," reproduction globe, 52" h, 15" w, 15" d 500

Pump Globe, Esso Ethyl, metal body, 2 lenses, 15.5" d 350

Pump Globe, Fleetwing, glass body, 1 lens, 14" d .350

Pump Globe, Gold Crown, milkglass, metal body, 1 lens, 16.5" h, 16" w 420

Salt and Pepper Shakers, pr, Phillips 66, plastic, 1-sided, 2.75" h, 1" w 80

Salt and Pepper Shakers, pr, Texaco, plastic, back mkd "Columbia Service Station 801 S. Wenatchee Ave. Wenatchee, Wash.," 2.75" h, 1" w, .75" d 55

Sign, diecut porcelain flange, Texaco, 2-sided, 23" h, 18" w 325

Sign, porcelain, "Mens Rest Room," 1 sided, green lettering, 5.5" h, 14.5" w . .12

Sign, porcelain, "Shell Gasoline," shell shaped, 2-sided, 25" h, 25" w 425

Sign, porcelain, "Standard Ethyl Gasoline," diecut, 2-sided 325

Sign, tin, "Do Not Clean With Gasoline," 1-sided, depicts man cleaning with gasoline, 6" h, 24" w 70

Thermometer, Gulf, metal, "Gulf No-Nox Gasoline and Gulfride Oil/The Best In Any Season," 26.75" h, 7.5" w 50

Thermometer, Texaco, diecut tin, "Compliments Forester Bros. Ser., Wabash 308, Mfg. Erickson-Des Moines," orig box, 6.25" h, 2.5" w 125

GAUDY ITALIAN

While not all items marked "Made in Italy" are gaudy, the vast majority are. They are collected for their kitsch, not aesthetic value.

The Mediterranean look was a popular decorating style in the late 1950s and early 1960s. Etruscan-style pieces, reproduction and copycats of Etruscan antiquities painted in light yellows and greens, often relief decorated with sea motifs including mythical sea creatures, and featuring a high gloss, majolica-type glaze, were the most popular. Production values were crude.

The Mediterranean look fell out of favor by the mid-1960s. Those gaudy Italians that did not wind up in the garbage dump were relegated to basements, attics, and other damp and foreboding places. Some wish they had stayed there.

Vases are the most commonly found form. The modestly decorated examples sell in the $15 to $25 range. A large elaborate example fetches $40 or more. The gaudiness of the piece affects its value—the more gaudy, the higher the perceived value.

GAY FAD GLASSWARE

In the late 1930s Fran Taylor and her husband, Bruce, founded the Gay Fad Studios, a firm that decorated glass and metal wares for sale in the tabletop market. The business flourished. In 1945 the Taylors transferred their operations from Detroit to Lancaster, Ohio, just across the street from the Anchor Hocking Glass Co.

Gay Fad glassware is found in hundreds of different designs. Many appeared as sets, e.g., the eight-glass Gay Ninety Family Portrait series. Look for decanters, juice sets, tea and toast sets, and waffle sets. Gay Fad glassware is usually marked with an interlocking "G" and "F" or "Gay Fad."

Cocktail Glass, Bentware, Beau Brummel ..8
Decanter, frosted, Bartender 8
Glass, Currier & Ives, hp, silk-screened ..3
Glass, 48 States 2
Pilsner Glass, Gay Ninety Family Portrait ..8
Salt and Pepper Shakers, pr, hp peaches, 3.5" h 18
Server, 3 sections, gold leaves dec, 8 x 22" 20
Server, rect, 3 pocket, gold and black leaves dec, sgd, 8 x 22" 20
Snack Tray, abstract pattern 15
Tray, white abstract design on clear glass, 8 x 22" 25
Tumbler, "Democrats/Say When," donkeys, 3 oz 3
Tumbler, Gal of Distinction, 12 oz 6
Tumbler, "Merry Christmas from Gay Fad," stylized dove 10
Tumbler, Rich Man, Poor Man 8
Tumbler, stylized cats 4
Tumbler, Vermont, 4.75" h, 2.5" d 3
Tumbler, Zombies 8

GEISHA GIRL

Geisha Girl porcelain is a Japanese export ware whose production began in the last quarter of the nineteenth century and still continues today. Manufacturing came to a standstill during World War II.

Collectors have identified over 150 different patterns from over one hundred manufacturers. When buying a set, check the pattern of the pieces carefully. Be on the lookout for "complete" sets with mix-and-match pieces.

Beware of reproductions that have a very white porcelain, minimal background washes, sparse detail coloring, no gold, or very bright gold enameling. Some of the reproductions came from Czechoslovakia.

Bamboo Tree, bread and butter plate, 6" d 10
Bamboo Tree, cup and saucer, mkd "Made in Japan" 8
Bamboo Tree, teapot 12
Bamboo Trellis, bowl, ftd, 7.5" d 35
Bamboo Trellis, chocolate set, pot, 6 cups and saucers, cobalt blue, latticework ground 225

Parasol Modern, toothpick holder, 2" h, $3.

Bird Cage, bread and butter plate, 6" d . . .12
Bird Cage, tete-a-tete, pot, 2 cups and
   saucers, red-orange, gold 8
Flat, bowl, red, gold trim, 6.5" d 25
Ikebana in Rickshaw, bowl, ftd, yellow,
   8" d 40
Ikebana in Rickshaw, teapot, cobalt
   blue, gold 35
Long-Stemmed Peony, creamer 12
Porch, cup and saucer, after dinner,
   dark green, Made in Japan 10
Porch, nut bowl, master, cobalt blue,
   Torii Nippon .25

G.I. JOE

   The first G.I. Joe 12" tall posable action figures for boys were produced in 1964 by the Hasbro Manufacturing Company. The original line was made up of one male action figure for each branch of the military. Their outfits were styled after World War II, Korean Conflict, and Vietnam Conflict military uniforms.

   The creation of the G.I. Joe Adventure Team made Joe the marveled explorer, hunter, deep-sea diver, and astronaut, rather than just an American serviceman. Due to the Arab oil embargo in 1976, the figure was reduced in height to 8" and was renamed the Super Joe. In 1977 production stopped.

   In 1982 G.I. Joe made his comeback—with a few changes. "The Great American Hero" is now a posable 3.75" tall plastic figure with code names corresponding to the various costumes. The new Joe must deal with both current and futuristic villains and issues.

Clubs: G.I. Joe Collectors Club, 225 Cattle Baron Parc Dr., Fort Worth, TX 76108; G.I. Joe: Steel Brigade Club, 8362 Lomay Ave., Westminster, CA 92683.

Periodical: *G.I. Joe Patrol,* P.O. Box 2362, Hot Springs, AR 71914.

ACTION FIGURE

Action Sailor, 1964 375
Black Adventurer 500
Land Adventurer 225
Man of Action 250
Sea Adventurer .425
Super Joe Commander 80
Talking Adventure Team Commander . .275
Talking Man of Action 325

CLOTHING AND ACCESSORIES

Air Manual 25
Ammo Box 10
Army Belt, with ammo pouches 30
Billy Club, no strap 10
Black Flippers 15
Crash Crew Belt, with axe and flash-
   light 25
Crash Crew Gloves 25
Deep Sea Diver Helmet 20
Dog Tag, no chain 20
Entrenching Tool 20
Flame Thrower Gun, 3 tanks 25
Green Belt, with 2 ammo packs 20
Hand Grenade 5

Foot Locker, green wooden box, orig contents, 5" h, 13.25" l, 6.5" w, $75.

Life Preserver 30
Machete and Sheath 20
Mess Kit, with knife and fork 15
Sailor Cap 10
Scabbard 3
Scuba Tank, no hoses 25
Space Boots, yellow 40
Space Suit, with 3 zippers, no flag,
   cloth boots, helmet 40
Survival Life Raft, with accessories 150
White Rifle 10

PLAYSETS AND VEHICLES

Action Man Jeep .325
Adventure Team Venicle Set, 1970 325
All-Terrain Vehicle, 1970s 55
Desert Patrol Attack Jeep Set 125
Helicopter Set, 1973 135
Motorcycle and Sidecar, 1967, 14" l . . .385
Official Jeep Combat Set, 1965 300
Shark's Surprise Set, with frogman,
   1969 550
Signal All-Terrain Vehicle, 1970s 50

GIRL SCOUTS

Girl Scout collectors started about twenty years behind Boy Scout collectors, but are catching up fast in knowledge and enthusiasm. So far, antique dealers are not in tune with their interests. However, there is a network of specialist Scouting dealers selling through the mail, and they are including Girl Scout items among their Boy Scout offerings. In addition, on-line auctions are selling a lot of Girl Scout collectibles.

Many active Girl Scout collectors are acquiring for their local Girl Scout Council Museums. They focus on different kinds of uniforms with suitable accessories. They need hats, belts, socks, and some badges but they don't need a complete set of all badges. They also like showy things like cameras and dolls.

Other Girl Scout collectors want a complete set of each type of badge and pin, plus all the calendars, and as many different Girl Scout dolls as possible. These are the true collectors.

The supply of Girl Scout collectibles is way below the demand. The problem is partly that people don't realize Girl Scout things have value. Some valuable things get discarded. Since antique dealers don't know the values of the various badges or uniforms, many of them steer clear of Girl Scout things. We need to get more information to those who can bring these items out of hiding and offer them for sale.

Advisor: Cal Holden, Box 264, Doylestown, OH 44230, (330) 658-2793.

Book, *Games For Girl Scouts*, 1969 2
Book, *Girl Scouts in the Rockies*, Lillian
   Roy, 1921 10
Book, *Juliette Low and the Girl Scouts*,
   green cloth cov with gold lettering,
   ©1928 GSA, 1944 20
Calendar, 1959 10
Camera, Girl Scout, 127, orig box 75
Coin, brass, 60th Anniversary 1912-1972,
   1" d 5
Coin Holder, plastic 5
Coin Purse, Brownie, "Koin-Bank"
   stamped in center, 2 x 4" 4
Cookbook, *Girl Scout Cookbook/Girl
   Scouts of the USA*, 160 pp, ©1971
   Henry Regnery Co 8
Cup, aluminum, collapsible, 2.5" h,
   2.375" d 5
First Aid Kit, tin, Johnson & Johnson . . .35
First Day Cover, Golden Jubilee 1912-
   1962, postmarked Burlington, VT,
   Jul 24, 1962 6
Handbook, *Charting the Course of a
   Girl Scout Mariner Ship*, 1942 55
Handbook, *Girl Scouts of the USA*, 13th
   printing, 1957, 6 x 9" 8

Chow Kit, green leather case, silver-plated folding knife, folding fork, and spoon, $30.

Book, The Girl Scouts Rally, *Girl Scout Series, Vol. 2,* Katherine Keene Galt, Saalfield Pub, hard cov, dj, 1921, $15.

Handbook, *Worlds To Explore–Handbook for Brownie and Junior Girl Scouts,* 1977 2

Magazine, *Life,* Mar 24, 1952 7

Magazine, *American Girl,* Aug 1939 10

Mess Kit, aluminum, cup, pot with bail handle, sauce pan, fry pan, dish dunking bag, nylon carrying case, Regal 7

Necktie, Brownie, cloth, snap-on, 1950s . .3

Pamphlet, "Girl Scouts Build Bridges to Other Lands," East West International Conference, HI 2

Patch, Community Olympics, 1987, 3" d . . .2

Photograph, camp scene, 3 x 4.75" 4

Pinback Button, "I'm For 'More' Girl Scouts," center trefoil symbol, green lettering on yellow ground, 1970s 3

Plate, "GS of EA" between 2 pine trees on white ground, mkd "Buffalo China," 9.75" d 30

Postcard, Girl Scout silhouette on front, logo on back, unused 45

Record, 33 1/3 rpm, recorded at Girl Scout Senior Roundup, Farragut, ID, Jul 1965, distributed by Maxwell House Coffee Co 5

Sash, Canadian, complete with 28 badges, 22" l 10

Sheet Music, *Girl Scouts Together,* 1941, 9 x 12" 10

Song Book, *Girl Scouts of Allegeny County,* PA, 64 pp, c1940-50s, 6.75 x 3.75" 2

Spoon, sterling silver, GS logo, 4.25" l . . .20

Tobacco Card, Miss Holder/The Policeman's Daughter, #13 from "Happy Family" series, Carreras Ltd, 1925, 1.5 x 2.5" 4

GOLD

Twenty-four-karat gold is pure gold. Twelve-karat gold is fifty percent gold and fifty percent other elements. Many gold items have more weight value than antique or collectible value. The gold-weight scale is different from our regular English pounds scale. Learn the proper conversion procedure. Review the value of an ounce of gold once a week and practice keeping that figure in your mind.

Take time to research and learn the difference between gold and gold plating. Pieces with gold wash, gold gilding, and gold bands have no weight value. Value rests in other areas. In many cases the gold is applied on the surface. Washing and handling lead to its removal.

Gold coinage is a whole other story. Every coin suspected of being gold should first be checked by a jeweler and then in coin price guides.

GOLF COLLECTIBLES

Golf was first played in Scotland in the fifteenth century. The game achieved popularity in the late 1840s when the "gutty" ball was introduced. Although golf was played in America before the Revolution, it gained a strong foothold in the recreational area only after 1890.

Most golf collectibles are common., so doing your homework pays, especially when trying to determine the value of clubs.

Do not limit yourself to items used on the course. Books about golf, decorative accessories with a golf motif, and clubhouse collectibles are eagerly sought by collectors. This is a great sports collectible to tee off on.

Clubs: Golf Collectors Society, P.O. Box 241042, Cleveland OH 44124; World Logo Ball Assoc., P.O. Box 91989, Long Beach, CA 90809.

Newsletter: *Golfingly Yours,* 5407 Pennock Point Rd., Jupiter, FL 33458.

Autographed Card, Ben Hogan, c1960-80 125

*Matchbook, Olympic Club, feature, 20 strike,
clubhouse image across sticks, $12.*
—Photo courtesy Ray Morykan Auctions.

Autographed Photo, Sam Snead,
  c1980-90s 40
Badge, enamel, mkd "N.F.L.G.C.," 1.25" h . .5
Ball, Black Bug Dimple, c1920 250
Ball, Chemico Triumph, concentric
  squares, c1920 175
Ball, Tee-Mee Mesh, 1930s 100
Ball Box, Dunlop, for mesh or dimple
  pattern balls, 1920-30s 75
Book, *Golf Club Trademarks*, paperback,
  99 pp, 1984 5
Book, *Golf Operators Handbook*, plan-
  ning, building, and operating for minia-
  ture putting courses, driving ranges,
  and par-3 golf courses, National Golf
  Foundation, 1959, 104 pp 10
Club, putter, Butchart-Nicholls, bamboo
  shaft, dot punched face, c1920s 60
Club, putter, D Anderson & Sons, bent
  neck, criss-cross with diamond-dot
  face scoring, c1900-10 100
Club, putter, Spalding, flanged back,
  Anvil mark, c1920 75
Game, Par-It Golf Game, 1930s 40
Magazine, *American Golfer*, 1905-16 75
Match Safe, sterling silver, ball and
  crossed clubs, c1900 450
Newspaper, *Dayton Daily News*, May
  23, 1921, headline "Yankee Bobby
  Jones Winner First Golf Tilt" 10
Pamphlet, Golf in Italy, Italian State
  Tourist Department, 1932 60
Pinback Button, "Joe Lewis/Open
  Contestant/Rackham Golf Club/July
  24-27, 1951," green lettering on
  white ground .25

Pinback Button, "Join Arnie's Army,"
  black and white Arnold Palmer photo,
  c1950-60s 40
Pinback Button, "Open Championship
  Tournament/No. 132 U.S.G.A./Aug
  10-13, 1920/Inverness Golf Club,
  Toledo," blue and red lettering on
  white ground .50
Spoon, sterling silver, golfer handle,
  c1900-30 75
Tee, Eterna, plastic, c1950s 50
Tee, No-Looz, rubber, weighted end,
  c1950-60s 90
Toothpick Holder, sterling silver, caddy
  in full swing, 2.75" h 100
Trading Card, 1981 PGA Tour, complete
  set (66) 35

GONDER POTTERY

In 1941 Lawton Gonder established
Gonder Ceramic Arts, Inc., at Zanesville,
Ohio. The company is known for its glazes,
such as Chinese crackle, gold crackle, and
flambé. Pieces are clearly marked. Gonder
manufactured lamp bases at a second plant
and marketed them under the trademark
"Eglee." Gonder Ceramic Arts, Inc. ceased
production in 1957.

Club: Gonder Collectors Club, 917 Hurl Dr.,
Pittsburgh, PA 15236.

Bookends, pr, prancing horse, 10"h 25
Bowl, #J-17, 4.5" h, 13" w 30
Candleholders, pr, #501-6, starfish, 8" d . .40
Candleholders, pr, #523C, 4" w 15
Candleholders, pr, #E-14, 1.75" h, 4.5" d . .10

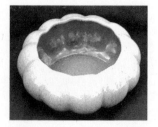

*Bowl, melon shape, turquoise ext, pink int,
imp "E-12/Gonder/U.S.A.," 7" d, $20.*

Cornucopia Vase, #414 18
Figure, #217, reclining panther, 15" l 45
Figure, #547, kneeling coolie, 5 x 3 x 2" . .55
Pitcher, #H-606, 9.25" h 30
Planter, #802, 9.5" h 50
Planter, #E-44 6
Vase, #319 15
Vase, #360, 7" h 15
Vase, #511, ming blue-green with black
　crackle glaze, 9.5" h, 10" w 10
Vase, #523, 9.625" h, 7.5" w 110
Vase, #E-49, 6" h .15
Vase, #F-373, 6" h, 3.5" w 15
Vase, #H-5 20
Vase, #H-56, 8.5" h 20
Vase, #H-79, 8" h .15
Vase, #H-601, gray-green gradiated ext,
　pink int, 10" h .20
Vase, #J-35, 10.25" h 25
Vase, #J-60, 8" h, 11.5" w 40
Vase, #J-69, 9.5" h, 8.5" w 10

GOOFUS GLASS

Goofus glass is a patterned glass on which the reverse of the principal portion of the pattern is colored in red or green and covered with a metallic gold ground. It was distributed at carnivals between 1890 and 1920. There are no records of it being manufactured after that date. Crescent Glass Company, Imperial Glass Corporation, LaBelle Glass Works, and Northwood Glass Company are some of the companies who made Goofus glass.

Value rests with pieces that have both the main color and ground color still intact. The reverse painting often wore off. It is not uncommon to find the clear pattern glass blank with no painting on it whatsoever.

Goofus glass is also known as Mexican Ware, Hooligan Glass, and Pickle Glass. Says a lot, doesn't it?

Newsletter: *Goofus Glass Gazette,* 400 Martin Blvd., Kansas City, MO 64118.

Bowl, apples, pears, and leaves, red
　and gold, 11" d .45
Bowl, carnations, 5 x 2" 5
Bowl, dogwood blossom, 9.5" d 15
Bowl, single rose, 4.5" d, 2" h 10
Bowl, water lilies, red and gold, 10.5" d . .50

Bowl, gold butterflies and red trim on clear glass, 10" d, $20.

Candy Dish, green and red flowers,
　6.5" d, 1.5" h 25
Compote, grapes, red, green, purple,
　and gold, 6" h, 4.25" w 50
Compote, red poppy, 5.5" h, 6" w 20
Compote, wild rose, 4.5" h, 5.5" d 25
Plate, 2 apples, red, 8.5" d 8
Plate, "An Easter Opening," chick
　coming out of egg, 6.25" d 30
Rose Bowl, fluted sides, rose, gold,
　green, and red .4
Vase, birds in dogwood tree, 13" h 50
Vase, double rose, pink and gold, 13" h . .30
Vase, sailing ship, red, gold, and green,
　9.25" h 35

GRANITEWARE

Graniteware, also known as agateware or enamelware, is the name commonly given to iron or steel kitchenware with an enamel coating. American production began in the 1860s and continues today.

White and gray are the most commonly found colors. However, graniteware can be found in shades of blue, brown, cream, green, red, violet, and yellow. Mottled pieces combining swirls of color are especially desirable.

Never lose sight of the fact that graniteware was inexpensive utilitarian kitchen and household ware. Modern prices should reflect this humble origin.

Club: National Graniteware Society, P.O. Box 10013, Cedar Rapids, IA 52410.

Bowl, blue swirl, 11.5" d, 3.25" h 35
Bucket, blue and white, rivetted handle,
    4.25" h, 4.25" d 75
Chamber Pot, blue and gray, 11.5" h 20
Coffeepot, blue and white, 9" h, 5.5" d . . .30
Coffeepot, brown and white, 8" h, 6.25" d .125
Coffeepot, red and white, drip-o-lator
    type 65
Coffeepot, white, black trim, 12" h, 8" w .25
Creamer and Sugar, red and white mot-
    tled, 3.375" h creamer, 5.5" h sugar . . .30
Cup, white, red trim, 4" d 8
Double Boiler, brown and white swirl,
    8.5" h, 8" d 375
Double Boiler, orange, 7" h, 5.75" d 30
Eggcup, blue, 2.75" h 40
End of Day Toothbrush Holder, dark
    brown, light brown, orange, burnt
    orange, and red swirl, dark brown
    trim, 3.5" d 225
Flour Canister, blue and white, 10.5" h,
    8" d 45
Kettle, blue and gray swirl, 9" h, 5" d 25
Ladle, gray, 9.5" l, 4.75" d bowl 10
Pan, red and white, 9.75 x 7" 7
Pie Plate, cream, red trim, 4.125" d 55
Pitcher, black speckled, 10.5" h, Vollrath
    Co 35
Refrigerator Dish, gray, 5.25 x 7.5 x 2.5" . . .9
Roaster, red, blue trim, wire insert,
    8.5" h, 14.25" l, 9" w 100
Salt Box, red and white, 7.5" h, 5.5" w . .115
Saucepan, cream and green, 4.5" h,
    5.75" d 18
Saucepan, teal and white swirl, 12" d . . .45
Soap Dish, green and white, mkd
    "GM 053" 35
Spoon, brown and white swirl, 13.375" l,
    2.25" bowl 135

Roasting Pan, cov, cobalt blue with white speckles, 13" l, $5.

Skimmers, cream colored, price each, $20.

Tea Kettle, red and white swirl, 6.25" h .165
Utility Bowl, cream and green, 11.25 x 4" .12
Wash Basin, tan and green, 13.5" d 20
Water Pitcher, green and white swirl,
    8" h, 4.125" d .325

GREETING CARDS

Greeting cards still fall largely under the wing of postcard collectors. They deserve a collector group of their own.

At the moment, high-ticket greeting cards are character-related. Someday collectors will discover Hallmark and other greeting cards as social barometers of their era. Meanwhile, enjoy picking them up for 25¢ or less.

Birthday, "Happy Birthday from the Walt
    Disney Film *Snow White and the
    Seven Dwarfs,* Valentine & Sons,
    1938 60
Christmas, "A Merry Christmas and
    Happy New Year," children and
    Christmas tree, c1870s 5
Christmas, girl by fireplace, Clapsaddle,
    artist sgd 8
Christmas, "Hail, Day of Joy," angel
    kneeling with dove on finger, Prang,
    c1870 20
Christmas, ice pond, boy putting skates
    on girl, fringed and embroidered,
    German 4
Christmas, "Merry Christmas to You All,"
    family in snowy woodland, c1880 4
Christmas, "Season's Greetings,"
    mechanical, boy with flowers, 19th C .20
Christmas, "Wishing You a Merry
    Christmas," fireplace, cat, and kittens,
    Prang, square, c1800s 18

Christmas, Sunshine Card, activity inside, 1960s, price each, 50¢.

Easter, 2 little angels putting flowers in front of cross, emb, postmarked 1909 . . .1
Easter, chicks and mountain climbers 6
Easter, cross on reef in sea, Carter & Karrick, 19th C 4
Easter, girl climbing out of egg shell, fringed, German, 19th C 7
Easter, "Shakespeare's Heaven Give You Many Merry Days," 19th C 3
Halloween, cats and pumpkin 20
Halloween, sleeping woman and fairies, Winsch, artist sgd, 1911 75
New Year, "Here Comes the New Year/ Lots of Good Cheer," child, tree, and toys, c1870 6
Thanksgiving, 2 children at table, Clapsaddle, artist sgd, Interntional Art Pub Co 12
Thanksgiving, Indian maiden on wagon, Winsch, 1911 .20
Valentine, Colonial dancers, emb, poem inside, 2.75 x 4.25" 6

GRISWOLD

Matthew Griswold purchased the Selden family interest in Selden & Griswold in 1884. Griswold became a cast iron king in the early 20th century under the leadership of Marvin Griswold, Matthew's son. Roger Griswold, son of Matthew, Jr., became president in 1926. The family's involvement ended in 1944. In 1957 the Griswold trade name was sold to Wagner Manufacturing Company, one of its major competitors. The additional sales eventually resulted in the company being part of the General Housewares Corporation.

Beware of reproductions and fantasy pieces. Many are made in India and imported with easily removable, country of origin paper labels.

Club: Griswold & Cast-Iron Cookware Assoc., P.O. Box 243, Perrysburg, NY 14129.

Newsletter: *Kettles 'n' Cookware*, 3007 Plum St., Erie, PA 16508.

Baking Pan, #81, red and cream 75
Chicken Pan, cov, Iron Mountain 60
Chicken Pan, cov, logo, smooth lid 70
Colonial Smokers Set, pattern #771, 772, 773 200
Dutch Oven, #9 65
Dutch Oven Skillet, #8, pressed aluminum 10
Food Chopper, #2 25
French Roll, #17 130
French Waffle Paddles, wood handles .125
Food Mold, rabbit 250
Food Mold, Santa 525
Griddle, #8, aluminum, wood handle 15
Griddle, #9, wood handle 125
Heat Regulator, #300 190
Muffin Pan, #15 175
Patty Mold Set, #72, orig box 85
Skillet, #2, smooth lid 375
Skillet, #4 450
Skillet, #5, Victor 475
Skillet, #7, shield pattern makers mark . .45
Skillet, #8, red and cream porcelain 35
Skillet, #9, star pattern makers mark 45
Skillet, #10, logo 35
Skillet, #15, oval 235
Skillet, #55, square 45
Skillet, pattern #769 200
Skillet Lid, #6, high dome, plain 100

Turk Head Mold, #140, 12 cavities, $200.

Skillet Lid, #9, pattern #469 85
Smokers Kettle, #773 45
Snack Skillet, #65 65
Toy Skillet, #775, square 150
Trivet, #7, pattern #205 75
Waffle Iron, Rev-O-Noc 35
Wheat Pan, #28 .235
Wheat Stick Pan, #2700 325

GUARDIAN SERVICE

In the mid-1930s, stainless-clad carbon steel cookware arrived on the scene. Development was rapid, albeit interrupted by WWII and the Korean War. By the 1960s, several manufacturers offered stainless steel clad aluminum cookware.

Century Metalcraft Corporation's Guardian Service cookware is popular, due largely to demand created by Internet sales. Initially, individuals seeking to complete sets inherited from their parents or to replace damaged pieces caused the price jump. Today, young "retro" collectors are driving the market.

Thus far, Guardian Service stands alone in the collecting realm. Stainless steel and aluminum cookware by companies such as Cory, Ekco, Mirro, and Revere are still garage sale merchandise.

Bacon Fryer, hostess gift, 18.5 x 9" 175
Casserole, metal lid, 8.75" d, 2.5" h 20
Cookbook, 72 pp, 5.75 x 8.5" 35
Cooker, metal lid, 1 qt 30
Double Boiler Set, two 10" glass lids, 3
    Bakelite handles, detachable handle,
    inner pot depth 3.75", outer 4.5" 75
Gravy Boat and Tray 20
Guardian Service Kit, 3 cans of Guardian
    Service Cleaner and Polish, utility
    handle, steel wool balls, missing
    lifters and cookbook, orig box 60
Omelet Pan 85
Omelet Pan, 10.5 x 5.5 x 3.5" 45
Pan, glass lid, 2.5 qt 12
Pot, domed glass lid, 7.75" d, 3.75" d 35
Pot, glass lid, 3 qt, 9.75" d, 4.5" d 40
Pot, glass lid, 10" d 20
Roaster, glass lid, 14.75" l, 8.75" h 65
Roaster, glass dome lid, 12" shallow pan .70
Roaster, metal lid, oval, 14.75 x 10 x 4" . . .80
Warming Tray, 14.75" l 30

HALL CHINA

In 1903 Robert Hall founded the Hall China Company in East Liverpool, Ohio. Hall produced refrigerator sets and a large selection of kitchenware and dinnerware in a wide variety of patterns. The company was a major supplier of institutional (hotel and restaurant) ware.

Hall also manufactured some patterns on an exclusive basis: Autumn Leaf for Jewel Tea, Blue Bouquet for the Standard Coffee Company of New Orleans, and Red Poppy for the Grand Union Tea Company. Hall teapots are a favorite among teapot collectors.

For the past several years, Hall has been reissuing a number of its solid-color pieces as the "Americana" line. Items featuring a decal or gold decoration have not been reproduced. Because of the difficulty in distinguishing old from new solid-color pieces, prices on many older pieces have dropped.

Club: Hall Collector's Club, P.O. Box 360488, Cleveland, OH 44136.

Note: For additional listings see Autumn Leaf.

Blue Bouquet, plate, D-style, 9" d 15
Blue Garden, casserole 55
Boston, creamer and sugar, maroon 80
Brown Eyed Susan, French baker 20
Drip-O-Lator, Cathedral 30
Drip-O-Lator, Rounded Terrace 20
Drip-O-Lator, Surfside, yellow, gold trim . .75

Chinese Red, ball jug, #3, $40. —Photo courtesy Ray Morykan Auctions.

Teapot, McCormick Tea Co, green and white with silver trim, 6-cup, $80. —Photo courtesy Ray Morykan Auctions.

Drip-O-Lator, Trellis 30
Flareware, cookie jar 55
Flareware, teapot .55
Gold Dot, bowls, nesting set of 3 40
Golden Glo, creamer and sugar 50
Harlequin, eggcup 15
Holiday, jug, 3 qt .15
Meadow Flower, casserole, ivory 50
Minuet, coffee server 35
Mums, cup and saucer 8
Old Crow, punch set, with 10 cups 175
Orange Poppy, bean pot 115
Orange Poppy, casserole, handled, oval . .60
Pastel Morning Glory, platter, D-sytle,
　11.25" l 12
Red Poppy, breadbox 20
Rose Parade, custard, straight sided . . .10
Royal Rose, casserole 20
Shaggy Tulip, coffee server 70
Sundial, sugar, cov, red 5
Target, coffee server 35
Taverne, mug 75
Teapot, Bird Cage, canary yellow 300
Teapot, Cleveland, green 65
Teapot, Connie, celadon green 55
Teapot, Hook Cover, yellow 35
Teapot, Moderne, ivory and gold 30
Teapot, Murphy, light blue 85
Teapot, New York, emerald green, gold
　dec, 2-cup 35
Teapot, Philadelphia, ivory, god dec,
　6-cup 150
Teapot, Streamline, red 170
Tulip, bowl, nesting set of 3 60
Tulip, platter, 13.25" l 15
Wildfire, mixing bowl, set of 3 70
Yellow Rose, French baker 12

HALLMARK ORNAMENTS

Hallmark Cards, Inc., was founded by Joyce C. Hall. Hallmark Keepsakes were first marketed in 1973 and these first-year ornaments are avidly sought by collectors. Handcrafted Keepsakes were added to the line in 1975, followed the next year by Baby's First Christmas and Bicentennial ornaments.

Collecting Hallmark Keepsake Ornaments became a popular hobby in 1987, leading to the creation of The Keepsake Ornament Collector's Club, whose membership roles now exceed 250,000. As with any contemporary collectible, keep in mind that secondary market values can be speculative.

Club: Hallmark Keepsake Ornament Collectors Club, P.O. Box 419034, Kansas City, MO 64141.

Newsletter: *Twelve Months of Christmas,* P.O. Box 97172, Pittsburgh, PA 15229.

Note: Prices listed are for ornaments MIB.

Amanda, #4321, 1984 25
Arctic Pals Row Kayak, #4822, Frosty
　Friends series, 1985 50
Bear with Candy Cane, #4792, Cinnamon
　Bear series, 1985 25
Bugs Bunny, #5412, Looney Tunes series,
　1993 25
Carolers, #5115, Cameo series, 1981 . . .30
Cat Naps, #5313, 1994 35
Cheerful Santa, #5154, 1992 25
Christmas, #1331, Betsy Clark series,
　1975 30
Coal Car, #5401, Christmas Skyline
　series, 1992 15

Tobin Fraley Carousel, 1983, $30.

Cozy Home, #4175, Nostalgic Houses
    and Shops series, 1993 40
Dancer Ice Skating, #4809, Reindeer
    Champs series, 1987 30
Donder's Diner, #4823, 1990 20
Favorite Santa, #4457, 1987 30
George Washington Bicentennial, #3862,
    1989 15
Hall Brothers Doll Shop, #4014, Nostal-
    gic Houses and Shops series, 1988 . . .50
King Klaus, #4106, 1990 15
Kringle Tours, #4341, Here Comes Santa
    series, 1992 35
Merry Old Santa, #4414, 1992 30
Old Fashioned Doll, #5195, 1985 35
Old Fashioned Santa, #4099, 1983 55
Peter Rabbit, #8071, Beatrix Potter
    series, 1996 70
Pup in Basket, #4484, Puppy Love series,
    1992 30
Rocking Horse, #6167, pewter, 1995 45
Santa and Friends, #4019, Carousel
    series, 1983 35
Snack, #7393, Chris Mouse series, 1994 . .15
Snoopy & Woodstock, #4741, 1988 40
Three French Hens, #3786, 12 Days of
    Christmas series, 1986 35
Timon-Pumbaa, #5366, Lion King series,
    1994 25
Vixen Tennis, #4562, Reindeer Champs
    series, 1989 20

HALLOWEEN

Halloween collectibles deserve a category of their own. There is such a wealth of
material out there that it nearly rivals
Christmas as the most-decorated holiday
season.

Remember how much fun it was to play
dress-up as a kid? Collectors have rediscovered children's Halloween costumes.
While you may be staggered by some of the
prices listed below, I see costumes traded
at these prices all the time.

Newletters: *Boo News,* P.O. Box 143,
Brookfield, IL 60513; *The Trick or Treat
Trader,* P.O. Box 499, Winchester, NH 03470.

Note: See costumes for additional listings.

Candlesticks, pr, black cat and jack-o-
    lantern, plastic, c1950, 2.5" h 20

Chocolate Mold, jack-o-lantern 35
Cookie Jar, jack-o-lantern, Abingdon,
    #674 300
Decoration, diecut cardboard, emb
    scene of frightened cats with "Go/
    Stop/Detour," orange, black, and
    green, c1930s, 8 x 9" 35
Decoration, diecut cardboard, emb
    scene of black cat in midst of multi-
    colored flowers, pinpoint glitter
    accent, lower left depicts seated
    cat, German, c1930s, 19" h, 20" w 35
Decoration, diecut stiff paper, large and
    small orange and black pumpkin, fig-
    ural black cat, black cat head, top
    center black silhouette of witch on
    broomstick, Dennison, 1930-40s 25
Eyeglasses, figural hissing black cats,
    plastic 30
Game, Whirl-O-Halloween Fortune and
    Stunt Game, card with spinner, 7 x 9" .40
Hat, paper, tissue paper constuction
    resembling jester, printed orange
    and black with headband design of
    black cat and jack-o-lantern, orange
    running cat, black witch on broom-
    stick silhouette, and flying bat, mkd
    "Made in Germany," c1930s, 8 x 13" . . .5
Ice Cream Mold, pumpkin, S & Co 40
Light, pumpkin, orange plastic, battery
    operated, c1950s, 2.5" d 40
Mask, clown, paper, red, black, and
    yellow, 8 x 9" 15
Noisemaker, litho tin and wood shaker
    rod, mkd "Kirchhof 'Life of the Party'
    Products," 2" l, 3" d 12

*Postcard, artist sgd by Ellen Clapsaddle,
$10.*

Hanger, emb cardboard, 1930s, 6.5" h, $18.

Noisemaker/Candy Stick, painted composition head mounted in crepe paper collar to wooden tube, paper illus of young girl and man merrymakers on front and back, attached to wooden dowel, paper wrapper sleeve with German inscriptions on both sides, c1930s, 7.5" h .... .75

Party Favor, black cat holding lollipop, orange plastic with black-striped jersey, c1950s, 5" h .... .20

Pinback Button, "Salem Tercentenary/ July 4-10, 1926," red and white illus of witch and cat flying on broomstick beneath crescent moon, blue lettering .15

Sign, paper, Imperial Ice Cream, "Special for Halloween/Imperial Harlequin/Orange Ice Cream With Apricots And Pineapples," witch on broom in front of full moon, flying bats, black cat with arched back, c1930s, 7.25 x 22" .... .50

HANGERS

You collect WHAT? Sure, I just got a whole bunch from the dry cleaners. Why, did you lock your keys in the car?

Be prepared for funny looks and odd replies if you go around asking for old clothes hangers. The search may be rewarded when you encounter the inventive mechanisms and ingenious designs answering the question of how to hang up articles of clothing.

Hangers designed for travel have employed folding sides, telescoping arms and accordion extensions. Others use wire coils, clamps, levers and spring action.

Hangers for drying may use a framework with clothespins or follow the contoured shape of a glove, stocking, sweater or pants.

Some antique hangers have patent dates from the early 20th and even late 19th centuries. Prices tend to rise as the construction and shape become more elaborate. Still, these collectibles are generally inexpensive and look great in an armoire or hung on the wall.

Advisors: Cheryl and Roger Brinker, PMB 165, 3140-B West Tilghman St., Allentown, PA 19104, (610) 434-4791.

Combination Hat and Garment Hanger, with wire loop extending horizontally from wall to support the hat by the brim, garment hook below, hat loop articulated to swing up against wall when not in use .... .75

Drying Hanger, wire hook above tubular aluminum hanger body contoured to outline of sweater, arms swing up to remove sweater and down for storage .... .35

Suit Hanger, wire loop shoulder supports, with wooden slats pant press opened by fold-down wire hook, circular logo of laurel leaves and possibly "Walker" stamped in wood . .12

Travel Hanger, delicate tubular metal shoulder supports with plastic pearl bead ends, hinged to triangular hub with thin wire hook, mkd "Featherweight patented 135680" 8

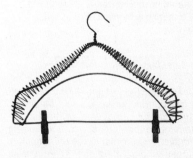

Coat Hanger, wire, graduated wire coil, semi-circular wire frame swings out to support back of jacket, $60.

Hat Hanger, 2 wooden supports joined by wire, $70.

Travel Hanger, sliding wire shoulder supports attached by double chain to wire hook, 10" closed to 15" extended . .6

Travel Hanger, sliding wire shoulder supports attached by double chain to wire hook, stamped "pat. 6-16-03 patspend," 11" closed to 16" extended . .6

Travel Hanger, wire hook supporting fold-down double hinged extension arms with ball pane hammered finish, metal arms stamped "Pronto D.R.G.M.," price for 2 travel hangers in leather case .18

Travel Hanger, wire hook with double hinged metal extension arms and push-in locking shoulder ends, 5" folded to 16" open 8

Travel Hanger, wire hook with double hinged metal extension arms and pull-out shoulder ends, stamped "Alsize," 5" folded to 15.5" open 7

Trouser Hanger, designed to hold trousers inverted by cuff, small flat metal hook with fold-down metal band arms 6

Trouser Hanger, with wire loop centered on thin horizontal rod wrapped by spring with metal clips at ends, 10" w 20

HANNA-BARBERA

How much is that gorilla in the window? If it's Magilla Gorilla, it could be pricey. Merchandise associated with Hanna-Barbera cartoon characters is becoming increasingly popular as baby boomers rediscover their childhood. Keep in mind that these items were mass-produced. Condition is a key element in determining value.

Boo Boo, stuffed toy, "I Am Boo Boo From the Huckleberry Hound TV Show," plush cloth body, vinyl face, orig string tag attached to arm, Knickerbocker, ©1959 Hanna-Barbera Productions, 9" h 35

Flintstones, Dakin figure, Barney Rubble, #2255, vinyl, 1970, 7.25 x 11", MIP 40

Flintstones, drinking glass, clear, brown, yellow, and white accent scenes of Fred pouring Barney a drink from dipper, Dino drinking from stone crock, Wilma and Betty talking, and Baby Puss next to palm tree, ©Hanna-Barbera Productions, 5" h, 2.875" d . . .35

Flintstones, paper dolls, "The Flintstones Betty & Barney," cover depicts Betty and Barney and Hoppy the Hopperoo smiling at each other in front of home, Wonder Books, #6689, 1974, 8.125 x 11.5" 20

Flintstones, premium, comic book, "March of Comics #341 The Flintstones with Pebbles," Child Life Shoes, cover depicts Dino singing as Pebbles helps Fred play base fiddle, 16 pp, ©1970, 5 x 6.875" 20

Flintstones, premium, lunch box with bottle, Denny's, blue hard vinyl box with attached paper label, 1989, 7.25 x 8.5 x 4" .25

Flintstones, salt and pepper shakers, pr, ceramic, image of Fred, Wilma, and Pebbles waving, red text "The Flintstones Bedrock City Kelowna B.C.," c1980, 2.875" h, 1.625" d 20

Flintstones, snowdome, Fred and Dino in Bedrock City, plastic, Fred holding large bones with Dino running toward him, both standing next to palm tree with volcano in background, 1980, 2.75 x 3.75 x 2.5" 20

Flintstones, *TV Guide*, Jul 1, 1961, Vol 9, #26, issue #431 .20

Flintstones, windup, litho tin, Fred on Dino, soft vinyl head, Marx, 1962, 2.5 x 7.75 x 5.25" 275

Hair Bear Bunch, stuffed toy, Bubi Bear, plush covering over pipe cleaner arms, stuffed head and body, wearing orange felt hat and Day-Glo fabric striped tunic, mkd "Sutton & Sons Inc, NY/Japan," 1971 5.75" h 35

Mr Jinks, soaky bottle, Purex, early 1960s, 10" h, $30

Huckleberry Hound, lamp, figural, vinyl head on plastic base, Arch Lamp Mfg, 1962, 12" h, 4" d 85

Huckleberry Hound, punch-out book, "Huckleberry Hound Sticker Fun," Whitman, #2178, ©1959 Hanna-Barbera Enterprises, 10.375 x 12" 15

Huckleberry Hound, thermos, metal, black cup, Quick Draw, Yogi and team of Hanna-Barbera characters in tug-of-war contest , 1961, 6.5" h . . .65

Huckleberry Hound and Yogi Bear, record, theme songs, cover depicts Huck and Yogi looking at top of large birdhouse stand with smiling crows and village in background, yellow vinyl, Golden Record, #550, 1959, 6" d .12

Jetsons, book, *Birthday Surprise*, Whitman Tip Top Tales, #2484, 1963, 6.5 x 7.5" 20

Jetsons, comic book, Gold Key, #2, Apr 1963, cover shows family flying along on 2 spacecrafts barbequing hotdogs and laughing 15

Jetsons, hand puppet, George Jetson, red, white, and blue fabric body, red felt collar, Knickerbocker, ©1960s Hanna-Barbera Productions, 9.25" h . .50

Jetsons, record, *Jetsons Theme Song/ Eep Opp Ork*, Golden Record, #R720A/B, yellow vinyl, cover depicts George out of control on flying carpet as family flies around in spacecraft, 1962, 6" d .10

Magilla Gorilla, doll, stuffed, brown felt body, vinyl head, wearing purple hat with green stripe, blue suspenders, purple bow tie, red shorts, brown shoes with blue trim, polka dot handkerchief in back pocket, ©1960s Ideal Toy Corp, 7.5" h 65

Mr Jinks, push puppet, black hat, red jacket and bow tie, holding white baton in right hand atop black base, Kohner, ©1960s Hanna-Barbera Productions, 4.5" h 35

Pebbles Flintstone, coloring book, Whitman, #1117, cover depicts Pebbles playing on back of Baby Puss who is trying to sleep as Fred and Wilma watch from living room, ©1963 Hanna-Barbera Productions, 8 x 10.875" 15

Pebbles Flintstone, ramp walker, Pebbles on Dino, Marx, 1960s, 1 x 3.75 x 3" 75

Peter Potamus, book, *Peter Potamus Meets the Black Knight*, Whitman Tell-A-Tale, #2506, 5.5 x 6.25" 15

Peter Potamus, coloring book, Whitman, #1133, cover depicts Peter sleeping in Magic Flying Balloon with So So nearby playing guitar, neatly colored pages, 1964, 8 x 10.875" 15

Quick Draw McGraw, pencil by number set, Transogram, #1403, 1961, orig 9.5 x 13.25 x .875" box 20

Quick Draw McGraw, premium, trading cards, Ovaltine, set of 12, Screen Gems trademark, c1960s, 2 x 3" 125

Rosie the Robot, ramp walker, Rosie standing in front of Astro, Marx, 1.25 x 2.5 x 3" .120

Secret Squirrel, frame tray puzzle, Whitman, #4559, 1967, 11.5 x 14.5" 20

Snagglepuss, punch-out book, " Snagglepuss Sticker Fun," Whitman, #1897-B, ©1963 Hanna-Barbera Productions, 10 x 11.875" 15

Squiddly Diddly, soaky bottle, Purex, late 1960s, 10" h 75

Huckleberry Hound, comic book, Dell, #14, Nov-Dec 1961, $10.

Wally Gator, doll, stuffed, cloth body,
smiling seated position, Playtime
Toys Inc, ©1970s Hanna-Barbera
Prod, 7.5" h 65
Yogi Bear, premium, punch-out puzzle,
Honey Fried Chicken, stiff cardboard,
image of Boo Boo with basket of
chicken drumsticks licking his lips
at dinner table and "Yogi's Chicken
Fills Your Tummy/It's Never Greasy…
Always Yummy," reverse image of
smiling Yogi and Cindy in frames,
1969, 8.875 x 10.375" 15
Yogi Bear, wristwatch, chrome case
with white face, blue numerals with
hands, full color center image of
smiling Yogi walking along carrying
knapsack on back, ©Hanna-Barbera
Prod, Swiss Made Bradley Time,
c1960s 65

HARKER POTTERY

In 1840 Benjamin Harker of East
Liverpool, Ohio, built a kiln and produced
yellowware products. During the Civil War,
David Boyce managed the firm. Harker and
Boyce played important roles in the man-
agement of the firm through much of its his-
tory. In 1931 the company moved to Chester,
West Virginia. Eventually, Jeannette Glass
Company purchased Harker, closing the
plant in March 1972.

Much of Harker's wares were utilitarian. The company introduced Cameoware in
1945 and a Rockingham ware line in 1960. A
wide range of backstamps and names were
used.

Colonial Lady, mixing bowl, pour spout, $25.

*Countryside,
scoop, $20.*

Antique Auto, snack set 10
Apple & Pear, cake lifter, 9.25 x 2.5" 35
Apple & Pear, cake set, 10" cake plate,
four 7" serving plates, cake server . . .60
Apple & Pear, utility plate, 11 x 12" 20
Blue Pansy, custard cup 18
Cameoware, bowl, Dainty Blue, 5.5" d . .12
Cameoware, bread and butter plate,
Dainty Blue, 6" d 5
Cameoware, cup and saucer, Dainty
Blue 10
Cameoware, demitasse cup, Dainty
Blue 15
Cameoware, lug soup, Dainty Blue 10
Cameoware, plate, Dainty Blue, 8.75" d . .12
Cameoware, plate, Dainty Blue, 9.5" d . . .10
Cameoware, platter, Dainty Blue, 11" d . .24
Cameoware, platter, Dainty Blue, 14" l . . .25
Cameoware, sugar, cov, Dainty Blue 18
Cameoware, utility plate, Dainty Blue,
11" d 20
Cherry Blossom, cereal bowl, green 40
Cherry Blossom, coaster, green 12
Cherry Blossom, soup bowl, green 75
Cock O'Morn, dinner plate, pink, 10" d . . .8
Colonial Lady, cup and saucer 10
Colonial Lady, dinner plate 10
Colonial Lady, platter 15
Dogwood, bowl, pink, 8.5" d 55
Dogwood, cake plate, ftd, pink, 13" d . . .140
Dogwood, creamer and sugar, pink 30
Dogwood, dinner plate, pink 35
Dogwood, sherbet, pink 30
Dogwood, tumbler, 12 oz 65
Gadroon, salt and pepper shakers, pr,
celadon 20
Oriental Poppy, casserole, cov 40
Pate Sur Pate, ashtray, Chesterton,
gray, 4.5" d 8
Pate Sur Pate, snack tray, gray, white
trim, 8.75" d 5
Petit Point Rose, fork, silver trim 12

Red Apple, bowl, swirl, 9" d 24
Red Apple, cake plate, 11" d 24
Red Apple, casserole lid, 8" d 18
Red Apple, cup .10
Red Apple, dinner plate, 9.5" d 20
Red Apple, pie baker, 9.25" d 25
Red Apple, salad plate 16
Red Apple, spoon 24
Red Apple, teapot, cov 60
Tulip, casserole, 8.375 x 4.75" 25
Tulip, fork, 8.75" l 5
Yellow Pansy, custard cup 10

HARMONICAS

As with most collectibles, unusual models are the most popular and therefore costly; those with bells or large brass horn attachments, or with cover plates made to look like airships, old cats, etc, will command three figure prices.

To anyone just getting started, we recommend a copy of the latest Hohner price list from Hohner, Inc, 1000 Technology Park, Glen Allen, VA, 23660, (804) 515-1900. Many harmonicas seen for sale as "antiques" or "old" are in Hohner's current line.

Most Hohner harmonicas are marked. Look for the trademark found on the side opposite the model name. Pre-1940 models are marked with a star in a circle held by two hands. On later models, the star is missing from the trademark.

Advisor: Harland Crain, 741 Cedar Field Ct., Chesterfield, MO 63017, (314) 576-6154; e-mail hcrain@harleysharps.net.

Clubs: Harmonica Collectors International, 741 Cedar Field Ct., Chesterfield, MO 63017; Society for the Preservation & Advancement of the Harmonica, P.O. Box 865, Troy, MI 48099.

Note: Prices listed are for harmonicas nice collectible condition with minimal dents, rust spots or other defects, and with original box in fine condition (unless otherwise indicated).

American Harmonica Co, U S Navy
   Band, 10 hole diatonic, 4 x 1" flags
   and anchor on cover plate, red, white,
   and blue box .25

BHI, The Koh-i-noor Boys Favourite,
   round cover plates, 14 double hole
   tremolo 5XI, with telescoping box 35
Borrah Minevitch, Radio Favorite, 10
   hole diatonic, all sides except back
   covered with metal, blue box with picture of Borrah on front and the
   Harmonica Rascals on back, 4.75 x
   1.25" 85
C A Seydel Sohne, The Music Master,
   14 hole diatonic, 6.875 x 1.125 red box,
   picture of band leader on box, same
   in tin box but 12 hole 55
Gretsch, The Varsity, 10 hole diatonic,
   with metal tongue protectors, silver
   box, made in Brazil, 4 x 1" 35
Hohner, 125th Jubilee, 1857/1982, 10
   hole diatonic, with box, 4 x 1" 35
Hohner, 3-tiered display case folds up
   to 10.75 x 9 x 6" box, picture on back
   of top lid shows people playing
   harmonicas, dark wood may or may
   not have clasp 570
Hohner, Centennial 1861/65–1961/65,
   standard Hohner international harmonica, 10 hole diatonic, blue-gray
   box with American and Dixie flags,
   with box, 4 x 1" 25
Hohner, El Centenario, 16 double hole
   tremolo, 6.75 x 1", wood extends .75"
   past cover plate, with 6-pointed star
   and box, celebration of Mexican
   independence 1810-1910, with box . . .55
Hohner, Larry Adler Professional, 16
   Chromatic, 16 double holes with silver
   latch case 125
Hohner, The Sportsman, 16 double hole
   tremolo, star on coverplate, picture
   of German hiker on box 60

Hohner, Trumpet Call, wooden resonator box with 5 brass horns, 10 hole tremolo, with box, $525.

Hohner, U S Navy Band, "Join the Navy See the World," plastic comb 10 hole diatonic, in blue pressed cardboard clam shell box, picture of U S Navy Band on box, 4 x 1" 30

Koch, Bugle Call, 10 hole diatonic, Model Y152, 4 tabs on cover plates, blue box with picture of Koch Kid with harmonica, 4 x 1" 35

Kostler, opera made in US zone, comes in tin box with pictures of dancers ...20

Kostler, Valencia (Kostler name not on box or harmonica), Tremolo comes in 4 different sizes, telescoping box pictures Spanish guitar player and woman, 10-12-14-16 double holes versions, price depends on size 35

Tombo, Unica Full Chromatic, 22 double holes, with red and white box, 7.5 x 1.5" 75

HARMONICA RELATED

Booklet, "How-to-Play the Harmonica," Hohner, cov scene of young man playing harmonica, with instructions, music, and pictures of US Marine Band, Navy Band, etc, 1925 15

Display Box, Hohner, wood, 3-tiered, folding, label on lid shows people playing harmonicas and annual sales figures, closed size 10.75 x 9 x 6" 570

HARTLAND PLASTICS, INC.

Although the Hartland trade name survives today, Hartland Plastic collectibles focus on plastic television cowboy and sports figures issued in the 1950s. The baseball figures were reissued in 1989. They have a "25" in a circle on their back just below the belt. Do not confuse them with the earlier figures.

Most figures came with accessories. These need to be present in order for the figure to be considered complete. There are two Lone Ranger figures, the second bearing a much closer resemblance to Clayton Moore.

After a period of rapid rise in the early 1990s, especially for sports figures, prices are now stable. In fact, commonly found figures are a hard sell at full book price.

Babe Ruth, holding bat and pointing to fence, Yankees, 7.5" h 165

Dan Troop, The Lawman, complete with hat and gun, 8" h 175

Dick Groat, at bat, Pirates, 7.375" h 400

Don Drysdale, pitching, Dodgers, 7" h .165

Duke Snider, at bat, Dodgers, 7" h 190

Eddie Mathews, throwing ball, Braves 7" h 140

Ernie Banks, at bat, Chicago Cubs, 7" h .165

Hank Aaron, at bat, Atlanta Braves, 7" h 165

Harmon Killebrew, at bat, Twins, 7" h ..165

Holy Mother, blue robe trimmed in gold over pearl white gown, molded brown hair flowing to waist at back, on black plastic base with gold accent, 11.25" h 45

Jim Hardie, Tales of Wells Fargo, movable arms, with gun and hat, 8" h ...175

Little Leaguer, 5.75" h 40

Lone Ranger and Silver, hands together at waist front, wearing cowboy chaps, blue outfit with black and silver accents, brass key chain inserted through muzzle as rein, 9.25" h 150

Luis Aparicio, fielding ball, White Sox, 7" h 165

Matt Dillon, Gunsmoke, complete with hat and gun 75

Minor Leaguer, 3.75" h 40

Nellie Fox, throwing ball, White Sox, 7" h 110

Rocky Colavito, at bat, Tigers, 7" h 200

Roger Maris, swinging bat, Yankees, 7.25" h 200

Stan Musial, at bat, Cardinals, 7" h 110

Mickey Mantle at Bat, NY Yankees, 6.75" h, $200.

Ted Williams, swinging bat, Red Sox,
7.5" h 165
Tonto and Scout, wearing plain belt
and brown headband, with head
feather and knife accessories, brass
key chain inserted through muzzle
as rein, 9.25" h 150
Vint Bonner, Restless Gun, with gun,
missing hat, 8" h 175
Warren Spahn, pitching, Braves, 7.5" h .140
Willie Mays, fielding position, Giants,
7.5" h 135
Yogi Berra, catching, removable mask,
6.5" h 110

HATPIN HOLDERS & HATPINS

Women used hatpins to keep their hats
in place. The ends of the pins were decorated in a wide variety of materials—ranging from gemstones to china—and the pins
themselves became a fashion accessory.
Since a woman was likely to own many hatpins and they were rather large, special
holders were developed for them.

Clubs: American Hatpin Society, 20
Montecillo Dr., Rolling Hills Estate, CA
90274; International Club for Collectors of
Hatpins and Hatpin Holders, 1013 Medhurst
Rd., Columbus, OH 43220.

HOLDERS

Art Nouveau, SS, 4 ring or neck-chain
holders, c1905, 6.5" h 150
Belleek, pink and maroon floral dec,
green leaves, gold top, mkd "Willets
Belleek," dated 1911, 5.25" h 125
China, hp, floral dec, artist sgd, Austria,
4.5" h 75
Figural, golf bag, SS, mkd "sterling 950,"
3" l 170
Limoges, grapes, pink roses, matte finish, sgd 60
Nippon, relief serpent dec, mottled
ground, 5" h 165
Royal Bayreuth, art nouveau lady, 16
pin holes, 4.5" h 475
Royal Rudolstadt, lavender and roses
dec 25
Schlegelmilch, RS Prussia, floral and
scroll dec, gold accents, ftd 170

Hatpin Holders, carnival glass, Northwood, Grape & Cable, purple ($425) and marigold ($350).

PINS

Advertising, Economy Stoves and
Ranges, 10" l 45
Art Deco, plastic, free-form design in
2-mold mottled color, c1925, 7" l
steel pin 25
Art Nouveau, gilt over brass, 2 polished
free-form amethysts on steel pin,
c1905, 8" l 80
Art Nouveau, SS, 4-sided, 12" l 85
Art Nouveau, SS, stylized woman, 1905,
8.75" l 80
Brass, openwork, amber setting 45
Carnival Glass, figural rooster, amber ...35
Figural, tennis racket, SP 25
Mercury Glass, elongated cased tear-
drop 70
Mother-of-Pearl, snake motif, ruby
head, gold top, USA 175
Porcelain, hp, gold overlay, Victorian
motif, c1890, 1.75" l 150
Porcelain, scenic design, ornate
mounting 35
St Louis World's Fair, enamel dec, 1904 .30

HATS, LADY'S VINTAGE

Stop! Don't think about throwing those
old hats away! Hats are a very important
part of fashion history. Hats can still be
found to purchase at reasonable prices
throughout the country and abroad.
However, condition is of great importance
as well as uniqueness and age. Millinery
items such as hat blocks, hat stands, hat
boxes, feathers, vintage ornamentation,
millinery advertisements and books are in
demand by collectors. There are many
unique and intriguing hats being designed
and constructed today for future collectors
of hats from the late 1900s.

As the new millennium has begun, the fashion industry is introducing many interesting hat styles in various materials. Watch out! There's much more to come. Happy hat hunting!

Advisor: Danielle Ware, Dulph & Dutch Antiques & Designs, 14 Laurel Dr., Tabernacle, NJ 08088, (609) 268-1967.

Club: The Costume Society of America, 55 Edgewater Dr., P.O. Box 73, Earleville, MD 21919.

HATS

Fabric, beige ribbed satin, patches of brown grosgrain "L" shaped designs, attached beige French knots grosgrain ribbon edge, no label, 1930s, fair condition 25

Fabric, denim cottonpoke bonnet, fabric ruffle across front, no label, late 1800s, good condition 75

Felt, black cap with black feathers gathered to 1 side in front, long black netting with black dots, Caprice, NY, 1940s, mint condition 125

Felt, black cap with strands of felt to 1 side, long black netting in front, New York Creations, 1950s, mint condition 65

Felt, gold 3" brim with 3.5" pleated satin ribbon around brim, bow in back, cream netting with chenille poofs, Joe Bill Miller, Paris, NY, 1970s, mint condition 35

Fabric, cream, pink, and green floral barkcloth with pleated band swirled around cap to one side, no label, mint condition, 1940s, $110.

Felt, mint green, felt plumes and white crescent buttons, Adolfo II, NY and Paris, 1960s, mint condition 95

Felt, yellow with black fish net overlay brimmed, banded with yellow grosgrain ribbon and sets of yellow belt closures, Margaret Longfellow, Prospect Park, PA, 1940s, good condition 45

Fur, beaver, lady's riding top hat with replacement netting, orig leather box, The Hatter Keeler, Patterson, NJ, late 1800s, good condition 245

Fur, black beaver cap, fan of feathers to 1 side in front, curls of black feathers on other with black dotted netting, black beads and sequins in shape of shamrock on top, no label, 1940s, mint condition 110

Fur, black, orange cloud-like swirls, 3.5" black grosgrain ribbon with flattened bow in front, no label, 1950s . . .45

Fur, black satin with mink trim and satin band, no label, 1930s, mint condition 35

Silk, black mourning bonnet, no label, early 1900s, good condition 65

Silk, pewter colored cap pointed down on both sides to ear, dark gray cut beads dec, iridescent sequin flowers with pearl centers, no label, 1950s . . .55

Silk, salmon colored 3" high round, 3 groups of leaves of iridescent sequins outlined with gray cut beads, Lit Brothers, Philadelphia, 1950s, good condition 65

Straw, natural colored, three 3" rings overlapped with centers open, large brown velvet bow and long brown netting in front with spiderweb-like circles throughout, Strawbridge & Clothier, 1930s, mint condition 95

Straw, natural colored turned up brim, multicolored fabric flowers across brim, Strawbridge & Clothier, Philadelphia, PA, 1940s, fair condition 25

Straw, red, 2.5" brim, allover bunches of fuchsia flowers, pink beads, and leaves dec, Kenderton Hat Shop, Sara Esposito, 1940s, good condition . .45

Velvet, brown cloche, black feather plumes in center front, Hattie Carnegie, 1930s 245

Feather, light rose pink cap, stylized to chin on one side, John Wanamaker, good condition, 1940s, $75.

RELATED MILLINERY ITEMS

Hat Stand, green painted wood, German composition doll head with felt trim hat at base, 12" h 95
Hat Stand, store, lavender painted with plaster dec on base, 54.5" h 125
Hat Stand, wood, natural color, 36" h 45
Millinery, feather dec, bird shaped, West Germany .65
Millinery, velvet and silk flowers, pastel colors .24

HEISEY GLASS

A. H. Heisey Company of Newark, Ohio, began operations in 1896. Its many blown and molded patterns were produced in crystal, colored, milk (opalescent), and Ivorina Verde (custard). Pieces also featured cutting, etching, and silver-deposit decoration. Glass figurines were made between 1933 and 1957.

Not all Heisey glass is marked. Marked pieces have an "H" within a diamond. However, I have seen some non-Heisey pieces with this same marking at several flea markets.

It is important to identify the pattern of Heisey pieces. Neila Bredehoft's *The Collector's Encyclopedia of Heisey Glass, 1925–1938* (Collector Books: 1986) is helpful for early items. The best help for post-World War II patterns is old Heisey catalogs.

Club: Heisey Collectors of America, 169 W. Church St, Newark, OH 43055.

Bread and Butter Plate, Empress Sahara, 6" d 14
Bread and Butter Plate, New Era, 6" d . .35
Candy Dish, cov, Plantation, 5" h 200
Celery, Empress Sahara, 10" 35
Celery, New Era .35
Cheese Plate, Twist Marigold, 6" d 40
Claret, New Era .20
Cocktail, New Era 18
Cocktail, Stanhope 30
Cocktail Shaker, Orchid, small 300
Cocktail Shaker, Orchid, sterling base, no plug 200
Compote, Rose, oval, 7" l 165
Cordial, New Era 45
Cordial, Savoy Plaza 100
Creamer, Orchid, ftd 35
Creamer, Twist, flamingo pink 50
Cup and Saucer, Empress Sahara 40
Cup and Saucer, New Era 65
Cup and Saucer, Rose 90
Decanter, Tally Ho, #4027 175
Goblet, Victorian, 9 oz 25
Juice Tumbler, New Era 23
Mustard, cov, Empress Sahara, with spoon 90
Nut Cup, New Era 60
Pilsner, New Era 60
Plate, Empress Alexandrite, 8" sq 95
Plate, Empress Sahara, 7" d 15
Plate, Empress Sahara, 8" d 20
Plate, Moonglow, #1230, 7" d 14
Punch Bowl, Lariat, 11 cup 100
Relish, 3 part, New Era 40
Sherbet, Duquesne, tangerine 180
Sherbet, Victorian 15

Berry Bowl, Beaded Swag, custard, mkd "Winsted, Conn.," 4.375" d, $50.

Candy Dish, cov, silver overlay and cutwork, 10.25" h, $175.

Sugar, Orchid, ftd 35
Syrup, Plantation 150
Tumbler, Thumbprint, ftd, 4 oz 4
Violet Vase, Orchid, 4" h 145
Water Goblet, Duquesne, tangerine ...210

HI-FI EQUIPMENT

Remember your "hi-fi" from the 1950s and 60s? The equipment used those glowing little bulbs called vacuum tubes, and music came from black vinyl discs called records, not CD's.

Well, now it's the 1990s, and some of that old hi-fi gear is now collectible. Items that are in demand are U.S. made vacuum tube type amplifiers, pre-amplifiers, AM/FM tuners and receivers. Also desirable are certain brands of speakers and record turntables from the U.S. and Europe. Certain old vacuum tubes if new and in the original boxes are also collectible.

The key to ascertaining an item's value is to know the manufacturer or brand, and the model number. Some of the amplifiers to look for include Audio Research, Conrad Johnson, McIntosh, Marantz, Western Electric, Altec, Acrosound, Heathkit, H. H. Scott, and Harmon Kardon. Speakers to look for include Altec, Tannoy, JBL, QUAD, and Lowthar. Record turntable names include Thorens and SME.

WARNING! NEVER plug old hi-fi gear into an AC outlet with the power on! Tube equipment uses high voltage circuits, and old power cords are almost always deteriorated—creating a potential hazard of shock or electrocution!

Advisor: Jeffrey Viola, 784 Eltone Rd., Jackson, NJ 08527, (732) 928-0666.

Audio Research, Model SP10, pre-amplifier, stereo, tubes 175
Brook, Model 10C3, amplifier, mono, 2A3 Triode tubes 100
Dynaco, Model ST-70, amplifier, stereo, EL34 tubes 100
Fisher, Model 80AZ, amplifier, mono, tubes, 30 watts 50
Fisher, Model 50A, amplifier, mono, tube, 50 watts 100
Heathkit, Model W7A, amplifier, mono, EL34 tubes 75
Langevin, Model "Cook Ultimate," amplifier, mono, 6550 tubes 150
Leak, Model Stero 50, amplifier, stereo, tubes, 50 watts 200
Marantz, Model 1 "Audio Consolette," pre-amplifier, tubes, wood case 150
Marantz, Model 2, amplifier, mono, tubes, 40 watts 200
Marantz, Model 9, amplifier, mono, 70 watts 500
McIntosh, Model MC275, amplifier, stereo, 6550 tubes 400
McIntosh, Model MC240, amplifier, stereo, 6L6 tubes 250
Tannoy, Model "Dual Concentric," speaker, 12" or 15" d 75
Thorens, Model TD124, photo turntable, 4 speed, belt drive 50
Vacuum Tube, Model EL34, GE, RCA, Mullard, Amperex, Telefunken 25
Vacuum Tube, Model 2A3, GE, RCA, Mullard, Amperex, Telefunken 50

Thorens, Turntable, 4 speeds, belt drive, wood base, $25.

Vacuum Tube, Model 6550, GE, RCA,
  Mullard, Amperex, Telefunken 25
Vacuum Tube, Model 12AX7, GE, RCA,
  Mullard, Amperex, Telefunken 10
Vacuum Tube, Model 300B, GE, RCA,
  Mullard, Amperex, Telefunken 75
Western Electric, Model 91, amplifier,
  mono, tubes, 2 chassis 500

HIGGINS GLASS

Michael Higgins and Frances Stewart Higgins were actively involved in designing and decorating glass in their Chicago studio by the early 1950s. Between 1958 and 1964, the couple worked in a studio provided for them by Dearborn Glass, an industrial company located outside Chicago. Pieces were mass produced. A gold signature was screened on the front of each piece before the final firing. During the period with Dearborn, the Higginses developed new colors and enamels for their double-layered pieces and experimented with weaving copper wire into glass, fusing glass chips to create crystalline forms, and overlaying colors onto glass panels.

After leaving Dearborn, the Higginses established a studio at Haeger. In 1966 they re-established their own studio. During the late 1960s and early 1970s, the Higginses manufactured large quantities of glass plaques, often framed in wood. In 1972 they purchased the building in Riverside, Illinois, that currently serves as their studio. Pieces made after 1972 have an engraved signature on the back. Unless stated otherwise, all of the listings below have a gold signature.

Ashtray, free form, blue and green fish,
  silver accents 55
Ashtray, free form, multicolored balloons
  and balloonists, gold signature, 9" l . . .60
Ashtray, free form, multicolored butter-
  flies, 9" l 85
Ashtray, rectangular, red, green, yellow,
  and white pocket watches with gold
  highlights, 7 x 10" 100
Ashtray, round, orange and yellow
  stripes radiating from center, 6.5" d . .35
Ashtray, seaweed growing in ocean
  water, multicolored, 5.875" d 50

Bowl, octagonal, yellow and green
  mums, 8.25" d 115
Bowl, round, light blue wheel spoke
  pattern in center, dark blue peacock
  feather motif around rim, 8.75" d 100
Bowl, round, red and gold Chinese
  calligraphy, 8.5" d 100
Bowl, round, red, orange, and peri-
  winkle blue flowers, 12.75" d 175
Bowl, round, yellow and white stripe,
  with gold water droplets, 6" d, 1.5" h . .65
Bowl, square, gold linear pattern, gold
  signature, 7 x 7" 65
Bowl, tapered rim, 8 alternating wide
  tapered panels in orange and salmon,
  clear scalloping around panels separating deeper orange from lighter
  orange, 8.25" d, 2.25" d base 90
Dish, stalks of leaves, scalloped, clear
  and opaque white and light blue-
  green dec, 7" d 70
Plate, free form, light blue, dark blue,
  and green mosaic tiles, 12 x 15" 125
Plate, round, orange and black Oriental
  tree, 8.5" d 85
Plate, round, red and orange flowers,
  7.5" d 125
Platter, clear, bands of red, orange,
  green, and white radiating from center, gold line spiraling from center
  to outer edge, gold signature, 17" d . .150
Tray, 8 abstract designs, white, clear,
  gray, black, and gold, 10 x 5" 90
Tray, blue and green spokes on purple
  ground, 7 x 14" 100

Bowl, free form, green, orange, and blue check with bubbles, gold signature, 9" h, $110. —Photo courtesy Jackson's Auctioneers & Appraisers.

Tray, radiating shades of yellow, alternating orange-yellow, yellow, and
green yellow edges, 14 x 14" 175
Tray, yellow and green flowers and
butterfly, 14 x 10" 50

HIPPIE MEMORABILIA

The "Hippies" continued the "Beatnik"
attitudes and conduct of rebellious, free-
thinking nonconformity during the tumul-
tuous 1960s. In 1964, students at the
University of California at Berkeley began
the first organized student protests, known
as "The Free Speech Movement." As the
Vietnam War escalated, a number of
groups such as the Students for a
Democratic Society (SDS), the Youth
International Party (Yippies), led by Abbie
Hoffman and Jerry Rubin, and the Weather
Underground formed to protest the war
with varying degrees of fervor.

The Haight-Ashbury area of San
Francisco became the center for the
emerging "counterculture." New and outrageous styles of clothes, music, art, theater, attitudes, behavior, and politics
emerged. Harvard professor Timothy Leary
began controlled experiments with hallu-
cinogenic drugs (legal at the time). The
watershed event of the counterculture,
which took place in August, 1969, was the
Woodstock Music and Art Fair, which
attracted at least 400,000 people. Rock
bands proliferated across the country.

The era produced many thousands of
highly collectible items. Basic categories
include books, records, posters, underground newspapers and comics, magazines, bumper stickers, pinback buttons,
etc.

Advisor: Richard M. Synchef, 208 Summit
Dr., Corte Madera, CA , 94925, (415) 927-
8844.

Note: Prices listed are for items in excellent
to near mint condition. All books are first
editions with dust jackets in near fine or
better condition.

Book, *Electric Kool Aid Acid Test, The,*
Tom Wolfe, NY, Farrar, Straus &
Girous, 1968, first printing 700

Book, *Hell's Angels*, Hunter S Thomp-
son, NY, Random House, 1967, first
printing 950
Book, *High Priest*, Timothy Leary,
Cleveland, OH, New American
Library, Inc, 1968, first edition 175
Book, *With the Weathermen*, Susan
Stern, NY, Doubleday & Co, 1975 85
Bumper Sticker, "Pat Paulsen for
President," Peter Geller Distributors,
red, white, and blue, 1968, 4 x 11" 80
Comic Book, Conspiracy Capers, under-
ground, The Conspiracy, Kathleen
Cleaver & Susan Sontag, Chicago, IL,
1969 250
Comic Book, Despair, underground,
Robert Crumb issue, The Print Mint,
Berkeley, CA, 1969, first printing 125
Figurine, hippie man with sign "Fight
Hate," Napcoware, 1970, 6" h 80
Handbill, Human Be-In, A Gathering
of the Tribes, Jan 14, 1967, Kelley,
Mouse*Bowen artists, The Bindweed
Press 500
Handbill, Quasar's Ice Cream Parlor,
Haight Ashbury, psychedelic, 1966,
9 x 5" 120
Handbill, Yippie!, Youth International
Party, Aug 1968, pre-Democratic
Convention in Chicago, red, white,
and blue, 8.5 x 11" 600
Jigsaw Puzzle, Richard Nixon/Spiro
Agnew, 2-sided, The Puzzle Factory,
1970, 22 x 15" 125
Magazine, *CAW!*, Students for a Demo-
cratic Society, Feb 1968, 1st issue ...250

Magazine, Evergreen Review, *No. 2*, "The
San Francisco Scene," NY, Grove Press,
Inc., 1959, $150.

Magazine, *Underground Digest*, Underground Communications, Inc, NY, first issue 150

Newspaper, *Sundance*, White Panther Information Service, Ann Arbor, MI, Vol 1, #1, Jul 4, 1970, first issue 300

Newspaper, *The Black Panther*, Oakland, CA, Mar 6, 1971, "Free Kathleen Cleaver and All Political Prisoners!" .100

Paperback Book, *Monday Night Class*, Stephen Gaskin, Santa Rosa, CA, Book Farm, 1970 90

Paperback Book, *The Jefferson Airplane and the San Francisco Sound*, Ralph S Gleason, NY, Ballantine, 1969 100

Pinback Button, "Free Angela," c1970, 1.5" d 60

Poster, "Can You Pass the Acid Test?," Norman Hartweg, artist, Ken Kesey & The Merry Pranksters, 1965 2,700

Record, *Wake Up America!*, Abbie Hoffman, Big Toe Records, 1969 250

Ticket, Woodstock Music & Art Fair, Globe Ticket Co, Aug 1969, 1 day or 3 day ticket 125

HOLIDAY COLLECTIBLES

Holidays play an important part in American life. Besides providing a break from work, they allow time for patriotism, religious renewal, and fun. Because of America's size and ethnic diversity, there are many holiday events of a regional nature. Attend some of them and pick up their collectibles. I have started a Fastnacht Day collection.

This listing is confined to national holidays. If I included special days, from Secretary's Day to Public Speaker's Day, I would fill this book with holiday collectibles alone. Besides, in fifty years is anyone going to care about Public Speaker's Day? No one does now.

Newsletter: *St. Patrick Notes,* 10802 Greencreek Dr., Suite 703, Houston, TX 77070.

Note: See Christmas, Halloween, and Valentines for additional listings.

Easter, pinback button, "Easter," white Easter lilies on dark blue ground, red lettering, 1920s 5

Father's Day, display, cardboard, "Father's Day Cards...say how much he means to you!," Gibson, 26" h, 23.5" w 20

Father's Day, label, White Owl Cigars, "Happy Father's Day," mother owl and 4 baby owls perched on branch, 8.5 x 6" 10

Father's Day, pinback button, St Joseph and young Jesus, black lettering on gray ground, 1920s 5

Fourth of July, pinback button, "Safe and Sane 4th of July," multicolored, patriotic symbols, eagle, Liberty Bell, Declaration of Independence, Independence Hall, Revolutionary War soldiers, blue lettering for 1910 celebration in Pittsfield, MA 15

Fourth of July, pinback button, Uncle Sam with firecrackers, multicolored, "Village Improvement Society So. Shaftsbury, VT," early 1900s 35

Memorial Day, brochure, Memorial Day services, Boulder City Central Labor Council, May 13, 1935 3

Memorial Day, postcard, "*The Monitor's Great Victory*," emb, postmarked Astoria, OR, Jul 4, 1910 4

Mother's Day, pinback button, mother and infant, single white carnation with green stem, 1920s 8

New Year's Day, postcard, bell with flocked fuchsia-colored flower, applied booklet opens to reveal greeting, mkd "Printed in Germany" 5

New Year's Day, sheet music, For the Sake of Auld Lang Syne, *1920, $10.*

Thanksgiving, postcard, Clapsaddle illus, 1909, $8.

St Patrick's Day, decoration, cardboard, dancing Irish girl, red hair, green with shamrocks on skirt, Dennison, 7"h ...10
St Patrick's Day, pinback button, "Erin Go Bragh," Irish flags and shamrock, black lettering, 1930s 8
St Patrick's Day, pinback button, "Guinness/Welcome to Ireland/Happy St Patrick's Day," 2.5" d 5
Thanksgiving, greeting card, "Here's hoping that you may have cause for thanks this day," emb turkey 1
Thanksgiving, postcard, Clapsaddle, boy and turkeys, Wolf & Co #1903, postmarked 1919 4
Thanksgiving, postcard, Tuck, Thanksgiving Day Post Cards Series #123, postmarked, 1907, used 5
Thanksgiving, postcard, "Today he's got me on the run, Tomorrow I will have the fun/Thanksgiving Greetings," turkey chasing girl, 1911 3

HOLT-HOWARD

A. Grant Holt and brothers John and Robert J. Howard formed the Holt-Howard import company in Stamford, Connecticut, in 1948. The firm is best known for its novelty ceramics, including the Cat and Christmas lines and the popular Pixie Ware line of condiment jars. Designed by Robert J. Howard and produced between 1958 and the early 1960s, these ceramic containers proved to be so successful that knock-offs by Davar, Lefton, Lipper & Mann, M-G, Inc., and Norcrest quickly found their way into the market. Kay Dee Designs purchased Holt-Howard in 1990.

Authentic Pixieware is easily identified by its single-color vertical stripes on a white jar, flat pixie-head stopper (with attached spoon when appropriate), and condiment label with slightly skewed black lettering. An exception is three salad dressing cruets which had round heads. All pieces were marked, either with "HH" or "Holt-Howard," a copyright symbol followed by the year "1958" or "1959," and "Japan." Some pieces may be found with a black and silver label.

Christmas Carolers, candleholder, 5" h, 8" d 15
Christmas Mouse, candleholder 10
Christmas Tree, napkin holder, 5" h 6
Coq Rouge, candleholder 10
Coq Rouge, cigarette box, 11.75" h 25
Coq Rouge, coffeepot 50
Coq Rouge, eggcup, 4 x 3 x 2" 10
Coq Rouge, napkin holder, 6" h, 5.5" d ...35
Coq Rouge, pitcher, ice lip, 9.5" h 9
Coq Rouge, recipe box, 5.5 x 3.25 x 4.25" .50
Coq Rouge, salt and pepper shakers, pr, 4.5" h 12
Coq Rouge, snack dish 8
Coq Rouge, spoon rest 15
Cozy Kitten, cottage cheese dish 18
Cozy Kitten, creamer and sugar 150
Cozy Kitten, instant coffee condiment ..100
Cozy Kitten, letter holder, 6.25"h 40
Cozy Kittch, match dandy 50
Cozy Kitten, soap shaker, 6.75" h 35
Cozy Kitten, string holder, 4.5" h, 5.25" w ..45
Daisy 'Dorables, box, cov, 5" d 30
Daisy 'Dorables, bud vase, 5.5" h 50
Dandy Lion, bank, nodder 50

Winter Green, candy dish, ©1959, 13.75" l, $15. —Photo courtesy Ray Morykan Auctions.

Holly Berry, creamer and sugar 20
Holly Berry, salt and pepper shakers, pr,
3.125" h 30
Li'l Old Lace, Granny, card holder, 5" h . .35
Li'l Old Lace, Granny, salt and pepper
shakers, pr, 4" h 30
Pixieware, candle hugger 15
Pixieware, cocktail onions jar 80
Pixieware, hanging planter 175
Pixieware, Italian dressing bottle, 6.5" h .50
Pixieware, jam and jelly jar 30
Pixieware, mustard jar 60
SS Noel, salt and pepper shakers, pr . . .90
Santa, pop-up candy jar, 6.5" h 100
Singing Angel, Christmas tree topper,
8.5" h 25
Winking Santa, eggnog pitcher, 6 cups . .50

HOME-FRONT COLLECTIBLES

Home-front collectibles emerged as a separate collecting category approximately three years ago. The fact that it took so long is surprising. However, many home-front collectibles have been sold for years in crossover categories such as postcards and magazines.

Club: Society of Ration Token Collectors, 618 Jay Dr., Gallipolis, OH 45631.

Activity Book, "Our Gallant Armed
Forces," ©1958 Samuel Lowe, 11 x
14" 25
First Day Cover, "Operation Crossroads,"
Jul 25, 1945, 3.5 x 6.5" 50
Handkerchief, sheer linen, red, white,
and blue, victory symbols, mkd
"Bloch Freres," 12.5 x 12.5" 40
License Plate, diecut tin, red "V" on
white enamel ground under blue
"Victory," Mayer Mfg Co, 3 x 10" 100
Matchcover, uniformed Hitler embrac-
ing world globe, "Strike at the seat
of trouble/Buy war bonds" 40
Match Holder, black plastic, black and
white MacArthur photo 40
Medal, bronze luster finish, raised Uncle
Sam profile and "Camp Dodge" on
front, reverse with fluttering US flag
above rising sun and "My Country,
'Tis of Thee," 2.5" d 8

Pin, gray metal, hanger bar with open
diecut "Victory" above "V" 30
Pin, savings stamps holder, plastic
eagle, red, white, and blue, gold
painted accents, bottom loop holding clear plastic slipcase, 1940s 20
Pinback Button, Japanese officer
squeezed in mechanical vise, "Beat
the Promise/Put the Squeeze on the
Japanese" 75
Pinback Button, Uncle Sam preparing
for war with balloon caption
"Preparedness/Let 'em Come," 1918 .75
Poster, "Pay-Day Bond-Day," paper,
1942, 37 x 51" .50
Ribbon, red fabric, white inscription
"Remember Pearl Harbor" with
image of falling bomb and tropical
island, .5 x 7.25" 25
Sheet Music, *Any Bonds Today?*, theme
song of National Defense Savings
Program, Irving Berlin, ©1941 Henry
Morgenthau Jr, 9 x 12" 8
Tumbler, clear, glass, frosted white ship
image with inscription "Blown Up in
Havana Harbor Feb 15, 1898, 3.5" h,
2.75" d 20
Tumbler, glass, clear, "We're In It—We'll
Win It," front full color decal of
Marine and girlfriend embracing,
reverse shows decal of blown skirt
of girlfriend to expose thighs, 4.75" h,
2.5" d 30

Poster, litho paper, Third Liberty Loan, sgd *"Lawrence S. Harris," archival backing, 29.75" h, 20" w, $150.* —Photo courtesy Collectors Auction Services.

Window Card, cardboard, red, white, and blue shield emblem circled by gold wheat ring, red inscription "Member Of" with blue inscription "United States Food Administration" on white ground, small inscription at bottom "Please hang this card in your front window," WWI, 5.5 x 9" 35

HOMER LAUGHLIN

Homer Laughlin and his brother, Shakespeare, built two pottery kilns in East Liverpool, Ohio, in 1871. In 1896 the firm was sold and new plants were built in Laughlin Station, Ohio, and Newall, West Virginia.

The original trademark used from 1871 to 1890 merely identified the products as "Laughlin Brothers." The next trademark featured the American eagle astride the prostrate British lion. The third mark featured a monogram of "HLC," which has appeared, with slight variations, on all dinnerware produced since about 1900. The 1900 trademark contained a number which identified month, year and plant at which the product was made. Letter codes were used in later periods.

REPRODUCTION ALERT: Harlequin and Fiesta lines were reissued in 1978 and marked accordingly.

Club: Homer Laughlin China Collectors Assoc., P.O. Box 26021, Arlington, VA 22215.

Note: For additional listings see Fiesta Ware.

Americana, platter, 15" l 15
Casualtone Gold, berry bowl 4
Casualtone Gold, bread and butter plate . .4
Casualtone Gold, cereal bowl 10
Casualtone Gold, cup 5
Casualtone Gold, dinner plate 15
Casualtone Gold, salad plate 5
Casualtone Gold, saucer 4
Conchita, platter, 11.5" l 50
Currier & Ives, cup and saucer 24
Eggshell Cavalier, creamer, 4.25" h 3
Eggshell Cavalier, sugar, cov, 4" h 2
Eggshell Georgian, dinner plate, 8" d 4
Eggshell Georgian, platter, 10" d 5
Eggshell Nautilus, platter, #J48NJ 20

Virginia Rose, cup and saucer, $3.

Harlequin, platter, red, 11" l 10
Harlequin, platter, red, 13" l 16
Jubilee, salad plate, 7.5" d 2
Kitchen Kraft, mixing bowl 35
Magnolia, soup bowl, 8" d 8
Oven Serve, bowl, 4.25" d 6
Oven Serve, bowl, 4.5" d 6
Oven Serve, bread and butter plate,
   6.5" d 8
Oven Serve, custard, pumpkin, 3.5" 5
Oven Serve, custard, pumpkin, 3.75" 5
Oven Serve, plate, 7" d 8
Oven Serve, plate, 9" d 15
Rhythm, salad bowl, yellow, 8.25" d 5
Riviera, dinner plate, 9.5" d 5
Riviera, gravy boat 15
Riviera, pitcher, 6.5" h 38
Virginia Rose, berry bowl 5
Virginia Rose, bread and butter plate 2
Virginia Rose, celery dish 25
Virginia Rose, dessert plate 4
Virginia Rose, dinner plate, 9.25" d 4
Virginia Rose, gravy boat 25
Virginia Rose, serving bowl 20
Virginia Rose, vegetable bowl 25

HORSE COLLECTIBLES

This is one of those collectible categories where you can collect the real thing, riding equipment ranging from bridles to wagons, and/or representational items.

The figurine is the most-favored collectible. However, horse-related items can be found in almost every collectible category from Western movie posters to souvenir spoons. As long as there is a horse on it, it is collectible.

A neglected area among collectors is the rodeo. I am amazed at how much rodeo material I find at East Coast flea markets. I never realized how big the eastern rodeo circuit was.

Book, *Smarty,* Katharine Newlin Burt, illus by Vic Donahue, cover depicts boy and girl with horses, hardcover, 136 pp, 1965 2

Bridle Rosette, price for pair 50

Doorstop, figural horse, cast iron, painted, 9.5" h, 11" l 12

Figurine, colt, black and white, Royal Doulton, 4" h, 3.5" l 25

Figurine, quarter horse, Hagen-Renaker, 3.25" l, 2.5" h 8

Figurine, Victorian horse and carriage, mkd "Made in Japan," 3.75" h, 4.5" l . . .8

Harness Strap, leather, 4 decorative brasses, 10" l 45

Hitching Post, black jockey, cast aluminum, old worn repaint, 31" h 250

Hoof Trimmer, iron 75

Horse Blanket, 1 side black, other side mottled brown .60

Horse Collar, leather covered wood, brass trim 125

Horseshoe Pouch, leather, mkd "Rawle London 1942" 10

Key Chain, attached miniature horse bit, 1.5 x 1.75" 3

Lasso, horsehair, rawhide covered tips, 1890s 250

Postcard, black man on horse, real photo 2

Poster, "Equestrian Equipment," horse with riding accessories, 3.75 x 4.5" . . .10

Saddle, McClelland type, large fenders, early 1900s 600

Saddle Stand, pine, red wash 65

Salt and Pepper Shakers, pr, ceramic, horse heads, orig foil label mkd "A Quality Product Japan," c1950s 10

Postcard, double wide, Anheuser-Busch adv, Clydesdales, color, 1944, 11 x 3.5", $30.

Coat Rack, horse head ends, brass, $25.
—Photo courtesy Ray Morykan Auctions.

Spurs, pr, steel chains 125

Tin, Cossack Tablets, "Save the Horse," man on horse, "A positive remedy for all acute & chronic ailments of the horse," Cossack Remedies Co, Montreal, Canada, c1915 20

HORSE RACING COLLECTIBLES

The history of horse racing dates back to the domestication of the horse itself. Prehistoric cave drawings show horse racing. The Greeks engaged in chariot racing as early as 600 B.C. As civilization spread, so did the racing of horses. Each ethnic group and culture added its own unique slant.

Horse racing reached America during the colonial period. The premier American horse race is the Kentucky Derby. Programs date back to 1924 and glasses, a favorite with collectors, to the late 1930s.

There are so many horse racing collectibles that one needs to specialize. Focuses include a particular horse-racing type or a specific horse race, a breed or specific horse, or racing prints and images. Each year there are a number of specialized auctions devoted to horse racing, ranging from sporting prints sales at the major New York auction houses to benefit auctions for the Thoroughbred Retirement Foundation.

Advertising Tear Sheet, Fleischmann's 90 Proof, jockeys on horses, "Big Favorite–3 Ways/No Other Whiskey …Only Fleischmann's Gives You The Big 3," *Collier'sMagazine,* 1951, 4.5 x 12.5" 5

Badge, Wangaratta Turf Club, Victoria, undated, c1970s 10

Book, *The ABC's of Horse Racing,* Dan

Parker, 216 pp, 1947 5
Book, *Trotting and Pacing Guide*, US
   Trotting Assoc, 148 pp, 1974 2
Cigar Box, wood, Marion Cigars, horse
   and jockey scene, late 1800s, 5.125
   x 8.375" 35
Game, Win, Place & Show, 3M, 1966 15
Lapel Pin, 112th Preakness Stakes, 1987 ..12
Magazine, *Quarter Horse Journal*, Apr
   1959, 152 pp 10
Pass, Riverside Jockey Club, 1932, 3.5
   x 2.125" 15
Pin, brass, center raised relief image
   of horse head above rim inscription
   "Bit & Bridle 1903" 8
Pinback Button, horse portrait with
   "Member Jockey Club," 1930s 10
Pinback Button, jockey portrait with
   "Webb, Celebrated American
   Jockey" 18
Program, Hollywood Park, Goose Girl
   Stakes, 1961 5
Program, Keeneland, Spring Meeting,
   Blue Grass Stakes, Apr 13-27, 1950 ...20
Program, Dunn County Fair, Menomonie,
   WI, 40th Annual race, 1928, 4 x 8.5" ...15
Ticket, Bowie Race Track, Maryland,
   Nov 26, 1936 8
Ticket, Santa Anita, 6th race, #3 to win,
   dated Jan 7, 1948 2
Tip Tray/Spinner, Fehr's Beer, Louisville,
   KY, jockeys on horses and numbers
   1-6, Behr's Beer logo in center,
   c1944, 4.125" d 70
TV Guide, Jun 10, 1950, horse racing

*Poster, sulky races, litho paper, archival
backing, mkd "Courier Litho, Buffalo, NY,"
c1890, 31" h, 45" w, $400.* —Photo courtesy
Collectors Auction Services.

*Tobacco Tin, Red
Jacket Smoking
Tobacco, 4.5" h, $25.*
—Photo courtesy
Gene Harris Antique
Auction Center, Inc.

cover 10
Windup, litho tin, jockey on horse,
   Occupied Japan 35

HOT WHEELS

   In 1968 Mattel introduced a line of two-
inch long plastic and diecast metal cars.
Dubbed "Hot Wheels," there were originally sixteen cars, eight playsets, and two collector sets.

   Hot Wheels are identified by the name
of the model and its year, which are cast on
the bottom of each vehicle. The most desirable Hot Wheels cars have red striping on
the tires. These early vehicles are the
toughest to find and were produced from
1968 to 1978. In 1979 black tires became
standard on all models. The most valuable
Hot Wheel vehicles are usually those with
production runs limited to a single year or
those in a rare color.

   Hop in your own set of wheels and race
to your nearest flea market to find your own
hot collectibles.

Newsletter: *Hot Wheels Newsletter,* 26
Madera Ave., San Carlos, CA 94070.

American Hauler, blue 8
Baja Bruiser, blue 12
Bugeye, red 20
Buzz Off, blue, yellow stripes 15
Classic Nomad, purple 40
Custom Cougar Redline, blue 18
Custom Volkswagen Redline, aqua 25
Deora, gold 60
Ferrari 312, red 6
Flintstones Flintmobile 8
Highway Rider 24
Iola, purple 15
Jeep Scrambler, red 10

Turboa 2061, yellow with green spots, 1986, $6.

Jet Thret, light green 55
King Kuda, blue .25
Lotus, green 5
Mantis, light blue 12
Mercedes Benz, green 18
Neet Street, chrome 15
Paddy Wagon, blue, with windshield . . .15
Rash One, blue .100
Rock Buster, chrome 8
Rolls Royce, gold 60
Sand Drifter, yellow, orange flames 12
Shelby Turbine, purple 30
Snake, yellow 50
Splittin' Image, green 20
Stingray Corvette 12
Torero, green 10
Twin Mill, chrome 25
Xploder, red 90

HOWARD JOHNSON'S

Howard Johnson assumed ownership of a patent medicine store in Wollaston, Massachusetts, in 1925. To expand the business, he started making his own ice cream. In addition to the usual flavors of vanilla, chocolate, and strawberry, he created ice cream flavors no one had heard of before. Business grew at a steady rate.

In 1929, Howard opened his first restaurant and expanded his line to 28 flavors of ice cream. The number of restaurants grew from 25 in 1935 to more than 800 by 1966.

During the 1950s Howard was a pioneer in the field of convenience frozen foods. He built commissaries in the Boston and Miami areas that delivered pre-portioned and pre-cooked foods to the Howard Johnson's up and down the East Coast.

Howard Johnson's Motor Lodges were established in 1954. The company opened a couple dozen Red Coach Grill restaurants through the 1960s. The Ground Round was added to the Howard's Johnson's family in 1969. The original company was sold and disbanded in 1979.

Advisor: Jeffrey C. McCurty, P.O. Box 882, Pleasant Valley, NY, 12569-0882.

Ashtray, clear glass, round, turquoise Lamplighter and Simple Simon motor-lodge logo in reverse plate image, c1960, 4.5" d 12
Bracelet, sterling silver chain with medallion of Simple Simon & The Pieman trademark in silver, black Bakelite background, Service Award, c1940, 7" l chain 75
Candy Container, cardboard, white, orange, and turquoise, box design of suitcase with various luggage stickers, mkd "Howard Johnson's Lollipops/6 Delicious Flavors/25¢/Net Wt 4.375 oz," Howard Johnson's, Quincy, MA, c1960-65, 6.75 x 1.25" 40
Charger, white maroon design, scalloped edge, Simple Simon and the Pieman trademark, Caribe China, Puerto Rico, USA, c1960s, 11.375" d . .60
Demitasse Cup and Saucer, white maroon design, scalloped edge, Pieman trademark, Syracuse China, c1960s, 4.5" d saucer 35
Drinking Glass, clear, Hojo Cola, roof dome trademark in orange and turquoise on white circle, "Hojo" in turquoise, "Cola" in clear cut-out letters, 8 oz, 1968-79 30
Food Bag, heavy paper, mkd "Howard Johnson's Hot R Cold Insulated Bag," features Simple Simon & The Pieman logo, white bag with orange and turquoise graphics, c1960, 14 x 5" 20
Ice Cream Container, heavy paper, round, "Howard Johnson's Ice Cream," Pieman logo, white, orange, and turquoise, Nestyle-Sealright Co, Fulton, NY, c1958-65, 4.5" h 25
Key Chain, formica, rect, white with orange and turquoise roof dome trademark on front, rear mkd "Howard Johnson's Motor Lodges" with address, 1968-79, 2.5 x 1.375" 5

Magazine, *MAD,* issue #106, spoof of
Howard Johnson's titled "MAD visits
a Typical Johnson Howard's Restau-
rant," Oct 1966 10
Menu, ice cream and desserts, heavy
paper, white, black, and turquoise,
lists sundaes, pies, cakes, thickshakes,
and ice cream sodas, c1940, 5 x 7.5" . .25
Pamphlet, lists 38 motor lodge locations
in 18 states, full color illus of room
designs and services available, c1958,
opens to 18 x 11.5" 20
Paperweight, gray marble cube with
oval brass and vinyl medallion on
top showing roof dome trademark,
orange and turquoise on white
ground, "Howard Johnsons" and
trim in gold, "Fine Marble Base Made
in Italy" sticker 1968-79, 2 x 2 x .75" . . .25
Platter, oval, white, maroon design,
Americana scenes with restaurant
and road sign, Caribe China, mkd
"Made Expressly for Howard
Johnson's Restaurants," Caribe
China, W C Ayres Co, Inc, c1950,
14" l 75
Playing Cards, deck of 52 plus 2 Jokers
in box, back design features
"Howard Johnson's" in black text
and view of cottage style restaurant
and automobiles in white, orange,
and turquoise, complete with instruction card for playing bridge and gin
rummy, Brown & Bigelow, St Paul,
MN, dated Apr 1943 75
Record, *Howard Johnson's Restaurants
and Motor Lodges,* 33 1/3 rpm,
features 7 different versions of radio
commercials promoting visiting
Howard Johnson's, background
music supplied for radio announcer
to add specific local information,
disc #D-743, World Broadcasting
System, Inc, Radio & TV Sales
Service, Philadelphia, PA, c1960-65 . .75
Sandwich Plate, Americana scenes
with 1930s cottage style restaurant
and automobiles, white and maroon,
smooth edge, Mayer China, Beaver
Falls, PA, mkd "Made expressly for
Howard Johnson Restaurants,"
8.125" d 40

*Sign, aluminum frame, Plexiglas panels,
fluorescent fixture, c1960-65, 20" w, $300.*

Sebastian Miniature, plaster, Simple
Simon and The Pieman with Wags the
Dog, multicolored, sticker mkd "A
Sebastian Miniature Designed by
Prescott W. Baston, Marblehead, MA,"
Stone Wall, 2.5" l, 1.375" w, 2.5" h 350
Service Pin, brass, round, gold-plated,
Simple Simon and The Pieman,
black background and gold border,
c1970, .625" d .25
Stirrer, plastic, transparent red, mkd
"Red Coach Grill," wagon wheel on
top, c1970, 6" l 4
Teapot, single serve, white and maroon,
Simple Simon and The Pieman,
Shenango China, c1960s, 3.5" h,
6.5" l, 4" d 60
Toy, ice cream van, diecast metal, 1/87
scale, 4 different models mkd
"Vanilla, Chocolate, Strawberry, or
Pistachio" with corresponding ice
cream cone graphic, white truck
with "Howard Johnson's," orange
and turquoise roof dome trademark,
Larami Corp, Philadelphia, PA, made
in Hong Kong, 1968-79, 2.75" l 20
Uniform, waitress, 1 pc design with
turquoise skirt, white blouse with
turquoise collar and rolled up sleeves,
Simple Simon and The Pieman logo
with shooting stars graphics, snap-up
front, Downs Bros, Boston, MA,
c1955-60 150
Weather Vane, steel, painted black,
Simple Simon and The Pieman with
lamp post, lamp post provides support for 3 figures, 20 lbs, 36 x 40",
c1947-55 1,000

Winross Truck, diecast metal, Simple
Simon and The Pieman in silhouette
graphic with "Howard Johnson's
Landmark For Hungry Americans,"
white, turquoise, and orange, 7.5" l . .100

HOWDY DOODY

The Howdy Doody Show is the most
famous of early television's children's programs. Created by "Buffalo" Bob Smith, the
show ran for 2,343 performances between
December 27, 1947, and September 30,
1960. Among the puppet characters were
Howdy Doody, Mr. Bluster, Flub-a-Dub, and
Dilly-Dally. Clarabell the clown and
Princess Summerfall-Winterspring were
played by humans.

There is a whole generation out there
who knows there is only one answer to the
question: "What time is it?"

Club: Howdy Doody Memorabilia Collectors
Club, 8 Hunt Ct., Flemington, NJ 08822.

Bib, Princess Summer-Fall-Winter-
Spring, terrycloth, printed name
separated by symbols of seasons,
©Kagran 1951-56, 11 x 13.5" 100
Book, *Howdy Doody in the Wild West,*
Big Golden Book, Simon & Schuster,
32 pp, ©Kagran 1952, 9 x 11" 20
Catalog, features Howdy lunch boxes,
puppets, records, shows, food, phon-
odoodle, and watches, illus, 1955 . . .575
Coloring Book, "Santa Visits Howdy
Doody's House," Filene's Chestnut
Hill premium,16 pp, ©Bob Smith
1951, 5.25 x 6.75" 50
Cue Sheets, typewritten paper sheets
serving as cue cards for show of
Wed, Jan 27, 1954, 7 x 7.5", price
for 6 40
Dixie Ice Cream Cup, waxed cardboard,
Howdy Doody head image with smaller
single head image of Mr Baluster,
Clarabell, Flub-a-Dub, and Dilly Dally,
©Kagran 1951-56, 2" h, 3" d 15
Doll, Howdy Doody, painted wood and
composition head, fabric neckerchief, "Howdy Doody" name decal
on chest with Bob Smith copyright,
c1948-51, 12.5" h 390

*Ventriloquist
Dummy, Ideal,
$300.*

Doll, Howdy Doody, plush body, rolling
eyes, "Howdy Doody" neckerchief,
Ideal, 1950s, 20" h 650
Game, Howdy Doody Ball-Rolling
Target Game, "Howdy Doody's Own
Game," Parker Bros, ©Bob Smith
1948-51, orig 1.25 x 7 x 15" box 125
Game, Howdy Doody TV Game, Milton
Bradley, ©Kagran 1951-56, orig 2 x
9 x 19" box 60
Ovaltine Shake-Up Mug, plastic, cap
inscription "Howdy Doody's Cold
Ovaltine Shake-Up Mug," decal on
side with Bob Smith copyright,
c1948-50, 5" h .80
Patch, fabric, for Buffalo Bob Smith
personal appearance, stitched
white "Tootsie Roll" on brown felt
fabric, red and white stitched border, reverse has brown leather
backing piece with needle post and
clutch fastener on each corner,
c1970-80s, 3 x 3.5" 20
Plates, china, Howdy image as cowboy
swinging lariat, mkd "Taylor, Smith,
Taylor, USA," 1950s, 8.5" d, price for
set of 5 375
RCA Howdy Doody Party Promotion Kit,
pennant with stick, ad mat, entry
blank, balloon, brochure, and orig
12 x 16" envelope 340
Salt and Pepper Shakers, pr, painted
hard plastic, applied thin vinyl neckerchief, cork stopper, ©Kagran,
Doodlings Inc, Cambridge, MA,
c1951-56, 3" h, 1.75" d base 200
Wrapping Paper, various repeating
Howdy party images and "It's Howdy
Doody Time," hundreds of feet in
length 650

HULL POTTERY

Hull Pottery traces its beginnings to the 1905 purchase of the Acme Pottery Company of Crooksville, Ohio, by Addis E. Hull. By 1917 a line of art pottery designed specifically for flower and gift shops was added to Hull's standard fare of novelties, kitchenware, and stoneware. A flood and fire destroyed the plant in 1950. When the plant reopened in 1952, the Hull products had a new glossy finish.

Hull is collected by pattern. A favorite with collectors is the Little Red Riding Hood kitchenware line, made between 1943 and 1957. Most Hull pieces are marked. Pre-1950 pieces have a numbering system to identify pattern and height. Post-1950 pieces have "hull" or "Hull" in large script letters.

Club: Hull Pottery Assoc., 15475 Hilltop Rd., Council Bluffs, IA 51503.

Newsletter: *Hull Pottery Newsletter,* 7768 Meadow Dr., Hillsboro, MO 53959.

Basket, Capri, green and yellow, 12" h . .12
Basket, Tulip, 102-33-6" 175
Bud Vase, Orchid, 306-6 3/4" 100
Candleholder, Iris, 411-5" 50
Candleholder, Magnolia, 27-4" 30
Cookie Jar, Little Red Riding Hood, full
    floral skirt, closed basket, 13" h 275
Creamer, Bow Knot, B-21-4" 75
Creamer and Open Sugar, Rosella,
    mkd "R-3-5 1/2"" and "R-4-5 1/2"" . . .100
Ewer, Camellia, 106-13 1/4" 400

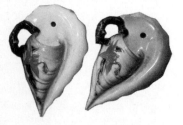

Wall Pockets, Woodland, W-13, price for pair, $150. —Photo courtesy Collectors Auction Services.

Ewer, Open Rose, pink, 105-7" 250
Ewer, Orchid, 311-13" 350
Jardiniere, Royal Imperial, pink and
    black, 75-7" 50
Jardiniere, Wild Flower, 64-4" 65
Salt and Pepper Shakers, pr, Little Red
    Riding Hood, 3.5" h 40
Shaker, Sun-Glow, 54, 2.75" h 10
Teapot, Magnolia Matte, pink and blue,
    emb "Hull Art U.S.A. 23," 6.5" h 85
Teapot, Serenade, S17, 5" h 90
Vase, Camellia, 102-8 1/2" 100
Vase, Magnolia Gloss, double cornu-
    copia, emb "Hull Art H-5," 12" h 40
Vase, Magnolia Matte, imp "Hull Art,
    U.S.A. 2," 8.5" h 115
Vase, Tulip, 100-33-8" 75
Vase, Wild Flower, yellow and dusty
    rose, mkd in relief "Hull Art USA, 59,"
    10.5" h 225
Vase, Woodland, dark green and blue,
    mkd in relief "Hull W7-5 1/2" USA" . . .65
Vase, Woodland, rose and chartreuse,
    emb "Hull W9 8 3/4" USA" 110
Wall Pocket, Poppy, 609-9" 175

HUMMEL LOOK-ALIKES, ERICH STAUFFER FIGURINES

Erich Stauffer figures were imported to the United States during the late 1950s through the 1980s. Often described as Hummel look-alikes, a Hummel collector can tell at a glance they are not the "real thing."

Most Stauffer figures are marked with a style number and the words "Designed by Erich Stauffer" in blue script. The mark is usually accompanied by either two crossed arrows or a crown motif. Some figures also have a blue triangular Stauffer tag and/or blue and gold "Original Arnart Creation, Japan" sticker. New figures were issued with a paper title strip attached at the front edge. Unfortunately, due to careless cleaning, this title strip is usually missing.

The same style number was sometimes used on up to six or eight different figures. This makes identification confusing for both potential and advanced collectors.

Figures measure from 4.25" up to 12" high. A guide to pricing today is $3 to $3.50

an inch, heightwise, for 4–5" figures, and $4 to $5 an inch, heightwise, for the taller figures, depending upon condition. Retention of the original title strip or blue tag is a bonus.

Advisor: Joan Oates, 685 S. Washington, Constantine, MI 49042.

44/63, Junior Prom, (Josef look-alike), with hangtag, pink dress with big bow, holding bouquet of flowers, 4.5" h 25

44/121, Picnic Time, boy, standing, with picnic basket, wearing white hat, 6.5" h 18

44/138, Picnic Time, girl, seated, with basket of flowers, 5" h 18

55/723, Napkins, napkin holder, boy chef with towel over arm 15

55/1057, Pet Time, boy brushing his dog on stool, 5" h 15

55/1556, Dancing Time, boy and girl, dancing side by side, 5.5" h 25

55/1581, no label, boy, standing, watermelon in each hand, blue jacket, long pants, 5" h 30

8316, Winter Time, nun in black habit, shoveling snow, 5" h 10

8326, Champion Collie, dog, seated, 6.5" h 20

8394, no label, boy, standing, umbrella over shoulder, knapsack over end of umbrella, 2 geese, 5" h 15

8543, Music Time, boy, seated, playing violin with bowler hat on, 6" h 18

S8442, Music Frolics, girl, standing, playing zither, goose by feet, 8.5" h ...25

S8517, Country Outing, boy, kneeling, holding closed umbrella in hand, 5" h .20

8213, Harvest Time, 5.125" h, $28.

U8542, Backyard Products, boy chef on fence, dog below, 5.25" h 20

S8543, Junior Nurse, girl, seated, with open nurse's bag, wearing white apron, holding scissors in hand, 6.25" h 35

HUMMELS

Hummel items are the original creations of Berta Hummel, a German artist. At the age of 18, she enrolled in the Academy of Fine Arts in Munich. In 1934 Berta Hummel entered the Convent of Siessen and became Sister Maria Innocentia. She continued to draw.

In 1935, W. Goebel Co. of Rodental, Germany, used some of her sketches as the basis for three-dimensional figures. American distribution was handled by the Schmid Brothers of Randolph, Massachusetts. In 1967 a controversy developed between the two companies involving the Hummel family and the convent. The German courts decided the Convent had the rights to Berta Hummel's sketches made between 1934 and her death in 1964. Schmid Bros. could deal directly with the family for reproduction rights to any sketches made before 1934.

All authentic Hummels bear both the M. I. Hummel signature and a Goebel trademark. There were various trademarks used to identify the year of production. The Crown Mark (trademark 1) was used from 1935–1949, Full Bee (trademark 2) 1950–1959, Stylized Bee (trademark 3) 1957–1972, Three Line Mark (trademark 4) 1964–1972, Last Bee Mark (trademark 5) 1972–1980, Missing Bee Mark (trademark 6) 1979–1990, and the Current Mark or New Crown Mark (trademark 7) from 1991 to the present.

Hummel material was copied widely. These copycats also are attracting interest among collectors. For more information about them, see Lawrence L. Wonsch's *Hummel Copycats With Values* (Wallace-Homestead: 1987).

Clubs: Hummel Collector's Club, 1261 University Dr., Yardley, PA 19067; M. I.

Hummel Club, Goebel Plaza, P.O. Box 11, Pennington, NJ 08534.

Apple Tree Boy, #142/1, trademark 5,
6" h 130
Apple Tree Girl, #141V, trademark 4,
10" h 500
Boy with Toothache, #217, trademark 5,
5.5" h 125
Chick Girl, #57/0, trademark 5 3.5" h 85
Crossroads, #331, trademark 5, 6.75" h .175
Doctor, #127, trademark 3, 4.75" h 100
Farewell, #65/1, trademark 5, 4.75" h . . .110
Favorite Pet, #361, trademark 5, 4.5" h . .140
Flower Vendor, #381, trademark 5, 5.25" h .130
Follow the Leader, #369, trademark 5,
7" h 450
Going to Grandma's, #52/0, trademark 5,
4.75" h 120
Good Friends, #182, trademark 5, 5" h . .120
Goose Girl, #47/0, trademark 3, 4.75" h . .170
Happy Days, #150 2/0, trademark 3,
4.25" h 110
Happy Traveler, #109/11, trademark 5,
7.5" h 175
Home From Market, #198, trademark 2,
5.5" h 190
Homeward Bound, #334, trademark 5,
5.25" h 140
Knitting Lesson, #256, trademark 5, 7.5" h .150
Latest News, #184, trademark 5, 7.5" h .120
Letter to Santa, #340, trademark 5, 7" h .130
Little Goat Herder, #200/1, trademark 5,
5.5" h 150
Little Helper, #73, trademark 5, 4.25" h . . .55
Little Tailor, #308, trademark 5, 5.5" h . . .120

Left: Kiss Me, #311, trademark 4, 6" h, $300. Right: Little Cellist, #89/1, trademark 6, 6" h, $180. —Photos courtesy Gene Harris Antique Auction Center, Inc.

Not For You, #317, trademark 5, 6" h 140
On Secret Path, #386, trademark 5,
5.25" h 150
Retreat to Safety, #201/2/0, trademark 3,
4" h 100
Ride Into Christmas, #396, trademark 5,
5.75" h 175
Signs of Spring, #203 2/0, trademark 5,
4" h 90
Sister, #98/0, trademark 3, 5.5" h 100

HUNTING COLLECTIBLES

The hunt is on and the only foxes are good flea market shoppers. It is time to take back the fields and exhibit those beautiful trophies and hunting displays. I do not care what the animal activists say. I love it. Old ammunition boxes, clothes, signs, stuffed beasts, photographs of the old hunting cabins or trips, and the great array of animal-calling devices. Oh yeah, this is the stuff that adventures and memories are made from.

Care and condition are the prime considerations when collecting hunting-related items. Weapons should always be securely displayed, insect deterrents and padded hangers are best for clothing or accessories, and humidity-controlled areas are suggested for paper ephemera. Good luck and happy hunting!

Clubs: Call & Whistle Collectors Assoc., 2839 E. 26th Place, Tulsa, OK 74114; Callmakers & Collectors Assoc. of America, 137 Kingswood Dr., Clarksville, TN 37043.

Periodical: *Sporting Collector's Monthly,* P.O. Box 305, Camden, DE 19934.

Newsletter: *Coykendall's Sporting Collectibles Newsletter,* P.O. Box 29, East Dorset, VT 05253.

Ammunition Box, Peters High Velocity, .410 gauge smokeless shotgun shells, image of flying duck, 1-pc box, full contents, 2.25 x 2.25 x 2.5" 140
Calendar, 1913 Winchester, Robert Robinson illus, image of hunter with rifle over shoulder, American Litho, NY, bands at top and bottom, Nov page only, dry mounted, 15.5 x 30" . . .950

Compass, celluloid, compass in center
of white celluloid disk with "Dave
Cook Sporting Goods..." in red, litho
by Parisian Novelty, Chicago, 1.5" d ..65
Counter Display Cabinet, Remington
"Hi Speed" .22, wood and glass,
16 x 10 x 6" 65
Counter Standup, American Field
Hunting Garments, diecut cardboard,
jump-out mallard with hunter in background, c1940-50, 14 x 16" 140
Game Call, crow, Green Head brand,
light green plastic stopper and horn,
brown plastic body, 3.25" 10
Game Call, deer, Dazy, mouth call, with
instructions, MIB 20
Game Call, duck, Cajun, walnut barrel
and stopper, plastic reed, ink
stamped name and address, 4.5" 12
Game Call, fox, Burnham Bros, brown
Bakelite, rubberband diaphragm,
orig box with papers 12
Pinback Button, Peter's Cartridges,
celluloid, image of duck flying
through letter "P," Bastian Bros,
Rochester, NY, .75" d 65
Poster, American Powder Mill, "Dead
Shot," duck falling from sky, litho by
George A Walker & Co, Boston,
framed and matted, 12.5 x 19.5" 500
Sign, Duxbak, "Serviceable clothes for
life in the open. Sheds water like a
Duck's Back.," tin over cardboard,
back view of duck landing on lake,
18.5 x 15" 325
Tin, Dupont, Schuetzen Smokeless,
paper label with hunter holding rifle
on green tin, 1 lb, 4 x 5.75 x 1.25" 65

*Envelopes, Dupont adv both sides, load
gauge chart on back, 3.75 x 6.5", price for
pair, $80. —Photo courtesy Collectors
Auction Services.*

*Stereograph, "Seven and One Hanging–
Team in the Wood for More," #12259,
Keystone View Co, orange border, "Game
Laws of Maine" on back, $8.*

Tin, Dupont Superfine HF Gunpowder,
brown and white label on red tin,
1 lb, 4 x 6 x 1.5" 45
Watch Fob, trap shooting, 1914 California State Championship, "5th Prize"
on back, eagles both sides, copper
plated, mkd "sterling," 1.25 x 1.75" ..140

ICE SKATING

I hope that I am not skating on thin ice
by adding this category to the book, but the
staff has found many skating-related items
and they were hard to ignore. Since ice
skating has been around for centuries and
is something I have never gotten the knack
of, I can only hope that this is better than
letting all these goodies go unnoticed.

Club: Antique Ice Skates Collectors Club,
70-104 Scott St., Meriden, CT 06450.

Advertising Trade Card, Huntley &
Palmers Buscuits, image of man
and woman on skating pond, c1900,
4.5 x 3" 3
Box, Indian Head ice skates, various
sports graphics, "A product of Indian
Head Shoe Co, Inc, Manchester, NH" .10
Exhibition Card, Dick Button, facsimile
signature "Richard Button," bottom
text "Englewood, NJ, World's Figure
Skating Champion and 1948 Olympic
Champion, Made in USA," 1948 8
Magazine, *Sports Illustrated*, "Olympic
Champion Peggy Fleming," Feb 19,
1968 15

Photograph, man and child on ice
   pond, sepia toned, 5.75 x 3.375" 8
Pie Plate, Currier & Ives, ice skating
   scene, 10" d 10
Postcard, ice skaters in Central Park,
   1900s, 3.5 x 5.5" 4
Postcard, man tying woman's skates,
   c1912...........................5
Program, Ice Cycles, featuring Walt
   Disney's Cinderella, 21 pp, 1953 10
Program, Skating Vanities, 12 pp,
   c1943, 8 x 11" 8
Program, Sonja Henie, Icetime of 1948
   with Sonja Henie and Arthur M Wirtz
   at Rockefeller Center 15
Sheet Music, *Pardon Me, Miss*, Harry
   Gershman, for ice revue "Rhythm on
   Ice," ©1950, 9 x 12" 5
Skates, Samuel Winslow, Worcester,
   MA, plain flat blade, wooden foot-
   plate, 1886 175
Skates, Union Hardware, Torpedo
   racing skate, small toe and heel
   plates, holes punched in for weight
   reduction, 1800s 210
Tobacco Card, Sonja Henie, #63, "The
   World of Sport" series 5

IMPERIAL GLASS

The history of Imperial Glass dates
back to 1901. Initially the company produced pattern and carnival glass. In 1916 an
art glass line, "Free-Hand," was introduced. However, Imperial's reputation rests
on a wide variety of household glassware
products, including Depression glass dinnerware patterns.

The company made a practice of
acquiring molds from firms that went out of
business, e.g., Central, Cambridge, and
Heisey. Imperial used a variety of marks
over time. Beware of an interlaced "I" and
"G" mark on carnival glass. This is an
Imperial reproduction.

Club: National Imperial Glass Collectors
Society, P.O. Box 534, Bellaire, OH 43906.

Note: See Candlewick for additional listings.

Beaded Block, pickle dish, 2 handles,
   amber, 6.5" 12
Beaded Block, sugar, amber 15

Lindburgh, comport, clear, 8.75" d, $15.
—Photo courtesy Ray Morykan Auctions.

Cape Cod, baked apple 8
Cape Cod, beer mug, 12 oz 45
Cape Cod, bitters bottle 60
Cape Cod, butter, cov, 160/144 35
Cape Cod, cake stand 55
Cape Cod, celery, 160/189 165
Cape Cod, cruet, 160/119 30
Cape Cod, goblet, 1602, 11 oz 10
Cape Cod, ice lip jug, 160/19, 40 oz 85
Cape Cod, punch cup, 160/37 5
Cape Cod, salad plate, 8" d 6
Cape Cod, sherbet, low, 1602 6
Field Flower, water pitcher, teal, 9" h 85
Grape, pitcher, #1950/473, orig label, 3 pt ..30
Grape, wine decanter, green, with
   stopper, 11.5" h 60
Jewels, plate, iridescent pale green,
   8" d 50
Marigold, creamer, stippled rays 25
Mount Vernon, cup and saucer 14
Mount Vernon, punch set, 15 pc 90
Nuart, ashtray 20
Old Williamsburg, candlesticks, pr, 7.5" ..20
Old Williamsburg, celery, 13" 25
Old Williamsburg, compote, 6" 20
Old Williamsburg, finger bowl, 4.5" 8
Old Williamsburg, individual creamer
   and sugar, amber 30
Old Williamsburg, juice, ftd 10
Old Williamsburg, nappy, 4" 10
Old Williamsburg, salad bowl, 9" 35
Old Williamsburg, water goblet, 6.75" ...8
Twist, claret, 4.875" 14
Twist, cordial, 3.625" 10
Twist, cup, 2" 12
Twist, juice, flat 8
Twist, plate, 8.325" 10
Twist, tumbler 8
Zodiac, bowl, ftd, 11" d 40
Zodiac, butter pats sweets server, 4.75" ..15

INK BOTTLES

In the eighteenth and early nineteenth centuries, individuals mixed their own ink. The individual ink bottle became prevalent after the untippable bottle was developed in the middle of the nineteenth century.

Ink bottles are found in a variety of shapes ranging from umbrella style to turtles. When the fountain pen arrived on the scene, ink bottles became increasingly plain.

Periodical: *Antique Bottle and Glass Collector,* P.O. Box 180, East Greenville, PA 18041.

Carter's Blue Black Ink, medium green, smooth base, tooled mouth, c1880-90, 6.125" h 175
F Kidder, aqua, pontil scarred base, flared lip, c1843-55, 2.5" h 65
Harrison's Columbian Ink, aqua, 8-sided, pontil scarred base, applied mouth, "Patent" on shoulder, c1840-60, 3.125" h 350
Harrison's Columbian Ink, aqua, 12-sided, pontil scarred base, "Patent" on shoulder, applied disc type mouth, c1850-60, 5.75" h 100
Hohenthal Brothers & Co Indelible Writing Ink, NY, deep olive amber, iron pontil, applied sloping collar with pour spout, c1845-55, 7" h 625
Hover, Philadelphia, blue green, open pontil, thin flared lip, c1840-60, 3" h . .400

Tea Kettle Shape, dark amber, 8-sided, smooth base, ground lip, brass neck ring and hinged lid, American, c1875-90, 2.25" h, $175. —Photo courtesy Gene Harris Antique Auction Center, Inc.

Master, medium yellowish amber, iron pontil, applied mouth with pour spout, 3-pc mold, c1835-55, 7.5" h . . .200
Milk Glass, opalescent powder blue, pontil scarred base, flared lip, c1810-20, 1.75" h 225
S O Dunbar, Taunton, MA, aqua, 12-sided, "Patent" on shoulder, pontil scarred base, applied mouth, c1835-55, 5.625" h 90
Stafford's Ink, medium blue green and aqua, smooth base, tooled mouth, c1890-1910, 9.75" h 40
Underwood's Ink, cobalt blue, smooth base, tooled mouth, c1890-1910, 9.75" h 30
Waters Ink, Troy, NY, umbrella, aqua, 6-sided, pontil scarred base, rolled lip, 2.625" h 675
Wood's Black Ink, Portland, cone, aqua, pontil scarred base, rolled lip, c1840-55, 2.5" h 225

INKWELLS

Inkwells enjoyed a "golden age" between 1870 and 1920. They were a sign of wealth and office. The common man dipped his ink directly from the bottle. The arrival of the fountain pen and ballpoint pen led to their demise.

Collectors seem to have the most fun collecting figural inkwells—but beware, there are some modern reproductions.

Club: The Society of Inkwell Collectors, 5136 Thomas Ave. South, Minneapolis, MN 55410.

Enameled Porcelain, white, light blue and multicolored floral alternating bands, brass neck collar and hinged lid, c1880-1910, 3.125" h 275
Figural, barrel, W E Bonney, aqua, smooth base, tooled mouth, c1855-70, 2.75" h 70
Figural, dog, clear pressed glass, hinged at collar, smooth base, orig red painted tongue, black lips and eyes, c1900-20, 3.75" h 110
Figural, fish, cast metal, orig paint, clear glass insert, hinged head and gills, c1875-95, 2.375" h 175

Master, brass, human busts on sides, winged creatures on handles and lids, leaf-form legs, 13.625" w, $150. —Photo courtesy Collectors Auction Services.

Figural, locomotive, aqua, smooth base, ground lip, c1875-80, 2" h 600

Figural, light blue majolica glaze, detailed woman and children scene on top, orig brass neck ring and hinged lid, c1875-95, 2.625" h 550

Figural, tea kettle, white porcelain, gold trim, melon shaped, c1875-95, 3" h . .350

Figural, turtle, purple amethyst, smooth base, ground lip, c1875-90, 2" h 650

Glass, yellow amber, geometric design, pontil scarred base, tooled disc mouth, c1810-30, 1.5" h 175

Pitkin, yellowish olive green, 36 rib pattern swirled to left, pontil scarred base, tooled disc mouth, c1778-1820, 1.875" h, 2.375" d 425

Soapstone, black, 4 quill holes and ink opening on top, c1780-1830, 1.5" h . . .200

Soapstone, black, square form, single filler hole on top, c1780-1820, 1.875" h 140

INSULATORS

Insulators were a trendy collectible of the 1960s and prices have been stable since the 1970s.

Insulators are sold by "CD" numbers and color. Check N. R. Woodward's *The Glass Insulator in America* (privately printed, 1973) to determine the correct CD number. Beware of "rare" colors. Unfortunately, some collectors and dealers have altered the color of pieces by using heat and chemicals to increase the rarity value. The National Insulator Association is leading the movement to identify and stop this practice. They are one of the few clubs in the field that take their policing role seriously.

Club: National Insulator Assoc., 1315 Old Mill Path, Broadview Heights, OH 44147.

Periodical: *Crown Jewels of the Wire,* P.O. Box 1003, St. Charles, IL 60174.

CD 102.4, N E Tel & Tel, blue-aqua 365
CD 103, Gayner #6 425
CD 106, Hemingray #9, jade green milk glass 12
CD 106, McLaughlin #9, olive green 9
CD 112, New Eng Tel & Tel Co 55
CD 121, B T Co/Canada, purple 35
CD 121, Brookfield, olive green, amber casts and swirls 30
CD 121, Gayner #160 12
CD 121, Maydwell 16W 35
CD 121, McLaughlin #16, emerald green .20
CD 122, McLaughlin #16, olive amber . . .25
CD 122, McLaughlin #16, teal 250
CD 126, Brookfield, #213, light green 5
CD 126, Whitall Tatum #512U, root beer . . .6
CD 130.1, Cal Elec Works Patent, aqua .475
CD 154, Dominion-42, light yellow 165
CD 154, Lynchburg #44, ginger ale 45
CD 156.1, Postal Telegraph Co, light green 40
CD 164, Maydwell-20, milk glass 20
CD 234, Pyrex #63, carnival 35
CD 275, F M Locke, Victor, NY, #2 65
CD 460, Verlica Belgium, BT48, clear 40
CD 640, Gingerbread Boy, dark green . . .45

White Ceramic, unmkd, 3.5 x 3.25", $2.

IRONS

Country and kitchen collectors have kept non-electric iron collecting alive. The form changed little for centuries. Some types were produced for decades. Age is not as important as appearance—the more unusual or decorative the iron, the more likely its value will be high. There are still bargains to be found, but cast iron and brass irons are becoming expensive. Electric irons are the iron collectible of the future.

Advisor: David Irons, 223 Covered Bridge Rd., Northampton, PA 18067, (610) 262-9335, fax (610) 262-2853, Internet: www.ironsantiques.com.

Club: Midwest Sad Iron Collectors Club, 24 Nob Hill Dr., St. Louis, MO 63138.

Newsletter: *Iron Talk,* P.O. Box 68, Waelder, TX 78959.

Note: David Irons is the author and publisher of *Irons By Irons*, *More Irons By Irons*, *Pressing Iron Patents*, and, published recently, *Even More Irons By Irons*.

Charcoal, Brittany, cut work on sides,
    handmade, early 1800 600
Charcoal, Junior Carbon Iron, 1911 300
Charcoal, The Marvel, side dampers,
    1924 140
Flat Iron, Keystone, double pointed 250
Flat Iron, slave iron, bell in handle,
    wrought 160
Flat Iron, Hoods patent 1867, soapstone
    insulator 200

Charcoal, New Plus Ultra, double spout, iron body, patented Jul 29, '02, $150.

Gasoline, Coleman, light blue enamel body, light blue wooden handle, $60.

Flat Iron, round back, Belgium 50
Fluter, machine, Manville, pyramid
    shaped 900
Fluter, rocker, Geneva 1866, 2 pc 90
Fluter, roller, American Machine Co,
    base holds heater 100
Fluter, combination smoother, wire clip
    closure 150
Goffering, double barrel, brass, tripod
    base 700
Goffering, wrought, tripod base, with
    heater 500
Liquid Fuel, Coleman, blue enamel 100
Liquid Fuel, Coleman, red enamel 500
Liquid Fuel, Improved Easy Iron, Foote
    Mfg Co 140
Liquid Fuel, Tilley, English, cream color .190
Liquid Fuel, revolving combination 500
Mangle Board, Danish, horse handle,
    carved, early 500
Sad Iron, Dover, 2 pc, cover over base . .30
Sad Iron, Enterprise, 2 pc, handle lifts
    off 25
Sad Iron, slant handle, handle at angle . .20
Slug, Austrian, brass, oxtongue, one
    post 190
Slug, Danish, brass, delicate posts 200
Slug, English, brass box iron, lift gate . .130
Small, French, cast, with rooster 150
Small, Gem 180
Small, German, box, charcoal iro 100
Small, goffering, "S" post, cast base . . .160
Small, Pearl 100
Small, Tri-bump handle, all cast 30
Smoother, Dutch, black glass, 1700s . . .200
Special Purpose, billiard table iron,
    London 150

Special Purpose, button hole, Santoy . .400
Special Purpose, polisher, Gleason,
   with heat shield 110
Special Purpose, sleeve, Sensible No. 1 . .50
Special Purpose, standing egg iron on
   tripod base 250

Tea Set, Tea Leaf, emb wheat-patterned body, Clementson Bros, c1860, $400.

IRONSTONE POTTERY

This was the common household china of the last half of the nineteenth century and first two decades of the twentieth century. This ceramic ware was supposed to wear like iron—hence the name "ironstone." Many different manufacturers used the term ironstone when marking their pieces. However, the vast majority of pieces do not bear the ironstone mark.

Pieces that are all white, including the pattern, are known as White Patterned Ironstone. A more decorative appearance was achieved by using the transfer process.

Club: White Ironstone China Assoc., Inc., P.O. Box 536, Redding Ridge, CT 06876.

Bowl, cov, white patterned, Leaf Fan,
   Alcock, 7.875" d 110
Cake Plate, transfer, Genoa, mkd
   "Genoa, W. Adams & Sons," 8.875" d . . .6
Creamer, white patterned, Ceres
   Wheat, mkd "Royal Patent Ironstone,
   Turner, Goddard & Co.," 5" h 15

Vegetable Tureen, white patterned, Fuchsia, mkd "Meakin Bros. & Co., 8.5" h, 13" l, 5" w, $185.

Creamer and Sugar, cov, Tea Leaf
   Lustre, rect, vertical ribbing on
   corners, mkd "Royal Ironstone China,
   Alfred Meakin, England," 6.375" h
   creamer, 6.5" h sugar 25
Dinner Plate, Tea Leaf Lustre, mkd
   "Royal Stone China, Wedgwood &
   Co., England," price for pair 5
Funnel, white patterned, bowl shaped
   top, small loop shaped handle, mkd
   "Sanitary Fruit Jar Funnel" in green
   on side, 4.75" d, 2.5" h 20
Gravy Boat and Underplate, Tea Leaf
   Lustre, oblong, vertical pleating on
   sides, mkd "Warranted Stone China,
   Mellor, Taylor & Co., England" 20
Plate, transfer, Buda, mkd "Buda,
   England," "W" in diamond within
   trademark, 8.75" d 8
Plate, transfer, corn design in bottom,
   fluted design sides, gallery type foot,
   8.625 x 5.75 x 3.875" 20
Plate, transfer, Seine, mkd "Seine,
   Wedgwood," 9.5" d 8
Plate, white patterned, Corn, Daven-
   port, 10.5" d 25
Platter, Tea Leaf Lustre, oval, mkd
   "Royal Ironstone China, Alfred
   Meakin, England," 11 x 7.875" d 12
Teapot, white patterned, Ivy, William
   Adams, 10" h .80
Toothbrush Box, cov, transfer, elon-
   gated oval shape, foliage design,
   mkd "Clementson Brothers, Hawley,
   Royal Patent Stone Ware," 8.5 x
   3.75 x 3.5" 20
Tray, white patterned, Moss Rose,
   handled, gold trim, Wedgwood, 9" l . . .20

ITALIAN GLASS

Italian glass, also known as Venetian glass, is glassware made in Italy from the 1920s into the early 1960s and heavily exported to the United States. Pieces range from vases with multicolored internal thick and thin filigree threads to figural clowns and fish.

The glass was made in Murano, the center of Italy's glass blowing industry. Beginning in the 1920s many firms hired art directors and engaged the services of internationally known artists and designers. The 1950s was a second golden age following the flurry of high-style pieces made from the mid-1920s through the mid-1930s.

Club: Murano Glass Society, 32040 Mt. Hermon Rd., Salisbury, MD 21804.

Newsletter: *Verti: Italian Glass News,* P.O. Box 191, Fort Lee, NJ 07024.

Bottle, attributed to Fratelli Toso, blue and white cane glass, unmkd, 18" h .100
Bottle, Simone Cenedese, clear glass, applied abstract green dec, sgd, 12 x 4.5" 125
Bowl, Barovier & Toso, designed by Ercole Barovier, rugiadoso, rounded leaf-form with serrated rim, clear with applied glass int segments, c1940, 4" h, 9" l 230
Bowl, Murano Studio, blue-red centered gold on white millefiori fused, against and within colorless disk form, 5.5" d 60

Figurine, dancer, red translucent glass with clear ornamentation and embedded gold flecks, "Paulus Products, Made in Italy," paper label, $300. —Photo courtesy Jackson's Auctioneers & Appraisers.

Vase, fazoletto, marbled vetro latimo and amethyst, blue iridescent int, 13" h, 15" w, $225.

Chandelier, Murano, clear glass, 4 electrified arms, opaque pink and blue flowers, unmkd, approx 18 x 15" 165
Compote, attributed to Salviati, ftd, lemon-yellow, green rim, 6.75" h, 8.75" d 275
Conch Shell, Barovier & Toso, iridescent, c1940, 3.75" h, 9" w 200
Decanter, Venini, designed by Tapio Wirkkala, beaker shaped, purple filigrana glass, clear glass cylindrical stopper, etched "Venini/Italia/TW," 9 x 5" 275
Ewer, attributed to Fratelli Toso, blue and white latticino glass with copper ribbons and gold leaf, unmkd, 1.52 x 6.5" .150
Figurine, Cenedese, pear, green and clear sommerso glass, sgd, 8.5 x 4.5" 100
Vase, Antonio Da Ros, sommerso glass, block shaped, off-center opening, cobalt, red, and yellow, 10.25 x 6.25" 1,100
Vase, Fratelli Toso, corseted, blue and beige acanne glass, unmkd, 11 x 4.5" .150
Vase, Raymor, cylindrical, abstract fish on striped white and yellow ground, ink mark "R729/Raymor/Italy," 11 x 3.75" 225
Vase, unknown maker, flared cylindrical form, clear, gold dust highlights, symmetrical trapped air bubbles and maroon pulled plaid design, 20th C, 4.75" h 175
Vase, Venini, designed by Fulvio Bianconi, fazzoletto, handkerchief form, green upright pulled and ruffled sides, paper label and acid-stamped mark "Venini Murano Italia," c1950s, 3" h 125

IVORY

Ivory is a yellowish-white organic material that comes from the teeth and tusks of animals. In many cases, it is protected under the Endangered Species Act of 1973, amended in 1978, which limited the importation and sale of antique ivory and tortoiseshell items. Make certain that any ivory you buy is being sold within the provisions of this law.

Vegetable ivory, bone, stag horn, and plastic are ivory substitutes. Do not be fooled. Most plastic substitutes do not approach the density of ivory nor do they have crosshatched patterns. Once you learn the grain patterns of ivory, tusk, teeth, and bone, a good magnifying glass will quickly tell you if you have the real thing.

Club: International Ivory Society, 11109 Nicholas Dr., Silver Spring, MD 20902.

Brooch, frontal bust of woman, carved
    ropetwist border, C-catch, tube
    hinge, brass safety chain and pin,
    1.125 x 1.375" .350
Brush Holder, carved, reticulated roses,
    Chinese, c1920, 3" h 175
Button, cutout girl and bird on blue
    ground 150
Button, painted cupid 75
Figure, 3 warriors, hardwood stand,
    Chinese, 7.5" h 350
Figure, beauty holding bouquet of flow-
    ers, hardwood stand, Chinese,
    12.25" h 375

Fan, ivory sticks, hp floral motif, c1770, 18.75" open width, $250.

Figure, Emperor and Empress on
    pedestals, sgd, c1900, 7.5" h 200
Figure, Japanese farmer resting on
    staff with gourd on back, c1920, 4" h .400
Incense Burner, cov, tripod base, low
    relief with dragons, stylized floral
    motifs, elephant and loose ring han-
    dles, pierced lid with turtle finial,
    antique finish embellished with
    beads, hardwood stand with silver
    wire inlay, Chinese, 8.5" h, 6.5" w 400
Puzzle Ball, 10 concentric circles with
    carved designs, Chinese, c1910,
    7.5" d 225
Vase, flowering branch with perched
    storks, phoenix, calligraphy and
    loose link chain, bas-relief, sgd,
    hardwood stand, Chinese 525
Vase, landscape with figures and build-
    ings, covered, low relief, with finial
    of figures in forest landscape, loose
    ring handles, hardwood stand,
    Chinese, 10" h 375
Wine Ewer, dragon spout, foliate han-
    dle, low relief carving, fitted loose
    link chains, hardwood stand,
    Chinese, 11.25" h 525

JEWELRY

In the current market, "antique" jewelry refers to pieces that are one hundred years old or older, although much of the jewelry from the 1920s and 1930s is passed as "antique." "Heirloom/estate" jewelry normally refers to pieces between twenty-five and one hundred years old. "Costume" refers to quality and type, not age. Costume jewelry exists for every historical period.

The first step to determining value is to identify the classification of jewelry. Have stones and settings checked by a jeweler or gemologist. If a piece is unmarked, do not create hope where none deserves to be.

Clubs: Assoc. for Collectors of Mourning Jewelry, P.O. Box 641, Burlington, WI 53104; American Society of Jewelry Historians, 1333A North Ave., Box 103, New Rochelle, NY 10804.

Periodical: *Ornament*, P.O. Box 2349, San Marcos, CA 92079.

Bracelet, 14k gold, 8 fine rope chains
completed by Florentine finish box
clasp surmounted by rose diamond
and pearl florets, 14.6 dwt, 6.5" l 350

Bracelet, SS, 7 oval stylized floral
plaques spaced by sterling links 125

Cufflinks, pr, 14k gold, Art Nouveau,
oval rose gold bar cuffs in repoussé
swirl design 350

Earrings, pr, SS, geometric tops suspending circular drops, stamped
sterling, Denmark, sgd "N.E. From" ..60

Hair Pin Chain, SS, trace-links spaced
by 8 sections of hair pin embellishment in shape of hearts, marquises,
and flowers, 33" l 150

Necklace, graduated faceted smoky
quartz beads suspending large oval
faceted pendant, 14k yellow gold
ball-form clasp, 24" l 200

Pin, 14k yellow gold, flower in bloom,
centered by cabochon emerald surrounded by cabochon rubies, foliate
frame dec with blue and green
translucent enamel and assorted
faceted emeralds, 12 dwt, 1.5" l 350

Pin, 18k white gold, man in the moon,
crescent shaped, sgd "Judity Ripka,"
4.9 dwt 275

Pin, 18k yellow gold, ribbon, embellished with multicolored enamel
Egyptian design, 5 dwt 125

Pin, 14k yellow and pink gold, stylized
bow, set to center with round purple sapphire and 2 small round
diamonds, hallmarked for Winthrop,
3.8 dwt 175

Ring, 5 split pearls edged with blue
enamel, pierced gallery, 14k yellow
gold mount 150

*Bar Pin, Victorian, enamel plaque on 14K
gold bar, bead and wire twist accents,
$864.* —Photo courtesy Skinner, Inc.,
Boston, MA.

Ring, 18k gold, double coil snake
design with rose-cut diamond eyes,
English, c1900, size 8 275

Ring, jadeite jade, collet-set marquise
shape within 14k yellow gold chased
mount, applied bead and wiretwist
dec, Chinese hallmarks, size 3.5 200

Suite, brooch and earclips, 14k yellow
gold, stylized fern set, 5 cultured
pearls and emeralds 350

Suite, brooch and earrings, with bezel-
set faceted citrine within 18k yellow
gold wiretwist frame, lever back
findings 250

JEWELRY, COSTUME

Diamonds might be a girl's best friend,
but costume jewelry is what most women
own. Costume jewelry is design and form
that has gone mad. There is a piece for
everyone's taste—good, bad, or indifferent.

Collect it by period or design—high-
brow or lowbrow. Remember that it is
mass-produced. If you do not like the price
the first time you see a piece, shop around.
Most sellers put a high price on the pieces
that appeal to them and a lower price on
those that do not. Since people's tastes differ, so do the prices on identical pieces.

Club: Vintage Fashion/Costume Jewelry
Club, P.O. Box 265, Glen Oaks, NY 11004.

Newsletter: *Glittering Times,* P.O. Box
656675, Flushing, NY 11365.

*Bangle, hinged, chased with foliate motif,
black enamel accents, Tiffany & Co, $575.*
—Photo courtesy Skinner, Inc., Boston, MA.

Bangle Bracelet, Bakelite, rounded
square red inlaid dots on black
ground, c1935 375

Bracelet, gold plated brass and enamel, 6 stamped brass filigree oval floral motif links, collet-set red rhinestones and blue enamel on small flowerheads, v-spring and box clasp, c1925-30, 7" l, .75" w 100

Brooch, figural plastic bulldog with wood carved details, black and white painted eyes, brass chain around neck with green plastic dog tag, 3" h, 2.25" w 125

Brooch, Hobé, goldtone filigree heart, inset green, clear, and pink rhinestones, 3 heart pendants with central rhinestone attached to bottom, 1938, 2.5 x 1.75" 175

Brooch, lucite, figural parrot, reverse painted orange beak, carved wood wing, 3.75" h, 1.25" w 100

Dress Clip, apple juice Bakelite, reverse carved, 2 swimming goldfish accented with seaweed, reverse painted detail .90

Earrings, pr, Christian Dior, simulated pearls, yellow crystals, and square cut faux brown gemstones, stamped "Chr. Dior 1961/Foreign," 1961 150

Earrings, pr, wood, figural cowboy boots, painted red and yellow, screwbacks, c1940, 1" l, .625" w 30

Necklace, Christian Dior, white and clear glass, pink crystal beads with large cluster pendant, stamped "Chr. Dior 1960" on pendant and clasp, 14.5" l .150

Pin, Trifari, silver airplane with pavé rhinestone body, red and blue enamel wings, tail, and nose, stamped, 1940s, 1.5" l 160

Charm Bracelet, silver, c1968, $40.

Ring, Miriam Haskell, gilded metal, round filigree top with attached multicolored stones hanging from short chains, stamped, 1.5" w 60

Suite, Hobé, bracelet and earrings, gold-plated, hinged, cluster of purple, lavender, ice blue, and yellow rhinestones, light blue stone, simulated pearls, stamped 150

Suite, Renoir, necklace, bracelet, and earrings, copper half-moons with blackened int, single strand short necklace, double strand bracelet, single half-moon clip earrings, stamped, 1950s 75

Suite, Trifari, brooch and earrings, leaf shaped, green, faux gemstones and goldtone stem and detail, clip earrings, 1960s .150

JOHNSON BROTHERS

The Johnson Brothers, Alfred, Frederick, and Henry, acquired the J. W. Pankhurst pottery located in the Staffordshire district of England in 1882 and began manufacturing dinnerware the following year. Another brother, Robert, joined the company in 1896 and took charge of American distribution.

Over the years the company produced hundreds of variations of patterns, shapes, and colors. One of the most popular and readily found patterns is blue and white Coaching Scenes, first introduced in 1963. Although it was also made in green and white, pink and white, and brown multicolored, only blue and white was shipped to the United States. Other popular patterns include Old Britain Castles and Friendly Village.

Coaching Scenes, bread and butter plate, pink, 6" d 8
Coaching Scenes, creamer and sugar, 4.75" h creamer, 5" h sugar 35
Coaching Scenes, dinner plate, 10" d . . .15
Coaching Scenes, platter, 12" l 25
Coaching Scenes, platter, 14" l 35
Coaching Scenes, soup bowl, 8.5" d 15
Devonshire, salad plate, 8" d 8
Dorchester, dinner plate 25
English Chippendale, dinner plate 18

English Chippendale, gravy boat 50
English Chippendale, salad plate,
    square, 7.5" d .10
English Chippendale, vegetable bowl,
    round 40
Friendly Village, cup and saucer, 2.5" h,
    5.75" d 10
Friendly Village, dinner plate, 10.5" d 15
Friendly Village, milk pitcher, 5.5" h 30
Friendly Village, salt and pepper
    shakers, pr 30
Harvest Time, creamer and sugar, 4" h . .25
Heritage Hall, platter, 12" l 15
Heritage Hall, vegetable bowl, 10" d 45
Indian Tree, dinner plate, 10" d 15
Old Britain Castles, bread and butter
    plate, blue, 6" d 8
Old Britain Castles, creamer and sugar,
    pink 12
Old Britain Castles, dinner plate, blue,
    10" d 15
Old Britain Castles, dinner plate, pink,
    10" d 15
Old Britain Castles, gravy boat, blue 45
Old Britain Castles, salad plate, red,
    8" d 8
Petite Fleur, bread and butter plate, 6" d . . .3
Petite Fleur, cup and saucer 10
Petite Fleur, salad plate, 7" d 8
Provincial, bowl, 6.5" d 6
Rose Chintz, cup and saucer 15
Rose Chintz, dinner plate, 10" d 25
Strawberry Fair, creamer and sugar 40
Strawberry Fair, dinner plate 5
Tulip Time, bowl, square, 6.25" d 6
Tulip Time, bread and butter plate, 6" d . . .3
Tulip Time, cup and saucer, 2.75" h cup,
    5.75" d saucer 12

Barnyard King, turkey platter, 20.5" l, $95.
—Photo courtesy Ray Morykan Auctions.

JOSEF FIGURINES

Josef Originals were designed and produced by Muriel Joseph George. She began sculpting ceramics in California during World War II. In 1959, in order to compete with cheap Japanese imitations, she formed a partnership with George Good's "George Imports" and began their own production in Japan. Muriel Joseph continued designing until 1984–85. George Good sold the company to Applause Co in 1985. While some lines continued to be made, no new designs have been produced under the Josef Originals name. Muriel passed away in 1995.

California Josef figurines are marked with a black oval paper label that reads "Josef Original California." In addition, the pieces may have an incised Josef Original marking on the bottom or sometimes merely an incised "X." The Japan pieces usually have two paper labels, an oval black label that reads "Josef Original," and a separate small oval sticker that reads "Japan." Some pieces were also ink stamped, and large pieces almost always have an incised Josef Original signature on the bottom.

Newsletter: *Josef Originals,* P.O. Box 475, Lynnwood, WA 98046.

Figurine, April, 4.25" h 50
Figurine, Bess, Musicale series, 6" h 65
Figurine, Birthstone Dolls series 20
Figurine, Bridal Shower, Special occa-
    sion series, 4.5" h 25
Figurine, bull, 2.75" h 20
Figurine, Buying a New Hat, A Mother's
    World series, 7.5" h 100
Figurine, camel, 2.5" h 25
Figurine, Church Belle 25
Figurine, Doll of the Month series 25
Figurine, German shepherd 20
Figurine, girl, Gigi series 100
Figurine, girl, Love Makes the World
    Go Round series, 9" h 100
Figurine, girl, Rose Garden series, 5" h . .60
Figurine, kangaroo, 6" h 35
Figurine, Lipstick, First Time series,
    4.5" h 45
Figurine, Louise, Colonial Days series,
    9.5" h 110

Figurine, mama elephant, $30.

Figurine, man with flower basket on
  shoulder .... .80
Figurine, Morning, Noon, and Night
  series, 5.75" h .... .35
Figurine, Party Dress, Sweet Sixteen
  series, 7.5" h 100
Figurine, penguin, 4.75" h .... .20
Figurine, Pennies from Heaven .... .25
Figurine, Penny, 4" h .... .50
Figurine, Pitty Sing, brown hat, 4" h .... .45
Figurine, School Belle .... .25
Figurine, Susan, First Formal series,
  5.25" h .... .45
Figurine, Victoria, 6" h .... .50
Figurine, Wu Cha, 10" h .... .80
Figurine, Yong Chee .... .55
Lipstick Holder, girl in purple dress .... .20
Music Box, Lara's Theme .... .80
Soap Dish, girl in green dress .... .20

JUGTOWN

Jugtown is the pottery that refused to
die. Founded in 1920 in Moore County,
North Carolina, by Jacques and Julianna
Busbee, the pottery continued under
Julianna and Ben Owens when Jacques
died in 1947. It closed in 1958 only to reopen
in 1960. It is now run by Country Roads,
Inc., a nonprofit organization.

The principal difficulty in identifying
Jugtown pottery is that the same glazes are
used on modern pieces as were used
decades ago. Even the mark is the same.
Since it takes an expert to distinguish
between the new and old, this is certainly
one category which novices should avoid
until they have done a fair amount of study.

Carolina pottery is developing a dedi-
cated core group of collectors. For more
information read Charles G. Zug III's
*Turners and Burners: The Folk Potters of
North Carolina* (University of North Carolina
Press: 1986).

Bowl, Chinese blue glaze, Jugtown
  Ware stamp, 4" h, 7.25" d .... .550
Bowl, flat rim, Chinese blue glaze, circular stamp mark, 4.5 x 7.25" ...... .825
Candlesticks, pr, corseted, gray speckled semi-gloss glaze, circular mark,
  11.5 x 4.75" .... .750
Candlesticks, pr, cup shaped bobeche
  and flaring base, blue semi-matte
  glaze, circular stamp mark, 11.5" h .. .100
Figurine, hen, salt-glaze stoneware,
  mottled brown and ochre glaze,
  1991, 7.5 x 8" .... .50
Jug, speckled beige semi-matte glaze,
  stamped "Jugtown Ware/1977," 5.75
  x 5" .... .70
Urn, 2 handles, olive green and ochre
  glaze over bisque brown body, circular mark, 9.5 x 7.5" .... .800
Vase, bulbous, 3 handles, orange,
  green, and yellow mottled glaze,
  stamp mark, 6 x 6" .... .675
Vase, ovoid, Chinese blue glaze, circular stamp mark, 4.5 x 3.25" ...... .375
Vase, ovoid, closed-in rim, dripping
  white semi-matte glaze over brown
  clay body, circular stamp mark, 6.5
  x 4.25" .... .500
Vessel, turquoise and red Chinese blue
  glaze, imp mark, 5.5 x 6.5" .... .850

Pitcher, tan, incised dec, 6.25" h, 7" w, $125.

KEWPIES

Kewpies are the creation of Rose Cecil O'Neill (1876–1944), artist, novelist, illustrator, poet, and sculptor. The Kewpie first appeared in the December 1909 issue of *Ladies' Home Journal*. The first Kewpie doll followed in 1913.

Many early Kewpie items were made in Germany. An attached label enhances value. Kewpie items also were made in the United States and Japan. The generations that grew up with Kewpie dolls are dying off. O'Neill's memory and products are being kept alive by a small but dedicated group of collectors.

Club: International Rose O'Neill Club, P.O. Box 668, Branson, MO 65616.

Doll, porcelain, Rose O'Neill copyright label on back, 4.25" h, $150.

Advertising Tear Sheet, Jell-O, "Cook or no cook, anybody can do that," Kewpies making dessert, Feb 1917, 5 x 6" 6
Book, *The Kewpies and the Runaway Babies*, Rose O'Neill, first edition, 111 pp, 1928, 8.25 x 6" 45
Doll, bisque, thinker, Germany, 4" h 225
Doll, bisque, thinker, Germany, 7" h 400
Doll, celluloid, Karl Standfuss, Germany, 2.5" h 25
Doll, celluloid, Karl Standfuss, Germany, 12" h 250
Doll, composition, 8" h 175
Doll, molded hard plastic, jointed arms, painted features, emb "Kewpie c. by Rose O'Neill," 1950s, 8" h 100
Doll, vinyl, Cameo Doll Co, 1960-70s, 16" h 125
Doll, vinyl, Effanbee, 8" h 25
Magazine, *Ladies' Home Journal*, Sep 1925, full page Cream of Wheat adv ..12
Magazine, *Woman's Home Companion*, Oct 1911, "The Kewpies & their new adventure verse & paintings by Rose O'Neill," 11 x 16" 25
Paper Dolls, Kewpieville Standups, ©1963, 1967, 1968 by Jos L Kallus, complete with 3 pp of dolls and 6 pp of clothing, uncut 15
Postcard, 3 Kewpies looking into basket of chicks, sgd, dated 1922 15
Postcard, "Merry Christmas," 1 Kewpie with painting pallet, 2 Kewpies around package with red ribbon, used 18
Tray, litho tin, Furnas Ice Cream adv, mkd "©Rose O'Neill, Parker-Brawner Co, Washington, DC, No. 2539," 13.375 x 13.375" 100

KEY CHAINS

Talk about an inexpensive collecting category. Most examples sell under $10. If you are really cheap, you can pick up plenty of modern examples for free. Why not? They are going to be collectible in thirty years and antiques in a hundred. Who knows, maybe you will live that long!

One of the favorite charity fundraising gimmicks in the 1940s and 1950s was the license plate key chain tag. There is a collectors' club devoted to this single topic.

Club: License Plate Key Chain & Mini License Plate Collectors, 888 Eighth Ave., New York, NY 10019.

AC Spark Plug, metal 8
Avia, plastic, clear, square 8
American Motorcycle Association, 1940 Gypsy Tour, brass, raised image of cycle rider, mail drop guarantee on back, 1.5 x 1.5" 45
Bayonne Motors, with tube to hold license, c1940 15
Chevrolet, brass, 50th anniversary 15
Dodge, enameled logo, leather 12

Texaco, mkd
"A.E. Co., Utica,
NY," 1" d, $45.
—Photo courtesy
Collectors Auction
Services.

Cabinet, silver-plated, 2.75" l, $15.

Esso Gasoline, gold finished metal,
  raised tiger head symbol, Esso logo
  under "Put A Tiger In Your Tank,"
  serial number on back for Happy
  Motoring Club, 1960s, 1.375" d 8
Good Luck, aluminum, 1946 penny
  insert, inscribed "Keep Me and
  Never Go Broke," "Parts Boys, Auto
  Specialty Co," 1.5" h 10
John F Kennedy, metal, brass finish,
  diecut initials, brass chain 15
Packard, metal key holder, attached
  metal ring, shades of gold and silver,
  blue, white, and black enameled
  convertible titled "Packard Panther,"
  brass Packard logo, late 1950s 20
Shell Oil, metal, seashells with "Shell"
  on back 12
Swift Premium Ham, enamel 12
World's Fair, New York, 1964, domed
  acrylic over silver and black unisphere, title, dates, flat silvered
  metal back 15

KEYS

There are millions of keys. Focus on a
special type of key, e.g., automobile, railroad switch, etc. Few keys are rare. Prices
above $10 are unusual.

Collect keys with a strong decorative
motif. Examples include keys with advertising logos to cast keys with animal or interlocking scroll decorations. Be suspicious if
someone offers you a key to King Tut's
Tomb, Newgate Prison, or the Tower of
London.

Cabinet, brass, 2.875" 12
Cabinet, bronze, 3.25" 25

Cabinet, iron, 1890s-1920s, 1.75" 4
Car, Cadillac, silver plated 35
Car, Esso, gold plated 10
Car, Oldsmobile, gold plated, colored
  enamel 14
Car, Pontiac, gold plated, Indian head . . .35
Chest, iron, 2.875" 18
Clock, brass, jewelers, 3" 32
Clock, steel, iron, Waterbury Clock Co,
  2.25" 16
Door, bronze, 4.25" 12
Door, iron, Lockwood Mfg, 2.75" 3
Door, steel, Norwalk, 3.25" 4
Door, steel, Reading Hardware, 4" 4
Gate, iron, 6" 7
Handcuff, iron, Taylor, 1.75" 2
Pocket Door, bronze, Sargent, 1.625" 14
Railroad, Erie & Lackawanna Railroad,
  mkd "LIRR," brass 10
Ship, bronze, bit type, foreign ship tags . . .6

KITCHEN COLLECTIBLES

Kitchen collectibles are closely linked
to Country, where the concentration is on
the 1860–1900 period. This approach is far
too narrow. There are a lot of great kitchen
utensils and gadgets from the 1900 to 1940
period. Do not overlook them.

Kitchen collectibles were used. While
collectors appreciate the used look, they
also want an item in very good or better
condition. It is a difficult balancing act in
many cases. The field is broad, so it pays to
specialize. Tomato slicers are not for me; I
am more of a chopping knife person.

Clubs: International Society of Apple Parer
Enthusiasts, 735 Cedarwood Terrace,
Rochester, NY 14609; Jelly Jammers, 110
White Oak Dr., Butler, PA 16001; Kollectors
of Old Kitchen Stuff, 354 Rte. 206 North,
Chester, NJ 07930.

Newsletter: *Kettles 'n Cookware,* P.O. Box 247, Perrysburg, NY 14129.

Apron, brown linen, printed design 4
Apron, purple, green, and yellow floral chintz, V-neck, bib style, scalloped edge with rick-rack trim around skirt 25
Book, *Kitchen Ideas*, Bantam Books, softcover, 110 pp, Mar 1979 2
Cheeseboard, wood, owl shaped, ceramic eyes and knife, Japan 6
Clock, stamped metal, figural teapot, electric, Sessions, 7" h, 8.5" w 35
Coffee Canister, metal, avocado, plastic wood type lid 2
Colander, ftd, yellow ware, 10" d 175
Corn Stick Pan, cast aluminum, cob shaped cups, Wearever, 13" l, 5.5" w ..15
Crimper, aluminum, Just-Rite 10
Dipper, red and white enamelware, solid red handle 175
Double Boiler, blue and white enamelware, iris swirl 300
Egg Scale, polished metal, mounted on wooden board, clip to hold egg, 20th C 60
Egg Timer, cast white metal, painted dec, John Wright, c1960s, 2" h, 3" w ..20
Flour Sifter, tin, "The Foster," tubular handle, squeeze action mechanism, 2 cups, 7" h 20
Food Mold, copper anodized aluminum, zodiac motif, 12" d 15
Funnel, blue and white enamelware, white int, strap handle 50
Knife Sharpener, iron, wood handle, Eversharp, Tungsten Tool Co, early 20th C 20

Lard Pail, Shamokin Packing Co, tin, bail handle, 2 lbs, $120.

Pot Holders, crocheted, red rose and border, green leaves, 7" sq, price each, $5. —Photo courtesy Ray Morykan Auctions.

Napkin Holder, acrylic resin, orange and yellow mushrooms 2
Nut Chopper, glass body, harvest gold plastic top, Federal Housewares 2
Oven Thermometer, painted wood, "Occident Flour," Russell-Miller Milling Co, Minneapolis, MN, early 20th C 30
Pastry Tube, tin cylinder, wooden plunger, star shaped opening, 10.5" l ..30
Pot Holder, embroidered cotton cutout, house motif, c1920-30s 10
Rolling Pin, maple, 27.5" l 35
Serving Basket, owl shaped, woven wicker, 12" l 2
Timer, Lux Minute Minder, styrene plastic, avocado 2
Trivet, cast iron, inlaid with acrylic resin, "Bless This Mess" 3
Whisk, gold daisies on avocado plastic handle, Travco, Made in Taiwan 2

KNOWLES DINNERWARE

In 1900 Edwin M. Knowles established the Edwin M. Knowles China Company in Chester, West Virginia. The company made semi-porcelain dinnerware, kitchenware, specialties, and toilet wares.

In 1913 a second plant in Newell, West Virginia, was opened. The company operated its Chester, West Virginia, pottery until 1931, at which time the plant was sold to the Harker Pottery Company. Production continued at the Newell pottery. Edwin M. Knowles China Company ceased operations in 1963.

In the 1970s the Edwin M. Knowles Company entered into a relationship with the Bradford Exchange to produce limited edition collector plates, with titles such as *Gone With the Wind* and *The Wizard of Oz* in addition to Norman Rockwell subjects.

Alice Ann, bowl, oval, 8" d 12
Alice Ann, creamer 5
Alice Ann, gravy boat 20
Alice Ann, plate, 8" d 8
Alice Ann, saucer 5
Arcadia, casserole 25
Arcadia, platter 10
Beverly, casserole 25
Beverly, cup 5
Beverly, eggcup, double 12
Beverly, plate, 8.5" d 6
Deanna, bread and butter plate, yellow,
   6" d 8
Deanna, butter dish, open, dark blue ...15
Deanna, coffee server, green 40
Deanna, creamer, red 10
Deanna, cup and saucer, yellow 12
Diana, bread and butter plate, 6" d 3
Diana, creamer 8
Diana, gravy boat 25
Diana, soup bowl 15
Esquire, fruit bowl, Sunflower, 5.5" d 12
Esquire, platter, Queen's Lace, 13" l 25
Fruits, berry bowl, 5.5" d 10
Fruits, bread and butter plate 6
Fruits, cup and saucer 10
Fruits, dinner plate 10
Fruits, platter, 11.75" l 25
Fruits, range shaker, 4" h 6
Fruits, serving bowl, 8.75" d 30

Tia Juana, bowl, 9.25" d, $15. —Photo courtesy Ray Morykan Auctions.

Fruits, vegetable bowl 15
Golden Wheat, platter, 12" l 6
Moss Rose, plate, 9.25" d 5
Tia Juana, berry bowl, 5" d 10
Tia Juana, plate, 9.25" d 20
Tulip, Utility Ware, bowl, oval, 9.5" d 8
Tulip, Utility Ware, coffeepot, 7.5" h 15
Tulip, Utility Ware, creamer and sugar ...8
Tulip, Utility Ware, gravy boat with
   underplate 10
Tulip, Utility Ware, soup bowl 4

KREISS CERAMICS

In 1946 Murray Kreiss founded Murray Kreiss and Company as an importer and distributor of Japanese-made ceramic figurines to the five-and-dime store and souvenir trade. Products covered a wide range from Santas and animals to Disney-like characters. As the 1960s ended, the company's focus shifted to fine furniture. Look for ashtrays, mugs, napkin ladies, and planters as well as figurines.

Ashtray, Christmas, rect, 3 children
   singing NOEL, rhinestone accents,
   6.125 x 2.625 20
Ashtray, Christmas, rect, dachshund
   with white beard and wearing Santa
   hat, "Have A Dog Gone Merry
   Christmas," 6 x 2.5" 15
Ashtray, Psycho, "I was born this way,
   what's your excuse??" on chain tag,
   blue, 4.75" h 20
Ashtray, Psycho, "This is worse than a
   dog's life," pink, rhinestone eyes 35
Bank, brown horse, felt saddle, 3.5" h,
   4.5" l 15
Bank, Christmas, pig wearing Santa hat
   with spaghetti trim, holding package,
   "A little money put away for Christmas
   Day," 7.5" h 25
Candleholder, Christmas, 2 small Santas
   balanced on larger Santa's shoulders,
   3 candles, 5.875" h, 5.25" l 35
Figurine, Boston terrier, 6" h, 7.5" l 30
Figurine, boxer dog, 5.75" h, 6.5" l 20
Figurine, Christmas, girl caroler wear-
   ing white fur coat and holding pack-
   age trimmed with red rhinestones,
   blue rhinestone eyes, 4.5" h 10
Figurine, circus tiger, with rhinestones ..10

Figurine, Psycho, purple, 5.25" h, $25.

Figurine, Elegant Heir, caveman holding club, blue rhinestone eyes, "You don't know the real me!," 6.375" h 15

Figurine, girl dog wearing pink tam and pink scarf with black polka dots, 3.125" h 8

Figurine, Green-eyed Monster, green dinosaur and 2 caveboys, 6.625" h 35

Figurine, Green-eyed Monster, yellow dinosaur and 2 caveboys, 6.875" h 35

Figurine, hillbilly, black fur hair and beard, holding jug, 6" h 20

Figurine, Moon Being, Dr Seuss look-alike, blue, with hair, orig "Moon Being" tag and sticker, 4.5" h, 3" l 60

Figurine, Psycho, blue, sad eyes, 10" h .110

Figurine, Psycho, screaming woman, wearing green dress, 5.5" h 25

Figurine, Psycho, "You think you're lucky? I run into accidents that started out to happen to someone else!," with hair, 4.625" h 25

Figurine, Psycho Christmas, Santa and Rudolph, "How did I ever get tied up with you??," 4.375" h 60

Figurine, skunks, yellow hat, fur tail, 3.5" h, price for pair 15

Mug, Psycho, "My mind's made up, don't confuse me with facts," purple 30

Napkin Lady, green candleholder hat, holding hors d'oeuvres tray, 10" h 40

Salt and Pepper Shakers, pr, cats, green rhinestone eyes, 5" h and 6" h 10

Salt and Pepper Shakers, pr, Christmas, Santa and Mrs Claus, blue rhinestone eyes, 3.375" h .20

Salt and Pepper Shakers, pr, cows, gold trim, 2.75" h kneeling cow, 3" h standing cow 8

LABELS

Labels advertising anything from cigars and citrus fruits to soaps and tobacco make great decorative accents. Properly framed and displayed, they become attractive works of art.

The first fruit crate art was created by California fruit growers about 1880. The labels became very colorful and covered many subjects. Most depict the type of fruit held in the box. The advent of cardboard boxes in the 1940s marked the end of fruit crate art and the beginning of a new collecting category. When collecting paper labels, condition is extremely important. Damaged, trimmed, or torn labels are significantly less valuable than labels in mint condition.

Clubs: American Antique Graphics Society, 5185 Windfall Rd., Medina, OH 44256; Cigar Label Collectors International, P.O. Box 66, Sharon Center, OH 44274; The Citrus Label Society, 131 Miramonte Dr., Fullerton, CA 92635; Florida Citrus Label Collectors Assoc., P.O. Box 547636, Orlando, FL 32854; The Fruit Crate Label Society, Rte. 2, Box 695, Chelan, WA 98816; International Seal, Label & Cigar Band Society, 8915 E. Bellevue St, Tucson, AZ 85715.

Newsletters: *The Cigar Label Gazette,* P.O. Box 3, Lake Forest, CA 92630; *Please Stop Snickering,* 4113 Paint Rock Dr., Austin, TX 78731.

Baking Powder, Betty Ann, Hastings, NB, redhead girl in pink dress skipping rope, white ground, gilt border, 6 oz 3.00

Beer, Bavarian, CA, Bavarian alps scene 15

Beer, Schoenling Draft Beer, OH, glass of cold beer 25

Bottle, Green Mountain Syrup, cabin, ox team, man making syrup, black family boiling cane syrup in iron kettle, 3.75 x 3.5" sq 1.00

Bottle, Joe De Marco, fat juicy strawberries, light blue leaves, 6" sq 50

Bottle, Raspberry Cordial, fancy oval with berries, 3.5 x 2.75" 50

Butter Box, Blue River Butter, cows
　on sides, blue, green, and yellow .. 2.50
Cigar, Abe Martin, cartoon character,
　scenes of Martin's farm 2.00
Cigar, Calsetta, redhead in green
　bodice, gilt coins 3.00
Cosmetic, Citrate of Magnesia, Victorian
　designs, 4.25 x 3" .... .75
Cosmetic, Cold Cream, white flowers,
　light purple accents, 6.25 x 1.875" .. .25
Cosmetic, Crown Hair Tonic, oval
　shape, florals, filt, art nouveau,
　3.25 x 2.25" .... .75
Cosmetic, Shave-Ease Cream, art
　deco, gold and black foil with red,
　1.5 x 2" .... .35
Fruit, Blue Goose, Los Angeles, orange
　ground 2.00
Fruit, Esperanza, Placentia, señorita
　wearing lace mantilla holding fancy
　lace fan, carnation in hair, blue
　ground 2.00
Fruit, Full O'Juice, Redlands, partially
　peeled orange, glass of orange
　juice, lavender ground 2.00
Fruit, Golden Circle, Redlands, wreath
　of oranges 2.00
Fruit, John & Martha, Reedley, oranges,
　white ground 1.00
Liquor, Golden Days, flying calendar
　pages .... .50
Liquor, Rocking Chair, old Mr Boston
　and rocking chair, 3.25 x 5" 1.50
Liquor, Royal Knight, knight and steed,
　castle, gilt .... .50
Sardine Can, Mermaid, long haired
　topless mermaid seated beside sea
　shell .... .25

Cigar, Wizard, 10 x 6.5", $30.

*Wine, "Tote, The Sportsman's Tonic," blue
and red, 3.25 x 4.25", $4.*

Soda, Ma Snaiders Strawberry Syrup,
　NY, cute little boy, 4.125 x 2.5" ..... .50
Soda, Waukesha Old Time Beverages,
　WI, sweet old granny, blue, red, gilt .50
Tin Can, Foodland, OH, cow, 3.5 x 10" . 2.00
Tin Can, Isaacs, forest, stream, moun-
　tains scene, asparagus on plate ... 1.00
Tin Can, June Peas, Baltimore, MD,
　bowl of peas, red roses and leaves 2.00
Vegetable, Abatti, vista ranches,
　homes, snowy mountains in blue
　shaded arch, 7 x 9" 1.00
Vegetable, Mo-Chief, Fresno, CA, bun-
　dle of asparagus, scenic ground .. 1.00

LACE

　While there are collectors of lace, most
old lace is still bought for use. Those buying lace for reuse are not willing to pay high
prices. A general rule is the larger the
amount or piece in a single pattern, the
higher the price is likely to be. In this
instance, the price is directly related to
supply and demand.

　Items decorated with lace that can be
used in their existing forms, e.g., costumes
and tablecloths, have value that transcends
the lace itself. Value for these pieces rests
on the item as a whole, not the lace. Learn
to differentiate between handmade and
machine-made lace.

Club: International Old Lacers, Inc, P.O. Box
554, Flanders, NJ 07836.

LADY HEAD VASES

Heart shaped lips and dark eyelashes mark the charm of the typical lady head vase. Manufactured in the early 1950s, head vases were produced in Japan and the United States. The decoration is thoughtfully done with a flare for the modeled feminine form. Many designs are enhanced with elaborate jewelry, delicate gloves, and a stylized hair-do or decorated hat. The majority of these vases are marked with the manufacturer's or importer's label and a model number.

Club: Head Vase Society, P.O. Box 83H, Scarsdale, NY 10583.

Inarco, E-5623, 6.5" h, $85.
—Photo courtesy Gene Harris Antique Auction Center, Inc.

Brinnis, Pittsburgh, PA, Made in Japan, 1-182, paper label, hand, pearl earrings and necklace, 7" h 225

Enesco, paper label, blue ribbon, pearl earrings, 7.25" h 300

Inarco, E-1066, Cleveland, OH, 1963 transfer and label, earrings missing, 4.5" h 45

Inarco, I-1068, 1963 transfer, paper label, hair comb, pearl earrings and necklace, lashes, 10" h 375

Japan, 56551/A, Fine Quality Japan, paper label, glossy, hand, bonnet, pearl earrings, lashes, 7" h 175

Japan, faint transfer, glossy, blonde ponytail, 5.75" h 15

Japan, label, long brown hair with flower, jeweled, lashes, 5.25" h 90

Japan, long blonde hair, crazed, 6.75" h .150

Lefton, 1843 transfer, paper label, lustre, lashes, hand, necklace, 5.75" h 50

Lefton, 1955 transfer and label, sgd "Geo. Z. Lefton," glossy, green checkered hat and bow, 5" h 50

Napcoware, C4897C 1960 transfer, imp mark, blue hat with rose, lashes, blonde hair, earrings, 4.75" h 55

Napcoware, C7471 transfer, partial National label, earrings, leaf pendant, 4.625" h .60

Napcoware, C7494 transfer, paper label, National Potteries, Made in Japan, blue hat, pearl earrings and necklace, 5.75" h 80

National Potteries Co, Cleveland, Made in Japan, C5036A Napco 1960 transfer, paper label, lashes, hand on upturned collar, coat and hat, 5.5" h .175

Relpo, K1932 transfer, paper label, black bows in hair, earrings, 5.75" h .175

Rubins Original, Japan, 499 transfer, paper label, pearl flowered shoulders and hat, earrings, lashes, 5.75" h . .65

Topling Imports Inc, Japan, 50/425, paper label, black ribbon, pearl necklace, 8.5" h 200

Trimontware Japan, paper label, hand, pearl earrings and necklace, lashes, 7" h 125

LAMPS

Collecting lamps can be considered an illuminating hobby. Not only is the collection practical, versatile, and decorative, but it keeps you out of the dark. Whether you prefer a particular lamp style, color, or theme, you will find a wonderful and enlightening assortment at any flea market.

Clubs: Fairy Lamp Club, 6422 Haystack Rd., Alexandria, VA 22310; Night Light Miniature Lamp Club, 38619 Wakefield Ct., Northville, MI 48167.

Newsletter: *Light Revival,* 35 West Elm Ave., Quincy, MA 02170.

Note: For additional listings see Aladdin and Motion Lamps.

Banquet, brass-washed, emb leaf motif, glass chimney and etched spherical globe, mkd "Bradley & Hubbard," 25" h, 6" sq base 180

Banquet, kerosene type, glass ball shade with hp flowers, kerosene burner on pedestal, brass knobs and white onyx rod above domed and pierced metal foot base, electrified, late 19th C, 29.25" h 190

Character, Huckleberry Hound, hard vinyl head, plastic base, ©Hanna-Barbera Productions, Arch Lamp Mfg Co, 1992, 12" h, 4" d 85

Character, Popeye, hollow soft vinyl, holding spinach can and fork, 1959 King Features Syndicate, Combex, England, 3 x 4 x 8.25" 100

Desk, ribbed bell form gold Aurene iridescent shade mounted on bronzed metal gooseneck base, molded shells on foot, shade shape #2524, sgd "Steuben," 4.75" l shade, 20" h overall .225

Desk, nickel-plated, oil, with chimney and white glass shade, mkd "Bradley & Hubbard," 22 x 9.5" 410

Floor, white enameled base with corseted shaft, bright chrome circular foot ring, unmkd, 42.5 x 7.5" 125

Hanging, Lightolier, teak arms, brass ceiling plate, 3 conical frosted glass shades, paper labels, 30 x 16" 50

Peg, cranberry optic ribbed onion form font with enameled white flowers, dotted gold center band, orig brass fittings and burner, 5.625" h, 3.375" h .100

Peg, satin glass font, shaded yellow MOP swirl pattern, orig brass fittings and burner, 6" h, 3.375" d 165

Student, brass, single arm, dome shaped open topped green overlay shade in ring above cylindrical font, adjustable metal standard with ring top and flaring round foot, electrified, late 19th/early 20thC, 21.25" h 325

Table, Arts & Crafts, oak and slag glass, 4-sided shaft and stepped base, pyramidal shade lined in caramel glass, unmkd, 22.5 x 15" 425

Table, brass, swing arm, plastic shade, unmkd, 11 x 8" .30

Table, ceramic, 4-sided, 2 incised sgraffito figures on copper against celadon ground, sgd "Marianna Von Allesch," 17 x 7.5", price for pair 100

Table, ceramic, emb leaf dec, fiber-glass shade, 29" h 35

Table, clear glass with gold fish design, cardboard shade, 31" h 100

Table, Italian glass, attributed to Seguso, fluted pink lustre glass, corseted body, domed base, cylindrical linen shade, unmkd, 19.5 x 9.5" base 100

Table, pressed glass, kerosene burner and brass collar, squatty ringed onion form blue opaline glass font above turned brass connector and flaring ringed pedestal, square white marble foot, c1860, 9" h 60

Left: Parlor Lamp, jeweled brass, 18.25" h, $450. Right: Fairy Lamp, ribbed vaseline dome, green pressed Clarke base, 3.5" h, $250. —Photo courtesy Gene Harris Antique Auction Center, Inc.

Miniature Lamps. Left: Bull's Eye pattern, amber colored glass font, clear chimney, $140. Center: Red satin glass, tulip-shaped shade and base, emb pattern, 9.75" h, $225. Right: Daisy & Cube pattern, green glass, $350.

Wall, swing arm, U-shaped chrome
arm, orange enameled shade and
wall mount, unmkd, 42" h, 8.5" d
shade 30

LAW ENFORCEMENT

Do not sell this category short.
Collecting is largely confined to the law
enforcement community, but within that
group, collecting badges, patches, and
other police paraphernalia is big. Most collections are based upon items from a specific locality. As a result, prices are region-
alized.

There are some crooks afoot.
Reproduction and fake badges, especially
railroad police badges, are prevalent. Blow
the whistle on them when you see them.

Newsletter: *Police Collectors News,* RR1,
Box 14, Baldwin, WI 54002.

Badge, "Deputy Sheriff," 6-point star,
nickel finish 90
Badge, "Police," eagle atop shield,
applied copper numbers, enamel
block letters 85
Badge, "Special Officer," 6-point star . . .25
Badge, "Special Police," shield with
pierced star center 35
Badge, "Watchman," C B & O Railroad .85
Billy Club, wooden 8
Bobby Helmet, England 100
Book, *Let's Go to the Police Station,*
1957 4
Book, *Story of the FBI, The,* 1954 12
Call Box, aluminum alloy, telephone and
telegraph sending unit, The Gamewell
Co, Newton, MA, late 1920s 350
Cap Badge, star shaped, Germany 8
Handcuffs, Harvard Lock Co 45
Handcuffs, Peerless Handcuff Co,
Springfield, MA 25
Kepi, French Police 35
Leg Irons, Tower Double Lock, late
1800s 200
License Plate, New Hampshire,
Department of Safety 25
License Plate, Wisconsin, Official
State Patrol 15
Model, Chevy Police Car, Monogram
Snap-Tite, 1/32 scale 5

Handcuffs, $20.

Model, Ford Interceptor Police Car,
AMT, 1970, 1/25 scale 20
Model, SWAT Command Van, Revell
Snap-Together, 1/32 scale 5
Nightstick, wooden 10
Patch, US Coast Guard Special Agent . . .4
Program, National Police Academy
Graduation Exercises, The Great
Hall, Jul 8, 1939 20

LEFTON CHINA

Lefton China was founded by George
Zoltan Lefton in Chicago, Illinois, in 1941.
The company markets porcelain giftware
from suppliers in Japan, Taiwan, Malaysia,
and China, with the bulk imported from
Japan.

Club: National Society of Lefton Collectors,
1101 Polk St., Bedford, IA 50833.

Bookends, pr, football, #H067, 5.5" h, 5" l ..10
Canister Set, Rustic Daisy, #4115 25
Cup, #E1660, double handle, purple
flowers, green foot, gold trim 15
Dish, #NE2347, blue paisley, gold trim,
3 x 6.5" 8
Figurine, birthday girl, #KW7227 5
Figurine, Bob White, #KW2002, price
for pair 20
Figurine, boy and cat, #03216, 2.25" h 5
Figurine, bride and groom, #05003, 4" h . .10
Figurine, girl, #403, wearing shamrock
green dress, 4" h 12
Figurine, lady's hands, #KW4198, 5.5" h ..12
Figurine, Siamese cat, #H4032, 3.5" h 5
Figurine, southern belle on stairs,
#CG6142 15

Figurine, Alcatraz 1909, Historic American Lighthouse series, George Z Lefton, 1998, $70.

Figurine, tabby cat, #80219, shades of
brown, black, and white, green eyes,
5" h, 4" w 15
Lady Head Vase, hand on face, mkd
"Japan, MR225103," 6" h 50
Planter, girl with basket, #YU50467,
5.5" h 15
Salt and Pepper Shakers, pr, Christmas
tree, #054 15
Salt and Pepper Shakers, pr, lambs,
#2009 8
Wall Hanging, Mother Goose, #1258,
6.5" h, 7.5" l 30

LENOX

Johnathan Cox and Walter Scott Lenox
founded the Ceramic Art Company, Trenton,
New Jersey, in 1889. In 1906 Lenox established his own company. Much of Lenox's
products resemble Belleek, not unexpect-
edly since Lenox lured several Belleek potters to New Jersey.

Lenox has an upscale reputation. China
service sets sell, but within a narrow price
range, e.g., $600 to $1,200 for an ordinary
service of eight. The key is Lenox gift and
accessory items. Prices are still reasonable. The category has not yet been truly
"discovered." Lenox also produces limited
edition items whose potential for long-term
value is limited.

Note: For additional listings see Limited
Edition.

Boullion Cup and Saucer, Rutledge 55

Bread and Butter Plate, Montclair,
6.5" d 8
Bud Vase, white, gold trim, pink flow-
ers and green leaves dec, mkd
"Barrington Collection, Lenox, made
in USA," 7.5" h 12
Cache Pot, white, bird on branch, gold
trim, gold paper sticker 20
Candlesticks, pr, cream, platinum trim,
3.75" h 10
Cereal Bowl, Country Holly, 6.25" d 6
Cornucopia Vase, white, 5" h 12
Cup and Saucer, Eternal 25
Dessert Plate, Liberty, 6.375" d 15
Dinner Plate, Hannah, 11" D 8
Dinner Plate, Moonspun 25
Dinner Plate, Princess, 10.5" d 15
Dish, leaf shape, green stamp mark,
6.25" l 10
Figurine, bird, green mark, 3" l 100
Fruit Bowl, Moonspun, 5.25" d 30
Ornament, carousel horse, 1989 50
Ornament, crystal, tree shaped, painted
gold holly leaves and red berries,
2.75" h 20
Perfume Bottle, clear, etched frosted
glass design, frosted crystal stopper,
5" h 15
Planter, bird, green, "Lenox Made in
USA" backstamp, 1939, 6 x 6" 85
Salad Plate, Dewdrops, Temperware,
8" d 10
Salad Plate, Hannah, 8.25" d 5
Salad Plate, Magic Garden, Temper-
ware, 8" d 3
Salad Plate, Rutledge, 8" d 15
Serving Bowl, Solitaire, 10" l, 6.25" w 70

*Poppies on Blue pattern. Cup, $10; oval
vegetable bowl, $25; oval platter, $35.*

Salt and Pepper Shakers, pr, RCA's Nipper, 1930s, 3" h, $50. —Photo courtesy Ray Morykan Auctions.

Vase, green, handled, mkd "Made expressly for Wiss Sons Inc, Newark, NJ" 100
Vase, white, allover daisy type flowers, gold trim, 12" h 40
Vase, white, emb roses, 6.5" h 12

L. E. SMITH

L. E. Smith Glass Company was founded in 1907 in Mount Pleasant, Pennsylvania, by Lewis E. Smith. Although Smith left the company shortly after its establishment, it still bears his name. Early products included cooking articles and utilitarian wares such as glass percolator tops, fruit jars, sanitary sugar bowls, and reamers.

In the 1920s, green, amber, canary, amethyst, and blue colors were introduced along with an extensive line of soda fountain wares. The company also made milk glass, console and dresser sets, and the always popular fish-shaped aquariums. During the 1930s, Smith became the largest producer of black glass. Popular dinnerware lines were Homestead, Melba, Do-Si-Do, By Cracky, Romanesque, and Mount Pleasant. Today, L. E. Smith manufactures colored reproduction glass and decorative objects.

Beverage Tray, black, 6" d 15
Bowl, Mt Pleasant, scalloped, 2-handled, pink, 8" d 20
Bowl, Mt Pleasant, scalloped, ftd, black, 9" d 30
Cake Plate, Do-Si-Do, handled 15

Powder Box, Ripple pattern, green, with matching flower block, 6" d, $25. —Photo courtesy Ray Morykan Auctions.

Cake Plate, Mt Pleasant, ftd, black, 10.5" d 40
Candleholder, Wigwam, black, 3.25" h ...20
Compote, Moon 'n Star, amberina 40
Console Bowl, black, 3 ftd, #1022/4, 9" d ..45
Creamer, Moon 'n Star, amberina 12
Creamer, Mt Pleasant, black 20
Cruet, Moon 'n Star, amberina 12
Cup and Saucer, Do-Si-Do, black 12
Cup and Saucer, Mt Pleasant, black 12
Fairy Lamp, Moon 'n Star, ruby 35
Figurine, goose girl, amber, 6" h 55
Figurine, lamb, black, 2.25" h 18
Flowerpot and Saucer, black, 4" h 25
Nut Dish, Mt Pleasant, black, #505, 8.25" d 25
Plate, Do-Si-Do, black, 8" d 12
Plate, Mt Pleasant, black, 8" d 12
Platter, Mt Pleasant, black, 13.5" d 85
Rose Bowl, Mt Pleasant, scalloped, 3 ftd, cobalt 35
Salt and Pepper Shakers, pr, Mt Pleasant, ftd, cobalt 40
Sandwich Tray, Mt Pleasant, black, 10" d 25

Candleholders, pr, Double Shield, #600, black, $60. —Photo courtesy Ray Morykan Auctions.

Sugar, cov, Do-Si-Do 8
Water Goblet, Moon 'n Star, amberina . .15

LETTER OPENERS

Isn't it amazing what can be done to a basic form? I have seen letter openers that are so large that one does not have a ghost's chance in hell of slipping them under the flap of a No. 10 envelope. As they say in eastern Pennsylvania, these letter openers are "just for nice."

Advertising letter openers are the crowd pleaser in this category. However, you can build an equally great collection based on material (brass, plastic, wood, etc.) or theme (animal shapes, swords, etc.)

Abraham Lincoln, copper, 11" l 35
Airplane, brass, "Washington DC,"
     8.25" l 45
Allard Express, stainless steel, 7" l 10
Alligator, copper coated metal, 7" l 30
Anchor, brass, 9" l 15
BankAmericard, plastic, 7.25" l 5
Bastian Bros Co, Rochester, NY, brass,
     plated steel coating, 9" l 50
Bird Head, celluloid, 7" l 10
Birds on Branch, painted brass, 7.75" l . .10
Canada, sterling silver, early 1900s,
     6.75" l 30
Capricorn, brass, 7.5" l 15
College Graduate, copper, 7.5" l 30
Connersville Casket Co Inc, Conners-
     ville, IN, stainless steel, 10" l 15
Cortland Standard, "Cortland's Home
     Newspaper," brass, stainless steel
     blade, 9.25" l 15

Dolphins, painted brass, 7" l 10
Duck, painted wood, 8.25" l 10
Fox Head, sterling silver, 7.25" l 55
Gates Rubber Co, "Vulco V-Belt,"
     bronze, Whitehead & Hoag, 8.25" l . . .20
Grand Chapter of Ohio, Order of the
     Eastern Star, bronze, c1937, 7" l 10
Gypsy, wood, hand carved, 4.5" l 10
Indian Chief, brass, 6.5" l 45
J B Ford Co, Wyandotte, MI, bronze,
     8.75" l 20
Kiwanis International, plastic, metal
     blade, 8" l 5
Male Dancer, bronze, chromed blade,
     9" l 20
Metropolitan Life Insurance Co, bronze,
     Whitehead & Hoag, 8.75" l 15
Miller High Life, painted plastic, 9" l 10
New Haven Register, bronze, Metal
     Arts Co, NY, 9" l 15
Old Sleepy Eye Collectors Convention,
     mkd "Japan, MR 225103," plastic,
     and stainless steel, 1981, 7.125" l 15
Owl, celluloid, 11.25" l 60
Peacock, bronze, 8.75" l 10
Scimitar, brass, trench art, 7.5" l 25
Seahorse, copper, gilded paint,9.25" l . . .15
Sea Shell, sterling silver, 6.5" l 50
Sickle, sterling silver, MOP handle,
     3.5" l 40
Squirrel, wood, hand carved, 5" l 10
Standard Varnish Works, celluloid,
     8.75" l 45
Uneeda Bread Co, litho tin, 8.25" l 45
Western Motif, silver-plated, 7.5" l 15
Williams "The Florist," plastic, metal
     blade, 8.625" l .10

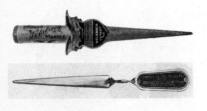

Top: Welsbach Company, Philadelphia, litho tin, 10.5" l, $45. Bottom: Briscoe Motor Sales Co, metal, 10" l, $10. —Photo courtesy Collectors Auction Services.

L. G. WRIGHT

Thanks to James Measell and W. C. Roetteis' *The L. G. Wright Glass Company* (Glass Press, 1997) collectors have the checklist they need to properly identify L. G. Wright Glass. The company's carnival glass, pattern, and overlay reproductions are collectible in their own right.

An auction was held in May 2000, to liquidate the L. G. Wright Glass Company holdings. Although some molds were bought by individuals, the majority were purchased by glass makers and importers including Fenton, L. E. Smith, Mosser Glass, Weishar

Enterprises, and an unidentifed importer planning Chinese production. Watch for reproductions in the near future.

Castor Bottle, cranberry opalescent . . .200
Compote, Moon 'n Star, ruffled top,
   blue 30
Covered Dish, Moon 'n Star, blue opal-
   escent 45
Cracker Jar, cov, floral dec, pink over-
   lay satin 400
Creamer and Sugar, Moon 'n Star,
   amber 7
Cruet, Daisy and Button, amber 45
Dish, Daisy and Button, vaseline 15
Pickle Castor, cranberry opalescent
   swirl 475
Pickle Castor, Daisy and Fern, cran-
   berry 400
Rose Bowl, Beaded Curtain, white and
   pink 160
Rose Bowl, Grape Delight, green
   iridescent 15
Rose Bowl, Peachblow, pink satin 35
Rose Bowl, pink satin 110
Salt and Pepper Shakers, pr, Daisy and
   Button, blue 12
Sugar Shaker, Moon 'n Star, amber 35
Sugar Shaker, Moon 'n Star, vaseline . . .18
Tumbler, Mary Gregory style, cobalt 20
Tumbler, Moon 'n Star, blue 8
Vase, Coin Spot, cranberry opalescent .200
Water Pitcher, Maize, amber overlay . .400
Water Pitcher, Moon 'n Star, crystal . . .260

LIBERTY BLUE

   In 1973 the Grand Union Company commissioned Liberty Blue dinnerware to be offered as a premium in grocery stores throughout the eastern United States. Ironically, though intended to celebrate America's Independence, the dinnerware was produced in Staffordshire, England.

   Liberty Blue dinnerware, introduced in 1975, portrayed patriotic scenes in blue on a white background. Original engravings depicted historic buildings and events from the American Revolutionary period. The Wild Rose border was reproduced from a design dating back to 1784.

   Liberty Blue is easy to identify. Most pieces contain the words "Liberty Blue" on the back and all are marked "Made in England." The back of each dish also contains information about the scene illustrated on it.

Baker, oval 40
Berry Bowl, 5" d .5
Bowl, 9" d 13
Butter Dish 40
Bread and Butter Plate, 6" d 1
Casserole, cov 80
Cereal Bowl, 7" d 14
Coaster, 4" d, price for set of 5 60
Creamer and Sugar 40
Cup 6
Fruit Bowl, 5" d. 1.125" d 5
Gravy Boat with Underplate 52
Luncheon Plate, 8.5" d 12
Meat Platter, 12" l 50
Mug, 3.75" h 20
Nappy, 5" l 5
Pie Plate, 10" d, 2.75" d 10
Pitcher, 7.75" h 80
Platter, 14" l 45
Salad Plate, 8.5" d 12
Salt and Pepper Shakers, pr 35
Saucer 3
Soup Bowl, flat rim, 8.75" d 18
Soup Tureen, cov 250
Sugar, cov 30
Teapot 120
Tray, 8" l 25
Turkey Platter, 18" l 45
Vegetable Bowl, oval, open, 9" l 35
Vegetable Bowl, round, cov 150
Vegetable Bowl, round, open 45

Dinner Plate, 10" d, $12. —Photo courtesy Ray Morykan Auctions.

LICENSE PLATES

License plates appeal to collectors because they are colorful, diverse, and can be found virtually anywhere, usually for minimal cost. Modern silkscreened graphics are now the rule rather than the exception on America's highways. These colorful specialty plates have transformed the lowly "number plate" into a 6 x 12" artist's palette.

Quality older issues continue to rise in value, but prices are often arbitrary, regional, and hard for the novice to accurately determine. Condition is primary; badly chipped porcelains or rusty metal plates with only traces of original paint remaining are usually of little value.

Plates from the industrialized North and East are most easily found; pre-war southern and western issues are much less common. Rare early issues still turn up on a regular basis, often from the unlikeliest of locations. Wartime scrap drives did not get them all—a good old "tag" can still be found by the treasure hunter or flea market frequenter, and the reward for a choice plate can be substantial.

Club: Automobile License Plate Collectors Assoc. (ALPCA), P.O. Box 7, Horner, WV 26372.

Newsletter: *The Plate Trader,* 21 Ridge Run SE, Apt D., Marietta, GA 30067.

Periodical: *PL8S: The License Plate Collector's Hobby Magazine,* P.O. Box 222, East Texas, PA 18046.

Alabama, 1960 8
Alaska, 1966, totem pole graphic ...... .20
California, 1976, Centennial .... .10
Colorado, 1958, skier graphic .... .35

California, 1914, porcelain, red and white, 4.5 x 16", $165. —Photo courtesy Collectors Auction Services.

Pennsylvania, 1935, blue and yellow, $6.

Connecticut, 1962, with tab .... .10
Connecticut, 1978, Dealer plate 8
Delaware, 1987 8
Florida, 1935, with tab .... .90
Florida, 1951, Keep Florida Green ...... .40
Florida, 1993, Superbowl XXV .... .75
Florida, 1997, University of Florida ..... .25
Idaho, 1940, "50th Anniversary 1890-
    1940" .... .75
Idaho, 1995, scenic graphic .... .10
Illinois, 1948, fiberboard .... .15
Indiana, 1978, map graphic 8
Iowa, 1965 6
Kansas, 1942, sunflower graphic ...... .50
Kansas, 1983, blue wheat .... .20
Maine, 1927 .... .30
Maryland, 1999, crane graphic .... .20
Michigan, 1997, Motor Capital .... .30
Montana, 1994, Big Sky graphic 4
Nebraska, 1972, Corn Husker 8
Nevada, 1958, Horseless Carriage ..... .175
New York, 1986, Centennial .... .30
Oklahoma, 1955 .... .35
Pennsylvania, 1914, porcelain .... .60
South Carolina, 1932 .... .100
Washington, 1916, porcelain .... .275

LIGHTNING ROD BALLS

Lightning rod balls are the ornamental portion of lightning rod systems typically found on the roofs of barns and rural houses from the 1840s to 1930s. The glass balls served only aesthetic purposes and did not contribute to the operation of the lightning rod system.

Glass balls were made in a rainbow of colors ranging from common white or blue milk glass to red and clear. Many clear glass balls turned shades of sun colored amethyst (SCA) through exposure to the sun. Mercury colored balls were created by silvering the interior surface of balls of different colors to produce silver, gold, cobalt, red, and green mercury colors. Lightning rod balls were also colored using flashing and casing techniques.

There are 34 standard shapes or styles of lightning rod balls.

Newsletter: *The Crown Point,* P.O. Box 23, Winfield, IL 60190.

Chestnut, white milk glass, 4.25"	.30
D&S, blue milk glass, 5.25"	.20
D&S, green	.275
D&S, white milk glass, 5.25"	.20
Diddie Blitzen, white milk glass, 4.25"	.30
Doorknob, sun colored amethyst	.75
Electra Cone, white milk glass	.10
K-Ball, blue milk glass	.40
Mast, white milk glass	.80
Moon & Star, amber	.50
National Round, sun colored amethyst	.100
National Round, white milk glass	.20
Patent '77, gold mercury	.325
Plain Round, amber, 4.5"	.25
Plain Round, blue milk glass, 4.5"	.25
Plain Round, dark green, 4.5"	.350
Plain Round, root beer, 4.5"	.15
Plain Round, sun colored amethyst, 3.5"	.20
Plain Round, vaseline, 5"	.15
Pleated Round, 7-Up green	.115
Pleated Round, cobalt blue	.75
Quilt Flat, teal	.400
Ribbed Grape, green-gray	.400
S Company, blue milk glass	.50
Shinn Belted, sun colored amethyst	.55
Shinn System, white milk glass	.25
SLR Company, cobalt blue, wide collar, no emb	.75
Thompson, cobalt blue	.70

Swirl, amber, 5.75", $45.

LILLIPUT LANE

Collectible cottages, also known as architectural collectibles, are the 1980/90s version of commemorative plates and whiskey bottles. The secondary market is highly speculative; and, there are more than ample signs that the bubble is bursting. Limited Edition and Collector Club models are among the most speculative.

In 1982 David Tate of Skirsgill, near Penrith, Cumbria, England, issued the first series of fourteen Lilliput Lane cottages, inspired by buildings in England's Lake District.

The company has used over a dozen different backstamps on its buildings, making them easy to date. Before buying on the secondary market, always check to see if the building is still in production and what its current suggested retail price is. A cottage needs to have its period box and certificate to be considered complete.

Club: Enesco Lilliput Lane Collectors' Club, 225 Windsor Dr., Itasca, IL 60143.

Balmoral Castle, L2288	.55
Bill & Ben's Cottage, 3" h	.35
Birthday Cottage, L2328	.25
Bridge House, 1991, 3" h	.20
Chatterbox Corner, L2333	.35
Chevrolet Dealership	.25
Chine Cottage, 2.75" h	.30
Cobbler's Cottage, 2.5" h	.30
Edinburgh Castle, L2247	.50
Fruits of Eden, 6" h	.40
Grandma and Grandpa's Cottage, L2321	.15
Hampton Court Palace, L2248	.65
Honeysuckle Cottage, 1992, 4" h	.70
Juliet's Tower, 2" h	.25
Make A Wish, L2342	.15
New Neighbors, L2229	.80
Out For A Duck Cottage, 3.25" h	.35
Pepper Mill Cottage, L2330	.25
Santa's Little Helper	.15
Smugglers Rest, L2331	.30
Sore Paws, L2022	.45
Summer Haze, 3.5" h	.40
Swan Princess Castle, 1988, 7.25" h	.50
Tanners Cottage, 1987, 2.25" h	.8
The Bobbins, L2178	.45
The Lion House, L2187	.30

The Planetarium, L2246 100
The Toy Shop 55
Wedding Bells, 1992, 3.125" h 20

LIMITED EDITION COLLECTIBLES

Collect limited edition collectibles because you love them, not because you want to invest in them. While a few items sell well above their initial retail price, the vast majority sell between twenty-five and fifty cents on the original retail dollar. The one consistent winner is the first issue in any series.

Whenever possible, buy items with their original box and inserts. The box adds another ten to twenty percent to the value of the item. Also, buy only items in excellent or better condition. Very good is not good enough. So many of each issue survive that market price holds only for the top condition grades.

Clubs: Collector's Society of America, 29352 Hoover Rd., Warren, MI 48093; International Plate Collectors Guild, P.O. Box 487, Artesia, CA 90702.

In addition, many companies that issue limited edition collectibles have company sponsored clubs. Contact the company for further information.

Periodicals: *Collector Editions,* 170 Fifth Ave., 12th Fl., New York, NY 10010; *Collector's Mart Magazine,* 700 E. State St, Iola, WI 54990; *Collectors News,* 506 Second St., P.O. Box 306, Grundy Center, IA 50638.

Architecture, Brandywine Collectibles, Boys School, Old Salem Collection, M Whiting, 1987 20
Architecture, The Cat's Meow, Craig Jeweler, Williamsburg Merchants, F Jones, 1994 12
Architecture, Cavanagh Group, Train Depot, Coca-Cola Brand Town Square Collection, 1992 250
Architecture, Dave Grossman Creations, Peggy's Point Light, Nova Scotia, Spencer Collin, 1996 40
Architecture, David Winter Cottages, Birthstone Wishing Well, Painting Event, D Winter, 1992 65

Architecture, David Winter Cottages, Hogmanay, Dickens Christmas Carol Collection, 1988, $100.

Architecture, Department 56, Grist Mill, Alpine Village Series, 1988 30
Architecture, Ertl Collectibles, Barn, Farm Country Christmas, L Davis, 1996 100
Architecture, Fitz & Floyd, Butternut Squash Dairy, Charming Tails Squashville Lighted Village, D Griff, 1995 45
Architecture, Geo Zoltan Lefton Co, Joseph House, Colonial Village, Lefton, 1993 50
Architecture, Harbour Lights, Cape Lookout NC, Tall Towers, 1996 60
Architecture, Lilliput Lane, Honeysuckle Cottage, Anniversary Collection, 1992 100
Architecture, Lowell Davis Farm Club, Chicken House, L Davis, 1985 50
Architecture, Reco, Outpost on Argaeus The Age of Exploration, V DiFate, 1997 35
Architecture, Courthouse, Williamsburg, S Thompson, 1990 20
Bell, Artists of the World, Los Ninos, T DeGrazia, 1980 45
Bell, Belleek, Cottage, third edition, 1992 30
Bell, Belleek, Four Calling Birds, Twelve Days of Christmas, 1994 30
Bell, Dave Grossman Creations, Faces of Christmas, Rockwell inspired, 1975 35
Bell, Fenton Art Glass Co, Christmas Morn, M Dickinson, 1978 50
Bell, Gorham, American Homestead, Currier & Ives, 1977 25
Bell, Greenwich Workshop, The Sound of Christmas, J Christensen, 1997 60
Bell, Kirk Stieff, Santa's Workshop, 1992 .40

Bell, Norman Rockwell Museum, Checking His List, 1982, 6.5" h, $45.

Bell, Lenox China, We Wish You A
　Merry Christmas, Songs of
　Christmas, 1991 50
Bell, Lladró, Christmas Bell, 1987 50
Bell, Lowell Davis Farm Club, "Kate"
　the mule, L Davis, 1993 75
Bell, Reed & Barton, Little Shepherd,
　Yuletide Bell, 1982 15
Bell, River Shore, Grandpa's Guardian,
　N Rockwell, 1981 50
Bell, Roman, Beach Buddies, F Hook,
　1985 25
Bell, Seymour Mann, Bluebird,
　Connoisseur Collection, Bernini,
　1995 15
Doll, Annalee Mobilitee Dolls, Thorndike
　Chicken, Doll Society, A Thorndike,
　1990, 7" h 90
Doll, Ashton Drake Galleries, Rachel,
　Amish Blessings, J Good-Krüger,
　1991 125
Doll, Cavanagh Group, Sissy Bar,
　Harley-Davidson, B Yaney, 1997 50
Doll, Columbus International, Smoky,
　Hermann-Spielwaren Annual Bears,
　U Hermann, 1998 140
Doll, Daddy's Long Legs/KVK Inc,
　Abigail the Cow, K Germany, 1990 . . .200
Doll, Georgetown Collection, Jennie
　Cooper, American Dairy Dolls,
　L Mason, 1990 130
Doll, Goebel of North America, Melvis
　Bumps, Dolly Dingle, B Ball, 1995 . . .100
Doll, Goebel of North America, Alice,
　Victoria Ashlea Originals, B Ball,
　1987 135
Doll, Gorham, Dollie's First Steps,
　Dollie and Me, J Pilallis, 1991 225
Doll, Gorham, Heather, Holly Hobbie,
　1983, 14" h 275

Doll, Jan Hagara Collectables, Adell,
　Danbury Mint, J Hagara, 1991, 19" h .200
Doll, Kurt S Adler, Nicholas on Skates,
　Royal Heritage Collection, J Mostrom,
　1994 120
Doll, Ladies and Friends, Emmy Lou
　Valentine, Lizzie High Dolls, B & P
　Wisber, 1989 .50
Doll, Lawtons, Wee Handful, W Lawton,
　994 300
Doll, Lee Middleton Original Dolls,
　Devan, Collector Series, L Middleton,
　1989 200
Doll, Seymour Mann, Pamela,
　Connossieur Doll Collection,
　E Mann, 1994 115
Doll, Seymour Mann, Cassie Flower
　Girl, Signature Doll Series, P Aprile,
　1992 175
Doll, Susan Wakeen Doll Co, Cynthia,
　The Littlest Ballet Company,
　S Wakeen, 1985 350
Figurine, Olivia, All God's Children/Miss
　Martha Originals, Collectors' Club,
　M Root, 1992 170
Figurine, American Artists, The Black
　Stallion, F Stone, 1985 175
Figurine, Anri, On My Own, Anri
　Collectors' Society, S Kay, 1995 175
Figurine, Armani, Clown with Dog,
　Clown Series, G Armani, 1984 100
Figurine, Artaffects, Cinderella, The
　Storybook Collection, G Perillo, 1981 .100
Figurine, Artists of the World, Littlest
　Angel, DeGrazia Annual Christmas
　Collection, T DeGrazia, 1994 150

Figurine, Museum Collection, Inc., Christmas Prayers, 1985, 5" h, $65.

Figurine, Byers' Choice Ltd, Dutch Girl, Children of the World, J Byers, 1992 .175

Figurine, Cast Art Industries, Wildflower, Dreamsicles Christmas, K Haynes, 1991 15

Figurine, Cavanagh Group, Gone Fishing, Coca-Cola Brand Heritage Collection, 1996 50

Figurine, Coyne's & Company, Winter Walk, David Frykman Christmas Collection, D Frykman, 1996 50

Figurine, Crystal World, Owl, Bird Collection, R Nakai, 1983 75

Figurine, Dave Grossman Creations, Mother's Touch, Embrace Series, T Snyder, 1998 40

Figurine, Department 56, Caroline Stringing Cranberries, All Through The House, 1992 15

Figurine, Duncan Royale, Banjo Man, Ebony Collection, 1990 80

Figurine, Eggspressions Inc, Little Angel, Angel Collection, S Arnett, 1996 150

Figurine, Enchantica, Sunfire, A Hull, 1993 35

Figurine, Fitz & Floyd, After Lunch Snooze, Charming Tails Everyday, D Griff, 1994 15

Figurine, Gartlan USA, Jerry Mathers, Leave It To Beaver, Noble Studio, 1995, 5" h 50

Figurine, Hallmark Galleries, Baby Raccoon, Tender Touches, E Seale, 1988 40

Plate, American Express, Scarlet Tanager, Songbirds of Roger Tory Peterson, 1982, $15.

Figurine, Hamilton Collection, King Rabbit, Camelot Frogs, S Kehrli, 1996 20

Figurine, Hudson Creek, Spangler's Spring, Chilmark Civil War, F Barnum, 1990 235

Figurine, Jan Hagara Collectables, Holly, Signature Series, J Hagara, 1985 75

Figurine, Kurt S Adler, Berwyn the Grand, Christmas Legends, P F Bolinger, 1994 175

Figurine, Lenox, Playtime, Lenox Classics/Crystal Cats, 1996 55

Figurine, Lowell Davis Farm Club, Company's Coming, Davis Cat Tales, L Davis, 1982 125

Figurine, Maruri USA, Single Great Horned Owl, Eyes of the Night, Maruri Studios, 1988 65

Ornament, Annalee Mobilitee Dolls, Elf Head, A Thorndike, 1982 30

Ornament, Artists of the World, White Dove, De Grazia Annual Ornaments, T De Grazia, 1987 75

Ornament, Dave Grossman Creations, Christmas Carol, inspired by E Kelly Sr, 1986 10

Ornament, Department 56, Bob & Mrs Cratchit, 1988 30

Ornament, Flambro Imports, Home For Christmas, Emmett Kelly Jr Christmas Ornaments, 1992 50

Ornament, Gorham, Victorian Heart, Archive Collectible, Gorham, 1988 60

Ornament, Hang in There, Charming Tails Deck the Halls, D Griff, 1993 50

Ornament, Harbour Lights, Holland MI, 1996 15

Ornament, Hudson Creek, Decorating the Tree, Sebastian Christmas Ornaments, PW Baston Jr, 1988 12

Ornament, Jan Hagara Collectables, Holly, Christmas Figural Ornaments, J Hagara, 1987 18

Ornament, June McKenna Collectibles Inc, Guardian Angel, Flatback Ornaments, 1988 40

Ornament, Kirk Stieff, Cat and Ornament, D Bacorn, 1992 10

Ornament, Kurt S Adler Inc, Allison Sitting in Chair, Christmas in Chelsea Collection, J Mostrom, 1992 .25

Ornament, Roman Inc, Cat in Bubbles
Jar, Animal Kingdom, D Griff, 1994 8
Ornament, Royal Doulton, Together For
Christmas, 1993 20
Ornament, United Design Corp, Angel
and Tambourine, Angels Collection,
1992 20
Plate, American Artists, Parakeets,
Feathered Friends, L Crouch, 1982 . . .30
Plate, American Greetings, A Mother's
Love Just Grows and Grows, Holly
Hobbie's Mother's Day, 1975 16
Plate, Anna-Perenna, Patience, Arctic
Spring, N Peter, 1983 75
Plate, Anri (Schmid), A Time For
Secrets, Sarah Kay Annual, S Kay,
1984 120
Plate, Armstrong's/Crown Parian, Under
Surveillance, Wells Fargo, McCarty,
1979 65
Plate, Artaffects, Sherlock Holmes,
Baker Street (Signature Collection),
M Hooks, 1983 55
Plate, Artists of the World, The Lord's
Candle, Celebration, T DeGrazia,
1993 40
Plate, B & J Art Designs, Laurel, Jan
Hagara, Old-Fashioned Country,
1985 42
Plate, Bareuther, Ribe Cathedral, Danish
Church, 1969 .25
Plate, Bing & Grøndahl, Bedtime,
Children's Day, C Roller, 1988 35
Plate, Bradford Exchange, Waltz of the
Flowers, Nutcracker, N Zaitseva,
1994 40

*Plate, Bing and Grøndahl, Danish Village
Church, Christmas Series, 1960, $120.*

*Plate, Zolan Fine Arts/Winston Roland,
Little Gardener, Country Friends, 1998, $10.*

Plate, Capo Di Monte, Petals, Memories
of the Heart, 1984 30
Plate, Crown Delft, Man By Fire,
Christmas, 1969 30
Plate, Danbury Mint, Hamming It Up,
Pigs in Bloom, 1997 30
Plate, Lowell Davis Farm Club, Right
Church Wrong Pew, Davis Cat Tales,
L Davis, 1982 .90
Plate, Delphi, '59 Red Ford Fairlane,
Fabulous Cars of the Fifties,
G Angelini, 1994 30
Plate, Fitz & Floyd, Father Frost, Myth
of Santa Claus, R Havins, 1993 70
Plate, Franklin Mint, A Stitch In Time,
Cobblestone Kids, D Bell Jarratt,
1983 65
Plate, Gartlan USA, Roger Staubach,
Roger Staubach Sterling Collection,
Charles Soileau, 1987, 3.5" d 20
Plate, WS George, Tango Dancers, Art
Deco, M McDonald, 1990 55
Plate, Kern Collectibles, Randy and Rex,
Portrait of Innocence, L Jansen, 1977 .55
Plate, Kirk, Mother and Child, Mother's
Day, 1972 75
Plate, Edwin M Knowles, Adoration of
the Shepherds, Eve Licea Christmas,
E Licea, 1989 .55
Plate, Lenox, Sea Lions, American
\Wildlife, N Adams, 1983 65
Plate, Lynell, Olde Country Inn, Betsy
Bates Annual, 1979 45
Plate, Pemberton & Oakes, Waiting to
Play, Children and Pets, 1986 35

Plate, Pickard, Green-Winged Teal and
Mallard, Lockhart Wildlife, J Lockhart,
1971 170

Plate, Reco International, Grandma's
Cookie Jar, Grandparent Collector's
Plate, S Kuck, 1981 40

Plate, River Shore, In Trouble Again,
Children of the American Frontier,
D Crook, 1986 .35

Plate, Rockwell Society, Angel with a
Black Eye, N Rockwell, 1975 50

Plate, Roman Inc, Little Children, Come
to Me, Child's World, F Hook, 1980 . . .45

Plate, Royal Bayreuth, Just Friends,
L Henry Series, 1976 60

Plate, Schmid, Bicentennial, Peanuts
Special Edition, C Schulz, 1976 30

Plate, Seymour Mann Inc, Hummingbird
Duo, Connoisseur Collection, Bernini,
1995 45

Plate, Spode, Sleigh Ride, Christmas
Pastimes, 1982 75

Plate, Sports Impressions, Babe Ruth
Sultan of Swant, J Catalano, 1996,
4.25" d 10

Plate, Wendell August Forge, Kennedy,
Great Americans, pewter, 1971 40

LITTLE GOLDEN BOOKS

Read me a story! For millions of children that story came from a Little Golden Book. Colorful, inexpensive, and readily available, these wonderful books are a hot collectible. You see them everywhere.

Be careful, you may be subject to a nostalgia attack because sooner or later you are going to spot your favorite. Relive your childhood. Buy the book. You won't be sorry.

Newsletter: *The Gold Mine Review,* P.O. Box 209, Hershey, PA 17033.

Baby Dear, #306-42, 1962 5
Baby Looks, #404, 1960, 4th printing,
1977 15
Big Brown Bear, The, #335, 1958 5
Christmas Carols, #26, 1946, 1st edition . .13
Fix It, Please, #32, 1947, "E" edition 15
Friendly Book, The, #199, 1954, "A"
edition 6

The Gingerbread Man, *#437, 1961, $6.*

Golden Egg Book, The, #304-11, 1962,
12th printing 1980 1
Grover's Own Alphabet, #109-51, 1978 . . .6
Hop, Little Kangaroo!, #558, 1965 1
*Hopalong Cassidy And The Bar 20
Cowboy,* #147, 1952, "A" edition 8
Howdy Doody and the Princess, #135,
1952 5
Howdy Doody In Funland, #172, 1953 8
Howdy Doody's Lucky Trip, #171, 1953 . . .5
Linda and Her Little Sister, #214, 1954,
"A" edition 55
Little Black Sambo, #57, 1948 55
*Little Golden Cut-Out Christmas Manger,
The,* #176, 1953, "B" edition 8
Little Gray Donkey, #206, 1954, "A"
edition 8
Little Yip-Yip and His Bark, #73, 1950,
"A" edition 9
Musicians of Bremen, The, #189, 1954,
"A" edition 4
Noises and Mr Flibberty-Jib, #29, 1947,
"D" edition 25
Peter Pan and Wendy, D24, 1952, "A"
edition 6
Roy Rogers and Cowboy Toby, #195,
1954 8
Roy Rogers and the Indian Sign, #259,
1956, "A" edition 15
Sailor Dog, The, #156, 1953, "A" edition . .3
Snow White and The Seven Dwarfs,
D4, 1949 6
Tiger's Adventure, #208, 1954, "A"
edition 5
Uncle Mistletoe, #175, 1953, "A" edition .12
Wiggles, #166, 1953, "A" edition 20

The Jolly Barnyard, *#67, 1972, $14.*

Wizard of Oz, The, #107-69, 1975 2
Yogi Bear, #395, 1960, "C" edition 4

LITTLE ORPHAN ANNIE

Little Orphan Annie is one of those characters that pops up everywhere—radio, newspapers, movies, etc. In the early 1930s "Radio Orphan Annie" was syndicated regionally. It went network in 1933. The show's only sponsor was Ovaltine. Many Little Orphan Annie collectibles were Ovaltine premiums.

Radio and cartoon strip Little Orphan Annie material is becoming expensive. Try the more recent movie- and stage-related items if you are looking for something a bit more affordable.

Belt, red, white, and blue striped fabric, bright luster brass buckle with emb eagle image above "Code Captain," Ovaltine premium, 1940, 1.25 x 2.75" .250
Book, *Little Orphan Annie and the Secret of the Well*, Whitman Better Little Book, #1417, 1947 35
Book, *Little Orphan Annie and the Ghost Gang*, Whitman Big Little Book, #1154, 1935 40
Booklet, Book About Dogs, 32 pp, full color front and back image of Annie and Sandy at billboard, inside front cover with black and white image of Annie and her radio friends on flying carpet, Ovaltine premium, 1936, 4.75 x 6.5" 35

Soaky Bottle, Lander, 1977, $30.

Box, Sunshine Biscuits, different scenes on panels, Annie feeding biscuits to circus elephant, shooting gallery scene, missing string handle, empty, c1930s, 1.5 x 3 x 5.5" 350
Coloring Book, Little Orphan Annie Crayon & Coloring Book, McLoughlin Bros, 1933, 10 x 13" 45
Comic Book, The Adventures of Little Orphan Annie, 16 pp, Quaker Puffed Wheat and Rice Sparkies premium, 7.5 x 10" 45
Decoder, brass, "1935 Radio Orphan Annie's S.S.," round, worn silver flash finish, 1.25" d 35
Decoder, "1936 ROA SS," secret compartment decoder, badge shaped, 1.25 x 1.75" 30
Decoder, brass, "1936 ROA Secret Code," Mysto-Matic decoder badge, round, plated brass, "ROA-Secret Code-1939," 1.75" d 55
Doll, Sandy, oilcloth, stuffed, tan, brown, and white, front image with "Sandy" on collar, reverse image with "Gray" on collar, 1930s, 8.5" h 100
Figure, Sandy, jointed wood, orange, black accents, "Sandy" name on 1 side, mkd "Made in USA," 1930s . . .40
Greeting Card, paper, folder, random glitter dots dec, colorful Christmas scene on front with "Annie and Sandy-Winifred and Harold Gray-Greens Farms Connecticut," dated 1942, 4.5 x 6.25" 150
Manual, "Radio Orphan Annie's Secret Society, 1937, Bigger and Better than Ever," together with Sunburst brass decoder badge, 1937, 1.75 x 2" .80

Ovaltine Shake-up Mug, beetleware white plastic cup, image of Annie and Sandy, "Leapin' Lizards! For a Swell Summer Drink There's Nothin' Like a Cold Ovaltine Shake-up–Eh, Sandy?," red top, 1931, 2.75 x 4.75" . . .45

Paperback Book, *Little Orphan Annie*, Whitman, 48 pp, 1928, 4 x 5.5" 350

Pinback Button, celluloid, image of Annie and "Orphan Annie Loves Red Cross Macaroni," Parisan Novelty Co, Chicago, 1.25" d 50

Punch-outs, "Little Orphan Annie Circus," brown paper mailing envelope with color stiff paper figures for "All-Star Action Show" display, Ovaltine premium, 1936, 10.5 x 15" . . .100

"Talking" Stationery, paper folder album with 12 stationery folders and matching plain white envelopes, folder front shows cover emblem for Radio Orphan Annie's Secret Society, diecut slit mouth opens and closes as folder is opened and closed, back cover shows 3 different scenes of Annie, Joe, and Sandy, Ovaltine premium, 1937 175

Trading Card, Wild West Bandanna, pictures and names of 26 western brand markings of the bandanna with instructions for wearing on front, reverse offers portrait ring premium, Ovaltine premium, 1934, 4.5 x 7" 60

LITTLE RED RIDING HOOD

On June 29, 1943, the United States Patent Office issued design patent #135,889 to Louise Elizabeth Bauer, Zanesville, Ohio, assignor to the A. E. Hull Pottery Company, for a "Design for a Cookie Jar." Thus was born Hull's Little Red Riding Hood line. It was produced and distributed between 1943 and 1957.

Early cookie jars and the dresser jars with a large bow in the front can be identified by their creamy off-white color. The majority of the later pieces have very white pottery, a body attributed to The Royal China and Novelty Company, a division of Regal China. Given the similarity in form to items in Royal China and Novelty

Company's "Old McDonald's Farm" line, Hull possibly contracted with Royal China and Novelty for production as well as decoration.

Variations exist in many pieces, e.g., the wolf jar is found with bases in black, brown, red, or yellow. Prices for many pieces are in the hundreds of dollars. Prices for the advertising plaque and baby dish are in the thousands.

Undecorated blanks are commonly found. Value them between 25 and 50 percent less than decorated examples.

Club: Red Riding Hood!, P.O. Box 105, Amherst, NH 03031.

REPRODUCTION ALERT: Be alert for a Mexican produced cookie jar that closely resembles Hull's Little Red Riding Hood piece. The Mexican example is slightly shorter. Hull's examples measure 13" high.

Batter Pitcher, 5.5" h 250
Butter, cov 550
Canister 900
Cookie Jar, open basket, gold stars on apron 400
Creamer and Sugar, ruffled skirt 550
Creamer, spout on top of head 200
Grease Jar, Wolf 950
Jar, cov, basket in front, 8.5" h 450
Jar, cov, basket on side, 9" h 400
Match Box 900
Mustard Jar, 4.5" h 550
Milk Pitcher, 8" h 325
Salt and Pepper Shakers, pr, 3.5" h 65
Salt and Pepper Shakers, pr, 5.5" h 135
Spice Jar 200

Cookie Jar, 13" h, $375.

Teapot, cov 575
Vase 375
Wall Pocket 450

LITTLE TIKES

Thanks to Beanie Babies, collector interest in infant and juvenile toys is growing. Rubbermaid's Little Tikes' toys and playtime equipment are one of the beneficiaries.

Little Tikes sturdy products are made of heavy-gauge plastic. They have proven virtually indestructible, one of the reasons they frequently appear in the garage sale, recyclable market. In fact, most are bought to be reused rather than collected.

While you should not expect to find examples that look factory new, do not buy pieces that are deeply scratched or incomplete.

LLADRÓ PORCELAINS

Lladró porcelains are Spain's contribution to the world of collectible figures. Some figures are released on a limited edition basis; others remain in production for an extended period of time. Learn what kinds of production numbers are involved.

Lladró porcelains are sold through jewelry and "upscale" gift shops. However, they are the type of item you either love or hate. As a result, Lladró porcelains from estates or from individuals tired of dusting that thing that Aunt Millie gave for Christmas in 1985 do show up at flea markets.

Club: Lladró Collectors Society, 1 Lladró Dr., Moonachie, NJ 07074.

Note: All figurines are complete with original box unless otherwise noted.

Afternoon Tea, #1428, 1982-99, 14.25" h .100
Agressive Duck, #1288, 1974-96, 8.5" h . .200
Bridal Bell, #6200, 1995, 8.5" h 150
Caught in the Act, #6439, 1997, 8.5" h . . .115
Daddy's Girl, #5584, 1989-97, 8.5" h 150
Dalmatian, #1260, 1974 325
Debutante, #1431, 1982-99, 14" h 115

Destination Big Top, #6425, 1996, 8" h . .225
Dreams of a Summer Past, #6401, 1997,
 9.5" h 150
Fawn and a Friend, 1990-97, 6" h 250
Flapper, #5175, 1982-96, 13.25" h 140
Flower Harmony, #1418, 1982-96, 8.5" h .130
For a Perfect Performance, #7641,
 1995, 10.5" h 140
Fragrant Bouquet, #5862, 1992, 8" h 150
From My Garden, #1416, 1982-98, 10" h .175
Gift of Love, #5596, 1989-99, 9.75" h 225
Grand Dame, #1568, 1987, 14" h 200
Guest of Honor, #5877, 1992-97, 8.5" h . . .80
Hi There, #5672, 1990-98, 6" h 250
How Do You Do?, #1439, 1983, 4.5" h . . .110
I Love You Truly, #1528, 1987, 13.5" h . . .300
Jesse, #5129, with base, 1982, 12" h 175
Julia, #1361, 1978 275
Lady of Monaco, #6236, 1995, 14" h 100
Modern Mother, #5873, 1992-97, 11.5" h .140
My Flowers, #1284, 1974, 9" h 250
My Goodness, #1285, 1974-96, 9" h 150
Nature's Bounty, #1417, 1982 300
Nostalgia, #5071, 1980-94, 6.5" h 100
Over the Clouds, #5697, 1990, 8" h 90
Pensive Clown, #5130, with base, 1982,
 11" h 180
Refreshing Pause, #6330, 1996, 3" h 60
Rose Ballet, #5919, 1992, 8" l 100
Spring Flirtation, #6365, 1997, 12.5" h . . .150
Summer Serenade, #6193, 1995, 12.5" h .300
Swan and the Princess, #5705, 1990-95,
 no box 180
Tailor Made, #6489, 1997, 7.75" h 80
Teatime, #5470, 1998, 14.25" h 150
Teruko, #1451, 1983, 10.5" h 225
Windblown Girl, #4922, 1974, 14" h 150

Alice in Wonderland, #5740, 1991, $300.

LOCKS & PADLOCKS

Padlocks are the most desirable lock collectible. While examples date back to the 1600s, the mass production of identifiable padlocks was pioneered in America in the mid-1800s.

Padlocks are categorized primarily according to tradition or use: Combination, Pin Tumbler, Scandinavian, etc. Fakes and reproductions are a big problem. Among the trouble spots are screw key, trick, iron lever, and brass lever locks from the Middle East, railroad switch locks from Taiwan, and switch lock keys from the U.S. Midwest. All components of an old lock must have exactly the same color and finish. Authentic railroad, express, and logo locks will have only one user name or set of initials.

Club: American Lock Collectors Assoc., 36076 Grennada, Livonia, MI 48154.

Combination, Karco, steel, 3 dials, 3.25" .55
Combination, Uneek US and Foreign Pats
    Pending, nickel-plated steel, 2.50" 65
Gate, iron and brass, 10" 70
Pin Tumbler, Best, Phil Fuels Co, brass,
    logo lock, keyhole cover, 1.5" 18
Pin Tumbler, Fraim, brass, 3" 15
Pin Tumbler, Reese US, brass, 1.75" 5
Pin Tumbler, USA Ordinance Dept,
    Corbin, brass, logo lock, 2" 18
Pin Tumbler, Yale, brass, push key 15

Left: Story Padlock, Skull & Crossbones, emb cast iron, John Gerard patent, National Hardware Co, 3.25" h, $175. Right: Lever Push Key, Franklin 6-Lever, brass, 2.25" d, $25.

Pin Tumbler, Yale, iron, push key, brass
    hasp, 2" 10
Push Key, Champion, 4-lever, brass, 2" . .60
Push Key, Cyclone, 6-lever, brass, 2.5" . .70
Push Key, Eagle Lock Co, 3-lever, 1.625" .120
Push Key, SB Co, 8 lever, brass, 2.375" .160
Railroad, C&NW RY, Eagle, steel, 3.5" . . .25
Railroad, CSTPM & O, Fraim, iron, 2.25" .20
Railroad, Milwaukee, Leoffelhotz &
    Prier, brass, 2.5" 100
Railroad, MSTP & SSM RY, Adlake,
    brass, switch, 2.75" 125
Trunk, Eagle Lock Co 5

LONGABERGER BASKETS

Collectors of antique and vintage baskets will tell you that Longaberger baskets are vastly overrated. While not something a Longaberger basket collector wants to hear, they may regret not paying attention when the current speculative bubble bursts.

Dave Longaberger founded The Longaberger Company, based in Newark, Ohio, in 1973. While the company stresses a handmade, craft ancestry for its baskets, the fact is they are mass produced. The company sold 7.7 million baskets in 1997, an indication that scarcity is a word that will not be used to describe a Longaberger basket, even fifty years from now.

Internet sales, especially on eBay, are fueling Longaberger basket speculative prices. The key is the price realized for the fifth example offered, not the first, assuming it is lucky enough to receive an opening bid or meet reserve.

Newsletter: *The Basket Collector's Gazette,* P.O. Box 100, Pitkin, CO 81241.

All American, All-Star Trio Combo, 1993 . .60
All American, Carry Along Combo, 1996 . .60
All American, Patriot, liner and protec-
    tor, 1997 60
All American, Picnic Pal Combo, protec-
    tor, 1998 50
All American, Pie, liner and protector,
    1998 125
Bee Basket, Bee, 1993 100
Bee Basket, Bee, liner and protector,
    1996 150

Bee Basket, Bee Combo, 1996 120

Bee Basket, Bee, liner and protector,
1997 130

Bee Basket, Bee, liner and protector,
1998 100

Booking Basket, Ambrosia, liner and
protector, 1993 .55

Booking Basket, Ambrosia, liner and
protector, 1996 .60

Booking Basket, Thyme Combo,
Garden Splendor, 1997 40

Booking Basket, Thyme, protector, 1998 . .30

Christmas Collection, Bayberry Combo,
1993 80

Christmas Collection, Christmas Cranberry, red, protector, 1995 130

Christmas Collection, Holiday Cheer,
liner and protector, 1996 90

Christmas Collection, Jingle Bell,
green, 1994 100

Christmas Collection, Memory, green,
1989 90

Christmas Collection, Mistletoe, red,
1989 110

Christmas Collection, Season's Greetings, red, SU plaid liner, protector,
1992 120

Christmas Collection, Snowflake, liner
and protector, 1997 90

Classics Collection, small laundry basket with protector, 1998 175

Collector's Club, 25th Anniversary Flag,
protector, 1998 130

Collector's Club, 25th Anniversary Flag
Combo, SU liner, 1998 175

Collector's Club, Charter Membership
Combo, with box, 1996 110

Collector's Club, Harbor, protector, 1998 .100

Collector's Club, Harbor Combo, 1998 . .120

Collector's Club, Harbor Combo with
Lid, 1998 150

Collector's Club, Membership, liner,
protector, box, and product cards,
1997 100

Collector's Club, Serving Tray Combo,
with box, 1996 250

Collector's Club, Welcome Home, liner,
protector, box, and product cards,
1997 150

Easter Series, Blue Easter, protector,
1989 90

Easter Series, Easter Combo, small,
matching fabric lid, 1997 45

Feature Basket, Boo Combo, 1994 110

Feature Basket, Horizon of Hope
Combo, Heritage Green, 1996 50

Feature Basket, Spoon, medium, custom weave with protector, 1996 50

LUGGAGE

Until recently luggage collectors focused primarily on old steamship and railroad trunks. Unrestored, they sell in the $50 to $150 range. Dealers have the exterior refinished and the interior relined with new paper and then promptly sell them to decorators who charge up to $400. A restored trunk works well in both a Country or Victorian bedroom. This is why decorators love them so much.

Collector interest is growing in old leather luggage. It is not uncommon to find early twentieth century leather overnight bags priced at $150 to $300 in good condition. Leather suitcases sell in the $75 to $150 range.

LUNCH BOXES

Lunch kits, consisting of a lunch box and matching thermos, were the most price-manipulated collectibles category of the 1980s. Prices in excess of $2,500 were achieved for some of the early Disney examples. What everyone seemed to forget is that lunch boxes were mass-produced.

The lunch kit bubble has burst. Prices dropped for commonly found examples. A few dealers and collectors attempted to prop up the market, but their efforts failed. If you are buying, it will pay to shop around for the best price.

Buy lunch kits. Resist the temptation to buy the lunch box and thermos separately. I know this is a flea market price guide, but lunch kits can get pricy by the time they arrive at a flea market. The best buys remain at garage sales where the kits first hit the market and sellers are glad to get rid of them at any price.

Action Jackson, Ohio Art, metal, with
thermos, 1973 .175

All American, Universal, metal, with
thermos, 1966 115

Astronaut Space, Thermos, dome top,
with thermos, 1960 350

Beany and Cecil Lunch Kit, Thermos,
vinyl, with thermos, 1961 175

Boating, Thermos, metal, with thermos,
1959 200

Bond XX Secret Agent, Ohio Art, metal,
1966 85

Bozo, Aladdin, dome top, 1963 160

Buccaneer, Aladdin, dome top, 1961 ...185

Bullwinkle Lunch Kit, Thermos, vinyl,
with thermos, 1962 290

Campus Queen, Thermos, metal, with
game pieces, 1967 125

Captain Kangaroo, Thermos, vinyl, with
thermos, 1964 200

Cartoon Zoo Lunch Chest, Ohio Art,
metal, 1962 175

Casper the Friendly Ghost, Thermos,
vinyl, with thermos 375

Colonel Ed McCauley Space Explorer,
Aladdin, metal, with thermos, 1960 ..175

Fess Parker Kaboodle Kit, American
Tradition, vinyl, 1964 160

Flags of the United Nations, Universal,
metal, with thermos, 1954 200

Globe-Trotter, Aladdin, dome top, 1959 .115

Gomer Pyle USMC, Aladdin, metal,
with thermos, 1966 200

Great Wild West, Universal, metal, with
thermos, 1959 525

Hector Heathcote, Aladdin, metal, with
thermos, 1964 140

Hogan's Heroes, Aladdin, dome top,
with thermos, 1966 200

H R Puffnstuf, Aladdin, metal, with
thermos and sticker, 1970 275

James Bond Secret Agent 007, Aladdin,
metal, 1966 250

Jet Patrol, Aladdin, metal, with thermos,
1957 200

Junior Nurse Lunch Kit, Thermos, vinyl,
with thermos, 1963 110

Lance Link Secret Chimp, Thermos,
metal, 1971 175

Peanuts, Thermos, vinyl, with thermos,
1965 225

Pink Panther, Aladdin, vinyl, with
thermos, 1980 60

Porky's Lunch Wagon, Thermos, dome
top, with thermos, 1959 175

Psychedelic, Aladdin, dome top, with
thermos, 1969 90

Roy Rogers, Thermos, vinyl, 1960 115

Sabrina, Aladdin, vinyl, 1972 110

Scooby Doo, Thermos, metal, with
thermos, 1973 175

Smokey Bear, Thermos, metal, 1975 ...350

Soupy Sales, Thermos, vinyl, with
thermos, 1965 325

The Brady Bunch, Thermos, metal, with
thermos, 1970 115

The Flintstones and Dino, Aladdin,
metal, with thermos, 1962 350

The Flying Nun, Aladdin, with thermos,
1968 110

The Monkees, Thermos, vinyl, with
thermos, 1967 225

The Pussycats, Aladdin, vinyl, with
thermos, 1968 80

The Road Runner, Thermos, metal,
1970 70

The Wild Wild West, Aladdin, metal,
1969 175

The World of Barbie, Thermos, vinyl,
1971 30

The World of Dr Seuss, Aladdin, vinyl,
with thermos, 1970 350

Tom Corbett Space Cadet, Aladdin,
metal, with thermos, blue, 1952 175

Twiggy, Aladdin, vinyl, with thermos,
1967 175

Underdog, Ardee, vinyl, with thermos,
1972 575

Wonder Woman, Aladdin, with thermos,
1977 115

Yogi Bear, Aladdin, with thermos, 1961 .350

*Marvel Comics' Super Heroes, Aladdin,
metal, $75.*

MAD COLLECTIBLES

What kid from the 1960s doesn't remember Alfred E. Neuman and his zany, irreverant humor? Alfred is getting older, as are many of his fans, but items adorned with his unforgettable face are very collectible.

Balloon, "What Me Worry?", yellow,
   red print 5
Book, *Completely Mad,* first printing,
   hardcover, dj, 1991, 10 x 10" 40
Calendar, 1976, Warner Books 10
Costume, Collegeville, 1960, MIB 350
Figure, Alfred E Neuman, bisque, 5.5" . .350
Game, Mad Magazine Card Game,
   Parker Bros, 1980 20
Game, What Me Worry?, Parker Bros,
   1979 25
Magazine, *MAD,* #122, Oct 1968, re-
   called, Robert Kennedy cov 100
Matchcover, Dick's Coffeehouse,
   Ashland, NE 15
Mug, Alfred E Neuman, 1988, MIB 20
Pen, Spy vs Spy, Applause, 1988 10
Poster, Uncle Sam image of Alfred E
   Neuman, Pandora Productions, 29 x
   23" 100
Record, *A Mad Record,* 33 1/3 rpm,
   1960s 12
Stationery, "485 MADison Ave," no
   watermark, 1980-90 5

Paperback Book, Like MAD, *Signet #1838, William M. Gaines, cover art by Freas, $8.*

MAGAZINES

Most magazines, especially those less than forty years old, are worth between 10 cents and 25 cents. A fair number of pre-1960 magazines fall within this price range as well. There are three ways in which a magazine can have value: the cover artist, the cover personality, and framable interior advertising. In these instances, value rests not with the magazine collector, but with the speciality collectors.

At almost any flea market, you will find a seller of matted magazine advertisements. Remember that the value being asked almost always rests in the matting and not the individual magazine page.

Newsletter: *The Illustrator Collector's News,* P.O. Box 1958, Sequim, WA 98382.

Periodical: *Paper Collectors' Marketplace (PCM),* P.O. Box 128, Scandinavia, WI 54977.

American Home 2
Boy's Life, Aug 1957 15
Country Home 75
Etudes, 1940s 4
Good Housekeeping, 1942 2
Life, Aug 25, 1941, Fred Astaire 10
National Geographic, Oct 1909, North
   Pole 45
National Geographic, Aug 1963, Walt
   Disney 10

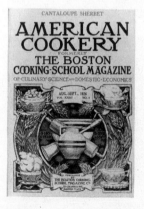

American Cookery, *Vol. XXXI, No. 2, Aug-Sep 1926, $3.*

Sports Illustrated, *Jul 17, 1972,* Olympic coverage from Munich, Germany, $5.

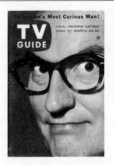

TV Guide, *Vol 4, No 12, Issue #156, Mar 24, 1956,* Dave Garroway cover, $10.

TV Times, *Aug 20-26, 1977, Alan Alda cover, $5.*

MAGIC COLLECTIBLES

Presto, chango—the world of magic has fascinated collectors for centuries. The category is broad; it pays to specialize. Possible approaches include children's magic sets, posters about magicians, or sleight-of-hand tricks.

When buying a trick, make certain to get instructions—if possible, the original. Without them, you need to be a mystic rather than a magician to figure out how the trick works.

Club: Magic Collectors Assoc, P.O. Box 511, Glenwood, IL 60425.

Newsletter: *Magic Set Collector's Newsletter,* P.O. Box 561, Novato, CA 94949.

Apparatus, Arab vase, brass, seems to levitate and mysteriously fill with water, with cork ball and levitating rope, 8.75" h, 5" d 160

Apparatus, billiard ball glass, brass-plated metal vase with spring push, missing lid, c1900, 5" h, 2.5" w 45

Apparatus, card box, nickel-plated metal, used for exchanging cards or making them disappear, Roterberg, c1900, 3 x 4.25 x .05" 110

Apparatus, cocktail shaker, removable cap and bottom panel, based on tea box substitution effect, Stull, 1935, 10.5" h, 3.5" d 115

Apparatus, disappearing wand, with orig paper covered and lined box, 2.5 x 15.25 x 1.25" box 115

Apparatus, foo can, chrome-plated, used to make liquids disappear and reappear, Burtini, 1947, 8" h, 5.5" d 45

Apparatus, goblets, set of 3, chrome-plated, used for moving small balls from one to another, Burtini, 1947, 4.75" h, 3" d 175

Apparatus, ticket changer, painted metal, red, early 20th C, 23" l 70

Apparatus, transformation box, cardboard covered with colored paper, used for transforming silks into doves, 1950, 3.5 x 4.75 x 4.25" 175

Book, *A Magician Among the Spirits,* Houdini, Harry, first edition, plates, cloth, NY, 1924, 5 x 7" 175

Book, *More Magic,* Professor Hoffman, illus, orig pictorial green cloth, ink stamped "De Vere," London, 1893, 5 x 7" 125

Book, *The Old and the New Magic,* Evans, Henry Ridgely, portrait frontispiece, orig pictorial cloth, first American edition, Chicago, 1906, 5 x 7" 175

Catalog, Max Andrew's "Vampire" Magic Catalogue, volumes 1 and 2, original wrappers, 1950s, 5 x 7" 110

Counter Display, "Blackstone/World's Greatest Magician," diecut, head of Blackstone looming over rectangular base, overprinted for Montreal performance at His Majesty's Theatre, 21.75 x 13.75" 275

Lobby Card, "Chasan Master Magician/smashing the Ghost Racket," red, blue, and black screenprint, ghost and skeleton cowering behind door, 1940-50s, 22 x 14" 115

Lobby Card, "Thurston/World's Famous Magician," color lithograph overprint for performance at Carolina Theatre, Durham, NC, Thurston with 2 red devils at his shoulders, Otis Litho Co, 1930s, 22 x 14" 300

Poster, "The Amazing Alma/On Stage," multicolored lithograph, nattily dressed magician levitating reclining woman while small red devil whispers in his ear, magic apparagus on table in background, c1915, 28.5 x 20" 350

Poster, "The Floyds/Unique Entertainers," color lithograph, oval portraits of Walter and Mary Floyd imposed on red ground, mkd "Boston: Libbie Show Print," c1915, 15 x 19.75" 200

MAGNIFYING GLASSES

The majority of magnifying glasses offered for sale at flea markets are made-up examples. Their handles come from old umbrellas, dresser sets, and even knives. They look old and are highly decorative—a deadly combination for someone who thinks he is getting an authentic antique. There are few collectors of magnifying glasses. Therefore, prices are low, often a few dollars or less, even for unusual examples. The most collectible magnifying glasses are the Sherlock Holmes type and examples from upscale desk accessory sets. These often exceed $25.

MARBLES

Marbles divide into handmade glass marbles and machine-made glass, clay, and mineral marbles. Marble identification is serious business. Read and re-read these books before buying your first marble: Paul Baumann, *Collecting Antique Marbles, Second Edition* (Wallace-Homestead, 1991) and Mark E. Randall and Dennis Webb, *Greenberg's Guide to Marbles* (Greenberg Publishing, 1988).

Children played with marbles. A large number are found in a damaged state. Avoid these. There are plenty of examples in excellent condition. Beware of reproductions and modern copycats and fakes. Comic marbles are just one of the types being reproduced.

Clubs: Marble Collectors' Unlimited, P.O. Box 206, Northborough, MA 01532; Marble

Collectors' Society of America, P.O. Box 222, Trumbull, CT 06611; National Marble Club of America, 440 Eaton Rd., Drexel Hill, PA 19026.

Handmade, end of day, onionskin 35
Handmade, Lutz, banded, 1" 250
Handmade, Lutz, end of day, onionskin, .75" 300
Handmade, mica, 1" 100
Handmade, sulphide, 1.25" 125
Handmade, swirl, banded, .75" 15
Handmade, swirl, peppermint, .625" 65
Machine-Made, Akro Agate, egg yolk and oxblood 60
Machine-Made, Akro Agate, lemonade corkscrew with oxblood 80
Machine-Made, Akro Agate, moonie, opalescent 3
Machine-Made, Akro Agate, Popeye corkscrew 25
Machine-Made, Akro Agate, sparkler . . .25
Machine-Made, Christensen Agate, cora 250
Machine-Made, Christensen Agate, green peewee 20
Machine-Made, Peltier, Christmas tree 60
Machine-Made, Peltier, comic, "Andy" .85
Machine-Made, submarine, cobalt blue, white, and brown swirls 175
Machine-Made, diaper folds, light green and orange opaque swirls 125
Machine-Made, Liberty 60
Machine-Made, Vitro Agate/Gladding-Vitro, blackie 50

Ribbon Swirl, red, white, and blue ribbon, yellow swirl ext, 2.5" d, $150.

MARILYN MONROE

In the 1940s a blonde bombshell exploded across the American movie screen. Born Norma Jean Mortonson in 1926, she made her debut in several magazines in the 1940s and in the movie *Scudda Hoo! Scudda Hey!* in 1948.

Now known as Marilyn Monroe, she captured the public eye with her flamboyant style and hourglass figure. Her roles in such films as *Bus Stop* and *Some Like It Hot* brought much attention to this glamour queen.

Marilyn's marriages to baseball hero Joe DiMaggio and famous playright Arthur Miller, not to mention her assorted illicit affairs with other famous gentlemen, served to keep her personal life on the front burner. It is commonly believed that the pressures of her personal life contributed to her untimely death on August 5, 1962.

Club: *Eternally Marilyn,* 3248 G South Holden Rd., Greensboro, NC 27407.

Calendar, 1954, "Golden Dreams/Posed by Marilyn Monroe," 9.5 x 15.5" 65
Limited Edition Plate, Forever, Marilyn, Milton H Greene: Up Close and Personal, 1997 .35
Limited Edition Plate, Graceful Beauty, Marilyn: The Golden Collection, M Deas, 1995 30

Sheet Music, Down In the Meadow, *from the movie* River of No Return, *c1954, $30.*

Limited Edition Plate, Marilyn Monroe/ *Seven-Year Itch,* Marilyn Monroe Collection, C Notarile, 1989 25
Limited Edition Plate, Opening Night 1954, Magic of Marilyn, C Notarile, 1992 . . .25
Magazine, *3D Movie,* Sep 1953, Vol 1, 8.5 x 10.75" 75
Magazine, *American Beauties,* Nov 1952, Vol 1, 52 pp, 9 x 11.75" 25
Magazine, *Man To Man,* May 1955, 8 x 10.5" 50
Magazine, *Movie World Magazine,* Jun 1955, "Earl Wilson says this is the new Marilyn" 30
Magazine, *People Today,* Dec 2, 1953, full color cover photo of Marilyn in red dress embracing column, 4 x 5.75" . . .45

MARX TOYS

The Marx Toy Company was founded after World War I when Louis and David Marx purchased a series of dies and molds from the bankrupt Strauss Toy Company. In the following years the Marx Toy Company produced a huge assortment of tin and plastic toys, including 60 to 80 playsets with hundreds of variations. These playsets, some with lithographed tin structures, are very collectible if complete. Marx also manufactured a number of windup and action toys like Rock-em Sock-em Robots and the very popular Big Wheel tricycle.

The company was bought and sold a number of times before filing for bankruptcy in 1980. The Quaker Oats Company owned Marx from the late 1950s until 1978, at which time it was sold to its final owner, the British toy company, Dunbee-Combex.

Bagatelle Game, Bazooka, plastic cover, litho tin playing surface, military type illus, 1950s, 6.5 x 12.5 x 1.75" 20
Bagatelle Game, Wild West, clear hard plastic cover, litho tin playing surface, firing mechanism launches ball bearings up and into separate plastic platform, wood boards with simulated bullet holes below, 1950s, 2.5 x 5 x 2" .20
Figure, 104 King's Knights, hard plastic, complete set, 1960s, 4 x 6.5 x 2.25" . . .25
Figure, Nutty Mads All Heart Hogan, soft plastic, red, 1963, 5.25" h 20

*Windup, milk wagon, litho tin, 1930s, 9.5" l,
$150.*

Figure, Treasure Island Pirate, soft
plastic, complete set of 6, 1960s,
3 x 9 x 1" box 35
Figure, Warriors of the World/Revolu-
tionary Soldiers, hard plastic, set of
6, 3" h, each in 2 x 3 x 1" box 60
Fix-All Wrecker Truck, hard plastic, red
and yellow, 4 storage compartments
in rear, complete with accessories,
1950s, 3.5 x 9 x 3.25" 40
Howitzer Cannon, hard plastic, complete
with 8 shells, 1950s, 5 x 12 x 5" box ...50
Irrigated Garden Set, Sears, 1960, 13.5
x 14 x 2" box 25
Jet Shot Repeater Airplane Water Pistol,
"Republic F-84 Thunderjet," hard plastic, 1950s, 9.5" l, 4 x 10 x 4" box 50
Playset, Army Training Center, litho tin,
complete with 6 soft plastic figures,
1950s, 7 x 11 x 6" 40
Playset, Super Circus, litho tin, complete, 1952, 11 x 28 x 3" box 175
Playset, The Untouchables, complete,
1961, 14.5 x 26.5 x 3" box 1,500
Ramp Walker, native on dinosaur, hard
plastic, 1960s, 3.75" l 35
Siren Signal Pistol, hard plastic, 1950s,
6.5" l, 3.5 x 7 x 2" box 50
Skin-Diver and Monsters of the Deep,
soft plastic figures and accessories,
1960s 50
Slot Car, hard plastic, #31, blue, red
and white accents, large exhaust
pipe attached to side, metal bars
attached behind drivers, 1960s,
2.25 x 6 x 2" 15
Thunderbird Car, friction, hard plastic,
Push and Go Toy series, 1950s, 2.25
x 5 x 1.5" 40

Train, Marx-Tronic Electric Train System,
hard plastic locomotive, 2 gondolas,
barrel loader with barrels, reversing
switch, flagman figure, track section
with double switch, 12 additional
track pieces, orig instruction sheet,
1960s, 9 x 20.5 x 3.5" box 35
Wheel of Chance, litho tin base with
attached number wheel, litho tin
wheel within clear plastic case,
"Midway/Wheel of Chance" with
circus theme illus, 1950s, 9 x 9 x
.25" base, 5 x 6.5 x 1" wheel 35
Windup, airplane, litho tin, 1930s, 7 x
8 x 3.5" box 250
Windup, Busy Miners, litho tin, car
travels up and down sloped track
between 2 buildings, 1930s, 2 x 16.5
x 4.25" 175
Windup, Charlie McCarthy, litho tin,
name repeated on car 4 times, "And
Edgar Bergen" on back, car spins in
circles as Charlie's head spins,
1930s, 3.5 x 7 x 6.5" 350
Windup, comical mailbox character,
hard plastic, tail spins as toy shakes,
©1969 D Dean, 3.25 x 4.5 x 6" 45
Windup, police cycle, litho tin, with
sidecar and litho tin policeman figure attached to handlebars, wooden
wheels, 1930s, 1.5 x 3.5 x 2.75" h 200
Windup, racer, litho tin car, plastic driver,
shield-shaped grille, exposed motor
with exhaust pipes, stylized wings on
rear, black rubber bumper attachment
on front, 1950s, 5.5 x 16.5 x .5" 275

*Windup, Strike Up The Band, Charlie
McCarthy, litho tin, $450.*

Windup, tractor, litho tin, rubber treads, $100.

Windup, Siren Fire Chief, litho tin,
   battery operated, 1930s, 5 x 15.5" 300

MARY GREGORY GLASS

Who was Mary Gregory anyway? Her
stuff certainly is expensive. Beware of
objects that seem like too much of a bargain. They may have been painted by Mary
Gregory's great-great granddaughter in the
1950s rather than in the 1880s. Also, watch
the eyes. The original Mary Gregory did not
paint children with slanted eyes.

Barber Bottle, blue, boy playing bugle,
   gold ring at neck and bottom, cut
   glass stopper, 10" h 150
Cruet, cranberry, silver enamel dec,
   maiden playing harp, 7" h, 3.5" w 175
Pitcher, green, child picking flowers,
   fluted, clear handle, 7.5" h 150
Plate, ruby, boy with rake and puppy,
   sgd "L Plues," Westmoreland type,
   8" d 35
Scent Bottle, cranberry, girl holding
   brush and paint palette, 6.75" h 85
Toothpick Holder, cranberry, Victorian
   girl pointing at woods, gold rim 160
Vase, amber, young girl and dragonfly,
   13.25" h 50
Vase, blue mist, boy flying kite,
   Westmoreland, 6.25" h 70
Vase, cobalt blue, cherubs and flowers,
   7.5" h, 3.25" w 100
Vase, pink ext, white int, boy with
   stick in hand and bag over shoulder,
   5.5" h 100

*Basket, scene of 3 children, metal frame
with raspberries and leaves at corners
and ornate feet, 9" h, 10" w, $275.* —Photo
courtesy Collectors Auction Services.

Vase, ruffled top, white enameled
   berries and leaves on cobalt blue
   ground, 9" h, 4.5" w, 3.75" d base 25
Water Set, pitcher and 4 tumblers,
   blue, girl and boy, 9" h 150

MATCHBOOKS

Don't play with matches. Save their
covers instead. A great collection can be
built for a relatively small sum of money.
Matchcover collectors gain a fair amount of
their new material through swapping. A few
collectors specialize in covers that include
figural shaped or decorated matches. If you
get into this, make certain you keep them
stored in a covered tin container and in a
cool location. If you don't, your collection
may go up in smoke.

Clubs: Casino Matchcover Collectors Club,
5001 Albridge Way, Mount Laurel, NJ 08054;
Rathkamp Matchcover Society, 432 N. Main
St., Urbana, OH 43078; The American
Matchcover Collecting Club, P.O. Box 18481,
Asheville, NC 28814. Note: There are over
thirty regional clubs throughout the United
States and Canada.

21 Club, 21 West 53nd St, NY, 1970s 2
American Airlines, "Largest Airline in
   the United States" on saddle, "Shell
   Aviation Products/Fly Safely with
   Shell" on front, red, white, and blue . .10

Atlanta Dairies, miniature carton 6

Bitucote Products, St Louis, MO, black
lettering on yellow ground 2

Buckeye Beer, bottle on back, waiter
on front, "The Buckeye Brewing Co.
Toledo, Ohio, Phone AD 7201" on
saddle, green, red, and white 5

Budweiser, back striker, "Budweiser
is for you" on front and back,
"Anheuser Busch Inc" on saddle,
red, white, and blue 5

Burlington Northern Railroad, "Burlington Northern" with logo on front and
back, blank saddle, green and white . .5

Bush, George, 30-strike, back striker,
"Bush for President," photo on front,
dated Nov 8, 1988 4

Coca-Cola, "Drink Coca-Cola" with
lollipop logo on front, "Drink Coca-
Cola"on saddle, "Take home a
Carton/Get That Refreshing New
Feeling" with 6-pack on back, yel-
low, red, green, and brown 10

Coon Chicken Inn, "Coon Chicken Inn,
2950 Highland Drive, Salt Lake City,
Phone 7-1062" on back, black bellhop on front, "Famous Coast to Coast"
on saddle, gold, red, black, white,
and pink 25

Crosley Refrigerators, "Only Crosley
Has The Shelvador" 8

Cotton Club Nightclub, "The World
Famous Cotton Club /Three Shows
Nightly /Never A Cover Charge/
Broadway at 48th Street" 12

Delta Air Lines, 30-strike, logo on front,
blank saddle, small jets on back,
red, white, and blue 8

Highway Service Station, Oakhall, VA 2

Indianapolis Motor Speedway, Haag's
Drug Store, c1930-40 3

International Trucks, 1940-50s, 3 x 1.75" . . .2

King George VI and Queen Elizabeth
Royal Visit to Canada, 1939, Eddy
Match Co 3

Kit Kat Club, Lion Match, "Kit Kat Club,
152 East 55th St, New York," with
black entertainers around name on
front and back, "Telephone Eld.
5-0543" on saddle, light green,
white, and black 15

Mammy's Chicken Farm, 30-strike,
back striker, "Mammy's" on footer,
"Black Mammy" on front and back,
"HI 5-4948" on saddle, "Fine Foods,
Cocktails, Capitol Drive at Teutonia,
Milwaukee"on back, map inside,
white, black, red, and yellow 15

Northwest Orient Airlines, tail of plane
on front, "Northwest Orient Airlines"
on saddle, "For Our Matchless
Friends" with logo and name on
back, red, white, and blue 5

Nixon/Agnew, 30-strike, "Nixon Agnew"
on front, red and white lettering,
elephant on back 10

Ozark Airlines, back striker, blank saddle, "We Make It Easy For You/Ozark
Airlines" on back, "Stop Lite" inside,
white, orange, and black 4

*Beachcomber, dancing zombie and drink
on display, Hawaiian dancer, shipwrecked
sailor, and monkey in palm tree across
sticks, $15.* —Photo courtesy Ray Morykan
Auctions.

*Flemington Glass Company, Lucky Sticks,
21 sticks each with card symbols for different poker hands, instructions inside
cover, Lion Match, $10.* —Photo courtesy
Ray Morykan Auctions.

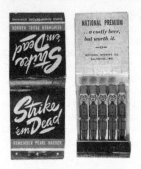

Strike 'em Dead, Remember Pearl Harbor, Japanese soldier on each stick, Feature Matchbook, Lion Match, $15. —Photo courtesy Ray Morykan Auctions.

Red Lion Inn, Hackensack, NJ, 21-feature, red lion logo on back, red lion logo across center 3 sticks, Lion Match 12

Reese's Peanut Butter Cups, "Reese's Peanut Butter Cups 1¢" on front, "H. B. Reese Candy Co, Hershey, PA" on saddle, box of candy on back, orange, green, white, and black 5

Schlitz Beer, front or back striker, "Schlitz, The Beer that made Milwaukee Famous" on front and back, blank saddle, brown, white, blue, and green 8

Southern Pacific Railroad, front or back striker, "Southern Pacific Streamlined Daylights" on front, blank saddle, Art Deco style train on back, yellow, red, green, white, and black 10

Stroh's, 30-strike, back striker, "Stroh's & Stroh's Light Official Beers 1982 World's Fair" on front, red, white, and blue 6

The Sands, Las Vegas, NV, "A Place In The Sun," Lion Match 5

Timken Roller Bearing Co, Canton, OH . . .8

Union Pacific Railroad, "Look, Listen and Live!/Safety First," "Avoid Crossing Accidents" on back 2

World's Fair, NY, 1939-40, "Don't Mark Time/4 Minute Crossings" 8

Yellow Cab, 1930-40s 2

MATCHBOX TOYS

Leslie Smith and Rodney Smith founded Lesney Products, an English company, in 1947. They produced the first Matchbox toys. In 1953 the trade name "Matchbox" was registered and the first diecast cars were made on a 1:75 scale. In 1979 Lesney produced over 5.5 million cars per week. In 1982 Universal International bought Lesney.

Clubs: American-International Matchbox Collectors & Exchange Club, 532 Chestnut St., Lynn, MA 01904; Matchbox Collectors Club, P.O. Box 977, Newfield, NJ 08344; The Matchbox International Collectors Assoc., P.O. Box 28072, Waterloo, Ontario N2L 6S8 Canada; Matchbox U.S.A., 62 Saw Mill Rd., Durham, CT 06422.

Aston Martin, #53-A, metallic light green, metal wheels, 1958 50

Austin Taxi Cab, #17-C, maroon, light gray int, gray plastic wheels, 1960 . . .65

Bedford Ambulance, #14-C, white, black plastic wheels, 1962 35

Bedford Low Loader, #27-B, light green cab, tan trailer, metal wheels, 1959 . . .75

Boat and Trailer, #9-D, bright blue deck, white hull, dark blue trailer, 1966 10

Caterpillar Bulldozer, #18-D, yellow, black plastic rollers, 1964 25

Caterpillar Tractor, #8-C, yellow, metal rollers, 1961 65

Chevrolet Impala, #57-B, metallic blue body, blue roof, silver plastic wheels, 1961 75

Cement Mixer, dark green body, unpainted wheels, 1948, Lesney 500

Ford Escort XR31 Cabriolet, #17-1, 1985, $4.

Caterpillar DW 20 Earth Scraper, #M-1-A, 1957, $25.

Covered Wagon, dark green body, white cover, brown horses, red barrels, Lesney, 1955 150

Daimler Ambulance, #14-B, cream, red cross decal on roof, metal wheels, 1956 65

Dodge Dumper Truck, #48-C, red, 1966 . .12

Dodge Stake Truck, #4-D, yellow cab, green stakes, 1967 10

Fiat 1500, #56-B, turquoise, brown luggage, black plastic wheels, 1965 . .15

Ford Cortina, #25-D, light brown, black plastic wheels, 1968 10

Ford Fairlane Station Wagon, #31-B, green, pink roof, red base, clear windows, silver plastic wheels, 1960 50

Ford Galaxie Police Car, #55-C, white, red dome light, black plastic wheels, 1966 35

Ford GT, #41-C, white, red wheels, #6 decal, 1965 300

Ford Refuse Truck, #7-C, orange, silver metal loader, gray plastic dump, 1966 . .10

GMC Tipper Truck, #26-C, red cab, green chassis, silver-gray dump, black plastic wheels, 1968 10

Hay Trailer, #40-C, blue, yellow stakes, black plastic tires, 1967 10

Horse Drawn Milk Float, #7-A, orange and white bottle load, metal wheels, 1954 75

John Deere Trailer, 51-B, green, black plastic wheels, 1964 20

Lincoln Continental, #31-C, metallic blue, black plastic wheels, 1964 15

London Trolley Bus, #56-A, red, metal wheels, 1958 65

Mercedes Trailer, #2-D, mint green, orange canopy, 1968 8

Mercury Police Car, #55-D, white, red dome light, black plastic tires, 1968 .250

Merryweather Marquis Fire Engine, #9-C, red, gold ladder, black plastic wheels, 1959 35

Pontiac Grand Prix Sports Coupe, #22-C, red, black plastic wheels, 1964 20

Road Tanker, #11-A, yellow, metal wheels, 1955 100

Refrigerator Truck, #44-C, red, turquoise container, black plastic wheels, 1967 .12

Rolls Royce Phantom V, 44-B, metallic tan, black plastic wheels, 1964 20

Volkswagen Microvan, #34-A, blue, metal wheels, 1957 75

MCCOY POTTERY

The Nelson McCoy Sanitary Stoneware Company was founded in 1910. Early production consisted of crocks, churns, and jugs. Pieces were marked with an "M" above a stenciled clover within a shield.

Molded artware was introduced in the mid-1920s; cookware, dinnerware, floral industry ware, gardenware, kitchenware, and tableware followed a decade later.

McCoy pottery is attractive and sought after by collectors unwilling to pay the prices commanded by Roseville and Weller pottery.

Newsletter: *The NM Xpress,* 8934 Brecksville Rd., Brecksville, OH 44141.

Bank, clown 25

Bank, Ernie the Keebler Elf, 9.5" h 45

Batter Bowl, blue and pink stripes, 8 x 4.5" 18

Lazy Susan, avocado and butterscotch, $35.
—Photo courtesy Ray Morykan Auctions.

Bud Vase, yellow rose, mkd "USA 1115,"
   5" h 15
Cookie Jar, chef with spoon, 10" h 25
Cookie Jar, Little Bo Peep 135
Cookie Jar, mammy, 11" h 40
Cookie Jar, owl, mkd "204 USA," 10.5" h ..10
Cookie Jar, rooster, 11" h 80
Cookie Jar, smiley face, 11.5" h 25
Cookie Jar, touring car 30
Cookie Jar, turkey 100
Ewer, emb cherries, brown, cream,
   and green, 9" h 18
Flowerpot, pale yellow, 3.5" h 10
Jardiniere, Pinecone, 6.5" h 35
Nesting Bowl Set, pink and blue striped,
   8", 7" and 6" d 30
Pitcher, grapes, green, 8.375" h 35
Planter, baby bootie, pink, 3" h 10
Planter, bamboo flowerpot, mkd "325
   USA," 4" h 10
Planter, bird bath, yellow and green,
   6" h 25
Planter, boot, 5" h 12
Planter, doe and fawn, 6.5 x 6" 15
Planter, lemon and leaf, 7 x 3.5" 60
Planter, pheasant, 7.25 x 3.25 x 2.5" 30
Planter, Scottie dogs, 7.5 x 4" 30
Planter, spinning wheel with cat and
   Scottie dog 12
Strawberry Planter, green and brown,
   #3021, 6.5" h 8
Vase, butterfly, yellow, 8 x 4.25" 25
Vase, Cabbage Rose, 8.25" h 70
Vase, double tulip, green and yellow 55
Vase, Floraline, seafoam green, 7.5 x 4" .10
Vase, tulip, 8 x 7" 65
Wall Pocket, daisy, 6" h 30
Wall Pocket, white lily, 7.5" h 85

MEDICAL ITEMS

   Anything medical is collectible. Doctors often discard instruments, never realizing that the minute an object becomes obsolete, it also becomes collectible. Many a flea market treasure began life in a garbage can. Stress condition and completeness. Specialize in one area. Remember some instruments do not display well.

Club: Medical Collectors Assoc., Montefiore Medical Park, 1695A Eastchester Rd., Bronx, NY 10461.

Newsletter: *Scientific, Medical & Mechanical Antiques,* P.O. Box 412, Taneytown, MD 21787.

Advertising Trade Card, Hood's Sarsaparilla, mother owl holding box of
   sarsaparilla on branch with 2 off-
   spring, "Food for the Wise..." 15
Aspiration Set, cherry wood case,
   complete with syringe, in-out nozzle,
   receptical cap with turnkey, hypo-
   dermic needles and tubing, c1880,
   12 x 4 x 11.5" 115
Baby Scale, white wicker basket,
   wooden base, white enameled base,
   c1930 50
Box, Grants Hygienic Crackers, c1930s ..8
Catalog, Bausch & Lomb Microscope,
   pocket folder, 8 panels, illus, c1905 ...15
Catalog, Spencer Dissecting Instruments,
   19 pp, Spencer Lens Co, c1920 15
Exploring Needle, cylinder serves as
   handle and holder for screw-ended
   needle, explores tumors and
   removes specimens, c1860-80 75
Eye Speculum, with retaining spring
   and lock, Bowmans, c1890 65
Eyelid Plate, hard rubber, flared ends,
   Jaeger, c1890 35
Hot Water Bottle, ceramic, c1880-1900,
   10" l 65
Leech Jar, flint glass, molded, c1850-70,
   6 x 6.5" 40
Medicine Case, black leather, with 6
   labeled vials, c1890 50

Almanac, Swamp-Root Almanac, Dream Book, *Dr. Kilmer & Co, Binghamton, NY, 32 pp, 8.25 x 5.5", $10.*

Medicine Bottle, clear glass, cork stopper, 5.25" h, $7.

Monaural Stethoscope, turned hard-
  wood, light brown, chestpiece
  removable from earpiece, inserts in
  side hole for carrying, 1800s 210
Pamphlet, What Is Chiropractic?, 71 pp,
  AMA, Chicago, 1920s 15
Quack Gadget, Thermocap, metal top,
  orig blue bulb, adjustable brown
  lower cardboard-type material
  allows fitting to head, Allied Merke
  Institutes, Inc, NY 225
Syringe, hard rubber, emb "I. R. Comb
  Goodyear 1861" 55
Tongue Depressor, ivory, c1820-60, 8" l ..50
Vaporizer, Vapo-Cresolene, gilt stand
  lamp, milk glass chimney, pan, and
  box, c1875 100

MELMAC

Durable Melmac dinnerware was all
the rage in the late 1960s and early 1970s.
Children could finally be assigned the chore
of washing the dishes without fear of loss
and breakage. Despite its claims of being
indestructable, continued dishwasher
washing takes its toll. If you plan to use the
Melmac you collect you'll have to revert to
hand washing.

Aztec, cup and saucer, mustard yellow ..4
Boonton, mixing bowl, pastel yellow 15
Boonton, serving bowl, cov, pink 25
Boonton Belle, cereal bowl, pink 5
Boontonware, cup and saucer,
  turquoise 10
Branchell, ashtray, mkd "Kay La Moyne"
  turquoise 10

Branchell, St Louis, MO, serving bowl,
  charcoal 10
Branchell Color-Flyte, bread and butter
  plate, coppertone 3
Branchell Color-Flyte, creamer, conical
  handles, chartreuse 8
Brookpark, Joan Luntz Modern Design,
  creamer, pink 6
Brookpark, Joan Luntz Modern Design,
  cup and saucer, black 8
Capac, creamer, pink 3
Flintwood, wine carafe, white and gold
  swirl 25
Florence, Prolon, dinner plate, lacquer
  red 8
Florence, Prolon, soup bowl, Chinese
  red 8
Holiday, Kenro, bowl, yellow, red
  specks 4
Imperial Ware, serving bowl, rect, pink,
  blue specks 6
Lifetime Translucent, water pitcher,
  light blue 25
Lucent, J & I Block Corp, dinner plate,
  translucent 8
Mallo-Ware, bowl, tab handle, pink 3
Meladur, Russel Wright, serving bowl,
  divided, yellow 20
Monterey Melmac, cup and saucer,
  brick red 4
Oneida, child's plate, white, Hanna-
  Barbera characters, 1964 15
Oneida Premiere, gravy boat with
  underplate, harvest gold 6
Residential, Russel Wright, berry bowl,
  sea mist 10

Vacron, Bopp-Decker Plastics, beverage set, 9.25" h pitcher and 4 tumblers, $45.

Residential, Russel Wright, butter, cov,
  salmon red 25
Residential, Russel Wright, serving
  bowl, divided, yellow 20
Rubbermaid, butter, cov, pink 10
Spaulding Ware, creamer, red 4
Talk of the Town, creamer, burgundy 6
Texas Ware, Plastic Mfg Co, mixing
  bowl, marbelized 15
Watertown, butter, cov, turquoise 15
Watertown, soup bowl, tab handle,
  brick red 6

METLOX

In 1921 T. C. Prouty and Willis, his son, founded Proutyline Products, a company designed to develop Prouty's various inventions. Metlox (a contraction of metallic oxide) was established in 1927. The company began producing a line of solid color dinnerware similar to that produced by Bauer. In 1934 the line was fully developed and sold under the Poppytrail trademark. New patterns were regularly introduced.

When Vernon Kilns ceased operations in 1958, Metlox bought the trade name and select dinnerware molds, establishing a separate Vernon Ware branch. This line rivaled the Poppytrail patterns.

Between 1946 and 1956 Metlox made a series of ceramic cartoon characters under license from Walt Disney. A line of planters and Poppets were marketed in the 1960s and 1970s. Recent production includes novelty cookie jars and Colorstax, a revival solid color dinnerware pattern. The company ceased operations in 1989.

California Ivy, bowl, divided, 11.25" d 30
California Ivy, cereal bowl, 6" d 14
California Ivy, creamer 20
California Ivy, dinner bowl, 10.25" d 12
California Ivy, fruit bowl, 5.25" d 12
California Ivy, gravy boat 35
California Ivy, jam and jelly relish 35
California Ivy, pitcher, 2.5 qt 65
California Ivy, salad bowl, 11.25" d 60
California Ivy, salt and pepper shakers,
  pr 25
California Ivy, sugar, cov 25
California Ivy, tumbler, 13 oz 25
California Ivy, vegetable bowl, 9" d 35
California Provincial, canister set, 3 pc .300
California Strawberry, bowl, 8.125" d 25
California Strawberry, bowl, 9" d 30
California Strawberry, butter, cov 40
California Strawberry, coffeepot 65
California Strawberry, gravy boat 25
California Strawberry, platter, 9.5" l 20
California Strawberry, platter, 11" l 25
California Strawberry, platter, 13" l 30
California Strawberry, salad bowl 50
California Strawberry, salad fork and
  spoon 40
California Strawberry, salad plate, 8" d . . .8
California Strawberry, salt and pepper
  shakers, pr 18
California Strawberry, soup bowl,
  6.75" d 12
California Strawberry, teapot 75
California Strawberry, vegetable bowl,
  cov, 1.25 qt 50
California Strawberry, vegetable bowl,
  cov, 2 qt 60
Ivy, bowl, 5" d 10
Ivy, bowl, 7" d 15
Ivy, vegetable bowl 20

California Strawberry, dinner plate, $10.

Red Rooster, dinner plate, $15.

Red Rooster, bread server 85
Red Rooster, canister set 275
Red Rooster, casserole, hen, small 55
Red Rooster, coffee carafe 110
Red Rooster, coffeepot 115
Red Rooster, cookie jar 75
Red Rooster, cruet set, 5 pc 200
Red Rooster, jug 80
Red Rooster, platter, 22" l 200
Red Rooster, salad bowl, 11" d 75
Red Rooster, teapot 145

MEXICAN COLLECTIBLES

Within the past year there has been a growing interest in Mexican jewelry. In fact, several new books have been published about the subject. Mexican pottery and textiles are also attracting collector attention. At the moment, buy only high-quality, handmade products. Because of their brilliant colors, Mexican collectibles accent almost any room setting. This is an area to watch.

MILITARIA

Soldiers have returned home with the spoils of war as long as there have been soldiers and wars. Many collectors tend to collect material relating to wars taking place in their young adulthood or related to re-enactment groups to which they belong.

It pays to specialize. The two obvious choices are a specific war or piece of equipment. Never underestimate the enemy. Nazi material remains the strongest segment of the market.

Reproductions abound. Be especially careful of any Civil War and Nazi material.

Clubs: American Society of Military Insignia Collectors, 526 Lafayette Ave., Palmerton, PA 18071; Assoc. of American Military Uniform Collectors, P.O. Box 1876, Elyria, OH 44036; Company of Military Historians, North Main St., Westbrook, CT 06498; Order & Medals Society of America, P.O. Box 484, Glassboro, NJ 08028.

Periodicals: *Militaria International,* Box 43400, Minneapolis, MN 55443; *Military Trader,* P.O. Box 1050, Dubuque, IA 52004;

North South Trader's Civil War, PO Drawer 631, Orange, VA 22960.

Armband, "US Army Air Force AWS Observer," blue felt, stitch insignia with gold stitched wings and title in gold, 4.5 x 16.5" 45
Aviator Map, WWII, silk-like fabric, "Eastern Asia" printed on both sides, detailed maps and villages plus flight routes and technical data, 1943, 6.5 x 6.5" folded size 60
Bank, white metal, dark bronze luster, bust portrait of Gen MacArthur, name incised on front, Milwaukee Avenue National Bank of Chicago, Ashland Division & Milwaukee, 2.25 x 3 x 5.75" 40
Banner, "Welcome Home," son in service, cloth, red, white, and blue, gold fringe, wooden rod, gold cord hanger, 9 x 13" 35
Blotter, "America's Finest Planes P-47 Republic Thunderbolt Army Fighter," Bond Bread premium, blue, plane image with loaf of bread on orange ground, unused, 3.5 x 6.5" 12
Book, *A Guide to US Army Insignia and Decorations,* brown, hardcover, red, white, and blue insignia on front cover corners, 62 pp, Whitman, #748, 1941, 3.5 x 5.5" 20
Bottle Stopper, figural, Gen MacArthur, brown composition head with gold accent hat, red mouth, gray accent hair, 2.25 x 2.75 x 3.75" 20

Child's Book, Allied Bomber and Fighter Aircraft of To-Day, *Series A151, pub by Offset Printing Ccy. Pty. Ltd., Sydney, Australia, c1947, 16 pp, 9.5 x 7.25", $16.*

Bank, General Eisenhower bust, cast white metal, Banthrico, 1940s, 5.5" h, $50.

Certificate, "Domain of the Golden Dragon Ruler of the 188th Meridian," green sea serpents around sides intertwined with sexy nude blondes with text "To All Sailors, Soldiers, Marines," issued for servicemen who have crossed international date line, ©1944 Lloyd Wooford, San Francisco, CA, 8.75 x 11.75" .... .25

Drinking Glass, clear, full inscription "Protect Our Shores," color decal depicting sailor and girlfriend embracing, reverse image shows blown skirt of girlfriend revealing upper thighs, 4.75" h, 2.5" d .... .30

Folder, leather, dark brown with gold eagle and text "United States Navy," sunburst accent and plane at top and bottom center edge, 7.25 x 8.5" ..... .20

Greeting Card, "Happy Birthday Soldier," diecut soldier on front wearing baggy uniform with "Happy Birthday Soldier! You're 1-A," opens to reveal smiling soldier wearing well-fitting uniform winking and "You're A-1 and You're 1-derful!," 4 x 5.125" .... .20

Hat, diecut cardboard, red, white, and blue, "V For Victory" on 1 side, large silver foil "V" stapled at left side, 3 x 11.5" .... .35

Magazine, *Time,* General Eisenhower cover, Sep 13, 1943, 108 pp, 8.25 x 11.5" .... .20

Magazine, *War Planes,* Dell Publishing, 34 pp, "Latest Fighting Planes of All Nations," 1942, 8.25 x 11" .... .20

Manual, Air Force, "Aircraft Recognition For the Ground Observer," silver accent bomber on front, 172 pp, #355-10, issued Apr 1955, 6.5 x 9.75" .. .30

Matchcover, "Ground Observer Corps," blue, silver accent relief text "Ground Observer Corps Civilian Auxiliary, United States Air Force Austinburg, Ohio, For the Time For Air Defense Is Now For America's Safety-Match Your Neighbors Hours Join The Ground Observer Corps" with wings logo, 1.5 x 4.5" .... .12

Mechanical Pencil, celluloid, white barrel inscribed with blue "V" and "Let US not forget Pearl Harbor," mkd "Falcon" on pencil clip, 5.25" l ...... .60

Noisemaker, litho tin, "Buy Defense Bonds," red wooden handle, American flag in center, eagle landing at left near Capitol building, Statue of Liberty on right, Mattel, 1951, 3.25 x 8.375 x .75" .... .35

Pin, enamel, "US Naval Service," red, white, and blue, gold accent anchors in center, .375 x .625" .... .15

Pinback Button, "Boycott Nazi Germany," cream and dark red litho, "Join Boycott Council," 1" d .... .40

Pinback Button, "Not A Nazi," cream and dark blue litho, 1" d .... .25

Pinback Button, "Out of Cambodia, Vietnam...All S E Asia!," black and white, gray outlines of various countries with text "Mass Action Memorial Day 1970," 1.75" d .... .20

Postcard, "Interior of Patton Museum showing War Trophies," full color, shows arillery, photo of Patton, Nazi flag, and other trophies in museum in Ft Knox, KY, 1940s, 3.5 x 5.5" ...... .30

Civil War Flag, cloth, 31 x 22", $440.
—Photo courtesy Collectors Auction Services.

Postcard, "Keep 'Em In Action-On Land, Sea, and in the Air," black and white photo, ships and tanks firing artillery, fighter planes, troops, truck convoys, Official Photographs US Army and Navy, Graycraft Co, Danville, VA, unused, 3.5 x 5.5" 15

Poster, "Buy War Bonds/Third War Loan," #54951, sobbing youngster wearing his dad's war medal while holding officer's cap, Victor Keppel art, 1943, 20 x 28" 45

Ribbon Badge, WWI, "Marshal Foch" cloth rosette suspending red, white, and blue individual ribbons, red ribbon inscribed in gold "Reception" and blue with gold "Committee," celluloid stick-pin depicts US and French flags plus inscription "Marshal Foch Entertainment Committee" 10

Sticker, "WAAC Women's Army Auxillary Corps US Army," brown center profile image of woman wearing Roman battle helmet, yellow ground with white stripes, black and white text on blue ground, 2 x 3" 20

MILK BOTTLES

There is an entire generation of young adults to whom the concept of milk in a bottle is a foreign idea. In another ten years we will need to include a chapter on plastic milk cartons. I hope you are saving some.

When buying a bottle, make certain the glass is clear of defects and the label and wording in fine or better condition. Buy odd sized bottles and those with special features. Don't forget the caps. They are collectible too.

Club: National Assoc. of Milk Bottle Collectors, Inc., 4 Ox Bow Rd., Westport, CT 06880.

Amador Goat Dairy, Glendale, AZ, square, maroon pyro, ribbed neck, 1 qt 30
Brookfield Dairy, Hellertown, PA, round, emb, 1/2 pt 40
Carnation Fresh Milk, Carnation Co, square, amber pyro, 1 qt 45
Clover Leaf, Stockton, CA, round, orange pyro, cream top, 1 qt 30

Colonial Dairies, Albany, GA, Golden Guernsey, emb, 1 pt 20
Coronet Gold Standard Milk, square, red pyro, 1 qt 20
Curly's Dairy, Salem, OR, round, green and brown pyro, Dutch Boy illus 65
Diamond's Cafeteria, round, emb, 1/2 pt .20
E C Earl Dairy Farm, Edward P Dubricki, Kalamazoo, MI, emb, 1 qt 30
East Greenwich Dairy Store, round, orange pyro, 1 qt 20
Fort Lewis A&M College, Hesperus, CO, round, red pyro, 1 pt 75
F W White Lone Pine, round, red pyro, 1 qt 25
G Rico, Cortez, CO, round, etched, 1/2 pt 10
Geo G Gillingham, Meadow Brook Park, Alexandria, VA, emb, 1 pt 25
Hall's Dairy, Millerstown, PA, round, maroon pyro, 1 qt 20
Heiss & Sons Dairy, Rochelle Park, NJ, round, orange pyro, barn scene, 1 qt .20
Highview Farms Dairy, Norwichtown, square, red pyro 25
Hollywood Dairy, Durango, CO, round, emb, 1/2 pt 35
Indian Hill Farm Dairy, Greenville, ME, round, orange pyro, 1 qt 20
Jarosz Milk Co, Chicago, IL, emb, pt 20
Kane Dairy Co-Operative Assoc, emb, 1 qt 30

Left: "Bangor Sanitary Dairy, Bangor, PA," emb lettering, 1/2 pt, $12. Right: Elsie the Cow, bank, "Save for a Rainy Day," 4.5" h, $25. —Photo courtesy Ray Morykan Auctions.

Landgren's Dairy, Kenosha, WI, square,
red pyro, cream top, 1 qt 40
Lantz's Dairy Pasteurized Milk, St Clairs-
ville, OH, round, 1 pt 75
Lippincott's Dairy Products, E Rochester,
OH, round, red pyro, 1 pt 65
Lobdell's Dairy Inc, Fairfield, CT, square,
gold pyro, 1 qt 20
Maplecrest, Maynard, square, green
pyro, 1 qt 15
Miller's Dairy, Frank B Miller, Watkins
Glen, NY, round, red pyro, 1 qt 35
Model Dairy, Corry, PA, round, green
pyro 30
Mortensen's Creamery, round, red pyro,
1 qt 30
Mountain Home Creamery, Lakeport,
CA, round, yellow pyro, 1 qt 35
Newsom's Pride Dairy, Albany, GA,
"Grade A, Milk and Cream, Phone
1729J," black pyro, 1 pt 20
Orofino Creamery Co, Orofino, ID, round,
red pyro, 1 qt 90
Parker's, Nichols, CT, square, orange
pyro, 1 qt 25
Pine Grove Dairy, Skaneateles, NY,
round, green and orange pyro, 1 qt ...25
Pleasant Dairy, Lewiston, ME, square,
red and yellow pyro, 1 qt 20
Putnam's Dairy, Ilion, NY, round, maroon
pyro, horse, wagon, and milkman, 1 qt .25
Raw Goat Milk, Earth-Bound Foods,
Glen Road, Sandy Hook, CT, orange
front, brown back 25
Ray's Crystal Dairy, NYC, round, maroon
pyro, 1 qt 20
Rosendahl Guernsey Farms, Hoosick
Falls, NY, J E Calhoun & Sons, round,
orange pyro, cow scene, 1 qt 20
Schwent Dairy, Southampton, LI, round,
maroon pyro, 1 qt 20
Sistersville Dairy, Sistersville, WV, emb,
1 pt 25
Snider's Grade Milk, Medford, OR, round,
black pyro 30
Southern Vermont 50th Anniversary
1945-1995, Dairy Goat Assoc, Inc,
Route 9, Marlboro, VT, square, 6 goat
heads on front, house on rear, green
pyro, 1 qt 30
Spencer Farms, Hiram, OH, emb, 1/2 pt ..10
Spurlin, Carlsbad, NM, square, orange
pyro, 1 pt 15

Upton's Farm, Bridgewater, MA, round,
black pyro, 1 pt 75
Valley Bell Ice Cream, round, red pyro,
1/2 pt 12
Wana Dairy Farms, Turner Wescott,
Wauregan Dairy, W T Burn's, round,
red and black pyro, cream top 75
Willow Farms, Frizellburg, MD, square,
maroon pyro, cream top, 1 qt 25

MILK GLASS

Milk glass is an opaque white glass that became popular during the Victorian era. A scientist will tell you that it is made by adding oxide of tin to a batch of clear glass.

Companies like Atterbury, McKee, and Westmoreland have all produced fine examples in novelties, often of the souvenir variety, as well as household items. Old timers focus heavily on milk glass made before 1920. However, there are some great pieces from the post-1920 period that you would be wise not to overlook.

Milk glass has remained in continuous production since it was first invented. Many firms reproduce old patterns. Be careful. Watch out for a "K" in a diamond. This is the mark on milk glass reproductions from the 1960s made by the Kemple Glass Company.

Club: National Milk Glass Collectors Society, 46 Almond Dr., Hershey, PA 17033.

Note: Items listed are white unless otherwise noted.

Bowl, Westmoreland, Paneled Grape, 11.25" l, $50. —Photo courtesy Ray Morykan Auctions.

Bowl, cov, Fostoria, Randolph, 1950s,
9.75 x 8.25" 35
Bowl, Westmoreland, Maple Leaf,
10" d 65
Cake Stand, Indiana, 1960s, 6.75" h,
10.375"sq 10
Candleholders, pr, Anchor Hocking,
ball edge, 1960s 8
Candlesticks, pr, dolphin, Westmoreland,
9.25" h 70
Compote, cov, Atterbury, basketweave,
c1880s, 10.25" h, 8" d 85
Covered Dish, cabbage, Portieux, blue . .40
Covered Dish, cat, Westmoreland, white
head, blue body, white wide ribbed
base, 5.5" l 45
Covered Dish, fish, Vallerysthal, blue . .425
Creamer and Sugar, Imperial, Grape,
3-toed, 1960s .25
Custard, McKee, yellow 170
Eggcup, Westmoreland, chick, 3.5" h 15
Figure, deer, reclining, Fostoria 38
Figure, jumping horse, Kemple 65
Fruit Bowl, Fostoria, Monroe, 1960s,
10.625" d 25
Honey Jar, Imperial, beehive shape,
4.875" h 35
Jar, cov, Scottie dog, pink 45
Jug, Fenton, #3965, squat 40
Match Safe, Bible, blue 25
Mayonnaise Liner, Fenton, #3803, 6" 10
Nappy, Vallerysthal, 3-toed, handled,
blue 30
Plate, Fenton, #3816, crimped edge,
8.25" d 20
Salt and Pepper Shakers, pr, Fenton,
#3806 15
Salt and Pepper Shakers, pr, Imperial,
Quilted, with basket holder, 1950s 30

*Miniature Lamp,
Pineapple in a
Basket pattern,
green dec, $325.*

*Perfume Bottle,
Carlton, clear
ruffled neck, gold
ribs, rose motif,
clear fluted stopper,
#4188, 7.25" h, $80.*

Toothpick Holder, Vallerysthal, boy with
basket, blue 70
Tumbler, Fenton, #3945, 5 oz 10
Vase, Imperial, Grape, lamp shaped,
1950s, 7.25" h 20

MODEL KITS

Manufacturers such as Aurora,
Horizon, and Revell/Monogram, produce
detailed model kits that let the builder's
imagination run wild.

Most model kits are packed in a cardboard box with an image of the model on
the surface. Pieces are snapped or glued
together. Painting and decoration is up to
the assembler. Model kits are produced
from plastic, resin, or vinyl, often requiring a
bit of dexterity and patience to assemble.

Buying model kits at flea markets
should be done with a degree of caution. An
open box spells trouble. Look for missing
pieces or lost instructions. Sealed boxes
are your best bet, but even these should be
questioned because of the availability of
home shrink wrap kits. Don't be afraid—
inquire about a model's completeness
before purchasing it.

Clubs: Kit Collectors International, P.O. Box
38, Stanton, CA 90680; Society for the
Preservation and Encouragement of Scale
Model Kit Collecting, 3213 Hardy Dr.,
Edmond, OK 73013.

3-D Scenic Sea Lab Kit, Eldon, 1970s,
12 x 23.5 x 3" box 20
'32 Skid-Doo, Aurora, 1963, 4 x 10.5 x
1.5" box 15
Alien, MPC, ©1970 20th Century Fox
Film Corp, 6.5 x 10 x 3" box 50

Astronaut In Space, Revell, 1969, 6.25 x
    10.25 x .5" 20
Batplane, Aurora, 10.5 x 14 x 3" h 50
BSA Lightning Rocket Motorcycle, Pyro
    Plastics Corp, 1966, 4.5 x 8 x 3" box . . .15
Columbia And Space Lab, Revell, 1980s,
    9.5 x 14.5 x 2.25" box 15
Cunard Line *RMS Queen Mary*, Revell,
    1962, 7.5 x 22 x 2" box 12
Dracula, Aurora, 1962, 4.5 x 7.5 x 8.25" h .35
Dracula's Dragster, Aurora, ©1964
    Universal Pictures Co, Inc, 5.25 x 13 x
    2.25" box 275
Ed "Big Daddy" Roth's Dragnut, Revell,
    1963, 6 x 9.5 x 2" box 85
Farrah's Foxy Vette, AMT, 1970s, 6 x 9.5
    x 3.75 " box 35
Ford '36 3-Window Coupe, Pyro Plastics
    Corp, 1950s, 4 x 8 x 2" box 8
Frankenstein, Aurora, ©1961 Universal
    Pictures Co, Inc, 3 x 8 x 9.75" 45
Fred Flintstone's Rock Cruncher, AMT,
    ©1974 Hanna-Barbera Productions,
    Inc, 5.5 x 7.5 x 3.5" box 15
Ghost of the Red Baron, Monogram,
    1969, 6.5 x 9.25 x 3.25" box 35
Glo-Monster/Terror, Lindbergh, glow-in-
    the-dark, 1971, 4.5 x 5.5 x 1.25" box . . .20
Human Skeleton, Renwal, glow-in-the-
    dark, 1950s, 10 x 17.25 x 1.25" 15
Indy 500 Winner Special Race Car, AMT,
    1960s, 4 x 8 x 2" box 8
Intrepid Civil War Balloon, AMT, 1970s,
    8.5 x 10 x 3" box 15
King Kong, Aurora, 1964, 6 x 8 x 9.5" h . . .50
Land of the Giants, Aurora, ©1968 20th
    Century Fox Television, Inc, 7 x 13 x
    2.5" box 175
Laurel & Hardy '25 T Roadster, AMT,
    1970s Larry Harmon Pictures Corp,
    6 x 9.25 x 4" box 35

1930 Ford Yellow Jacket, Monogram,
#PC-76, 1962, $75.

1963 Ford Galaxie Convertible, promotional
model, champagne color, 8.25" l, $150.

Madam Tussaud's Chamber of Horrors
    La Guillotine, Aurora, 1964, 2 x 9 x
    9.5" h 75
Mr Hyde/Monsters of the Movies,
    Aurora, 1975, 4.75 x 7.75 x 3" box 50
Pepsi Skateboard Van, Revell, 1979,
    9.5 x 13.5 x 4.25" 15
Phantom and Voo Doo Witch Doctor,
    Revell, ©1965 King Features Syndi-
    cate Inc, 8.25" h phantom, 7" h witch
    doctor 50
Phantom of the Opera, Aurora, 1963,
    4 x 5.5 x 1.25" h 65
Robin the Boy Wonder, Aurora, ©1966
    National Periodical Publications, Inc,
    4 x 5.5 x 8" h 50
Science Educator Kit/Neanderthal Man,
    Ringo Toy Corp, 1967, 8.5 x 15 x 1.75"
    box 12
Six Million Dollar Man Evil Rider, MPC,
    ©1975 Universal City Studios, Inc,
    6.25 x 9.25 x 3.5" box 15
Space Shuttle Challenger, Revell, 1980s,
    9.5 x 14.5 x 2.25" box 15
Superboy and Krypto, Aurora, 1965,
    5.5 x 9 x 6.5" h .65
Superman, Aurora, 1964, 5.5 x 8 x
    8.25" h 45
The Bionic Woman Bionic Repair, MPC,
    1976, 6.5 x 9.25 x 3.25" 15
The Creature, Aurora, 1963, 7 x 7 x 8" h . .50
The Forgotten Prisoner of Castle-Mare,
    Aurora, 1966, 4 x 4.5 x 8.5" h 60
The Frog, Aurora, 1966, 7 x 8 x 7.25" h . . .50
The Hunchback of Notre Dame, Aurora,
    1963, 5 x 5 x 6.25" h 35
The Incredible Hulk, Aurora, 4.5 x 6.5 x
    3.75" 50
The Strange Changing Vampire, MPC,
    1970s, 7 x 10 x 3" box 15

Walt Disney's Haunted Mansion/Grave Robber's Reward, MPC, ©1974 Walt Disney Productions, 8.25 x 11 x 3" box 40

Walt Disney's Haunted Mansion/The Vampire's Midnight Madness, MPC, ©1974 Walt Disney Productions, 8 x 11 x 3" box 35

Weird-Ohs Sling Rave "Curvette" the Way Out Spectator, Hawk Model Co, 1964, 4.5 x 9 x 1" box 30

World War II Japanese Medium Tank, Aurora, 1964, 5.25 x 13 x 1.5" box 15

MONSTERS

Collecting monster related material began in the late 1980s as a generation looked back nostalgically on the monster television shows of the 1960s and horror movies of the 1960s and 1970s. Fueling the fire was a group of Japanese collectors who were raiding the American market for material relating to Japanese monster epics featuring reptile monsters such as Godzilla, Rodan, and Mothra. This spurred a collecting revival for Frankenstein, King Kong, and the Mummy.

While an excellent collection of two-dimensional material, e.g., comic books, magazines, posters, etc., can be assembled, stress three-dimensional material. Several other crazes, e.g., model kit collecting, cross over into monster collecting, thus adding to price confusion.

Club: Munsters & The Addams Family Fan Club, P.O. Box 69A04, West Hollywood, CA 90069.

Newsletter: *Dark Shadows Collectables Classifieds,* 6173 Iroquois Trail, Mentor, OH 44060.

Addams Family, bank, The Thing, battery operated, box opens and green hand reaches out to grab coin 25

Addams Family, comic book, The Addams Family Comic Book, Hanna-Barbera, 1975 4

Addams Family, doll, Morticia, soft vinyl head, hard plastic body, Filmways TV productions, Inc, 1964, 5" h 40

Addams Family, game, The Addams Family Card Game, Milton Bradley, 1964 10

Addams Family, model kit, Addams Family Haunted House, glow-in-the-dark, Polar Lights 15

Addams Family, paperback book, *Addams and Evil,* Charles Addams, Pocket Cardinal 3

Addams Family, record, 45 rpm, *Addams Family Theme/Uncle Fester's Blues,* Hector Records 2783 20

Creature From the Black Lagoon, movie still, black and white, 8 x 10" 55

Creature From the Black Lagoon, trading card, Comic Monsters series, 1970-80 .2

Creature From the Black Lagoon, wind-up, litho tin, Japan 60

Dark Shadows, autograph, Frid, Jonathan, PS, waist-up, color, Frid as Barnabas Collins, gold ink signature, 8 x 10" 35

Dark Shadows, Barnabas Collins Dark Shadows Game, Milton Bradley, 1969 .50

Dark Shadows, comic book, Gold Key, #15, 1972 8

Dracula, lobby card, *Brides of Dracula,* 1960, 11 x 14" 35

Dark Shadows, magazine, *Who's Who in Daytime TV, #3,* 4 pp article, Jonathan Frid on back cover, 1969 ...20

Dracula, photo, Bela Lugosi as Dracula, black and white, 8 x 10" 6

Dracula, playbill, starring Frank Langella at the Martin Becky Theatre, NY, 1978 .3

Elvira, model kit, Elvira, Mistress of the Dark...Macabre Mobile, Monogram, 1988, 1/24 scale 10

Frankenstein, figure, Universal Monsters series, Hasbro, 12" h 15

Godzilla, model kit, Aurora #149, 1964, $425.

Frankenstein, soaky bottle, Colgate-Palmolive, 1965, $90.

Frankenstein, magazine, *Castle of Frankenstein Monster Annual Fearbook,* 1967 10

Frankenstein, photo, *Frankenstein Meets the Wolfman,* sgd by Jane Adams, black and white, 8 x 10" 15

Godzilla, lobby card, Bandai, 1985, price for set of 24 25

Godzilla, micro figure, Rodan, 1956 6

Godzilla, model kit, Godzilla vs King Kong, Billiken Models, Japan 35

Hunchback of Notre Dame, blotter, Lon Chaney, pictorial scene 40

Karloff, Boris, magazine, *Famous Monsters of Filmland,* #121, Dec 1975 6

King Kong, figure, soft plastic, with removable 1.25" woman figure, Palmer Plastics, 1960s, 3" h 35

King Kong, magazine, *London Illustrated News,* May 13, 1933, 2 pp article on making of *King Kong,* photos and illus 250

King Kong, movie still, black and white, Jessica Lange, from *King Kong,* Paramount Pictures, 1976, 8 x 10" 10

Mummy, pinback button, "Remember Mummy's Day" 12

Munsters, autograph, Yvonne DeCarlo, PS, as Lily Munster, black and white, black ink signature, 8 x 10" 50

Munsters, hand puppet, Mattel, 1964 ...45

Munsters, model kit, Drag-U-La, AMT, #905-170, 1964, 1/25 scale 75

Munsters, paperback book, *The Munsters and the Great Camera Caper,* Whitman, 1965 6

Munsters, paper dolls, Whitman, 1966 ..20

Phantom of the Opera, pin, Lon Chaney, United States Post Office "Classic Monster Stamps" promo 2

Wolfman, pencil topper, plastic head, brown, white and red accents, mkd "Hong Kong" 1.25" h 10

MORTON POTTERIES

Morton is an example of a regional pottery that has a national collecting base. Actually, there were several potteries in Morton, Illinois: Morton Pottery Works and Morton Earthenware Company, 1897–1917; Cliftwood Art Potteries, 1920–1940; Midwest Potteries, 1940–1944; and, Morton Pottery Company, 1922–1976.

Prior to 1940 local clay was used and fired to a golden ecru. After 1940 clay was imported and fired white. Few pieces are marked. The key to identifying Morton pieces is through the company's catalogs and Doris and Burdell Hall's books, *Morton's Potteries: 99 Years,* (published by the authors, 1982), and *Morton Potteries Vol. 2,* (L-W Book Sales, 1995).

American Art Potteries, figure, rearing horse, 11.5" h 30

American Art Potteries, figure, squirrel, 5.5" h 15

American Art Potteries, flower frog, tufted titmouse, 8" h 15

American Art Potteries, planter, quail, 9.5" h 25

American Art Potteries, planter, swan, 10.25" h 20

Cliftwood Art Potteries, boudoir lamp, cobalt blue, orig maroon felt base, 6" h, 8.5" h to top of fixture 15

Cliftwood Art Potteries, clock, donut shape, green, Lux Clock Works, Waterbury, CT, 8.5" h 75

Cliftwood Art Potteries, figure, cat, cobalt blue, 5.75" h 30

Cliftwood Art Potteries, grease jar, orchid and pink drip over white 20

Cliftwood Art Potteries, pretzel jar, barrel shape 50

Cliftwood Art Potteries, sweetmeat bowl, turquoise and pink drip over white ...20

Cliftwood Art Potteries, wall pocket, tree trunk, 8" h 70

Midwest Potteries, figure, Afghan dog, 7.25" l 30

Midwest Potteries, figure, crane, $25.

Midwest Potteries, figure, cowboy on
bucking bronco, black, gold highlights,
7.5" h 25
Midwest Potteries, figure, deer, 12" h . . .35
Midwest Potteries, figure, Irish setter,
4" h, 8" l 30
Midwest Potteries, planter, duck,
5.75" h 10
Morton Pottery Co, ashtray, Rival Crock-
Pot, 5.625" l, 3.875" w 40
Morton Pottery Co, ashtray, Statler Hotel,
5.25" d 10
Morton Pottery Co, bank, kitten, white,
yellow stripes .15
Morton Pottery Co, eagle, light brown
and white, 6" h, 3.75 x 3.25" base 30
Morton Pottery Co, bookends, pr, parrot,
rose, yellow, green, and blue over
white 25
Morton Pottery Co, cookie jar, olive
green, mkd "USA-3539," 11.5" h 15
Morton Pottery Co, creamer, hp rooster
on black ground, 5.5 x 4.5 x 2.75" 20
Morton Pottery Co, flower holder, woman
with jug 10
Morton Pottery Co, match holder, Statler
Hotel, 5.25" d 10
Morton Pottery Co, planter, bulldog, light
green, 3.75 x 3.75", price for pair 10
Morton Pottery Co, planter, camel, black
eyes, red mouth and nose, 3" h, 4.5" l .10
Morton Pottery Co, planter, old woman
in shoe, 6" h, 6.5" l 5
Morton Pottery Co, wall pocket, nesting
love birds, green leaf dec, 6.75" h,
4.25" w 10
Morton Pottery Co, wall pocket, peacock,
blue 15

MOTHER'S DAY COLLECTIBLES

It's not fair. The amount of Mother's
Day memorabilia is about ten times that of
Father's Day memorabilia. It has something
to do with apple pie. A great deal of the
Mother's Day memorabilia seen at flea markets is "limited edition." The fact that you
see so much is an indication that few of
these issues were truly limited. Insist on
excellent or better condition and the original box when buying.

Since so many collectors are focusing
on limited edition material, why not direct
your efforts in another direction, for example, greeting cards or pinback buttons. Your
costs will be lower, and your collection will
be one of a kind, just like your mother.

Limited Edition Figurine, A Song for
Mother, Hamilton Collection, W Henry,
1997 20
Limited Edition Figurine, horse, Noritake,
Mother's Day 1975, 3.5" h, 5" l 50
Limited Edition Figurine, Mother's Angel,
G Armani, 1997 175
Limited Edition Plate, A Tender Moment,
Rockwell Museum, N Rockwell, 1982 .70
Limited Edition Plate, Canada Geese,
Fleetwood Collection, D Balke, 1983 . .50
Limited Edition Plate, Just Like Mother,
Avondale, F Taylor Williams, 1984 75
Limited Edition Plate, Mother's Day, Count
Agazzi, 1972 35

*Limited Edition Plate, Cat and Kitten,
Mother's Day series, Bing and Grøndahl,
1971, $12.*

Limited Edition Plate, Special Memories,
 Tom Newsom, Creation of Love, 1985 . .8
Limited Edition Ornament, Stitched With
 Love, Carlton Cards, 1993 12
Pinback Button, "Anna Jarvis Founder,
 Philadelphia, Mother's Day" with
 carnation, multicolored, 7.5" d 3
Pinback Button, "Mother, May, 2nd
 Sunday, Mothers Day," carnation
 behind heart, red and white, 1.25" d . . .5
Pinback Button, mother and infant, single
 white carnation on green stem, 1920s .8
Pinback Button, religious icon of mother
 and son, c1920s 5

MOTION LAMPS

Motion lamps feature a scene that lights and gives the illusion of motion. They first appeared in the 1920s and are still produced today, but their popularity peaked in the 1950s. Early lamps were constructed of metal and glass, while later lamps were primarily plastic. All feature some type of rotating cylinder that spins from the power of the heat produced by the bulb.

Early lamps used a complex system of animation sleeves to produce sophisticated motions like water running, wheels turning, or fire blazing. Today's motion lamps use simple colorful cylinders whose moving images project onto the surface of an outer shade. Besides scenic lamps, psychedelic, advertising, and figural lamps are among others that are collectible.

Note: Values listed below are for complete lamps in very good condition that are free of cracks, dents, and scratches, and have good color. Perfect or restored examples will be more valuable.

Asian Scene, L A Goodman, brass base,
 1957 200
Bar Is Open, 1950s-60s, 11" h 35
Bathing Beauties, L A Goodman, Bake-
 lite base 275
Beacon Light Lighthouse, National Lamp
 Co, 1930s 300
Butterflies, Econolite, 1954 175
Christmas Tree, Econolite, blue, 1948-52,
 10" h 100

Church and Mill Snow Scene, Econolite,
 1957 200
Circus, blue enamel base, 1940s-50s,
 11" h 170
Don't Drink the Water, Lacolite, 1971 . . .100
Elbe River Stream, Germany, 8" h 130
Forest Fire, Econolite, 1955 150
Forest Fire, Roto Vue Jr, Econolite, 1949,
 10" h 90
Fountain of Youth, Econolite, 1950 150
Fountain of Youth, Roto Vue Jr, Econolite,
 1950, 10" h 100
Hopalong Cassidy Camp Fire, Roto Vue
 Jr, Econolite, 1950, 10" h 350
Japanese Twilight, National Lamp Co,
 1930s 225
Lighthouse, L A Goodman, 1956 210
Molson's Keg, adv, 1950s, wooden keg
 base, train and ship on shade, 1950s .115
Mountain Waterfall, L A Goodman,
 1956 140
Niagara Falls, Econolite, brass base,
 1955 125
Niagara Falls, Lacolite, 1970s 65
Niagara Falls, National Lamp Co, wood
 and gesso frame, 1930s, 12" h 200
Niagara Falls, Scene In Action Corp,
 9.25" h 150
Ocean and Fish, pleated cylinder 40
Old Mill, Econolite, 1956 125
Psychedelic, Visual Effects, 1970s 90
Sailing Ships *Old Ironsides, Mayflower,*
 and *Windjammer,* Econolite, 1958 . . .175
Seagram's 7, adv, 1970s, 14" h 80
Ship and Lighthouse, L A Goodman,
 1956 100
Trains, Econolite, 1956 200
Village Blacksmith, Gritt Lamp Co,
 1920s, 12" h .210

*Hopalong
Cassidy Bar-20
Ranch,
Econolite, red
plastic shade
and base, $350.*

MOTORCYCLE COLLECTIBLES

Motorcycles are generational. My father would identify with an Indian, my son with the Japanese imports, and I with a Harley.

Some of these beauties are as expensive as classic and antique cars. If you see a 1916 Indian Power Plus with sidecar for a thousand or less, pick it up. It books at around $15,000.

Do not overlook motorcycle related items.

Clubs: American Motorcyclist Assoc., 13515 Yarmouth Dr., Pickerington, OH 43147; Antique Motorcycle Club of America, P.O. Box 300, Sweetser, IN 46987.

Periodicals: *Motorcycle Shopper Magazine,* 1353 Herndon Ave., Deltona, FL 32725; *Old Bike Journal,* 6 Prowitt St., Norwalk, CT 06855.

Advertising Tear Sheet, "Express Yourself...Suzuki '69," 2 men on motorcycles with inset motorcycle image and text, 8 x 11" 4

Catalog, Spare Parts For Harley-Davidson Motorcycles and Sidecars, 1930-1933 Models, Aug 1, 1932, 84 pp, 9.25" h, 6.25" w 20

Engine, Harley-Davidson, serial #56G1933, 1956 475

Knife Clip, chromed metal, "Buffalo Harley-Davidson," swing-out blade at top, fingernail blade at bottom, gold luster inset with red sponsor name and black buffalo silhouette . . .45

Catalog, Guaranteed Motorcycle Supplies, illus, 1916, 10.5 x 7.5", $165. —Photo courtesy Collectors Auction Services.

Trophy, metal with wood base, American Motorcycle Assoc. logo on plate, 14.5" h, $5. —Photo courtesy Collectors Auction Services.

License Plate, British Columbia, dealer's, 5 x 8" 8

License Plate, Idaho, 1967 20

Pin, brass, "Coventry Eagle," flying eagle holding streamer, red porcelain enamel accent 50

Pin, brass, "Lea Bridge Speedway/ Supporters Club," figural wings above circle center image of motorcyclist against black and white checkered ground, Birmingham, England, 1930s .60

Pin, brass, "Harley-Davidson 50 Years," brass, c1954 50

Pin, silvered brass, figural laughing head Indian Motorcycles, 1920-30s, .875" h .50

Pin, silvered brass, figural tank with red incised "Davidson," c1941, 1" l 50

Pinback Button, Indian Motorcycles, center profile head portrait, "Hendee Mfg Co, Springfield, Mass." rim inscription, 1920-30s .50

Postcard, "Be Not Afraid," BMW Motorcycles promo, white lettering, BMW logo 1

Poster, model sitting on vintage Harley-Davidson, 34 x 22" 5

Record Book, vinyl, Indian Motorcycle Co, Springfield, MA, contains maintenance hints, sidecar pointers, speed table, and information about Indian Motorcycles, 1929-30, 4.25" h, 2.75" w 100

Tab, diecut brass, figural wings with "Davidson," blue enamel accent, 1920s 20

Trophy, metal and wood, American Motorcycle Association logo on slide-out plate, 14.5" h, 3.5" w 5

MOVIE MEMORABILIA

The stars of the silent screen have fascinated audiences for over three-quarters of a century. In many cases, this fascination had as much to do with their private lives as their on-screen performances.

This is a category where individuals focus on their favorites. There are superstars in the collectibles area. Two examples are Charlie Chaplin and Marilyn Monroe.

Posters are expensive. However, there are plenty of other categories where a major collection can be built for under $25 per object. Also, do not overlook present-day material. If it's cheap, pick it up. Movie material will always be collectible.

Club: The Manuscript Society, 350 N. Niagara St., Burbank, CA 91505.

Periodicals: *Big Reel,* P.O. Box 1050, Dubuque, IA 52004; *Movie Advertising Collector,* P.O. Box 28587, Philadelphia, PA 19149; *Movie Collector's World,* Box 309, Fraser, MI 48026.

Book, *Shirley Temple Treasury,* Random House, 206 pp, 1959, 8.5 x 11.25" 20
Checkerboard, *Follow the Fleet,* RKO pictures promo, litho paper over cardboard, starring Fred Astaire and Ginger Rogers, black and white montage of 9 film scenes on 1 side, red and black checkers playing board with "It's Your Move To Start Telling Your Public About" on reverse, 1936, 9 x 10.5" 90

Lobby Card, A Very Special Favor, *Rock Hudson, Leslie Caron, Charles Boyer, color, 11 x 14", $25.*

Arcade Card, John Mack Brown, greentone, 1950s, 3.25 x 5.25", $12.

Comic Book, Helen of Troy, Dell, #684, 1956 Warner Bros 40
Dish, white china, center color portrait image of Jay Smith, tan rim, underside stamped gold signature "Hal Roach/ Our Gang/The Sebring Pottery Co," 1930s, 5.25" d 75
Game, The Singing Bone Movie Adventure Game, Hasbro, from *The Wonderful World of the Brothers Grimm,* MGM, 1962, 1.5 x 8.5 x 16.5" box 20
Lobby Card, *Korea Patrol,* Jack Schwarz Productions, Pathe Industries, full color, 1951, 11 x 14", price for set of 8 40
Lobby Card, *Lad, A Dog,* Warner Bros, full color, 1962, 11 x 14" 10
Lobby Card, *My Little Chickadee,* Universal Pictures, starring W C Fields and Mae West, 1940, 11 x 14" 20
Lobby Card, *Underground,* Warner Bros, full color, 1941, 11 x 14", price for set of 3 40
Magazine, *Modern Movies Hollywood Exposed,* 1975 8
Magazine, *Movie Story,* 1945 10
Magazine, *Movie Time Magazine,* Grace Kelly on cover, 1955 5
Magazine, *Silver Screen,* 1972 3
Movie Book, *The Poor Little Rich Girl,* Saalfield, 32 pp, 27 black and white movie scenes, 9.5 x 10" 25
Movie Herald, "James Cagney in *Great Guy,*" 2-sided, color scenes of Cagney with Mae Clarke, 8 x 10.375" 12
Movie Poster, *Old Yeller,* starring Dorothy McGuire and Fess Parker, 1957, 27 x 40" 8
Movie Poster, *The Thrill of It All,* Doris Day and James Garner, 30 x 13" 10

Movie Poster, The Belle of New York, *Fred Astaire, Vera Ellen, 1952, $500.*
—Photo courtesy Collectors Auction Services.

Movie Poster, *Who's Minding the Store,* starring Jerry Lewis and Jill St John, 30 x 13" 20

Movie Script, *Invaders From Mars,* orig screenplay by John Tucker Battle, dated "9-5-50" 50

Movie Still, Bob Hope and Signe Hasso in scene from *Where There's Life,* ©1947 Paramount Pictures, 8 x 10" ...15

Paper Dolls, Shirley Temple Dolls and Dresses, Saalfield, 1938, 11 x 12.5" ..175

Photograph, Dean Martin and Jerry Lewis, browntone image of smiling Martin and Lewis, white facsimile signatures, Paramount Pictures, 1953, 8 x 10" 12

Photograph, Hedy Lamarr, sepiatone, pensive looking Lamarr with hand at forehead looking off to right, 1938, 11 x 14" 20

Pinback Button, *Blazing Saddles,* 1974, 3" d 15

Pinback Button, "*Chicago Times* Shirley Temple Club," litho tin, dark blue and white with bluetone photo, 1930s 95

Pinback Button, "Mickey Rooney as Young Tom Edison/King of the Movies," bluetone photo and lettering on light blue ground with "921," 1.25" d 15

Pinback Button, "Spanky Hal Roach Our Gang," redtone photo on red ground, 1930s, .875" d 25

Playing Cards, The Brown Derby, complete deck of 52 plus 2 Jokers, back design of sepia 5-photo montage of int and ext views, 1940-50s, .75 x 4 x 5.25" box 15

Program, *Seven Wonders of the World,* 24 pp, c1950s, 9 x 12" 15

Program, *The Old Man and the Sea,* Warner Bros, starring Spencer Tracy, 16 pp, center full color and monotone stills, 1958, 9 x 12" 20

Ruler, *The Nutty Professor,* white plastic, black and white Jerry Lewis caricature, 1963, 1.5 x 12" 25

Sheet Music, *Sweetheart of Mine,* full color Mary Pickford illus, lower right facsimile signature "My official song, Sincerely Mary Pickford," 1914, 10.5 x 13.5" 15

Window Card, *The Big Mouth,* Columbia Pictures, starring Jerry Lewis, 1967, 14 x 22" 35

Window Card, *The Ugly American,* Universal Pictures, starring Marlon Brando, 1963, 14 x 22" 15

MUGS

The problem with every general price guide is that it does not cover the broad sweeping form categories, e.g., wash pitchers and bowls, any longer. A surprising number of individuals still collect this way.

If you stay away from beer mugs, you can find a lot of examples in this category for under $10. Look for the unusual, either in form or labeling. Don't forget to fill one now and then and toast your cleverness in collecting these treasures.

Club: Advertising Cup and Mug Collectors of America, P.O. Box 680, Solon, IA 52333.

A & W Root Beer, emb, 3.125" h 3

A & W Root Beer, Mama Burger, special edition, 3.25" h 3

A & W Root Beer, orange and brown oval logo, 4.25" h 3

Air Force, pewter, wings on front and inscription "1968-1972" 5

Budweiser, lizards and "We could've been huge!," 16 oz, 1991 Anheuser-Busch Inc, 6" h 3

Coca-Cola, World of Coca-Cola, Las Vegas, silver metallic, 5.5" h 8

Coors Light, dog racing, clear, 5.5" h 6

Dad's Root Beer, barrel shaped, emb, 5.25" h 8

Pan-American Expo, stoneware, emb dec, imp "Whites Pottery Utica, N.Y.," 5" h, $140. —Photo courtesy Collectors Auction Services.

Dayton Hudson, aviator Santa Bear and Mrs Bear, 1987 5
Dunkin Donuts, "The Big One," 3.25" h . .10
Fred Flintstone, Canada Wonderland, milk glass 2
Freestate Raceway at Laurel–Breeders Crown, ceramic 5
Garfield, "Here's to you, and here's to me, here's to health and herbal tea," Enesco, 3.75" h .3
Happy Birthday, milk glass, balloons and clown face, Pyrex 5
McDonald's, Mac Tonight on each side, clear, emb 90
McDonald's, New London & Waupaca, WI, clear, arches, 5.5" h 26
Mighty Ducks, metallic emblem, 5.875" h .5
New York Region Sports Car Club of America, "Renault LeCar Grande Fanale, Lime Rock, Oct. 15, '77" 8
Outhouse, mkd "Rumph Pottery 1973," 5.5" h 25
Pepsi, Mickey Through the Years–The Mickey Mouse Club, milk glass 4
Pinocchio, Pinocchio on front, information on movie on back 15
Pluto, glass, 5.5" h 4
Star Wars, Obi-Wan Kenobi, Rumph Pottery, 1977 60

MUSICAL INSTRUMENTS

Didn't you just love music lessons? Still play your clarinet or trumpet? Probably not! Yet, I bet you still have the instrument. Why is it that you can never seem to throw it out?

The number of antique and classic musical instrument collectors is small, but growing. Actually, most instruments are sold for reuse. As a result, the key is playability. Check out the cost of renting an instrument or purchasing one new. Now you know why prices on "used" instruments are so high. Fifty dollars for a playable instrument of any quality is a bargain price. Of course, it's a bargain only if someone needs and wants to play it. Otherwise, it is fifty dollars ill-spent.

Clubs: American Musical Instrument Society, RD 3 Box 205-B, Franklin, PA 16323; Automatic Musical Instrument Collectors Assoc., 2150 Hastings Court, Santa Rosa, CA 95405; Miniature Piano Enthusiast Club, 633 Pennsylvania Ave., Hagerstown, MD 21740.

Periodicals: *20th Century Guitar,* 135 Oser Ave., Hauppauge, NY 11788; *Vintage Guitar Classics,* P.O. Box 7301, Bismarck, ND 58507.

Note: See Harmonicas for more listings.

Advertising Tear Sheet, Gibson Mandolin-Guitar Co, 1915, 6.5 x 9.75" 5
Advertising Tear Sheet, The Randolph Wurlitzer Co, Feb 1920, "All musical instruments with complete outfits free trial," 12 x 7" 3
Book, *Old Musical Instruments Pleasures and Treasures,* Rene Clemencic, G P Putnam's Sons, NY, printed in Germany, 120 pp, full color illus, hard cov, 1968, 8.25 x 8.5" 9
Book, *Picture Book of Musical Instruments,* Marion Lacey, Lothrop, Lee & Shepard Co, 1942, 11.25 x 8.5" . . .4
Catalog, F E Olds & son, 17 pp, custom built brass instruments, 1941, 7.5 x 10.25" 7
Catalog, Fender Musical Instruments, 45 pp, color illus, 5 x 4" 15
Fife, English, boxwood, 5 brass keys with round covers, ivory fittings, 11.75" l . .315
Flute, unmkd, bamboo, pierce-carved holes, 16.5" l 60
Guitar, Favilla Guitars, Inc, style C-5 overture, mahogany body and neck, rosewood fingerboard, labeled "Made in U.S.A. Est. 1890 Original Herk Favilla Ser. No. 126862," with case, 19" l 145
Guitar Pick, Bob Dylan 1992 world tour logo on 1 side, reverse with "It ain't me babe B.D.," white print on tortoise ground 30
Maracas, wood, hp dec, 11" h, 3" d 10

Piano Rolls, for player piano, $5 each.

Oboe, Austrian, H Schuck, Vienna, maple, stamped "H. Schuck Wien," 2 silver keys with square covers, c1900, 22" l 575

Tenor Recorder, German, labeled with decal "Johannes Adler," 1 brass key, modern, 24.25" l 45

Token, obverse with bust of Handel and "Handel Instruments Tun'd & Lent To Hire," reverse with lyre and "Dodd's Cheap Shop for Musical Instruments New Street Covent Garden," 1790s, half-penny size 25

Tom Drum, Ludwig, stamped "Jul 11 1967," 12" 45

Traverse Flute, unmkd, blackwood, nickeled keys and fittings, 26" l 200

NAPCO

David Rein, Irwin Garber, and a Mr. Payner established the National Potteries Corporation (NAPCO) in 1939. Initially, it was an importer and manufacturer of floral containers. NAPCO ended its manufacturing operations after World War II.

NAPCO imported products include decorative accessories, kitchenware, and other ceramic items. The company moved its operations from Cleveland, Ohio, to Jacksonville, Florida, in 1984.

Beware of NAPCO look-alikes. Few early designs were copyrighted. A NAPCO label or solid reference book documentation are keys to identification.

Bank, Ellie Fant, 3.75" h 15
Bell, Santa, 4BX3739, 4" h 20
Bell, Saturday, S1291F, Bell of the Week, 3.25" h 25

Beverage Set, juice pitcher and 6 cups, C6240 30
Candleholders, pr, snowmen, X8830, 3.75" h 25
Canister Set, owls, C7812, 4 pcs 30
Cheese Jar, K2969 30
Cookie Jar, mushroom, 8544, 8.25" h 20
Creamer and Sugar, Miss Cutie Pie, A3507/YE, 4.5" h 75
Cup and Saucer, Provincial, C8817 10
Figurine, angel playing concertina, C6351, 2.75" h 12
Figurine, April Daisy, 1C1931, Flower of the Month, 4.5" h 25
Figurine, Casey, A3163, 3.25 h 20
Figurine, girl with candy cane umbrella, 1CX4408, 4" h 20
Figurine, March, C5763, Calendar Cutie, 5.25" h 20
Figurine, Matchpoint, A2715/5, 4.5" h ...25
Figurine, schnauzer, 9854, 7.5" h 35
Figurine, Scorpio, S980, Zodiac angel, 2.75" h 25
Lady Head Vase, C3307, 5.5" h 55
Lady Head Vase, C5047, 6" h 50
Mug, Aries, C8322, 4" h 5
Mug, Hollyday, X7455, 3.5" h 15
Music Box, Christmas carolers, X7645, 6.5" h 30
Pitcher, C7815, floral dec, 7.25" h 20
Planter, basset hound, C7087, 6.25" h ...20
Planter, dachshund, C6717, 4.5" h 15
Planter, January, Planter of the Month, S624, 4.25" h 30
Planter, kitten, 6917, 5.75" h 20

Wall Plaques, set of 4 fruit, #B3761, paper labels, 5.75" l grape cluster, price for set, $10. —Photo courtesy Ray Morykan Auctions.

Planter, Little Miss Muffet, A1721D,
7.25" h 80
Planter, praying boy, A4697A, 5.5" h 20
Planter, Virgo, S1259, Zodiac angel,
4.25" h 35
Salt and Pepper Shakers, pr, June Rose,
1C3125, Flower of the Month, 3.5" h . . .30
Salt and Pepper Shakers, pr, Santa on
bell, X6047, 3.25 h 20
Wall Plaque, springer spaniel, B3871,
5" sq 25

NAPKIN RINGS

If you really get lucky, you may find a
great Victorian silver-plated figural napkin
ring at a flea market. Chances are that you
are going to find napkin rings used by the
common man. But do not look down your
nose at them. Some are pretty spectacular.
If you do not specialize from the beginning,
you are going to find yourself going around
in circles. Animal shaped rings are a
favorite.

Acorn, SS, Georg Jensen, 2" w 65
Angel, Avon, 1983, 2.25" w 3
Art Deco, woman, Noritake, 1.25" h,
2.125" w 90
Art Nouveau, SS, scroll design, unmkd . .60
Bunny, metal, full figure bunny on front,
basket on rear .25
Bunny, SS, engraved "Marjorie," Webster
Co, North Attleboro, MA, 1.625" d 40
Cherub, SP, seated on anvil and forging
2 connected rings, allover scroll
design, 4.5" h .250

*Emu and Kangaroo, silver plated, stamped
with hallmarks and "Made in Australia,"
4.25" l, $120.*

Dachshund, bone china, gold leaf edging,
Staffordshire, 2 x 1.5" 6
Elephant, green Bakelite, red eyes, 3 x
2.125" 60
Elephant, yellow Bakelite, balancing
green ball on forehead, painted green
eyes, 3 x 2.25" .50
English, SS, machine turned dec, mkd
"Birmingham," 1926-27, 1" d 35
Flowers and Leaves, SP, 1.625" d 8
Hobnail, white, 2" d 10
Ornate, SS, beaded style, engraved "JK,"
1.75" d 45
Oval, SS, engraved name on side,
Gorham, 2.5" l .25
Penguin, green Bakelite, ivory beak,
white eyes, 2.75 x 2" 200
Rectangular, SS, engraved lettering on
side, 2.5 x 1.5" 10
RMS Majestic, electroplated nickel
silver, enamel on bronze crest, mkd
"EPNS," 1.75 x 1.5" 12
Rooster, metal 2
Scottie Dog, ceramic, black, white eyes,
red ribbon, 2.75 x 1.25" 8
Victorian Woman, SP, hands behind back
holding barrel, 4.5 x 3" 40

NAUTICAL

There is magic in the sea, whether one
is reading the novels of Melville, watching
Popeye cartoons, or standing on a beach
staring at the vast expanse of ocean.
Anyone who loves water has something
nautical around the house. This is one case
where the weathered look is a plus. No one
wants a piece of nautical material that
appears to have never left the dock.

Periodical: *Nautical Collector,* One Whale
Oil Rd., New London, CT 06320.

*Hurricane Lamp,
brass, red and green
lenses, Wilcox
Crittenden and Co.,
6" h, $130.* —Photo
courtesy Collectors
Auction Services.

Ship's Wheel, brass, wood handle, 24" d, $200. —Photo courtesy Collectors Auction Services.

Bill of Sale, Schooner *Mariah Meresa,* Dec 1848, transferring title of 1/16th of the schooner to new owner, 10.5 x 17" .... .50

Bookends, pr, "Let 'er Blow," George Mulligan, Rehberger Mfg Co, Chicago, 1927, 8" h, 6.75 x 5.25" base .... .50

Booklet, The America's Cup International Race, Holbrook Mfg Co premium, emb trophy cup on front cov, 28 pp, 1899 . .30

Compass, brass, John Hand, Philadelphia, c1900 .... .175

Map, St John's River, FL, hand drawn, 1893, 16 x 22" 5

Pin, red, white, and blue fabric bow with suspended brass pendant, center image of ocean liner approaching wine bottles and grape clusters, inscription "Goodwill Tour To Italy/ April 1938" .... .10

Pin, brass, figural ship's tiller wheel, over- laid small brass flag with "the National Tours," red enamel ground, 1920-30s . .5

Pinback Button, American Cup Cruise, blue anchor with red "1934" 6

Pinback Button, Easthampton Boat Club, blue and white pennant symbol with inset small white triangle, c1890s 6

Pinback Button, Maritime Union, black and white center transport ship with initials "A.G.G.L/M.T.F.," 1919 8

Pinback Button, Rotary Yacht Contest, blue and silver, 1920s 6

Stickpin, metal, dark charcoal luster, figural racing yacht, on choppy waters above inscription "Reliance," c1900 . .15

Telescope, brass, single-draw, orig black leather grip, sliding lens cov, remov- able lens cap and sliding lens shade, Bardou Fils et Cie, France, 19th C, 28.5" l .... .450

Thermometer, figural lighthouse, mar- bleized red and gray, bone tempera- ture gauge, mounted on rockwork stone base, 13.5" h .... .375

NEMADJI POTTERY

The Nemadji Pottery was located in Moose Lake, Minnesota. Founded by C. J. Dodge in 1923, it made swirl-decorated earthenware pottery similar in appearance to Niloak. In addition to vases and other decorative accessories, the company also made tiles. Nemadji Pottery ceased opera- tions in 1973.

Bowl, #187 .... .30
Candlestick, #116 .... .35
Urn, #105 .... .50
Urn, #126 .... .35
Urn, #127 .... .50
Vase, #128 .... .25
Vase, #139 .... .50
Vase, #160 .... .35
Vase, #201 .... .30
Vase, #202 .... .40
Vase, #203 .... .50
Vase, #204 .... .40

Vase, blue and green swirled pattern, mkd "Nemadji Pottery U.S.A.," 7" h, $25.

NEWSPAPERS

"Extry – Extry, Read All About It" is the cry of corner newspaper vendors across the country. Maybe these vendors should be collected. They appear to be a vanishing breed. Some newspapers are collected for their headlines, others because they represent a special day, birthday, or anniversary. Everybody saved the newspaper announcing that JFK was shot. Did you save a paper from the day war was declared against Iraq? I did.

Club: Newspaper Collectors Society of America, Box 19134, S. Lansing, MI 48901.

Newspaper: *Newspaper Memorabilia Collectors Network,* P.O. Box 797, Watertown, NY 13601.

Periodical: *Paper Collectors' Marketplace (PCM),* P.O. Box 128, Scandinavia, WI 54977.

1967, The Indianapolis Star, *JFK assassination,* $25.

1712, *The Examiner,* criticizing Queen
and war in Europe, 2pp 25
1731, *The London Gazette,* royalty and
appointments, printed half-penny
stamp at bottom, 2 pp, 7 x 12" 25
1822, *The Independent Chronicle &
Boston Patriot,* shipping, politics,
foreign and national news, 4pp 8
1835, *New York Mirror,* literature and
fine arts, 8 pp 8
1917, Feb 1, *Chicago Daily Tribune,* "Sink
All Ships," 4 pp 25
1918, Nov 12, *Boston Herald,* "German
Surrender Most Complete Ever Known;
Wilson Stretches Hand To Prostrate
Enemy," 12 pp .15
1918, Nov 13, *Boston Herald,* "Armistice
Amended; Germany Must Yield All
Submarines," 14 pp 12
1927, May 21, *Dayton News,* Dayton, OH,
Lindbergh over Ireland 25
1933, Jan 5, *Lancaster Daily Eagle,*
Lancaster, OH, Coolidge dies 15
1940, Aug 12, *Daily Journal-Gazette,*
Mattoon, IL, Nazis open aerial battle . .5
1945, Apr 13, *The Springfield Democrat,*
"Roosevelt Dies; Pres. Truman To
Continue Predecessor's Policies,"
8 pp 12

1945, Apr 15, *Boston Sunday Globe,*
"Roosevelt Goes Home/Fallen Chief
Starts His Last Journey To Hyde Park
After Capitol Services" 12
1945, May 7, *Buffalo Evening News,*
Buffalo, NY, War Victory issue 4
1956, Jul 27, *San Francisco Examiner,*
Andrea Doria sinks 20
1962, Feb 20, *New Bedford Standard
Times,* "Glenn Orbits Earth," front
page photos and article, 12 pp 8
1968, Jun 6, *Williamsport Gazette,* PA,
Robert Kennedy killed 15
1976, Apr 6, *San Jose Mercury,* CA,
Howard Hughes dies 15
1977, Aug 17, *Boston Herald,* "Elvis Is
Dead," 44 pp 15

NILOAK POTTERY

When you mention Niloak, most people immediately think of swirled brown, red, and tan pottery, formally known as Mission Ware. However, Niloak also made items in a host of other designs through 1946. These included utilitarian wares and ceramics used by florists that can be bought for a reasonable price. If Niloak prices follow the trend established by Roseville prices, now is the time to stash some of these later pieces away.

Club: National Society of Arkansas Pottery Collectors, 2006 Beckenham Cove, Little Rock, AR 72212.

Bud Vase, Ozark Dawn II, 4" h 25

Vase, Mission Ware, yellow, blue, and brown swirl, imp mark, 5.25" h, $75.

Candlesticks, pr, classical shape, rolled rim, flaring foot, scroddled brown, blue, terra cotta, and sand, stamped mark, 8" h, 5" d 150

Console Set, Mission Ware, center bowl and pr candlesticks, bowl and 1 stick mkd, 10" d bowl, 8.5" h candlesticks, price for set 300

Cornucopia, cream, 6" h 20

Figure, canoe, brown, 8" l 35

Figure, frog 20

Humidor, Mission Swirl, 5" h 450

Pitcher, yellow, 3.25" h 15

Planter, boxing kangaroo, tan, 5" h 30

Planter, duck, pink and white, 5" h 20

Pot, Mission Swirl, 2.75" h 100

Strawberry Jar, Ozark Dawn II, 7" h 40

Vase, baluster shape, scroddled brown, blue, terra cotta, and sand, stamped mark, 9.5" h, 5" d 300

Vase, classical shape, semi-ovoid form, scroddled brown, ivory, and terra cotta, stamped mark and paper label, 12" h, 7.5" d 500

Vase, corseted cylinder, scroddled brown, blue, and terra cotta, stamped mark, 10" h, 4.5" d 225

Vase, figural shoe, blue, 2.5" h 25

Vase, Mission Ware, classical shape, scroddled brown, tan, and blue, unmkd, 9.5 x 5" 250

Vase, Mission Ware, classical shape, scroddled tan and brown, stamped mark, 15 x 6" 975

Vase, Ozark Dawn II, overlapping leaves, 7" h 45

Vase, pear shape, flared rim and ring foot, scroddled brown, blue, terra cotta, and sand, stamped mark, 9.75", 4.75" d 375

Vase, spherical, closed-in rim, scroddled brown, blue, terra cotta, and sand, stamped mark and paper label, 5.75" h, 7" d 250

Vessel, scroddled brown, beige, and terra cotta, stamped mark, 6" h, 8" d .450

NIPPON

Nippon is hand painted Japanese porcelain made between 1891 and 1921. The McKinley tariff of 1891 required goods imported into the United States to be marked with their country of origin. Until 1921, goods from Japan were marked "Made in Nippon."

Over two hundred different manufacturer's marks have been discovered for Nippon. The three most popular are the wreath, maple leaf, and rising sun. While marks are important, the key is the theme and quality of the decoration.

Nippon has become quite expensive. Rumors in the field indicate that Japanese buyers are now actively competing with American buyers.

Club: International Nippon Collectors' Club, 9101 Sulkirk Dr., Raleigh, NC 27613.

Bowl, Kingfisher, matte and high glaze finish, green "M" in wreath mark, 3.625" h, 7.25" w 925

Bowl, pink flowers on green ground, gold beading, 10" d 30

Bowl, relief molded, green "M" in wreath mark, 7.75" w 110

Nut Set, 7 pcs, $165. —Photo courtesy Gene Harris Antique Auction Center, Inc.

Vase, floral and gold dec, unmkd, 8.625" h, $300.
—Photo courtesy Ray Morykan Auctions.

Bowl, scalloped edge, Mt Fuji in center with flying cranes, 3 ladies playing game with paddles, butterflies, and flowers, 10.25" d 50

Chocolate Pot, swan medallions, cobalt blue and gold with enamel jewels, green maple leaf mark, 9.5" h 225

Cup, painted roses and leaf design, raised dots, gold trim 5

Demitasse Set, rose and gold dec pot, 4 cups and saucers, 11.75" l tray, red and green "RC" mark, price for set . .135

Dresser Set, moriage dragon, powder box, hair receiver, and 8.375" l tray, green "M" in maple leaf mark, 5.5" h 250

Fernery, triangular form with pillars and scenic painted sides, green "M" in wreath mark, 3.625" h, 6" w 110

Hair Receiver, pink roses and floral design, gold bead dec, green maple leaf mark 30

Marmalade and Dipper, scenic painted, green "M" in wreath mark with "Made in Japan," 5.25" h 55

Nappy, Woodland, shield and lion border, green maple leaf mark, 7" l 275

Nut Dish, cobalt floral and leaf design, green "M" in wreath mark, 3.5" l 5

Pin Tray, ftd, floral design, gold trim 2 x 3.75" 25

Smoke Set, Phoenix Bird on tan ground, 7" l tray, green "M" in wreath mark, price for 3 pc set 110

Talcum Powder Shaker, floral and gold dec, green "M" in wreath mark, 4.75" h 125

Toothpick Holder, 3 handles, rose and gold dec, green maple leaf mark 88

Vase, owl on branch, gold trim, green maple leaf mark, 8.5" h 880

Vase, pink roses and green leaves, 2 handles, shaded brown to gold, 8.25" h 100

Vase, Tapestry, Gold Royal, rising sun mark, 3.5" h 185

Vase, woman on cottage path, green "M" in wreath mark, 9.25" h 210

NON-SPORT TRADING CARDS

Based on the publicity received by baseball cards, you would think that they were the only bubble gum cards sold. Wrong, wrong, wrong! There is a wealth of non-sport trading cards.

Prices for many of these card sets are rather modest. Individual cards often sell for less than $1. Classic cards were issued in the 1950s. More recently released sets are also collectible, as witnessed by prices realized for Beatles and television-related cards from the 1960s.

Club: United States Cartophilic Society, P.O. Box 4020, St. Augustine, FL 32085.

Periodicals: *Non-Sport Update,* 4019 Green St., P.O. Box 5858, Harrisburg, PA 17110; *The Wrapper,* 1811 Moore Ct., St. Charles, IL 60174.

Note: Prices listed are for sets in excellent condition.

Bowman, Frontier Days, 1953, 128 cards 750

Cardz, Tales From the Crypt, 1993, 110

Champs, American Vintage Cycles, 1992, 100 cards 18

Bowman, US Presidents, 1952, 36 cards, $25.

Comic Images, Excalibar, 1989, 45 cards .15
Comic Images, Shadowhawk, 1992, 90
  cards 10
Comic Images, The Melting Pot, 1993,
  100 cards 20
Comic Images, Unity, 1992, 90 cards 8
Dart, Vietnam Fact Cards, 1988, 66 cards 25
Donruss, All Pro Skateboard, 1978, 44
  sticker cards 12
Donruss, Andy Gibb Posters, 1978, 42
  posters 60
Donruss, Awesome All-Stars, 1988, 127
  sticker cards .18
Donruss, Elvis Presley, 1978, 66 cards . . .25
Donruss, King Kong, 1965, 55 cards 300
Donruss, Magnum P I, 1983, 66 cards . . .16
Donruss, Oddest Odd Rods, 1970, 66
  sticker cards 165
Donruss, Rock Stars, 1979, 66 cards 30
Donruss, Space:1999, 1976, 66 cards 18
Donruss, Zero Heroes, 1984, 66 sticker
  cards 10
Fleer, Beautiful People, 1978, 50 stickers,
  14 cards 35
Fleer, Dumb Dads, 1983, 63 stickers 15
Fleer, Gong Show, 1979, 66 cards, 10
  stickers 25
Fleer, Kustom Cars I, 1974, 9 cards, 30
  stickers 75
Fleer, Marvel Metal, 1995, 138 cards 35
Fleer, Three Stooges, 1966, 66 black and
  white cards .425
Fleer, Yule Laff, 1960, 66 cards 75
Frostick, Animal Cards, 1930s, 44 cards .185
Gum, Inc, 1956, Adventure, #86
  Schmelling .300
Imagine, You Slay Me, 1992, 60 cards . . .10
Impel, X-Men, 1992, 100 cards 30
Leaf, What's My Job?, 1965, 72 cards . . .85
Lime Rock, Spy vs Spy, 1993, 55 cards . .10
Mother's Cookies, Beauty and the Beast,
  1987, 16 cards 15
Philly, Dark Shadows, 1968, Series 1, 66
  cards 325
Rosan, Famous Monsters Series, 1963,
  64 cards 125
Rosan, John F Kennedy, 1964, 64 cards .60
SkyBox, Mortal Kombat, 1995, 90 cards .10
SkyBox, Nightmare Before Christmas,
  1993, 90 cards 20
SkyBox, Pagemaster, 1994, 90 cards . . .12
SkyBox, Return of Superman, 1993, 100
  cards 20

SkyBox, Snow White and the Seven
  Dwarfs, 1993, 90 cards 10
SkyBox, Toy Story, 1995, 90 cards 15
SkyBox, Youngblood, 1995, 90 cards 25
Star Pics, Troll Force, 1993, 50 cards, 10
  stickers 12
Topps, Astronauts, 1963, 55 cards, 3-D
  backs 300
Topps, Battlestar Galactica, 1978, 132
  cards, 22 stickers 40
Topps, Brady Bunch, 1969, 88 cards . . .950
Topps, Bring 'Em Back Alive, 1950, 100
  cards 540
Topps, Civil War News, 1962, 88 cards .450
Topps, Close Encounters, 1978, 66 cards,
  11 stickers 14
Topps, Dinosaur Attack, 55 cards, 11
  stickers 13
Topps, Evel Knievel, 1974, 60 cards 140
Topps, Flag Midgee Cards, 1963, 99
  cards 100
Topps, Flags of the World, 1956, 80
  cards 175
Topps, Funny Valentines, 1959, 66 cards .90
Topps, Gilligan's Island, 1965, 55 cards .825
Topps, Good Times, 1975, 55 cards, 21
  stickers 70
Topps, Goonies, 1985, 88 cards, 15
  stickers 12
Topps, Hit Stars, 1957, 88 cards 650
Topps, Laugh-In, 1968, 77 cards 175
Topps, Perlorian Cats, 1983, 55 stickers . .9
Upper Deck, Street Fighter, 1995, 90
  cards 15

NORITAKE AZALEA

Noritake china in the Azalea pattern
was first produced in the early 1900s.
Several backstamps were used. They will
help date your piece.

Azalea pattern wares were distributed
as a premium by the Larkin Company of
Buffalo and sold by Sears, Roebuck and
Company. As a result, it is the most commonly found pattern of Noritake china. Each
piece is hand painted, adding individuality
to the piece. Hard-to-find examples include
children's tea sets and salesmen's samples.
Do not ignore the hand painted glassware
in the azalea pattern that was manufactured to accompany the china service.

Creamer, $12.

Berry Bowl, 5.25" d 4
Bon Bon, 5.625" d 30
Bouillon Cup, with underplate 115
Bowl, 5.75" d 15
Bowl, 8" d 10
Bowl, 9.625" d 15
Bread and Butter Plate, 6" d 40
Butter Dish, with insert 25
Butter Tub, 5" d 35
Cake Plate, 2 handles, 9.75 x 9.5" 15
Casserole, 8.5" d 80
Celery Dish, 13" l 45
Condiment Bowl, 3 ftd, with underplate
    and ladle, 4.5" d 25
Cream Soup Bowl, ...90
Cruet 140
Cup and Saucer, 2" h cup, 5.5" d saucer . .5
Eggcup 45
Fruit Bowl, 5.25" d 6
Gravy Boat 40
Jam Pot, 5" h, 3.5" w 55
Ladle, 6" l 15
Luncheon Set, 20 pcs, creamer and cov-
    ered sugar, six 7.5" d plates, six 5.5" d
    saucers, and five cups 55
Mayonnaise Set, 3 pcs 15
Milk Pitcher, 5.625" h 140
Nappy 20
Plate, 9.75" d 20
Platter, 11.625" l 12
Platter, 13.5" l 30
Relish Dish, 2 part ....
Salt and Pepper Shakers, pr, 3.75" h 20
Serving Plate, 2 handles, 9.75" d 25
Snack Set 35
Snack Tray, 8.5" l 15
Soup Bowl, 7.25" d 30
Sugar, cov 15
Tea Tile, 5.75" d 50
Teapot, 4" h 70
Toothpick Holder, 2.5" h, 1.625" d 100
Vegetable Bowl, 2.5" h, 9.375" d 15

NORITAKE CHINA

Noritake is quality Japanese china imported to the United States by the Noritake China company. The company, founded by the Morimura brothers in Nagoya in 1904, is best known for its dinnerware lines. Over one hundred different marks were used, which are helpful in dating pieces. The Larkin Company of Buffalo, New York, issued several patterns as premiums, including the Azalea, Briarcliff, Linden, Savory, Sheridan, and Tree in the Meadow patterns, which are readily found.

Be careful. Not all Noritake china is what it seems. The company also sold blanks to home decorators. Check the artwork before deciding that a piece is genuine.

Club: Noritake Collectors' Society, 145 Andover Pl., West Hempstead, NY 11552.

Asian Song, creamer 10
Asian Song, cup and saucer 12
Asian Song, dinner plate, 10.625" d 10
Asian Song, salad plate, 8.375" d 10
Asian Song, serving bowl, 10" d 45
Asian Song, serving platter, 16.25" l 75
Bancroft, dessert plate 10
Elysian, dessert plate 2
Elysian, salad plate, 7.5" d 4
Fairfax, place setting, 40 pcs, twelve
    7.5" d soup bowls, eleven teacups,
    fifteen saucers, one 8.5" tray, five
    8" d dessert plates, one 7.5" d covered
    dish, five 10" d dinner plates, and five
    5.5" d fingerbowls 100

Art Deco pattern, Bowl, silver-gray, blue, red, and white on green ground, 1920-30s, 3.125" h, $55.

Syrup and Underplate, green M in wreath mark, c1911, 3.75" h, $65. —Photo courtesy Ray Morykan Auctions.

Gravy Boat, attached underplate 15
Grayburn, creamer 10
Grayburn, plate, 10.25" d 4
Grayburn, serving bowl, 3" h, 10.5" l,
   7.5" w 3
Holly, coffeepot, 10" h 45
Holly, salt and pepper shakers, pr 10
Holly, serving bowl, 9" d 40
Holly, soup tureen, 10.5" d 115
Homage, bread and butter plate 3
Homage, creamer 8
Homage, cup and saucer 8
Homage, sugar, cov 10
Homecoming, place setting, 5 pcs, cup
   and saucer, 5.5" d berry bowl, 6.25" d
   dessert plate, 10.5" d dinner plate 15
Limerick, place setting, 5 pcs, bread and
   butter plate, dinner plate, salad plate,
   cup and saucer 45
Lorelei, sugar, cov 6
Lorento, bowl, 8" d 10
Lorento, dinner plate, 10" d 15
Lorento, platter .35
Luxoria, dinner plate, 10" d 15
Milroy, bread and butter plate, 6.25" d 4
Milroy, salad plate, 8.5" d 10
Monteleone, bread and butter plate 10
Monteleone, creamer and sugar 10
Monteleone, dinner plate 10
Monteleone, teacup 10
Nanarosa, bowl, 7.5" d 8
Ontario, place setting, 5 pcs, bread and
   butter plate, dinner plate, salad plate,
   cup and saucer 40
Oxford, bread and butter plate, 6.25" d . . .3
Oxford, gravy boat 15
Oxford, plate, 7.75" d 4
Oxford, plate, 9.75" d 8
Oxford, platter, 11.75" l, 8.75" w 15
Oxford, soup bowl, 7.25" d 10
Reverie, dinner plate, 8.25" d 10

Ridgewood, gravy boat 15
Rosebud, serving bowl, divided,
   10.125" d 20
Southern Lace, plate, 10.5" d 10
Weyburne, bread amd butter plate,
   6.25" d 6

NORITAKE
TREE IN THE MEADOW

If you ever want to see variation in a dinnerware pattern, collect Tree in the Meadow. You will go nuts trying to match pieces. In the end you will do what everyone else does. Learn to live with the differences. Is there a lesson here?

Tree in the Meadow was distributed by the Larkin Company of Buffalo, New York. Importation began in the 1920s, almost twenty years after the arrival of azalea pattern wares. Check the backstamp to identify the date of the piece.

Basket 40
Bowl, 8 x 3" 30
Cake Set, 5 pcs .45
Celery Dish, 11" l, 5.5" w 35
Chocolate Set, chocolate pot with 6 cups
   and saucers .175
Creamer and Sugar 35
Cup and Saucer .30
Dinner Plate, 8.5" d 6
Nappy, 5.5" d 10
Olive Dish, 9 x 4" 20
Plate, 10" d 50
Relish Dish, divided, 8.5 x 5" 15
Soup Bowl, flat, 7.25" d 12
Teapot, 4.5" h 45

Salt and Pepper Shakers, pr, $30.

Vase, 8.5" h .... .30
Wall Pocket, 8" h .... .50

NUTCRACKERS

With the computer age in full swing it seems online auction sites are taking center stage making it easier to find our most precious collectibles. Ebay, a favorite, has driven the price of nutcrackers sky high. I have been known to bid on a nutcracker not knowing if I really want it or if it is the mere fact that I don't want anyone else to buy it. It's definitely a consolidated market with an inventory that seems bottomless. The never ending challenge of winning a bid on Ebay keeps the thrill in the game with an open invitation to return that could be referred to "addicting."

Tracking down nutcrackers for a collection can become a real treasure hunt, and a fun one indeed. While no formal invention date has ever been assigned to the nutcracker we do know that in an early inventory of the contents of the Louvre in Paris (1420) a gilded silver nutcracker is listed. Furthermore, King Henry VIII gave Anne Bolyn a gift of a nutcracker. The first nutcrackers were probably nothing more than two large stones, the nut placed on the bottom stone was hit with a heavier rock. This type is very easy to find. You may have several right in your own backyard. Nutcrackers, in fact, are as versatile as people themselves. They come in all shapes, colors, sizes, weights, and types. There are three basic types of nutcrackers. The first is the screw type. A nut is placed in a hollowed out interior and a wooden screw is turned into it. The pressure of the end of the screw against the nut will break or crack the nut open. The second type has a handle that serves as a lever and pivots at one end. Some of this type have even been reinforced with metal and are not uncommon. Finally, there is the sort which works on indirect pincer action. Two levers are pivoted off center with the short end jaws closing as a result of pressure on the long ends of levers. Many of this kind are animals that crack the nuts. Nutcrackers can be as small as two inches and as tall as a six foot man. Some of the most beautiful nutcrackers are made of wood and are one-of-a-kind specimens. Nutcrackers are made of wood, metal, porcelain, or even glass. Some are even made of ivory. Painted nutcrackers in the form of people often have folklore elements. They feature the costumes of a region and are brightly colored. Most of these are from Germany. The most popular makers are Christian Steinbach and Christian Ulbricht. Each year there are new editions and new series. These are true collectibles, some of them becoming quite valuable.

Wooden soldier type nutcrackers are brightly painted and dressed in very fine costumes made in Germany. These are very popular in the collector market. Collectors suggest that you keep the box they come in. They range in size from one inch to six feet tall, the most common being about twelve to eighteen inches high. Most are made in Germany by very fine craftsmen. The new ones on the market range in price from $99 to $750. Like any collectible there are the ones that have sold out and have soared to the $3,500 mark like the limited edition Steinbach wooden Merlin nutcracker holding an owl. Each have their own character and each carry their own value to the buyer and to the collecting market. Have fun collecting, or should I say "GO NUTS."

Advisor: Claudia J. Davis, 2550 Finch Rd., Hayden Lake, ID 83835.

Club: Nutcracker Collectors' Club, 12204 Fox Run Dr., Chesterland, OH 44026.

Wood, man's head, hat bill forms lever, 10.5" d mahogany bowl, mkd "Germany, Christmas 1948," $70.

Wood, man holding umbrella, 9.125" h, $100.

Cast Iron, alligator, 7-16" h 75
Cast Iron, Knee Knocker, formed to sit
   on top of thigh over knee, indented
   spot to place nut, with hammer, 7" l,
   5" w 125
Mickey Mouse, mounted on round base,
   The Walt Disney Co, made in China,
   14" h 45
Porcelain, painted flowers, screw-type,
   6" h 175
Wood, African woman, ebony, short red
   leather skirt, beaded eyes, legs provide pliers action, removable head has
   corkscrew, made in France, 10" h 50
Wood, bears head, glass eyes, mouth
   opens to crack nut, 6-9" h 125
Wood, man, mounted on semi-circular
   horse, made in German Republic,
   10" h 150
Wood, sailor, screw type, Taiwan 10
Wood, soldier, brightly painted, made
   in China, 4-24" h 5
Wood, squirrel, screw type, 7" l 100
Wood, troll's head, red stocking cap,
   carved swirls on handle, made in
   Norway 75

OCCUPIED JAPAN

America occupied Japan from 1945 to 1952. Not all objects made during this period are marked "Occupied Japan." Some were simply marked "Japan" or "Made in Japan." Occupied Japan collectors ignore these two groups. They want to see their favorite words.

Beware of falsely labeled pieces. Rubber-stamp marked pieces have appeared on the market. Apply a little fingernail polish remover. Fake marks will dis-

appear. True marks are under glaze. Of course, if the piece is unglazed to begin with, ignore this test.

Club: The Occupied Japan Club, 29 Freeborn St., Newport, RI 02840.

Bookends, pr, colonial ladies 30
Bowl, fish dec, blue reticulated rim, light
   blue "Made in Occupied Japan," 4" h .10
Cigarette Box, with 2 ashtrays, mkd
   "Rosetti, Chicago USA, Hand-Painted,
   Made in Occupied Japan" 25
Cup and Saucer, dragon pattern, blue
   and white, blue "Made in Occupied
   Japan" 20
Figure, angel busts, pr, bisque, mkd,
   "Made in Occupied Japan Lamore
   China #432," 2.75" h 55
Figure, boy wearing large slippers,
   Hummel look-alike, blue-green, "Made
   in Occupied Japan" 20
Figure, cherub, on pedestal, bisque, red
   "Made in Occupied Japan," 7" h 45
Figure, clown sitting on pig, mkd "Ardalt,
   Occupied Japan," 5" h, 4.375" w 100
Figure, colonial man carrying flowers,
   bisque, red "Made in Occupied Japan,"
   7.375" h 25
Pin, double Scottie, celluloid, mkd "Made
   in Occupied Japan" on pin back 10
Planter, Dutch clog shoe 10
Planter, pig, mkd "SS, Made in Occupied
   Japan," 3.375" h 15
Salt and Pepper Shakers, pr, flowers
   and butterflies, 3.25" h shakers mkd
   "Japan," 4" w holder mkd with blue
   "R" and "Made in Occupied Japan" .20

Salt and Pepper Shaker Set, tomatoes on leaf tray, mkd "Maruhon Ware, K (in circle) Hand Painted Japan" on shakers, "Made in Occupied Japan" on tray, 5.625" l tray, $20.
—Photo courtesy Ray Morykan Auctions.

Salt and Pepper Shakers, pr, Indian and
squaw in canoe, 3" h, 6.25" w 15
Toby Mug, MacArthur, mkd "Merit, Made
in Occupied Japan," 4.25" h 50
Vase, girl, with raised arm, bisque, mkd
"Paulux, Made in Occupied Japan,"
7.5 h 25
Wall Pocket, lady with full skirt, red
"Made in Occupied Japan," 6" h 35
Windup, Baby Pontiac, litho tin, blue,
gold grille, yellow headlights, silver
wheels, Modern Toys, mkd "Made in
Occupied Japan," 1940s, 1.25 x 3.25
x 1" h 40

OCEAN LINER COLLECTIBLES

Although the age of the clipper ships
technically fits into this category, the period
that you are most likely to uncover at flea
markets is that of the ocean liner. Don't
focus solely on American ships. England,
Germany, France, and many other countries
had transoceanic liners that competed with
and bested American vessels. Today is the
age of the cruise ship. This aspect of the
category is being largely ignored. Climb
aboard and sail into the sunset.

Clubs: Steamship Historical Society of
America, Ind., 300 Ray Dr., Suite #4,
Providence, RI 02906; Titanic Historical
Society, P.O. Box 51053, Indian Orchard, MA
01151; Titanic International, Inc, P.O. Box
7007, Freehold, NJ 07728.

Advertising Tear Sheet, Mobilgas adv
featuring *Queen Mary* and "200,000
H.P. Under Her Hood," 6.5 x 10" 5
Ashtray, ceramic, *Holland America Line*,
stylized bow of vessel with yellow,
green, and white funnels and sailing
ship below, 4" d 20
Baggage Tag, *Cunard White Star Line*,
white lettering on red ground, 3.5" d . . .4
Booklet, passenger list for *Cunard White
Star Georgic*, 14 pp, dated Jun 13,
1936, 3.5 x 5.75" 10
Medallion, *Ile De France*, dark silver
luster finish, profile of ocean liner on
global waters with inscription "French
Line," reverse depicts symbolic woman
reclining in lower gown and bared
upper torso, holding flower in hand
and resting historic sailing boat on
forearm, crest symbols, c1920s 15
Menu, *MS Lafayette*, dated Mar 3, 1937 . .8
Model Kit, *Queen Mary*, Revell 25
Pinback Button, *Conte Di Savoia*, black
and white photo, 1920-30s 15
Pinback Button, *The Rex*, black and white
photo, 1920-30s 15
Postcard, *RMS Aquitania Cunard White
Star*, ocean liner in harbor, printed in
England, unused, 1930s 8
Postcard, "Liner at Landing Stage
Liverpool," postmarked Dec 17, 1918,
5.5 x 3.5" 10
Puzzle, cruise ship, interlocking wood
pcs, bottom stamped "Japan," 4.75" l .10

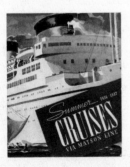

*Booklet, "Summer 1936-1937 Cruises Via
Matson Line," 8 pp, black and white photo
illus, 7.875 x 9.5", $35.*

*Handbook, "P&O Royal Mail Liners Tourist
Class Handbook of Information," black and
white photo illus, 24 pp, 1934, 5.625 x
8.875", $45.*

OLYMPIC COLLECTIBLES

Why has the collecting of Olympic memorabilia lagged behind other sports collectibles?

There are several reasons: the frequency of the Olympics; the international flavor of the event; the "baggage" of social, political and economic factors: and the failure, with few exceptions, to develop and market the super athletes that have participated.

Since the 1984 Los Angeles Olympics, pin collecting has been the driving force bringing the Olympics to public attention. In most cases the initial expense is small and the pin collectors trade frequently, putting the emphasis on pin collecting as a hobby, rather than an investment.

Olympic items can be found at garage sales, flea markets, auctions, and antique shows. Beginners should focus on a specific collecting category.

Club: Olympic Pin Collector's Club, 1386 5th St., Schenectady, NY 12303.

1984, Los Angeles, XXIII Summer Games, plush toy, Sam the Olympic Eagle mascot, $50.

1928, Amsterdam, IX Summer Games, ashtray, brown glass, "Olympiade–1928/Amsterdam," mkd "KK," 6 x 6" . .90

1932, Lake Placid, III Winter Games, ticket, Grandstand Season Ticket, Feb 4-13, section 5, seat 165 100

1932, Los Angeles, X Summer Games, booklet, Medical Report of the Xth Olympic Games, 40 pp, black and white photos, 8.5 x 6" 35

1956, Melbourne, XVI Summer Games, ashtray, clear glass, 4.75" w, $30.

1940, Helsinki, XII Summer Games, souvenir scarf, silk, Olympic stadium between 2 Finnish flags and legend in Finnish, 9 x 9" 75

1948, London, XIV Summer Games, luggage sticker, Hungarian team, in English and Hungarian, unused 40

1948, London, XIV Summer Games, NOC team pin, Czechoslovakia, tombac silver, struck, rectangular, "CS. Vybor Olymp." on white ground, Bohemian lion on red ground, "1948" on blue ground, and multicolored Olympic rings, 35 x 25mm 165

1952, Oslo, VI Winter Games, magazine, *Ski/Olympic Preview*, Feb 1952, 36 pp .25

1956, Melbourne, XVI Summer Games, commemorative plate, Olympic torch over map of Australia within legend, "Olympic Games/Melbourne Australia. 22 Nov-8 Dec. 1956," mkd "Superior Quality/Made in Japan," 8" d 150

1968, Grenoble, X Winter Games, NOC team pin, Soviet Athletes, tombac gilt, cloisonne, square, "CCCP/1968" and Olympic rings within stylized snowflake, flat surface with plain ground, 31mm 75

1972, Munich, XX Summer Games, belt buckle, bronze, "Munich 1972" within wreath 20

1972, Munich, XX Summer Games, NOC team pin, Great Britain, tombac gilt, cloisonne, shield shape, red and blue British flag over Olympic rings with "Great Britain" above and "Munich/1972" below, white ground, 33 x 27mm 55

1972, Sapporo, XI Winter Games, pin, nickel copper, cloisonne, Sapporo games logo, skier, and Japanese flag in wreath, obverse "Sapporo/1972" . .50

1976, Montreal, XXI Summer Games, license plate, Quebec, La Belle Province, Olympic rings 35

1984, Los Angeles, XXIII Summer Games, poster, gymnast above parallel bar surrounded by small banners above "Games of the XXIIIrd Olympiad, Los Angeles, 1984," Signature series 100

1988, Calgary, XV Winter Games, ski hat, acrylic, white, Olympic emblem with stylized snowflake and maple leaf ...25

1988, Seoul, XXIV Summer Games, NOC team pin, Bangladesh, post with military clutch, tombac gilt, epoxy, round, NOC logo and Olympic rings above "Bangladesh/1988/XXIV Olympiad," 18mm 40

OWL COLLECTIBLES

Most people do not give a hoot about this category, but those who do are serious birds. Like all animal collectors, the only thing owl collectors care about is that their bird is represented.

Bank, brass, Napier 4
Book, *The Owl and the Bee,* Saalfield, 1915, 6 x 11" 10
Bottle Opener, brass, mkd "Made in Italy," 5.5" h 10
Bracelet, silver owl with amber rhinestone eys, silvertoned mesh band, Sarah Coventry 4

Left: Soaky Bottle, Woodsy Owl, Lander, $70. Right: Mechanical Bank, cast iron, head turns, c1880, 7.5" h, $500. —Photo courtesy Collectors Auction Services.

Cookie Jar, Norcrest, stamped "T208," orig sticker 10
Cookie Jar, Treasure Craft, 10" h 25
Creamer, golden yellow body, cream face, rosey pink cheeks, gold highlights, Shawnee 15
Label, Wise Bird Brand, West Orange Citrus Growers Assoc, 1930s 3
Matchcover, New York World's Fair 1939-40, "White Owl Cigar Exhibit/ New White Owl Blended With Havana" 8
Music Box, pair of owls cuddled together on stack of logs, plays *Love Makes the World Go Round,* Gorham, made in Japan 12
Needle Book, Red Owl Store, "A Gift For You From Your Red Owl Store," 5.5" h ..5
Ornament, Hallmark Keepsake Ornament, 1984 5
Salt and Pepper Shakers, pr, made in Japan, 3" h 4
Stein, porcelain and metal, brown owl with green-blue eyes, green and brown base, blue Hachiya Bros mark, Japan, c1950-60s, 8.5" h, 4" d 15
Toothpick Holder, owl seated on tree stump, shades of green, yellow, and orange, mkd "Made in Occupied Japan," 2.5" h 8
Wall Pocket, made in Japan, 7" h 5

PADEN CITY GLASS

The Paden City Glass Manufacturing Company, Paden City, West Virginia, was founded in 1916. The plant closed in 1951, two years after acquiring the American Glass Company. Paden City glass was handmade in molds. There are no known free-blown examples. Most pieces were unmarked. The key is color. Among the most popular are opal (opaque white), dark green (forest), and red. The company did not produce opalescent glass.

Club: Paden City Glass Society, Inc., P.O. Box 139, Paden City, WV 26159.

Banana Split Dish, green 20
Bowl, Black Forest, rolled edge, green, 13" d 300
Bowl, Cupid, rolled edge, pink, 11" d ...400

Bowl, Maya, ftd, blue, 10" d 55
Bowl, Peacock & Wild Rose, ftd, pink . .175
Bowl, Peacock & Wild Rose, rolled
   edge, green .180
Cake Plate, Cupid, ftd, pink 175
Cake Plate, Orchid, yellow 70
Candy Dish, Ardith, square, green 150
Candy Dish, Nora Bird, cov, flat, pink . .325
Comport, Cupid, pink 325
Console Bowl and Candlesticks, Crow's
   Foot, blue 300
Cordial Decanter, Party Line, with
   stopper 20
Creamer and Sugar, Black Forest, pink .135
Cup, Ardith, yellow 35
Figure, bird, blue, 5" h 165
Figure, chanticleer, blue 175
Figure, Chinese pheasant, blue, 13.75" l .175
Figure, pheasant head, blue, 12" l 175
Figure, rooster, black 450
Figure, rooster, head down, blue 225
Ice Bucket, Cupid, green 325
Ice Bucket, Peacock & Wild Rose, no
   bail 275
Mayonnaise and Spoon, Nora Bird, ftd,
   green 120
Mayonnaise Underplate, Cupid, green .230
Pitcher and Tumbler, Ardith, green 575
Plate, Ardith, 2 handles, pink 135
Plate, Largo, blue, ftd 20
Sherbet, Penny Line, red 8
Soda Glass, green 12
Tray, Black Forest, center handle, green .80
Tray, Cupid, pink, oval 380
Tumbler, Penny Line, red, 6" h 12
Vase, Peacock & Wild Rose, black,
   10" h 300
Vase, Peacock & Wild Rose, green 360

Candlesticks, Echo, #116, ebony, 10" h, $20.
—Photo courtesy Ray Morykan Auctions.

PAINT-BY-NUMBER

Paint-by-number pictures are most frequently collected according to subject matter. Crossover collectors are the biggest customers. A modest interest is building for paint-by-number metal crafts such as kitchen trays and other accessories.

April in Paris, Craft Master 75
Ballerinas, Craft Master 40
Blue Boy, Craft Master, Masterpiece
   Series 40
Conflict at Sea, Craft Master 75
Fisher's Cove, Craft Master, 1964 8
Holly Hobbie, Craft Master, 1974 5
K-9, Craftint Animal Series, 2 sketches,
   oil colors, brushes and brush cleaner .5
Nude, Craftint Big 3 Set, 1950-60s 90
Pinocchio, Craftint 50
Playtime, Hallmark, complete with instruc-
   tions, pre-sketched and numbered
   deep pile Martin woven French velvet
   panels, brushes and brush cleaner,
   1960s 5
Polar Bears, Paint Works 8
Royal Award, Studio-Size Numbered Oil
   Paint Set, 2 pictures, Sunset at Sea
   and Home Voyager, Art Award Co,
   Brooklyn, NY .15
Stallion, Craft Master 20
Tales of Wells Fargo, Transogram 25
The Gold of Autumn, Craft Master, 16 x
   20" sketch, 30 oil colors 10
The Last Supper, Craft Master 30
Wyatt Earp, Transogram, 1958 55

*Tray, Metal Artcraft Co, floral design,
kit includes 16.25 x 11" tray, paints,
instructions, and box.*

PAINT CANS

Paint signs, thermometers and give-aways have been collected for many years, however the old paint can has been over-looked...or at least until now. Wonderful old paint cans come in all sizes and shapes. Their labels show America in miniature... life styles, automobiles, interior design and changing times in lavish colors and graphics. In addition to larger name brand companies such as Sherwin-Williams, there were many smaller local companies throughout the United States. Their labels were designed to attract the attention of the buyer, as well as to show the buyer how the paint was to be used. Paint can collecting is fresh and affordable and they can be displayed beside your "John Deere" tractor or your "Black Americana" collection. They are still available at local flea markets and antique shops.

Look for unusual sizes and shapes. The more complex the design, the more desirable and valuable the can will be.

For a complete look at this collecting field covering paint items from the 1800's through 1980 check out *Collecting Paint Advertising and Memorabilia* (Schiffer Publishing, Ltd, 2000) by Irene Davis.

Advisor: Irene Davis, P.O. Box 63, New Church, VA 23415, (757) 824-5524, web: www.creekhouseantiques.com.

Atlaslac, Geo C D, Wetherill & Co, paper label showing Atlas with earth on his back, 1 qt 95

Bay State Varnishes, Wadsworth, Howland & Co, printed litho label, square can with bail wooden handle, shows pilgrim holding can of paint and brush, 1 gal 45

BPS Blackboard Slating, The Patterson-Sargent Co., paper label, 1/2 pt 10

Bright Wagon Paint, John Lucas & Co Inc, paper label shows wooden wagon, 1 qt 65

Carter White Lead Co, metal pail with bail handle, decal type label, 25 lbs . .40

Chi-Namel Kitch-n-Tint, The Ohio Varnish Co, paper label shows little Chinese men painting kitchen, 1 qt 45

Cook's Rapidry Enamel, Cook Paint & Varnish Co, paper label shows little boy painting can, 1 pt 20

Crow Black Enamel, Frank Bownes Co Inc, paper label shows 2 black crows perched on branch, 1/4 pt 35

Dinah Black Enamel, Boston Varnish Co, paper label showing black mammies walking around can with can of paint in 1 hand and brush in other, 1 qt . . .225

Eagle Pure White Lead, The Eagle-Pitcher Lead Co, printed litho label on 60 lb metal panel with bail handle 125

Effecto Auto Enamel, Pratt & Lambert Inc, paper label shows antique auto, 1/2 pt 95

Fixall Automobile Finish, Louisville Varnish Co, paper label shows antique auto, 1 pt 145

Glos-Tone, The Martin-Senour Co, orange paper label shows 2 room setting of furniture, 1/16 gal 25

Kyanize, Boston Varnish Company, 1/2 pt, $125.

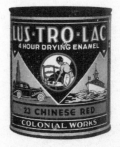

Lus-Tro-Lac, Colonial Works, paper label, 1 qt, $50.

Jap-A-Lac, The Glidden Varnish Co,
printed litho label shows 2 Japanese
ladies in Oriental setting, 3.25 x 6"
rectangular can with screw-off top .175

Kyanize White Enamel, Boston Varnish
Co, applied paper label, rectangular
can with screw-off top, 1/2 pt 90

LiqUidEne Decorative Enamel, Yarnall
Paint Co, orange paper label shows
lady painting dressing table, 1/16 gal ..25

Little Trojan Four Hour Enamel, The
Tredennick Paint Mfg Co, paper label
shows line drawing of house with
green roof 20

Oriole Lead and Zinc, August Miller &
Son, applied paper label shows Oriole
in flight, 1 gal 45

Par-O-Keet Lacquer, The Lowe Brothers
Co, paper label shows 2 parakeets,
1/2 pt..........................35

Red Devil Quick Drying Enamel, Technical
Color & Chemical Works Inc, dark blue
paper label with devil head in center,
1 qt 15

Regatta Vinyltex 59, Jotum-Baltimore
Copper Paint Co, paper label shows
sailboat and cabin cruiser on water,
1 qt 30

Rutland Roof Coating, Rutland Fire Clay
Co, red and green checkered printed
litho label with 2 circles, 1 shows work-
men coating factory roof, other shows
gentlemen coating house roof, 1 gal ..75

Satin-Glo Enamel, British America Paint
Co Ltd, green and yellow paper label
shows little black boy with large paint
brush, 3 oz 50

Wizard Automobile Enamel, Western Auto Supply Co, paper label, 1/2 pt, $50.

United States Standard Ready Mixed Paints, paper label, 1 qt, $45.

Socony Paints, Socony Paint Products
Co, paper label shows flying pegasus,
1 gal 45

Unico Products Super Barn Paint, United
Cooperative Inc, printed litho label
shows farm scene and wraps around
can, 5 gal 125

PAPERBACK BOOKS

This is a category with millions of titles
and billions of copies. Keep this in mind
before paying a high price for anything.

A great deal of the value of paperbacks
rests in the cover art. A risqué lady can
raise prices as well as blood pressure.
Great art can make up for a lousy story by
an insignificant author. However, nothing
can make up for a book's being in poor condition, a fate which has befallen a large
number of paperbacks.

For a detailed listing, I recommend consulting Kevin Hancer's *Hancer's Price
Guide to Paperback Books, Third Edition*
(Wallace-Homestead, 1990, out-of-print)
and Jon Warren's *The Official Price Guide
to Paperbacks* (House of Collectibles, 1991).
Both are organized by company first and
then issue number. Hence, when trying to
locate a book, publisher and code number
are more important than author and title.

The vast majority of paperbacks sell in
the 50¢ to $2.50 range.

Periodical: *Paperback Parade,* P.O. Box 209,
Brooklyn, NY 11228.

PAPER DOLLS

Paper dolls have already been through one craze cycle and appear to be in the midst of another. The publication of Mary Young's *A Collector's Guide To Magazine Paper Dolls: An Identification & Value Guide* (Collector Books, 1990) is one indication of the craze. It also introduces a slightly different approach to the subject than the traditional paper doll book.

The best way to collect paper dolls is in uncut books, sheets, and boxed sets. Dolls that have been cut out, but still have all their clothing and accessories, sell for fifty percent or less of their uncut value.

Paper doll collectors have no desire to play with their dolls. They just want to admire them and enjoy the satisfaction of owning them.

Club: The Original Paper Doll Artists Guild, P.O. Box 14, Kingfield, ME 04947.

Newsletters: *Paper Doll News,* P.O. Box 807, Vivian, LA 71082; *Yesterday's Paper Dolls,* 808 Lee Ave, Tifton, GA 31794.

Periodical: *Paperdoll Review,* P.O. Box 14, Kingfield, ME 04947.

21 Nations, Saalfield, #2179 10
American Family of the Civil War, Tom
　　Teirney 2
Archie, Whitman, 1969 10
Ballet, Whitman 15
Barbie and Ken, Mattel, 1962 25
Barbie Rockers, Whitman, 1986 10
Bill Clinton and His Family, Tom Tierney . .5
Bill Gates 99, Chris Alpine 5

Tricia Paper Doll, Artcraft, 6 pp, 1970, 8.25 x 12.25", $25.

Bridal Party, Whitman, 1968 5
Buffy, Whitman, 1968 8
Carmen Miranda, B Shackman Co 10
Dinah Shore and George Montgomery,
　　Whitman, 1959 .35
Disney's Annette, Whitman, #1958, 1956 .75
Dolls of the 1930s, Athena Publishing Co,
　　1976 5
Glamour Models, Stephens Publishing
　　Co, #177 20
Happy Birthday, Saalfield, #2772 15
Happy Bride, Whitman, 1966 10
Happy Family Paper Dolls, Whitman,
　　#1984 5
Heavenly Blue Wedding, Merrill, 1955 . . .5
Here's the Bride, Whitman, #2109 5
June Allyson, Whitman, #970, 1950 45
Lana Turner, B Shackman 10
Mary Poppins, Whitman, 1966 15
Midge, Whitman, 1963 20
Movie Starlets, Stephens Publishing Co,
　　#178 15
Paper Dolls on Parade, Saalfield, #2295 .25
Petal Dolls, Uneeda, 1969 5
Raggedy Ann & Andy, Whitman, 1974 . . .12
Storyland, Merrill, #1549 5
Tammy and Family, Whitman, 1964 30
Teen Town, Merrill, #3443, 1946 30
The Nurses, Whitman, 1963 20
White House, Pat, Tricia, and Julie Nixon,
　　Saalfield, 1969 .20
Wishnik Trolls, Uneeda, 1960s 8

PAPER MONEY

People hide money in the strangest places. Occasionally it turns up at flea markets. Likewise early paper money came in a variety of forms and sizes quite different from modern paper currency. Essentially, paper money breaks down into three groups—money issued by the federal government, by individual states, and by private banks, businesses, or individuals. Money from the last group is designated as obsolete bank notes.

As with coins, condition is everything. Paper money that has been heavily circulated is worth only a fraction of the value of a bill in excellent condition. Proper grading rests in the hands of coin dealers. Krause Publications (700 East State Street, Iola, WI 54990) is a leading publisher in the area of coinage and currency. *Bank Note Reporter,* a Krause newspaper, keeps collectors up-to-date on current developments in the currency field. There is a wealth of information available to identify and price any bill that you find. Before you sell or turn in that old bill for face value, do your homework. It may be worth more than a Continental, which by the way, continues to be a real "dog" in the paper money field.

PAPERWEIGHTS

This is a tough category. Learning to tell the difference between modern and antique paperweights takes years. Your best approach at a flea market is to treat each weight as modern. If you get lucky and pay modern paperweight prices for an antique weight, you are ahead. If you pay antique prices for a modern paperweight, you lose and lose big.

Paperweights divide into antique (prior to 1945) and modern. Modern breaks down into early modern (1945 to 1980) and contemporary (1980 and later). There is a great deal of speculation going on in the area of contemporary paperweights. It is not a place for amateurs or those with money they can ill afford to lose. If you are not certain, do not buy.

Clubs: International Paperweight Society, 761 Chestnut St., Santa Cruz, CA 95060; Paperweight Collectors Assoc., Inc., P.O. Box 40, Barker, TX 77413.

Advertising, Dewick & Flanders Insurance, glass, tinted color illus of office front, Cruver Co, Chicago, 1 x 2.5 x 4" .35
Advertising, Hartley Grain Co, glass, black and white photo image of farm grain service structure and office building, dated Oct 14, 1901, 1 x 2.5 x 4" 30
Advertising, Lawrence Cement Co, glass, inscription "Hoffman Rosendale" with adv text for other products, mkd "Barnes & Abrams Co, Grapeville, PA" under 1882 patent date, 1 x 2.5 x 4" ...30
Advertising, Provident Life & Trust Co, glass, black and white illus of corner office building, 1.25 x 2.5 x 4" 35

Advertising, Safety Fund National Bank, glass, black and white engraving style illus of office building in Fitchburg, MA, mkd "Abrams Co, Pittsburgh" under 1892 patent date, 1 x 2.5 x 4" ...30
Advertising, Westinghouse Union Battery Co, metal, figural car battery, dark charcoal finish, 1 side inscribed "Westinghouse Union Battery Co, Pittsburgh, PA U.S.A.," other side inscribed "Buck & Colvin" with street address in Oakland, CA, 1930s, 1 x 1.25 x 1.5" 20
Commemorative, Popsicle 50th Anniversary, marble, enameled brass attachments, red, white, blue, and orange design of Twin Popsicle on red ground, black text on brass rim "1923-1973/The Red Sicle Ball/Sign of the Real Thing," rect attachment with "Popsicle 50th Anniversary Celebration," 2 x 3 x .75" 15
Contemporary, F Whittemore, small mushroom spray on dark blue ground, signature cane in bottom, 2" d 165
Contemporary, Perthshire, millefiori on deep blue ground, signature cane, 1973, 2.75" d 120
Contemporary, Peter Holmes, 2 love birds and heart on blue flash ground, red and white millefiori outer circle, scratch signed, limited 103/250, 1982 .65
Contemporary, St Louis, American eagle sulphide on deep blue ground, red and white double overlay, limited 400, 1976 175

Contemporary, green and yellow swirls with controlled bubbles, 3.75" h, $60.

Contemporary, Crider, blue and white swirls, sgd, $75.

Souvenir, 1893 Columbian Expo, glass, horticulture building and inscription" Worlds Columbian Exposition, Chicago, 1893," Barnes & Abrams Co, Grapeville, PA, .75 x 2.5 x 4" 35

Souvenir, 1901 Pan-American Expo, glass, view of Mfg & Liberal Arts Building, 1 x 2.5 x 4" 35

Souvenir, The Milwaukee Road, hollowed white metal, figural streamlined engine, copper luster finish with yellow and black decal on front edge, 1930s, 1.25 x 1.5 x 6.5" 35

PARKING METERS

I have seen them for sale. I have even been tempted to buy one. The meter was a lamp base, complete with new lamp wiring and an attractive shade. To make the light work, you put a coin in the meter. I'm not sure why, but they are rather pricey, usually in the $50 to $100 range. Maybe it has something to do with the fine that you will pay if you obtain one illegally. Might be a good idea to stash a few coin-operated meters away.

PATRIOTIC COLLECTIBLES

Americans love symbols. We express our patriotism through eagles, flags and shields, the Liberty Bell, Statue of Liberty, and Uncle Sam. We even throw in a few patriots, such as Benjamin Franklin.

Club: Statue of Liberty Collectors' Club, 26601 Bernwood Rd., Cleveland, OH 44122.

Note: For addition listings see Flags and Flag Collectibles.

Constitution, bread and butter plate, clear glass, Constitution signer's names, emb "1776-1876" 80

George Washington, plate, Royal Doulton, c1920s 85

Eagle and Shield, ice cream mold, pewter, 5" h 125

Flag, stickpin, diecut celluloid, red, white, and blue flag on brass stickpin, reverse "Liberty Plows/Rock Island Plow Company/Rock Island, Ill" 15

Flag, stuffed toy, Garfield, plush, holding flag, red, white, and blue hat, Dakin, 1978, 8 x 7" 30

Flag, tie, red, white, and blue, "Wilson/ Marshall," black, white embroidered names 50

Liberty Bell, candy container, blue glass, early 20th C 75

Liberty Bell, painted brass, metal clapper, McGovern/Shriver, raised inscription "Proclaim Liberty Throughout All the Land," 2.5 x 2.75" 8

Shield, pinback button, "Chicago-American Herald & Examiner" above shield, "Olympic Champions Club," below, c1932 15

Shield, Union Pacific Railroad, red, white, and blue shield logo, white lettering on blue ground, 1940s 12

Statue of Liberty, dime bank, celluloid, blue and white, center Statue of Liberty image on side, opposite side with text for youthful savers 50

Pillow Sham, entitled "Daughter of the Regiment," silk print, labeled "©1904 by Bernhard Ulmann & Co.," first quarter 20th C, 22.75" sq, $75.

Uncle Sam, bank, painted composition,
bust of Uncle Sam wearing red, white,
and blue striped jacket and hat, front
base with raised text "I Want You,"
1960s, 3.5 x 4.25 x 7" 35
Uncle Sam, candy container, composition,
removable base, 1930s 85
Uncle Sam, marionette, composition,
wood, metallic thread, red, white, and
blue, sequined top hat, metallic shoes,
Macy & Co, 36" h 150
Uncle Sam, ornament, Uncle Sam
Keepsake Ornament, pressed tin,
Hallmark, 1984 25

*Drinking Glass,
"Civilization Is
Overrated!,"
Camp Snoopy,
McDonald's
premium, 1983,
$2.*

PEANUTS

Peanuts is a newspaper cartoon strip
written and illustrated by Charles M.
Schulz. The strip started about 1950 and
starred a boy named Charlie Brown and his
dog, Snoopy. Its popularity grew slowly. In
1955, merchandising was begun with the
hope of expanding the strip's popularity. By
the 1970s Charlie Brown and the gang were
more than just cartoon strip characters.
They greeted every holiday with TV specials; their images adorned lunch boxes,
pencils, pins, T-shirts, and stuffed toys.

While Peanuts collectibles have been
gaining momentum over the years, Charles
Schulz's recent death has triggered a tem-
porary increase in values.

Club: Peanuts Collector Club, Inc., 539
Sudden Valley, Bellingham, WA 98226.

*Limited Edition Plate, Christmas Eve at the
Fireplace, Peanuts series, Schmid, 1974,
$35.*

Alarm Clock, Snoopy, as baseball player,
orange face, white numerals, black
and white image of Snoopy on mound
wearing yellow cap, Model 594, orig
box, Equity Industries, VA, ©1958
United Features Syndicate, c1970s . . .25
Book, *Peanuts Revisited,* Charles M
Schulz, hardcover, Weekly Reader
Children's Book Club Edition, Holt,
Rinehart, and Winston, 1959 3
Costume, Snoopy, plastic mask, vinyl
costume, orig box, 1960-70s 20
Figure, Snoopy, as WWI Flying Ace,
jointed, plastic, removable flying
helmet, made in Hong Kong, 7.25" h . .25
Game, Snoopy Come Home, Milton
Bradley, #4304, 1970s, 9.5 x 19, x 1.5"
box 20
Limited Edition Plate, Linus and Snoopy,
Mother's Day series, C Schulz, Schmid,
1976 35
Limited Edition Plate, Snoopy and the
Beaglescouts, Peanuts Annual, C
Schulz, Schmid, 1984 20
Lunch Box, metal, dome top, "Have Lunch
With Snoopy," doghouse design,
yellow, Snoopy on front lying down
eating sandwich, back shows Snoopy
lying down reading book, 6.5" h metal
thermos with tan top, Thermos, ©1968
United Features Syndicate, 4.25 x
8.625 x 6.5" 40
Lunch Box, vinyl, Lucy listening to
Schroeder playing piano as Snoopy
and Woodstock dance and Charlie
Brown and Linus look on, King-Seeley
Thermos Co, 1972, 6.75 x 9 x 3.75" 65
Magazine, *Life,* 1967, "The great Peanuts
craze/Charlie Brown and Snoopy
winners at last" 15

Music Box, Snoopy, wood and composition, Snoopy as WWI aviator holding baton in air, plays *It's a Long Way to Tipperary*," Anri, Italy, ©1968 United Features Syndicate, c1970s, 4.25" w .150

Pennant, felt, Linus, sucking thumb and holding blanket, "I Love Mankind, It's People I Can't Stand," mkd "A Peanuts Pennant, Copyright 1967 United Features Syndicate" 10

Pinback Button, Linus, holding blanket, "I Believe in Statehood, Countryhood, Cityhood, and Neighborhood," black figure and lettering on yellow ground, 1964 8

Pinback Button, Snoopy, wearing astronaut outfit, "I'm on the Moon!" 12

View-Master Set, Peanuts, B536, ©1966 United Features Syndicate 15

Wastebasket, metal, Peanuts gang, "Cheese" 15

PENCIL CLIPS & PAPER CLIPS

Paper clips clip pieces of paper together. Pencil clips hold pencils in one's pocket. Both were popular; both were used to advertise products. Neither form is used much today. After seeing several hundred examples, I think they should be missed.

The listings below are for paper clips with celluloid buttons and metal spring clips, all dating from the early 1900s. Pencil clips have celluloid buttons with metal pencil holders.

PAPER CLIPS

Arthur Chapin Co, "Your Spring Farm Evaporated Milk Distributor" 2

Bissel Co, multicolored, red inscription, 1" l 30

Eureka Jewelry Co, sepia photo of woman wearing pearls and white gown, light green and white inscription, dark brown border, 1.25" l 40

Harrison & Smith Co, "Minneapolis, Since 1871/The B Line of Greetings & Booklets" 2

Lane Mfg Co, Montpelier, VT, black and white sawmill, c1900, 2.5" l 25

Peacock Condoms, litho tin, yellow, green, and red, c1940, 2 x 2" 35

Paper Clip, L F Grammes & Sons, Allentown, PA adv, brass, 3.125" h, $25.

PENCIL CLIPS

"Barreled Sunlight," image of barrel, black and white 25

"Conn," brown and white 20

"Drink 7-Up," black, white, and red 10

"Drink Coca-Cola," red and white 10

"Formay, Ask Me," blue and white 30

"Krueger Beer & Ale," red and white 1

"Ortho Chevron," red 2

"Pepsi," red, white, and blue, 1950s . . .8

"Pepsi-Cola," red, white, and blue 10

"Red Cross Ranges, Co-Operative Foundry," red, green, and white 20

"Royal Crown Cola," red, blue, and yellow 10

"Starrett Tools," red and gold 8

Victor, "Use Victor Flour," red, yellow, and white 25

"White House Coffee," image of White House, black, blue, and white 35

PENCIL SHARPENERS

Pencil sharpeners divide into two distinct groups: (1) mechanical counter, desk, and wall models and (2) miniature handheld novelty sharpeners. The first group is expensive, the second still affordable.

When buying a mechanical sharpener, make certain it is complete. The period box and instruction sheet add value.

Novelty sharpeners were produced in vast quantities. Comparison shopping keeps the cost low. Do not buy any example that is not in fine or better condition.

1964-65 New York World's Fair, plastic, figural blue unisphere on orange base, white inscription, 1.75 x 1.75 x 2.5" 35

Lampwick, Catalin, figural, full color
decal on dark yellow ground, ©1939
Walt Disney, 1.75" h 125

National Cash Register, diecast metal,
dark bronze luster finish, paper replica
inserts in upper display windows front
and back, cash drawer opens forward
for emptying pencil shavings, 2.25" h .15

Our Gang, butterscotch Catalin, octagon,
applied brass circle holding inset
miniature black and white photo
beneath clear celluloid of "Spanky/
Hal Roach 'Our Gang' Comedies,"
1930s, 1.1875" .100

Panchito, Catalin, full color decal on
orange ground, 1.125" d 60

Pot Belly Stove, brass 6

Pterodactyl, cast metal, dark bronze
finish, 3-D figure attached to base,
1984, 1.5 x 2.25 x 2" 25

Rolltop Desk, diecast brass, Hong Kong . .8

Sailing Ship, celluloid, dark turquoise
blue sail, light yellow mast topped
by red flag, black hull 30

Saxophone, metal, white, gold luster
finish, mkd "Germany" 55

Soccer Player, cast metal, purple, black,
orange, and green, Japan, 2" h 10

PENNANTS

Pennants were produced in large
enough quantities for collectors to be picky.
Buy pennants only if they are in good condition. Images and lettering should be crisp
and the pennant should show no signs of
moth or insect damage.

When storing pennants, keep them flat
or roll them on a cylinder. Do not fold!
Creases left from years of folding can be
very difficult to remove.

1940 New York World's Fair, black and
white, Trylon and Perisphere accented
by light blue on white, yellow-gold
trim band, 3.5 x 8.5" 40

Ali-Frazier, "A Thrilla in Manila/Oct 1,
1975," white and green, alternating
Ali and Frazier heads in red repetition,
6.5 x 12" 40

Apollo 11, lunar exploration scene and
designs, yellow, red, black, white,
and blue, 3.5 x 6.5" 20

Baltimore Bullets, dark blue, orange and
white, small orange NBA copyright
symbol at upper left corner, orange
felt band and streamers, 12 x 29.5" . . .12

Baltimore Orioles, insert paper full color
team photo with identifications, center
design of overlay orange fabric arc
slotted through white fabric extending
beyond pennant edge, white, orange,
and black, 1969, 12 x 30" 20

Brooklyn Dodgers, inked portrait of
Ringling Bros Emmett Kelly, 5 x 12" . .150

Gene Autry, "Back in the Saddle Again/
Gene Autry and Champ," blue and
white, 11 x 27.5" 35

Hopalong Cassidy, Hoppy on horse at
left, black and white, white strip,
black streamers, c1950, 7.5 x 17.5" . . .15

Miami Dolphins, "World Champions,"
orange, white and turquoise blue,
1992-93, 12 x 30" 12

Neil Armstrong, "Wapakoneta, Ohio
Home of Astronaut Neil Armstrong,"
red, white lettering and trim strip,
insert black and white photo of
Armstrong, c1969, 9 x 19.5" 60

Ronald Reagan, "Inauguration Day/
Jan 20, 1981," red, white, and blue,
bluetone image of Reagan at left,
12 x 30" 12

*"Beech Bend International Raceway,
Bowling Green, KY," orange felt, white
band, multicolor design, $50.*

*Ohio Turnpike, emblem and "I Travelled
Ohio," red felt, gold strip, red streamers,
multicolor roadside scenes, 27" l, $5.*

"Truman-Barkley Inauguration, Washington DC, 1949," red, white, and gold, 11 x 29" 60
Vancouver BC, Royal Canadian Mounted Police officer at left, brown, blue streamer strips, 1940-50s, 5 x 12" 10

PENNSBURY POTTERY

Henry and Lee Below established Pennsbury Pottery, named for its close proximity to William Penn's estate, in 1950. The Belows had previously worked for Stangl Pottery, thus the similarity in styles.

Pennsbury motifs are heavily nostalgic, farm and Pennsylvania German oriented. The pottery made a large number of commemorative, novelty, and special-order pieces. Many of these relate to businesses and events in the Middle Atlantic States, thus commanding their highest price within that region.

Pennsbury Pottery was sold at auction in December, 1970.

Look-Alike Alert: The Lewis Brothers Pottery, Trenton, New Jersey, purchased fifty of the lesser Pennsbury molds. Although they were supposed to remove the Pennsbury name from the molds, some molds were overlooked. Further, two Pennsbury employees moved to Lewis Brothers when Pennsbury closed. Many pieces similar in feel and design to Pennsbury were produced. Many of Pennsbury's major lines, including the Harvest and Rooster patterns, plaques, birds, and highly unusual molds, were not reproduced.

Amish, plate, #1029-37, 11.5" d 45
Amish, sugar bowl, open 12
Angel, plate, 19708.25" d 12
Barbershop Quartet, coaster, 4" d 2
Barbershop Quartet, creamer, 11 x 8" ...20
Barbershop Quartet, mug, 4" h 15
Bird, Audubon Warbler, #122 215
Bird, Magnolia Warbler, #112, 4" h 145
Bird, Redstart, #113 25
Black Rooster, bowl, divided, 9.5" d 20
Black Rooster, bowl, heart shape, 6" d ..25
Black Rooster, pitcher, 5.5" h 15
Black Rooster, plate, 8" d 8

Black Rooster, snack set 25
Black Rooster, tray, divided 35
Commemorative, plate, Doylestown Trust Co, 5" d 5
Dutch Talk, bowl, 9" d 15
Eagle, pitcher, 6.5" h 5
Eagle, plaque, 12.25 x 4.5" 60
Eagle, plate, 8" d 20
Eagle, tankard, 4.5" h 20
Family, plate, 11.5" d 50
Folk Art, cup and saucer 35
Hex, coffeepot, 2cup, 5.5" h 60
Hex, creamer, 2.5" h 10
Hex, gravy boat, 4" h 20
Hex, powder jar, 6.5" d 50
Holly, serving tray 55
Mother Serving Pie, pie plate, 9" d 85
Outen the Light, trivet, 4.375" d 10
Railroad, plaque, "Baltimore & Ohio RR 1837/Lafayette," 7.75 x 5.75" 20
Railroad, plaque, "Pennsylvania RR 1856/Tiger" 25
Red Barn, plate, 8" d 35
Red Barn, pretzel bowl 45
Red Rooster, bowl, 5" d 30
Red Rooster, bread and butter plate, 6.5" d 3
Red Rooster, candleholder, 5" h, price for pair 50
Red Rooster, creamer, 4" h 5
Red Rooster, dish, heart shape, 5.5" d ..30
Red Rooster, pitcher, 6.25" h 20
Red Rooster, tray, 5.5 x 7.5" 20
Tulip, tray, 7.5 x 5.5" 20
Two Birds Over Heart, desk basket, 5" ..50
Walking to Homestead, pie plate, 9" d ..20

Railroad, plaque, Central RR of New Jersey, 1870, imp "Pennsbury Pottery, Morrisville, Pa" on bottom, 7.875" l, $30.

PENS & PENCILS

Forget the ordinary and look for the unusual. The more unique the object or set is, the more likely it is that it will have a high value. Defects of any kind drop value dramatically. When buying a set, try to get the original box along with any instruction sheets and guarantee cards (you will be amazed at how many people actually save them).

Clubs: American Pencil Collectors Society, 640 Evergreen Dr., Mountain View, WY 82939; Pen Collectors of America, P.O. Box 821449, Houston, TX 77282.

Newsletter: *Pens,* P.O. Box 64, Teaneck, NJ 07666.

Periodical: Pen World International, 3946 Glade Valley Dr., Kingwood, TX 77339.

PENS

Esterbrook, fountain pen, metallic green, black end tips, 5" l 20
Moore, fountain pen, black, "Loyal Order of the Red Men," 14K "Junior 4" nib, gold emb Indianhead with initials, 5" l 25
Floaty Pen, "Manned Spacecraft Center," space center in Houston flanked by images of space capsule and recovery helicopter, c1960s, 5.75" l 40
Floaty Pen, cruise line souvenir, "*Digby,* Nova Scotia to Saint John, New Brunswick," transparent chamber depicts full color steamship route across "Bay of Fundy," c1950s, 5.75" l .12
Parker, Blue Diamond Vacumatic, gold pearl stripes, 1940s 90

Parker, Duofold Senior, red-orange, "Big-Red," 1920s 150
Parker, Model 75, fountain pen, polka-dot cap and barrel 100
Sheaffer, emerald pearl stripes, 1939 . . .60
Sheaffer, Lifetime Demi, roseglow radite, lever fill, 1937 200
Wahl, Skyline, plastic, black, c1940 100
Waterman, Corinth Taperite, blue, chrome cap, gold-filled trim, lever fill,1949 50
Wearever, ballpoint, plastic, blue and yellow, 5" l 20

PENCILS

1901 Pan-American Expo, wood, lead, brass 0cap holding insert metal loop ring, barrel segmented into red, white, and blue sections, silver lettering inscription "Souvenir of Pan American Exposition 1901," mkd "American Pencil Co, NY," 12" l 20
Atlantic Oil, mechanical, celluloid, brass point and pocket clip, barrel with marble insert depicting red, white, and blue example oil can, inscription "Film Strength/Years of Research/Can Was Filled and Sealed at Our Refinery," state of Florida image with "Motor Oil Quota Maker/Fall Campaign 1940," Parker, 5.75" l .15
Coca-Cola, mechanical, silvered metal and celluloid, red barrel with silver inscription "Drink Coca-Cola in Bottles" with imprint for local bottler, figural bottle pencil clip, 1940s, 5.25" l .50
Parker, Parkette, mechanical, marbleized ruby, 4.75" l 30
Pearl Harbor, mechanical, celluloid, white barrel inscribed by blue letter "V" and "Let US not forget Pearl Harbor," mkd "Falcon," 5.25" l 6

"Tiolene Motor Oil, Made from Cabin Creek Crude," mechanical pencil, oil samples in plastic base, "Jerry's Pure Oil Station, Park River, North Dakota" adv, 5.875" l, $100.
—Photo courtesy Collectors Auction Services.

Sheaffer, fountain pen, black, white, and gray, 4.75" l, $30.

Popeye, wood, lead, turquoise blue,
white inscription, mkd "Linton 210
No. 2," 7.5" l 5
Tarco, mechanical, marbleized gold and
green, 4.75" l 30

PEPSI-COLA

Caleb D. Bradham, a pharmacist and
drugstore owner in New Bern, North
Carolina, developed "Brad's Drink," a soda
mix, in the mid-1890s. By 1898, Brad's Drink
had become Pepsi-Cola. Six years later he
sold his first franchise.

Pepsi-Cola's fortunes soared in 1933
when the company doubled its bottle size
and held its price to a nickel. Pepsi challenged Coca-Cola for the number one spot
in the soda market. One of the most popular
advertising jingles of the 1950s was "Pepsi-
Cola Hits The Spot, Twelve Full Ounces
That's A Lot."

Beware of a wide range of Pepsi-Cola
reproductions, copycats, fantasy items, and
fakes. A Pepsi and Pete pillow issued in the
1970s, a Pepsi glass-front clock, and a 12"
high ceramic statue of a woman holding a
glass of Pepsi are a few examples.

Club: Pepsi-Cola Collectors Club, P.O. Box
817, Claremont, CA 91711.

Advertising Tear Sheet, *Ladies' Home
Journal,* Apr 1958, "The Fine Art of
Staying Lovely," 10.5 x 14" 4
Bank, diecast metal, 1940 tanker truck,
yellow, 1:18 scale 15
Bottle Opener, wall mount, metal, emb
"Pepsi-Cola" 10
Bottle Opener, wall mount, metal,
engraved "Pepsi-Cola Bott. Co.,
Malden, MO," 2" l 9
Calendar, 1943, "Pepsi-Cola Presents
Famous American Paintings" 35
Clock, light-up, plastic and metal, 1950s,
17 x 13" 275
Matchboook, "Drink Iced Pepsi-Cola/
It's Chock-Full of Goodness," early
6-pack container on back, saddle
shows 1/5 cent excise tax paid stamp
used on Canadian matches exported
from 1918 through 1949, different
games or puzzles on inside 10

Napkin Holder, metal, blue 15
Flange Sign, masonite and metal, bottle
cap, "Pepsi-Cola," red, white, and
blue, 1940s, 11 x 13" 475
Pencil Clip, "Pepsi-Cola," red, white,
and blue, 1.5" h, 1" d 3
Pencil Holder, silvered tin, bullet shaped,
red, white, and blue celluloid wrapper
with product name, inscription "Bigger
Drink/Better Taste" and "5¢," bullet
nose removes and holds sharpened
stub pencil, 1950s, 4" l 30
Serving Tray, oval, nostalgic woman at
bar holding glass, 14.5 x 11.5" 8
Sign, celluloid, "Ice Cold Pepsi-Cola
Sold Here," red, white, and blue,
1950s, 9" d 125
Sign, celluloid, "Pepsi-Cola/More Bounce
to the Ounce," gold ground, 1950s,
9" d 240
Sign, masonite, "Drink Pepsi-Cola,"
1950s, 15 x 15.75" 20
Sign, plastic and metal, light-up, bottle
cap, "Drink Pepsi-Cola Ice-Cold,"
1950s, 16" d 275
Sugar Shaker, glass, clear, metal top ...15
Thermometer, wood, woman saluting
and holding glass of Pepsi, 23" l,
7" w 15
Toy Truck, friction, Linemar, 5" l 100
Zippo Lighter, brushed chrome, attached
metal emblem depicting delivery truck
and "Pepsi-Cola," orig case, 2.25" h,
1.5" w 25

*Left: Bottle, painted label, Duraglas 951-G,
12 oz, 9.75" h, $20. Right: Thermometer,
emb metal, 27.25" h, $200.* —Photo
courtesy Collectors Auction Services.

PERFUME BOTTLES

Perfume bottles come in all shapes and sizes. In addition to perfume bottles, there are atomizers (a bottle with a spray mechanism), colognes (large bottles whose stoppers often have an application device), scents (small bottles used to hold a scent or smelling salts), and vinaigrettes (ornamental boxes or bottles with a perforated top). The stopper of a perfume is used for application and is very elongated.

Today's collectors are also interested in commercial bottles. They enjoy the pretty shapes and colors as well as the sexy names.

Clubs: International Perfume Bottle Assoc., 3314 Shamrock Rd., Tampa, FL 33629; Miniature Perfume Bottle Collectors, 28227 Paseo El Siena, Laguna Niguel, CA 92677.

Cologne, bellow form with crown and emb fleur-de-lis design, sheared lip, pontil scarred base, c1840-60, 3.25" h 150

Cologne, electric blue, tapered 12-sided cylindrical form with sloped shoulders, rolled lip, smooth base, c1860-80, 6.125" h 85

Cologne, milk glass, vertical rib and star in banner, smooth base, rolled lip, American, c1865-85, 5.75" h 70

Cologne, opalescent powder blue milk glass, pontil scarred base, flared lip, orig blown ground glass stopper, c1845-65, 5.25" h 55

Figural, Bunker Hill, clear glass, smooth base, tooled mouth, 11.75" h 55

Figural, crystal palace, clear glass, smooth base, tooled mouth, 13.375" h .55

Harrison's Columbian Perfumery, clear glass, smooth base, flared lip, American, c1855-65, 5.125" h 35

Perfume, green, mold blown heart shape, short neck and rolled lip, emb "Penslar, 5.75" h 60

Scent, aqua pinwheel, pontil scarred base, rolled lip, c1845-55, 2.125" h 90

Scent, cobalt blue, mold blown with crown and plumage design, sheared lip, pontil scarred base, c1830-55, 3" h 300

Scent, Sandwich, fiery opalescent milk glass, smooth base, ground lip, missing cap, American, c1865-75, 3" h 40

Scent, sapphire blue, mold blown ovoid form, 18 swirled ribs pattern, sheared lip and pontil, 19th C, 2.375" h 80

Scent, sunburst, medium cobalt blue, pontil scarred base, tooled lip, American, c1850-60, 2.75" h 375

Toilet Water, clear, mold blown 8-panel design, flattened flanged lip, pontil scarred base, Boston & Sandwich Glass Co, 2.375" h 55

Toilet Water, sapphire blue, blown 3-mold cylindrical shape with vertical ribbing, flared lip, smooth neck with lower neck ring, pontil scarred base, c1815-30, 5.25" h 130

Left: Perfume, silver overlay on opaque body, crown finial, $125. Right: Scent, red jasper effect, silver cap, 2.25" h, $160.

PETER MAX COLLECTIBLES

Peter Max has been creating collectibles since 1967. He's the quintessential pop icon whose works symbolized the colorful 1960s hippie era. Interest in Peter Max collectibles has escalated since the first Psychedelic Show in New York City in 1995.

Collectors should note that items dated pre-1973 are most in demand. Unsigned Peter Max look-alike items should be avoided. Find the Peter Max signature on the item before purchase. Since Peter Max owns the copyrights to all his designs, he has not authorized any reproductions or reprints to his works. Prices continue to rise in this area, as well as the entire psychedelic era field.

Beach Towel, cotton, man walking on
   planet with stars and mushroom
   images, 56 x 36" 30
Book, *Peter Max the Land of Yellow*,
   Franklin Watts, 32 pp, full color cover
   and story art throughout, hardcover,
   ©1970 Peter Max, 8.75 x 11.25" 20
Cookie Jar, smiling man's head, red hair,
   large eyes, black bowtie, hat shaped
   lid, 9.5" h 50
Inflatable Pillow, vinyl, 2-sided design
   of winged man in green, pink, and
   yellow surrounded by small abstract
   designs and white stars on blue
   ground, c1970, 15 x 15" 15
Jell-O Shaker, yellow plastic cup, black
   and red wrap-around illus of man
   surrounded by planets and stars,
   missing lid, 1972, 7.25" h 20
Pinback Button, celluloid, black, deep
   pink, blue, and yellow abstract floral
   design on white ground, bar pin on
   back with pop-out easel and hanger
   tab, c1970, 9" d 25
Poster, glossy paper, 2-sided, horizontal
   format on front shows identical black,
   white, and red smiling mouth images
   on gray ground surrounded by orange
   and blue rings, black and white striped
   background, vertical format on back
   shows full color side portrait surrounded by planets, stars, and rays, address
   ink stamp for "Slax N' Jeans Meriden,
   Conn.," 12.5 x 20.5" 45
Poster, glossy paper, "Graham Nash's
   Children of the Americas Radiothon,"
   Sat, Nov 12, 1988, shows girl riding
   on back of winged woman holding
   flower in 1 hand and wand in other,
   24 x 36" 45
Puzzle, *Life* Mini-Max Puzzle, butterfly
   and faces, Series PM2, 126 pcs, 1970,
   6.75 x 11" assembled size 15
Puzzle, Prism-Kaleidoscope, 500 pcs,
   Springbok, 1967 12
Scarf, silk, 3 graduated circles design
   with large Peter Max copyright, c1970,
   21 x 21" 65

PEZ DISPENSERS

   The Pez dispenser originated in Germany and was invented by Edvard Haas in 1927. The name "Pez" is an abbreviation of the German word for peppermint—pfefferminz. The peppermint candy was touted as an alternative to smoking.

   The first Pez container was shaped like a disposable cigarette lighter and is referred to by collectors as the non-headed or regular dispenser.

   By 1952 Pez arrived in the United States. New fruit flavored candy and novelty dispensers were introduced. Early containers were designed to commemorate holidays or favorite children's characters including Bozo the Clown, Mickey Mouse, and other popular Disney, Warner Brothers, and Universal personalities.

   Collecting Pez containers at flea markets must be done with care. Inspect each dispenser to guarantee it is intact and free from cracks and chips. Also, familiarize yourself with proper color and marking characteristics.

Club: The Fliptop PEZervation Society, P.O. Box 124, Sea Cliff, NY 11579.

Angel, with feet 75
Annie 185
Aral Pez Pal, with body part 20
Baloo, no feet 40
Baloo, with feet 30
Bambi, black nose, with feet 55
Batgirl, soft head 200
Batman, with cape, no feet 100

*Tweety Bird and
Sylvester, $10 each.*

Captain America .120
Clown with Collar, no feet 85
Cockatoo, yellow face, red beak 85
Cool Cat, no feet 85
Cool Cat, with feet 75
Cow, blue face, horns 100
Crocodile, neon green 150
Daffy Duck, with feet 25
Dalmatian Pup, no feet 75
Dalmatian Pup, with feet 65
Daniel Boone 275
Dog Whistle, no feet 40
Dog Whistle, with feet 25
Droopy Dog, moveable ears 25
Duck, red flower, white face 120
Dumbo, with feet 35
Foghorn Leghorn, no feet 100
Gorilla, brown face 110
Icee Bear, purple stem 6
Indian Chief, gray headdress 150
Indian Whistle, with feet 20
King Louis, with feet 30
Koala Whistle, with feet 30
Li'l Bad Wolf, with feet 30
Li'l Lion, red hair 75
Majarajah, light green turban 50
Merlin, with feet .25
Miss Piggy, with lashes 25
Monkey Sailor, no feet 55
Mowgli, with feet 30
Octopus, orange 100
Petunia Pig, with feet 45
Pig Whistle, no feet 85
Pirate, no feet 60
Pony, orange head, no feet 85
Speedy Gonzalez, with feet 15
Wile Coyote, with feet 65

PFALTZGRAFF

The name Pfaltzgraff is derived from a famous Rhine River castle, still standing today, in the Pfalz region of Germany. In 1811, George Pfaltzgraff began producing salt-glazed stoneware in York, Pennsylvania.

Initial production consisted of stoneware storage crocks and jugs. When the demand for stoneware diminished, the company shifted to animal and poultry feeders and red clay flowerpots. The production focus changed again in the late 1940s and early 1950s as the company produced more and more household products, including its first dinnerware line, and giftwares.

Club: Pfaltzgraff America Collectors Club, 2536 Quint Ln., Columbia, IL 62236.

America, platter, 14" l 20
Aura, platter, 14 x 10.25" 5
Christmas Heirloom, candy dish, 7" l,
　4.75" w 12
Christmas Heirloom, mug, 5" h 8
Folk Art, butter crock, half stick 8
Folk Art, casserole, individual 8
Folk Art, cup and saucer 2
Folk Art, vegetable bowl, 8.5" d 10
Gourmet, butter, cov 8
Gourmet, canister, 6.5" h 15
Heritage, creamer and sugar 10
Heritage, pitcher, 5" h 6
Heritage, vegetable bowl, 10.75 x 8.75 x
　2.75" 12
Spring Song, cereal bowl 8
Village, casserole, 2 qt 10
Village, coffee canister 8
Village, honey pot, with dipper, 16 oz 20
Village, teapot, cov 6
Village, utensil caddy 10
Yorktowne, baking dish, 12 x 8.25" 25
Yorktowne, berry bowl, 5.75" d 3
Yorktowne, bowl, heart shaped 10
Yorktowne, candleholder, 4.25" h 5
Yorktowne, clock, 10.5" d 25
Yorktowne, creamer and sugar 4
Yorktowne, Lazy Susan, wood, 13" d 25
Yorktowne, mixing bowl, 8" d 5
Yorktowne, salt and pepper shakers, pr . .8
Yorktowne, serving bowl, 10" d 8
Yorktowne, soup mug, 5" d 5
Yorktowne, trivet, 8.5 x 8.5" 12

Yorktowne, cup and saucer, $4.

PICTURE FRAMES

We have reached the point where the frame is often worth more than the picture in it. Decorators have fallen in love with old frames. If you find one with character and pizazz at a flea market for a few dollars, pick it up. It will not be hard to resell. Who said picture frames have to be used for pictures? They make great frames for mirrors. Use your imagination.

Club: International Institute for Frame Study, 443 I St. NW, P.O. Box 50156, Washington, DC 20091.

Blue Glass, Art Deco style, metal corners, cardboard back, c1948, 4 x 5" .... .30
Brass, Art Deco, half circle projection on sides, easel back, 6 x 8" .... .75
Brass, Egyptian motif, 3.5 x 6" .... .100
Cast Iron, Art Nouveau, oval, gilded, folding stand, openwork scrolls and leaves, 10.5 x 8" .... .50
Glass, twisted glass with red internal striping, Italian .... .200
Ivory, pierced and carved floral design, 1.25 x 2.25" .... .75
Mahogany, deep well, black inner border with gilt edge, 12.5 x 15 ..... .65
Mahogany, folk art, laminated, pyramid dec, old varnish finish, 9 x 12.75" .... .45
Silver-Plated, dragon motif, Japan, 6 x 8" .... .200
Silver-Plated Brass, beaded edge with applied corners, 3.75 x 6" .... .60

Wood, tramp art, star motif, notch-carved, 26 x 20", $350.

Thermoplastic, overall mother-of-pearl effect, c1937, 5 x 5" .... .125
Wood, tramp art, rect, chip-carved, diamond shape projections at each corner, 1915, 17.25 x 19.5" .... .65
Wood and Glass, Art Deco, black and white diagonal stripes .... .75

PIE BIRDS

Pie birds and pie funnels continue to be a hot collectible and functional kitchen novelty. The basic criteria for pie birds are: ceramic pottery (e.g. stoneware, porcelain), glazed inside and outside, 3 to 5 inches tall, arches (cutouts) at the base to allow steam to enter and exit through a top vent hole. There are Pyrex and aluminum (non-US) pie funnels.

Many novelty pie vents have found their way into the market in the last 25 years. Beware of figural pie vents from England that are stained with brown gook that allude to age and usage. Note: age crazing is a process that can be applied to new pie vents.

Club: Pie Bird Collectors Club, 158 Bagsby Hill Ln., Dover, TN 37058.

Newsletter: *Piebirds Unlimited Newsletter,* 14 Harmony School Rd., Flemington, NJ 08822.

2-Headed Bird, Barn Pottery, Devon, England .... .65
Benny the Baker, 1950-60s .... .70
Blackbird, Clarice Cliff, c1930-60s ...... .20
Blackbird, seated on log, Artone Pottery, England .... .50
Bird on Nest, with chicks, Artisian Galleries .... .350
Chef, Pierre, holding spoon, black face, yellow smock .... .85
Chick, yellow, Josef Originals, 1970s .... .60
Duckling, American Pottery Co .... .25
Elephant, pink and gray, Cardinal China Co .... .125
Funnel, ceramic, England .... .10
Rooster, Blue Willow pattern, new ..... .15
Rooster, Marion Drake .... .65
Rooster, pastel colors, Cleminson Pottery, 1940s .... .20
Songbird, American Pottery Co, 1940s .. .15

Roosters, Pearl China Co, $40 each.

Songbird, multicolored patches, Morton
    Pottery 18
Walrus, black, mkd "Made in Japan" ..125

PIERCE, HOWARD

Howard Pierce established his pottery
studio in LaVerne, California, in 1941.
Initially he produced small pewter animal
figurines. A lack of metal supplies during
World War II forced him to close. He
reopened in 1945 and produced a line of
contemporary ceramic figurines.

Pierce's work was sold in high-end gift
shops and department stores. A satin-matte
brown on white combination glaze was his
favorite. In 1956 he introduced a line of
Jasperware products.

Pierce entered semi-retirement in 1968
when he moved to Joshua Tree, a desert
community near Palm Springs. He still produces a small range of limited production
pieces that are sold through select outlets.

Figurine, African woman's head, beige
    and brown speckled hair, 7" h 30
Figurine, bear, 3" h, 6" w 15
Figurine, bird on tree stump, 5.75" h 50
Figurine, cat, brown and white, 8" h 45
Figurine, chipmunk, 7" l 45
Figurine, coyote, 6" h 100
Figurine, dachshund, 10" l, 3.25" h 135
Figurine, dove, 7" l, 4.5" h 20
Figurine, duck, dark brown, brown speck-
    led chest, 9 x 4" 70
Figurine, gazelle, mkd "100P," 11.25" h ...75
Figurine, girl holding open container
    beside 2 jugs, 9" h 50

Figurine, girl reading book, 7" h 75
Figurine, mouse, 2.25" h, 2.75" l 20
Figurine, penguin, 6.625" h 40
Figurine, pelican, 8.5" h 60
Figurine, raccoon, 9" l, 3.75" h 65
Figurine, roadrunner, 9" l, 5" h 25
Figurine, seal, black, 5" h, 6" w 50
Figurine, snow owl, gray and cream,
    4" h 30
Figurine, sparrow, tail down, 3.5" h 30
Flower Frog, quail, 8" h 75
Nativity Set, Joseph 7.25" h, Mary hold-
    ing baby Jesus, 4.25" h, lamb 2.25" h .250
Planter, green, white deer nestled into
    side, imp "80P," 10" l, 2.5" h 30

PIG COLLECTIBLES

This is one animal that does better as a
collectible than in real life. Pig collectibles
have never been oinkers.

Established pig collectors focus on the
bisque and porcelain pigs of the late 19th
and early 20th centuries. This is a limited
view. Try banks in the shape of a pig as a
specialized collecting area. If not appeal-
ing, look at the use of pigs in advertising. If
neither please you, there is always Porky.
"That's All, Folks!"

Club: The Happy Pig Collectors Club, P.O.
Box 17, Oneida, IL 61467.

Ashtray, Stangl 50
Bank, cast iron, "Buy at Norco and
    Save/Norco Foundry & Specialty Co,
    Pottstown, Pa," 5" l 25
Bank, Corky Pig, Hull, 5.25" h, 7" l 45

Bank, cast iron, $80. —Photo courtesy
Gene Harris Antique Auction Center, Inc.

Creamer, gray, Royal Bayreuth, c1900, 4.25" h, $500. —Photo courtesy Ray Morykan Auctions.

Book, *The Tale of the Grunty Pig,* Arthur
   Scott Bailey, 114 pp, ©1921 Grosset
   & Dunlap 8
Book, *The Three Little Pigs,* Stampkraft,
   Barse & Hopkins, NY, 4.5 x 6" 12
Chocolate Mold, pig playing horn, 2 pc,
   Anton Reiche, 5.5" h 130
Comic Book, Porky Pig, Dell, #35, Jul-
   Aug 1954 3
Cookie Jar, pig wearing yellow shirt,
   gray pants, pink and black highlights,
   mkd "USA" 90
Creamer, pink pig wearing brown hat,
   yellow tail/handle, Royal Copley,
   4.5" h, 6" l, 2.75" w 10
Figurine, cobalt iridized, Fenton, 3" l 20
Figurine, composition, stick legs,
   German, 2.5" l, 1.5" h 15
Figurine, farmer pig, smiling, gold trim,
   unmkd, 6" h 8
Figurine, piglet, Goebel, 3" h, 2.75" w 10
Figurine, sleeping mama pig with 5
   piglets feeding, mkd "Hand Painted
   Pacific Japan" 15
Food Mold, copper, 4" l 6
Little Golden Book, *The Party Pig,* Simon
   & Schuster, 1954 10
Pitcher, standing pig, majolica, 7.75" h ..12
Salt Shaker, "I'm Salt," Japan, 3" h 5
Shot Glass, emb green glass, "A Pig
   Shot" 5
Toy, Pudgy Pig, Fisher-Price, #478 35
Zippo Lighter, pig in uniform emblem 8

PINBACK BUTTONS

Around 1893 the Whitehead & Hoag Company filed the first patents for celluloid pinback buttons. By the turn of the century, the celluloid pinback button was used as a promotional tool covering a wide spectrum, ranging from presidential candidates to amusement parks.

This category covers advertising pinback buttons. To discover the full range of non-political pinbacks consult Ted Hake and Russ King's *Price Guide To Collectible Pin-back Buttons 1896–1986* (Hake's Americana & Collectibles Press: 1986).

American Gentlemen Shoe, "Sold
   Everywhere," center image of early
   American man, black and white, red
   lettering, white rim 12
Colonial Bread, bread loaf in blue and
   white wrapper with red and gold
   spots on each end, 1930s 12
Dakota Gold Turkey, "Fancy Turkey,"
   turkeys in front of sunrise, blue and
   yellow, red lettering, 1940s 12
Davis OK Baking Powder, red, yellow,
   black, and white bottle, white ground,
   c1896 15
Dry Yeast Baking Powder, yellow, black,
   and white canister, c1896 15
Dustbane Sweeping Compound, center
   canister image, black and yellow 15

McKinley/Roosevelt/Van Sant, Minnesota 1900 trigate, celluloid, 1.25" d, $65. —Photo courtesy Gene Harris Antique Auction Center, Inc.

Uncle Sam hanging Hitler, mechanical, litho metal, 1940s, $30. —Photo courtesy Gene Harris Antique Auction Center, Inc.

Good Humor, "Know America Club," center American flag, red, white, and blue, 1930s .... .45

Hankey's Farm Boy My-t-Fine Bread, boy, cow, milk can, and chicken, red lettering, white ground, 1900s ...... .35

Maltese Cross Rubbers, red logo on white ground, blue lettering outer rim inscription ..../......10

Maxwell House Coffee, red and white band with "The People's Choice," 1950-60s 8

"Mr Zip," image of zip code symbol figure above name in black lettering, 1960s . .5

Old Master Coffee, elf wearing red cap, green ground 20

Patton's Sun-Proof Paints, "Five Year Guarantee," yellow smiling sun face emitting yellow rays to outer brown rim, blue lettering 15

Peck-Williamson Furnace, "Sawrie– The Man Who Made the Underfeed Famous in Nashville" 75

Philco, "It's Philco Week," red and white, 1930s 8

Reddy Kilowatt, "The Mighty Atom," red portrait, blue lettering, white ground, 1960s 20

Statwood Home Detective, "Earnest Ernest," cartoon image of beaver as home inspector, 1950s 20

Sunny Jim-Bran Dandies, "Be a Regular Fellow," 1900s 35

Westinghouse, center "W" above "Westinghouse X-Ray," orange and black, 1930s 8

PINUP ART

The stuff looks so innocent, one has to wonder what all the fuss was about when it first arrived upon the scene. Personally, I like it when a little is left to the imagination.

George Petty and Alberto Vargas (the "s" was dropped at Esquire's request) have received far more attention than they deserve. You would be smart to focus on artwork by Gillete Elvgren, Billy DeVorss, Joyce Ballantyne, and Earl Moran. While Charles Dana Gibson's girls are also pinups, they are far too respectable to be included here.

Newsletters: *Glamour Girls: Then and Now,* P.O. Box 34501, Washington, DC 20043; *The Illustrator Collector's News,* P.O. Box 1958, Sequim, WA 98382.

Blotter, Moran, cardboard, full color portrait, "Called In the Draft," "Sox Appeal," "Figures Don't Lie," "Special Extra," "Pretty Foxy," Brown & Bigelow, 1950s, 4 x 9", price for set of 5 40

Calendar, 1946, Mozert, "Fairest Flower," 10 x 17.5" 100

Calendar, 1947, Petty, "Petty Girl," spiral bound, 9.25 x 12.5" 40

Calendar, 1947, Varga, *Esquire,* horizontal format, 8.5 x 12" envelope 65

Calendar, 1952, Thompson, "Studio Sketches," spiral bound, 8.75 x 12.25" .70

Calendar, 1957, Frahm, "The Shake-Down," ©1955 A Fox, 10 x 16.75" 60

Calendar, 1958, Frahm, "Going Down," ©1956 A Fox, 10 x 16.75" 60

Ashtrays, litho tin, blue ground, Texaco Service adv, 4.25" w, $65 each. —Photo courtesy Collectors Auction Services.

Calendar, 1966, Elvgren, "A Fair Shake," orig envelope, 5 x 10", $35.

Calendar Card, MacPherson, 1949, "Stocking Up," 4.75 x 10" 6

Calendar Top, Moran, "Maid in Baltimore," Brown & Bigelow, 1940-50s, 16 x 20.5" 60

Greeting Card, Munson, fold-out, full color illus progress from clothed secretary through various stages of undress to final illus posed in sheer transparent upper body covering, health food practice theme text on panel, mkd sponsor name "Nunemaker Artist Bureau, Reading, PA," 1944, 6.25 x 8.25" closed size 45

Magazine, *Wink-A-Fresh Magazine*, Jan 1946, Vol 1, #5, blonde-haired model in black swimsuit taking waist measurement while winking eye at viewer, red ground, 64 pp, 8.5 x 11" 20

Memo Booklet, Elvgren, "Keep 'em Flying," "A Christmas Eve," 4.5 x 8", price for set of 2 25

Memo Booklet, Elvgren, "Peace Offering," "Sweet Presentation," "Neat Trick," "What's Cookin?," "Sailor Beware," inside cover has 1965-66 calendar, Brown & Bigelow, 3.25 x 6", price for set of 5 60

Playing Cards, 52 cards plus 2 Jokers, Arctic view of model in red and white Santa outfit admired by 2 penguins, imprint for sponsor "Graceflo Dra-Pul Curtains," sgd "Elvgren," Brown & Bigelow, 1 x 4 s 5" plastic case 25

Playing Cards, 52 cards plus 2 Jokers, model in yellow outfit with green spots riding carousel pony, dark blue ground, sgd "Erbit," 1950s 20

Portrait, Armstrong, "June," model posed in soft lush scenic setting, framed, 1920-30s, 12 x 14" 60

PLANTERS

A planter is any container suitable for growing vegetation. It may be constructed of any number of materials ranging from wooden fruit crates and painted tires found on suburban front lawns to ceramic panthers stalking 1950s television sets. If you thought all those planters you got from the florist were junk, read on. Too bad you threw them out or sold them for a dime each at your last garage sale. This category deals with the figural ceramic variety found in abundance at all flea markets.

Baby Ballerina, Haeger, 5.5" h 8
Baby Buggy, pastel colors, unmkd, 7.5" l . .8
Basketweave, McCoy, 5" h, 5.5" d 10
Bird, head down, white, Shawnee, 5.5" l . .8
Bluebird, rhinestone eyes, Lefton, #288, 6" h 10
Boxing Gloves, McCoy, 5.5" h 15
Boy, standing next to tree stump, Shawnee, #533, 6.5" h 10
Canary, perched by flower, Royal Copley, 3.5" h, 4" d 20
Children in Shoe, Czechoslovakia, 4" h . .10
Cow, reclining, Japan, 5.5" l 5
Dachshund, howling to moon, tail up, attached planter to side 10
Davy Crockett, American Bisque, 5" h . . .45
Donkey, pulling cart, 6" h, 6.5" l 5
Dutch Boy, carrying buckets on shoulders, stamped "Made in Japan," 4" h 8
Elephant, seated beside pot, gold trim, American Bisque, 3.75" h 12

Geometric pattern, olive green, mkd "CP-1318 USA," 8.5" l, $10.

Baby, holding football, Ardco, 5.5" h, $8.

Elephant, standing on ball, Royal Copley, 7.5" h .... .25

Fire Engine, pastel colors, American Bisque, 6" l .... .25

Fish, black and white, Stanford Pottery .10

Hat, Fenton, 3.25" h, 4.5" w 5

Hobnail, milk glass, Fire-King, 4.5" h, 4" d .2

Horse Head, Lefton, H1953, 6.25" h ...... .15

Mammy, seated on stoop, McCoy, 7" l ...25

Monkey, holding nut, Brush, 5" h .... .20

Monkey Head, white, McCoy, 5.5" h 10

Oaken Bucket and Pump, Inarco, 5.25" h 10

Santa, hp, "Japan" paper label, 5.5" h ...2

Seal, mouth open, bow around neck, 5.25" h .... .10

Tree Stump with Mushrooms, American Bisque, 4.5" h .... .12

Wagon Wheel, McCoy, 8.25" h .... .20

Watering Can, basketweave and floral dec, Shawnee, 5.5" h .... .15

PLANTERS PEANUTS

Amedeo Obici and Mario Peruzzi organized the Planters Nut and Chocolate Company in Wilkes-Barre, Pennsylvania, in 1906. The monocled Mr. Peanut resulted from a trademark contest in 1916. Standard Brands bought Planters only to be bought themselves by Nabisco. Planters developed a wide range of premiums and promotional items. Beware of reproductions.

Club: Peanut Pals, P.O. Box 652, St. Clairsville, OH 43950.

Advertising Tear Sheet, "Planters Fall Fiesta/Fall Time is Planters Nut Time," shows various Planters products, 1953, 10 x 14" 4

Advertising Tear Sheet, *Ladies' Home Journal,* Apr 1948, "Let's Have a Party/ Underwood Deviled Ham," 5.5 x 14" ...3

Alarm Clock, red body, yellow face with Mr Peanut in center, black hands and numbers, c1960s .... .250

Bag, glassine, "Planters Pennant Salted Peanuts/The Nickel Lunch," c1940s ..10

Bank, figural, plastic, removable hat, blue, green, red, and tan, 7" h ...... .15

Book, *The World of Mr Peanut,* softcover, 12 pp, 9 x 11" 4

Cookbook, *Cooking–The Modern Way,* 1948 3

Flatware, 4 forks, 3 spoons, 3 knives, plastic, red, figural Mr Peanuts handles .... .40

Jar, clear glass, "Fish Globe Planters Salted Peanuts," tin lid, fish shaped label .... .375

Jar, clear glass, "Planters," hexagonal, clear glass lid with peanut handle, yellow lettering and Mr Peanut figure .... .155

Light Pull, figural, molded plastic, c1960s .... .15

Mechanical Pencil, figural, molded plastic, Mr Peanut on top, yellow and blue .... .20

Paperweight, figural, pot metal ...... .775

Pen and Pencil Set, "Mr Peanut's 75th Birthday" gold filled, Mr Peanut engraved on clip .... .200

Punchboard, Planters Salted Cashews/ Cocktail Peanuts, 5¢, 10.5 x 10.125" ...35

Toy Train, orig box, Tyco, 1977 .... .50

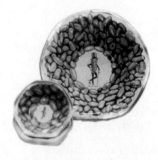

Nut Set, tin, 6 x 9" master dish, four 3" d individual dishes, price for set, $20.

Peanut Chopper, premium, unused, $25.

Ashtray, black Femlin on orange ground, $5.

Tumbler, "Mr Peanut 75th Anniversary,"
   price for set of 6 250
Windup, figural Mr Peanut, black and
   tan 400

PLAYBOY COLLECTIBLES

Playboy memorabilia, from magazines to calendars to Playboy Club items is a popular collecting category, especially now since all the clubs have closed. Hugh M. Hefner began his empire in 1953 with the debut of the first issue of *Playboy Magazine.* Marilyn Monroe graced its cover and centerfold. Many Playboy collectibles can be found at yard sales, swap meets, flea markets, collectible shows, and antique malls. Value on items listed are in good condition, but will be higher if they are in excellent condition and/or unopened or unused such as sealed puzzles and playing cards.

Club: Playboy Collectors Assoc., P.O. Box 653, Phillipsburg, MO 65722.

Magazine, Australian Playboy, *Feb 1979, Australia's first playmate issue, $65.*

Ashtray, clear glass, white center with
   gold "VIP"and rabbit logo, 3.75" sq . . .20
Book, *The Playboy Cartoon Album,*
   Playboy Press, 192 pp, 1963, 8.5 x 11" .20
Bracelet, gold link, center diecut gold
   metal rabbit head symbol within
   heart symbol, attached tag "Playboy
   jewelry is designed by skilled artisans
   with an eye to the '80s," 6" l, hinged
   black case 20
Calendar, 1963, orig envelope 40
Calendar, 1970, orig envelope 20
Calendar, 1972, orig envelope 20
Calendar, 1964, with subscription page,
   orig 8.5 x 12.75" envelope 40
Candleholder, glass, black Femlin image
   on opposite sides circled by repeated
   inscription "The Playboy Club," 1960s,
   6.25" h 30
Drinking Glass, clear, tapered, weighted
   bottom, black Femlin within inscription
   "The Playboy Club," c1960, 6" h, 2" d . .10
Lighter, metal, black, gold luster trim,
   tiny white rabbit head symbol at lower
   left corner, with black vinyl snap fasten-
   er pouch, 1960s, .25 x 1 x 1.375" 20
Magazine, Jun 1958 2
Magazine, Apr 1966 3
Pinback Button, "The Bunny Open Disco
   Championships," 1979, 3" d 12
Purse, vinyl, yellow, repeated black
   Playboy rabbit image with repeated
   "Bunny Bag," 1960s, 5 x 7" 20
Puzzle, full figure Playmate, with en-
   closed guide paper, 1972, 5.5 x 4"
   canister 20
Puzzle, Playboy Playmate of the Year,
   500 pcs, centerfold photo of Miss
   January Liv Lindeland, with guide
   paper, 6.5 x 5.25" canister 35

On the Rocks
Glass, $5.

Rust-Oleum,
Brown & Bigelow,
boxed set, $7.

Shot Glass, clear, printed Femlin with
inscription "The Playboy Club," 3" h,
price for set of 6 40

PLAYING CARDS

The key is not the deck, but the design
on the deck surface. Souvenir decks are
especially desirable. Look for special decks
such as Tarot and other fortune-telling
items.

Always buy complete decks. There are
individuals who just collect Jokers and
have a bad habit of removing them from a
deck and then reselling it. Prices listed are
for complete decks.

Clubs: Chicago Playing Card Collectors,
Inc., 1826 Mallard Lake Dr., Marietta, GA
30068; 52 Plus Joker, 204 Gorham Ave.,
Hamden, CT 06514; International Playing
Card Society, 3570 Delaware Common,
Indianapolis, IN 46220.

Bicentennial Flags, double deck, 1976 ...2
Birds, Fireside Game Co, 1899 10
Buster Brown, miniature, cartoons on
    each card, USPC, 1906 100
Cheer-up, hospital cartoons, Stancraft,
    1960 5
Cunard Line, Forman & Sons, steamship,
    1900 75
Dark Shadows, double deck 12
Dewar's Scotch Whiskey, Goodall &
    Son, London 4
Fortune Telling, Whitman, 1931 6
Hank Williams Jr 3
Harvard Club, New York 10
Hershey's Chocolate Syrup 2
Joe Camel, 1980s 2
Kennedy Kards, caricature courts,
    Humor House, 1963 15

Kent Feeds, Brown & Bigelow 10
Long Lost Sinking Ships, American
    President Lines Ship Co, 1950s 18
Midway Airlines 2
Mohawk Airlines, 20th Anniversary
    1945-65 25
Night's Gallery, nudes, Japan, 5 x 7" 15
Peanuts, miniature, Hallmark 5
Planters Tavern Nuts 6
Pla-More Playing Cards 40
Princeton University, The Princeton
    Club, NY, USPC, 1923 15
Raffles Hotel, Singapore 5
Raggedy Andy, miniature, Hallmark 4
Singapore Airlines 5
Swiss Air 5
Tang Dynasty, Chinese 20
Tarot, DeLawrence, 1950 35
TWA Lockheed 749, standard, USPC,
    1970 4
Van Camp's, c1911 85
Vargas Girls, different pin-up color
    drawings on each card, Stancraft,
    1953 100
Victory, patriotic courts, Arrco, 1945 80
Wisconsin, Wisconsin Historical Society,
    double deck, c1950 8

Edison Mazda
Lamps, Maxfield
Parrish illus "The
Waterfall," 2931,
full deck, $275.
—Photo courtesy
Gene Harris
Antique Auction
Center, Inc.

POLITICAL ITEMS

Collect the winners—time does not treat losers well. Do not pay much for items less than thirty years old. Also concentrate on the non-traditional categories. Everyone collects pinbacks and posters. Try something unusual. How about political ties, mugs, or license plates?

Clubs: American Political Items Collectors, P.O. Box 340339, San Antonio, TX 78234; Third Party & Hopefuls, 1901 Ridgeway, Apt. #8, De Pere, WI 54115.

Newsletter: *The Political Bandwagon,* P.O. Box 348, Leola, PA 17540.

Periodical: *The Political Collector,* P.O. Box 5171, York, PA 17405.

Agnew, Spiro, trash can, litho tin, 1 side shows Agnew playing tennis with hardhat in hand inscribed "God Bless America," other side shows Agnew playing golf with balloon caption "But I Did Say...Fore!," 13" h 35
Carter, James E, hand puppet, hollow rubber head, stuffed fabric hands, blue cloth coat, red, white, and blue header "Puppet President/I Never Promised You a Rose Garden," "I Am Jimmy" sticker, 6 x 9" 20
Dukakis, Michael, pinback button, "Dukakis for President 1988," blue-tone photo surrounded by outline of Wisconsin state, blue lettering on white ground .10

Eisenhower, Dwight D, sheet music, *All for the USA,* Henry Dellafield, ©1954 Bach Music Co, 9.25 x 12" 15
Kennedy, John F, flicker, black and white plastic sheet, photo of Kennedy profile with "The Man for the 60s," 1.125 x 1.25" .12
Nixon, Richard M, game, Who Can Beat Nixon?, 9 x 11.5 x 2" box 15
Reagan, Ronald, autographed card, "To Blaine Howard with very best wishes Ronald Reagan," black ball-point pen signature, c1979, 3 x 5" . . .100
Reagan, Ronald, pocket watch, brass, raised image of Reagan, inscription "40th President" on hinged lid, opens to reveal full color eagle, garland, and crossed flags on dial, raised image of White House on reverse watch cover, Nicolet, 4.5 x 4.5" blue felt-lined box with presidental seal . . .75
Republican, program, "Republican Victory Kick-Off Dinner," diecut football, 8 pp, for Covnention Hall, Philadelphia, PA, Tue Oct 4, 1955, sepia illus 25
Republican, ribbon badge, "Republican National Convention Delegate," Kansas City, MO, Aug 1976, attached brass hanger bar, blue fabric ribbon 25
Roosevelt, Franklin D, sheet music, *The Road Is Open Again,* Irving Kahal and Sammy Fain, 9 x 12" 18
Roosevelt, Theodore, pinback button, "For President Theodore Roosevelt," color portrait on dark gold ground, black lettering, 8" d 20

Roosevelt, Franklin D, stereograph, "Franklin Delano Roosevelt, President of the United States, at His Desk in the Executive Office, Washington, D.C.," #5*33535, Keystone View Co, $70.

Smith, Al, watch fob, "For President Al Smith," celluloid button in emb brass fob, $40. —Photo courtesy Gene Harris Antique Auction Center, Inc.

Roosevelt, Theodore, watch fob, brass, incised black lettering "Roosevelt 1904 Fairbanks/Washington," 1.375 x 1.5" 20

Truman, Harry S, letter, "Harry S. Truman/ Federal Reserve Bank Building/Kansas City Six, Missouri" letterhead, dated Oct 21, 1955, letter thanking person for requesting signed copy of Truman's memoirs, black ink signature, 7.25 x 10" 150

POODLE COLLECTIBLES

People who collect dog and cat memorabilia are a breed apart. While most cat collectors collect items with any cat image (except Siamese collectors), dog collectors tend to specialize. Poodle collectors are more fortunate than most because the poodle was a popular decorating motif during the 1950s and 1960s. Poodles were featured on everything from clothing to lamps.

Action Figure, Peteena the Pampered Poodle, Hasbro, 6 outfits, 1966 50

Advertising Tear Sheet, Old Gold Cigarettes, 2 poodles sitting at table with ashtray and cigarettes 5

Advertising Tear Sheet, Pepsi, man and woman walking 2 poodles illus 5

Ashtray, pink poodle design, Lefton 12

Book, *Playtime Poodles,* Helen Wing 6

Brooch, Bakelite, figural 35

Canister Set, 4 pcs, emb, Ransburg of Indianapolis 40

Creamer and Sugar, cov, Enesco 20

Figure, ceramic, California Ceramics, 14.5" h 70

Tea Towel, linen, gray, turquoise, and green, "Parisian Prints All Pure Linen" paper label, 28.75 x 16.25", $10.

Figure, pink poodle lady, mkd "KB80552 Lefton China Hand Painted" 20

Lamp, ceramic, pink, paper shade 30

Pattern, child's poodle skirt, Simplicity, 1950s 3

Purse, wicker, leash handle, mkd "Maybelle Marie Birch California" ...40

Purse, woven, white, 2 black poodles dec, "Princess Charming by Atlas Hollywood Fla" label 20

Skirt, clown with poodle jumping through hoops dec 25

Tea Towel, linen, hand embroidered 5

TV Lamp, chalkware, 1950s 40

Vase, black poodle with pink rose illus, Josef Originals paper label 20

POSTCARDS

This is a category where the average golden age card has gone from 50¢ to several dollars in the last decade. Postcards' golden age is between 1898 and 1918. As the cards have become expensive, new collectors are discovering the white border cards of the 1920s and 30s, the linens of the 1940s, and the early glossy photograph cards of the 1950s and 1960s.

It pays to specialize. This is the only way that you can build a meaningful collection. The literature is extensive and can be very helpful.

Clubs: Deltiologists of America, P.O. Box 8, Norwood, PA 19074; Postcard History Society, P.O. Box 1765, Manassas, VA 20108.

Periodicals: *Barr's Post Card News,* 70 S. 6th St., Lansing, IA 52151; *Postcard Collector,* P.O. Box 1050, Dubuque, IA 52004.

Note: *Barr's* and *Postcard Collector* list over fifty regional clubs scattered across the United States.

Advertising, Acker's "Atlantic City's Sweetest Attraction," mermaid in sea presenting box of candies, inset storefront view, monotone view on back of Atlantic City beach and bathing beauty, c1904 85

Advertising, Ginger Mint Julep, photo of truck from the Emerson Drug Co, Baltimore, MD, black and white 100

Christmas, hold-to-light, $250.

Valentine, #265, divided back, $3.

Advertising, Indian Motorcycles, "Come over and see for yourself! The greater comfort, efficiency, cleanliness in 1927 Indians/28 Big Improvements," man on motorcycle 125

Advertising, Longines Pocket Watches, fantasy woman montage, factory, and pocket watch, hand-colored, A Witnauer Co, NY 150

Advertising, New Home Sewing Machine, cartoon image of grandma sewing up pants of grandson while he is wearing them, French, English text, c1910 85

Christmas, "Merry Christmas," artist's rendition of Christmas tree decorated with candles, German 65

Christmas, Santa figure, emb, brown robe with gold highlights, twig crown, and pine tree staff, with angel sitting on shoulder, PFB #9103 45

Fourth of July, emb, Miss Columbia sitting atop Liberty Bell and fire-crackers 40

Halloween, emb, child lifting top off jack-o'-lantern, design by Freixas, Winsch, 1914 125

Hold-To-Light, "A Happy Christmas to You," child chasing turkey, diecut, illuminates fruit, clothing, and decora-tive elements 15

Hold-To-Light, dressed rabbit family painting Easter eggs, illuminates eggs, lantern, and light rays 75

Hold-To-Light, New Year, diecut year "1910," illuminates numbers 75

New England Singing Festival, Fitchburg, MA, emb, chorus sings as cherubs and goddess in heaven join in, German text, 1909 100

Real Photo, Santa Claus, holding Kewpie doll, toy train, and toy horse, c1908 . .100

Real Photo, Burton's Tea Store, ext store front view of grocer's with window display of products, British, c1910 . . .125

Real Photo, dentist treating soldier, "Camp Hospital, Camp Kearny, California," c1925 100

Real Photo, Orville Wright, inscription "Orville Wright in his aeroplane in Berlin, September 1909," M Vogel, Berlin, Germany 125

Real Photo, William Taft, sepia photo of Taft speaking from back of rail car, "Taft 10/3 '08 Newton," unused 40

Red Cross Doll, Japanese girl with wounded soldier dolls, medical ban-dages and bottles in background, Japanese, c1918 85

Thanksgiving, emb, woman in pumpkin patch, gold frame, brown border, attributed to S Schmucker, Winsch . .100

Artist Sgd Postcards. Left: "Snow Birds," Philip Boileau, $12. Right: children at wedding, A. Bertiglia, $8.

Valentine's Day, printed on silk, "St. Valentine's Greeting" in heart and Victorian woman carrying tray of fruit, Winsch 40

POSTERS

Want a great way to decorate? Use posters. Buy ones you like. Concentrate on one subject, manufacturer, illustrator, or period. Remember that print runs of two million copies and more are not unheard of. Many collectors have struck deals with their local video store and movie theater to get their posters when they are ready to throw them out. Not a bad idea. But why not carry it a step further? Talk with your local merchants about their advertising posters. These are going to be far harder to find in the future than movie posters.

Because so many people save modern posters, never pay more than a few dollars for any copy below fine condition. A modern poster in very good condition is unlikely to have long-term value. Its condition will simply not be acceptable to the serious collector of the future.

"*Angel's Holiday,*" Jane Withers, "When it's 'Angel's' day off…trouble's in the offing!," Fox, 1937, 27 x 41" 100
"Automobile Needs," paper, family on picnic, 37 x 23.5" 90
"*Bonzo Goes to College,*" Maureen O'Sullivan, Edmund Gwenn, Bonzo as football star, Universal, 1952, 27 x 41" 90

*Left: "Mayo's Plug" adv, linen, 17.75 x 30", $775.
—Photo courtesy Past Tyme Pleasures.*

Ringling Bros and Barnum & Bailey Circus, "Goliath the Monster Sea Elephant," 28 x 31", $225.

Boy Scouts of America, "Character Development Americanization Citizenship Training," smiling scout above "Do A Good Turn Daily," Anon, c1917, 18 x 24" 175
"*Butch Cassidy and the Sundance Kid,*" Paul Newman, Robert Redford, full color, "Coming May 20th," Fox, 1969, 14 x 22" 150
Concert, Mothers of Invention, James Cotton Blues Band, Apr 1920, 1968, abstract illus of trees, sun surrounded by clouds, stars, and doves, 14 x 22" . .40
Concert, The Grateful Dead, Jan 20, 1979, Shea's Buffalo Theater, Buffalo State University, NY, large wooly mammoth skull against checkered ground, 3 pyramids at bottom, second printing, ©1988 Grateful Dead Merchandising, 17 x 22" 20
Concert, Vietnam Veterans Benefit, May 28, 1982, George Mascone Center, San Francisco, Earth with large rose lying across Vietnam, featuring Boz Scaggs, Jefferson Starship, Grateful Dead, and Country Joe McDonald, "From Vietnam Veterans to the World A Night of Peace and Healing/A Benefit for The Vietnam Veterans Project," sgd by artists in silver ink at bottom right, 13.25 x 21.25" 125
"Conquer Fear of Insecurity and War," fearful man, woman, and child, blue and brown, issued by "World Economic Co-operation," Baldridge, c1937, 16 x 21" 150
District of Columbia Motor Club, "Keep From Between Parked Cars," paper, giraffe standing on sidewalk between parked cars, ©1935 Safety & Traffic Engineering Dept, American Automobile Assoc, 22 x 17" 100

"It's Your America/1940 Census," Uncle Sam scribbling in ledger, red, white, and blue, Anon, 25 x 36" 175

"Let's Keep The I Can In American," silkscreen design of wartime pilot and workers, Anon, 24 x 36" 275

"Round-The-World By Clipper," crowd, globe, Pan Am Clipper wing and props flying across top, Mark von Arenburg, c1949, 25 x 42" 275

"Smokey Says–Burned Timber Builds No Homes–Prevent Forest Fires," Albert Staehle, Smokey Bear as construction worker smiling and pointing to post-war house under construction," 1946, 13 x 18" .175

"...Step Ahead Mighty Amoco," cardboard, smiling marching band drummer, Amoco logo at right, sgd "G. Brehm," 28 x 61" 110

"The Man Without A Button Is A Slacker," fingers pointing to slacker man with appeal to "Get Into the Ranks of the Fighting Fourth," black and white, distributed by *The Boston Post* Oct 17, 1918, 18 x 23" 125

"The Smartest Ford Car Ever Built!," paper, "Smart New Interior," 3 people seated in car on left, car interior on right, 35 x 46" .90

"Time To Change Summer Golden Shell Motor Oil 25¢," litho cardboard, clothesline with crying baby face and diaper, mkd "01005-Litho in USA," 58 x 40" 100

"Visit Spain," Pan-American Airlines, stylized image of caballero and woman amid palms, Cernay, c1948, 24 x 39" .250

Anti-Vietnam War, march and rally, San Francisco, $50.

PRAYER LADIES

Prayer Ladies were manufactured by Enesco in the mid 1960s. Originally marketed under the name Mother-in-the-Kitchen, the figurines were made of highly glazed porcelain and modeled with reddish brown hair swept up into a bun, bowed head, closed eyes, hands folded or holding a household object, and wearing a high-necked dress. A prayer is inscribed on the white apron.

Pink is the dress color that is most commonly found. Blue is much harder to find, and white with blue trim is the scarcest of all. Forms range from common napkin holders, toothpick holders, and salt and pepper shakers to elusive sprinkler bottles and canister sets.

Air Freshener, pink 150
Bank, pink 140
Bell, blue 90
Bell, pink 80
Bud Vase, pink .125
Candleholders, pr, pink 150
Canister, pink 300
Cookie Jar, blue 500
Cookie Jar, pink 300
Cookie Jar, white, blue trim 425
Crumb Sweeper Set, brush and tray, pink 150
Egg Timer, pink 130
Flat Spoon Rest. blue 45
Flat Spoon Rest, pink 35
Flat Spoon Rest, white, blue trim 50
Instant Coffee, blue 140
Instant Coffee, pink 35
Instant Coffee, white, blue trim 160
Mug, blue 140
Mug, pink 130
Napkin Holder, blue 35
Napkin Holder, pink 25
Napkin Holder, white, blue trim 40
Photo Holder, pink 130
Planter, pink 125
Ring Holder, pink 45
Salt and Pepper Shakers, pr, blue 20
Salt and Pepper Shakers, pr, pink 15
Salt and Pepper Shakers, pr, white, blue trim 20
Soap Dish, blue 45
Soap Dish, pink 40

Tea Set, Enesco, blue, 6.5" h teapot, 4.25" h creamer and sugar, price for 3-pc set, $275.

Spoon Holder, blue .... .55
Spoon Holder, pink .... .45
Tea Set, teapot, creamer, and sugar,
    pink .... .250
Toothpick Holder, blue .... .30
Toothpick Holder, pink .... .20
Toothpick Holder, white, blue trim ..... .35
Wall Plaque, pink .... .100

PRINTS

There are many types of prints. Artist prints are original works of art. Mass-produced prints can be a reproduction of an artist's paintings, drawings, or designs or feature illustration art developed for mass appeal as opposed to an aesthetic statement.

When evaluating a framed print, think of two values: (1) the print outside the frame and (2) the matting and framing. All too often, there is more value in the matting and framing than the print itself.

Clubs: American Antique Graphics Society, 5185 Windfall Rd., Medina, OH 44256; American Historical Print Collectors Society, P.O. Box 201, Fairfield, CT 06430; Arthur Szyk Society, Inc., 1200 Edgehill Dr., Burlingame, CA 90410; Gutmann Collectors Club, 24A E. Roseville Rd., Lancaster, PA 17601; The Harrison Fisher Society, 123 N. Glassell, Orange, CA 92666; Hy Hintermeister Collectors Group, 5 Pasture Rd., Whitehouse Station, NJ 08889; Kate Greenaway Society, P.O. Box 8, Norwood, PA 19074; Philip Boileau Collector's Society,

1025 Redwood Blvd., Redding, CA 96003; R. Atkinson Fox Society, 8141 Main, Kansas City, MO 64114; Rockwell Society of America, P.O. Box 705, Ardsley, NY 10502.

Newsletters: *Fern Bisel Peat Newsletter,* 20 S. Linden Rd., Apt. 112, Mansfield, OH 44906; *The Illustrator Collector's News,* P.O. Box 1958, Sequim, WA 98382.

Periodical: *Journal of the Print World,* 1008 Winona Rd., Meredity, NH 03253.

Audubon, John James, "Black & White Creeper," #18, plate 90, hand colored and printed by R Havell, London, 1830, 25 x 17" sight, framed .... .350
Erté, Romain DeTirtoff, "La Serenade," lithograph, printed in colors on wove paper, with blindstamp of publisher, margins, framed, 20 x 14.5" sheet ...575
Fink, Aaron, "Smoker," lithograph, yellow and black on gray paper, sgd "Aaron Fink" in pen lower right, inscribed "B.A.T." in pencil lower left, 14.75 x 11.5" image, matted .... .225
Gorman, R C, "The Earring," lithograph, brown, blue, and black on paper, sgd and dated "R.C. Gorman 1975" in pencil lower left, numbered "44/50" in pencil lower right, drystamps lower center, edition of 50, 1975, 30 x 21.75", framed .... .450

Adriano Manocchia, "Mt. Katahdin – Moose," commemorative color print from orig oil painting, limited to 350, sgd and numbered, 14 x 19", $135. —Photo courtesy Collectors Auction Services.

Icart, Louis, "Mignon," etching and
aquatint with touches of hand-coloring,
wove paper, sgd, artist's blindstamp,
copyrighted and dated in plate, water
staining in image area, 1928, 20.25 x
13.5", 25.5 x 18" sheet 800
Mazur, Michael, "Bird's Nest Fern,"
mono-type, green and brown on paper,
sgd "Mazur" in pencil lower right,
titled in pencil lower left, inscribed
and dated in pencil lower center,
17.5 x 25.5" image, framed 550
Motherwell, Robert, "Untitled" from the
New York Portfolio, color photolitho-
graph with embossing on paper, sgd
and inscribed "Motherwell/TP" in
pencil lower right, printer's/publisher's
drystamp lower right, edition of 250
plus proofs, 1982, 30 x 22.5" image . . .520
Rauschenberg, Robert, "Statue of Liberty,"
color photo-screenprint with collage
on charcoal hand-made paper, sgd,
numbered and dated "Rauschenberg
202/250 85" in pencil lower left, edition
of 250, 1983, 35.5 x 24" image 635
Tworkov, Jack, "L.F.-S.F.-E#4," etching
with aquatint on BFK Rives paper with
watermark, printed and published by
Landfall Press, Inc, Chicago, signed
and dated "Tworkov/79" in pencil lower
right, titled in pencil lower center, numbered "53/100" in pencil lower center,
printer's drystamp lower left, edition
of 100, 1979, 14.5 x 14.5" plate 425

PUNCHBOARDS

Unpunched punchboards are collectible. A punched board has little value
unless it is an extremely rare design. Like
most advertising items, price is determined
by graphics and subject matter.

The majority of punchboards sell in the
$8 to $30 range. The high end is represented by boards such as Golden Gate Bridge at
$85 and Baseball Classic at $100.

Punchboards are self-contained games
of chance made of pressed paper containing holes with coded tickets inside each
hole. For an agreed amount the player uses
a "punch" to extract the ticket of his or her
choice. Prizes are awarded to the winning

ticket. Punch prizes can be 1¢, 2¢, 3¢, 5¢,
10¢, 20¢, 50¢, $1 or more.

Not all tickets were numbered. Fruit
symbols were used extensively as well as
animals. Some punchboards had no printing at all, just colored tickets. Other ticket
themes included dice, cards, dominoes,
words, etc. One early board had Mack
Sennett bathing beauties.

Punchboards come in an endless variety of styles. Names reflected the themes of
the boards. Barrel of Winners, Break the
Bank, Baseball, More Smokes, Lucky Lulu,
and Take It Off were just a few.

At first punchboards were used to
award cash. As legal attempts to outlaw
gambling arose, prizes were switched to
candy, cigars, cigarettes, jewelry, radios,
clocks, cameras, sporting goods, toys, beer,
chocolate, etc.

The golden age of punchboards was
the 1920s to the 1950s. Attention was
focused on the keyed punchboard in the
film *The Flim-Flam Man.* This negative publicity hurt the punchboard industry.

Advisor: Clark Phelps, Amusement Sales
Co, 7610 S. Main St., Midvale, UT 84047,
(801) 255-4731.

Baker's Dozen, baker wearing chef's
hat watches thirteen $20 winners,
10 x 14" 45
Barrel of Cigarettes, Lucky Strike green
and others, 10 x 10" 44
Beat the Seven, card tickets determine
winners, 10 x 10" . . . . : . .35

Best Hand, poker hand tickets, 6.5 x 11", $35.

Bell of Victory, picture of bell for jackpot, 5 x 7" 35

Big Game, 8 x 10.5" 30

Candy Bars Put & Take, trade stimulator to sell candy bars, 7 x 7" 32

Candy Special!, penny candy board, 4.5 x 7.5" 24

Cash In, sack of money, 8.5 x 9" 18

Cigar Game, small board to sell cigars, 4 x 3.5" 15

Extra Bonus, unusual dice tickets, 13 x 12" 40

Five On One, 11 x 11" 18

Girlie Board, prize space to be filled in by operator, 9 x 13" 32

Good As Gold, gold foil, cash board, 12 x 15" 35

Good Punching, cowboy theme, 9.5 x 10" 35

Hit the Barrel, old wooden barrel as jackpot, 9 x 11" 35

Joe's Special Prize, 11 x 14" 20

Little Sawbuck, cash jackpot board, 7.5 x 8.5" 28

Lu Lu board, colored tickets, 10 x 11" ...28

Musical Monkey, thick, 12 x 14" 43

Nickel Charley, 10 x 9" 18

Nickel Play, cash board, 5 x 7" 28

Old Pennies, 2¢ and 3¢, 6.75 x 11" 45

Open Field Board, diecut opening for operator's prizes, 11 x 16.5" 12

Pocket Board, cartoon graphics, 2 x 2.75" 8

Pots-A-Plenty, 11 x 17.5" 26

Premium Prizes, 10 x 12" 20

Section Play, 8.5 x 10" 18

Johnson's Chocolates, Elvgren pin-up illus, boxes of chocolate for prizes, 9 x 11", $35.

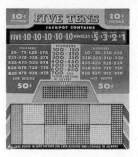

Five Tens, typical cash board, 10 x 13", $18.

Speedy Tens, 10 x 13" 18

Three Sure Hits, 10 x 14" 24

Tu Pots, 12 x 18" 44

Win A Buck, 4.5 x 7.5" 12

PUPPETS

No, somebody is not pulling your strings, there really is a category on puppets. This category covers marionettes and related jointed play toys, as well as finger and paper puppets. There are bound to be a few of your favorite character collectibles hanging around this new category.

Note: See Ventriloquist Dummies for additional listings.

HAND PUPPET

Captain Kangaroo, soft vinyl head, heavy ribbed black fabric body, white felt hands, red felt bow tie, painted white hair, black hat, mkd "Captain Kangaroo" on back of neck with The Rushton Co copyright, non-working inside squeaker mechanism, 1950s, 10" h 35

Dutch Boy, painted soft vinyl head, fabric handcover body, blue hat, white shirt overlaid by blue felt fabric apron with white inscription lettering on chest, 1960s, 12" h 25

Gabby Hayes, painted soft rubber head, fabric body, blue hat, chocolate brown face, molded white beard, "Gabby Hayes" name and copyright symbol at back of neck, 1950s, 9" h 100

Goofy, soft vinyl head, fabric body, red,
white, and orange plaid design on
body with tiny flowers, white felt
hands, red hat, red fabric bow tie,
non-working squeaker mechanism,
Gund Mfg Co, 1950s, 10.25" h 45
Lone Ranger, painted soft rubber head,
light blue fabric body, red felt fingers,
unmkd, 1950s, 9" h 65
Mister Ed, soft vinyl head, plush body,
yarn mane, simulated reins, open
mouth, inside talking mechanism,
Mattel, 1962, 11" h 75
Sweet Tooth Sam, painted green soft
vinyl head, black fabric body,
black top hat and rear collar, 1960s,
10.5" h 25
Teddy Snow Crop, applied gray vinyl
shell face with blue eye accents,
fabric handcover with white plush
finish, red smile line, red fabric tag
attached to chest with silver inscription "Teddy Snow Crop," Snow Crop
Orange Juice premium, orig 6 x 9"
brown paper mailing envelope, 1950s,
7 x 8.5" 40

MARIONETTE

Dorothy, plastic head with painted
accents, glued artificial blonde hair,
jointed wood body under checkered
pink and white fabric outfit, white
gauze fabric apron with light blue
needlepoint trim, Hazell's Marionettes,
Kansas City, 1950s, orig box, 13" h . . .100

*Hand Puppet, monkey, long brown fur,
43" l, $7.*

*Marionette, black
boy, wood and
cloth, 15" h, $90.
—Photo courtesy
Collectors Auction
Services.*

Dutch Girl, hp face, molded plastic
hands, yellow yarn hair, white felt
collar over striped blue and white
cotton outfit, light blue felt cap with
white rickrack trim, blue wooden bead
shoes, Pelham, 9" h, 12.5 x 6" box 25
Gretel, orig box, Pelham, 13" h 50
Jiminy Cricket, plastic head, hands, and
shoes, cloth outfit, felt vest and bow
tie, tag mkd "Jiminy Cricket copyright
Walt Disney Prod. Pat. #2509135. Gund
Mfg. Co. Swedlin Inc.," back of head
mkd "WDP Gund," 13" h 30
Oliver Hardy, "Push Button Marionette,"
Knickerbocker, 1970s, 10.5" h, 6.5 x 17"
box, ...50
Wonder Woman, vinyl head, hard plastic
body, fabric outfit, attached hand con-
trol unit, orig box, "String Puppet" by
Madison Ltd, ©1977 DC Comics Inc . .35

PUSH BUTTON

Bozo the Clown, #3991, Kohner, 5" h 20
Casper, Kohner 12
Frisky the Barking Dog, wood, orig box,
Avenue Mfg & Sales Co, 5" h 60
Huckleberry Hound, holding baton in
right hand, black hat, red jacket and
bow tie, black base, Kohner, 1960s,
4.5" h 35
Jack-O'-Lantern, wood, 4.5" h 3
Joe Cool, Ideal, 1977 35
Magilla Gorilla, Kohner 25
Mr Jinks, holding smiling mouse in right
hand, Kohner, 1960s, 4" h 35
Pebbles Flintstone, Kohner 10
Peter Pan, Kohner, 1950s, 6" h 45
Popeye, Kohner 10
Ricochet Rabbit, Kohner 15
Santa Claus, Kohner, #3992, 3.75" h 10

PURINTON POTTERY

Bernard Purinton founded Purinton Pottery in 1936 in Wellsville, Ohio. In 1941 the pottery relocated to Shippenville, Pennsylvania. Dorothy Purinton and William H. Blair, her brother, were the chief designers for the company. Maywood, Plaid, and several Pennsylvania German designs were among the patterns attributed to Dorothy Purinton. William Blair designed the Apple and Intaglio patterns.

Purinton did not use decals, as did many of its competitors. Greenware was hand painted and then dipped into glaze. A complete dinnerware line and many accessory pieces were produced for each pattern.

The plant ceased operations in 1958, reopened briefly, and then closed for good in 1959.

Newsletter: *Purinton News & Views,* P.O. Box 153, Connellsville, PA 15425.

Apple, chop plate, scalloped border,
   12" d 60
Apple, cookie jar, wooden lid, square . .150
Apple, cup and saucer 10
Apple, Dutch jug, 2 pt 30
Apple, Kent jug, 1 pt 45
Apple, oil cruet 80
Apple, sugar, cov 55
Apple, salt and pepper shakers, pr,
   range size 30
Apple, tumbler 20
Brown Intaglio, honey jug 110
Brown Intaglio, Kent jug 45
Daisy, coffee canister, cobalt trim 160
Fruit, canister, oval, blue trim 30
Fruit, creamer and sugar, miniature 25
Fruit, Dutch jug, 2 pt, 5.75" h 70
Fruit, Kent jug 20
Fruit, oil cruet, 5" sq 50
Fruit, sugar, cov 8
Heather Plaid, chop plate 60
Heather Plaid, cookie jar, oval 110
Heather Plaid, spaghetti bowl 125
Mountain Rose, basket planter, 6.25" h . .80
Mountain Rose, teapot, 2 cup, 4" h 75
Mountain Rose, Rebecca jug, 7.5" h 15
Normandy Plaid, candleholder, with
   insert 475

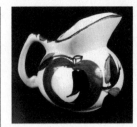

Apple, creamer, 4.5" h, $15.

Normandy Plaid, cookie jar 55
Normandy Plaid, Dutch jug, 5 pt 50
Normandy Plaid, jug, 8 oz, 4.75" h 75
Normandy Plaid, oil and vinegar cruet,
   round 75
Normandy Plaid, oil and vinegar cruet,
   square 22
Normandy Plaid, roll tray 25
Normandy Plaid, spaghetti bowl 100
Normandy Plaid, tumbler, 12 oz, 5" h 20
Normandy Plaid, vegetable bowl,
   divided 30
Palm Tree, dinner plate 375
Palm Tree, honey jug 120
Pennsylvania Dutch, cookie jar, wooden
   lid, square 350
Pennsylvania Dutch, tea and toast plate,
   8.5" d 75
Red Ivy, coffeepot, 6 cup 50
Red Ivy, Dutch jug, 2 pt 30
Red Ivy, honey jug 35
Red Ivy, teapot, 6 cup, 6" h 80
Tulip and Vine, coffee server 75

PURSES & ACCESSORIES

It is amazing what people will carry draped over their shoulders! Remember those alligator purses, complete with head and tail? Or how about those little metal mesh bags that held a lady's hankie and a book of matches, at most? As impractical as they were, these are are some of the most collectible purses on the market. Where value is concerned—think unusual.

Items found inside a purse are also hot collectibles. Forget about compacts. Everyone knows they are collectible. Keep your eyes open for lipsticks, mirrors, and solid perfumes.

Value is in the shape of the container. Competition is strong from crossover collectors, e.g, cat collectors.

Club: California Purse Collector's Club, P.O. Box 572, Campbell, CA 95009.

PURSES

Beaded, black, machine-strung plastic beads, Japan, 1950s, 7.5 x 0.25" 20

Beaded, cottage on water scene, snap closure, 6.5 x 8.5" 140

Beaded, floral and abstract motif, beaded fringe, snap closure, German, 7.25 x 11.25" 170

Beaded, reticulate, geometric motif, draw string closure, 5.25 x 7.25" 65

Beaded, hand-embroidered work made from an antique Mallorcan paisley shawl, Odette, 1930s, 5 x 9" 125

Beaded, machine embroidered dec, woman in center wearing puffy skirt surrounded by floral dec, gold metal frame and clasp, made in Austria, 1940s 70

Beaded, peacock and floral dec, snap closure, 7.5 x 10" 100

Beaded, pouch style, yellow, red, and black geometric motif, accordion closure, 7.25 x 8.5" 85

Beaded, rose motif, snap closure, German, 6.25 x 9.25 100

Beaded, swag style, black and crystal, drawstring closure, 7.5 x 7.5" 100

Beaded, swag style, turquoise, snap closure, 7.25 x 7" 85

Box, "Night Owl," Enid Collins 75

Lucite, white, $40.

Beaded, floral design, crocheted top, green, rose, yellow, and white, $60.

Camel, pouch shaped, allover metallic nail head embellishment, silver closure clasp, tan grosgrain int with matching change purse, retractable double shoulder strap, int silver plate stamped "Judith Leiber," 1980s, 16 x 10 x 3" . .170

Clutch, burgundy leather envelope, black trim, double "C" logo at center flap, burgundy leather int with optional goldtone chain shoulder strap, "Chanel" stamped in gold on lining, 1970s, 12 x 9 x 2.5" 115

Linen, "It Grows on Trees," Enid Collins .60

Shoulder, red leather, square, front flap, long thin shoulder strap, black leather lining, plate on int stamped "Bottega Veneta, Made in Italy," 1974, 5.25 x 5 x 3" 80

Tote Bag, quilted leather bottom and leather int, long goldtone chain and leather strap with round tag and double "C" logo, stamped "Chanel" on lining, 1980s, 14 x 14 x 3.5" 160

ACCESSORIES

Lipstick, black baked enamel tube, painted girl and mushrooms glitter dec, 2.25" l 35

Lipstick, Elizabeth Arden, goldtone tube, pearls and rhinestones dec on lid, letter "E" repeated around lower rim, 2.5" l 20

Lipstick, Halston, goldtone and silvertone, stylized heart shaped tube, 2.75" l 35

Lipstick, Tangee, red and white plastic tube, 2" l 10

Lipstick Holder, ceramic, figural poodle, 6 x 3" 15

Lipstick Holder, "Do Re Mi," red enamel holder, 3 lipstick tubes, 2 x 1.5" 35

Vanity Case, Illinois Watch Case Co, goldtone, powder case, Weldwood watch, puff with logo, and mirror, 2.75" sq, $200.

Mirror, goldtone, brown marbleized lid with pearl dec, lipstick concealed in handle, 2.375 x 2.125" 25

Mirror, goldtone filigree, pink cabochon stones dec, beaded mirror retainer, 3.75 x 1.5" 30

Mirror, goldtone, green enamel, red flowers dec, 5.5 x 2.25" 35

Mirror, goldtone, petit-point design, decorative wire mirror retainer, 3.75 x 1.25" 20

Mirror, silvertone, raised leaf design with inset colored stones, beveled mirror, 4 x 1.625" 15

Perfume Compact, figural parrot, yellow, green, and gold, White Linen fragrance fragrance, 1 x 2.5" 50

Scent Container, ring, goldtone, inset pearls dec, 8 x 1.5" 15

Scent Container, figural frog, polished goldtone, scroll design dec, pearl eyes, 1 x 1.5 x 1.125" 45

PUZZLES

The keys to jigsaw puzzle value in order of importance are: (1) completeness (once three or more pieces are missing, forget value); (2) picture (no one is turned on by old mills and mountain scenery); (3) surface condition (missing tabs or paper or silver fish damage causes value to drop dramatically); (4) age (1940 is a major cutting off point); (5) number of pieces (the more the better for wood); and (6) original box and label (especially important for wooden puzzles). Because of the limitless number of themes, jigsaw puzzle collectors find themselves competing with collectors from virtually every other category.

Puzzle collectors want an assurance of completeness, either a photograph or a statement by the seller that he actually put the puzzle together. Unassembled cardboard puzzles with no guarantees sell for $1 or less, wooden puzzles for $3 or less. One missing piece lowers price by 20 percent, two missing pieces by 35 percent, and three missing pieces by 50 percent or more. Missing packaging (a box or envelope) deducts 25 percent from the price.

Club: Assoc. of Game & Puzzle Collectors, PMB 321 197 M Boston Post Rd. West, Marlborough, MA 01752.

Note: The following prices are for jigsaw puzzles that are complete, in very good condition, with their original box.

Abraham Lincoln, Einson-Freeman, #17, Ray Morgan illus, 10.625 x 14.5" 20

American Bank and Trust Co of PA, BankAmericard, "Takes the puzzle out of your banking," diecut cardboard, 16 pcs, 4 x 5" 10

Animal Puzzles, Samuel Gabriel Sons & Co, #T218, diecut cardboard, mother cat and 2 kittens playing in shoe on box, c1940s 15

Baseball, Tuco, Upson, ABC's Wide World of Sports, #8244, diecut, early 1970s, 252 pcs .8

Chess Players, Parker Bros, hand cut, drawing room scene of gentlemen at game table, 200 pcs, 17 figurals, late 1930s 30

Chicago World's Fair Picture Puzzle, 1933, 300+ pcs, $25.

Hibiscus Time in Bermuda, Parker Bros for Miss Josephine Flood's Picture Puzzle Mart, NY, 266 hand-cut plywood pcs, figural pcs, 1940s, 16.5 x 10.5", $75.

Dawn's Early Light No. 305, Consolidated Paper Box Co, #25, 375 pcs 10

DeMartini Macaroni Co, Martini Brand Spaghetti, The Zoo in Puzzles, Series #1, "Giraffe" 20

Dick Tracy Kiddies Jigsaw Puzzle, Jaymar Specialty Co, 1950s 35

Doc Savage Jigsaw Puzzle, Whitman Publishing Co, #4610, diecut cardboard, 100 pcs 10

Dr Kildare Jigsaw Puzzle, Milton Bradley, #4318, over 600 pcs, includes 14 x 12" color portrait for framing, 1962 20

Folger's Coffee Co, Folger's can with ocean liner in center medallion, 56 pcs, cardboard and metal container resembling coffee can, 1980. 8 x 10.5" .5

Gypsy Love Call, E E Fairchild Corp, Finesse Picture Puzzle, #647, diecut, over 250 pcs, approx 11 x 14" 6

Happy Birthday Miss Jones, Parker Bros, Norman Rockwell illus, 1973, 11 x 14" 10

Hospitality, Built-Rite, Interlocking Picture Puzzle, over 350 pcs 5

Johnson Wax, Raid Picture Puzzle, diecut cardboard, bugs interrupted in their feasting, Don Pegler illus, 156 pcs, 11.75" sq, 3" d cardboard, metal, and plastic tube can 20

Kitty-Cat Picture Puzzle Box, Saalfield Publishing Co, #567, 6 puzzle set, Fern Biesel Peat illus, each puzzle approx 8 x 10" 50

Lux Toilet Soap, The Wayside Inn, 150 pcs, paper envelope with picture guide, 1930s, 12.5 x 10.5" 12

Old Woman & Pig Picture Puzzle, McLoughlin Bros, 1890 250

Paul Revere's Ride, Leisure Hour Puzzle Co, hand cut, F M Stone artist, 589 pcs, 16 x 19" 60

Pip the Piper Frame Tray Puzzle, Whitman Publishing Co, 17 pcs, 11.375 x 15" ...15

Proof Positive, Consolidated Paper Box Co, #250-29, diecut, boy photographing dog holding fishing float, 375 pcs, 1950s, approx 19.5 x 15.5" 6

Red Riding Hood, Daintee Toys, Inc, masonite tray puzzle, c1940 15

Santa Inez Valley, Milton Bradley, #4730, diecut, 468 pcs, mid 1930s 10

Shall We Go Sailing?, Regent Specialities, Inc, diecut, 391 pcs, 19.125 x 15.5" 12

Son of Hercules, Milton Bradley, #4572-X8, 43 pcs, 1966, 14.25 x 10.125" 20

Super Bowl Sunday, Hallmark Cards, Springbok, diecut, over 500 pcs, 18 x 23.5" 5

The Case of the Snoring Skinflint, by Henry Slesar, Janus Games, Inc, The Janus Mystery Jigsaw Puzzle, #1 of 4, over 500 pcs, story on back of cardboard box, 1973, approx 22 x 15" 20

The Circus, Milton Bradley, The Dover Jig Picture Puzzle, #4728, diecut, guide picture on box, 1930s 15

The Rug Merchant, Glad Houser, hand cut, Near Eastern woman showing rug to elderly gentleman buyer, Balesio Roman Tivol artist, 100 pcs, c1920, 8 x 6" 15

The Tavern, Selchow & Righter Co, Pandora Jig Saw Puzzle, abstract figural pcs, 72 pcs 20

Tony Sarg's Puzzles, Transogram Co, 1930s 45

Hood's Four-in-One Puzzle, C E Hood Co, 34 diecut cardboard pcs, 32 pp booklet, ©1896, 11.25 x 18.5", $65.

Treasure Hunters, Pine Tree Puzzle,
   strip cut, 64 pcs 15
Tree Island, Glencraft/Glendex, hand cut,
   New England landscape, interlocking,
   304 pcs, 1960s, 14 x 10" 30
White Rose Tea, Puzzle #1, untitled,
   cardboard, boy taking sick dog to vet,
   49 pcs, envelope with guide picture,
   1932-33, 7 x 9" .20

PYREX

    I'll bet everyone has at least one piece
of Pyrex glassware in his/her house. This
heat resistant glass can be found in many
forms, including casserole dishes, mixing
bowls, sauce pans, and measuring cups.
Pyrex was manufactured by Corning Glass
Works.

Bowl, Bluebelle 6
Bowl, delphite, 10" d 25
Canister, floral dec lid, 4" h, 6.25" d 10
Canister, green lid, 3.75" h, 4.75" d 8
Carafe, with candle warmer, #4612 30
Carafe, plastic lid, 10" h 10
Carafe, turquoise diamonds, 48 oz,
   9.5" h 12
Casserole, blue stripe 20
Casserole, Butterprint 20
Casserole, Daisy 20
Casserole, Gold Acorn 5
Casserole, Golden Honeysuckle 15
Casserole, Town and Country 20
Casserole, yellow, mkd "Pyrex brand
   tableware by Corning, 700-10 oz,"
   7" d 5
Chip and Dip Set, Cinderella shape,
   white on turquoise 20

Mixing Bowl, Butterprint Cinderella, #443,
$8. —Photo courtesy Ray Morykan Auctions.

Pie Baker,
clear, orig
paper label, $5.

Cruet Set, gold stripes 10
Cup and Saucer, Bluebelle 8
Dinner Plate, Bluebelle 8
Mixing Bowl Set, 3 pcs, delphite 60
Mixing Bowl Set, 3 pcs, Town and
   Country 12
Nesting Bowl, Bluebelle, 2.5 qt 10
Nesting Bowls, set of 3, Early American .15
Nesting Bowls, set of 4, Butterprint,
   Cinderella shape 35
Percolator, 6 cup, Flameware 30
Percolator Pump, Flameware, rangetop,
   4 cup 15
Platter, oval, 14" l 12
Refrigerator Dish, Early American 8
Refrigerator Dish, red, 1.5 cups 10
Refrigerator Dish, Town and Country 8
Refrigerator Dish, turquoise 12
Refrigerator Dish, Verde 8
Salt and Pepper Shakers, pr, plastic lid . .8
Trivet, crystal, 9" d 12

RADIO CHARACTERS & PERSONALITIES

    Radio dominated American life
between the 1920s and the early 1950s.
Radio characters and personalities enjoyed
the same star status as their movie counterparts. Phrases such as "The Shadow
Knows" or "Welcome Breakfast Clubbers"
quickly date an individual.

    Many collectors focus on radio premi-
ums, objects offered during the course of a
radio show and usually received by sending
in proof of purchase of the sponsor's product. Make certain an object is a premium
before paying extra for it as part of this
classification.

    Many radio characters also found their
way into movies and television. Trying to

separate the products related to each medium is time consuming. Why bother? If you enjoyed the character or personality, collect everything that is related to him or her.

Clubs: Friends of Vic & Sade, 7232 N. Keystone Ave., Lincolnwood, IL 60646; National Lum 'n' Abner Society, #81, Sharon Blvd., Dora, AL 35062; North American Radio Archives, 134 Vincewood Dr., Nicholasville, KY 40356; Old Time Radio Collectors Assoc., Rt. 1, Box 197, Belpre, OH 45714; Pow-Wow (Straight Arrow), P.O. Box 24751, Minneapolis, MN 55424; Radio Collectors of America, 28 Wolfe St., Unit #1, West Roxbury, MA 02132.

Newsletter: *Hello Again,* P.O. Box 4321, Hamden, CT 06514;

Periodical: *Old Time Radio Digest,* 10280 Gunpowder Rd., Florence, KY 41042.

Amos 'n Andy, sheet music, *Three Little Words,* from movie *Check and Double Check,* 4 pp, ©1930 Harms Inc, 9 x 11.75" 20

Benny, Jack, record, *The Jack Benny Album,* cover shows Benny playing violin with body depicted as potted plant 25

Burns & Allen, record, *George Burns & Gracie Allen,* cover shows portraits of Burns and Allen 25

Captain Midnight, book, *Joyce of the Secret Squadron, A Captain Midnight Adventure Book,* Whitman, #2376, 1942, 5.75 x 8" 30

Amos 'n Andy, map, Eagle's View of Weber City, orig Pepsodent mailer, 5.5 x 8.25" envelope, $50.

Kitty Kelly, pinback button, 1930s, $7. —Photo courtesy Gene Harris Antique Auction Center, Inc.

Captain Midnight, booklet, "Captain Midnight's Air Hero Stamp Album," Skelly Oil premium, blue accent cover with purple Capt Midnight image and plane in background, artist signature "Ted Hawkins" in lower right, 8 pp, 1939, 5 x 6.75" 75

Captain Midnight, patch, Ovaltine premium, "Captain Midnight Squadron Member 1989," blue cloth, blue and silver accent stitched jet in center on light blue ground, red and yellow lettering, with letter signed by Capt Midnight, orig 6.5 x 9.5" envelope 50

Charlie Chan, booklet, "Charlie Chan's Chinese Proverbs," Chas E Sullivan Florist & Binyon Optical Company premium, adv for radio program "Coming over KJR," 12 pp, ©1935 American Radio Features Syndicate, 4 x 5.75 " 140

Don Winslow, pin, silvered brass, "Don Winslow Squadron of Peace–Ensign," Kellogg's premium, 1939, .75" l 20

Frank Buck's Adventure Club, neckerchief, cotton, Pepsodent premium, silkscreened design, 27 x 30.5" 150

Jimmie Allen, letter and membership card, letter with text "To the Parents of Jimmie Allen Club Members," 2-sided stiff paper membership card with text "Royal Bread Flying Club," wings design, and facsimile Allen signature, orig mailing envelope with return address for "Royal Baking Company," dated 1937 90

Jimmie Allen, movie herald, *The Sky Parade,* front shows photo fo Allen, herald opens to reveal bluetone photo collage of scenes from film with airplane silhouette featuring film text, ©1936 Paramount Productions Inc, 6 x 9" 100

Kate Smith, cookbook, $8. —Photo courtesy Collectors Auction Services.

Little Orphan Annie, "Radio Orphan Annie's Secret Society," Ovaltine premium, 12 pp, 5 x 7.25" 75
Sgt Preston, book, *Sgt Preston and Yukon King*, Rand McNally, ©1955 Sgt Preston of the Yukon Inc, 6.75 x 8" 20
Speed Gibson, fan postcard, front shows browntone photo with facsimile signature and Gorman's Bread adv, reverse shows inked mailing address and postmark date 1938, 3.5 x 5.5" 100
The Shadow, pinback button, "The Shadow Secret Society," color portrait on purple ground, yellow lettering, black rim, c1970s. 1.5" d 20
Vernon Grant, booklet, "The Cow and the Silver Cream," J A Wright & Co Silver Cream premium, discovery of silver polish featuring Vernon Grant characters, 12 pp, 1944, 4.75 x 6.5" . . .20

RADIOS

If a radio does not work, do not buy it unless you need it for parts. If you do, do not pay more than $10. A radio that does not work and is expensive to repair is a useless radio.

The radio market went through a number of collecting crazes in the 1980s and 1990s. It began with Bakelite radios, moved on to figural and novelty radios, and now is centered on early transistors and 1940s plastic case radios. These crazes are often created by manipulative dealers. Be suspicious of the prices in any specialized price guide focusing on these limited topics.

There are several general guides that do a good job of keeping prices in perspective.

Clubs: Antique Radio Club of America, 81 Steeple Chase Rd., Devon, PA 19333; Antique Wireless Assoc., Box E, Breesport, NY 14816.

Periodicals: Antique Radio Classified, P.O. Box 802, Carlisle, MA 01741; The Horn Speaker, P.O. Box 1193, Mabank, TX 75147.

Admiral, 5R11, tabletop, Bakelite, square-lined, c1948 15
Admiral, 6P32, portable, alligator leatherette, front drops, palm trees on grill, double handle at top, 1940s . .40
Air Castle, 211, tabletop, plastic, over-sized tuning knob, 1940s 25
Air King, A400, tabletop, "Minstrel," Bakelite, 1947 .25
Arvin, 140P, portable, suitcase-style, cloth covered, gray metal trim, large handle at top, 1947 15
Atwater Kent, 188, console, 4-legged, arc shaped dial with 4 knobs, 1932 . .100
Belmont, 770, console, Art Deco style, oval dial with 4 knobs below, 1935 . .150
Bendix, 687A, portable, leatherette and plastic, 5 tubes, 1946 15
Crosley, 9-104W, table top, Bakelite, painted white, metal grill, dial with 3 knobs below 35
Crosley, 10-304, portable, "Playtime," plastic handle on top, circular dial, concentric grill, 1950 15
DeWald, 503, tabletop, Bakelite, dial at top edge, 1946 25

Addison, A2A, Catalin, maroon body and knobs, yellow trim, c1940, $700. —Photo courtesy Gene Harris Antique Auction Center, Inc.

Emerson, 380, portable, Bakelite, knobs
and dial below leather strap, 1940 . . .50
Emerson, AX211, tabletop, "Little Miracle,"
Bakelite, c1938 .35
Emerson, 671, alarm, circular clock face
. at right, elongated dial at left, 1950 . . .15
Fada, 110, table top, wood, Art Deco
style, 4 tubes, 1930s 65
Fada, 454, tabletop, Bakelite, molded
Z-shaped grill bars, 1938 50
Farnsworth, CT41, tabletop, brown
Bakelite, 1941 .35
General Electric, 546, clock, plastic,
vertical grill bars, center square clock
face, 1953 15
King, 71, tabletop, wood, 1926 75
Magnavox, TRF5, tabletop, wood, large
dial and 3 knobs 150
Motorola, 45P, "Pixie," portable, plastic,
coat-pocket style, 1956 75
Motorola, 50Z1, tabletop, Bakelite, round-
ed corners, square dial at right, 1941 .15
Olympic, 450, portable, plastic, coat-
pocket style, fold-down handle, 1955 .35
Philco, 37-630T, tabletop, 6 tubes, 3 bands,
circular dial above tuning lever and
3 knobs, 1937 .100
RCA, 8BX6, portable, aluminum and
Bakelite, 1948 .50
RCA, 9BX56, portable, plastic, alligator
trim, 1949 25
Sentinel, 294, tabletop, wood, rounded
sides and top, AM/shortwave bands,
1940s 35
Silvertone, 3001, tabletop, rectangular,
tuning wheel over large V-shaped
speaker cloth with logo and knob 30
Sparton, 100, tabletop, Bakelite, elongated dial at top edge, 1947 25

*Arvin, #840T, metal case, plastic knobs,
1954, $65.* —Photo courtesy Gene Harris
Antique Auction Center, Inc.

*Baldwin,
Baldwinette,
tombstone,
wood, AC, 1930,
$150.* —Photo
courtesy Gene
Harris Antique
Auction Center,
Inc.

Sparton, 1037, radio/phono, pull-down
radio at right, pullout phono at left,
1948 15
Stromberg-Carlson, 61H, tabletop, wood,
octagonal dial above 3 knobs and
lever, 1935 55
Sylvania, 510H, tabletop, Bakelite, horizontal louvers across front, 1950 35
Tele-Tone, 165, tabletop, plastic, large
round dial at right, 1948 15
Troy, tabletop, mahogany, 1935 55
Truetone, D3300, portable, plastic, coat-
pocket style, fold-down handle on top,
circular dial in center, 1953 35
Westinghouse, 190, console, square
lined, pullout phono behind center
door, 1949 50
Westinghouse, 523T4, tabletop, "Star
Value," plastic, square, oversized knob
at front right, 1955 15
Zenith, 5D011, tabletop, wood, square,
circular dial 15

RADIOS, TRANSISTOR

In the early 1960s transistor radios
were the rage. Music was now both
portable and convenient. Today, the transistor has gone the way of the early hand held
calculator—both are clumsy and obsolete.

Newsletter: *Transistor Network,* 32 W. Main
St., Bradford, NH 03221.

Admiral, 743, white, right round tuning
knob, left volume, slotted chrome grill,
leather case, top handle, 1959 25
Airline, GEN-1146A, upper sliderule dial,
right side dual thumbwheels, lower
perforated grill, wrist strap, 1965 10

Americana, Super DX Model FP80, plastic with metal grill, 8 transistors, c1962, $30.

Aiwa, AR-670, upper right peephole dial, lower perforated chrome grill, right side thumbwheel tuning, left side thumbwheel volume, 1964 5

Crosley, JM-8MN, "Fantasy," figural book, maroon, opens to reveal tuning and volume knobs, metal grill, 1956 . .225

Emerson, 855, upper round large dial, brick grill cutouts, leather case, top handle, 1956 50

General Electric, 917A, thumbwheel tuning and volume, lower perforated chrome grill, 1963 15

Hitachi, KH903, sliderule dial, louvered plastic grill, top handle, telescopic antenna, 1964 .10

Novelty, Care Bear Cousins, blue, colorful decal, slide controls, Playtime Products Inc, ©1985 American Greeting Cards 10

Novelty, Folger's Coffee, figural coffee can, 1980s .30

Novelty, green apple, Hong Kong, 1970s .20

Novelty, He-Man, Nasta, 1984 20

Novelty, ladybug, wings open as volume control is turned up, Hong Kong, 1970s 30

Novelty, Miracle Whip, "The Bread Spread," ©1980 Kraft Foods 35

Novelty, My Little Pony, ©1983 Hasbro Industries 10

Novelty, owl, yellow, black eyes are controls, Stewart, 1970s 15

Novelty, Safeguard Soap, gold and white, mkd "Deodorant Soap" along bottom, 1980s 25

Realtone, Tr1053, upper sliderule dial, right and left side thumbwheels, lower mesh plastic grill, 1964 5

Silvertone, 2214, "Medalist," swing handle, 1962 45

Truetone, DC3316, upper sliderule dial, right and left thumbwheels, lower perforated chrome grill, 1963 10

RAGGEDY ANN

Johnny Gruelle registered the trademark and patented a Raggedy Ann doll pattern in 1915. Three years later, he published *The Raggedy Ann Stories,* the first of twenty-five books about Raggedy Ann that Gruelle wrote before his death in 1938. Andy first appeared in 1920.

The first Raggedy Ann dolls were produced by Volland in 1915. When Volland went bankrupt in 1934, the Exposition Doll Company took over production for a year. Molly-'es, owned by Mollye Goldman, produced an unlicensed Raggedy Ann doll between 1935 and 1938. Gruelle sued for trademark and patent infringement and won. Gruelle contracted with Georgene Novelties Company to resume production. Knickerbocker Toy Company became the licensee in late 1962. In 1982, Warner Communications, owner of Knickerbocker, sold the company to Hasbro. In 1993, Applause issued a Raggedy Ann, Andy, and Baby Ann doll based on the unauthorized Molly-'es.

Advertising Tear Sheet, doll offer with magazine subscription, 1941, Curtis Publishing Co 10

Bank, plastic, Bobbs-Merrill Co, 7" h 12

Book, *Raggedy Ann and Raggedy Andy's Very Own Fairy Stories,* Johnny Gruelle, published by The Bobbs-Merrill Co, 1960s 25

Book, *Raggedy Ann and the Paper Dragon,* Johnny Gruelle 40

Book, *Raggedy Ann in the Deep Deep Woods,* The Bobbs-Merrill Co, 1960 . .25

Costume, Ben Cooper, 1989 5

Doll, Dress Me Raggedy Ann, Knickerbocker, 20" h 30

Dolls, Raggedy Ann & Andy, Playskool, 11" h 10

Doll, Raggedy Andy, Georgene Novelties New York, ©1957, 22" h, $110. —Photo courtesy Collectors Auction Services.

Game, "Who Am I?," Hallmark, 1978 20
Lamp, Raggedy Ann with orange yarn-like hair, wearing blue skirt, pink shirt with white ruffles by wrists, white collar and apron with buttons, Lefton sticker 20
Limited Edition Plate, Christmas Morning, Raggedy Ann Christmas, Schmid, 1977 25
Limited Edition Plate, The Raggedy Shuffle, Raggedy Ann Annual, Schmid, 1981 45
Little Golden Book, *Raggedy Ann & Andy Help Santa Claus,* June Goldsborough illus, ©1977, third printing, 1979 3
Paper Dolls, Raggedy Ann & Raggedy Andy, The Bobbs-Merrill Co, 1968 10
Puppet, Applause, 1987, 15" h 40

RAILROADIANA

Most individuals collect by railroad, either one near where they live or grew up or one for which they worked.

Railroad collectors have been conducting their own specialized shows and swap meets for decades. Railroad material that does show up at flea markets is quickly bought and sent into that market. Collectors use flea markets primarily to make dealer contacts, not for purchasing.

Railroad paper from timetables to menus is gaining in popularity as railroad china, silver-plated flat and hollow wares, and lanterns rise to higher and higher price levels. The key to paper ephemera is that it bear the company logo and have a nice displayable presence.

Clubs: Key, Lock and Lantern, Inc., P.O. Box 66, Penfield, NY 14526; Railroadiana Collectors Assoc., Inc., P.O. Box 4894, Diamond Bar, CA 91765; Railway & Locomotive Historical Society, P.O. Box 193552, San Francisco, CA 94119.

Periodical: *The Main Line Journal,* P.O. Box 121, Streamwood, IL 60107.

Ashtray, C&NW, glass, square, 2 rests, Chicago and North Western Line logo on clear bottom, 3.5" d 15
Blotter, Missouri Pacific Lines, red logo with black steam train and "A Service Institution," 3.25 x 6" 8
Bond, Mississippi and Tennessee Railroad Co, pays 5¢ to bearer, American eagle in center circle, Indian figure at left, dated Feb 20, 1862 8
Bread and Butter Plate, New York Central Railroad, Dewitt Clinton pattern . .20
Bread and Butter Plate, Northern Pacific Railroad, Monad pattern 30
Brochure, Santa Fe, Grand Canyon Outings, 62 pp, Mar 1927, 4 x 9" 10
Calendar, C&NW, streamliner "400" crossing stone arch bridge, 1941 30
Candy Container, figural lantern, glass, red, tin base, wire handle, 3.75" h 15
Cap Badge, metal, brakeman, Missouri, Kansas & Texas Railway 60
Dinner Plate, Denver & Rio Grande Western Railroad, Blue Adam pattern 50
Juice Tumbler, Union Pacific Railroad . . .12
Key, switch-type, St Louis & San Francisco Railway 60
Lantern, clear globe, raised lettering "Canadian Pacific Railroad," wood handle 50

Conductor's Hat, L.I.R.R., current production, $40.

Map, folding, The Garden of Canada, Niaraga St. Catharines and Toronto Railway, c1910, 4 x 9.25" closed size, $15.

Lantern, clear etched globe, Chesapeake & Ohio Railway 60

Lighter, M&NS, stainless steel, raised red diamond logo, Halco 55

Match Safe, pewter, figural locomotive, emb ornate designs on sides 50

Napkin, cloth, Union Pacific, streamliner motif printed in corner, yellow border on white ground, 11 x 16" 10

Pencil, wood, "Friendliness is a Milwaukee Road Tradition," no eraser 3

Pinback Button, brown railroad mail bag on white ground, "Pioneer Assn. of the Old L.S. & M.S. RY," 1921 8

Pinback Button North Western Railroad, "Alfalfa The Great Wealth Producer," black, white, and red log on chartreuse ground, 1900s .12

Plate, New York Central Railroad, Mohawk pattern 50

Platter, Pennsylvania Railroad, Liberty pattern 25

Platter, Union Pacific Railroad, Challenger pattern 20

Sign, porcelain, emb, self-framed, French, 36.5" h, 37" w, $150. —Photo courtesy Collectors Auction Services.

Playing Cards, Burlington Route, 2 horseback riders watching train go by, silver box 25

Print, Pennsylvania Railroad, multicolored, sgd "Grif Teller," framed, 1933, 20 x 26.5" 175

Ruler, CGW, plastic, center Chicago Great Western Railway logo, black printing on white ground, 12 l 18

Sheet Music, *I've Been Working on the Railroad,* Calumet Music Co, Chicago, 1935 12

Shot Glass, Union Pacific, frosted shield logo, 2.5" h 10

Sign, "M-K-T/Missouri-Kansas-Texas-Lines," diecut porcelain, 24 x 27" 500

Sign, "Railway Express Agency," porcelain, diamond shaped, 8 x 8" 125

Soup Bowl, Union Pacific Railroad, Harriman Blue pattern 20

Step Stool, metal, Panama Limited 225

Stock Certificate, Chicago, Burlington and Quincy Railroad, 100 shares, Capital, locomotive vignette, brown border, 1895 15

Ticket, Central Vermont Railroad, 500 miles, 1886, 3.5 x 4.25" 15

Ticket, Fitchburg Railroad, Troy to Rochester, first class, 1880. 2.25 x 4.5" 10

Timetable, Chicago Great Western Railroad, Mar 1, 1940 8

Timetable, Great Northern Railway, Oct 28, 1962 5

Tray, Burlington Northern logo in green border with white cattle brands, gold and white center longhorn motif, 4.75 x 11.75" 35

RAMP WALKERS

These comical toys have waddled their way into many toy collections. While you may find some ramp walkers made from metal, wood, or celluloid, the majority of those available are plastic. Subjects vary from advertising figures to generic animals to popular television cartoon characters.

Bear, Marx 10

Bonny Braids, orig box, Charmore Co, NJ, 1951 110

Camel, blue, Marx 15

Chipmunks in Band, Marx 25
Circus Elephant 20
Clown, Wilson, 5.25" h 25
Dachshund, 3.75" l 10
Donald Duck, with wheelbarrow, 3.5" l . .15
Duck, 3" h 15
Figaro, Marx 12
Fred Flintstone, Burger King premium 5
Goofy Grape, Pillsbury, 1971 25
Hap and Hop, Marx 15
Indian Woman with Child, 3.5" h, 3"l 15
Kangaroo, Marx 10
Little King, Marx .50
Milking Cow, Marx 25
Monkeys Carrying Bananas, Marx 10
Mother Goose, Marx 35
Pluto, Marx 8
Popeye, Hong Kong 15
Santa Claus, Marx 25
Stegasaurus, black native on back,
    Marx 35
Three Little Pigs, Marx 50
Top Cat and Benny, Marx, 3" h 55
Vikings, 1.5" h, 1.75" l 5
Woman Pushing Roller-Type Vacuum,
    3.25" h, 3.25" l 20

RANSBURG

Harper J. Ransburg founded a glass cutting firm in Indianapolis, Indiana, in 1911. Following World War I, he introduced two decorated candles and hand-decorated glassware to his product line. Hand-decorated stoneware followed in 1931; then hand-decorated metalware in 1933.

The period from 1945 to the end of the 1960s was the Golden Age of Ransburg kitchen and bathroom hand-decorated metal and stoneware products. Designs are very period driven from the Fab Fifites to the Psychedelic Sixties.

Ball Jug, Dutch girl 65
Ball Jug, red, flowers 20
Bowl, ceramic, blue, fruit motif 80
Breadbox, cream, pineapple dec 10
Breadbox, pineapple dec 16
Breadbox, pink and copper 18
Breadbox, yellow, toleware 50
Cake Keeper, fruit motif 8
Canister Set, blue-speckled, 4 pcs 18
Canister Set, copper top, 4 pcs 20

Cookie Jar, globe, red, asters, 10" h, $45.

Canister Set, orange-red, 3 pcs 12
Canister Set, rooster, yellow, 4 pcs 20
Canister Set, roosters, 2 pcs 5
Cookie Jar, crock, asters 20
Cookie Jar, globe, hollyhocks 50
Cookie Jar, green, flowers 15
Creamer and Sugar, green, flowers 35
Mixing Bowl, red, flowers 18
Pitcher, blue, flowers 42
Pitcher, yellow toleware 35
Recipe Box, asters 45
Teapot, green, flowers 65
Tissue Box, pink, poodle 18
Trash Can, Bath Bouquet 20
Trash Can, roosters 30
Tray, white, toleware 45
Wax Paper Dispenser, red, asters 25

REAMERS

Finding reamers in mint condition is next to impossible. The variety of materials from which they were made is staggering, ranging from wood to sterling silver. As in many other categories, the fun examples are figural.

Reamers are identified by a number system developed by Ken and Linda Ricketts in 1974. This cataloging system was continued by Mary Walker in her two books on reamers. Edna Barnes has reproduced a number of reamers in limited editions. These are marked with a "B" in a circle.

Club: National Reamer Collectors Assoc., 47 Midline Court, Gaithersburg, MD 20878.

Cambridge, glass, green 200
Federal, glass, pink 75
Fry, glass, amber, orange 450
Fry, glass, rose 275
Grapefruit, glass, jadeite 400
Hazel Atlas, glass, cobalt, 2 pc 300
Hazel Atlas, glass, Criss Cross, cobalt .350
Hazel Atlas, glass, pink, tab handle 40
Hazel Atlas, glass, yellow, 2 cup 475
Hazel Atlas, milk glass, tab handle 75
Handy Andy, aluminum, table model,
   crank handle, red base 18
Hocking, transparent green 30
Nasco-Royal, metal, scissor type 8
Japan, ceramic, citrus fruit, mkd "Trico,
   Hand Painted, Made in Japan," 5" h .175
Japan, ceramic, clown, mkd "Mikori
   Ware, Hand Painted, Made in Japan,"
   7.25" h 300
Japan, ceramic, duck, lusterware,
   3.5" h 200
Japan, ceramic, floral motif, 5.25" h 125
Jeannette, glass, blue 125
Jennyware, glass, ultramarine 150
Sunkist, glass, #331-B 115
Sunkist, glass, carmel 375
Sunkist, glass, crown tuscan 375
Sunkist, glass, custard 65
Sunkist, glass, fruit bowl, ftd, pink 300
Sunkist, glass, opalescent 200
Sunkist, milk glass 25
Tufglas, green 100
US Glass, glass, clambroth 75
US Glass, glass, grapefruit, green 575

RECORDS

Most records are worth between 25¢ and $1. A good rule to follow is the more popular the record, the less likely it is to have value. Who does not have a copy of Bing Crosby singing "White Christmas"? Until the mid-1980s the principal emphasis was on 78 rpm records. As the decade ended 45 rpm records became increasingly collectible. By 1990 33^1/3 rpm albums, especially Broadway show related, were gaining in favor.

By the way, maybe you had better buy a few old record players. You could still play the 78s and 45s on a 33^1/3 machine. You cannot play any of them on a compact disc player.

Clubs: Assoc. of Independent Record Collectors, P.O. Box 222, Northford, CT 06472; International Assoc. of Jazz Collectors, P.O. Box 518, Wingate, NC 28174.

Periodicals: *DISCoveries,* P.O. Box 1050, Dubuque, IA 52004; *Goldmine,* 700 E. State St., Iola, WI 54990.

Boone, Pat, *Star Dust,* 33^1/3 rpm, Dot
   Records 2
Captain Kangaroo, *Dear Lisa,* 45 rpm,
   Kenro Production Concept, ©1977
   My Name Records 4
Cash, Johnny, *Orange Blossom Special,*
   Columbia CS-2309, 1065 20
Charlie Moore and the Dice Partners,
   Truckin', LP, Leather Records 8
Cheech & Chong, *Santa Claus and
   His Old Lady,* Ode Records, #66021,
   45 rpm 3
Cooke, Sam, *Tammy/The Bells of Saint
   Mary's,* Keen Records B-2001, EP,
   orig picture sleeve 30
Daniels, Joe, *Blue Rhythm of the Blues
   & Solitude,* 78 rpm, Decca 2
Drysdale, Don, *One Love,* Reprise Records
   R20-162, 45 rpm, promotional label,
   orig picture sleeve 10
Dukes of Dixieland, *Struttin' at the
   World's Fair,* Columbia CS-8994, 1964 .12
Eddy, Duane, *The Lonely One,* 45 rpm 2
Harris, Marion, *Oh, Judge! (He Treats
   Me Mean/He Done Me Wrong),* 78
   rpm, Columbia A2968 10

Eddie Fisher, "I Love You" 2-record set, So In Love/My One and Only Love *and* The Girl That I Marry/What Is This Thing Called Love!, *45 rpm, RCA Victor, #EPB-1097, 1955, $7.*

The Four Lads, Moments to Remember/ Dream On, My Love, Dream On, *45 rpm,* Columbia, #40539, 1955, $3.

Hope, Bob, *Bob Hope in Russia and Other Places,*Decca DL-4396, 1963 . . .20
Jerry Lee Lewis and Friends, *Duets,* LP, Sun Records, yellow vinyl 8
Jones, Quincy, *Bossa Nova,* Mercury MG-20751, 1962 15
Joplin, Janis, *In Concert,* LP, CBS, 1972 . .3
Nelson, Ricky, *Songs By Ricky,* Imperial Records IMP-162, 45 rpm 40
Scott, Ray, *Boppin Wig Wam Willie,* Erwin Records E-700 15
Snow, Hank, *Let Me Go, Lover/I've Forgotten You,* RCA Victor 20-5960 2
Soundtrack, *Every Whick Way But Loose,* Elektra 5E-503, 1979 10
The Chipmunks, *Sing Again with the Chipmunks,* LP, Liberty LST-7159, 1961 .8
The Miracle, *Way Over There,* Tamla Records 54028, 45 rpm 30

RED WING

　　Red Wing, Minnesota, was home to several potteries. Among them were Red Wing Stoneware Company, Minnesota Stoneware Company, and The North Star Stoneware Company. All are equally collectible. Red Wing has a strong regional base. The best buys are generally found at flea markets far removed from Minnesota. Look for pieces with advertising. Red Wing pottery was a popular giveaway product.

Club: Red Wing Collectors Society, Inc, 2000 West Main St., Ste. 300, Red Wing, MN 55066; The Rumrill Society, P.O. Box 2161, Hudson, OH 44236.

Art Pottery, candleholder, #576, RumRill Athenian Group, nude, 10.5" h 250
Art Pottery, figurine, "The Muse," DeLuze Line, bronze, 7.5" h, 13.75" l 70
Art Pottery, planter, dachshund, #1342, matte green, 7.5" l, 1.5" w 65
Art Pottery, planter, giraffe, #896 325
Art Pottery, planter, lamb, blue, Red Wing sticker 125
Art Pottery, planter, swan, #239, pink . . .20
Art Pottery, vase, #174, Georgia Rose Line, ivory with pink int, 5" h 110
Art Pottery, vase, #1183, eggshell ivory antiqued with brown, 6" h 70
Art Pottery, wall planter, M-1484, black violin, with sticker and sealed instruction packet of strings 50
Ashtray, "Minnesota Twins 1965 World Series Ashtray" 150
Ashtray, Red Wing Potteries 75th Anniversary, wing shaped 150
Bed Warmer, designed by Rehder, Pat 1901 175
Bowl, Gray Line, 10" d 100
Bowl, Paneled, sponged dec, 10" d 175
Bowl, Saffron, bottom mkd 140
Cookie Jar, Cattails, blue and tan 250
Cookie Jar, Jack Frost 325
Cookie Jar, Round Up 425
Crock, Birchleaf Beehive, blue, 3 gal . . .400
Cup, Bob White .4
Dessert Bowl, Tampico 8
Fruit Jar, Stone Mason, black, 1/2 gal. . .275
Hot Water Bottle, brown leaf design . . .225
Jug, "Red Wing Liquor Co," 1/2 gal 575
Lamp Base, cattail with flowers 250
Milk Pan, white, bottom mkd, 15.5" d . . .100
Mixing Bowl, Brides, green and white, 7" d 100

Jug, red wing logo, blue"5" and stamp, 5 gal, 18.5" h, $35. —Photo courtesy Collectors Auction Services.

Mixing Bowl, Saffron, "Koehn's Grocery,
Parkston, SD" .... .80
Mug, barrel shaped, "G" in 6-pointed
star, mkd "Gluek Brewing Co." on
bottom 180
Pantry Jar, cov, "Your Store–Pitts Bros.
–Alexandria, S.D." .... .475
Pitcher, CherryBand, "Compliments of
Olsen & Son, Frederic & Lewis, Quality,
Price, Service" .... .475
Pitcher, Random Harvest, 12" h .... .40
Plate, Bob White, 8" d .... .15
Plate, Hearthside, 11" d .... .12
Plate, Magnolia, 10.375" d 5
Platter, Bob White, 20 x 11" .... .20
Platter, Lotus, Concord Line, 13 x 11" ... .15
Salad Plate, Tampico, 6.75 x 6.375 ..... .20
Spice Test Plate, pink, 11" d 110
Spittoon, Albany slip dec, bottom mkd
"Minn. Stoneware" .... .450
Spittoon, zinc glaze .... .325
Water Cooler, wing and oval mark,
hand turned, 4 gal .... .675

ROAD MAPS

The majority of collectible road maps
were issued after 1910. Previously, maps
were issued by railroads, and from the turn
of the century to 1920, guide books were
issued for bicycle routes and brave early
automobile owners.

In the mid-1920s a uniform national
highway marking system was adopted,
roads got better and America became
mobile. Maps were published and given
free to motorists by oil companies and state
governments. Although other private interests published atlases and special maps,
the oil company and state issues have the
largest following among collectors.

Scarce maps issued by obscure or
regional oil companies and those with interesting graphics command the highest
prices. Maps published by major oil companies after World War II are plentiful and
their value has remained modest.

As in all collectibles, especially paper
items, condition is all important. Prices listed are for road maps in excellent condition.

Advisor: Peter Sidlow, 5895 Duneville St.,
Las Vegas, NV 89118, (702) 873-1818, fax
(702) 248-4288.

Club: Road Map Collectors of America, 5832
NW 62nd Terrace, Oklahoma City, OK 73122.

Amoco, 1932 100
Associated, 1930 .... .85
Barnsdall, 1928 125
Colonial, 1928 .... .85
Champlin, 1927 150
Cities Service, 1929 125
Covey, 1939 150
Derby, 1925 200
Diamond DX, 1937 .... .50
Dixie, 1931 100
Freedom, 1936 .... .85
Gulf, 1940 .... .20
General, 1928 175
Humble, 1946 .... .25
Magnolia, 1932 100
Marathon, 1940 .... .50
Mobil, 1946 .... .25
Pan-Am, 1937 .... .50
Pan Handle, 1952 .... .60
Pure, 1928 .... .80
Richfield, 1930 .... .80
Shell, 1931 .... .60
Standard Oil, 1933 .... .50
State Issue, Arizona, 1936 .... .75
State Issue, Nevada, 1936 .... .85
State Issue, New Mexico, 1936 ..... .40
State Issue, Wyoming, 1947 .... .35
Sterling, 1933 .... .75
Sunset, 1940 150
Tydol, 1927 100
White Eagle, 1928 300
White Star, 1931 150

*Shell Motor Oil, 1929,
$100.* —Photo courtesy
Collectors Auction
Services.

ROBOTS

This category covers the friction, windup, and battery operated robots made after World War II. The grandfather of all modern robot toys is Atomic Robot Man, made in Japan between 1948 and 1949.

Robots became battery operated by the 1950s. Movies of that era fueled interest in robots. R2D2 and C3PO from Star Wars are the modern contemporaries of Roby and his cousins.

When buying at a flea market, take time to make certain the robot is complete, operational, and has its original box. The box is critical.

Boxer Ding-A-Ling, Topper, battery operated, plastic, orange body, black arms, blue legs, orig box, 1970s, 5.5" h 25
Commando The Amazing Mike Controlled Robot, Ideal, remote control, hard plastic, walks forward and turns right or left, with 4 hollow plastic ball missiles which are dropped into openings at shoulders and fired when arms swing, missing rubber-tipped plastic rockets, orig box, 1961, 18" h 150
Jupiter Robot, Kanto Toys, windup, hard plastic, Robbie-style, red, black arms, full color litho tin panels on chest and back, silvered metal antennas on head and face plate with red transparent plastic insert, walks forward, orig box, 1960s, 7" h 125

Rock 'Em – Sock 'Em Robots, Marx, #5015MO, $150.

Space Robot, Y, Japan, battery operated, light-up plastic dome, robot driver, 1955-60, 9.5" l, $275.

Lost In Space, Remco, battery operated, hard plastic, red body, black arms and legs, cardboard panel attachments on right and left sides of base, ©1966 Space Productions, 6 x 9 x 12"400
Mechanical Mighty Robot, Japan, windup, litho tin, metallic green body, black, red, silver, and yellow accents, dial, switches, and missile insignias on each arm, see-through plastic cover on chest, walks forward as sparks are visible through chest cover, orig box, 1960s, 5.5" h 75
Mr Machine, Ideal, windup, plastic, aluminum built-in key, orig box, 1960, 18" h 160
Robert the Robot, Ideal, battery operated, remote control, hard plastic, gray, red arms, clear plastic eyes, antenna on top of head, moves forward, movable hands with spring activated claw-like hands, crank on back activates voice mechanism, eyes light up, orig box, 1950s, 14" h 150
Robot Dog, KO, Japan, windup, litho tin, coil spring tail with plastic tip, transparent plastic cover on back, plastic google eyes, antennae on top of head serves as on/off switch, 1950s, 5.5 x 8 x 5" 475
Space Explorer, Yonezawa, battery operated, litho tin, screen on chest lowers to reveal 3-D scene of spaceman behind control panel, waddles back and forth as it walks forward, stops and retracts into box form before repeating action, orig box, c1959, 11.75" h 1,000

Television Spaceman, Alps, battery
operated, litho tin, hard plastic hands,
transparent cover on front of half of
head, attached metal chain with silvered metal antenna unit that attaches to top of head with on/off switch,
walks forward as eyes spin, orig box,
c1959, 15" h 650
Whistling Mr Machine, Ideal, windup,
plastic, red head, arms, and legs,
gears and windup mechanism visible
through clear plastic see-through
body, orig box, 1977 60
Zoomer the Robot, Nomura, battery
operated, walks forward as eyes
light-up, orig box, c1954, 7.5" h 850

ROCK 'N' ROLL

Most collectors focus on individual
singers and groups.   The two largest
sources of collectibles are items associated with Elvis and the Beatles. As revivals
occur new interest is drawn to older collectibles. The market has gotten so big that
Sotheby's and Christie's hold Rock 'n' Roll
sales annually.

Club: Kissaholics, P.O. Box 22334, Nashville,
TN 37202.

Note: See Beatles and Elvis for additional
listings.

Clark, Dick, American Bandstand Yearbook, 42 pp, black and white and color
photos, center fold-out for "Annual
Dance Contest," c1959, 9 x 12" 25

*Jukebox,
Wurlitzer 1050,
$6,775.*—Photo
courtesy
Auction Team
Köln.

Rolling Stones, record album, Tattoo You,
LP, $15.

Freed, Alan, concert ticket, "The Alan
Freed Show," tan stiff paper, black
printing, Apr 22, 1960, Carnegie Music
Hall, Pittsburgh, PA, 1.5 x 3.75" 75
Grateful Dead, backstage pass, set of 6,
fabric patch with adhesive back, for
concert events 1990 to 1994, 4 depict
skeletons wearing roses, female on
elephant, pilot in plane, and cowboy,
2 depict panther and eagle with lightning bolt design above eyeballs,
unused, 2.5 x 3.75" 50
Grateful Dead, poster, Feb 27-28 and
Mar 1-2, 1969 concerts at Fillmore
West featuring Grateful Dead,
Pentangle, and Sir Douglas Quintet,
center band portraits surrounded by
abstract design, 14 x 21" 85
Hendrix, Jimi, badge, plastic, safety pin
back, photo sticker on front, small
name sticker on back, Anabas Ltd,
1973, 4 x 4.5" cellophane bag 15
Jackson, Michael, puzzle, A Shining
Star, Colorforms, ©1984 MJJ
Productions, Inc, 13 x 14 x 1.5" box 8
Jones, Tom, switchplate cover, card-
board, black and white photo of Jones
with arms crossed wearing leather
jacket, Kakamamie Co, 1968, 5 x 8" ...10
Joplin, Janis, poster, Jan 17-22, 1967
concert at Matrix, San Francisco,
Big Brother and The Holding Company,
photo of Joplin and band, 13.75 x 20" .40
Kiss, model kit, Custom Chevy Van, AMT,
1977, 6 x 9.25 x 4" box 65
Nelson, Ricky, autograph, CS, center
"Hi Rick Nelson" black felt tip pen
signature 85

Partridge Family, coloring book, Saalfield, 1971, 8.25 x 10.75" 20

Presley, Elvis, lobby card, *It Happened at the World's Fair,* MGM, 1963, 11 x 14" 20

Presley, Elvis, record, *Shake, Rattle and Roll,* RCA Victor EPA-830, 45 rpm, sleeve depicts Elvis dancing and playing his guitar, photo on reverse with short biography, 1956 65

The Monkees, program, 32 pp, black and white photos, full page Pontiac adv with Monkees in Monkeemobile, ©1967 Raybert Productions, Inc, 12 x 12" 25

Tiny Tim, autograph card, inscribed "To Blaine," black felt tip pen signature . .25

Zappa, Frank, pinback button, "We Will Bury You," image of Zappa wearing sunglasses, 1960s, 3" d 45

ROCKWELL, NORMAN

The prices in this listing are retail prices from a dealer specializing in Rockwell and/or limited edition collectibles. Rockwell items are one of those categories for which it really pays to shop around at a flea market. Finding an example in a general booth at ten cents on the dollar is not impossible or uncommon.

When buying any Rockwell item, keep asking yourself how many examples were manufactured. In many cases, the answer is tens to hundreds of thousands. Because of this, never settle for any item in less than fine condition.

Club: Rockwell Society of America, P.O. Box 705, Ardsley, NY 10502.

Advertising Tear Sheet, GM Financing adv, 10 x 13" 8

Book, *Air Sea Trail Rangers Handbook,* 1969 10

Christmas Card, textured painted image of Mr and Mrs Rockwell, inside red ballpoint pen inscription "Merry Christmas from the Rockwells Molly & Norman," 4.75 x 6.5" white envelope postmarked Stockbridge, MA, Dec 19, 1968, addressed to "Charlie Robert & Family, Arlington, Va," 4.5 x 6.125" . . .225

Cookbook, *Saturday Evening Post Album of Better Health Family Cookbook,* Vol 2, #1, 144 pp, Curtis Publishing Co, 1979, 8.5 x 11" 4

Limited Edition Bell, Checking His List, The Norman Rockwell Museum, 6.25" h 4

Limited Edition Figurine, Going Out, 2.25" h 15

Limited Edition Plate, Baby's First Steps, American Family I, Rockwell Museum, N Rockwell, 1979 50

Limited Edition Plate, Dreamboats, Norman Rockwell Collection, Dave Grossman Creations, Rockwell-inspired, 1983. 8.5" d 30

Limited Edition Plate, It's Your Move, Norman Rockwell Clowns, Hoyle Products, N Rockwell, 1978 65

Magazine, *Saturday Evening Post,* Jun 27, 1925, 192 pp 130

Mug, set of 4, The Cobbler, The Lighthouse Keeper's Daughter, The Toymaker, and For a Good Boy, gold trim on handle, 4" h, 2.75" w 5

Music Box, Springtime, boy playing flute surrounded by animals, plays *In the Good Old Summertime,* Hallmark Galleries, 8 x 6 x 3.5" 20

Necktie, girl and boy going to doctor's office 5

Poster, Maxwell House Coffee adv, 1932-32 325

Sheet Music, *Little French Mother, Goodbye,* 1919 45

Limited Edition Plate, Dreaming in the Attic, Rediscovered Women series, Edwin M Knowles, $15.

ROOSTER COLLECTIBLES

Country has always had a barnyard favorite. Pigs were popular in the late 1980s and early 1990s. Cows commanded Country stylists' loyalties in the mid-1990s.

The rooster reigned supreme from 1946 through the end of the 1950s. Rooster images flooded the kitchen on everything from metal bread boxes and canister sets to dish towels and trays. Several American pottery manufacturers made dinnerware featuring a rooster motif, e.g., Metlox's California Provincial and Red Rooster patterns. Japanese manufacturers followed suit with inexpensive imports. Several of the Japanese patterns featured rose motifs surrounding the rooster.

Bread and Butter Plate, Stangl, Country
   Life 25
Breadbox, wood, dovetailed, 15 x 8" 10
Butter, cov, Pyrex, Butterprint, aqua,
   6.75" l, 3.75" w 5
Cake Plate, glass, hp roosters on side,
   metal lid with copper handle, 14" d,
   7" h 10
Candy Dish, Westmoreland, 9" h 15
Canister Set, 4 pcs, sugar, flour, tea, and
   coffee, Rooster and Roses 55
Condiment Dish, Fitz & Floyd, Coq Du
   Village, 5.25" d 15
Condiment Server, Rooster and Roses,
   mkd "Early Provincial Under Glaze
   Hand Painted in Japan" 30
Cup and Saucer, Pennsbury Pottery,
   Black Rooster 8
Cup and Saucer, Taylor, Smith & Taylor,
   Reveille Rooster 3

Weathervane, emb tin, 23.5" l, $275. —Photo courtesy Collectors Auction Services.

Dinner Plate, Homer Laughlin, Brown
   Rooster, 10" d 4
Dinner Plate, Rooster and Roses, mkd
   "PY," 10.25" d 20
Dinner Plate, Taylor, Smith & Taylor,
   Reveille Rooster 5
Figurine, green, Fenton, 2.75" h 10
Flour Canister, Metlox, Red Rooster 35
Jar, glass, figural milk can with inscrip-
   tion "Milk," reverse hp rooster with
   flower dec, Enesco, 6.5" h 2
Jelly Mold, copper, 8" d 80
Pitcher, Pennsbury Pottery, Black
   Rooster, 5.5" h 30
Pitcher, Rooster and Roses, Ucagco,
   5" h 12
Platter, Homer Laughlin, Brown Rooster .6
Refrigerator Dish, rooster and cornstalks,
   1.5 cups, 3.25" h, 4.25" l, 3.5" w 4
Salt and Pepper Shakers, pr, Metlox,
   California Provincial 15
Salt Shaker, Rosemeade, 3.25" h 20
Spaghetti Bowl, Watt, Rooster pattern .175
Tidbit Tray, cov, Rooster and Roses 25

Pitcher, Watt Pottery, Rooster pattern, "Porter's Gas/Miller, S.D." adv, 4" h, $65. —Photo courtesy Collectors Auction Services.

Cookie Cutter, tin, strap handle, early 20th C, $20.

Vegetable Bowl, Homer Laughlin, Brown
　Rooster 2
Wall Plaques, pr, fighting roosters,
　Norcrest 25
Wall Pocket, figural teapot, Rooster and
　Roses, Ucagco, 5" h, 6" d 50
Wall Pocket, Royal Copley, 6.75" d 15

Wall Pocket,
4-H Club,
green, 4.25" h,
$85.

ROSEMEADE

If you live in the Dakotas, you probably
know about Rosemeade. If you live in
California, Georgia, or Maine, I am not so
sure. Rosemeade is one of the many regional pottery manufacturers that American
collectors rediscovered in the past decade.

Rosemeade is actually a trade name for
ceramic pieces made by the Wahpeton
Pottery Company between 1940 and 1953
and Rosemeade Potteries between 1953
and 1961. Production included commemorative and souvenir pieces and household
and kitchen wares.

Rosemeade prices are stronger in the
Midwest and Plains states than elsewhere
across the country. Figurines and figural
pieces command top dollar.

Club: North Dakota Pottery Collectors
Society, P.O. Box 14, Beach, ND 58621.

Ashtray, applied pheasant, "South
　Dakota/Pheasant State" 40
Bank, black bear, 3.75 x 6" 375
Bookends, pr, Russian Wolfhounds,
　black, 6.75" h 225
Candleholders, pr, bird, 4 x 3" 50
Candy Dish, shell, pink and white, 2.75" h,
　4.5" l 45
Commerative Plate, Dakota Territory
　Centennial, 7.25" d 25
Creamer, brown, 2.25" h 10
Creamer and Sugar, blue tulip dec 30
Figurine, deer, pink, 7.75" h 10
Figurine, duck 25
Figurine, monkey, cream, 3" h 390
Flower Holder, heron, 6.75" h 60
Pitcher, speckled pink, 5.5" h 15
Planter, grapevine, 6 x 4" 20
Planter, swan, lavender, 5" h 20
Plaque, applied fish, "Pike Lake Resort,"
　6 x 3.75" 300
Salt and Pepper Shakers, corn 30

Salt and Pepper Shakers, pr, flamingos .55
Salt and Pepper Shakers, pr, Pekinese .100
Shaker, elephant, 2.75" h 20
Shaker, quail 5
Spoon Rest, pheasant 45
Watering Can, rabbit motif, 4" h 50

ROSEVILLE POTTERY

Roseville rose from the ashes of the J.
B. Owen Company when a group of
investors bought Owen's pottery in the late
1880s. In 1892 George F. Young became the
first of four succeeding generations of
Youngs to manage the plant.

Roseville grew through acquisitions of
another Roseville firm and two in
Zanesville. By 1898 the company's offices
were located in Zanesville. Roseville art
pottery was first produced in 1900. The
trade name Rozane was applied to many
lines. During the 1930s Roseville looked for
new product lines. Utilizing several high
gloss glazes in the 1940s, Roseville revived
its art pottery line. Success was limited. In
1954 the Mosaic Tile Company bought
Roseville.

Pieces are identified as early, middle
(Depression era), and late. Because of limited production, middle period pieces are
the hardest to find. They also were marked
with paper labels that have been lost over
time. Some key patterns to watch for are
Blackberry, Cherry Blossom, Faline, Ferella,
Futura, Jonquil, Morning Glory, Sunflower,
and Windsor.

Clubs: American Art Pottery Assoc., P.O.
Box 834, Westport, MA 02790; Roseville's of
the Past Pottery Club, P.O. Box 656,
Clarcona, FL 32710.

Bookends, pr, Snowberry, blue, raised
  mark, 5.5 x 5 x 4.5" 140
Centerbowl, Fuchsia, brown, imp mark,
  4 x 12.5" 225
Floor Vase, Bushberry, green, raised
  mark, 18" h 875
Jardiniere, Futura, protruding shoulder,
  stylized yellow, green, blue, and lavender leaves on burnt-orange ground,
  unmkd, 6 x 8.5" 250
Pillow Vase, Futura, 4-sided, pink and
  green glossy glaze, buttressed handles, emb geometric pattern, unmkd,
  8.5 x 6.25" 775
Pitcher, Pinecone, blue, imp mark,
  10" h 775
Planter, Blackberry, oblong, 3.5 x 13.5" .475
Squat Vase, Cherry Blossom, pink,
  unmkd, 5.25 x 7" 600
Squat Vessel, Cherry Blossom, brown,
  unmkd, 4" h 275
Triple Wall Pocket, Primrose, brown,
  imp mark, 8" h 650
Urn, Cosmos, blue, raised mark, 8" d . .250
Urn, Foxglove, pink, imp mark, 8" h 250
Vase, Falline, bulbous, brown, unmkd,
  6.5 x 6.5" 650
Vase, Jonquil, bulbous, 2-handled,
  unmkd, 6.75" .415
Vase, Montacello, corseted, brown,
  stylized pattern, black paper label,
  4.24 x 5.5" 350
Vase, Wisteria, tapered, brown, but-
  tressed base, foil label, 8.25" h 475
Vase, Zephyr Lily, blue, squat base,
  flaring rim, imp mark, 12" d 225

*Basket, Water Lily, #382-12, 1940s, 12" h,
$350. —Photo courtesy Collectors Auction
Services.*

*Bookends, pr, Peony, #11, 1942, 5.75" h,
$200. —Photo courtesy Ray Morykan
Auctions.*

Vessel, Blackberry, bulbous, 6" h 650
Vessel, Luffa, beaker shaped, brown,
  unmkd, 6.25" h 300

ROYAL CHINA

  Royal China began operations in 1934.
The company produced an enormous number of dinnerware patterns. The backs of
pieces usually contain the names of the
shape, line, and decoration. In addition to
many variations of company backstamps,
Royal China also produced objects with private backstamps. All records of these
markings were lost in a fire in 1970.
  In 1964 Royal China purchased the
French-Saxon China Company, Sebring,
Ohio, which it operated as a wholly-owned
subsidiary. On December 31, 1969, Royal
China was acquired by the Jeannette
Corporation. When fire struck the Royal
China Sebring plant in 1970, Royal moved its
operations to the French-Saxon plant. The
company changed hands several times,
until operations ceased in August 1986.
  Collectors concentrate on specific patterns. The two most favored are Currier and
Ives (introduced 1949–50) and Willow Ware
(1940s). Because of easy availability, only
purchase pieces in fine to excellent condition.

Club: The Currier & Ives Dinnerware
Collectors Club, RD 2, Box 394,
Hollidaysburg, PA 16648.

Blue Willow, berry bowl 2

Blue Willow, chop plate, 12.25" d, $18. —Photo courtesy Ray Morykan Auctions.

Blue Willow, bowl, 8" d 8
Blue Willow, creamer and sugar 25
Blue Willow, cup and saucer 5
Blue Willow, dinner plate, 10" d 15
Blue Willow, flat soup 30
Blue Willow, gravy and underplate 30
Blue Willow, platter, 12" l 20
Blue Willow, vegetable bowl, 10" d 20
Bucks County, berry bowl 8
Bucks County, butter, cov 35
Bucks County, cereal bowl 20
Bucks County, vegetable bowl 25
Colonial Homestead, butter, cov 40
Colonial Homestead, casserole 90
Colonial Homestead, cereal bowl, tab
    handle 40
Colonial Homestead, gravy, with under-
    plate 45
Colonial Homestead, pie plate 50
Colonial Homestead, platter 30
Colonial Homestead, teapot, flat spout .100
Currier & Ives, bread and butter plate ...4
Currier & Ives, cake plate, tab handles ..20
Currier & Ives, calendar plate 20
Currier & Ives, cereal bowl 20
Currier & Ives, chop plate, 12" d 30
Currier & Ives, creamer and sugar 25
Currier & Ives, cup and saucer 2
Currier & Ives, dinner plate 3
Currier & Ives, fruit bowl 2
Currier & Ives, iced tea tumbler 16
Currier & Ives, juice tumbler 12
Currier & Ives, luncheon plate, 9" d 18
Currier & Ives, old fashioned tumbler ...12
Currier & Ives, pie plate 20
Currier & Ives, platter, 13" l 30
Currier & Ives, salad plate 10
Currier & Ives, soup bowl 12
Currier & Ives, teapot, cov 145
Currier & Ives, vegetable bowl, 9" d 20
Currier & Ives, water tumbler 15

Fair Oaks, berry bowl 8
Fair Oaks, bread and butter plate 8
Fair Oaks, cereal bowl 20
Fair Oaks, vegetable bowl, 9" d 25
Memory Lane, plate, tab handles 10
Memory Lane, soup bowl 6
Memory Lane, tumbler, 3.25" h 10
Old Curiosity Shop, ashtray 25
Old Curiosity Shop, berry bowl 5
Old Curiosity Shop, bread and butter
    plate 3
Old Curiosity Shop, butter, cov 40
Old Curiosity Shop, platter 50
Old Curiosity Shop, salad plate 13
Old Curiosity Shop, vegetable bowl 25
Pink Willow, cup and saucer 15
Pink Willow, soup bowl, 8" d 20
Pink Willow, vegetable bowl, 8.25" d 30

ROYAL COPLEY

Royal Copley ceramics were produced by the Spaulding China Company located in Sebring, Ohio. These attractive giftware items were most often marked with a paper label only, making identification a challenge. For hints on identifying unmarked Royal Copley, refer to Leslie C. and Marjorie A. Wolfe's *Royal Copley (plus Royal Windsor and Spaulding)* published by Collector Books, 1992.

Newsletter: The Copley Courier, 1639 N. Catalina St., Burbank, CA 91505.

Ashtray, leaf, applied bird, 5.375" d 5
Ashtray, mallard duck, 3.5 x 6" 15
Bank, pig, 7.35" h 35

Figurines, 5.5" h hen and 6" h rooster, price for pair, $30.

Pitcher, daffodil design, yellow and pink, 8" h, $20.

Bank, teddy bear, gold dec, unmkd,
  7.5" h 65
Bud Vase, warbler, 5" h 10
Creamer and Sugar, leaf 25
Figurine, airedale, 6.5" h 15
Figurine, cat, black and white, pink bow
  tie, 8" h 25
Figurine, cocker spaniel, 6" h 20
Figurine, dancing lady, 8.25" h 50
Figurine, flycatcher, 8" h 20
Figurine, lark, 6.5" h 10
Figurine, sparrow, 5" h 5
Lamp Base, wren 30
Mug, emb "Baby," fish handle, 4.125" h .30
Planter, coach 10
Planter, deer and fawn, 9.5" h 20
Planter, dog pulling planter, 6" h 20
Planter, elf and stump, 6.5" h 15
Planter, girl leaning on barrel 15
Planter, mallard duck and wagon,
  3.75" h 15
Planter, resting poodle, gray, gold dec ..75
Planter, Siamese cats, 9.5" h 100
Planter, tanager on stump 10

ROYAL DOULTON

The chance of finding a piece of Royal Doulton at a flea market is better than you think. Often given as a gift, the recipient seldom realizes its initial value. As a result, it is sold for a fraction of its value at garage sales and to dealers.

Check out any piece of Royal Doulton that you find. There are specialized price guides for character jugs, figures, and toby jugs. A great introduction to Royal Doulton is the two-volume video-cassette entitled *The Magic of a Name*, produced by Quill Productions, Birmingham, England.

Clubs: Royal Doulton International Collectors Club, 700 Cottontail Ln., Somerset, NJ 08873; Royal Doulton International Collectors Club (Canadian Branch), 850 Progress Ave, Scarborough, Ontario M1H 3C4 Canada.

Periodical: Collecting Doulton, B.B.R. Publishing, Elsecar Heritage Centre, Nr Barnsley, S. York, S74 8H5 U.K..

Cereal Bowl, Letterbox, Bunnykins, with
  signature 50
Character Jug, The Viking, D 6496,
  7.25" h 325
Character Jug, Town Crier, D 6537,
  3.25" h 185
Figurine, Affection, HN 2236 70
Figurine, Babie, HN 1679 40
Figurine, Bedtime, HN 1978 35
Figurine, Cherie, HN 2341 50
Figurine, Darling, HN 1985 30
Figurine, Daydreams, HN 1731 90
Figurine, Enchantment, HN 2178 95
Figurine, Janet, HN 1537 80
Figurine, Lambing Time, HN 1890 145
Figurine, Nicola, HN 2804 35
Figurine, Old Balloon Seller, HN 1315 ..145
Figurine, Peggy, HN 2038 50
Figurine, Rose, HN 1368 145
Figurine, Valerie, HN 2107 60
Limited Edition Plate, America, Christmas
  Around the World, 1978 55
Limited Edition Plate, Artful Dodger,
  Charles Dickens Plates, 1980 65
Limited Edition Plate, Christmas In
  England, Beswick Christmas, H Sales,
  1972 35

Character Jug, Robinson Crusoe, D 6539, 1959, 4" h, $75. —Photo courtesy Gene Harris Antique Auction Center, Inc.

Figurine, Christine, style 2, HN 2792, 7.5" h, $250. —Photo courtesy Gene Harris Antique Auction Center, Inc.

Limited Edition Plate, Sisterly Love, All
  God's Children, L DeWinne, 1984 95
Limited Edition Plate, While Shepherds
  Watched, Childhood Christmas,
  N Faulkner, 1984 40
Plate, Orange Vendor, Bunnykins, with
  signature, 7.25" d 65
Toby Jug, Blacksmith, D 6571, 7.25" h . .100
Toby Jug, Major Green the Golfer,
  D 6740, 4" h .125
Toby Jug, Monsieur Chasseur the Chef,
  D 6769, 4" h .125
Toby Jug, Mrs Loan the Librarian,
  D 6715, 4" h 90

ROYAL HAEGER

David H. Haeger founded Haeger Potteries in Dundee, Illinois, in 1871. The company produced its first art pottery in 1914. The Royal Haeger line was introduced in 1938. Haeger Potteries began production for the florist trade and organized the Royal Haeger Lamp Company in 1939.

Many Haeger pieces can be identified by molded model numbers. The first Royal Haeger mold was assigned the number "R-1," with subsequent numbers assigned in chronological order. Giftware in the Studio Haeger line, designed by Helen Conover, have an "S" number. Royal Garden Flower wares, produced between 1954 and 1963, have an "RG" number.

The initial collecting craze that established Royal Haeger as an independent col-lecting category is over. Prices have stabilized for commonly found pieces. Speculative price prevails for high-end pieces.

Club: Haeger Pottery Collectors Club of America, 5021 Toyon Way, Antioch, CA 94509.

Ashtray, #155 clam shell, 8 x 14" 15
Ashtray, #1003, butterfly, 9 x 14 45
Ashtray, R 1719, 12" l 10
Basket, R 386 10
Centerpiece Bowl, R 182, palm leaf
  shaped, 26" l 35
Compote, #3003, turquoise and white,
  4.5" h 20
Daisy Bowl, mauve agate, mkd "Royal
  Haeger by Royal Hickman, Made in
  USA," 12" d 125
Figurine, black panther, 13" l 55
Figurine, elephant, chartreuse and
  honey, 6" h 15
Figurine, mermaid, pearly white satin
  glaze, 10" h 25
Figurine, mother and child, 11.5" h 20
Pitcher, H6 608, Persian blue, rooster
  handle, 9" h 40
Planter, R G79, black pedestal, 5" h 6
Planter, brown drip, scalloped edges,
  6 x 13" 10
Table Lamp, mare and foal, ...60
TV Lamp, gazelle, 8" h 65
Urn, R6-150, 8" h 12
Vase, #412, green, hp scroll work 15
Vase, R 182A, swan, 7.5" h 65
Vase, R 301, 9" h 35
Vase, R 1702, 12.25" h 10

Ashtray, Cotton White, freeform, pebbled surface, mkd "Royal Haeger ©153 USA," 11 x 8", $15. —Photo courtesy Ray Morykan Auctions.

ROYAL WINTON

Royal Winton is more than chintz, a fact appreciated by collectors familiar with Eileen Busby's *Royal Winton Porcelain: Ceramics Fit For A King* (Glass Press, 1998). Royal Winton production includes commemorative and patriotic ware, handpainted ware, an assortment of luster wares, mottled ware, mugs and jugs, pastel ware, souvenir ware, and transfer ware.

In 1885 Sidney and Leonard Grimwade founded the Grimwade Brothers Pottery in Stoke-on-Trent. The firm became Grimwades, Ltd., when it acquired the Winton Pottery Company and Stoke Pottery in 1900. Atlas China, Rubin Art Pottery, Heron Cross Pottery, and Upper Hanley Pottery were added in 1906–07. The "Royal" attribution grew out of the company's promotion of a visit to the plant in April 1913 by King George V and Queen Mary.

Royal Winton's first chintz patterns were introduced in the late 1920s and flourished in the 1930s. In 1997 the company began making limited reproductions of some of its most popular 1930s chintz pieces.

Club: Royal Winton International Collectors' Club, Dancer's End, Northall, Bedfordshire LU6 2EU U.K.

Box, cov, Pastel Ware, cream, gilded
    edge 95
Box, oval, mkd "Churchill July 1965" 65
Cake Plate, Transfer Ware, coral center
    with Egyptian motif on yellow band,
    8.5" d 65
Candy Dish, mkd "Elizabeth II Crowned
    June 2, 1953" 65
Candy Dish, mottled pink 60
Cheese Keeper, cov, Cottage Ware, Ye
    Olde Mill 350
Compote, Leaf Ware, light orange and
    green, metal base 45
Condiment Set, white floral design on
    blue 90
Creamer and Sugar, mottled green 75
Cup, Byzanta, silhouette of dancers on
    yellow, blue-gray tree and city in
    background, mkd "Watteau" on
    bottom 85

Fruit Bowl, ftd, mottled green, gilded
    edge 110
Jardiniere, blue, floral band, mkd
    "Rubian Art" 150
Mug, musical, horse and buggy scene,
    plays *I Love to Go a'Wandering* 225
Mug, King George VI, 2.75" h 200
Mug, Pip the Panda illus 100
Plate, crossed British and American flags
    over Canadian flag, mkd "Canada,"
    7" d 75
Teacup and Saucer, "Queen Elizabeth
    II Crowned June 2, 1953" 55
Teapot, Cottage Ware, red roof, mkd
    "Ye Olde Inne" 300
Vase, Byzanta, orange, black bands
    around top and bottom, black classical musical scene in center, 7.5" h ...225

RUGS

You have to cover your floors with something. Until we have antique linoleum, the name of the game is rugs. If you have to own a rug, own one with some age and character. Do not buy any rug without unrolling it. Hold it up in the air in such a way that there is a strong light behind it. This will allow you to spot any holes or areas of heavy wear.

Periodical: Rug Hooking, 500 Vaughn St., Harrisburg, PA 17110.

Hooked, animals, multicolored, brown
    ground, mounted on stretcher, 26 x
    41" 300

Hooked, Disney's Bambi and Thumper, brown, blue, red, yellow, pink, and green, 22 x 40", $85. —Photo courtesy Collectors Auction Services.

Hooked, birds and flowers, Waldoboro
type sculptured flowers, elaborate
scroll border, red, pink, yellow, blue,
and green, beige ground, olive border,
30 x 50" 200

Hooked, carriage with horse, driver,
passenger, and footman, black, olive,
and gray silhouette on beige stripe
ground, 24.5 x 45.5" 275

Hooked, dog, leaf border, attached to
larger piece of wool felt, 25 x 40.5" ..175

Hooked, flowers in center on green
diamond surrounded by darker green
and gray conforming shapes, black
ground, variegated border, late 19th C,
36 x 59" 450

Hooked, geometric pendant in center
surrounded by border of American
Indian good luck symbols, shades of
red, tan, gray, and black, burlap backing, late 19th C, 33 x 60" 175

Hooked, "Home Sweet Home," maroon,
green, olive, and brown, floral designs
in corners, red scroll border, 28 x 40" .150

Navajo, 6-pointed star, dark red center,
whirling log design with arrows at top
and bottom, gray ground, 23 x 25.5" ...75

Navajo, geometric, black triangular
design, tan ground, red border, c1920,
27 x 49" 140

Navajo, hourglass, central design, ser-
rate border diamonds with old style
cross design, hand-carded wool in
tan, black, red, and natural white,
c1950, 37 x 60" 75

Navajo, storm, rust, brown, and white,
53 x 77" 90

Oriental, Anatol Turkish, ivory border,
gold spandrels, red ground, added
fringe, 41 x 49" 165

Oriental, Sparta, runner, dark blue border,
dark mauve ground, 34 x 100" 190

Oriental, Turkoman, ivory border, brown
ground, color bleeding, 30 x 45" 135

Penny, circles, gray wool and olive twill,
red felt centers on white flannel
ground, tab border, 27.5 x 51.5" 150

Rag, geometric, olive, red, and maroon
earth tones, corners and center with
checkerboard type design, 25.5 x
34.5" 150

Rag, stripes, red and green on beige
ground, 37 x 158" 35

RUSSEL WRIGHT

Russel Wright was an American industrial engineer with a design passion for
domestic efficiency through simple lines.
Wright and his wife, Mary Small Einstein,
wrote *A Guide To Easier Living* to explain
the concepts.

Some of his earliest designs were exe-
cuted in polished spun aluminum. These
pieces, designed in the mid 1930s, included
trays, vases, and teapots.

Russel Wright worked for many different companies in addition to creating material under his own label, American Way.
Wright's contracts with firms often called
for the redesign of pieces which did not
produce or sell well. As a result, several
lines have the same item in more than one
shape. Among the companies for which
Wright did design work are Chase Brass &
Copper, General Electric, Imperial Glass,
National Silver Company, and the Shenango
and Steubenville Pottery Companies.

Though most collectors focus on
Wright's dinnerware, he also designed
glassware, plastic items, textiles, furniture,
and metal objects. His early work in spun
aluminum often is overlooked, as is his later
work in plastic for the Northern Industrial
Chemical Company.

ALUMINUM

Cheeseboard 75
Ice Fork 75
Tidbit Tray, single 85
Wastebasket 125

CHINA

American Modern, after dinner cup and
saucer, coral 25
American Modern, after dinner cup and
saucer, seafoam 30
American Modern, bread and butter
plate, chartreuse, 6" d 5
American Modern, chop plate, char-
treuse 30
American Modern, cup, cedar 10
American Modern, cup, coral 10
American Modern, pitcher, chartreuse .100
American Modern, plate, coral, 8" d 14

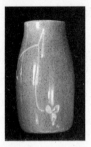

White Clover, vase, $30.

American Modern, plate, coral, 10" d ...12
American Modern, vegetable bowl, 2
  handles, white 90
Iroquois, bread and butter plate,
  avocado, 6" d 5
Iroquois, carafe, nutmeg 150
Iroquois, casserole, cov, divided,
  avocado 60
Iroquois, casserole, open, ice blue, 8" d .25
Iroquois, cereal bowl, avocado, 5" d 10
Iroquois, gumbo flat soup,
  nutmeg 35
Iroquois, plate, avocado, 10" d 10
Iroquois, platter, avocado, 14.5" l 35
Iroquois, vegetable bowl, divided, ice
  blue, 10" d 40
White Clover, casserole, cov, 2 qt 45
White Clover, dinner plate, 10" d 10
White Clover, sugar, cov 15

GLASS

American Modern, cordial, 2.25" h 15
American Modern, water goblet, char-
  treuse, 4.125" h 25
Bartlett Collins, Eclipse, cocktail, 3" h ...10
Bartlett Collins, Eclipse, ice tub 40
Imperial, Flair, juice tumbler, 6 oz 45
Imperial, Flair, water tumbler, 11 oz 50
Imperial Twist, iced tea tumbler 35
Old Morgantown, goblet, 11 oz 35

PLASTIC DINNERWARE

Meladur, cereal bowl, almond 8
Meladur, cup and saucer, almond 12
Meladur, salad plate, almond, 7" d 8
Residential, cup and saucer, sea mist
  gray 15
Residential, dinner plate, sea mist gray .10
Residential, platter, aqua 25

Residential, salad plate, salmon red 10
Residential, vegetable bowl, divided,
  turquoise 35

SALT & PEPPER SHAKERS

Hang on to your hats. Those great figural salt and pepper shaker sets from the
1920s through the 1960s have been discovered by the New York art and decorator
crowd. Prices have started to jump. What
does this say about taste in America?

When buying a set, make certain it is a
set. Check motif, base, and quality of work-
manship. China shakers should have no
cracks or signs of cracking. Original paint
and decoration should be present on china
and metal figures. Make certain each shaker has the right closure.

Salt and pepper shaker collectors must
compete with specialized collectors from
other fields, e.g., advertising and black
memorabilia. I have been searching for a
pair shaped like jigsaw puzzle pieces. So
far I have neither seen a pair nor found a
dealer who has seen one but I will not give
up.

Club: Novelty Salt & Pepper Shakers Club,
P.O. Box 677388, Orlando, FL 32867.

Basket of Blueberries, ceramic 4
Black Boy and Watermelon, Japan 85
Black Chef and Mammy, ceramic 6
Boy and Girl, Shawnee 15
Boy and Girl Mice, Japan 20
Calico Dogs, Japan 15

Amish Couple, painted cast iron, $8.
—Photo courtesy Ray Morykan Auctions.

Campbell Soup Kids, F & F Mold & Die
  Works, 4.5" h .80
Cowboy and Cowgirl in Boots, Japan,
  4" h 35
Cowboys, Josef Originals 35
Crabs, "Japan" paper label, 1.5" h, 3" l . . .7
Crystal Salt, 3" h 30
Duck and Egg, 3.25" h 25
Ducks, nodder .35
Elephants, cork stopper, stamped
  "Japan," 2" h .4
Exxon Tiger, plastic 15
Football Player, Ucagco, 4.75" h 45
Grannies, Napco 15
Horse Heads, Rosemeade 85
Horses, incised "Japan," 3.75" h 20
Idaho Spuds, Japan 85
Indians, nodder, round drum base 95
John F Kennedy, in rocking chair, mkd
  "Copyright, Arrow 1962, NYC, Japan" .75
Kangaroo, Japan, 4.5" h 50
Light Bulbs, glass, cobalt and forest
  green, 3.5" h .35
Mr Peanut, plastic 15
Mushroom, with tray, 3 pcs, Japan 15
Owls, Lefton 15
Parrots, Fitz & Floyd 35
Peter Pumpkin Eater, Japan 35
Poodles, Goebel, 3.5" h 35
Poppin' Fresh and Poppie, plastic, mkd
  "Copyright Pillsbury 1974," 4" h 40
Quaker Hurricane, sterling silver, 6.5" h .35
RCA Nipper 30
Rustic Daisy, Lefton, 3.25" h 10
Seagram's 7, plastic, 3.5" h 25
Siamese Cats, blue rhinestone eyes, 4" h .12
Snuggle Hug Bears, Regal China, 3.5" h .35
Squirrels, Goebel 60
Swans, ceramic, dark brown, 2.5" h 10

*Plastic, clear top, turquoise base, mkd
"Deka, Elizabeth, N.J. No. 120," 4" h, $12.*

Skulls, ceramic, long necks rest in teeth base, heads nod, mkd "Patent T.T.," 3.5" h, 3.5" w, $55. —Photo courtesy Collectors Auction Services.

Urn, ceramic, white, gold trim, Japan 8
Watering Cans, Rooster and Roses 25

SAND PAILS

The illustrations found on litho tin sand pails are truly works of art. Innumerable child's themes from animals to cartoon characters have graced the sides of these seashore toys. Despite the fact that sand and salt water are natural enemies of tin toys, concentrate on pails in very good condition with little surface damage. Pails were mass-produced in large quantities, making condition an important part of value.

Club: Ohio Art Collectors Club, 18203 Kristi Rd., West, Liberty, MO 64068.

Boy, puppy, and beach ball, plaid design
  around top and bottom, Ohio Art,
  1950s, 3" h 65
Circus Theme, performing animals,
  Chein, 1960s, 5" h 125
Circus Theme, ringmaster, lion, clown,
  and tiger 65
Comic Farmer, farmer strumming banjo
  for cows and pigs in pasture, Ohio
  Art, 1970s, 5" h 55
Disney, characters from *Pinocchio* film,
  1940, 6.5" h .225
Drum Majorette, boy pumping weights,
  and little girl handing out ice cream
  cones at circus, designed by Elaine
  Ends Hileman, Ohio Art, 1950s, 8" h . . .95
Fishing, boys fishing from boat while
  riding large fish, red plastic handle,
  shield logo, Chein, 1950s, 8" h 65
Flipper, children with trick performing
  dolphin, "World's Best Toys" logo,
  Ohio Art, 1960s 95

Children Playing Musical Instruments, patriotic motif, red, white, and blue, T Cohn, $85.

Garden, boy and girl playing in wheelbarrow one side, girl chasing chicken and boy feeding lamb other side, "World's Best Toys" logo, Ohio Art, 1960s 125

Kids at Beach, little boy and girl playing under beach umbrella on both sides, red plastic handle, Chein, 1950s, 8" h .65

Kids in Boat, anchor border, Ohio Art, 1950s 150

Kids on Carousel, designed by Elaine Ends Hileman, #117, Ohio Art, 1950s .150

Peter Rabbit, story written around sides with illus inserted in text, light blue and pink ground, Chein, 1960s, 8" h . .145

Shirt Tales, TYG and Pammy, Ohio Art, 1981 25

Signs, various road signs and patch pockets on denim ground, Ohio Art, 1970s, 8" h 45

Tiger Cubs, playing in grass, Ohio Art, 1970s, 5" h 65

SCHMOOS

Al Capp (Alfred Gerald Caplin) introduced the world to Li'l Abner and the residents of Dogpatch on August 20, 1934. The comic strip ran until 1977. The enormous popularity of the strip led to an amusement theme park, a Broadway musical, several Fleischer cartoons, a wealth of comic books and softcover paperbacks, two movies, and Kickapoo Joy Juice (a short-lived soft drink). The March 1952 Sunday strip in which Li'l Abner married Daisy Mae holds the record for the most widely read comic strip of all time.

Capp's fertile imagination created Fearless Fosdick, a strip within a strip, and a host of classic comic characters from The Bald Eagle to the ham-shaped Schmoo. The Schmoo lived in a Garden of Paradise. Capp had no qualms about licensing the images of his characters. Look for Schmoo banks, drinking glasses, paperbacks, salt and pepper shakers, sheet music, and more.

Balloon, figural, black, white face and name, cardboard platform with ink design on top of shoes designed to hold figural balloon, 4 x 6.25" bag reads "Toss-Up Balloon Lands On Its Feet" .70

Barrette, plastic, figural running Daisy, blonde hair, red blouse, black shorts, Occupied Japan, 1.5" h 8

Bat and Ball Paddle, wooden, "Li'l Abner's Schmoo-Fly," diecut yellow plywood, black accent smiling Schmoo, ©1948 UFS, 5.625 x 10.25 x .25" 50

Beanie, wool and cotton, 1 side shows Injun Joe and Washable Jones being followed by Schmoos, reverse has stiff paper tag with stitched red ground showing Abner and other characters, Plymouth Hat Mfg Co, c1950, 7" d 75

Bottle, glass, figural, smiling boy Schmoo, metal cap, mkd "Baldwin laboratories, Saegertown, PA," 7" h 75

Coupon, offering 6 comic books for 15¢ and box top from Oxydol or Dreft or 2 wrappers from Ivory Soap, offer expired Aug 31, 1950, 3.25 x 6.5" 8

Figure, plaster, boy and girl Schmoo, 4.75" boy, 4.25" girl 175

Frame Tray Puzzle, Li'l Abner, Jaymar, 35 pcs, 14 x 11", $20.

Magnet, plastic figural, c1948, 1.5" h 40
Nesting Figures, set of 6, plastic, white,
  black inked smiling face on front,
  removable bottom, 1.75" to 5.25" h . . .175
Pin, plaster, figural Schmoo, unmkd, 1 x
  2 x .5" 75
Pin, brass, figural Schmoo, black accents
  on face, late 1940s, 1.5" h 30
Tumbler, set of 8, different images on
  each tumbler, UFS, 1949, 5.25 x 10.75
  x 5.25" box 175

Teacher's Valentine, bi-fold, 1960s, 4.375 x 5.375", $1.

SCHOOL MEMORABILIA

"School Days, School Days, good old golden rule days." I've been singing this refrain ever since I moved into the former Vera Cruz elementary school in Pennsylvania.

Bell, brass, wooden handle, 1890s, 5" h .45
Book, *Beginner's History,* 1916 5
Book, *Eclectic Geography,* 1888 10
Book, *Dick and Jane Reader,*
  hardcover 35
Chalk Holder, wooden 10
Clock, Stromberg master regulator,
  1915, 60" d 575
Desk, student's, oak, drawer under seat
  with pencil tray, 18 x 22 x 20" 75
Schoolmaster's Desk, cherry, 32 x 39 x
  30" 525
Student's Desk, wooden, pegged, slant
  lid, 36 x 30 x 24" 200
Game, Geography Lotto, 1956 25
Globe, litho tin, Chein, 1930s 40
Map, canvas, pull-down type, Universal,
  NY 25

Educational Scroll, Richmond School Furniture Co, Muncie, IN, oak case, ©1928, 40 pictures, 11" h, 21" w, $70.

Paper Dolls, School Days, Gabriel &
  Sons 35
Pencil Box, 5 storage compartments,
  Leatherette Novelty Co 5
Pencil Box, litho tin, Red Goose Shoes . .45
Pencil Sharpener, celluloid, Scottie
  dog 35
Postcard, Lincoln Building, Quakertown
  Schools, PA, black and white 5
Postcard, Spring Grove Minnesota High
  School, real photo, 1931 5
Report Card, Pupil's Report, neatly filled
  in, 1900 3
Reward of Merit, Excelsior, 50 merits,
  white and blue, gold trim, 1866 10
Sheet Music, *Little Old Red Schoolhouse,*
  Wheeler & Durham, 1890 12
Valentine, "To My Teacher," bi-fold,
  1930s 5
Watercolor Paints, Felix the Cat, pam-
  phlet detailing history of American
  flag, Hassenfeld Bros Inc, 1950s 50

SECONDHAND ROSES

This is a catchall category—designed specifically for those items which are bought solely for their utilitarian use. Anyone who regularly attends country auctions, flea markets, or garage sales has undoubtedly seen his fair share of "recycled" household goods. Ranging from wringer washers to electronic video games, these products and appliances are neither decorative nor financially lucrative. They are strictly secondhand merchandise.

There is not much reason to focus on brand names, with two exceptions—Maytag and Craftsman. First, Maytag, widely regarded as the Cadillac of washers and dryers, consistently realizes higher prices than any other brand. Second, Craftsman hand tools, distributed by Sears, generally bring higher prices due to the company's generous replacement policy.

As a result of advances in technology and space constraints in modern homes, several larger sized appliances have little or no value on today's market. For example, console stereos and large chest freezers can often be had free for the hauling.

All items listed below are in good, clean condition. All parts are intact and appliances are in working order. The prices are designed to get you in the ballpark. Good luck in getting a hit.

Lamp, ceramic, turquoise with gold highlights, parchment shade, 1960s, 30.5" h, price for pair, $75.

Air Conditioner, purchased in Fall or
   Winter 50
Air Conditioner, purchased in Spring 75
Air Conditioner, purchased in Summer .100
Air Mattress, double 8
Attaché Case, leather, fitted int, locking .10
Answering Machine 15
Barbecue Grill, charcoal 8
Barbecue Grill, propane gas 50
Bedroom Suite, French Provincial, white
   with gold trim, single bed, nightstand,
   chest of drawers, and dresser with
   mirror 175
Bicycle, 16", coaster brakes 15
Big Wheel, plastic, 3 wheels 4
Bird Bath, concrete, bowl and pedestal .10
Booster Seat 5
Camp Stove, Coleman, 2-burner 20
Can Opener, electric 2
Car Seat 10
CD Player, multiple disc 50
Coffee Table, wood, modern 25
Computer, with monitor, 2-5 years old . .150
Computer, with monitor, 5+ years old . . .40
Dehumidifier, 15 pt 25
Diaper Bag 2
Dishwasher, portable, 5 years old 50
Dutch Oven 5
Exercise Bicycle, stationary 15
Extension Ladder, aluminum, 40' 60
Fan, battery operated, hand-held 1
Fan, window, puchased in Spring, Fall,
   or Winter 10
Fan, window, purchased in Summer 20
Filing Cabinet, metal, 4 drawers 40

Freezer, upright, full size, 5 years old . . .100
Garden Tools, hoe, rake, shovel, etc. 5
Grill Cover 4
Grill Utensils, fork, spatula, and brush . . .4
Hair Dryer, hand held, full size, multiple
   settings 3
Highchair, metal, plastic, and vinyl 12
Kerosene Heater, purchased in Spring,
   Summer, or Fall 35
Kerosene Heater, purchased in Winter . .50
Lawn Mower, electric, purchased in
   Fall or Winter .15
Lawn Mower, electric, purchased in
   Spring or Summer 20
Lawn Mower, gas, purchased in Fall or
   Winter 35
Lawn Mower, gas, purchased in Spring
   or Summer 50
Microwave Oven, large, 1-5 years old . . .45
Mixer, counter top, 2 bowls 12
Movie Projector, 8mm or Super 8 2
Playpen 8
Pots and Pans, 8 pc set, SS 40
Refrigerator, bar size 50
Refrigerator, full size 100
Rug Shampooer .15
Sewing Machine, portable, electric 25
Snow Shovel, purchased in Spring,
   Summer or Fall 5
Snow Shovel, purchased in Winter 10
Space Heater 15
Stemware, 3 sizes, 24 pcs 65
Step Ladder, wooden, 5' 30
Stereo, turntable/cassette, receiver
   and 2 speakers 50
Stroller 15
Television, color, console 75
Television, color, portable, 19" 50
Television Stand, casters 10

Toaster Oven 12
Trailer Hitch 12
Traveling Liquor Cabinet, complete 20
Typewriter, electric 2
Vacuum Cleaner, canister or upright 25
VCR, 5 years old 65
Wardrobe, metal 20
Weight Lifting Bench 15

SEWING ITEMS

This is a wide open area. While many favor sterling silver items, only fools overlook objects made of celluloid, ivory, other metals, plastic, and wood. An ideal specialty collection would be sewing items that contain advertising.

Collecting sewing items received a big boost as a result of the Victorian craze. During the Victorian era a vast assortment of practical and whimsical sewing devices were marketed. Look for items such as tape measures, pincushions, stilettos for punchwork, crochet hooks, and sewing birds (beware of reproductions).

Modern sewing collectors are focusing on needle threaders, needle books, and sewing kits from hotels and motels. The general term for this material is "20-Pocket" because pieces fit neatly into 20 pocket plastic notebook sleeves.

Clubs: International Sewing Machine Collectors Society, 551 Kelmore St., Moss Beach, CA 94038; National Button Society, 2733 Juno Pl., Apt. 4, Akron, OH 44313; Thimble Collectors International, 2594 E Upper Hayden Lake Rd., Hayden, ID 83835; The Thimble Guild, P.O. Box 381807, Duncanville, TX 75138; Toy Stitchers, 623 Santa Florita Ave., Millbrae, CA 94030.

Newletters: *That Darn Newsletter*, 461 Brown Briar Circle, Horsham, PA 19044; *Thimbletter*, 93 Walnut Hill Rd., Newton Highlands, MA 02161.

Glove Darner, sterling silver, ornate,
   4.25" l 70
Match Safe, silvered brass, detailed lid
   design including lion "King of Tailors"
   logo, standing Indian warrior and
   symbolic commerce lady, 1904 patent
   year mkd inside lid 35

Needle Book, dog holding needle while
   cat tries to thread it, West Germany,
   6.5" w 6
Needle Book, Happy Home Needle Book .4
Needle Book, J E Foisy Music Stores,
   MI, profile of woman on cover, 1911
   calendar around book 6
Pinback Button, White Sewing Machine
   Co, Cleveland, OH, celluloid 20
Sewing Box, cedar, carved hinged doors,
   int spool tray on both ends, 10 x 7" ...40
Sewing Kit, brass and celluloid tube
   holder, brass thimble cap with orange
   enamel collar, contains small double
   spool of black and white threads, mkd
   "Parisian Novelty Co, Chicago/Dairy
   and Ice Cream Industry For More
   Than 34 Years" 15
Sewing Machine, Davis, electric 25
Sewing Machine, Eldredge, electric 45
Sewing Machine, Greyhound Electric ...45
Sewing Machine, Howe, treadle, cast
   iron base, drop-leaf work surface,
   A B Howe, NY, c1880 100
Sewing Machine, Singer, "New Family,"
   treadle, c1872 100
Sewing Scissors, ornate, mkd "USA,"
   3.5" l 25
Sewing Scissors, silverplated, figural
   crane, mkd "H Morley & Sons,
   Germany," 4" l 10
Sock Darner, glass, blue, 5" l 80
Stocking Darner, Singer Sewing Machine
   attachment #35776 ....
Tape Measure, Fox's Guernsey Dairy ...15

Toy Sewing Machine, Singer #20, chain stitch, cast iron, with table clamp and orig box, c1950, $150. —Photo courtesy Gene Harris Antique Auction Center, Inc.

Advertising Trade Card, Clark's O.N.T. Cotton Thread, $10.

Planter, fawn and fern, #737, $20. —Photo courtesy Ray Morykan Auctions.

Tape Measure, metal, Reddy Kilowatt, San Diego Gas & Electric Co, 1.5" w . .35
Tape Measure, "Singer Sewing Machine 1851-1951 A Century of Sewing Service" 60
Toy Sewing Machine, Sewhandy, #20, black, orig box, c1952 85

SHAWNEE POTTERY

The Shawnee Pottery company was founded in Zanesville, Ohio, in 1937. The plant, formerly home to the American Encaustic Tiling Company, produced approximately 100,000 pieces of pottery per working day. Shawnee produced a large selection of kitchenware, dinnerware, and decorative art pottery. The company ceased operations in 1961.

Club: Shawnee Pottery Collectors Club, P.O. Box 713, New Smyrna Beach, FL 32170.

Ashtray, Cameo, #205, boomerang shape, shell pink 8
Bud Vase, #1168 12
Casserole, cov, King Corn, individual, 9" .125
Cookie Jar, drum major, #10 315
Cookie Jar, owl 100
Cookie Jar, Puss 'n Boots, short tail . . .125
Cookie Jar, Puss 'n Boots, tulip decals, gold trim 200
Cookie Jar, Smiley, yellow neckerchief, floral decals, gold trim 265
Creamer, elephant 40
Creamer, Puss 'n Boots 40
Creamer and Sugar, King Corn 40
Flowerpot, Daisy .12
French Casserole, Kenwood Lobster, #904 30

Jardiniere, Petit-Point, #2908, yellow, 5" sq 8
Mixing Bowl, King Corn, #6 35
Mug, King Corn, #69 40
Pitcher, miniature, yellow, 2.75" h 10
Planter, basket, #640 10
Planter, black bull, pink leaf planter 30
Planter, dog in row boat, #736 20
Planter, hound and Pekingese, #611 15
Planter, rooster, #1503, bronze 15
Planter, squirrel, pink 8
Salt and Pepper Shakers, milk cans, small 15
Salt and Pepper Shakers, pr, owl, small .10
Salt and Pepper Shakers, pr, Puss 'n Boots, gold trim, large 80
Salt and Pepper Shakers, pr, Puss 'n Boots, small 20
Teapot, Daisy 60
Vase, Confetti, #2102, 8" h 6
Wall Pocket, bow, #434, yellow, 4 x 5" . . .18
Window Box, Petit-Point, #1905, rect, orange, 8" l 10

Salt and Pepper Shakers, pr, Winnie and Smiley, large, $125. —Photo courtesy Gene Harris Antique Auction Center, Inc.

SHEET MUSIC

The illustrated covers of 19th and 20th century sheet music provide for a fun and fine collectible. Since any subject or personality can be found on sheet music, it provides a remarkable look at popular culture and history. Whether your interest is Women's Suffrage or Bill Haley and the Comets, your alma mater or home state, ethnic groups or transportation, Sophie Tucker or Madonna, sheet music covers abound. A too-little recognized facet of collecting sheet music is that many collectors are musicians, and interested in preserving and celebrating America's musical heritage as well.

Prices vary widely according to venue. The same sheet may turn up at a flea market for $1, at a shop for $10, and on ebay for $20. At this writing there are no reliable price guides for sheet music. There is a very nice series of books about sheet music (with researched and documented prices) by Marion Short that approaches collecting by category.

Sheet music can be easily stored flat on shelves, but should not be repaired with any over-the-counter tape, as none of the popular brands are of archival quality.

Advisor: Wayland Bunnell, 199 Tarrytown Rd, Manchester, NH 03103.

Clubs: National Sheet Music Society, 1597 Fair Park Ave., Los Angeles, CA 90041; New York Sheet Music Society, P.O. Box 354, Hewlett, NY 11557; Remember That Song, 5623 N. 64th Ave., Glendale, AZ 85301.

Newsletter: *The Rag Times*, 15222 Ricky Ct., Grass Valley, CA 95949.

Periodical: *Sheet Music Magazine*, 333 Adams St., Bedford Hills, NY 10507.

Africana, Berliner, 2/4 march, 2-step, rag, tribesman dancing around fire and idol, 1903 25
Dickey Bird Song, The, Fain, Dietz, *Three Little Darlings,* Iturbi, Jeanette MacDonald, Jane Powell, purple, pink, and white, 1947 6
Drifting, Polla, Lamb, Rolf Armstrong illus of pretty woman in sailor hat, 1920 6

Always and Always, *Joan Crawford, 1937, 9 x 12", $12.*

Deep Purple, DeRose, Parish, fuchsia dec graphic above large photo of Donny and Marie Osmond on lattice background, 1967 5
Faithful Forever, Robin/Rainger, *Gulliver's Travels,* Paramount Pictures cartoon scenes on film strip, 1939 6
Heart and Soul, H Carmichael, Loesser, Four Aces photo in red heart, 1938 5
Hello Ma Baby, Emerson, drawing of black man upper left and woman lower right on phones, 1899 15
Mammy's Little Kinky Headed Boy, Trinkaus, White, drawing of Mammy with child in rocking chair, 1926 8
Melody In Spring, Gensler, Thompson, *Melody In Spring,* Lanny Ross, Ann Sothern, romantic circle photo, 1934 .10
My Cairo Maid, Foster/Schonberg, DeSylva, vivid Egyptian woman by water, columned building, 1917 12
Night Over Shanghai, Warren, Mercer, *The Singing Marine,* Dick Powell, Doris Weston, 1937 8
Shades of Gray, Mann/Cynthia Weil, full color photo of The Monkees, 1966 ...15

Drake's Cake Walk, *black and white, red logo, c1909, 10.5 x 14", $30.*

Sheridan's Ride March-Gallop, *litho cov,* A Hoen & Co, 1922, 9 x 12", $55.

Shortnin' Bread, Wolfe, Wood, stylized African American woman with large pan of bread on her head, red, black, and white, 1928 5

Sister Susie's Sewing Shirts for Soldiers, Darewski, Weston, blackface photos of Al Jolson in large "S" on green ground, 1914 12

Softly As I Leave You, DeVita, Calabreste/ Shaper, Elvis Presley photo, 1962 15

Stay In Your Own Backyard, Udall, Kennett, white children playing, black child looking on, cabin, mother behind, inset Louise Dresser, 1899 10

Time Will Tell, W Donaldson, Jones, full color pretty woman holding locket with long chain, wearing orange off-shoulder dress, 1920 10

You Needed Me, Goodrum, photo of Anne Murray, 1978 4

Waiting For the Robert E Lee, Gilbert, Muir, green and black riverboat, cotton, chickens, dice, African American man palying banjo, 1930 10

Ziegfield Follies, Berlin, *Mandy,* full color Henry Clive drawing of pretty woman Bevo in song list, 1919 12

Travelin' Man, Ricky Nelson, Golden West Melodies, c1960-61, $20.

SHOE RELATED COLLECTIBLES

This is a category with sole. Nothing more needs to be said.

Advertising Trade Card, A S Kreider Co, "Advanced Styles," 1923 3

Advertising Trade Card, The Factory Shoe Store, 617 Penn St, Reading, PA. 5.75 x 4" 4

Clicker, Triangle Brand Shoes, emb text "All Heel Leather/Counter Innersole," triangle logo for McElwain, 1930s 15

Flip, 2 In 1 Shoe Polish, diecut celluloid, multicolored illus of man holding product can, overlaid red band with white lettering, Whitehead & Hoag, 1905 . . .12

Pinback Button, Buster Brown Hose Supporter, multicolored illus, black lettering, early 1900s 15

Pinback Button, Buster Brown Shoes Radio Club, multicolored Buster and Tige portraits on white gorund, red and blue lettering, 1930s 20

Pinback Button, K-Z Shoes, child in bib overalls above inscription "I Wear K-Z Elk Brand Shoes," 1920s, .75" d . .20

Pinback Button, Ohio Reservation School Shoes, "Can't Wear Them Out," sepia portrait of boy wearing patriotic top hat, brown lettering, early 1900s 12

Pinback Button, Pony Stockings For Boys and Girls, 1920s 10

Pocketknife, Bakelite, figural lady's shoe, 2" l 20

Shoe Horn, celluloid, figural lady's leg, marbleized moss green, applied black plastic on bottom with "BPOE," 8" l . . .20

Shoe Horn, celluloid, green, 7" l 8

Calendar, Snag Proof Shoes & Boots, litho cardboard, 1903, 10.25 x 6.75", $150. —Photo courtesy Collectors Auction Services.

Shoe Horn, vulcanized fiber, Merkel Bobbin Co adv, 4.625" l, $8.

Shoe Horn, sterling silver, rope twist handle, engraved script "Elsie" on horn, Whiting hallmark on back, 5.5" l .12
Shoe Polish Kit, electric, Iona, 1960s 25
Shoe Stretcher, metal, mkd "Lefcourt Gentleman's Shoes, 400 Madison Ave, New York City" .8
Sign, Red Wing Shoes, metal, raised lettering, 24 x 18 75
Tin, Shinola Shoe Polish, sample, 1.75" d 40
Whistle, litho tin, Weatherbird Shoes, diecut, 4-reed, yellow paint with red and black logo symbol, 1930s 15
Whistle, litho tin, yellow paint with image of elfin-like character, inscription "For Girls and Boys/Made by Hamilton-Brown Shoes," Japan, 1930s 15
Toy, windup, litho tin, cobbler holding plastic headed hammer and nail, fabric hair, cloth shirt, Japan 45

SILHOUETTE PICTURES

Eighteenth- and nineteenth-century silhouettes (shades) are profiles produced by hollow cutting or mechanical tracing. Additional detail was often added by painted highlights.

Marlys Sellers' *Encyclopedia of Silhouette Collectibles on Glass* (Shadow Enterprises, 1992) introduced collectors to colored pictures in a silhouette style that were painted on the back of a piece of flat or convex glass and were popular from the 1920s through the early 1950s. They are usually found with a paper scenic or tinted background or a background of textured foil. A popular promotional giveaway, examples are found with an imprinted advertising message. Forms range from a simple two-dimensional picture to a jewelry box.

HOLLOW CUT

Family Portrait, mother, father, son, and daughter, mounted together in bird's-eye maple frame, 11 x 9" frame size .500
Gentleman, ink details on black cloth, 5.5 x 4.5" frame size 200
Couple, man and woman, ink details, sgd "Doyle, Cyrus and Polly Balkam," period brass oval frames, 6.5 x 5.5" frames, price for pair 300
Woman, ink hair and dress details, sgd "D. Hubbard," oval brass frame, 5.75 x 4.75" frame size 150

PAINTED ON GLASS

Colonial Couple, one with couple holding hands, other with gentleman pushing lady in swing, rect, curved glass, Benton Glass Co, 8" h, 6" w, price for pair .70
Colonial Couple, dancing minuet, in garden, cellist and flutist in background, tan ground, black-painted wood frame, "The Dance," Buckbee-Brehem Co, 1930s 25
Colonial Couple, one with gentleman helping lady as she descends on ladder from window, other with gentleman serenading lady beneath her window, angel hair and dried flowers behind, oval, 6.5" h, 4.5" w, price for pair 75
Colonial Ladies, one standing next to table and gazing in mirror, other seated next to table with lamp, round, curved glass, sgd "Ann Priest, Baltimore, Md," 5" d, price for pair . . .25

Autumn scene, painted on glass, cut-out trees, moonlit landscape of log cabin and stream, with thermometer and 1956 calendar, 8.125 x 4.125", $12.

Colonial Ladies, one walking her Scotty dog, other seated at table and writing a letter, round, curved glass, white metal frames, mkd "Hand Painted," 5" d, price for pair .... .25

Colonial Room Setting, mother seated on bench, daughter on floor teasing cat with string, drapes, fireplace, and table with potted plant in background, rect, curved glass, copper frame, 6" h, 8" w .... .35

Ducks, taking flight from pond, ducks and autumn woodland setting in background, rect, adv for "Dick's Café Manchester, Maryland," with thermometer, gold metal frame, 4" h, 5" w ...15

Early American Room Setting, two women sitting before hearth flanked by portraits, one woman in rocking chair knitting, other seated at spinning wheel, adv for "The Butcher Boy Food Market," with thermometer at right and 1941 slide-out calendar at bottom .... .40

Family, camping and fishing, trees in background, rect, adv for Sam Amendola, Massena, NY, gold metal frame .... .20

Southern Belles, one holding parasol and sniffing flower, other bending and picking flower, rect, curved glass, 5.125" h, 4.125" w, price for pair ..... .35

Dining Room Setting, painted on glass, family seated at table, yellow, brown, and black painted silhouette, window looks out on rolling hills, with 1956 calendar pad, Forever #6841, 8.125 x 6", $10.

SILVER PLATED

G. R. and H. Ekington of England are credited with inventing the electrolytic method of plating silver in 1838. In late nineteenth-century pieces, the base metal was often Britannia, an alloy of tin, copper, and antimony. Copper and brass also were used as bases. Today the base is usually nickel silver.

Rogers Bros., Hartford, Connecticut, introduced the silver-plating process to the United States in 1847. By 1855 a large number of silver-plating firms were established.

Extensive polishing will eventually remove silver plating. However, today's replating process is so well developed that you can have a piece replated in such a manner that the full detail of the original is preserved.

Identifying companies and company marks is difficult. Fortunately there is Dorothy Rainwater's *Encyclopedia of American Silver Manufacturers, 4th Edition* (Schiffer Publishing, 1998).

Bonbon, 2 flat handles, ftd base, engraved "Hotel Statler," Reed & Barton, 9" l, 4.5" w .... .20

Bread Basket, wire sides, 11 x 8", 3" h 5

Butter Spreaders, set of 8 in box .... .12

Coaster Set, glass coasters with SP rims, price for set of 4 .... .12

Coffee Server, Crown Sheffield, on ftd stand, 14" h, 9.5" w .... .60

Condiment Holder, US Navy, detachable center handle, eagle and "U.S.N." on one side, mkd "Reed & Barton, Silver Solder, #2901," 10" l, 3.75" w ...25

Dish, shell shape, mkd "Wallace 471" 8

Goblet, figural lady holding cup with scrolled handles balanced atop her head, gold-washing cup int, 7.125" h .. .40

Grapefruit Spoons, violet patterned handles, Wm Rogers & Son, price for set of 4 .... .18

Ice Tongs, claw ends, England, mkd "E.P.N.S." with 3 stars in clover leaf .. .18

Mirror, Art Nouveau, openwork irises and leaves design, hook for hanging, 12" h, 6.5" w .... .35

Match Safe, Art Nouveau design, 2.5" l, $55.

Pickle Castor, 4" h clear glass insert,
12" high SP frame 35
Tequila Shot Glasses and Tray, Alpaca
Plateada, six 1.5" h shot glasses,
6.5 x 5" tray 15
Water Pitcher and Tray, pitcher mono-
grammed "M" and mkd "Madison
Roger," rect tray mkd "Silver Plate
Epon Steel China" 20

SKATEBOARDS

Scooters were the predecessors to skateboards and that is where the similarity ends. When you are riding skateboards there isn't any handle or brakes. The first production skateboards were made of plywood around 15 inches long and 4 inches wide and had metal roller skate wheels. Road rash is the mother of invention so by the mid-60's clay wheels were tried out with great success. The boards started to break as well so the plywood turned to solid maple, oak, and ash.

Due to the hazards involved with skateboarding, the authorities, moms, and politicians silenced the revolution until the 1970s. Some renegade outlaw skaters still practiced their craft in back alleys and under the cover of darkness. When plastic or urethane wheels were introduced no governing body could stop this growing movement. Riding on them was so smooth and the control was unbelievable. Other great innovations at the time were better trucks (the bracket that the wheels are attached to). The boards became wider and longer and riding with pads and a helmet was required if you wanted to visit a skate park. A few companies were trying out fiberglass and platic skateboard decks. There are thousands of plastic skateboards from the 70's still around that are a dime a dozen. Fiberglass on the other hand is gold.

In the 80's the people who were pushing the limits on this now extreme sport were heroes to young skaters. And as such a pro would design his own board, put his name on it and sell a ton. Look for lots of dragons and swords for graphics as well. During this time no name manufacturers in the 80's also put out boards that sold for cheaper than ones that you would get at the specialty shops.

Skateboards can be broken up into five eras: 30's–50's-Fruitcrate Skate Scooter, 60's-Sidewalk Surfing, 70's-Punk & Skateboard Parks, 80's-Ramps & Street, and 90's-Grundge.

Advisor: Thomas J. VanderHorst, 9011 West End Dr, Kalamazoo, MI 49002, (616) 327-6248, e-mail: uncletom@net-link.net.

Ampul "The Surfer" Motorcross Down-
hill 400
Banzi Aluminum Double Kicktail 50
Duke Kahanomoku 180
Grassboard Tank Treds 100
Hang Ten 40
Hobie Sundancer/2 Wide Wheels 200
Kneeboard, 18" w 40
Maharajah 40
Makaha Blue Clay Wheels 80
Roller Derby Blue Mustang #15 30
Sears & Roebuck Skee-Skate 30
Solo Sundancer/2 Wide Wheels 180
Surfbird 30
Tony Hawk (the Tiger Woods of skate-
boarding) 100
Val Surf 40
Zipees Surfboard on Wheels 60

Sims Pure Juice, 36" l, $40.

SLEDS

Sleds divide into two basic groups: (1) clippers with pointed runners and (2) cutters with runners that curl upward in a bow-like fashion.

By the mid-1930s, Flexible Flyer, headquartered in Philadelphia, dominated the sled market. Its lines include The Airline Series, Flexy Racer, Ski Racer, and the Yankee Clipper. Other sled manufacturers included: American Toy and Novelty Works/American Acme (Emigsville, PA); Buffalo Sled Company/Auto Wheel Coaster (North Tonawanda, NY); Ellington Turing Co. (South Paris, ME); Garton Toy Company (Sheboygan, WI); Kalamazoo Sled Company (Kalamazoo, MI); and, Standard Novelty Works (Duncannon, PA).

Sledding lost its popularity in the late 1960s. Balzon-Flexible Flyer filed for Chapter 11 bankruptcy in 1975. The Roadmaster Corporation revived the company in 1993 and continues to manufacture sleds.

Fleetwing Racer, model 350, black lettering on red ground, wings on steering bar, safety runners, rounded bumper, c1940, 51.5" l 35

Fleetwing Spring Top Flash, model 41, red lettering and stripes on deck, red stripes on steering bar, rounded wood bumper, 1940, 41" l 65

Flexible Flyer, Admiral Byrd model 5G, trademark eagle, ribbon, and sled and scrolling vines on deck, pinstriped steering bar, metal bumper, 1928, 63" l 150

Flexible Flyer, safety runners, chrome bumper, 45" l, $20.

Flexible Flyer, Airline Ace 37H, trademark eagle, ribbon, and sled with arrow on deck, wings on steering bar, safety runners, chrome bumper, 1955, 37" l . .40

Flexible Flyer, Airline Racer 60, trademark eagle, ribbon, and sled and "Airline Racer" pierced by arrow on deck, wings on steering bar, safety runners, metal bumper, 1936, 60" l 75

Flexible Flyer, model 2C, steel frame, trademark eagle, shield, and ribbon and scrollwork on deck, pinstriped steering bar, metal bumper, 1914, 42" l 125

Flexible Flyer, model 3E, steel frame, trademark eagle, ribbon, and sled flanked by diamonds and pinstripes on deck, metal bumper, 1921, 45" l . . .100

Flexoplane, "Flexoplane," stripes, and arrowheads on deck, pinstriped steering bar, rounded bumper, c1920s 60

King of the Hill, lettering and scrollwork on deck, no bumper, c1935, 32" l 50

Lightning Guider, model 125, lettering and lightning bolts on deck, metal bumper, 1950s, 56" l 50

SLOT CARS

Aurora, the premier name in slot car racing, marketed its first electric slot car play set in the fall of 1960. Since then, slot cars have successfully competed with electric trains for their share of the model hobbyist's dollars.

Clubs: National Slot Car Racing Club, 1903 Middlefield Rd. #3, Redwood City, CA 94063; United Federation of H.O. Racers Assoc., 6800 W. Kilgore Ave., Yorktown, IN 47396.

Newsletter: *Lots of Slots,* 503 Boal St., Cincinnati, OH 45210; *Slot Car Trader,* 127 Island Dr., Elyria, OH 44035.

AFX, BMW M1, #11, white, red, and blue 35

AFX, Dodge Magnum, #14, red, white, orange, and yellow 30

AFX, Express Trailer, gray 10

AFX, Fall Guy Pick-Up, brown and tan . . .55

Aurora, '63 Corvette, yellow, split window 40

Aurora, '67 Thunderbird Hardtop, turquoise 75

Aurora, Dino Ferrari 1381, blue and white, 1967-72, $35.

Aurora, Ford GT, Wild One, #5, white and
  orange .... .25
Aurora, Ford J Car, blue and white .... .35
Aurora, Ford J Car, turquoise .... .50
Aurora, Indy Racer, #2, yellow .... .70
Aurora, Mangusta Mongoose, yellow .. .35
Aurora, McLaren Elva Flamethrower,
  black and white .... .35
Aurora, Thunderjet Chaparral 2-F, #1,
  black and white .... .20
Aurora, Thunderjet Chaparral
  Flamethrower, #1, black and white .. .20
Aurora, Tow Truck, white .... .50
Aurora XKE Jaguar, black .... .70
Aurora XKE Jaguar, turquoise .... .30
Aurora XKE Jaguar, white .... .35
Aurora, XLerator Chaparral 2-F, lime,
  black, and silver .... .25
Aurora, XLerator Ford J, #3, orange,
  black, and silver .... .20
Bachman, Chaparral 2-F, red .... .75
Bachman, Dodge Charger, white, #70 .. .225
Cox, Ford GT, blue .... .100
Eldon, '64 Corvette, turquoise .... .35
Eldon, '68 Corvette, lime green .... .40
Ideal, Nova Glow Lighted, #41, blue,
  white, and red .... .10
Marx, '64 T-Bird, #2, gray and white .... .65
Marx, '64 T-Bird, #2, red and white ..... .45
Strombecker, Ford Stock Car, blue,
  copper accents, 1/32 scale .... .30
Strombecker, Pontiac, red, black and
  white roof, 1/32 scale .... .45
Tyco, Ferrari F1, #12, red, white, and
  silver .... .15
Tyco, Funny Mustang, orange and yel-
  low flames .... .30
Tyco, Lamborghini Countach, red ..... .12
Tyco, Wrangler Stock Car, #2, blue and
  yellow .... .190

SMOKEY BEAR

It is hard to believe that Smokey Bear
has been around for more than fifty years.
The popularity of Smokey started during the
Second World War, as part of a national
awareness campaign for the prevention of
forest fires. The National Forest Service ran
slogans like "Keep 'Em Green; Forests Are
Vital to National Defense" in an attempt to
keep the public's attention on the war
effort.

From then to now Smokey has been
more than just a crusader for fire awareness and prevention; he has been a collectible character and a source of enjoyment to many admirers. There was a wide
variety of Smokey collectibles produced:
watches, radios, toys, posters, and many
games and books. Most had short production runs and were used as Forest Service
giveaways or were sold by a select number
of department store chains.

Good luck in your collecting and
remember only you can prevent forest fires.

Bank, figural Smokey holding removable
  shovel, brown plastic, yellow hat, blue
  pants, silver belt buckle, orig box,
  c1960, 7.75" h .... .125
Coloring Book, Whitman, 1960s, 8 x
  10.5" .... .12
Game, Smokey Bear Game, Milton
  Bradley, 1973 .... .30
Lunch Box, Thermos, vinyl, 1960s ..... .100
Nodder .... .50

*Soaky Bottle,
Lander, c1970,
10.75" h, $25.*

Salt and Pepper Shakers, ceramic,
figural .... .100
Wristwatch, metal case, full figure
Smokey Bear and "Smokey" on dial,
watch hands are shovels, Bradley,
1970s, 1.25" d dial .... .60

SNACK SETS

The earliest snack sets (originally called tea and toast sets) were porcelain and earthenware examples manufactured overseas. Glass sets produced in the United States were a popular hostess accessory during the boom years following World War II. American dinnerware manufacturers of the time, such as Purinton and Stangl, also produced sets to match their most popular dinnerware patterns.

Newsletter: *Snack Set Searchers' Newsletter,* P.O. Box 908, Hallock, MN 56738.

Note: The following prices are for eight piece sets unless noted otherwise.

CERAMIC

Pennsbury, Red Rooster .... .25
Steubenville, Woodfield, gray .... .45
Made In Japan, Cherry China, violet
chintz, 2 pc .... .25
Made In Japan, Empress China, leaf
chintz, 2 pc .... .20
Made In Japan, Hakusan China, pine
cones, 2 pc .... .10
Made In Japan, Lefton, Brown Heritage
Floral, 2 pc .... .35
Made In Japan, Noritake, Azalea, 2 pc . .45
Royal Albert, Old Country Rose, 2 pc ... .25
Royal Albert, Petit Point, 2 pc .... .40
Royal Winton, Pink Petunia, 2 pc ...... .45

GLASS

Anchor Hocking, Mosaic .... .70
Anchor Hocking, Classic, milk glass ... .25
Anchor Hocking, Colonial Lady, with
crystal cups .... .20
Anchor Hocking, Early American
Prescut, MIB .... .50
Anchor Hocking, Fan, with red cups ... .30
Anchor Hocking, Fleurette .... .25

Federal, Blossom, $18.

Federal, Gold Halo .... .20
Federal, Patio Set .... .20
Federal, Yorktown, iridescent .... .20
Hazel Atlas, Beads & Ribs .... .25
Hazel Atlas, Fancy Apple .... .20
Hazel Atlas, Seashell Moroccan,
amethyst .... .50
Indiana, Button & Daisy, crystal .... .20
Indiana, Harvest, lime green .... .60
Indiana, Harvest, milk glass .... .35
Jeannette, Dewdrops .... .20

PLASTIC

Arrowhead Plastic, 12 pc .... .12
Gothamware .... .12
Lennoxware .... .25
Monopoly .... .30
Monsanto Thermal .... .15

SNOWBOARDS

Snowboards, small surfboards for snow, have been around since a Viking broke one of his skis and had to make it back to his village on just the remaining one. There is also a story that says ancient Hawaiians took their surf and paddleboards up to the tallest volcanos and mountains on the island and surfed down in a sideways stance.

Fast forward to the 1960s when millions of people were being entertained with either surfing, if you lived on a coast, or sidewalk surfing for us land-locked individuals. It was just a matter of time until somebody took the wheels off a skateboard and tried it in the snow.

Christmas 1965 Sherm Poppen did it with a pair of children's snow skis fastened together, then with a waterski. He turned that idea into the Snurfer which was the predecessor to the modern day snowboard. Jake Burton Carpenter was innovating in Vermont. His snowboard company is the biggest in the industry today. Tom Sims was doing well with skateboards and was the first to ride down on a snowy hill in 1963. Other people on the cutting edge were Cris and Beverly Sanders, Chuck Barfoot, Jack Smith, Demitre Milovitch, and Mervin Manufacturing.

People look for boards they had when they first started riding. The demand for old wooden snowboards has risen dramatically in the last few years. Some ways to date snowboards include:

1. Wood. The first boards were all wood. Later plastic was adhered to the bottom to make them go faster.

2. Foot Traction—Staples or Straps. The earliest boards had staples or plastic pegs to keep your feet from slipping off. Then came bungee cords and straps that resembled water ski bindings. Finally, hard plastic bindings with ratchet straps were invented for a more stable ride.

3. Skegs and Metal Edges. Riding on soft fluffy snow requires no means of control. That is what the first Snurfer style boards were like. Once the sledding hill became icy we needed a way to keep from sliding out. One skeg was placed at the back in the middle, then two, then three until they had edges from tip to tail like snow skis have had for 50 years.

4. Shape. Long skateboards with a rope. Long, wide skateboards with a rope and a V-tail.

Advisor: Thomas J. VanderHorst, 9011 West End Dr, Kalamazoo, MI 49002, (616) 6248. email: uncletom@net-link.net.

Arrow Ski Board, Creative Playthings,
　Princeton, NJ 80
A-Team, Jeff Smith Model 300
Avalanche Freestyle & Slalom 300
Barfoot, FE 400
Barfoot, WE 250
Burton, Backyard 400
Flite, 140cm, 150cm, 180cm 300

Snurfer, Jem, yellow with black pad, $100.

Flying Banana 150
Jem, Red Decca 60
Jem, SRM, white pads 20
Jem, yellow, 3 stripe 20
Lib Tech Doughboy Shredder, 79" l 100
Marina Black 60
Sims, FGE 300
Sims, WGE 200
Skiboard 150
Skifer, brown, with foot pads 50
Skifer, red and yellow 20
Snow Skimmer, Bec-Mar, black, brown,
　or red 40
Snowtech Pulsar Comp SL 150 250
Snurfer, Brunswick, yellow, 1 stripe 30
Snurfer, Brunswick, yellow, 5 stripe 20
Snurfer, Made in Canada-Staples 100
Snurfer, Red Decca 30
Snurfer, SRM, white pegs 20
Snurfer, SRM, wood pegs 50
Star Surfing Co 60
Ultimate Air Snowboard 200

SNOW GLOBES

The majority of plastic and glass snow globes found at flea markets are imported from the Orient. A few are produced in France, Germany, and Italy. There are no American manufacturers, but rather dozens of large gift companies who design and import an array of styles, shapes, and themes. Enesco Corporation of Elk Grove Village, Illinois, is one of the largest.

Club: Snowdome Collectors Club, P.O. Box 53262, Washington, DC 20009.

Boy and Dog, glass globe, black ceramic base, painted ceramic figure of boy wearing red snowsuit and brown dog by his side, Atlas Crystal Works, 1940s, 3.75" h 15

Deer, clear dome, white base, deer
   standing in front of red house with
   snow-covered roof, pine tree behind,
   needs water, 4" h 8
Dreamsicles, clear globe, snowy mound
   base with trees, birds, Dreamsicle
   cherub, and north pole, boy and girl
   ice skaters and pine tree inside, musical, skaters spin as "Winter Wonder-
   land" plays 30
Empire State Building, clear glass globe,
   black ceramic base, white building,
   gold decal "Empire State Building,
   New York" 12
McDonald's, clear globe, wood music
   box base, Ronald McDonald and 5
   friends holding hands around
   Christmas tree with McDonald's
   arch topper, plays "Jingle Bells,"
   5.75" h 25
Pez, clear dome, base has purple,
   orange, and yellow stripes above
   "PEZ" on yellow, ringmaster and
   elephant Pez dispensers in front of
   blue archway with "PEZ," 4" h, 3" d . . .15
Polar Bear, clear glass globe, black
   ceramic base, white bear standing
   upright, 4" h, 3" d 25
Rockefeller Center, glass globe, black
   ceramic base, white building, light
   brown snow, gold decal label
   "Rockefeller Center–Radio City,
   New York," 1945, 3.75" h, 3" d 75
Santa, clear dome, white base, Santa
   emerging from chimney, holding
   small tree, blue background, needs
   water, 2" h 30

*Puerto Rico, clear plastic dome, blue
plastic base, 2 frogs on seesaw, palm tree
and rainbow in background, $8.*

*Santa, plastic, 2-pc,
2 molded panels
and white snow in
globe, late 1980s,
4.875" h, $25.*

Santa, figural Christmas tree with clear
   globe set in center, waving Santa
   standing next to bag loaded with toys
   in globe, 1950s, 5.75" h 15
Snoopy, clear plastic globe, red plastic
   base, wearing red and white striped
   stocking cap, pulling sled laden with
   toys, needs water, 3.5" h 10
Tweety Bird, clear globe, ice cream
   dish-shaped base, wearing blue ear-
   muffs, holding large spoon, sitting on
   and eating from large mound of ice
   cream, 5" h 30

SOAKIES

In the early 1960's two companies,
Colgate-Palmolive and Purex, began inten-
sive marketing of children's bubble bath in
bottles shaped like cartoon characters.
Purex called their product "Bubble Club"
and Colgate-Palmolive called theirs
"Soaky." The Purex bubble club bottles
were fashioned almost exclusively after
Hanna-Barbera characters, while the
soakies featured Disney, Warner Bros.,
Terrytoons, Harvey and other characters.

Since then, many other companies
have packaged children's soap products in
containers that have a figural shape. The
name Soaky has evolved into a generic
term for any of these types of containers
whether they are bubble bath or shampoo
and whether they contain liquid or powder.
It is the consensus of most collectors that
what makes a container a "Soaky" is that it
is shaped like a character or object and that
its function was to contain a soap product.

Collecting Soakies is great fun since they are colorful, relatively inexpensive, and span a time period from the boomer years of the 1950s and 1960s to the present. It is a collection that is open ended, as new bubble bath containers are brought to the market every year.

Advisor: Joseph Pizzo, 1675 Orange St., Beaumont, TX 77701-5315.

Bamm-Bamm, Flintstones, Purex, 1960s .10
Batman, Colgate-Palmolive, 1966 40
Bert, Sesame Street, Minnetonka, 1995 . .3
Broom Hilda, Lander Co, 1977 45
Buzz Lightyear, Toy Story, Johnson &
   Johnson, 1999 3
Care Bear, AGC, 1984 5
Darth Vader, Star Wars, Omni, 1981 10
Dick Tracy, Colgate-Palmolive, 1965 25
Elmer Fudd, Colgate-Palmolive 10
Ernie, Sesame Street, Minnetonka, 1995 . .3
G.I. Joe, 5 variations, DuCair Bioescence,
   1980s 8
Pebbles, Flintstones, Purex, 1960s 10
Popeye, Colgate-Palmolive, 1965 20
Marvin the Martian, Warner Bros.
   Stores, 1996 12
Mighty Mouse, 1-pc, Colgate-Palmolive,
   1960s 5
Mighty Mouse, head screws off,
   Colgate-Palmolive, 1960s 12
Mouseketeer Girl, red and blue varia-
   tions, Colgate-Palmolive, 1960s 15
My Little Pony, Benjamin Ansehl, 1990 . .10

Left: Pinocchio, Colgate-Palmolive, 1960s, $10. Right: Incredible Hulk, Benjamin Ansehl Co, 1990, $15.

Pluto, Avon, 1970 7
R2D2, Star Wars, Omni, 1981 10
Ringo Starr, Colgate-Palmolive, 1965 90
Squiddly Diddly, Purex, 1965 30
Teenage Mutant Ninja Turtles, 4 differ-
   ent characters, Kid Care, 1991 3
Woody, Toy Story, Johnson & Johnson,
   1999 3

SOAP COLLECTIBLES

At first you would not think that a lot of soap collectibles would survive. However, once you start to look around you'll see no end to the survivors. Many Americans are not as clean as we think.

There is no hotel soap listed. Most survivors sell for 50¢ to $2 per bar. Think of all the hotels and motels that you have stayed at that have gone out of business. Don't you wish you would have saved one of the soap packets?

Advertising Tear Sheet, Fairy Soap, little
   girl in basket, "Have you a Little Fairy
   in your home?/To be healthy, children
   must be clean/To be clean, the use
   of perfectly pure soap is essential,"
   1913 3
Advertising Tear Sheet, Goblin Soap, 4
   children washing hands, box of Goblin
   soap in corner, 1919 5
Advertising Tear Sheet, Ivory Soap,
   Egyptian girl with "A Beauty Secret
   3000 Years Old," from Feb issue of
   The American magazine, 1922 3
Advertising Trade Card, for French
   laundry soap, Kendall Mfg Co,
   Providence, RI, diecut, figural frog on
   rock in pond, 3.75 x 3" 2
Box, Ivory Soap, wood, hinged top, metal
   straps on sides, 8.75 x 5.75" 25
Milk Cap Extractor, celluloid covered
   metal disk, green lettering "West
   End Laundry Co" on white, "Using
   Ivory Soap," 1920-30s 15
Pin, Bee Soap, diecut brass, figural bee,
   early 1900s 15
Pinback Button, Bee Soap, multicolored,
   bee with product name and gauze-
   like wings, blue inscription "Save the
   Big Black Bees" 15

Book, Elizabeth Harding, Bride, *Ivory Soap* premium, 1900s, 5.5 x 7.5", $60.

Pinback Button, Wool Soap, multicolored, children comparing length of nightshirts, "My Mamma Used Wool Soap!/I Wish Mine Had" 10

Pocket Mirror, Lava Soap, celluloid, center image of gray soap bar in opened container box, early 1900s . . .20

Sign, Fairbank's Soaps, metal, "the cheapest & best in the whole world," 11 x 16.5" 8

Sign, Ivorine Soap, metal, 11 x 14" 10

Sign, Triple A Soap, metal, little boy cowboy getting into bathtub wearing only cowboy hat and holster, "…at the end of a dusty trail, it's the soap of choice for even the toughest cowboy" 25

SOCIAL CAUSE COLLECTIBLES

Social cause collectibles are just now coming into their own as a collecting category. Perhaps this is because the social activists of the 1960s have mortgages, children, and money in their pockets to buy back the representations of their youths. In doing so, they are looking back past their own protest movements to all forms of social protest that took place in the twentieth century.

Great collections can be built around a single cause, e.g., women's suffrage or the right to vote. Much of the surviving material tends to be two-dimensional. Stress three-dimensional items the moment you begin to collect. As years pass, these are the objects most likely to rise in value.

Club: American Political Items Collectors, Labor History Chapter, P.O. Box 407, Dallas, NC 28034.

Booklet, The Chicago Conspiracy Trial, The Chicago Conspiracy vs The Washington Kangaroos 20

Matchbook Cover, "He Needs Your Help!," bluetone photo of prisoner of war, red text on white ground, issued by VIVA, text on inside explaining mission, unused, 1970s 15

Medal, "Protest Against the Wilson Tariff Bill," brass, front depicts arms with rolled up sleeve and ribbon in hand mkd "Labor," reverse text "National Working Men's Protective Tariff League Washington 1894 April 20-21," 1" d 15

Pinback Button, "Angela Is Free/Free All Political Prisoners T. U. A. D.," black on orange, 1.75" d 20

Pinback Button, "Black Panther Party," black silhouette against black and white striped pattern, "Death to the Fascist Pigs," c1968 15

Pinback Button, "In Union There Is Strength," multicolored, clasped hands above eagle with pink ribbon in beak, perched on red, white, and blue shield with gold outline, light yellow and blue ground, c1920 15

Pinback Button, "United Labor May-Day," white on red, "1886-1936 50th Anniversary" 15

Pinback Button, "Vote Socialist 60 After 60," blue on white, red numerals, late 1930s 15

Pocket Mirror, "Buy American/Hammered Rings/Insure the Job," celluloid, red, white, and blue, 1930s 15

Postcard, real photo, women standing beside "The Girls Friendly Society" truck, c1910 .100

Poster, National Peace Action Coalition, "Demonstrate against the war Nov. 6," 23 x 32", $65.

Postcard, "Stand Up For Your Rights," independent woman declining seat in trolley car, red, white, and blue, 1908 15

Ribbon, fabric, "May 1st/Unite-Fight Fascism Hunger War!/United Front May Day Committee," late 1930s, 1.75 x 3.25" 20

Sticker, "Votes For Women," yellow on black 25

SODA FOUNTAIN & ICE CREAM COLLECTIBLES

The local soda fountain and/or ice cream parlor was the social center of small town America between the late 1880s and the 1960s. Ice cream items appeared as early as the 1870s.

This is a category filled with nostalgia—banana splits and dates with friends. Some concentrate on the advertising, some on the implements. It is all terrific.

Clubs: National Assoc of Soda Jerks, P.O. Box 115, Omaha, NE 68101; The Ice Screamer, P.O. Box 465, Warrington, PA 18976.

Badge, "Ass'n of Ice Cream Mfrs of Penna & New Jersey," celluloid, center clear display opening for insertion of name paper in back slots, 1930-40s, 2.5" d 20

Hot Fudge Machine, Nestles, metal, Helmco Lacy, Chicago, IL, with ladle, orig guarantee and instructions, 12" h, 9.75" d 130

Ice Cream Cone Holder, glass jar with metal lid and holder, 14.25" h 465

Key Chain Tag, Velvet Ice Cream, white celluloid, red lettering, 1920s 15

Malted Milk Dispenser, Hamilton Beach, metal and acrylic top, porcelain base, 18.5" h, 7.5" d 325

Milk Shake Mixer, Multimixer, Model 9-B, stainless steel, Sterling Multi-Products, Sterling, IL, 18" h, 13" w, 11.5" d 285

Pinback Button, "Ice Cream King of Food," litho tin, "National Ice Cream Week," copyright for *Ice Cream Review* magazine on rim curl, 1930s ..15

Pocket Mirror, Reid's Champagne Ice Cream, black and gold lettering on white, gold rim accent 20

Scoop, Gilcrest, #31 60

Serving Tray, litho tin, "Drink Orange Julep" acrosss top and bottom, woman on beach holding parasol and glass, mkd "American Art Works Inc, Coshocton Ohio," 13.25" h, 10.25" w 165

Sign, "Bezile," ice cream cone with logo on both sides, ©Dairy Products Advertising, Weston Ontario," 28" h, 22" w .110

Sign, "Chapman's Ice Cream," porcelain, arrow with double heart and "Perfectly Delicious," 1940s, 30 x 40" 175

Sign, "Cherry Ice Cream Bon Bons," paper, 14 x 18" 4

Sign, "Enjoy Some Now–it's Anamosa's Ice Cream," cardboard, 1940-50s, 16 x 29" 100

Sign, "Mom Always Buys Monticello Ice Cream," cardboard, 1950s, 23 x 36" ..175

Sign, "On Ice/Long Green Ko-Nut Red Rock In Bottles 5¢," tin, emb, Red Rock Co, 27.5" h, 19.25" w 100

Spinner Top, red inscription under celluloid "The Velvet Kind-Cream of Ice Cream" on ivory white ground 15

Straw Container, glass, metal lid and bottom, 12.5" h, 3.2" d 185

Straw Container, pressed glass, square shaped, with paper straws, 9.5" h ...110

Tin, Sweetheart Sugar Cones, S & S Cone Corp, 15.5" h, 12.5" d 250

Hanging Rack, "Ice Cream, 10¢," brass and copper, glass insert behind cut-out letters, twisted wire hooks and hanger, 18" h, 18" d, $700. —Photo courtesy James D. Julia, Inc.

SOFT DRINK COLLECTIBLES

National brands such as Coca-Cola, Canada Dry, Dr Pepper, and Pepsi-Cola dominate the field. However, there were thousands of regional and local soda bottling plants. Their advertising, bottles, and giveaways are every bit as exciting as those of the national companies. Do not ignore them.

Clubs: The Cola Club, P.O. Box 392, York, PA 17405; Crown Collectors Society International, 4300 San Juan Dr., Fairfax, VA 22030; Dr Pepper 10-2-4 Collector's Club, 3100 Monticello, Suite 890, Dallas, TX 75205; Grapette Collectors Club, 2240 Hwy. 27N, Nashville, AR 71852; National Pop Can Collectors, 19201 Sherwood Green Way, Gaithersburg, MD 20879; ; New England Moxie Congress, 445 Wyoming Ave., Millburn, NJ 07041; Painted Soda Bottle Collectors Assoc., 9418 Hilmer Dr., La Mesa, CA 91942.

Newsletters: *Painted-Label Soda Bottles,* 1055 Ridgecrest Dr., Goodlettsville, TN 37072; *Root Beer Float,* P.O. Box 571, Lake Geneva, WI 53147.

Periodical: *Club Soda,* P.O. Box 489, Troy, ID 83871.

Note: For additional listings see Coca-Cola and Pepsi-Cola.

Door Push, 7-Up, aluminum, "Come in, 7-Up likes you," 1940s, 9" h 165
Door Push, Orange Crush, porcelain, "Come Again/Drink Orange Crush/ Thank You," 1930-40s, 3.5 x 9" 375
Clock, Dr Pepper, light-up, metal body, glass face and cover, 15.5" sq 132
Clock, Royal Crown Cola, light-up, cardboard body, glass face and cover, "Drink Royal Crown Cola/Best By Taste-Test," 15" d 300
Clock, Sun Crest, light-up, glass face, metal case, Telechron Inc, 15.25" d . .325
Figure, Wink, vinyl, inflatable, yellow and green, red domed nose, applied soft yellow artificial hair, Alvimar, ©1965 Stoessel Graphics Inc, 30" h . .20
Flange Sign, "7-Up Likes You," 1946, 10 x 12" 110

Hanging Flower Basket, 7-Up, cardboard, multicolored 4-sided 3-dimensional diecut, 7-Up logo each side, 1940s, 20" h, 14" w .325
Kick Plate, 7-Up, heavily emb, hand holding bottle of soda with "Your 'Fresh Up' 7-Up," 1947, 11" h, 31" w . .350
Menu Board, 7-Up, framed glass, "Real 7-Up sold here," 1930-40s, 17" h, 10" w 130
Menu Board, Squirt, "Enjoy...Squirt never an after-thirst!," 20 x 28" 275
Menu Board, Orange-Crush, cardboard, 1941, 17 x 27" 200
Menu Sign, Cherry Smash, 2 pc, tin over cardboard, "Drink Cherry Smash/A True Fruit Blend," 1940-50s, 9 x 18" . .500
Menu Sign, Cherry Up, tin, bottle pouring into glass, "A Delightful Drink/A Real Super-Charged Beverage, 1940-50s, 9 x 18" 450
Mug, Moxie, clear glass, emb lettering, 5" h 20
Puzzle, Hood's Sarsaparilla, cardboard, double horse-drawn buggy carrying doctor away from laboratory and factory buildings, 15 x 10" 100
Sidewalk Sign, 7-Up, vertical, "Fresh Up! with 7-Up," 1953, 28" h, 20" w . . .120
Sign, 7-Up, diecut bottle, "7-Up , You Like It, It Likes You" on label, 1962, 45" h, 13" w .100
Sign, Ma's Root Beer, emb tin, 6-pack at left, "Thank You Call Again/The Kind That Mother Used To Make," 1930-40s 150

Serving Tray, Cherry Sparkle, Graf's Soft Drinks, Northwestern Extract Co, Milwaukee, WI, yellow lettering, red soda, green ground, 10.5 x 13.25", $150.

Sign, Nichol Kola, tin, 12 x 29", $75. —Photo courtesy Gene Harris Antique Auction Center, Inc.

Sign, NuGrape, emb tin, hand holding
bottle, "Drink NuGrape/Demand It In
This Bottle," 1930s, 5 x 14" 385
Sign, Nu Icy, emb tin, bottle, "Drink Nu
Icy/Assorted Flavors You Can't Forget,"
1930s, 9 x 20" 525
Sign, Orange Crush, emb tin, bottle at
left, "Drink Orange Crush," 1930s,
9 x 20" 350
Sign, Squirt, emb tin, "Enjoy Squirt Never
An After Thirst," 1959 100
Sign, Whistle, emb tin, hand holding
bottle,"Thirsty? just Demand the
Genuine Whistle," 1930s, 10 x 28" . . .475
Thermometer, Dr Pepper, tin, "Dr Pepper
Hot or Cold," 26.5" h, 7.25" w 110
Thermometer, Frostie Root Beer, tin,
"Drink Frostie Root Beer/A Real Taste
Treat," 1940s, 8.5 x 36" 475

SOUVENIR BUILDINGS

Souvenir buildings are three-dimensional replicas of famous buildings and monuments. They were originally made as souvenirs for travelers or to commemorate a particular building, occasion, or person. Many are still being made today for the same reasons. Since nearly every location has at least one building or monument that symbolizes that place, the numbers of existing souvenir buildings worldwide runs into the thousands.

Collectors prefer metal buildings, especially pot metal with a high lead content, which produces replicas with fine detail. First made in 1876 to commemorate the hundredth anniversary of the U.S. Revolution, souvenir buildings became especially popular in the early 20th century, again after World War II and now as an item for collectors. Buildings include churches, cathedrals, skyscrapers, mosques, castles, banks, bridges, and office buildings. They are often the only three-dimensional representation of an architectural structure other than the structure itself.

Age is not as important as rarity, condition, detail, and architectural interest. Most souvenir buildings measure between 1" and 7" high.

Advisor: Dixie Trainer, P.O. Box 70, Nellysford, VA 22958-0700, (804) 361-1739, e-mail: souvenirbu@aol.com, web: SBCollectors.org; free copy of club newsletter *Souvenir Building Collector* available upon request.

Club: Souvenir Building Collectors Society, 63 Claremont Ave., Orinda, CA 94563.

Note: Prices listed are for metal buildings unless noted otherwise.

Agriculture Bank of China, Dalian
Branch, copper finish, 7.75" h 360
Boston Cityscape, made in Japan,
antique brass finish, 2.25" h 250
Combined Insurance Company of
America, coin bank, mfg by A.C.
Rehberger, brass finish 350
Corn Exchange Bank, Chicago 460
Easton National Bank & Trust Co,
Banthrico, pewter finish 50
Federal Building, Chicago World's Fair,
table lamp 310
Fort Snelling 10
Hoosac Tunnel, Banthrico coin bank
made for Adams Co-op Bank, Adams,
MA, pewter finish 38

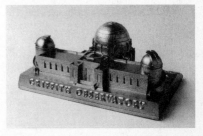

Griffith Observatory, Los Angeles, CA, $125.

Castle Sirmione, Italy, $350.

Leaning Tower of Bologna, Italian vil-
lage, Cleveland Exposition, 1936 125
Liberty Corporation, Greenville, SC,
paperweight made for 1982 opening
ceremonies, pewter, 3" d 50
Lincoln Memorial, Washington, DC, mfg
by Bates & Klinke, pewter 25
Lincoln Memorial, Washington, DC, mfg
by Bates & Klinke, 24K gold finish 35
Mackinac Island Bridge, MI, made in
Japan, silver finish 50
Notre Dame, Paris, large 40
Notre Dame, Paris, small 8
Nuremberg Castle, Nuremberg, Germany,
jewelry box, silver finish, pink silk
lining 55
Parliament Building, Budapest, Hungary .100
Prudential Building, Chicago, bank,
missing trap and antenna, silver
finish, 6.25" h 125
Reading Pagoda, Reading, PA, hp alu-
minum 25
Safeco Field, Seattle, WA, inaugural
game souvenir 95
Santa Rosa Savings and Loan, coin
bank, Banthrico, copper finish 75
Speyer Dom (Cathedral), Speyer,
Germany, copper on pot metal 60
Superga Cathedral, Italy, ashtray, silver
finish 70
Tower of David, Wailing Wall, Jerusalem,
silver finish 85
Victory Column, Rajasthan, India 85
Vladimir's Golden Gate, Russia, solid
brass, green marble base 125
Will Rogers' Shrine of the Sun, Colorado
Springs, CO, salt or pepper shaker,
silver 12
Yomei Gate, Toshogu, Japan, cigarette
box, painted white metal 85

SOUVENIRS

This category demonstrates that, given
time, even the tacky can become collectible. Many tourist souvenirs offer a
challenge to one's aesthetics. But they are
bought anyway.

Tourist china plates and glass novelties
from the 1900 to 1940 period are one of the
true remaining bargains left. Most of the
items sell for under $25. If you really want to
have some fun, pick one form and see how
many different places you can find from
which it was sold.

Club: Statue of Liberty Collectors' Club,
26601 Bernwood Rd., Cleveland, OH 44122.

Bank, Portsmouth Trust Co, tin canister
with celluloid top and bottom, bank
image, Parisianne Novelty Co, Chicago,
1919 patent date, 2.5" d 25
Bank, Howard Johnson's, restaurant
replica, white plastic, orange roof,
1950s, 5" w 20
Guide Book, Freedomland, New York
City, "World's Largest Entertainment
Center," describes 40+ attractions on
205+ acres, 20 pp, ©1960, 8 x 11.5" ...60
Handkerchief, 12th Olympiad, Helsinki,
Finland, 1940, cancelled due to WWII,
mostly blue printing on white fabric,
Olympic torch, rings, tower, and flags
of Finland, 9.5 x 10.5 85
Paperweight, Brooklyn Bridge, clear
glass over tinted color photo of
bridge, early 1900s, 2.25 x 4 x 1" 30

*Creamer, "Souvenir of Greensburg, Pa.,"
ruby-stained glass, 4.25" h, $40.*

Handkerchief, embroidered "Souvenir of France, 1919," $12.

Pendant, 1898 Agriculture Fair, Richfield, NY, celluloid, 3 horse heads surrounded by "Annual Fair Agricultural Society, Richfield, N.Y., Sept. 26-28, 1898," harvest fruits on back, red, white, and blue hanger ribbon, 2.25" d 25

Pinback Button, 4th Annual Water Carnival hosted in Orr, MN, 1941, celluloid, hydroplane image, red, white, and blue, .875" d 10

Plate, Salt Lake City, UT, litho tin, Mormon Temple Block in center surrounded by other scenic views, ©1911 by Souvenir Novelty Co, Salt Lake City, 10" d 60

Salt and Pepper Shakers, pr, Trader Vic's, ceramic, figural Polynesian idols, made in Japan, 1970s 12

Tumbler, 1939 visit to Canada by Queen Elizabeth I and George VI, blue and red portraits and text on clear glass, stylized flower cut in base, 3.75" h ...15

View Book, Buffalo Bill's Memorial Museum, Lookout Mountain, CO, 18 full color views, 1920s, 4.25 x 6" closed size 35

SOUVENIR SPOONS

Collecting commemorative spoons was extremely popular from the last decade of the 19th century through 1940. Actually, it has never gone completely out of fashion. You can still buy commemorative spoons at many historical and city tourist sites. The first thing to check for is metal content. Sterling silver has always been the most popular medium. Fine enamel work adds to value.

Clubs: American Spoon Collectors, 7408 Englewood Ln., Raytown, MO 54133; The Scoop Club, 84 Oak Ave., Shelton, CT 06484.

1893 World's Columbian Exposition, Columbus bust on handle, ship in bowl, Isabella on handle reverse, sterling, demitasse 25

1894 California Mid-Winter International Exposition, bar at top of twisted handle, "Midwinter Exposition, San Francisco, 1894" in bowl, silverplate, demitasse, 4.5" l 25

1895 Cotton States and International Exposition, Manufacturers and Liberal Arts Building in bowl, silverplate, demitasse 25

1898 Grand Army of the Republic, bridge and logo on handle, monument in bowl, "32nd National Engagement 1898" silverplate, demitasse 25

1901 Trans-Mississippi Exposition, Mines and Mining Building in bowl, Crown Silverplate Co, demitasse 11

1904 Louisiana Purchase Exposition, Jefferson bust on handle, Palace of Electricity in bowl, Cascades & Monument on handle reverse, silverplate, demitasse 10

1904 Louisiana Purchase Exposition, Machinery Hall in bowl, "World's Fair St. Louis 1904" below, Imperial, silverplate 20

1907 Jamestown Ter-Centennial Exposition, pier, boats, etc in bowl, Extra Coin Silverplate, demitasse 12

1915 Panama-Pacific International Exposition, shovel design handle, inscription regarding President Taft turning first spadeful of dirt to start building fair, sterling, sugar spoon ...65

1933 Century of Progress International Exposition, logo on handle, Science Building in bowl, Winthrop, silverplate, teaspoon 5

"Allentown Crockery Co., 37 South 7th St., Allentown, PA," factory image in bowl, silver plated, $20. —Photo courtesy Gene Harris Antique Auction Center, Inc.

"Charles W. Cramsjaw, Atlantic," black man on handle, watermelon in bowl, enameled sterling silver, $412. —Photo courtesy Collectors Auction Services.

1939 New York World's Fair, Trylon, Perisphere, and flags on handle, Fair name in bowl, silverplate, demitasse, 4.5" l 40
1964 New York World's Fair, from Vatican Pavilion, shepherd at top of handle, building interior and Fair name in bowl, "Th. Marthinsen Sterling Norway" on handle reverse, demitasse, 4" l 15
Big Timber, MT, flower on handle, city name in bowl, toned, sterling, 3.5" l 3
Brooklyn Bridge, bridge on handle, church in bowl, 1746 scene on handle reverse, name and "Christmas '93" engraved on back of bowl, C C Adams & Co, sterling, demitasse 25

SPACE COLLECTIBLES

This category deals only with fictional space heroes toys. My father followed Buck Rogers in the Sunday funnies. I saw Buster Crabbe as Flash Gordon in the movies and cut my teeth on early television with Captain Video. My son belongs to the Star Trek generation. Whichever generation you choose, there is plenty to collect.

Club: Galaxy Patrol, 144 Russell St., Worcester, MA 01610.

Battlestar Galactica, game, Parker Bros, ©1978 Universal City Studios, Inc, 9.25 x 18.25 x 1.5" box 20
Buck Rogers, book, *Buck Rogers 25th Century A D,* Whitman Big Little Book, #742, ©1933 John F Dille Co 35
Buck Rogers, Buck Rogers Space Ranger Kit, Sylvania premium, punch-out, unused, orig 11.25 x 15" envelope 75

Buck Rogers, catalog, "Buck Rogers Caster," 12 pp, casting sets and accessories, includes comic strip reprints, Rapaport Bros, 1935, 5 x 8" 175
Buck Rogers, figure, cast metal, Dr Huer, unpainted, 1930s, 2" h 15
Flash Gordon, book, *Flash Gordon in the Forest Kingdom of Mongo,* Whitman Better Little Book, #1492, ©1938 King Features Syndicate, Inc 35
Flash Gordon, pencil box, paper cov cardboard, slide-out tray with pencil, rulers, crayons, etc, Flash and Dale battling "Space-Dragon" on front, Flash "Commandeers A Sand-Car" on back, Eagle Pencil Co, ©1951 King Features Syndicate, Inc, 4.5 x 8 x 1" ..50
Outer Limits, book, *The Outer Limits Annual,* 96 pp, full color reprints from Dell comic book series ©1965 United Artists Television, 7.5 x 10.5" 50
Planet of the Apes, puzzle, General Aldo, Aldo on horseback, 96 pcs, H-G Toys, ©1967 Apjac Productions, Inc, 6.25" h cardboard canister 25
Space: 1999, model, Hawk, MPC, ©1977 ATV Licensing Ltd, 5.25 x 8 x 2.5" box .20
Space Patrol, advertising trade card, Wheat and Rice Chex premium, set of 7, full color scene, from Rockets, Jets and Weapons series, includes Space Station, Monorail Liner, Saucer Attack, War of The Planets, Emergency in Space, Rocket Over Canali, and Space Refueling," 2.5 x 3.5" each ...135

Tom Corbett, book, Stand By For Mars, *Tom Corbett Space Cadet Story, #1, by Carey Rockwell, illus, Grosset & Dunlap, NY, 216 pp, ©1952, hard cov, dj, $15.*

Bank, composition, "Save Now For Your Trip To The Moon," c1970, 4.75" h, $40.
—Photo courtesy Ray Morykan Auctions.

Space Patrol, drink shaker, figural rocket-ship, 2-pc translucent plastic shaker, opaque vinyl straw, Steri-Lite United Plastic Corp, early 1950s, 2.75 x 2.75 x 8.5" box .... .75

Tom Corbett Space Cadet, wrist compass, high relief hard plastic attachment at center holding compass, upper body of Corbett with pair of rockets and planet at bottom surrounding compass with rocket illus, straps with repeated images of spaceman, rocket, planets, and name logo, unmkd, 1950s, 7.25" l .50

SPACE EXPLORATION

There can be no greater thrill than collecting an artifact of man's greatest adventure. Space exploration collecting covers a wide range of items from rocket models to autographs of men who walked on the moon! Autographs from astronauts can be had for free by writing to NASA and making a request. Autographs from former astronauts can be had by making a request to the astronaut or from an autograph dealer.

Mission patches from the earliest days of space exploration are also highly collectible. Mission patches are small works of art depicting the goals and members of a particular mission. Mission patches can be found at flight museums or through mail order or home retailers.

One of the most exciting areas of space collecting is that of items actually used to help send Man to the moon. These items include hardware, manuals, and almost anything used in the quest for space. While these items can be hard to find, they can still be had from many of the people who

were involved with, but have retired from, the space program. Other space items include presentation and manufacturer models, art, books, space collector cards, postal covers, medallions, coin sets, and collector pins.

Advisor: Dennis Kelly, P.O. Box 9942, Spokane, WA 99209 (509) 456-8488.

First Day Cover, commemorates launch of "Shuttle Mission 51-L" (Challenger shuttle—postmarked before launch and explosion), Kennedy Space Center postmark .... .250

Flicker Badge, astronauts planting flag on moon, Avri-Vue Productions, 3" d 25

Magazine, *Popular Mechanics,* Aug 1959, "Race To the Moon" cover article, artist renditions of Soviet and U.S. spacecrafts on cover 8

Matchbook Cover, moon landing scene, "Space Age—U.S.A.," c1969 6

Medal, Apollo 11, commemorates "Man's First Lunar Landing July 20-21, 1969," silver, Medallic Art Co, 999+ silver, 2.5" d, .125" thick, orig box .... .18

Mug, "Apollo," white glass, blue mission emblem, modules, astronaut names, and date, 3.25" h .... .12

Pass, NASA Space Shuttle Flight 51-1, "Distinguished Guest," laminated plastic with spring clip fastener, for return of shuttle mission Aug 27-Sep 3, 1985, 2.5 x 4" .... .35

Pen, Astronaut Porous Point Pen, Duro Pen Co, Brooklyn, "NASA Approved," on unopened blister pack, 5.25" l .... .20

Stereograph, "Full Moon from negative taken by Prof. H. Draper, with his silvered glass telescope," C Bierstadt, Niagara Falls, NY, $6.

Badge, "26th IAM Convention Delegate, Miami Beach, 1964," emb scene with space capsule, moon, palm trees, and beach, $20.

Pinback Button, Apollo 11 Moon Landing, eagle landing on moon, Earth in background, pale blue and black, 1.5" d ...12

Pinback Button, "First M(ichael Collins) E(dwin E. Aldrin) N(eil A. Armstrong) On The Moon July 21st 1969," celluloid, blue and red lettering, white ground, 3.5" d 30

Pinback Button, portrait of astronaut wearing helmet, rim inscription " 'Great, Scott!' U.S.A., Astronaut Scott Carpenter," 1.75" d 20

Plaque, portrait of astronaut John Glenn, rim inscription "The New Frontier, Man of the Year, Astronaut John Glenn," first U.S. orbital flight, Feb 1962, celluloid, black and white, 6" d . .35

View-Master Reel Set, "Apollo Moon Landing," 3-reel set, 16 pp booklet ...12

SPARK PLUGS

Over 4,000 different plug names have been identified by collectors, the most common of which are Champion, AC, and Autolite. Spark plugs are classified into six types: name plugs, gadget plugs, primer plugs, visible plugs, coil plugs, and quick detachable (QD) plugs.

There is no right or wrong way to collect spark plugs. Some people collect a certain style of plug, while others grab any plug they can find.

Use care when examining old spark plugs. Many have fragile labels which can be destroyed through improper handling.

Club: Spark Plug Collectors of America, 9 Heritage Ln., Simsbury, CT 06070.

Auto Par 6
Autolite, orig black and yellow box, 10mm 3
Beru, plug logo, purple porcelain, MM ...8
Bethlehem Aviation, MM 20
Champion, 10MM 2
Champion, 33 gas engine special, .5" l ...30
Chryco 6
Excelsior, MM 45
Genuine Soot-Proof, blue logo 20
Gulf 6
Hi-Speed 10
Hitachi 6
Holley 8
Improved Long Distance, .5" 35
Jewel, brass/mica, .5" 40
J-M, licensed 40
Mosler Vesuvius, genuine vitite 20
Motor Meter, type F for Fords 20
Rex, brass gland nut, .5" l 15
Splitdorf, green hex 25
Standard, odd base, MM 25
Tuner 6
Valley Forge 6

SPORTS & RECREATION

There has been so much written about sport cards that equipment and other sport-related material has become lost in the shuffle. A number of recent crazes, such as a passion for old baseball gloves, indicates that this is about to change. Decorators have discovered that hanging old sporting equipment on walls makes a great decorative motif. This certainly helps call attention to the collectibility of the material.

Since little has been written outside of baseball and golf collectibles, it is hard to determine what exactly are the best pieces. A good philosophy is to keep expenditures at a minimum until this and other questions are sorted out by collectors and dealers.

Clubs: Boxiana & Pugilistica Collectors International, P.O. Box 83135, Portland, OR 97283; The Tennis Collectors Society, Guildhall Orchard, Mary Lane North, Great Bromley, Colchester, Essex, C07 7TU U.K.

Periodical: *Boxing Collectors News,* 3316 Luallen Dr., Carrollton, TX 75007.

Boating, magazine, *Popular Boating,*
Mar 1962 4

Bowling, cocktail shaker, glass, red
plastic center connection, "Wild
Turkey" with turkey image, 9.25" h,
3" d 10

Bowling, cuff links and tie tack, 2 bowling pins and 1 ball, gold finish, brushed
silver face, unused 5

Boxing, pinback button, celluloid, "Punch
With Patterson/Polo Grounds July 29,"
center photo of Floyd Patterson, red
on cream, early 1960s 50

Boxing, postcard, "Won't It Be a Dark
Fourth of July If the Eclipse Looks Like
This?," inset photo of Jack Johnson
and Jim Jeffries, used, New York,
1910 175

Drag Racing, jacket, York US 30, red
nylon, York US 30 and Superstock
patch 75

Drag Racing, poster, 1972 Superstock
Nationals, York, 13 x 20" 45

Drag Racing, program, Superstock
Nationals, 1969 18

Drag Racing, trophy, Vargo Dragway,
1962 Roadster top, 6" h 40

Hockey, photograph, 1910 Freshmen
Hockey Team, Yale University, New
Haven, CT, black and white, matted
and framed 15

Hockey, trading card, Parkhurst, #9, Ron
Stewart, 1953-54 2

Horse Shoes, postcard, men playing
horse shoes in St Petersburg, FL,
"Barn Yard Golf/Williams Park,"
dated 1932 3

Bowling, change purse, leather, $8.

Marbles, pinback button, celluloid, "*The
Baltimore Daily Post*" around rim,
center "I am in The Marble Contest,"
red rim, white lettering, 1930s, .75" d . .75

Skiing, booklet, A Guide to Skiing, Fred
Pearson, illus, 70 pp, 5 x 7" 35

Swimming, postcard, Springbrook
Swimming Pool, Lima, OH, divided
back, unused 5

Table Tennis, book, *Modern Table Tennis,*
Jack Carrington, revised edition, G
Bell & Sons, London, 136 pp, 1960 5

Table Tennis, Harvard Table Tennis Set,
contains 4 paddles, 2 nets with mounting brackets, and "Laws of Table
Tennis," booklet, orig box, c1950-60s . .5

Track, postcard, "5th Avenue Theatre
Week of September 14th," John J
Hayes photo above "John J. Hayes/
Winner of The Marathon, 1908" 150

Walking, pinback button, "Los Angeles
Examiner's Walking Club," participant's
name in center, Wm H Hoegee Co,
early 1900s 10

STAMPS, MISCELLANEOUS

A secondary market is being established for trading stamps such as S&H
Green Stamps and Gold Bond Stamps; look
for listings under "Trading Stamps."

Other nonpostage stamps of interest to
collectors include revenue stamps (often
collected by philatelists), savings bond
stamps, and war ration stamps.

Clubs: American Revenue Assoc., P.O. Box
56, Rockford, IL 50468; State Revenue
Society, 27 Pine St., Lincroft, NJ 07738.

*Boxing, ringside bell, brass and heavy
metal, 15.5" h, 12" w, $110. —Photo courtesy
Collectors Auction Services.*

STAMPS, POSTAGE

When I was a boy, everybody and his brother had a stamp collection. In today's high tech world that is not often the case. Most stamps found at flea markets will be cancelled and their value is negligible. They can usually be bought in batches for a few dollars. However, there are rare exceptions. Who knows? If you look long and hard enough you may find an "Inverted Jenny."

Club: American Philatelic Society, P.O. Box 8000, State College, PA 16803.

Periodicals: *Linn's Stamp News,* P.O. Box 29, Sidney, OH 45365; *Scott's Stamp Monthly,* P.O. Box 828, Sidney, OH 45365; *Stamp Collector,* 700 E. State St., Iola, WI 54990.

STANGL POTTERY

Stangl manufactured dinnerware between 1930 and 1978 in Trenton, New Jersey. The dinnerware featured bold floral and fruit designs on a brilliant white or off-white ground.

The company also produced a series of three-dimensional bird figurines that are eagerly sought by collectors. The bird figurines were cast in Trenton and finished at a second company plant in Flemington. During World War II the demand for the birds was so great that over 60 decorators were employed to paint them. Some of the birds were reissued between 1972 and 1977. They are dated on the bottom.

Club: Stangl/Fulper Collectors Club, P.O. Box 538, Flemington, NJ 08822.

BIRD FIGURES

Bluejay, #3276 25
Canaries, pr, #3746 and #3747 350
Cerulean Warbler, #3456 25
Ducks, "Stangl 22kt gold" label, 4.5" l
    drinking duck, 4" h duck with head up,
    price for pair 45
Hummingbirds, #3626 and #3628, price
    for pair 55
Hummingbirds, #3599, price for pair . . .210

Bird Figure, Blue Birds, $160.
—Photo courtesy Collectors Auction Services.

Kentucky Warbler, #3598 30
Key West Quail, #3454 130
Magpie Jay, #3758, 10.5" h 1,350
Oriole, #3402 40
Parrot, #3449 50
Pheasant Cock, #3492 200
Prothonotary Warbler, #3447 50
Rivoli Hummingbird, #3627 110
Warbler, #3597 25

DINNERWARE & ACCESSORIES

Antique Gold, vase, #1905 24
Apple Delight, dessert plate, 8" d 4
Canadian Goose, ashtray, 1950s, 8 x 10" .18
Colonial, cereal bowl, #1388, blue, 6" 8
Colonial, cereal bowl, #1388, yellow, 6" d .8
Colonial, pepper shaker, #1388,
    tangerine 25
Colonial, salad plate, #1388, yellow, 7" d .12
Concord, cup and saucer 10
Country Garden, cereal bowl, 5.5" d 6
Country Garden, salt and pepper
    shakers, pr 20
Dogwood, salad plate, 7.875" d 4
Fruit, bread and butter plate, 6" d 12
Fruit, dinner plate, 10" d 20
Fruit, salt and pepper shakers, pr,
    cherries 25
Fruit, teapot 65
Fruit, vegetable bowl, divided, 10.25" d . .25
Fruit and Flowers, bread and butter
    plate, 6" d 10
Garden Flower, fruit bowl 4
Gold Brushed, bud vase, #5096 12
Golden Blossom, pitcher 25
Golden Harvest, pitcher, 2 qt 25
Gold Lyric, tidbit tray, center handle,
    10" d 15
Granada Gold, tidbit tray, #3151, center
    handle, 5.25" h, 10" d 10

Town and Country, creamer and cov sugar, brown, $40. —Photo courtesy Ray Morykan Auctions.

Harvest, salad plate, 7" d 15
Magnolia, cup and saucer 8
Magnolia, dinner plate, 10" d 8
Magnolia, lug soup 12
Magnolia, luncheon plate 8
Orchard Song, cov sugar 10
Orchard Song, cup and saucer 10
Orchard Song, fruit bowl, 5.5" d 12
Sculptured Fruit, comport 20
Star Flower, cup and saucer 8
Sunflower, coaster 12
Terra Rose, cigarette box 15
Thistle, bread and butter plate 6
Thistle, cup and saucer 6
Thistle, dinner plate, 10" d 10
Thistle, lug soup .10
Town and Country, creamer, blue 65
Town and Country, dish, cov, blue,
    8.25" d 100
Town and Country, gravy boat, blue 90
Town and Country, salt and pepper
    shakers, pr, blue 75
Town and Country, sugar, cov, blue 15

STANLEY TOOLS

Mention the name Stanley to a carpenter and the first tool that comes to mind is a plane. While Stanley planes are the best documented and most widely collected planes on the market, Stanley also produced many other tools, many of which are becoming desirable to tool collectors.

Periodical: *Stanley Tool Collector News,* 208 Front St., P.O. Box 227, Marietta, OH 45750.

Adjustable Bevel, #18, 6" 45
Bevel, #30 100

Block Plane, #65 .130
Block Plane, #140 140
Box Scraper, unused 40
Butt Gauge, #95 .45
Carpenters Boxwood and Brass Caliper
    Rule, #62C 200
Carpenters Boxwood Rule, #621/2, 24" . .50
Chamfer Shave, #65 85
Chisel Plane, #97, rejapanned 250
Compass Plane, #20, black japanned,
    orig box 540
Dowelling Machine Cutter Head, 3/4" . . .75
Lever Cap, #604, Stanley Rule and Level
    Co 25
Plane Cutter, #55, price for 8 85
Plane Iron, #8, 2.625" 70
Reeding Cutter, #55, price for 8 130
Rounding Plane, #1441/2 265
Rule, #86, Stanley Rule & Level Co, 4-fold
    folding rule, ivory and German silver,
    Geo W Hill, 24" 300
Scraper, #283 415
Scraper Blade 65
Scraper Plane, #112 215
Toothing Iron 70

STAR TREK

In 1966, a new science fiction television show aired that introduced America to a galaxy of strange new worlds filled with new life forms. The voyages of author Gene Roddenberry's starship *Enterprise* enabled the viewing audience to boldly go where no man had gone before. These adventures created a new generation of collectors: "Trekkies." From posters, costumes, and props to pins, comic books, and model kits, there is no limit to the number of Star Trek collectibles that can be found.

With the release of Paramount's *Star Trek: The Motion Picture* in 1979, the Star Trek cult grew. The *Enterprise*'s new devotees inspired the inevitable new sequels: *Star Trek II: The Wrath of Khan, Star Trek III: The Search for Spock, Star Trek IV: The Voyage Home, Star Trek V: The Final Frontier, Star Trek VI: The Undiscovered Country, Star Trek: Generations,* and *Star Trek: First Contact.*

In 1988, Trekkies demanded the return of the *Enterprise* to television and were rewarded with *Star Trek: The Next*

Generation. A new starship, manned by a new crew, continued the quest for the unknown. More recent spinoffs include *Star Trek: Deep Space 9* and *Star Trek: Voyager.* Whether you are an old Trekkie or a Next Generation Trekkie, keep seeking out those collectibles. May your collection live long and prosper.

Clubs: International Federation of Trekkers, P.O. Box 242, Lorain, OH 44052; Starfleet, 200 Hiawatha Blvd., Oakland, NJ 07436; Star Trek: The Official Fan Club, P.O. Box 111000, Aurora, CO 80042.

Comic Book, Gold Key #90210-302, No. 17, 1972, $12.

Action Figure, Borg, Playmates, 1992 . . .15
Action Figure, Captain Kirk, *Star Trek V*, Galoob 35
Action Figure, Decker, Mego, 1979, 3.75" h 25
Action Figure, Dr McCoy, Mego, 1974, MOC 125
Action Figure, Dr McCoy, Mego, 1979, 3.75" h 25
Action Figure, Ilia, Mego, 1979, 12" h, MOC 60
Action Figure, Kirk, Mego, 1974, MOC . . .60
Action Figure, Klingon, Mego, 1974, MOC 60
Action Figure, Lieutenant Commander Data, Playmates, 1992 10
Action Figure, Mr Spock, Ertl, 1984, 3.75" h 35
Action Figure, Mr Spock, *Star Trek V*, Galoob 35

Child's Book, Star Trek Mission to Horatius, *Whitman Authorized TV Adventure, #1549, hard cov, 210 pp, 1968,* $50.

Book, *Star Trek Star Fleet Technical Manual,* vinyl covered cardboard cover, gold title, Ballantine, ©1975 Franz Joseph Designs, 8.5 x 11" 15
Coloring Book, Planet Ecnal's Dilemna, Whitman, 60 pp, unused, ©1978 Paramount Pictures Corp, 8 x 11" 15
Lunch Tote, blue nylon, *Star Trek: The Next Generation,* carrying handles and shoulder strap, Thermos, ©1988 Paramount Pictures, 6.5 x 13 x 9" 35
Model, Mr Spock, AMT, ©1968 Paramount Pictures Corp, 8.5 x 10 x 3" box 65
Model, *USS Enterprise Command Bridge,* AMT, ©1976 Paramount Pictures Corp, 8.5 x 10.5 x 3" box 35
Paperback Book, *The Making of Star Trek,* Ballantine Books, 416 pp, 1968, 4.25 x 7" 8
Paperback Book, *The Trouble With Tribbles./The Story Behind A Star Trek Show,* Ballantine, 278 pp, 4.25 x 7" 15
Pencil Tablet, full color cover of William Shatner as Captain Kirk with *Enterprise* in background, unused, c1967, 8 x 10" .20
Phaser Ray Gun/Space Flashlight, hard plastic, black and silver, Zarak-Hamway, ©1976 Paramount Pictures Corp, 3.75" l, MOC 30
Pinback Button, "The Star Trek Convention 1975," *Enterprise* and New York City skyline, ©Tellurian Enterprises, Inc, 2.5" d 10
Playset, *Enterprise,* Mego 400
Puzzle, "The Alien," series 2, H-G Toys, ©1976 Paramount Pictures Corp, 7.5 x 9 x 1.5" box .10

Ring, McDonald's Happy Meal premium,
plastic, raised designs on lids of
secret compartments, Kirk, Spock,
Enterprise, and insignia, 1979, 1.5 x
4", price for set of 4 150
TV Guide, Mar 4, 1967, Vol 15 #9,
Philadelphia edition, 4 pp article on
Leonard Nimoy, color cover photo of
Kirk and Spock 20
Vehicle, *USS Enterprise Starship, Star
Trek: The Next Generation,* diecast,
detachable saucer section, Galoob,
©1988 Paramount Pictures Corp,
5.75" l, MOC 15
View-Master Set, set of 3 reels with
story booklet, ©1968 Paramount
Pictures Corp, 4.5 x 4.5" 35

STAR WARS

It was in a galaxy not so long ago that
author/director George Lucas put into
motion events that would change the way
we think of space. In 1977 a movie was produced that told the story of an evil Empire's
tyrannical rule over the galaxy and of the
attempts of a young man from a distant
world to end this tyranny. Luke Skywalker's
adventures became the Star Wars saga
and spanned six years and three separate
movies: *Star Wars, The Empire Strikes
Back,* and *Return of the Jedi.*

The enormous success of the *Star
Wars* movies inspired the release of a wide
range of movie-related products including
toys, games, costumes, records, and comic
books. "May the Force Be With You"as you
travel through the flea market aisles in
search of Star Wars treasure.

Club: Official Star Wars Fan Club, P.O. Box
111000, Aurora, CO 80042.

Action Figure, Darth Vader, Kenner,
1977, 4" h, MOC 150
Action Figure, Gredo, Kenner, 1977,
3.75" h, MOC .100
Action Figure, Princess Leia Organa,
Kenner, orig box, 1977, 11.5" h 100
Playset, Darth Vader's Star Destroyer,
Kenner, 1980 85
Earring Set, full figure R2D2, Weingeroff
©1977, MOC 8

*Belt Buckle, emb silvered metal, C-3PO
and R2-D2, mkd "1096," 3.25" l, $15.*

Game, Star Wars Destroy Death Star,
1978 15
Hand Puppet, Yoda, vinyl, white hair,
orig box, Kenner, ©1980 40
Laser Rifle Carrying Case, gray hard
plastic, holds 19 figures and accessories, with see-through scope,
Kenner, ©1984, 2 x 25 x 11" 15
Light Saber, battery operated, black plastic saber handle, yellow vinyl inflatable
sword, Kenner, orig box with photo
of light saber battle between Darth
Vader and Ben Kenobi and inset of
boy with light saber, ©1977, 35" l 100
Lunch Box, metal, C-3PO and R2-D2
decal on plastic thermos, King-Seely,
1977 85
Play-Doh Set, Ice Planet Hoth, includes
molds for Darth Vader, Storm Trooper,
R2-D2, Skywalker, and Leia, plastic
space vehicle, play mat, and 3 cans
of Play-Doh, Kenner, ©1980 20
Playset, Hoth Turret Defense, Micro
Collection, consists of white plastic
ice base, gray rotating turrets, 6 diecast figures, instructions, and decal
sheet, Kenner, ©1982 20

Star Wars
Official Poster
Magazine,
*magazine folds
out to poster,
Issue Six,
Artoo, 8.5 x
11.25", $10.*

Postage Stamp Collecting Kit, includes
48 pp album, 24 Star Wars seals,
postage stamps, hinges, magnifier,
and orig box, ©1977 12
Tie Fighter, diecast metal, Kenner,
©1978, 3.5" h, MOC 40
Tie Interceptor Vehicle, gray plastic,
flashing laser light, space sound,
removable wing panels, orig Jedi box,
Kenner, ©1983 80
Trading Card Set, *Return of the Jedi,*
consisting of 132 cards and 33 stickers,
color photo fronts, character illus and
text on back, Topps, ©1983 18

STEIFF

At the age of two, Margarete Steiff contracted polio, which left her paralyzed and
confined to a wheelchair. Despite her hand-
icap, she became a wonderful seamstress.
While working as a dressmaker in 1880,
Margarete used scraps of felt to make several elephant pin cushions which she gave
as gifts to family and friends. The first Steiff
toy was born. Soon she was making donkeys, horses, camels and even a pig. By
1897, her five nephews had joined her company and the now famous identification
"Button in Ear" was created. Her nephew
Richard Steiff designed and exhibited the
first teddy bear at the Leipzig trade fair in
1903. The bear was a great success. During
the 1950s, known as "the Golden Age of
Steiff," the company experienced their
most productive years. Exportation of the
button in ear brand quality playthings was
at its highest. As a result, many examples of
these detailed fine toys can be readily
found today. These are avidly sought by collectors. The Margarete Steiff Company still
remains in existence, a tribute to its
founder.

Advisor: Bety B. Savino, The Toy Store, 5001
Monroe St, Franklin Park Mall, Toledo, OH
43623.

Clubs: Steiff Club, 425 Paramont Dr,
Raynham, MA 02767; Steiff Collectors Club,
P.O. Box 798, Holland, OH 43528.

Army Donkey, 1957, 6" 350

*Navy Goat, #5717 on yellow ear tag, button
in ear, 6" h, $350.*

Clownie, #714 on wrist tag, button on
wrist band, 1956-57, 5.5" 125
Clownie, #719 on wrist tag, button on
wrist band, 1956-58, 7.5" 170
Duke University Devil, #7128 on yellow
ID tag, button on collar, 11" 800
Princeton University Tiger, button in ear,
1957, 6" 400
Snobby Poodle, #5314 on yellow ear tag,
chest tag, button in ear, black, 6" 120
Snobby Poodle, #5322 on yellow ear tag,
chest tag, button in ear, gray, 1953-
58, 9" 140
Zotty Bear, #6317, #1 on ear tag, 1951-58,
11" 200
Zotty Bear, #6328, #1 on ear tag, 1951-
58 325

STEMWARE

There are two basic types of stemware:
(1) soda-based glass and (2) lead- or flint-
based glass, often referred to as crystal.
Today crystal is also a term synonymous
with fine glassware and used to describe
glass that is clear. Lead crystal, which must
contain a minimum of 24% lead oxide, has a
brilliant clarity, durability, and a bell-like
tone that emanates when the glass is
struck.

Free blown, mold blown, and pressed
are the three basic methods used to make
stemware. Decorating techniques include
cutting and etching. Color also is used to
create variety.

There are thousands of stemware patterns. If you do not know your pattern, consider sending a drawing of the stem and a rubbing of its decoration to Replacements, Ltd. (P.O. Box 26029, Greensboro, NC 27420). Replacements has an excellent research staff. Also check Harry L. Rinker's *Stemware of the 20th Century: The Top 200 Patterns* (House of Collectibles, 1997) and/or Bob Page and Dale Frederiksen's *Crystal Stemware Identification Guide* (Collector Books, 1998). If you do not find your specific pattern, you will find ample comparables.

The following is a simple approach to determining a quick price per stem for your stemware: (1) soda glass stem, plain, $2 to $4; (2) soda glass stem, pressed, $5 to $8; (3) soda glass stem, elaborately decorated, $12 to $15; (4) lead glass stem, plain, $15 to $18; (5) lead glass stem, simple decoration, $20 to $25; (6) lead glass stem, elaborate decoration, $25 to $30; and (7) lead glass stem, streamline modern or post-war modern design style, $15 to $20. Add a 20% premium for patterns from Baccarat, Gorham, Lenox, Waterford, and Wedgwood.

Tiffin, King's Crown, water goblet, cranberry flashed, 5.625" h, $10.

Duncan & Miller, Willow, champagne, crystal, 4.75" h .18
Duncan & Miller, Willow, cocktail, crystal, 4.5" h 18
Duncan & Miller, Willow, cordial, crystal, 4.5" h 30
Duncan & Miller, Willow, highball, crystal, 5.625" h 24
Duncan & Miller, Willow, old fashioned, crystal, 3.25" h 24
Fostoria, Heritage, champagne, crystal, 5.125" h 10
Fostoria, Heritage, highball, crystal, 5.25" h 10
Fostoria, Heritage, iced tea, ftd, crystal, 7.125" h 12
Fostoria, Heritage, water goblet, crystal, 7.25" h 10
Fostoria, Heritage, wine, crystal, 6.125" h .10
Gorham, First Lady, champagne, crystal, platinum trim, 4.625" h 18
Gorham, First Lady, cocktail, crystal, platinum trim, 4.125" h 18
Gorham, First Lady, cordial, crystal, platinum trim, 3.75" h 20

Gorham, First Lady, juice, crystal, platinum trim, 6.5" h .18
Mikasa, Arctic Lights, brandy, crystal, 5.75" h 16
Mikasa, Arctic Lights, champagne, crystal, 6.5" h 16
Mikasa, Arctic Lights, cordial, crystal, 7" h 16
Mikasa, Jamestown, champagne, fluted, crystal, gold trim, 8" h 10
Mikasa, Jamestown, iced tea, crystal, gold trim, 8.125" h 10
Noritake, Paris, brandy, crystal, platinum trim, 5.5" h 12
Noritake, Rhythm, champagne, crystal, platinum trim, 4.375" h 18
Noritake, Virtue, champagne, crystal, etched, 5.275" h .30
Tiffin, King's Crown, champagne, cranberry flashed, 3" h 10
Tiffin, King's Crown, champagne, ruby flashed, 3" h 6
Tiffin, King's Crown, claret, cranberry flashed, 4.375" h 18
Tiffin, King's Crown, claret, ruby flashed, 4.5" h 10
Tiffin, King's Crown, cocktail, cranberry flashed, 4" h 12
Tiffin, King's Crown, cocktail, ruby flashed 10
Tiffin, King's Crown, highball, cranberry flashed, 5.5" h .12
Tiffin, King's Crown, iced tea, cranberry flashed 12
Tiffin, King's Crown, iced tea, ruby flashed 10
Tiffin, King's Crown, juice, cranberry flashed, 4" h 10
Tiffin, King's Crown, juice, ruby flashed, 4" h 8

STRADIVARIUS VIOLINS

In the late 19th century inexpensive violins were made for sale to students, amateur musicians, and others who could not afford older, quality instruments. Numerous models, many named after famous makers, were sold by department stores, music shops, and by mail. Sears, Roebuck sold "Stradivarius" models. Other famous violin makers whose names appear on paper labels inside these instruments include Amati, Caspar DaSolo, Guarnerius, Maggini, and Stainer. Lowendall of Germany made a Paganini model.

All these violins were sold through advertisements that claimed that the owner could have a violin nearly equal to that of an antique instrument for a modest cost; one "Stradivarius" sold for $2.45. The most expensive model cost less than $15. The violins were handmade, but by a factory assembly line process.

If well cared for, these pseudo antique violins often develop a nice tone. The average price for an instrument in playable condition is between $100 and $200.

STRING HOLDERS

I have fond memories of the plaster face of a Dutch girl with a piece of string coming out of her mouth that hung in my mother's kitchen. I also remember saving string, attaching accumulated pieces and wrapping them into a ball.

Few save string any longer. It is a lost art. Fortunately, plenty of collectors are saving the string holders that were found in virtually every kitchen from the 1920s through the 1950s.

Beware of fake string holders made by hollowing out the back of a figural head wall plaque and drilling a hole in the mouth, e.g., a Chinese or Siamese man or woman, or altering a figural wall lamp, e.g., a pineapple or apple face.

Apple House and Worm, chalkware 30
Bonzo the Dog, detachable head, bisque,
    5.5" h 175

Chef, red hat, green collar, chalkware, 8" h, $50. —Photo courtesy Ray Morykan Auctions.

Canister, silhouette of granny in rocking
    chair, tin 15
Cozy Kitten, Siamese cat head, ceramic,
    orig box, Holt-Howard 55
Fox Head, ceramic, Philip Laureston,
    Babbacombe Pottery, England, 8" h ..15
Girl, curly hair, huge eyes, blue kerchief
    in hair, chalkware, mkd "Artist-Bello,
    Copr. 1942 by Universal Str. Co,"
    7.75" h 185
Girl, wearing bonnet, ceramic, Napco ..40
Kitten on Ball of Yarn, white kitten with
    green eyes and pink ears, yellow
    yarn, ceramic, Lefton sticker 75
Little Red Riding Hood, ceramic, 6" h 30
Mammy Head, coconut with painted fea-
    tures, white fabric bandanna, 4" h 20
Mammy, ceramic, wearing polka dot
    dress and plaid apron, 6.5" h 100
Pear, with leaves and grapes, chalkware,
    mkd "Turiddi Art Milw Wis," 7.5" h .....
Pig with Flowers, ceramic 50
Sphere, pedestal base, cast iron 50
Sphere, suspended from wall mount
    bracket, cast iron 75

Beehive, cast iron, 4.5" h, 6.5" d, $60.

Strawberry, with leaves and white blossoms, chalkware .... .90
Woman, brown hair in bun, hands in apron pockets, wearing green dress and white apron with blue flowers and "I Hate House Work," chalkware .... .30

STUFFED TOYS

Stuffed toys is a generic term for plush toys. Normally one thinks first of the teddy bear when considering stuffed toys. Yet, virtually every animal and a fair number of characters and personalities have appeared as stuffed toys. Margarette Steiff's first stuffed toy was not a bear but an elephant.

By the early 1920s, many companies, e.g., Gund, Ideal, and Knickerbocker, were competing with Steiff for their share of the stuffed toy market. Collectors pay a premium for examples from these companies. The 1970s stuffed toys of R. Dakin Company, San Francisco, are a modern favorite.

Following World War II, stuffed toys became a favorite prize of carnival games of chance. Most are inexpensive Asian imports and hold only modest interest for collectors. Do not pay more than a few dollars for these poor quality examples.

Periodical: *Soft Dolls & Animals,* 30595 Eight Mile, Livonia, MI 48152.

Note: See Steiff and Teddy Bears for additional listings.

Aunt Jemima and Youngsters, oilcloth-like, bonded seams, 12" h Aunt Jemima, 9" h Diana, 8.5" h Wade ..... .75
Boo Boo Bear, plush, vinyl face, orig string tag mkd "I Am Boo Boo Bear From The Huckleberry Hound TV Show,"Knickerbocker, ©1959 Hanna-Barbera Productions, 9" h .... .35
Bubi Bear, plush, orange, stuffed head and body, pipe cleaner arms, felt hat, Sutton & Sons, Inc, NY/Japan, ©1971 Hanna-Barbera Productions, 5.75" h .... .35
Calypso Joe, plush, orange felt hat, yellow felt pants, attached bongo drum at lower chest, Dakin Dream Pets, c1970, 8" h .... .15

Kermit the Frog, plush, green, ©1985 Henson Associates .... .15
Little Lulu, cloth, smiling, full figure, yarn hair, label mkd "Handmade by Hazel," 1940s, 17" h .... .75
Magilla Gorilla, cloth, smiling full figure, vinyl head, purple hat with green stripe, brown felt cloth body, wearing blue suspenders, purple bow tie, red shorts, brown shoes with blue trim, polka dot handkerchief in back pocket, Ideal, 1960s, 7.5" h .... .65
Platter Puss, American Bandstand Official Autographed Mascot, cloth, felt ears, tail, and underbelly, diecut facial accents, plastic whiskers, bow around neck holding cardboard tag designed like a record, ©1959 Merrimag Toy Co, unused, 13.5" h .... .75
Sandy, oilcloth, dark tan with brown accents, white tail tip, muzzle, and eye voids, name on collar, 1930s, 8.5" h .... .100
Surfing Frog, plush, orange fabric with white corduroy underside, attached yellow wooden surfboard, Dakin Dream Pets, c1970, 9.25" l .... .15
Wally Gator, cloth, smiling, seated, Playtime Toys, Inc, ©1970s Hanna-Barbera Productions, 7.5" h .... .65
Winnie The Pooh, plush, pull-string talker, removable felt shirt, Sears, 1964, 6.5 x 12 x 6" box .... .50

The Cat in the Hat, Dr Seuss, Coleco, 1983, 25" h, $25.

SUGAR PACKETS

Do not judge sugar packets of the 1940s and 1950s by those you encounter today. There is no comparison. Early sugar packets were colorful and often contained full color scenic views. Many of the packets were issued as sets, with a variety of scenic views. They were gathered as souvenirs during vacation travels.

There is a large number of closet sugar packet collectors. They do not write much about their hobby because they are afraid that the minute they draw attention to it, prices will rise. Most sugar packets sell for less than $1. It's time to let the sugar out of the bag. Get them cheap while you can.

Club: Sugar Packet Clubs International, 15601 Burkhart Rd., Orrville, OH 44667.

SUPER HERO COLLECTIBLES

Super heroes and comic books go hand in hand. Superman first appeared in Action Comics in 1939. He was followed by Batman, Captain Marvel, Captain Midnight, The Green Hornet, The Green Lantern, The Shadow, Wonder Woman, and a host of others.

The traditional Super Hero was transformed with the appearance of The Fantastic Four—Mr. Fantastic, The Human Torch, The Invisible Girl, and The Thing.

It pays to focus on one hero or a related family of heroes. Go after the three-dimensional material. This is the hardest to find.

Clubs: Air Heroes Fan Club (Captain Midnight), 19205 Seneca Ridge Ct., Gaithersburg, MD 20879.

Newsletter: *The Adventures Continue* (Superman), 1935 Fruitville Pike #105, Lancaster, PA 17601.

Aquaman, pinback button, "Aquaman Official Member Super Hero Club," #15, Button World Mfg, ©1966, MIB . .40
Aquaman, "Super Candy & Toy" box, cardboard, Aquaman image, Phoenix Candy Co, © 1967, 2.5 x 3.75 x 1" 60

Flash Gordon, puzzles, Milton Bradley, figural pcs, 1951, price for 3-pc set, $110.

Captain Marvel, film, super 8, "Captain Marvel and the Death Ship," from 1941 Republic Pictures serial "Adventures of Captain Marvel," silent, c1960s .20
Captain Marvel, tattoo transfers, single sheet with 6 images and Captain Marvel portrait, 1940s, with orig envelope, 3.75 x 7.25" 200
Flash Gordon, belt, Ming the Merciless, blue leather, repeated illus of "Flash Gordon," portrait, rocketship, and sword fight scene between Flash and Ming, orig store hanger hook, Lee, 1979, 27.5" l, unused 20
Flash Gordon, Better Little Book, *Flash Gordon and the Tyrant of Mongo,* Whitman, #1484, 1941 65
Flash Gordon Sparkling Ray Gun, transparent blue hard plastic, red, white, and yellow flame stickers, purple "Flash Gordon," ©1976, 4" l, MOC 25
Green Hornet, photograph, radio fan club, Britt Reid leaning on desk, Green Hornet insect shadow behind, glossy, black and white, adv for radio program and greeting from cast on back, 8 x 10" .250
Marvel Super Heroes, hand puppets, set of 4 including Spider-Man, Captain America, Thor, and The Hulk, molded vinyl heads, thin vinyl bodies, Imperial Toy Corp, ©1978, 8" h 50
Mighty Comics, game, Mighty Comics Super Heroes Game, ©1966 Archie Comic Publications, characters include The Shield, The Hood, Captain Flag, Mr Justice, Fly Man, Fly Girl, and others 75

Phantom, Better Little Book, *The Phantom and the Girl of Mystery,* Whitman, #1416, 1947 50

Phantom, patch, purple felt, Phantom's face and name embroidered in black, white, and blue, 1970s, 3" d 15

Shazam, night light, painted ceramic Shazam figurine on round base, ©1978, 7.5" h, 4" d 70

Spider-Man, night light, plastic, figural, eyes light up, Electricord, ©1978 Marvel Comics Group, 3" h, MOC 15

Superman, cereal box with comic strip, Kellogg's Pep, #12 in series, ©1947 . .100

Superman, coloring book, "Superman Coloring Book," Saalfield, ©1940, 8 x 12", partially colored 300

Superman, coloring cloth, vinyl, with orig box and crayons, Howe Plastics, 1960s, 28 x 32" 65

Superman, comic book, #11, Jul-Aug 1941 75

Superman, picture frame, "Superman's Superfriend," image of Superman bending down to look at inset picture frame, mirrored ground, goldtone metal frame, ©1977 DC Comics, 8 x 10" 20

Superman, playsuit, Funtime Playwear, 3-pc outfit with shirt, pants, and cape, child's size 12, orig box, 1950s 250

Superman, "See-A-Show Stereo Viewer Set," Kenner, plastic viewer and 5 film cards for Superman, Daffy Duck, Alvin & The Chipmunks, Captain Kangaroo, and Gentle Ben, orig unopened box, 1969 35

Spider-Man, book and record set, Power Records #PR10, 45 rpm, ©1974 by Marvel Comics Group, $20.

Fantastic Four, comic book, Marvel Comics Group, Vol 1, No 100, Jul 1970, $50.

Superman, trading cards, Topps, 9 cards from set of 66, from series with "Watch Superman On T.V." text on backs, includes #1, 6, 14, 15, 21, 24, 26, 38, and 44, 1965 10

Superman, toy tank, windup, lighto tin, built-in key, Marx, ©1940, 2.75" h, 4" l 600

Superman, valentine, diecut stiff paper, Superman from chest up with young boy and girl on opposite sides of a brick wall, ©1940, 4.25 x 6.5" 45

Superman, wristwatch, chromed metal case, Superman image on yellow dial, blue vinyl straps, Bradley, c1962 75

Thor, mask, molded plastic, Ben Cooper, late 1960s, 11" h 20

Wonder Woman, Magnetic Maze Chase Game, Nasta Industries, ©1980 DC Comics, 10 x 13" 20

SWANKYSWIGS

Swankyswigs are decorated glass containers that were filled with Kraft Cheese Spreads. They date from the early 1930s. See D. M. Fountain's *Swankyswig Price Guide* (published by author in 1979) to identify pieces by pattern.

Most Swankyswigs still sell for under $5. If a glass still has its original label, add $5.

Club: Swankyswigs Unlimited, 201 Alvena, Wichita, KS 67203.

Antique #1, brown 3
Band #2, red and black,, 3.375" h 4
Band #2, red and black, 4.75" h 5
Band #2, red and black, 5" h 10
Band #2, red and black, 5.25" h 15

*Forget-Me-Not,
royal blue, 1948, $3.*

Bustling Betsy, green, 3.75" h 3
Cornflower #1, light blue, 3.5" h 4
Cornflower #2, cornflower yellow, 3.5" h . .3
Cornflower #2, dark blue, 3.5" h 4
Cornflower #2, light blue, 3.5" h 4
Cornflowr #2, red, 3.5" h 4
Daisy, 3.75" h 4
Daisy, 4.5" h 15
Daisy, 5.75" h 20
Forget-Me-Not, red, 3.5" h 4
Forget-Me-Not, yellow 3
Forget-Me-Not, yellow and green, 3.5" h .3
Kiddie Cup, blue, 3.75" h 3
Kiddie Cup, orange, 3.75" h 3
Sailboat, red and black 15
Texas Centennial, cobalt 40
Tulips, black, 3.5" h 4
Tulips, blue 4

SWAROVSKI CRYSTAL

Swarovski introduced its crystal decorative accessories in the 1970s. They were an immediate success. High lead content, stringent quality control and remarkable design sophistication are hallmarks of Swarovski crystal pieces which set them apart from crystal bibelots produced by other manufacturers.

Most pieces are marked with a variation of the Swarovski logo. Occasionally you will find a piece bearing the artist's signature in script. Some collectors are willing to pay an additional 10% for this feature, but it is subjective and somewhat controversial among Swarovski enthusiasts. Collectors of Swarovski crystal are very keen on obtaining complete original packaging, without which prices are compromised 10–25%. Only the annual and numbered limited editions came with certificates of authenticity.

Clubs: Swan Seekers Network, 9740 Campo Road, Suite 134, Spring Valley, CA 91977, Swarovski Collectors Society (company-sponsored), 1 Kenney Dr., Cranston, RI 02920.

Beads, tourmaline, #5301, 4mm, price for
  lot of 50 10
Christmas Ornament, octagonal pendant
  with "Peace 1988" above wreath, 1988,
  orig box and certificate 85
Christmas Ornament, snowflake, 1996,
  2.125" w 60
Christmas Ornament, snowflake, 2000 . . .56
Figurine, bald eagle perched on branch,
  white head, yellow beak, orig box
  and certificate 185
Figurine, chicken, black eyes, silver
  metal feet, #7651NR20, retired Jan
  1998, orig box and certificate 55
Figurine, grand piano with stool,
  #7477NR000006, orig box and certifi-
  cate 150
Figurine, pouncing beagle, 1.75" l 40
Figurine, rabbit, #7652NR45, retired Jul
  1988, orig box and certificate 260
Figurine, Siamese fighting fish, crystal
  body, green fins and tail 100
Figurine, sitting ballerina, frosted head
  and torso, orig box and certificate . .125
Figurine, snowman, black buttons,
  orange carrot nose, frosted face
  and scarf, 2000 75
Figurine, wolf, Fairy Tales, black eyes
  and nose, frosted tail, #7550000002 . .110
Maxi Flower, floral bouquet, orig box
  and certificate 365

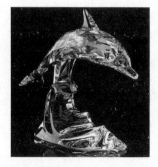

Figurine, dolphin, #7644NR000001, $210.

Paperweight, New Life egg, cut flowers and crosshatching, orig box, certificate, and Biblical verse card, 3.5 x 2.25" 20

Pillbox, figural owl with crystal face and jeweled eyes, perched on leafy branch, opens at center 45

Tennis Bracelet, tanzanite, sixteen 3mm stones set with 8 Swarovski crystal diamonds, size 7 30

Vase, Gemini, conical body with red jewels around top and red ring above crystal base 185

SWIZZLE STICKS

There is no end to the number of ways to collect swizzle sticks—advertising, color, motif, region, time period, and so on.

You can usually find them for less than $1. In fact, you can often buy a box or glass full of them for just a few dollars. Sets bring more, but they must be unusual.

Club: International Swizzle Stick Collectors Assoc., P.O. Box 1117, Bellingham, WA 98227.

Cane, bamboo handle, 7.5" l, price for 6 ..3
Cats, glass, black and white, set of 6 ...20
Chili Peppers, glass, set of 6, 8" l 10
Dolphin, glass, light blue and clear, price for 6............................14
Four-Leaf Clover, brass and glass, set of 4 8
Gilbey's Gin, plastic, cobalt blue 5.25" h pitcher, 9 matching swizzle sticks 6
Jack Daniels, plastic, 6.75" l, price for 6 ..4
Ohio State University, plastic, "Go Bucks," red and white, 6" l, set of 14 5

Swizzle Sticks, souvenir, plastic, 75¢ each.

Sterling Silver, retractable, jump ring on end, mkd "Silver," 4.75" l, $25.

Pink Flamingos, glass, set of 6 18
Seagram's Seven, plastic, set of 6 4
Sun Valley Idaho, plastic, set of 4 5
University of Michigan, plastic, 6" l, set of 3 4
Whizzle Sticks, plastic, "Whistle for your drink," 6" h, MIP 8
Wurlitzer, plastic, "Johnny One Note," red, price for 6 12
Zulu Lulu, plastic, 6" l, set of 6 4

SYROCO

In the 1890s, Adolph Hostein, owner of the Syracuse Ornamental Company, developed a formula of wood compound and casting liquids that could be poured into molds. The resulting casting appeared to be hand carved. The company manufactured a wide range of decorative accessories ranging from ashtrays to wall sconces. The Syracuse Ornamental Company became Syroco, Inc., in the 1930s.

In 1943 Walt Disney licensed Multi-Products of Chicago to produce a set of comic figures from Pinocchio. Multi-Products did them in Syroco wood. Collectors insert a second "c," Syrocco, to indicate a figure or object made by the parent company, Syroco, Inc. In addition to the Disney figures, Multi-Products did a series of twenty-four figures based on comic characters from the King Features Syndicate which were distributed as premiums by Pillsbury.

Bookend, "Ye Old Inn," stagecoach with 4 horses, rooster perched on sign, tree in background, antique leather look, 6" h, 5" w 6
Bookend, Scottie dog head and paws, 6.5" h, 5.5" w 8

Tie Rack, scottie dog, 8 swiveling wire hangers, Syroco Wood label, $20. —Photo courtesy Ray Morykan Auctions.

Bookends, iris design, 7" h, 5" w, price
   for pair 20
Bowl, feather design, Syroco Wood
   label, 12.5" l, 8.5" w 12
Bowl, oblong, oranges, leaves, and
   blossoms design, 10.25 x 7.75" 15
Figure, Mammy, wearing turban, yellow
   dress, and green apron, holding tea
   set, mkd "Famous Louisiana Mammy"
   on base, 5.5" h 45
Figure, phoenix bird, gold finish, Syroco
   Wood label, 8" h, 12" l 25
Figures, bears, realistically modeled, 5" l
   mother bear, 2" long baby bear, price
   for pair 15
Pipe Holder, leaf design, holds 6 pipes,
   Syroco Wood label 25
Powder Box, round, antique white with
   gold, scrollwork on lid, corseted and
   fluted sides, Syroco Wood label, 2" h,
   7" d 20
Radio, souvenir of 1939 New York
   World's Fair, RCA Victor, 9 x 6 x 6" 85
Shelves, antique white with gold trim,
   ornate scrollwork below shaped shelf,
   Syroco Wood label, 10" w, price for
   pair 30
Souvenir Bowl, "Alaska," Alaskan flag,
   dog sled, and totem pole in center,
   fluted sides, scalloped rim, mkd
   "Taco" with arrow on base, 7 x 5" 20
Souvenir Bowl, "Franconia Notch, New
   Hampshire," rect, Flume, Aerial
   Tramway, Old Man of the Mountain,
   and 3 spruce trees in center, woody
   border with 2 pine cones in each
   corner, mkd "Anco," 8 x 11.5" 15

Souvenir Bowl, Washington, DC, Capitol
   in center, scalloped rim, wood branch
   handle, 10 x 8" 12

TARGET BALLS

Glass target balls, used by hunters to sharpen their shooting skills, arrived on the scene in the mid-1870s. They were often filled with feathers so that when hit, they gave the impression a live bird had been shot. Fields covered with glass were a problem. Target balls made from pitch were an improvement.

Target balls are collected by manufacturer, glass pattern, and color. Their reign was short. George Ligowski invented the clay pigeon in 1880. Target balls faded from the scene as the nineteenth century ended.

Cobalt Blue, fishnet design, "Van Custem,
   A St. Quentin" 140
Cobalt Blue, diamond pattern, "Van
   Custem - A St. Quentin," 2.375" d 130
Golden Yellow Amber, overall dot pattern
   on both sides, horizontal lines on both
   seams, rough sheared mouth, blown
   3-pc mold, c1880-1900, 2.625" d 400
Golden Yellow Amber, rough sheared
   mouth, "Ira Paine's Filled/Ball Pat.
   Oct. 23, 1877," 2.625" d 150
Light Green, fishnet design, NB Perth
   Glass Works 235
Moss Green, man shooting motif, over-
   all diamond pattern, 2.625" d 175
Olive Yellow, rough sheared mouth,
   blown 3-pc mold, c1880-1900,
   2.625" d 150

Cobalt Blue, sheared lip, c1880-90, 2.875" d, $100 each.

Pink Amethyst, diamond pattern, rough
  sheared mouth, "W.W. Greener St
  Marys Works Birmm & 68 Haymarket
  London," c1880-90, 2.375" d 450
Purple Amethyst, man shooting motif,
  overall diamond pattern, 2.625" d 375
Sapphire Blue, diamond pattern,
  "N.B. Glass Works Perth," 1880-90,
  2.625" d 130
Yellow Amber, diamond pattern, "B.
  Bogardus Glass Ball Patd Apr 10th
  1877," 2.625" d 475

TAYLOR, SMITH & TAYLOR

W. L. Smith, John N. Taylor, W. L. Taylor,
Homer J. Taylor, and Joseph G. Lee founded
Taylor, Smith, and Taylor in Chester, West
Virginia. In 1903 the firm reorganized and
the Taylors bought Lee's interest. In 1906
Smith bought out the Taylors. The firm
remained in the Smith family's control until
it was purchased by Anchor Hocking in
1973. The tableware division closed in 1981.

One of Taylor, Smith, and Taylor's most
popular lines was Lu-Ray, produced from
the 1930s through the early 1950s. Designed
to compete with Russel Wright's American
Modern, it was produced in Windsor Blue,
Persian Cream, Sharon Pink, Surf Green,
and Chatham Gray. Coordinating colors
encouraged collectors to mix and match
sets. Taylor, Smith, and Taylor used several
different backstamps and marks. Many
contain the company name as well as the
pattern and shape names.

A dating system was used on some dinnerware lines. The three number code
included month, year, and crew number.
This system was discontinued in the 1950s.

Note: See Russel Wright for additional listings.

Boutonniere, butter dish, cov 15
Boutonniere, carafe, wood lid, metal
  warming stand, 12" h 30
Boutonniere, creamer and cov sugar . . .10
Boutonniere, lug soup, 8" w 10
Boutonniere, salt and pepper shakers, pr .20
Boutonniere, soup bowl, 6.75" d 6
Boutonniere, serving bowl, 8.25" d 12
Boutonniere, serving bowl, 9" d 8

Boutonniere, dinner plate, 10.25" d, $4.
—Photo courtesy Ray Morykan Auctions.

Empire Roses, casserole, cov, bud finial,
  platinum trim, 8" d 55
Empire Roses, creamer and sugar 10
Empire Roses, platter, 11.5" l 30
Empire Roses, platter, 15" l 18
Empire Roses, sauce boat and under-
  plate 20
Empire Roses, serving bowl, 9" d 12
Holiday Wreath, plate, 7.25" d 8
Holly Spruce, dinner plate, 10.5" d 10
Luray, bread and butter plate, blue,
  6.75" d 4
Luray, butter dish, cov, yellow 65
Luray, casserole, cov, green, 10" w
  handle to handle 95
Luray, chop plate, blue, 14" d 30
Luray, coffeepot, cov, yellow, 7" h 265
Luray, coupe soup, yellow, 8" d 20
Luray, creamer and sugar, pink 25
Luray, dinner plate, green, 10" d 10
Luray, dinner plate, yellow, 9.25" d 12
Luray, epergne, yellow, 8.5" h 110
Luray, lug soup, green 28
Luray, platter, oval, pink, 13.5" l 15
Luray, serving bowl, oval, yellow, 10.25" l .24
Luray, serving bowl, round, yellow, 9.5" d .28
Luray, tumbler, pink 64
Pebbleford, cookie jar, PA Dutch potted
  plant decal, 9" h, 7.5" d 200
Pebbleford, pitcher, ice lip, pink, 8.5" h . .60
Petit Point, cake plate 15
Platinum Blue, partial dinner service,
  consisting of 5 dinner plates, 8 salad
  plates, 2 soup bowls, 6 dessert bowls,
  14 cups and saucers, 4 round serving
  bowls, and 1 each cov oval casserole,
  cov sugar, creamer, cov coffeepot,
  and gravy boat 75

Luray, platter, green, 13.5" l, $12. —Photo
courtesy Ray Morykan Auctions.

Reveille, bread and butter plate, 6.75" d   .5
Reveille, cup and saucer 4
Reveille, dinner plate, 10.25" d 6
Rooster, 5-pc place setting 30
Rose, dinner plate, 10.25" d
Versatile, blue flowers, platinum trim,
    dinner plate, 10.5" d 6
Versatile, blue flowers, platinum trim,
    platter, 11.25" l 12
Versatile, blue flowers, platinum trim,
    vegetable bowl, 9" d 12

TEDDY BEARS

The name "Teddy" Bear originated with
Theodore Roosevelt. The accepted date of
their birth is 1902–1903. Early bears had
humped backs, elongated muzzles, and
jointed limbs. The fabric was usually
mohair; the eyes were either glass with pin
backs or black shoe buttons.

The contemporary Teddy Bear market
is as big or bigger than the market for
antique and collectible bears. Many of
these bears are quite expensive. Collectors
speculating in them will find that recouping
their investment in ten to fifteen years will
be a bearish proposition.

Club: Good Bears of the World, P.O. Box
13097, Toledo, OH 43613

Periodicals: *Teddy Bear & Friends,* P.O. Box
420235, Palm Coast, FL 32142; *Teddy Bear
Review,* 170 Fifth Ave. 12th Flr., New York,
NY 10010.

Hermann, brown tipped gold mohair,
    fully jointed, glass eyes, shaved muz-
    zle, black embroidered nose and
    mouth, excelsior stuffing, clipped
    mohair pads, 1940s, 19" h 230
Ideal, light gold mohair, fully jointed,
    glass eyes, brown embroidered nose,
    mouth and claws, excelsior stuffing,
    replaced pads, spotty fur loss, fabric
    wear, c1919, 23" h 375
Ideal, yellow mohair, fully jointed, glass
    eyes, black embroidered nose, mouth
    and claws, felt pads, excelsior stuffing,
    1920s, 25" h 625
Schuco, Windup Teddy on Roller Skates,
    beige mohair head, glass eyes, embroi-
    dered nose and mouth, cloth and metal
    body and legs, cotton shirt, felt over-
    alls, hands, and boots, rubber wheels,
    8.25" h 485
Schuco, yellow mohair, 2-faced, fully
    jointed, black steel eyes, embroidered
    nose and mouth, comic face with
    plastic tongue, metal nose, metal
    eyes backed with plastiform ringlets,
    1955, 3.5" h 575
Steiff, blonde mohair, fully jointed, under-
    scored button, black steel eyes, pad-
    less paws, c1906, 3.5" h 375
Steiff, dark brown mohair, fully jointed,
    glass eyes, black embroidered nose,
    mouth, and claws, excelsior stuffing,
    felt pads, some fur loss and matting,
    mid 20th C, 11" h 230

*Steiff, Zotty Bear, #6343, 1951-58, 17" h,
$500.*

Steiff, gold mohair, fully jointed, glass eyes, felt pads, excelsior stuffing, remnants of embroidered nose, mouth, and claws, spotty fur loss, button missing, c1951, 11.5" h 200

Tara Toys, Ireland, gold mohair, fully jointed, plastic eyes, Rexine pads, mouth opens and closes by squeezing knobs on back of head, cloth label, pads worn, fur loss, replaced nose, early 1950s, 16" h 175

Unknown Maker, aqua rayon mohair, fully jointed, glass eyes, embroidered nose and mouth, excelsior stuffing, cotton pads, 1920-30s, 22" h 115

Unknown Maker, cream mohair, fully jointed, black steel eyes, embroidered nose, mouth, and claws, excelsior stuffing, felt pads, fur loss, early 20th C, 13.5" h 175

Unknown Maker, gold brown mohair, fully jointed, glass eyes, embroidered nose and mouth, kapok and excelsior stuffing, felt pads, wearing dress, bonnet, and glasses, 1920s, 24" h 350

Woodnough, black mohair, "Honey Bear," jointed head, glass eyes, open pink velvet lined mouth, pink embroidered nose, stubby tail, jointed head, light yellow V-shaped insert on chest, c1930, 9.75" h .85

TELEPHONE CARDS

Telephone cards, commonly known as telecards, have been big in Europe for years. Telecards are credit cards issued by major telephone companies and many private companies. You purchase a card and then use up the credit each time you place a call. Once the credit value of the card is exhausted, you have an instant collectible.

Some telecards are produced as part of a series, some are limited editions. Most stand alone. The cards are issued in quantities that start in the hundreds and continue into the tens of thousands. Collector value rests in a card's graphics, issuing telephone company, and the number issued. Prices are highly speculative. Only time will tell how this collectible will "reach out and touch" collectors.

Prices listed here are from current sales lists issued by several individuals selling directly to collectors. The market has yet to determine if a premium is to be paid for cards with unexpended credit balances.

Access Telecom Inc (ACT), Earthline/US Electronics, 15 units 12

Access Telecom Inc (ACT), Walter Mercado Psychic 20

ACMI (ACI), Smokey Bear, $6 value 14

AT&T (ATT), Nabisco/Oreo Cookie, 10 units 8

ATS, Hammermill Papers, 20 minutes . . .12

American National Phone Card (ANP), Guardian Angel Xmas, 10 units 8

Ameritech (AMT), Season's Greetings, 5 units 2

American Express Telecom (AMX), Lighthouse, $10 value 12

AmeriVox (AVX), Folger's coffee, 10 minutes 13

Argo City Company (ARG), Broken Silence, 10 units 12

Bell Atlantic (BAT), James Earl Jones, green, $5 value 10

Bell Canada (BEL), Air Ontario/Windsor, 5 minutes 12

Bell South (BST), Mobility: Beach, $30 value 10

Cable & Wireless (C&W), TelePUCK/ Anaheim Sports Show, 5 minutes 10

Canada Telecom Network (CTN), Greyhound log, 20 minutes 20

Communication Design Group (CDG), Red Dog-It's Your Call, 15 minutes 12

Creative Communications (CCI), Milky Way Lite, 15 minutes 15

Pour Téléphoner Choisissez Votre Heure, French, remote type chip, unused, $20.

Destiny Communications (DES), Rollie
    Fingers, 10 units 10
GTE, Monday Night Football, 5 minutes .20
GTI, Luke & Landspeeder, $5 value 5
Karis Communications (KAR), Karis logo,
    10 minutes 5
NYNEX (NYN), Lillehammer Olympic Luge,
    $5 value 25
OmniTel (OMN), Cam Neeley, $8 value . .10
Pacific Bell (PAC), Soccer/Cobi Jones,
    $20 value 20
Sprint (SPR), Monsters of the Gridiron,
    $3 value 10
USACard Corporation (USA), Wish You
    Were Here, $5 value 8

TELEPHONES & RELATED

Although Alexander Graham Bell filed his telephone patent in 1876, rude telegraph and sound-operated devices existed prior to that date.

Beware of reproduction phones or phones made from married parts. Buy only telephones that have the proper period parts, a minimum of restoration, and are in working order. No mass-produced telephone in the United States made prior to 1950 was manufactured with a shiny brass finish.

Concentrating on telephones is only half the story. Telephone companies generated a wealth of secondary material from books to giveaway premiums.

Clubs: Antique Telephone Collectors Association, P.O. Box 94, Abilene, KS 67410; Telephone Collectors International, Inc., 3207 E. Bend Dr., Algonquin, IL 60102.

Advertising Tear Sheet, "SOS–a signal
    with a double meaning," stand phone
    with "Western Electric Purchasers
    Manufacturers Distributors Since 1882
    For the Bell System, 4.5 x 12.125" 4
Advertising Trade Card, Rocky Mountain
    Bell Telephone Co 10
Almanac, American Telephone &
    Telegraph Co, 1934 5
Bond, New England Telephone &
    Telegraph Co, $1000, ornate border,
    image of woman using push-button
    phone by side of road 3

Candy Container, glass, figural candle-
    stick phone, wooden receiver 15
Magazine, *Telephone Topics,* Dec 1925 . .6
Novelty Telephone, Hershey's Chocolate
    Milk Container, Model 6000, touch-
    tone dialing, Arrow Trading Co, made
    in Taiwan, 1985 100
Novelty Telephone, Jolly Green Giant,
    touch-tone dialing, Hong Kong, 1984 .75
Novelty Telephone, mallard duck, wood,
    eyes light-up, Telemania 10
Novelty Telephone, Pepsi-Cola, candle-
    stick style, pulse dialing, American
    Telecommunications Corp, 1974 100
Pin, figural bell, diecut celluloid 20
Pin, figural telephone, goldtone 4
Planter, ceramic, hands around candle-
    stick phone, Hull, #90, gray, black,
    and pink 50
Playing Cards, Yellow Pages, pinochle
    deck, Redi-Slip 8
Postcard, girl wearing bonnet holding
    candlestick phone, "Hello! How are
    you?" 3
Salt and Pepper Shakers, pr, receiver
    end is salt, mouthpiece is pepper,
    dial lifts off to reveal sugar bowl,
    complete with spoon, mkd "Victoria
    Ceramics, Japan," 1950s 8
Telephone, Connecticut Telephone &
    Electric Co, desk set, metal, c1949 . . .40
Telephone, Eastern Telephone Co,
    upright desk stand, tapered style,
    early 1900s 500
Telephone, L M Ericsson, desk style,
    c1905 100

Telephone, Automatic Electric Co, Chicago, wall mount, metal, rubber handpiece and speaker, 9.5" h, 10" w, $175. —Photo courtesy Collectors Auction Services.

*Sign, 2-sided flange, porcelain, 18" sq,
$275. —Photo courtesy Collectors Auction
Services.*

Telephone, Monarch Telephone Mfg
Co, upright desk stand, cast iron
base, c1904, 11.5" h 200
Telephone, Stromberg Carlson, model
1543W, desk style, 1963 ....:.40
Telephone, Western Electric, Lucite
buttons, 1960s 50
Telephone Directory, Seattle, WA, Mar
1961 10
Wall Pocket, antique phone, 5 x 4.5 x 2" .10

TELEVISION CHARACTERS & PERSONALITIES

The golden age of television varies
depending on the period in which you grew
up. Each generation thinks the television of
its childhood is the best there ever was. TV
collectibles are one category in which new
products quickly establish themselves as
collectible. The minute a show is cancelled,
anything associated with it is viewed as
collectible.

The golden age of TV star endorse-
ments was the 1950s through the 1960s. For
whatever reason, toy, game, and other
manufacturers of today are not convinced
that TV stars sell products. As a result,
many shows have no licensed products
associated with them.

Periodicals: *Big Reel,* P.O. Box 1050,
Dubuque, IA 52004; The TV Collector, P.O.
Box 1088, Easton, MA 02334.

Note: Consult the most recent edition of
Maloney's Antiques & Collectibles
Resource Directory, by David J. Maloney,
Jr., for information about fan clubs for spe-
cific television shows.

Andy Griffith, record, *Andy Griffith Just
For Laughs,* 33¹/₃ rpm, Capitol
Records, 1958 20
Banana Splits, record, *The Tra-La-La-
Song,* 45 rpm, Kellogg's premium,
©1969 Hanna-Barbera Productions . .30
Ben Casey, pencil case, cardboard,
paper label on lid depicts color photo,
Hasbro, ©1962 Bing Crosby
Productions, 4 x 8.5 x 1.25" 35
Bionic Woman, Action Club Kit, 9 x 12"
orig mailing envelope includes color
illus of Jaime Sommers, membership
card, and certificate with center
portrait images and facsimile signa-
tures, Kenner, ©1975 Universal City
Studios 35
Captain Kangaroo, View-Master Set, 3
reels, ©1957 Sawyer's Inc, 4.5 x 4.5"
envelope 20
Charlie's Angels, puzzle, Farrah Fawcett,
wearing sleeveless shirt, blue jeans,
holding flower in hand, American
Publishing Corp, ©1977 Pro Arts Inc,
8.5 x 14 x 1.5" box 12
Dallas, pinback button, "J. R. For
President," 1.75" d 5
Dragnet, Flashlight Whistle Gun, hard
plastic, raised "Badge 714" design
on side of handle, whistle on gun
butt, Transogram, ©1955 Sherry TV
Inc, 3.5" l, MOC 50

*Bonanza, book, by Basil Deakin, illus by
R Walker, printed in Great Britain by Purnell
& Sons Ltd, 93 pp, 1965, 8.375 x 11", $18.*

Hopalong Cassidy, alarm clock, US Time, 5.5" h, $250.

Dukes of Hazzard, paint-by-number set, Craftmaster, ©1980 Warner Bros, 8.5 x 10 x 1" box 25

Fantasy Island, autograph, script sgd by Herve Villechaize, 60 pp final draft script for Oct 28, 1981, episode "Funny Man/Tatto, The Matchmaker," black felt tip pen signature "Love Tattoo Herve Villechaize" with hand-drawn heart with arrow, 8.5 x 11" 75

Get Smart, pinback button, black and white photo of Don Adams as Maxwell Smart with text "I'm A Smartie! Agent 86," red and blue on white ground, 1970s, 3" d 20

Highway Patrol, star shaped badge, plastic, "Watch Highway Patrol Starring Broderick Crawford/Purity, Body, Flavor" with Ballantine Beer logo, 1950s, 3 x 3.25" 50

Jackie Gleason, pinback button, "Jackie Gleason, Mmmm! Boy," black and white, 1.25" d 12

Jack Parr, pinback button, "Welcome Back Jack Parr," black and white photo of Parr resting his head on his hand in center of large white heart, mkd "Empress Specialty Co," 1950-60s, 3.5" d 15

Laugh-In, View-Master Set, 3 reels, ©1968 George Slatter-Ed Friendly Productions and Romart Inc, 4.5 x 4.5" envelope 15

Leave It To Beaver, coloring book, Saalfield, c1958, 8.25 x 10.75" 20

Leave It To Beaver, magazine, *Children's Playmate Magazine,* Jan 1961, Vol 32, #7, 2 pp article on Jerry Mathers and his pet monkey Fuzzy, 6 x 9" 20

Magnum PI, model kit, GTS Ferrari, Revell, ©1982 Universal City Studios Inc, 7 x 10 x 3.5" box 8

Man From UNCLE, sheet music, *Theme From the Man From UNCLE,* black, white, and purple cover with cast photo of Vaughn, McCallum, and Carroll, black felt tip pen Robert Vaughn signature, Hastings Music Corp, ©1964 MGM Inc, 9 x 12" 30

Monte Hall, necktie, cotton, blue, red, white, and yellow stripes, tag mkd "Monte Hall" 8

Ozzie Nelson, autograph, PS, black and white, black ink signature "To Miss Tassia, with memories of a very pleasant evening, Best Wishes Ozzie Nelson," 10 x 12.75" 50

Pee-Wee Herman, doll, stuffed, hard vinyl head and hands, pull-string talker, Matchbox, ©1987 Herman Toys, 10 x 20.5 x 4.5" box 40

Red Skelton, *TV Digest,* Oct 4, 1952, Vol 6, #40, Philadelphia edition 30

Dukes of Hazzard, lunch box, Aladdin, 1980, $20.

Ralph Edwards, game, Ralph Edwards' This Is Your Life, 1950s, $30.

The Partridge Family, sheet music, I Think I Love You, *pub by Leeds Music, Australia, c1970, $10.*

Swan, ceramic, white, Maddux, mkd "Calif USA 828 ©59," 12" h, $75. —Photo courtesy Ray Morykan Auctions.

Six Million Dollar Man, game, Parker
 Bros, ©1975 Universal City Studios,
 9.25 x 18.25 x 1.5" box 15
The Fall Guy, lunch box, emb metal,
 plastic thermos, full color illus, Aladdin
 Industries, ©1981 20th Century Fox,
 7 x 8 x 4" 20

TELEVISION LAMPS

What 1950's living room would be complete without a black ceramic gondola slowly drifting across the top of the television set? Long before the arrival of VCRs, Home Box, and Nintendo systems, figural lamps dominated the tops of televisions. The lamps were made of colorful high gloss ceramics and the subject matter ranged from the relatively mundane dog statue to the more exotic (tasteless?) hula dancer.

A collection of ten or more of these beauties will certainly lighten up the conversation at your next party. On second thought, it does not take ten. The pink poodle lamp on my TV is more than adequate.

Antique Convertible, Buckingham
 Ceramics, 5.5" h 45
Ballet Dancers 8
Basset Hound, painted plaster, 9" h 45
Colonial Couple, candy dish, 12.5" h 85
Comedy and Tragedy Masks, Royal
 Haeger, 9.5" h 50
Covered Wagon, Marcia of California,
 11" l 55
Cowboy on Bronco, 12" h 55
Crowing Rooster, white, gold trim, Lane,
 15" h 65
Duck, planter, Hollywood Ceramics,
 7.5" h 45

Elephant, 6.5" h 45
Flamingo, planter, LaVelle, 9.5" h 45
Flower, maroon 55
Greyhound, planter, ceramic, brown,
 Royal Haeger, 6.25" h, 11.5" w 75
Island Girl, leaning against palm tree,
 ceramic, green, screen background . .40
Jesus, plaster, fiberglass back shade . .120
Kissing Fish 75
Owl, Kron, 11.5" h 100
Peacock, planter, Royal Fleet of
 California, 10" h 55
Pea Fowl, Royal Fleet of California, 10" h 50
Sailboat, bronze, 13" h 50
Sailboat, painted plaster, Garland
 Creations, 13.5" h 50
Ship, plaster, reverse painting on glass
 background, mkd "Duquesne
 Statuary" 125
Siamese Cats, Midwest Potteries, Kron
 Line, 1940-44, 13.25" h 40
Swan, planter, Maddux of California,
 10" h 70
Swordfish, 10.5" l 45

Oriental Girl, kneeling on bridge, ceramic, turquoise, molded fiberglass shade, unmkd, 7.125" h, 9.5" l, $250.

TELEVISIONS

Old television sets are becoming highly collectible. It is not unusual to see a dozen or more at a flea market. Do not believe a tag that says "I Work." Insist that the seller find a place to plug it in and show you. A good general rule is the smaller the picture tube, the earlier the set. Pre-1946 televisions usually have a maximum of five stations, 1 through 5. Channels 7 through 13 were added in 1947. In 1949 Channel 1 was dropped. UHF appeared in 1953.

In order to determine the value of a television, you need to identify the brand and model number. See *The Official Rinker Price Guide to Collectibles* (House of Collectibles) for a more detailed list.

Club: Antique Wireless Assoc., Box E, Breesport, NY 14816

Periodical: *Antique Radio Classified,* P.O. Box 2, Carlisle, MA 01741.

Admiral, 20X11, tabletop, Bakelite, square lines, ribs molded into sides, 10" screen 65
Air King, A1001A, console, flat front, screen over 4 knobs, large grill cloth, 1949, 10" screen 75
Andrea, CVK15, wooden, 13 channel tuner, FM radio dial below screen, 1948, 15" screen 75
Arvin, 2161, square lined, 2 knobs below screen, 16" screen 35

Philco, Predicta 21, with stand, $250.
—Photo courtesy Gene Harris Antique Auction Center, Inc.

Bendix, 3051, square lined console, 16" screen 35
Capehart/Farnsworth, 8C215, wooden console, 2 large knobs below screen, 21" screen........................15
CBS-Columbia, 20C3, console, French Provincial style, double doors, 1951, 20" screen........................25
Crosley, 10-401, tabletop, Bakelite, plastic mask around screen, 1950, 10" screen 50
Emerson, 644, tabletop, porthole type screen, 4 knobs, 12" screen 75
Fada, 925, tabletop, 1949, 16" screen 65
General Electric, 24C101, console, double doors, 24" screen, 1951 20
Motorola, 10T2, tabletop, gold bezel around screen, 1950, 10" screen 75
Norelco, PT200, console, fixed plastic projection screen, 1948 50
Philco, 51-T1601, tabletop, metal, rounded top, screen over 4 knobs, 1951 15
Sony, TV-500U, portable, UHF dial and controls, 1961, 5" screen 20
Sparton, 4920, console, double doors, 1949, 12" screen 50
Stromberg-Carlson, TC-19-LM, console, double doors, 1949, 19" screen 45
Tele-King, T-510, tabletop, square-lined front screen over 4 knobs, 1949, 10" screen 75
Westinghouse, H-610, tabletop, 4 knobs, 1948, 10" screen 65
Zenith, G2322, tabletop, brown Bakelite, 1950, 12" screen 65

TENNIS BALL CANS

Tennis balls originally came in bags and cardboard boxes. In 1926, Wilson introduced the first metal tennis ball can. It opened with a small key like a can of ham and had a flat lid that would not stay on the can after it was opened. After 1942, the lid was improved so that it could be put back on the can after opening to hold the balls securely. This lid was slightly dome-shaped. Dome lid cans were also of the key wind opening type. Most English key wind cans had flat lids, regardless of when they were made and should not be confused with the rare United States flat-lid cans. However, the older English cans had a small solder spot either on the lid or the bottom of the can, and four sets of ridges in groups of two to four horizontally around the can. The newer English cans had no solder spot and only one ridge near the top.

Around 1972, easy opening pull-ring cans were introduced. The best cans are the big 12-ball cans, four-ball cans, and flat-lid cans made in the United States, and cans with a famous player on them. The newer pull-ring cans are still very common and are only worth 50¢ to $10. Some balls are still sold in boxes. Pre-1960 boxes are hard to find and are worth $50 to $200. Boxes that predate cans are extremely rare and can cost $100 or more.

Advisor: Larry Whitaker, 1337 Joplin Dr. #2, San Jose, CA 95118, (408) 723-4665. e-mail: LWhita@aolcom.

Club: The Tennis Collectors Society, Guildhall Orchard, Mary Lane North, Great Bromley, Colchester, Essex, C07 7TU U.K.

Bancroft, "Professional," red and gold
  with white lettering, USA dome lid . . .45
Borden, Chris Evert picture on can,
  paper label, USA pull tab 40
Dunlop, white, red lettering, USA dome
  lid 15
Dunlop, olive drab, black lettering, USA
  flat lid 175
Dunlop, 4 ball disc lid can, red and
  white, English 175
Faultless, 1 ball cardboard box, all
  weather ball 100
Macy's, white and black with gold USLTA
  emblem, USA dome lid 40
Nassau, green and white with palm
  trees, Korea 40
Pennsylvania, old country club and
  antique car, USA flat lid 225
Po-Do, 12 ball can, green with silhouette
  of dog's head .600
Rex, brown with white lettering, USA
  dome lid 40
Slazenger, yellow at top and bottom
  with green middle, "Nylon Armoured,"
  English 15
Spalding, red with white diagonal
  lettering, USA dome lid 35
Spencer Moulton, light blue with white
  lettering, 6 ball English box, 1933 100

Left: Dunlop, Championship Yellow, USA, dome lid, $15. Right: Slazenger, England, "Nylon-Armoured," $15.

Victor, blue with white ball on front,
  USA dome lid .80
Wards, cardboard can, red with black
  lettering 180
Wilson, "Thos. E Wilson," multicolored,
  "Patented July 20, 1926," USA flat
  lid 800
Wilson, cardboard can, white with blue
  lettering, "1946" 150
Wilson, 12 ball can, International, Don
  Budge, black, orange, blue, white . . .800
Wright & Ditson, clear plastic bag
  holding 3 balls, 1945 200

TEXTILES

Period fabrics are hot. Individuals are buying bolts of cloth from the 1920s through the 1970s and using them to create a wide range of "period" decorative accessories ranging from draperies to slip covers. The more the pattern speaks decade, i.e., you cannot help thinking Forties, Fifties, etc., when you see it, the higher its value.

Every type of fabric is hot—from chenille to polyester. Every form is hot—from bedspreads to table linens. Do not worry who made or designed it. If it has pizzazz, that is enough.

This category is about using, not displaying.

Bedroom Set, chenille matching bed
  spread, 4 curtain panels, and rug,
  cowboy motif with bucking bronco,
  corral fencing, branding irons, boots,
  pistols, horseshoes, and longhorn
  steer heads, multicolor on light butterscotch ground, 100 x 105" bedspread,
  86 x 38" curtain panels, 43 x 25" rug,
  price for set .300

Bedspread, chenille, multicolored on light beige ground, central cowboy wearing green hat, red neckerchief, yellow shirt, blue pants and holding rifle mounted on brown and white palomino, pistol and horseshoe at pillow, red rope border, twin size 40

Bedspread, chenille, pink and white, center snowflake and flower medallion, floral spray at foot, swags and bows on sides, full size, few minor tears 25

Bedspread, chenille, rows of curlicues arranged in a diamond pattern, dark brown and white on lighter brown ground, full size, 90 x 100" 35

Bedspread, miniature mint green and light blue rosebuds arranged in a checkerboard pattern on white ground, white fringe, 80 x 112" 150

Bedspread, pale yellow chenille design on darker yellow satin ground, star and scroll medallion in center and at pillow, swags and bows border, full size, few minor tears 50

Curtains, 2 panels, broadcloth, collage of safari animals in gold and brown tones, 1960s-70s, 24 x 46" panel 30

Curtains, 4 panels, bark cloth, ivory lining, large flowers and leaves design, ivory lining, 1950s, 43 x 42" panel 30

Curtains, 6 panels, blue and white fern design, 44 x 74" panel 150

Dresser Scarf, multicolored embroidery on white ground, 2 southern belles holding flower garlands, 43 x 18" 15

Dresser Scarf, multicolored embroidery on white ground, dog sitting beneath flower arbor and looking up at bluebird, crocheted border, 36 x 17" 15

Tablecloth, cotton, printed blue, red, yellow, and green on white ground, cross stitched design with trains and flowers, 48" sq 20

Tablecloth, linen, orange and yellow sailboats and lighthouses on white ground, 44 x 47" 35

Tablecloth, linen, red and gray grapes, leaves, and wheat stalks on white ground, 45 x 48" 12

Tablecloth, printed blue, red, yellow, and green on white ground, center checkerboard design with fruits, flowers, and teapots, wide border with couples engaged in various homey activities such as cooking, cleaning, napping, etc., outer blue band border with fruits, flowers and a coffeepot in each corner, 1950s, 50.5 x 46" 20

Tea Towel, linen, black and gray dogs on bright pink ground, sgd "Tammie S. Keefe" 15

Tea Towel, linen, souvenir of Edinburgh, map of Edinburgh with tourist attractions, 1950s, 22 x 31" 6

Tea Towel, linen, turquoise and white, hanging teacups and saucers design, 1950s-60s, 15.5 x 30" 8

Throw Rug, chenille, rect, red, brown, yellow, and green light beige ground, saddle in center, boot in each corner, rope border, 46 x 24" 35

Tea Towel, cotton, multicolored print, man playing banjo, 1950s, 28 x 16", $10. —Photo courtesy Ray Morykan Auctions.

Tablecloth, cotton, fruit and flowers motif, c1940s, 45" sq, $15. —Photo courtesy Ray Morykan Auctions.

THERMOMETERS

The thermometer was a popular advertising giveaway and promotional item. Buy only thermometers in very good or better condition that have a minimum of wear on the visible surface. Remember, thermometers had large production runs. If the first example you see does not please you, shop around.

Club: Thermometer Collectors Club of America, 6130 Rampart Dr., Carmichael, CA 95608.

Cherry Smash, tin, "Drink Cherry Smash/ A True Fruit Blend," 1940-50s, 9" d . . .375
Coca-Cola, tin, "Drink Coca-Cola/Sign of Good Taste," 1950s, 8 x 30" 425
Double Cola, tin, "Drink Double Cola/ You'll like it better," 5 x 17" 140
David Harum Flour, wooden, "David Harum Flour/David Harum Feed," dated 1937, 3 x 12" 65
Fin & Feather Boots and Shoes, emb tin, 4.5 x 14" 110
Frostie Root Beer, tin, "Drink Frostie Root Beer/A Real Taste Treat," 1940s, 8.5 x 36" 425
Golden Sun Coffee, porcelain, "Golden Sun Coffee Is Always Good/Buy Coffee Of Your Grocer Only" dated 1915, 2.75 x 11.5" 385
Kurtz Bros School Supplies, copper plated housing, scene of Clearfield PA factory, 9" d 225

Silhouette Picture, multicolor portraits on black ground, thermometer in center, adv at bottom, 1960 calendar pad on back, DL Line, 6 x 8", $12.

Peter's Weatherbird Shoes, porcelain, c1915, 27" h, $175. —Photo courtesy Collectors Auction Services.

Mail Pouch Tobacco, porcelain, "Chew Mail Pouch Tobacco/Treat Yourself To The Best," 1930-40s, 5 x 14" 425
Nature's Remedy, porcelain, "NR To-Night Tomorrow Allright/Come In/If you get it here it's good," 7 x 27" 175
Sunbeam Bread, tin, "Reach For Sunbeam Bread/Let's Be Friends," 1957, 12" d 575
Tums, aluminum, "Tums for the Tummy/Tums Quick Relief for Acid Indigestion Heartburn," 4 x 9" 55
Vaughn's Bread, tin, "Vaughn's Dainty Bread/Sign of Quality/Sanitary Bakery," 1940-50s, 6 x 24" 140
Waller Bros, metal, "Waller Bros. Judsonia Ark./Phone 78F2/The Honest Strawberry Plant Growers, 6 x 15" . . .250

TICKET STUBS

Next time you attend a paying event, don't throw away that ticket stub! It may be worth something in twenty years.

Abbott & Costello, ABC radio program, blue printing on dark blue ground, late 1940s, 1.5 x 4" 10
Alice Cooper, May 13, 1973 concert at San Diego Sports Arena, black printing on light red ground, 1.5 x 3.5" 15
Batman's Adam West, All Star Show, Shea Stadium, Flushing, NY, Jun 25, 1966, blue printing on off-white ground, , 1.5 x 6.25" 75
Biehl's Moving Pictures, black printing on orange cardboard, pre-1920s, 1.75 x 3.5" 10
Cardinals vs Montreal Expos, Busch Stadium, St Louis, Sep 27, 1998 35

Baseball, 1924 World Series, 7th and deciding game, $450.

Muhammad Ali vs George Foreman, reserved seat for closed circuit TV viewing in Convention Hall, Miami Beach, Sep 24, 1974, black printing on green ground with image of each boxer 40

New York Yankees, American League Baseball Club of New York, grand-stand, 1930s 5

Reagan/Bush Inauguration, Jan 21, 1981, stiff paper, red, blue, and black letter-ing on silver ground, red outlined eagle in center, 2.75 x 7.25" 20

Rocky Marciano vs Jersey Joe Walcott, Chicago Stadium, Apr 10, 1953, upper ringside seat, blue and red on pink ground with bluetone photo, 2 x 6" ...40

The Adventures of Ozzie and Harriet, CBS radio program, Jun 9, 1948, black printing on green ground 20

The Mel Blanc Show, CBS radio program, "Colgate Toothpowder Presents The Mel Blanc Show," Sep 24, 1946, blue printing on front, black printing on back, pink ground 20

TINS

The advertising tin has always been at the forefront of advertising collectibles. Look for examples with no deterioration to the decorated surfaces and little or no signs of rust on the insides or bottoms.

The theme sells the tin. Other collec-tors, especially individuals from the trans-portation fields, have long had their eyes on the tin market. Tins also play a major part in the Country Store decorating look. Prices for pre-1940 tins are still escalating. Before you pay a high price for a tin, do your home-work and make certain it is difficult to find.

Club: Tin Container Collectors Assoc., P.O. Box 440101, Aurora, CO 80044.

Astor House Coffee, 1 lb, screw top, 4 x 6.25" 185

Beech-Nut Coffee, sample key wind, 3.25 x 2.5" 55

Bomb-Buster Popcorn, paper label, 2.5 x 5" 65

Cavalier Plug Tobacco, attached labor union sticker, 6.25 x 3 x 1.5" 90

Dupont Superfine HF Gunpowder, 1 lb, 4 x 6 x 1.5" 45

Eagle Coffee, continental Can Co, screw top, 4 x 6" 100

Farmers Pride Rubbed Sage, paper label, 2.25 x 3 x 1" 45

Golden West Coffee, Closset & Devers, Portland, OR, 2 lb, keywind, dated 1927, 5 x 7" 150

Heart's Delight Coffee, Scoville, Brown & Co, Wellsville, NY, 1 lb 90

Himyar Cigarette Tobacco, cigarette papers under tax stamp, 14 oz, 5.25 x 6.5" 125

Lady Adams Oysters, Mebius & Drescher Co, Sacramento, CA, paper label, 2.75 x 4.25" 90

Light Sweet Burley Tobacco, 8.5 x 10.75" 215

McCormick's Tea, 1 lb, dated 1936, 3.75 x 3.75 x 6" 45

Monadnock Peanut Butter, The Holbrook Grocery Co, Keene, NH, 3.75 x 3.5" ..200

Parrot and Monkey Baking Powder, Sea Gull Specialty Co, Baltimore & New Orleans, paper label, 2.5 x 5" 55

Ox-Heart Peanut Butter, Oswego Candy Works, 1 lb, 3.75 x 3.75", $265. —Photo courtesy Past Tyme Pleasures.

Uncle Sam Shoe Polish, 3.75 x 1.5", $130. —Photo courtesy Past Tyme Pleasures.

Perfect Coffee, A H Perfect & Co, 1 lb, screw top, dated 1923, 4 x 6" 75

Popeye White Hulless Pop Corn, dated 1949 King Features, 3 x 4.75 x 2" 75

Red Wolf Coffee, Ridenour Baker Grocer Co, Kansas City, MO, 1 lb, 5 x 4" 225

Sam Toy Talcum, Metal Pkg Co, Brooklyn, NY, 2.5 x 4.5 x 1.75" 75

Ward's Talcum Powder, Bullock Ward Co, Chicago, 2.5 x 4 x 1.5" 150

Winchester After Shave Talc, Jolind Dist, NY, man and dog graphics, 2.75 x 4.75 x 1'" 200

TOBACCO COLLECTIBLES

The tobacco industry is under siege. Fortunately, they have new frontiers to conquer in Russia, Eastern Europe, Asia, and Africa. The relics of America's smoking past, from ashtrays to humidors, are extremely collectible. Many individuals are not able to identify a smoking stand or a pocket cigar cutter. Today, tobacco growing and manufacturing have virtually disappeared. Is it possible that there will be a time when smoking disappears as well?

Clubs: Cigar Label Collectors International, P.O. Box 66, Sharon Center, OH 44274; International Seal, Label, and Cigar Band Society, 8915 E. Bellevue St, Tucson, AZ 85715; Society of Tobacco Jar Collectors, 3011 Falstaff Rd. #307, Baltimore, MD 21209; Tin Tag Collectors Club, Rte. 2 Box 55, Pittsburg, TX 75686.

Newsletter: *The Cigar Label Gazette,* P.O. Box 3, Lake Forest, CA 92630.

Charm, diecut brass, raised relief image of trademark bull for Bull Durham Tobacco, early 1900s 8

Cigar Box, Monte Carlo, 7.5 x 5.75 x 3.25" 10

Cigar Box Label, Amo Ortiz, Tampa, FL ..10

Cigar Box Label, Mississippi River Crooks 3

Cigar Box Opener, metal, R G Sullivan Inc, Manchester, NH, 8" l 10

Cigarette Album, Duke's Cigarettes, Governors, Coats of Arms, 16 pp 95

Cigarette Card, Allen and Ginter, World's Racers, 15 cards, 1888 85

Cigarette Card, D Buchner & Co, Police Inspectors, Capts and Chiefs of Fire Dept, 14 cards, 1888 350

Cigarette Card, Duke's Cigarettes, Yacht Colors of the World, 25 cards, 1890 ..110

Cigarette Dispenser Case, metal, Art Deco, black enamel with silver accent motif, 1930s, .75 x 3 x 4" 45

Display, Zig Zag Cigarette Papers 10

Lapel Stud, celluloid on metal, "Stop at Yates Hotel and Smoke High Admiral," c1896...........................8

Money Clip, white enamel on chromed steel, replica Chesterfield Cigarettes pack on each side, Robbins Co, 1950s 20

Pinback Button, "I Smoke Zephyrs," central red sun background, 1930s ...12

Pinback Button, Willie Penguin separating political party symbols of donkey and elephant under inscription "In Either Case-Keep Kool," 1930s 18

Pocket Mirror, Mascot Tobacco, multi-colored dog image, red lettering on white 60

Pocket Mirror, "Smoke Union Made Cigars," celluloid, blue union label on tan ground, black lettering, Cigar Makers Union #33 on rim curl ..85

Tin, Pedro Smoking Tobacco, lunch box type, 4.5 x 7.75 x 5", $125. —Photo courtesy Gene Harris Antique Auction Center, Inc.

Display, Philip Morris Cigarettes, diecut cardboard stand-up, 44" h, 16.5" w, $185. —Photo courtesy Collectors Auction Services.

Tin, Union Leader Smoking Tobacco, red, gold and white lettering, repeated eagle emblem, 6" h 20
Tin, Van Bibber Pipe Tobacco, 2.5 x 4.5 x 1" 65

TOKENS

Token collecting is an extremely diverse field. The listing below barely scratches the surface with respect to the types of tokens one might find.

The wonderful thing about tokens is that, on the whole, they are very inexpensive. You can build an impressive collection on a small budget. Like match cover and sugar packet collectors, token collectors have kept their objects outside the main collecting stream. This has resulted in stable, low prices over a long period of time in spite of an extensive literature base. There is no indication that this is going to change in the near future.

Clubs: American Numismatic Assoc, 818 N. Cascade Ave., Colorado Springs, CO 80903; Token and Medal Society, Inc., P.O. Box 366, Bryantown, MD 20617.

B Stotts Pool Hall, Cody, NE, bronze 10
Buzzards Roost Cigar Store, Hilger Bros, aluminum 4
Centennial, Liberty Bell/Independence Hall 35
Co-Operative Cigar Star, York, PA, bronze 10
Duval Jewelry Co, 1937, aluminum 25
Exchange Hotel, Oil City, PA, 5¢ Bottle Check, aluminum 5

Duquesne Brewing Co, Pittsburgh, PA, aluminum keychain, "Keep Me And Never Go Broke, 1948D penny, $12.

Farmers National Bank, Pennsburg, PA, 1926 Anniversary, gilt bronze 8
Keystone Dairy, New Kensington, PA, 3¢ Bottle Return, aluminum 6
New York City Transit 1
Ohio Bar, Parkersburg, WV, bronze 4
Oklahoma Railway Co, white metal, "Good For One City Fare," holed, 17mm 2
Owls Social Club, York, PA, aluminum 5
Polk Co, Haines City, FL 5
Souvenir of Dan River Queen, Stuart, VA, nickel 8
Union Dairy Co, bronze 35
Whitehead's Bakery, "5¢ Loaf Bread," aluminum 18
Yacht Club, Chicago, IL, 25¢ In Drinks Only, bronze 8

TOOLS

Every flea market has at least a half dozen tables loaded with tools. The majority are modern tools sold primarily for reuse. However, you may find some early tools thrown in the bunch. Dig through tool boxes and the boxes under the tables. Decorators like primitive tools for hanging on walls in old homes. Other desirable tools include those that are handwrought or heavily trimmed with brass. Names to look for include Stanley, Keen Kutter, and Winchester. Refer to the Stanley and Winchester listings for further information on these brand names.

Club: The Early American Industries Assoc., 167 Bakersville Rd., South Dartmouth, MA 02748.

Newsletter: *Tool Ads,* P.O. Box 33, Hamilton, MT 59840.

Periodical: *The Fine Tool Journal,* 27 Fickett Rd., Pownal, ME 04069.

Bowsaw, beech, boxwood handles,
ebony winder .125
Block Plane, carriage maker's, tapered,
8" l 20
Bullnose Plane, #2509, Preston 50
Chamfer Plane, beech, Preston type,
Sorby 65
Corner Chisel, James Swan 60
Hammer, #1, double headed shoe ham-
mer, patented Jan 7, 1868, graphic,
J Vigeant, Marlboro, MA, 12" l 75
Handrail Plane, McKenzie, 2.375" 50
Level and Plumb, hand wrought, maho-
gany and brass, 43" l stylized arrow
carved on 1 side, 48" l 15
Nail Header, hand wrought by black-
smith, 13.75" l 40
Pianomaker's Brace, French, mahogany
head, full brass baluster 160
Plane, #105, boxed bead molding plane,
Casey and Co, Auburn, NY, 9.5" l 25
Plane, dovetail, with snicker iron and
orig brass skate, Mathieson 150
Plumb Bob, surveyor's, brass, C L Berger
& Sons, Boston, MA, 3" l 60
Rule, hook rule with lumber scales,
Esborn Lumber Corp, NY, adv on
back, 24" l 75
Screwdriver, brass handle inlaid with
ebony and red Bakelite, 9.5" l 10
Sickle, wood handle, iron blade, 21" l . . .20
Spokeshave, nickel plated, Preston, 7" l 100
Stringing Router, with 6 cutters, Preston .65

"American Combined Level and Grade Finder," patented and mfg by Edward Helb, Railroad, York Co., PA, July 12, 1904, 24" l, $285.

Ratchet Wrench, Reliable, 12.5" l 60
Timber Scribe, beech handle, Timmins . .45

TOOTHBRUSH HOLDERS

Forget your standard bathroom cup or mounted wall toothbrush holders. They have no pizzazz. No one collects them.

Collectors want the wonderful ceramic figural toothbrush holders from the 1930s through the 1960s. Images are generation-driven, from a 1920s bisque boy seated on a fence and holding an umbrella to a 1950s high-glazed seated elephant. Licensed characters from comic strips, children's literature, and cartoons, especially Disney, are plentiful. Prices for pre-1940 examples begin around $60 and extend into the hundreds.

If you find these vintage toothbrush holders pricey, consider modern plastic examples, many of which are found in the shapes of licensed characters from children's television shows and comics. Do not overlook figural electrical toothbrush sets. I already have several in my collection.

Boy, playing violin, dog at side, Japan,
5" h 35
Boy, riding spotted elephant, Japan,
6.25" h 50
Cowboy, Japan, 5.25" h 40
Duck, Japan, 5.25" h 50
Frog, playing banjo, Japan, 6" h 50
Humpty Dumpty, bisque, Japan, 5.25" h . .50
Kissing Dutch Couple, Japan, 6" h 50
Little Orphan Annie and Sandy, bisque,
Japan, 4" h 125
Man, wearing derby hat, hands in pock-
ets, Japan, 5" h 50
Oriental Woman with Vase, Japan,
5.25" h 55
Penguin, Japan, 5.5" h 50
Scottie Dogs, Diamond Cleaners adv,
Japan, 5.25" h 70
Soldier, green, red, and black, Japan,
6.75" h 50
The Baker, 2 holes, Japan, 5.25" h 60
The Butcher, 2 holes, Japan, 5.25" h 60
The Candlestick Maker, Japan, 5" h 60
Three Little Pigs, mkd "S155©Walt
Disney," 5.25" h 300
Uncle Walt and Skeezix, Japan, 4" h . . .150

TOOTHPICK HOLDERS

During the Victorian era, the toothpick holder was an important table accessory. It is found in a wide range of materials and was manufactured by American and European firms. Toothpick holders also were popular souvenirs in the 1880 to 1920 period.

Do not confuse toothpick holders with match holders, shot glasses, miniature spoon holders in a child's dish set, mustard pots without lids, rose or violet bowls, individual open salts, or vases. A toothpick holder allows ample room for the toothpick and enough of an extension of the toothpick to allow easy access.

Club: National Toothpick Holder Collectors Society, P.O. Box 417, Safety Harbor, FL 34695.

Carnival Glass, red, tulip shaped, scalloped rim with sawtooth edge, hobstars design, Imperial, 2.5" h, 2.5" d . . .30
Ceramic, figural crowing rooster, red comb, green and red feathers, green base, holes in tail feathers for inserting toothpicks, 4.25" h, 3.75" w 8
Ceramic, figural locomotive, brown glaze, 2" h, 2.5" l 5
Ceramic, red transfer, Quail pattern, oval, Furnival, 2.375" h, 2.625" w 35
Glass, amber, pressed hobstar pattern, goblet shaped, hexagonal pedestal base, mkd "Prescut," 3" h, 2" d 8
Glass, chocolate slag, Cactus pattern . . .20
Glass, cobalt blue with white swirls, sgd "Loetz Austria," 1940s, 2.5" h, 2" d 30

Glass, clear, figural goat-drawn cart, $175.
—Photo courtesy Gene Harris Antique Auction Center, Inc.

Glass, amberina, Thumbprint pattern, 6-sided, 2.25" h, $175.

Glass, jadite, sawtooth edge, raised Indian head above "Saratoga" on front, crossed tomahawks on back, 4-ftd, mkd "Pittsburgh, Pa. 1903," 2.5" h 15
Glass, vaseline, figural bird with holder on its back, 2.75" h 10
Glass, vaseline, Shriners' commemorative, emb and hp emblem and "Pittsburgh 1905" 35
Plastic, clear cylinder with turquoise lid and base, gold finial, plastic toothpicks, 4" h, 1.75" d 6
Soapstone, "See No Evil" monkeys squatting around semi-ovoid holder, China, 2.25" h .12

TORTOISE SHELL ITEMS

It is possible to find tortoise shell items in a variety of forms ranging from boxes to trinkets. Tortoise shell items experienced several crazes in the 19th and early 20th centuries, the last occurring in the 1920s when tortoise shell jewelry was especially popular. Anyone selling tortoise shell objects is subject to the Endangered Species Act and its amendments. Tortoise shell objects can be imported and sold, but only after adhering to a number of strict requirements.

Dresser Set, mirror, comb box, covered jar, and shoe horn, floral motif 25
Fingernail Guard, ornate gold filled mounting, 3.75" l 22
Hand Mirror, oval 110
Humidor, tortoise shell knob on top, 6.5" h 35
Match Safe, pocket, emb sides 65
Pin, pique, yellow gold, silver, domed circle, flat hollow back, floral design, c1860 325
Pocketknife, Dixon, 2.5" l blade 15

Scent Bottle Case, Georgian, arched
cover, convex front and back, 2.5" h .110
Side Comb, cut steel, crown motif, late
Victorian 185
Trinket Box, rect, lacquered, hinged lid,
single drawer, 9.5" l 250

TOYS

The difference between men and boys
is the price of their toys. At thirty one's
childhood is affordable, at forty expensive,
and at fifty out of reach. Check the following
list for toys that you may have played with.
You will see what I mean.

Clubs: Diecast Toy Collectors Assoc., P.O.
Box 1824, Bend, OR 97701; The Antique Toy
Collectors of America, Inc., Two Wall St.,
13th Flr., New York, NY 10005; Toy Car
Collectors Club, 33290 W. 14 Mile Rd. #454,
West Bloomfield, MI 48322.

Periodicals: *Antique Toy World,* P.O. Box
34509, Chicago, IL 60634; *Toy Shop,* 700 E.
State St., Iola, WI 54990.

Note: *Maloney's Antiques & Collectibles
Resource Directory* by David J. Maloney,
Jr., lists many collectors' clubs for specific
types of toys. Check your local library for
the most recent edition.

Alps, Japan, Electric Car with Siren,
friction, litho tin, produces siren noise,
orig box, 1950s, 1.5 x 6 x 2.75" 40
Bandai, 1959 Cadillac, friction, litho tin,
green and light blue, detailed dash-
board, white plastic steering wheel,
3.5 x 11.25 x 3" 350
Chein, Busy Mike Sand Toy, litho tin,
1950s, 2.5 x 7 x 7.25" 40
Courtland, Fire Truck, windup, litho tin,
plastic wheels, 1950s, 3 x 8.5 x 3.25" .100
Haji, Japan, Torpedo Boat, friction, litho
tin, 1950s, 1.25 x 3.5 x 1" 15
Hubley, US Army Plane, cast metal, red
and silver, nickel-plated propeller,
folding wheels, cockpit opens, black
rubber wheels, 1950s, 6 x 8 x 3" 65
James Industries, Slinky Elephant, 2-pc,
hard plastic body, pink, black hat,
soft red plastic wheels, orig box,
1960s, 5.5 x 9.5 x 7.25" 60

*Alps, Japan, Indian Joe, battery operated,
4 actions, orig box, 1960s, 12" h, $90.*

Japan, Central Railway Express Train,
friction, litho tin, 1950s, 1 x 8.5 x 2" . . .35
K, Japan, Torpedo Boat, friction, litho
tin, sparking action, orig box, 1950s,
1.5 x 6 x 1.75" 45
Kanto Toys, Japan, Volkswagen, friction,
litho tin, blue, produces siren noise,
orig box, 1950s, 2.5 x 6 x 2.5" 75
Linemar, Jet, friction, litho tin, USAF/
F-102, repeated star insignia, pilot
in cockpit, 1960s, 3 x 3.5 x 1.5" 30
Mattel, Switch 'N Go Dump Trailer, hard
plastic, orig box, 1966 25
Modern Toys, Xylophone Player, windup,
celluloid xylophone player attached
to painted tin xylophone unit, orig box,
1950s, 3.5 x 4 x 5.75" 175
Nomura Toys, Japan, Combat Soldier,
windup, litho tin, vinyl head, holding
brown plastic rifle, 1960s, 2.5 x 3 x
5.5" 45
Nylint, Street Sprinkler, pressed steel,
white, black and orange decals, 1960s,
6 x 16 x 7" 100
Ohio Art, Coney Island Roller Coaster,
litho tin and plastic, 1960s, 15 x 21 x
3.75" 125
Remco, Johnny Reb Authentic Civil War
Cannon, hard plastic, complete with
accessories, orig box, 1961, 11 x 30
x 12" 100
Taiyo, Japan, Ford Mustang, battery
operated, litho tin, orig box, 1960s,
4 x 10 x 3" 75
TT, Japan, 1909 Ford Touring Car, battery
operated, litho tin, red, black and
gold accents, orig box, 1960s, 3.75 x
6.5 x 4.25" 30

Wyandotte, Humphrey Mobile, litho tin, windup, 7" h, $400. —Photo courtesy James D. Julia, Inc.

Redemption Catalog, S&H Green Stamps, 1927, $15.

Tonka, Pick-Up Truck, pressed steel, dark metallic blue, black rubber tires, plastic windshield and headlights, decal on doors, 5.5 x 13 x 5.5" .... .45

TPS, Japan, Happy Hippo, windup, litho tin, 1950s, 2 x 6 x 5.5" 175

Unique, Gertie the Galloping Goose, windup, litho tin, orig box, 1930s, 3.5 x 9.5 x 4" 100

Western Germany, Longshoreman, windup, litho tin, longshoreman wearing bib overalls and checkered shirt, diecut arms with anchor tattoo, 1950s, 2 x 4.5 x 4.25" 175

Yone, Japan, Happy Grandpa with Ringing Mill, windup, litho tin, parasol spins, bell rings, grandpa rocks back and forth, chickens move, orig box, 1960s, 4" h, 4" d base 100

TRADING STAMPS & RELATED

Trading stamps were offered by retail stores to attract customers and increase sales. The more money spent, the more stamps you could earn. The stamps could be redeemed for merchandise, either from the store that issued the stamps or from redemption centers that offered catalog merchandise. The first independent trading stamp company was set up in 1896. The use of trading stamps has declined, but some companies still give them out to stimulate sales.

Redemption Catalog, Big M Stamps, 1950s 8

Redemption Catalog, Buccaneer Stamps, 1961 8

Redemption Catalog, Double M Trading Stamps, 1958 12

Redemption Catalog, Frontier Saving Stamps, 1957 16

Redemption Catalog, Gold Bond Stamps, 1973 4

Redemption Catalog, Plee-zing Groceries, 1950s 11

Redemption Catalog, S&H Green Stamps, 1958 8

Redemption Catalog, S&H Green Stamps, 1983 6

Redemption Catalog, Top Value Stamps, 1959 6

Redemption Catalog, United Trading Stamps, 1968 4

Redemption Catalog, Yellow Stamps, 1956 10

Sign, Gift Bond, electric, light-up, Aalco Sign Co, 18.5" w, 7.5" h 30

Stamp Saver Books, Quality Stamps, price for 12 6

Stamp Saver Box, wood, wall mount, "Trading Stamps" on top, brass eagle on front, 12" h, 6.75" w 10

TRAINS, TOY

Toy train collectors and dealers exist in a world unto themselves. They have their own shows, trade publications, and price guides. The name you need to know is Greenberg Books, now a division of Kalmbach publishing, 21027 Crossroads Circle, Waukesha, WI 53187. If you decide to get involved with toy trains, write for a catalog. The two most recognized names are American Flyer and Lionel, and the two most popular gauges are S and O. Do not overlook other manufacturers and gauges.

The toy train market has gone through a number of crazes—first Lionel, then American Flyer. The current craze is boxed sets. Fortunately, the market is so broad that there will never be an end to subcategories to collect.

Clubs: American Flyer Collectors Club, P.O. Box 13269, Pittsburgh, PA 15243; Lionel Collector's Club of America, P.O. Box 479, La Salle, IL 61301; Train Collectors Assoc., P.O. Box 248, Strasburg, PA 17579.

Periodical: *Classic Toy Trains,* 21027 Crossroads Circle, P.O. Box 1612, Waukesha, WI 53187.

Note: See the most recent edition of *Maloney's Antiques & Collectibles Resource Directory* by David J. Maloney, Jr., for additional information on other specialized train collector clubs.

American Flyer, boxcar, #33513, B&O, blue and orange 30

American Flyer, caboose, #5160, Union Pacific 15

American Flyer, cattle car, #4020, standard gauge, green and blue 75

American Flyer, double street lamp, #580 20

American Flyer, gondola, #920, Southern, S gauge, black 10

American Flyer, locomotive, #4321, O gauge, 0-6-0, black and white, nickel trim, with tender 70

American Flyer, passenger station, #258, HO gauge 70

American Flyer, Silver Flash Passenger Set, orig box 225

American Flyer, Trestle Bridge, #750, black and yellow 75

Buddy L, stock car, #1004, 3.25" gauge, red 375

Dorfan, coach, Seattle, red and yellow ..20

Dorfan, gondola, #600, narrow gauge ...20

American Flyer, engine and tender, #4663, $330. —Photo courtesy Collectors Auction Services.

Plasticville, School House Kit SC-4, $15.

Dorfan, tank car, light blue 140
Ives, baggage car, #50 75
Ives, bridge, #92-3, standard gauge 50
Ives, gondola, #20, standard gauge 135
Ives, tender, #25, O gauge 150
Ives, transformer, #204 8
Lionel, crossing gate, #152 8
Lionel, Fort Knox Gold reserve car, #6445, silver 65
Lionel, Lamp, #58, cream, orig box 15
Lionel, LV 44 Ton Switcher, #627, red ...70
Lionel, Missile Firing Car, #6544, with 4 rockets, blue, white lettered console .55
Lionel, Santa Fe Blue Stripe Set, O gauge 160
Marklin, Electric Locomotive, #3036, green, orig box 45
Marklin, Swiss Electric Locomotive, #3050, green, orig box 65
Marklin, luggage van, #4017, green, orig box 45
Marx, engine, Wabash boxcar, Southern Pacific passenger car, and cargo car with sliding doors 20
Marx, gondola, tin, Joy Line 30
Marx, hopper, plastic, Huron Portland Cement 2
Marx, locomotive, 0-4-0, plastic 40
Marx, tank car, #256, litho tin 5
Plasticville, Bridge and Pond Unit, BL-2, orig box 15
Plasticville, Colonial Church, 1803, orig box 30
Plasticville, Diner, DE-7, orig box 35
Tootsietoy, Freight Train Set, 4620 locomotive, 4621 tender, 4695 box car, 4696 gondola, 4697 caboose 135
Tootsietoy, tank car, Sinclair Oil 12
Tootsietoy, wrecking crane 15
Tootsietoy, Zephyr Railcar 5
Williams, SP Daylight Streamlined Passenger Car Set, #2612, orig box ..140

TRANSPORTATION

Cars, planes, and trains are the obvious transportation collectibles. They each have their own separate collecting category.

What about the other forms, such as buses and trolleys? They deserve a place in the sun as well. This is a catchall category. Put your token in the box and hop aboard.

Club: National Assoc. of Timetable Collectors, 125 American Inn Rd., Villa Ridge, MO 63089.

Calendar, Greyhound, paper, bus driver and 3 bathing beauties at beach, Greyhound bus in background, "Biscayne Key, Miami, Florida, Color Photo by Ardean R Miller," framed, October 1953 pad, 32" h, 19.5" w 40

Chauffeur's Badge, bronzed metal, rim inscription "Licensed Chauffeur– New York 1913," serial number incised in center, threaded post and disk wheel fastener 15

Game, Toonerville Trolley, Milton Bradley, #4838 120

Pin, taxi telephone number, celluloid, green lettering on white ground, needle post and clutch fastener, 1930s-40s 12

Pinback Button, Gordon Bennett International Balloon Race and Carnival, Cleveland, red, white, and blue, issued for concession worker, 1930 60

Child's Book, Monarchs of the Road, *No. 896, illus by T E North, pub by Birn Bros Ltd, England, 12 pp, c1947, 10.5 x 8.25", $15.*

Advertising Tear Sheet, Greyhound Lines, "Pioneers of Highway Travel 1835 and 1935," 26" h, 20" w, $130. —Photo courtesy Collectors Auction Services.

Pinback Button, "Greater New York Taxi League, blue and white emblem with vintage auto and "Founded 1919" on white ground, white lettering on maroon rim, 1" d 20

Pinback Button, Penboss Bus Tours, turquoise on white, 1950s tour bus image, 1.25" d 5

Sign, Greyhound Lines, paper, "Pioneers of Highway Travel 1835 and 1935," bus image, framed, 20" h, 26" w 125

Ticket, trolley, commemorates Aug 15, 1914 Panama Canal opening, ticket good Aug 9-15, 1937, 3.5 x 2" 80

Toy, double decker bus, battery operated, painted tin, mkd "Bumper Car" on front bumper, Japan, 1960s, 14" l 500

TRAPS

Although trapping is not a well thought of occupation this day and age, we must admit the American trappers of bygone days were the men who opened the West and after whom many towns are named. Trap collecting today is a growing hobby and condition means everything on those old traps. A rusty old Victor trap has very little value, yet please don't sand blast or paint traps that you plan to sell. Let the buyer decide how he wants to clean it. Value is determined by the maker of the trap, condition, and readability of lettering on the pan (where the animal places its foot).

Trap collecting encompasses mouse and rat traps, glass fly and minnow traps, and steel traps from small to large bear traps, as well as paper ephemera such as fur company catalogs and trapping magazines.

Advisor: Tom Parr, P.O. Box 94, Galloway, OH 43119, (614) 878-6011.

Club: North American Trap Collectors Assoc., P.O. Box 94, Galloway, OH 43119.

Bear Trap, Herter's No. 41 AX, 1960s . . .600
Bear Trap, Mackenzie Dist Fur Co,
    currently produced 175
Bear Trap, Newhouse No. 6, with teeth,
    Animal Trap Co 1,500
Catalog, F C Taylor Fur Co, St Louis, MO,
    1923 45
Fish Trap, Swedish Ringsak 500
Hawk Trap, Gibbs, with perch 300
Minnow Trap, Camp, glass, cone-shaped
    holes in glass .95
Mouse Trap, "Delusion" wood box with
    compartment, screen front 50
Mouse Trap, mason jar lid, several types .20
Mouse Trap, Wigington Glass 40
Mouse Trap, wood snap trap with writing .3
Muskrat Stretcher Board, wood, usually
    handmade, uniform, shows use 5
Scent Bottle, with label and wood or
    cardboard shipping container 20
Trap, Victor No. 1, long spring trap 3
Trap, Victor No. 3, double long spring,
    Animal Trap Co 5
Wolf Trap, Newhouse No. 4 1/2, double
    long spring, Animal Trap Co 125

Bear Trap, Triumph #415X, $200.

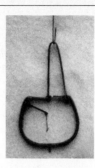

Fish Trap, Gabriel, $300.

Wolf Trap, Newhouse No. 4 1/2, double
    long spring, Oneida Community 300

TRAYS

Tin lithographed advertising trays date back to the last quarter of the 19th century. They were popular at any location where beverages, alcoholic and nonalcoholic, were served.

Because they were heavily used, it is not unusual to find dents and scratches. Check carefully for rust. Once the lithographed surface was broken, rust developed easily.

Smaller trays are generally tip trays. Novice collectors often confuse them with advertising coasters. Tip trays are rather expensive. Ordinary examples sell in the $50 to $75 range.

Arctic Ice Cream, serving tray, polar
    bear, round 975
Bellevue Ice Cream, Green Bay, WI,
    serving tray, ice cream party with
    10 children and puppy, round 675
Buffalo Brewing Co, tip tray, litho by
    Kaufman & Straus, NY, round 275
Burdan's Ice Cream, serving tray, young
    woman holding tray with ice cream,
    round 725
Deer Run Whiskey, serving tray, elk by
    stream, round 275
Fairfield Butter Co, serving tray, 2 children at table with lace cloth, round,
    1915 700
Hires Root Beer, serving tray, "Things
    is getting higher, but Hires are still
    nickel a trickle," round, 1920s 130

Utica Club, West End Brewing Co, Utica, NY, 12" d, $20.

Hoefler Ice Cream, serving tray, young woman eating ice cream, oval, c1915 425

Jersey-Creme, serving tray, round, 12" d .110

Moxie, tip tray, "Drink Moxie/Very Healthful," round, 6" d 90

NuGrape, serving tray, litho by American Art Works, Coshocton, OH, hand holding bottle, rectangular 100

Pepsi-Cola, serving tray, bottle of Pepsi in front of US map, rectangular, 1940s 170

Purity Ice Cream, serving tray, woman eating ice cream, square, 1913 425

Red Raven, serving tray, woman hugging large red raven, round, 12" d . . .100

Sanitary Ice Cream, serving tray, Haskell Coffin artwork, woman serving ice cream, round .500

Velvet Ice Cream, change tray, young woman eating ice cream, oval 275

Zipp's Cherri-o, serving tray, bird sipping drink through straw, round 775

TROPHIES

There are trophies for virtually everything. Ever wonder what happens to them when the receiver grows up or dies? Most wind up in landfills. It is time to do something about this injustice. If you plan on collecting them, focus on shape and unusual nature of the award. Set a $5 limit—not much of a handicap when it comes to trophy collecting. Always check the metal content of trophies. A number of turn-of-the-century trophies are sterling silver. These obviously have monetary as well as historic value. Also consider sterling silver when the trophy is a plate.

TURTLE COLLECTIBLES

Turtle collectors are a slow and steady group who are patient about expanding their collection of objects relating to these funny little reptiles. Don't you believe it! My son is one of those collectors, and he's not at all slow when it come to expanding his collection. Turtle collectibles are everywhere. Like all animal collectibles, they come in all shapes and sizes. Candles, toys, storybooks, jewelry, and ornaments featuring turtles can be found at almost any flea market. Watch out for tortoise shell items. This material is subject to the provisions of the Federal Endangered Species Act.

Note: See Tortoise Shell Items for additional listings.

Ashtray, metal, shell opens to reveal tray, 2.5" h, 8.5" l 30

Brooch, plastic, brown and yellow 3

Cookie Jar, Donatello, Teenage Mutant Ninja Turtles, Mirage Studios 35

Covered Dish, Anchor Hocking, 4.5" l, 3.25" h 4

Doorstop, cast iron, Wilton, 3 x 8.75" 65

Figure, earthenware, brown, Japan 1

Flask, ground top, 6" l 65

Paperweight, cast iron, Fire Insurance adv on celluloid insert on hinged shell lid, int mirror, early 1900s, 4" l . .150

Pin, red Bakelite, brass wire accents, 1940s, 2.75 x 1.375" 25

Planter, white, McCoy, 5.5" h, 4" w 15

Salt and Pepper Shakers, pr, metal 10

Covered Dish, turtle finial, white milk glass, $210. —Photo courtesy Gene Harris Antique Auction Center, Inc.

Figurine, green sea turtle, Red Rose Tea premium, Wade, $3.

String Holder, cast iron, 6" l, 4.5" h ..... .35
Toothpick Holder, child holding umbrella
 seated on turtle, SP, Pairpoint ..... .175

TYPEWRITERS

The number of typewriter collectors is small, but growing. Machines made after 1915 have little value, largely because they do not interest collectors. Do not use the patent date on a machine to date its manufacture. Many models were produced for decades. Do not overlook typewriter ephemera. Early catalogs are helpful in identifying and dating machines.

Clubs: Internationales Forum Historishe Burowelt, Postfach 500 11 68, D-5000 Koln-50, Germany; Early Typewriter Collectors Assoc., P.O. Box 641824, Los Angeles, CA 90064.

Newsletters: *Ribbon Type News,* 28 The Green, Watertown, CT 06795; *The Typewriter Exchange,* P.O. Box 62607, Philadelphia, PA 19115.

Advertising Tear Sheet, "Shh! The New
 Royal Electric Speaks Softly," woman
 with hand behind ear standing behind
 typewriter, 10 x 13" 3
Letterhead, Chicago Writing Machine
 Co, "Manufacturers of 'The Chicago'
 Typewriters, 151-153 Wabash Avenue,
 Chicago, USA," dated 3-23-1905 ..... .10
Pamphlet, "The Business Economy of
 the Typewriter" 5
Ribbon Tin, Osborn 5
Ribbon Tin, Remtico 8
Typewriter, Carissima, Bakelite housing
 and lid, 1934 ..... .200
Typewriter, Corona Folding, #3, 1912 .... .90
Typewriter, Densmore, #4, 1898 ..... .365
Typewriter, Erika Folding, 1910 ..... .35
Typewriter, Empire, 1892 ..... .200

Ribbon Tin, Serv-U, 2.625" d, $75. —Photo courtesy Wm. Morford.

Typewriter, Harris Visible, #4, c1913 .... .315
Typewriter, International Electromatic,
 IBM, 1930 ..... .120
Typewriter, LC Smith & Bros, 1904 ..... .60
Typewriter, Macy's Portable, 4-row,
 1920 ..... .50
Typewriter, Monarch Pioneer, 1932 .... .100
Typewriter, Rem-Blick, 1928 ..... .325
Typewriter, Remie Scout, 1932 ..... .325
Typewriter, Remington Noiseless, #6,
 1925 ..... .125
Typewriter, Royal Model 1, 1906 ..... .225
Typewriter, Smith Premier, #10, 1907 .... .50
Typewriter, Woodstock, 1914 ..... .45

UMBRELLAS

Umbrellas suffer a sorry fate. They are generally forgotten and discarded. Their handles are removed and collected as separate entities or attached to magnifying glasses. Given the protection they have provided, they deserve better.

Look for umbrellas that have advertising on the fabric. Political candidates often gave away umbrellas to win votes. Today baseball teams have umbrella days to win fans.

Seek out unusual umbrellas in terms of action or shape. A collection of folding umbrellas, especially those from the 1950s, is worth considering.

Advertising, *The Morning Call,* Allentown,
 PA, newspaper, comic strip characters,
 unused ..... .25

UNITED STATES MARINE CORPS

Recruiting
Poster,
WWI, $350.

A recent survey indicated that there are currently over 2,000,000 former United States Marines. Not many of these former (never "ex") Marines can—or will—allow the U.S.M.C. insignia, commonly referred to as the "Eagle, Globe and Anchor," to go unnoticed when they see it today. It may be found on the cover of a book or magazine, the side of a toy truck or train, on a recruiting or movie poster, printed or embroidered on wall hangings or tapestries or on many other formats. A great many of these former Marines and countless other militaria collectors are constantly in search of almost any items that relate to or were used at some point by U.S. Marines. Toy soldiers, Guidebooks for Marines, toys of all types, U.S.M.C. or the Eagle, Globe and Anchor are all in demand to these collectors. Some of these items have little monetary value, but whether it be monetary or sentimental worth, collectors of United States Marine memorabilia are out in great numbers. If you have any of the above mentioned items or others not listed and would like to dispose of them, please let me know. Semper Fidelis!

Advisor: Stan Clark, 915 Fairview Ave, Gettysburg, PA 17325, (717) 337-1728, Fax (717) 337-0581, e-mail: scmb@blazenet.net

Autograph, General Smedley D Butler . .75
Book, *Guidebook for Marines,* 1952 65
Book, *Marine: Life of Chesty Puller,*
   1st edition 35
Book, *The Old Breed: History of 1st*
   Marine Division in WWII 100
Bookends, pr, Iwo Jima 35

Helmet, WWI with painted patch and
   EGA 200
Movie Poster, *Come on Leathernecks,*
   27 x 41" 250
Movie Poster, *Gung Ho,* 27 x 41" 150
Movie Poster, *Halls of Montezuma,* 27
   x 41" 65
Photograph, sgd by Commandant 25
Photograph, yard-long, WWI Marines
   in training 75
Postcard, real photo, marines in uniform,
   1906-30s 15
Ring, man's, WWI era, Tun Tavern/Iwo
   Jima 40
Identification Bracelet, marine's, WWII .45
Recruiting Poster, "We Don't Promise
   You A Rose Garden" 75
Toy Soldier, AIM Mounted Marines, orig
   box 150
Trench Art, sketched USMC emblem
   on shell 100

Recruiting
Poster,
WWI, $250.

UNIVERSAL POTTERY

Universal Potteries of Cambridge, Ohio, was organized in 1934 by The Oxford Pottery Company.

Three of Universal's most popular lines were Ballerina, Calico Fruit, and Cattail. Unfortunately, the Calico Fruit decal has not held up well over time. Collectors may have to settle for less than perfect pieces.

Not all Universal pottery carried the Universal name as part of the backstamp. Wares marked "Harmony House," "Sweet William/Sears Roebuck and Co.," and "Wheelock Peoria" are part of the Universal production line. Wheelock was a department store in Peoria, Illinois, that controlled the Cattail pattern on the Old Holland shape.

Upico, water jug, blue and white, red cap, 8.25" h, $35.
—Photo courtesy Ray Morykan Auctions.

Ballerina, bread and butter plate, dove gray	.4
Ballerina, chop plate, dove gray, 13" w	.12
Ballerina, creamer and open sugar, forest green	.10
Ballerina, cup and saucer, black	.6
Ballerina, dinner plate, dove gray, 10" d	.5
Ballerina, luncheon plate, jade green, 9" d	.4
Ballerina, salt and pepper shakers, pr, burgundy salt, dove gray pepper	.10
Ballerina, serving bowl, periwinkle	.15
Ballerina Magnolia, creamer	.8
Ballerina Magnolia, cup and saucer	.8
Ballerina Magnolia, dinner plate, 10.125" d	.8
Ballerina Mist, cup and saucer	.3
Ballerina Mist, dinner plate, 10" d	.8
Ballerina Mist, pitcher, 7.5" h	.20
Ballerina Mist, salt and pepper shakers, pr, 3" h	.15
Ballerina Woodvine, berry bowl, 5.5" d	.2
Ballerina Woodvine, luncheon plate, 9.125" d	.25
Bittersweet, casserole	.20
Bittersweet, pitcher	.15
Bittersweet, salt and pepper shakers, pr, range size	.20
Bittersweet, tilt pitcher	.55
Calico Fruit, bowl, 4" d	.12
Calico Fruit, cake plate	.30
Calico Fruit, pie plate	.35
Calico Fruit, shaker	.8

Cattail, casserole, cov	.65
Cattail, creamer	.15
Cattail, gravy and underplate	.55
Cattail, pie plate	.12
Cattail, salad fork and spoon	.30
Cattail, vegetable, 9.5" d	.20
Circus, bowl, 6.5" d	.18
Circus, milk pitcher, 5" h	.30
Circus, platter, oval, handled, 13" l	.18
Hollyhock, chop plate	.25
Hollyhock, dinner plate	.8
Hollyhock, vegetable	.20
Upico, ball jug, brown and white, 7" h	.25
Upico, casserole, cov, blue and white, 8.5" d	.15
Upico, salt and pepper shakers, pr, blue	.10
Upico Ivory, bowl, cov, triple rose decal, 5" d	.15
Upico Ivory, dinner plate, floral decal, 10.25" d	.4
Upico Ivory, dinner plate, triple rose decal, 10.5" d	.4
Upico Ivory, serving bowl, floral decal, 8" d	.4

URINALS

When you gotta go, you gotta go—any port in a storm. You have been in enough bathrooms to know that all plumbing fixtures are not equal.

The human mind has just begun to explore the recycling potential of hospital bedpans. Among the uses noted are flower planters, food serving utensils, and dispersal units at the bottom of down spouts. How have you used them? Send your ideas and pictures of them in action to the Bedpan Recycling Project, 5093 Vera Cruz Road, Emmaus, PA 18049.

VALENTINES

There is far too much emphasis placed on adult valentines from the 19th century through the 1930s. It's true they are lacy and loaded with romantic sentiment. But, are they fun? No!

Fun can be found in children's valentines, a much neglected segment of the valentine market. Focus on the 1920 through 1960 period penny valentines. The artwork is bold, vibrant, exciting, and a tad corny. This is what makes them fun.

There is another good reason to collect 20th century children's valentines. They are affordable. Most sell for less than $2, with many good examples in the 50¢ range. They often show up at flea markets as a hoard. When you find them, make an offer for the whole lot. You won't regret it.

Club: National Valentine Collectors Assoc., P.O. Box 1404, Santa Ana, CA 92702.

Greeting Card, baseball player, mechanical, "I catch for keeps, My Valentine," arms move, easel back 10
Greeting Card, boy playing harmonica mechanical, eyes move, "If my Valentine you'll be, we'll have perfect harmony" 5
Greeting, donkey, mechanical, lower jaw moves, "Hee-Haw say I because you're wise, you've shaken all the other guys" 5
Greeting Card, fan, mechanical, fold-out, girl on heart, Gabrial & Sons 25

Catalog, Comic Valentines For 1881, black and white, 12 pp, 8.25 x 5.25", $60. —Photo courtesy Collectors Auction Services.

Puzzle, "A Valentine For You," Hallmark, 1940s, 6.5 x 5.25", cloth mailing sack, $40.

Greeting Card, figural heart, cover plain 2-tone red, opens, girl with basket of flowers, gold gild 20
Greeting Card, girl with dog, diecut, easel back, unsgd, Twelvetrees 20
Greeting Card, girl with rose cheeks seated on chair, easel back, "To Cora from Maynard," 5.25 x 5.75" 8
Greeting Card, "Happy Valentine's Day from Dick, Jane, and Sally" 20
Greeting Card, Lov-O-Gram, opens, pig pops up, ring master, unsgd, Twelvetrees 12
Greeting Card, Victorian boy in clover with heart, diecut 15
Postcard,"Valentine's Greetings," band across center with emb hearts and flowers, John Winsch, ©1912, printed in Germany, postmarked Feb 13, 1913, Milwaukee, WI 8

VENTRILOQUIST DUMMIES

Ventriloquist dummies have been very popular throughout the last sixty years. Although ventriloquism dates back to ancient times, it really wasn't popular until Edgar Bergen and Charlie McCarthy made their debut in the 1930s. Ironically their show aired on the radio.

Charlie's popularity prompted the production of many licensed articles including tin toys by Marx, puppets, dummies, glasses, spoons, books, soap, records, pins, paddle balls, and games. While all these items are collectible, the composition dummies and puppets are especially desirable. Objects depicting Mortimer Snerd and Effie Klinker, two more of Edgar's creations, are also sought after by collectors.

Paul Winchell's television series, Winchell/Mahoney Time, was broadcast during the 1950s. Following his success with Jerry Mahoney, Winchell added sidekick Knucklehead Smiff. Ventriloquist Jimmy Nelson introduced Danny O'Day and Farfel (later the Nestle's Chocolate dog) on the Milton Berle Texaco Star Theatre Show. Both these popular shows resulted in a host of licensed products.

A wide range of ventriloquism memorabilia, from photos and playbills to dummies and toys, can be found at flea markets and antiques shows.

Advisor: Andy Gross, P.O. Box 6134, Beverly Hills, CA 90212-1134, (310) 820-3308, e-mail: pop@LAmagictoy.com.

Note: Listings are for items MIB.

VENTRILOQUIST DUMMIES

Charlie McCarthy, Juro 75
Daniel Boon Dummy Dan, moving eyes .285
Danny O'Day, Texaco uniform, composition, Brooklyn Mass Co 800
Howdy Doody, Ideal 350
Humphrey Higsby, composition, Brooklyn Mass Co 800
Jerry Mahoney, moving eyes, Juro, c1955 950
Jerry Mahoney, Paul Winchell Co, ©1966, 24" h .575
Knucklehead Smiff, composition, Juro 1,900
Knucklehead Smiff, Paul Winchell Co, ©1966, 24" h .575
Mortimer Snerd, Juro 75

RELATED ITEMS

Book, *Ventriloquism for Fun and Profit*, by Paul Winchell, hard cover, dj, c1954 100
Brooch, Charlie McCarthy, mechanical .275
Carnival Chalkware Statue, Charlie McCarthy 170
Flexi Doll, Mortimer Snerd, Ideal, c1938 300
Hand Puppet, Charlie McCarthy, composition, Ideal 175
Hand Puppet, Farfel the dog, Juro Co . .325
Hand Puppet, Jerry Mahoney, Paul Winchell Co, 1966 130

Ventriloquist Dummy, Gerry Gee, composition, Australia, $800.

Hand Puppet, Knucklehead Smiff, Paul Winchell Co, 1966 130
Hand Puppet, Mortimer Snerd, composition, Ideal 200
Puppet, Mortimer Snerd, cardboard, moving mouth and eyes, c1938 160
Soap, Charlie McCarthy 100
Toy, Charlie McCarthy, windup, tin, Marx, c1937 .650
Toy, Mortimer Snerd, windup, tin, Marx, c1937 650
Toy, Mortimer Snerd Trick Car, windup, tin, Marx, c1938 600

VERNON KILNS

Founded in Vernon, California, in 1912, Poxon China was one of the many small potteries flourishing in southern California. By 1931 it was sold to Faye G. Bennison and renamed Vernon Kilns.

The high quality and versatility of its product made Vernon ware very popular. Besides a varied dinnerware line, Vernon Kilns also produced Walt Disney figurines and advertising, political, and fraternal items. Another popular line was historical and commemorative plates, which included several plate series featuring scenes from England, California missions, and the West.

Surviving the Depression, fires, earthquakes, and wars, Vernon Kilns could not compete with the influx of imports. In January, 1958, the factory was closed. Metlox Potteries of Manhattan Beach, California, bought the trade name, molds, and remaining stock.

Newsletter: *Vernon Views,* P.O. Box 945, Scottsdale, AZ 85252.

1860, coffeepot, 8 cup 50
1860, dinner plate, 10.5" d 12
1860, saucer 4
1860, soup bowl, 8" d 15
Arcadia, bread and butter plate, 7" d 3
Brown Eyed Susan, cup and saucer 5
Brown Eyed Susan, salad plate 5
Commemorative Plate, General Douglas
    MacArthur 5
Commemorative Plate, Lions Club
    International Convention, 1950 4
Commemorative Plate, state of Indiana .15
Cypress Gardens, plate, 10.25" d 8
Gingham, butter, cov 35
Gingham, salt and pepper shakers, pr . . .4
Hibiscus, coffeepot, cov 75
Homespun, berry bowl 3
Homespun, bowl, flat tab handles 10
Homespun, cup .2
Homespun, pitcher, 2 qt, 11.5" h 35
Homespun, porridge bowl 50
Homespun, sugar, cov 8
Homespun, vegetable bowl, divided 10
Lei Lani, bowl, 5.625" d 15
Lei Lani, saucer, 6" d 18
Monterey, creamer 5
Monterey, cup 6
Orchard, creamer, 3" h 8
Orchard, cup and saucer 4
Orchard, soup bowl 6
Organdie, bread and butter plate 4
Organdie, chop plate 5
Organdie, creamer and sugar 6
Organdie, fruit bowl, 5.5" d 3
Organdie, luncheon plate, 9.5" d 4
Rio Verde, chop plate 20

1860 Pattern, soup tureen, San Fernando shape, brown transfer of 1860s American canal scene, 1944, 13" d, $300.

Commemorative Plate, Will Rogers, red transfer dec, 10.5" d, $16.

Tickled Pink, dinner plate 8
Tickled Pink, pitcher, 2 qt, 9.75" h 45
Tickled Pink, salad plate 10

VIDEO GAMES

At the moment, most video games sold at a flea market are being purchased for reuse. There are a few collectors, but their numbers are small.

It might be interesting to speculate at this point on the long-term collecting potential of electronic children's games, especially since the Atari system has come and gone. The key to any toy is playability. A video game cartridge has little collecting value unless it can be played. As a result, the long-term collecting value of video games will rest on collectors' ability to keep the machines that use them in running order. Given today's tendency to scrap rather than repair a malfunctioning machine, one wonders if there will be any individuals in 2041 that will understand how video game machines work and, if so, be able to get the parts required to play them.

Next to playability, displayability is important to any collector. How do you display video games? Is the answer to leave the TV screen on twenty-four hours a day?

Video games are a fad waiting to be replaced by the next fad. There will always be a small cadre of players who will keep video games alive, just as there is a devoted group of adventure game players. But given the number of video game cartridges sold, they should be able to fill their collecting urges relatively easily.

What this means is that if you are going to buy video game cartridges at a flea market, buy them for reuse and do not pay more than a few dollars. The more recent the game, the more you will pay. Wait. Once a few years have passed, the sellers will just be glad to get rid of them.

VIEW-MASTER

William Gruber invented and Sawyer's Inc., of Portland, Oregon, manufactured and marketed the first View-Master viewers and reels in 1939. The company survived the shortages of World War II by supplying training materials in the View-Master format to the army and navy.

Immediately following World War II a 1,000-dealer network taxed the capacity of the Sawyer plant. In 1946 the Model C, the most common of the viewers, was introduced. Sawyer was purchased by General Aniline & Film Corporation in 1966. After passing through other hands, View-Master wound up as part of Ideal Toys.

Do not settle for any viewer or reel in less than near-mint condition. Original packaging, especially reel envelopes, is very important. The category is still in the process of defining which reels are valuable and which are not. Most older, pre-1975, reels sell in the 50¢ to $1 range.

Club: National Stereoscopic Assoc., P.O. Box 14801, Columbus, OH 43214.

Stereoscope Light Attachment, orig box, instructions, and reel list, c1950, 5.625" h, $20.

Reel, Casper the Friendly Ghost, B-533, $6.

Reel Set, Six Million Dollar Man, 1974 . . .10
Reel Set, Star Trek, 1968 35
Reel Set, Television Shows at Universal
 City, "Scenes from McHale's Navy,
 The Virginian, Wagon Train" 25
Reel Set, War Between the States,
 1961 20
Reel Set, Wizard of Oz, B3611-13, Land
 of Oz, The Emerald City, The Wizard's
 Secret, 1957 20
Viewer, Charlie's Angels, hard plastic,
 set of full color action slides, Fleet-
 wood Toys, 1977 20
Viewer, Michael Jackson's Thriller View-
 Master Gift Set, ©1984 Optimum
 Productions, orig box 15
Viewer, Sawyer's, metal viewer, hard
 plastic case, hinged lid 12

VOGUE PICTURE RECORDS

Vogue Picture Records are attracting
the interest of a growing number of collectors. They were invented by Tom Saffady
and manufactured by his company Sav-
Way Industries in Detroit, Michigan, in
1946–47. These innovative high quality 78
rpm records were constructed with a central aluminum core for durability. A colorful
paper illustration covering the entire record
was applied to the core and then sealed in
clear vinyl.

The beautiful multi-colored pictures are
often romantic, at times whimsical, and frequently represent the song title. A small
black and white photo of the artist appears
as an insert at the margin of the illustration.
The regular production Vogues were issued
with a number in the range R707 to R786.

A wide variety of music can be found on
Vogue Picture Records including big band
swing, jazz, country, Latin, fairy tales for
children, and even dance instructions.
Seven albums each containing two records
are known to have been released.
Unfortunately, the record division of Sav-
Way Industries was forced into bankruptcy
after only fifteen months of production
somewhat limiting the availability of these
attractive and highly collectible records.

Please be aware that some Vogue
Picture Records have been reproduced by
Bear Family Records. These new records

play at 45 rpm and are easily distinguished
from the originals by their lighter weight
and black edge rim.

Advisor: John Coates, 325 Woodland Dr,
Stevens Point, WI 54481, (715) 341-6113, e-
mail: jcoates@coredcs.com.

Note: Prices listed are for records in good
average used condition. An asterisk (*) indicates Vogue Picture Records that have
been reproduced.

*R707, *Sugar Blues/Basin Street Blues,*
 Clyde McCoy and His Orchestra 40
*R712, *Atlanta GA/Aren't You Glad You're*
 You, Shep Fields & His Orchestra . . .110
*R718, *Some Sunday Morning/In The*
 Dog House Now, Lulu Belle & Scotty .65
R721, *You're Only In My Arms/When I*
 Gets To Where I'm Goin', Patsy
 Montana 85
*R723, *Wave To Me, My Lady/You Won't*
 Be Satisfied ('til You Break My Heart),
 Art Kassel & His Orchestra 95
*R724, *Everybody Knew But Me/ Sweet*
 I've Gotten On You, Frankie Masters
 & His Orchestra 125
R731, *You Took Advantage of Me/*
 Between the Devil and the Deep Blue
 Sea, Marion Mann 95
R733, *Blue Skies/Seville,* The Hour of
 Charm All Girl Orchestra directed by
 Phil Spitalny 55
R735, *Welcome to My Dream/Anybody*
 Home, Frankie Masters & His Orches-
 tra 85
*R736, *Out Where the West Winds*
 Blow/Who's Gonna Kiss You When
 I'm Gone, Kenny Roberts with The
 Down Homers 75

*R714, Doodle Doo Doo/All I Do Is Wantcha,
Art Kassel & His Orchestra, $55.

R734, Sweetheart/A Little Consideration,
Art Kassel & His Orchestra, $75.

R739, *Rhumba Lesson No. 1/Rhumba
Lesson No. 3,* Paul Shanin 85
R740, *I Dreamed About You Last Night/
Rhumba Lesson No. 2,* Paul Shanin . .110
R745, *The Trial of Bumble The Bee-
Part 1/The Boy Who Cried Wolf-
Part 1,* The Jewell Playhouse directed
by James Jewell 95
R750, *Shoo Fly Pie and Apple Pan
Dowdy/Who's Got A Tent For Rent,*
The King's Jesters 150
R751, *Mean To Me/Humphrey, The Sweet
Singing Pig,* The King's Jesters 110
R753, *At Sundown./Way Down Yonder
In New Orleans,* Clyde McCoy & His
Orchestra 55
R754, *She's Funny That Way/Dizzy's
Dilemma,* The Charlie Shavers Quintet .80
*R758, *You're Gonna Hate Yourself in the
Mornin'/Long, Strong and Consecutive,*
Marion Mann .75
*R766, *G'Wan Home, Your Mudder's
Callin'/Sepulveda,* The King's Jesters .85
R770, *The Whiffenpoof Song/If That
Phone Ever Rings,* Art Kassel & His
Orchestra 60
R771, *If I Could Be With You/Jeannine,*
Art Kassel and His Orchestra 75
R774, *Desert Fantasy/Save Me a Dream,*
Sonny Dunham & His Orchestra 75
R779, *A Man, A Moon and A Maid/Cuban
Yodelin' Man,* Enric Madriguera and
His Orchestra .95
R780, *Let's Get Married/Touch Me Not,*
Art Kassel & His Orchestra 45
R782, *What Am I Gonna Do About You/
Maybe You'll Be There,* Joan Edwards .95
*R786, *Boogie Woogie Yodel/Baby I
Found Out All About You,* The Down
Homers 150

WADE CERAMICS

Red Rose Tea issued several series of
small Wade figurines. I will not be happy
until I have multiple sets. "Drink more tea"
is the order of the day at my office. How
much simpler it would be just to make a list
of the missing Wades and pick them up at
flea markets.

Club: Wade Watch, 8199 Pierson Ct.,
Arvada, CO 80005.

Decanter, Mackinlay's Very Old Scotch
Whisky, thistle design 40
Dish, basket shape with Alsatian puppy
lying inside, 1974-81 15
Figurine, angel fish, English Whimsies,
set 9, dark gray, blue base, 1978 18
Figurine, bluebird, Miniature Animals,
1st issue, beige body and tail, blue
wings and head, Red Rose Tea pre-
mium, 1967-73 6
Figurine, corgi, Miniature Animals, 4th
issue, honey brown, black nose, Red
Rose Tea premium, 1982-84 6
Figurine, Dr Foster, Miniature Nurseries,
2nd issue, light brown, yellow tie,
blue puddle, Red Rose Tea premium,
1972-79 8
Figurine, Dumbo, Hat Box Series, set 2,
1st issue, Dec 1957 50
Figurine, Jill, Miniature Nurseries, 2nd
issue, yellow hair, beige dress, blue
bucket, Red Rose Tea premium,
1972-79 6
Figurine, kitten with yarn, Miniature
Animals, 1st issue, dark and light
brown kitten, pink yarn, Red Rose Tea
premium, 1967-73 8
Figurine, Lady (Disney's Lady and the
Tramp) Hat Box Series, set 1, 1st
issue, Jan 1956 25
Figurine, Little Boy Blue, Miniature
Nurseries, 2nd issue, blue hat and
coat, brown pants, Red Rose Tea
premium, 1972-79 9
Figurine, Mary Mary, Nursery Favourites,
yellow hair, blue dress, pink shoes . . .45
Figurine, mongrel, Miniature Animals,
1st issue, dark brown back, light
brown front, black nose, Red Rose
Tea premium, 1967-73 5

Figurine, pony, Circus Animals, 5th issue, beige, Red Rose Tea premium, 1993-98, $5.

Figurine, Old Woman Who Lived In A
   Shoe, Miniature Nurseries, 2nd issue,
   honey brown with red-brown roof,
   Red Rose Tea premium, 1972-79 6
Figurine, Pied Piper, Miniature Nurseries,
   2nd issue, pink and brown coat, green
   bush, Red Rose Tea premium, 1972-79 .6
Figurine, pig, English Whimsies, set 6,
   beige, green base, 1975 18
Figurine, The Pink House, Village of
   Broadlands, pink, gray roof, 1988 30
Stein, Budweiser/Ski 93, 5" h 35
Teapot, paisley chintz pattern, green,
   blue, rose, tan, and yellow on beige
   ground, 7" h, 8" w 55

WALLACE NUTTING

Wallace Nutting (1861–1941) was
America's most famous photographer of the
early twentieth century. A retired minister,
Nutting took more than 50,000 pictures,
keeping 10,000 of his best and destroying
the rest. His most popular and best-selling
scenes included exterior scenes (apple
blossoms, calm streams, and rural
American countrysides), interior scenes
(usually featuring a colonial woman working near a hearth), and foreign scenes (typically thatch-roofed cottages). His poorest
selling pictures, which have become
today's rarest and most highly collectible
pictures, are classified as miscellaneous
unusual scenes and include categories not
listed above: animals, architecturals, children, florals, men, seascapes, and snow
scenes. Process prints are 1930s machine-
produced reprints of twelve of Nutting's

most popular pictures. These have minimal
value and can be detected by using a magnifying glass. Nutting sold millions of his
hand-colored platinotype pictures between
1900 and his death in 1941.

While attempting to seek out the finest
and best early American furniture as props
for his colonial interior scenes, Nutting
became an expert in early American
antiques. He published nearly twenty books
in his lifetime, including his ten-volume
State Beautiful series, and various other
books on furniture, photography, clocks,
and his personal biography. He also
became widely known for his reproduction
furniture. His furniture shop reproduced
hundreds of different furniture forms, all
clearly marked with a distinctive paper
label glued directly to the piece or his block
or script signature brand.

The overall synergy of the Wallace
Nutting name—pictures, books, and furniture—has made anything Wallace Nutting
quite collectible.

Club: Wallace Nutting Collectors Club, 2944
Ivanhoe Glen, Madison, WI 53711.

Book, *Ireland Beautiful*, 2nd ed, dj 60
Book, *New Hampshire Beautiful*, 1st ed .50
Print, A Barre Brook, blue stream rippling
   towards tall trees and stone wall,
   Barre, MA, 13 x 22" 240
Print, A Berkshire Brook, shallow rocky
   stream winding around rail fence, pink
   blossoms, and corner of field, MA,
   orig copyright label on back, 13 x 16" .200
Print, A Bit of Sewing, girl sews while
   sitting beside Nuttingolme fire,
   Southbury, CT, 9 x 12" 200
Print, A Dahlia Jar, floral picture with
   dark red and yellow dahlias arranged
   in handled stoneware pitcher/vase,
   orig copyright label on back, 8 x 10" .625
Print, A Little River, country road running
   along rock swift-running stream, Mt
   Washington in background, NH, sgd
   lower right, copyright lower left, orig
   copyright label on back, 20 x 30" 400
Print, A Story of Chivalry, girl reading
   book while sitting beside Webb House
   fire near wall, Revolutionary War
   pictorial wallpaper, Wethersfield, CT,
   10 x 12" 300

Print, Penzance, $1,500. —Photo courtesy Michael Ivankovich Antiques, Inc.

Print, An Elaborate Dinner, girl stirring black kettle while standing beside large Nuttinghame fireplace, South-bury, CT, script 1909 copyright on image lower left, 22 x 28" 900

Print, Birch Hilltop, hillside birch cluster overlooking blue lake, NH, 9 x 11" ...165

Print, Bonny Dale, narrow blue stream winding past orange flowers, green fields, and tall trees, Derry, Ireland, hand-colored, 13 x 16" 300

Print, Decked As a Bride, country road running past colorful pink blossoming apple orchard, Berkshires, MA, 18 x 22" 300

Print, Dream and Reality, farm path winding through orchard's stone wall into blossoming apple orchard, MA, 10 x 16" 200

Print, Harmony, girl playing harp while sitting in formal Webb House parlor, Wethersfield, CT, 14 x 17" 375

Print, miniature foreign exterior scene, Larkspur, narrow path leads past girl in flower garden to thatch-roofed cottage, 4 x 5" 115

Print, Red Eagle Lake, fall-colored trees reflecting in still blue lake, tall moun-tain rising in distance, NH, orig copy-right label on back, 16 x 20" 325

Print, The Goose Chase Quilt, girl sew-ing quilt while sitting beside red brick fireplace, MA, 10 x 18" 375

Print, The Heart of Maine, calm shallow rocky stream flowing past fall-colored trees, ME, 16 x 20" 425

Print, untitled exterior scene, country road winding around birch trees and rail fence, 5 x 7" 75

Print, untitled interior, girl wearing long dress and bonnet standing beside hanging mirror in Nuttingholme parlor, Framingham, MA, 7 x 9" 150

Print, untitled miniature exterior scene, rippling blue pond beside hillside with autumn foliage, 4 x 5" 100

Silhouette, girl holding pearl necklace over open jewelry box, 7 x 8" 50

Silhouette, girl standing by armless statue 50

Silhouette, girl wearing puffy dress and standing by large cheval mirror, 7 x 8" .65

WALL POCKETS

What is a wall pocket? My mother used them for plants. A "rooter" she called them. Now they are used as match holders and places for accumulating small junk.

Most common wall pockets were pro-duced between the 1930s and 1960s; though there are some that date to the Victorian era. Wallpockets can be made of wood, tin, glass or ceramic. Ceramic examples have been produced both domestically and abroad. Wall pockets come in all shapes and sizes, but all have a small hole on the back side for the insertion of the wall hook.

Club: Wall Pocket Collectors Club, 1356 Tahiti, St. Louis, MO 63128.

Apple on Leaves, McCoy, 7" h 65

Arrowhead, dark green, Creek Pottery, Checotah, OK, 1970s, 8" h 45

Snowberry, Roseville, #1WP-8, 8" h, $250. —Photo courtesy Gene Harris Antique Auction Center, Inc.

Girl's Head, unmkd, 5.125" h, $55. —Photo courtesy Gene Harris Antique Auction Center, Inc.

Baby Face on Peace Lily, mkd "Oy-NC Japan," 6" h 25

Betty Boop on Cone, white, gold luster, mkd "Betty Boop Des. L Copp by Fleischer Studios, Made in Japan," 5" h 125

Bird, multicolored green, long tail, mkd "Fulper 375" .300

Black Chef on Stove, Hollywood Ceramics, 6" h 75

Bucket with Roses, brown, Woodrose pattern, Weller Pottery 100

Bullet, Tiffin satin glass, pointed base, US Glass, Tiffin, OH, #16258, 9.5" h . . .100

Butterfly, light yellow, Nelson McCoy, incised "NM," 1940s, 5.75" h 300

Canoe, vaseline glass, Daisy and Button, unmkd, 8" l 80

Chinese Girl, smiling, wearing wide brimmed hat, Royal Copley, 7.5" h 45

Cone, amber, Fostoria, style #1881, 8.25" h 125

Cornucopia, light pink, mkd "Red Wing 441," 7" h 50

Elf, sitting on bananas, mkd "Gilner 1950 Calif," 1950s, 7.5" h 45

Fish, dark pink, black highlights, mkd "Ceramicraft San Clemente, California," 8.5" h, 11" l 30

Flour Scoop, yellow, emb flowers, mkd "USA Camark N-45," 10" l 25

Grapes on Leaf, purple and chartreuse, mkd "Treasure Craft, Compton, California," 6" h 25

Harlequin Man and Woman, mkd "Made in Japan," 6" h, price for pair 85

Horse Collar, brown, mkd "Royal Duran, Calif," 10" h 50

Iron, yellow, pastel accents, Hull, Sun Glow pattern #83, 1950s 90

Pigtail Girl, eyes closed, brown hair, aqua bonnet and collar, Royal Copley, 7" h .45

Scottie Dog, Shawnee, 9.5" h 60

Shell, mkd "Stangl USA 3238," 6" h 125

Violin, white, pink rose with green leaves, gold trim, #369, Lefton, 7.5" h 30

WASHDAY COLLECTIBLES

Washday material is a favorite of advertising collectors. Decorators have a habit of using it in bathroom decor. Is there a message here?

Advertising Trade Card, Lavine For Washing, 3.125 x 4.275" 10

Box, Fairbank's Gold Dust Washing Powder, unopened 10

Clothes Dasher, heavy tin, wood handle, Rapid Vacuum Washer, c1920 45

Dusting Brush, horsehair, turned wood handle, 9" l 20

Dust Pan, graniteware, gray speckled .100

Ironing Board, poplar, folding, single board top, 4 turned legs, old green paint on base, 59.5" l, 30" h 150

Laundry Basket, woven splint, oblong, ribbed, open rim handles, 24" l, 20" w, 11" h 120

Pinback Button, child peering from galvanized steel tub,"Atlantic Stamping Co" 35

Pinback Button, "Domestic Vacuum Sweeper Company," multicolored, cleaning lady emptying sweeper bag .70

Pinback Button, girl operating hand-crank washing machine, "The Vandergrift Rotary Clothes Washer" . .40

Laundry Bag, muslin, red and blue print, black embroidery, blue binding, 17 x 23", $12. —Photo courtesy Ray Morykan Auctions.

Pinback Button, Gold Dust Washing
Powder 40
Pocket Mirror, Fairbank's Gold Dust
Washing Powder, 2.125 x 3.125" 3
Sadiron, round back, 5.75" l, 4.5" h 20
Salt and Pepper Shakers, pr, washing
machine, wringer style, plastic 2
Soap Saver, tin frame, twisted wire
handle, hanging loop, wire mesh
container, 3.5 x 2.5", 7" l handle 20
Whisk Broom, mammy handle, 4.5" l 20

WASHING MACHINES

For collecting purposes clothes washing machines fall into two distinct categories; automatic and wringer. This category pertains to vintage automatic washers, which fill themselves with water, wash and rinse the clothes, extract the water from both the clothes and the machine and turn themselves off without any help from the operator.

Bendix sold the very first automatic washer in 1938. It had to be bolted to the floor to keep it from jumping during the spin cycle. Blackstone and Westinghouse were about to market their very first automatic washers in 1941 when World War II forced a halt in domestic appliance production as factories converted to supply materials for the war effort. In 1947 automatic washers from Frigidaire, Thor, Blackstone, GE, Westinghouse, Launderall, AMC, Kenmore and the 1900 Corporation (soon to become Whirlpool) appeared. They were extremely expensive and long waiting lists formed to purchase one of these new machines.

Bendix pioneered another first in 1953, the combination washer/dryer, which was a front loading machine. It did both washing and drying in one machine. In the 1950s the styling of automatics was similar to cars, with heavy usage of chrome, lighted dials, audible signals, windows in the lids, and cabinet colors such as pink, turquoise, pastel yellow, and sea foam green (the yellow and green colors of the 1950s were very different than the harvest gold and avocado colors of the 1970s).

Vintage 1940s and 50s automatic washers are now extremely rare. They were complicated machines that tended to break down more frequently than other home appliances. Modern restoration is time consuming and expensive. Most vintage parts haven't been available for over thirty years. To maintain its value, restoration should be performed by an expert in this field. While having the matching dryer will add to the washer's value, vintage dryers were less complicated and are still readily found.

Advisor: Robert Seger, 3629 15th Ave. South, Minneapolis, MN 55407, (612) 729-7561, e-mail: Unimatic1140@Yahoo.com.

Clubs: Maytag Collectors Club, 960 Reynolds Dr., Ripon, CA 95366; Yahoo Classic Appliances, www.clubs.yahoo.com /clubs/classicappliances.

Note: Prices listed are for machines in complete, unrestored condition. They are in good shape aesthetically and mechanically.

ABC-O-Matic, windowless lid, 1950-58 .200
ABC-O-Matic, window lid, 1950-58 400
AMC/AMC Coronado, round glass lid,
1947 200
Apex Wash-A-Matic & Universal
(Bouncing Basket Automatic), 3000
Series models, 1949 600
Apex Wash-A-Matic & Universal
(Bouncing Basket Automatic),
windowless lid models, 1950-56 400
Apex Wash-A-Matic & Universal
(Bouncing Basket Automatic),
window lid models, 1950-56 500
Bendix/Philco Bendix, pre-war front
loading, bolt-down, 1938-41 400
Bendix/Philco Bendix, Duomatic front
loading washer/dryer combination,
1953-58 300

*Bendix,
Model S,
1947, $100.*

Bendix/Philco Bendix, wobbling agitator automatic, perforated basket, 1960s .100
Blackstone, Model 50, 50A, 1947 400
Blackstone, Model 150, 250, 350, agitator drain models, 1950-57 300
Blackstone, solid tub models, 1958-60 . .100
Easy, 30" models with fluid drive, 1952-57 200
Easy, combination washer/dryer, any model, 1956-63 350
Easy, Velvapower direct drive transmission models, 1958-64 100
Frigidaire, Model WJ-60, white perforated tub and hamonizer, 1947 700
Frigidaire, Model WL-60, rimless black speckled solid tub and harmonizer, 1949 300
Frigidaire, Pulsamatic Models WV-35, WS-56, WD-56, WS-57, WD-57, WS-58, WD-58, 1955-58 100
Frigidaire, Multimatic Models, 1959-64 .100
General Electric, AW6 Models, direct drive transmission, 1947-50 600
General Electric, single belt drive model, with Filter-Flow, 1953-55 200
General Electric, combination washer/dryer, 1954-64 300
Hotpoint, Coaxial transmission model, 1953-59 100
Hotpoint, combination washer/dryer Model LY-1, 1957 500
Kelvinator, window lid, 1950-58 400
Kelvinator, windowless lid, 1950-58 300
Kelvinator, 1959-66 100
Kenmore, combination washer/dryer, 1957-60, 33" w 300
Kenmore, Lady Kenmore, 1957-62 200
Launderall, 1947-51 400
Maytag, Model AMP, 1948-52 300
Maytag, Helical drive Models 142, 160, 1958-60 25
Maytag, combination washer/dryer 340W, 440C, 1958-65 500
Montgomery Ward/Wardomatic, Apex design, bouncing basket, 1954-56 . . .500
Montgomery Ward/Wardomatic, front loading, Westinghouse design, 1957-64 150
Norge/Hamilton, Time Line washer, 1952-58 200
Norge/Hamilton, Dispensomat, 1959-60 .100
Norge/Hamilton, combination washer/dryer, 1958-64 500

Speed Queen, fluid drive, AMC design, stainless steel basket, 1954-59 200
Thor, semi-automatic washer/dishwasher with both tubs, 1947-52 600
Thor, 1953-55 400
Westinghouse, front loading, B-1-3, B3, C-1-3, C3, 1950-53 350
Westinghouse, combination washer/dryer, WD-1. WD-2, Wd-3, 1956-60 . .500
Whirlpool, bolt-down model, 1947-50 . . .300
Whirlpool, Imperial/Mark XII Model, 1957-62 100
Whirlpool, combination washer/dryer, 1961-65, 29" w 200

WASTEBASKETS

Wastebaskets are not just for garbage. Many collectors are just beginning to appreciate the great lithographed artwork found on many character cans.

Bobby Orr, litho tin, mkd "Copyright National Hockey League Services Inc 1971/Cheinco Housewares, J Chein & Co, Burlington, NJ, 16" h, 8.75" d 20
Charlie Brown and Snoopy, metal, ©1950, 1958, 1965, United Feature Syndicate, Inc, 13" h 10
Floral Motif, metal, pink and black, 13" h . .6
Floral Motif with Polka Dots, blue ground, litho tin 12
Ivy and Berries, litho tin, 12.5" h 10
Pink, plastic, rippled, iridescent white and blue flowers, rhinestone accents, 9.5" h 15
Poodles, litho tin, black and white, 12.5" h 35
Raggedy Ann & Andy, litho tin, Chein, 1972 25

Black Hole, litho tin, ©1979 Walt Disney Productions, Chein, 13" h, $18.

Scottie Dogs, pressed paper cardboard,
   tin bottom, 1940-50s, 13" h 30
Star Motif, clear acrylic, metal corner
   brackets, cut glass type design with
   stars motif, Trelawney, 12.25" h 8
Thomas the Tank Engine, litho tin 10
Tweety Bird, litho tin, 10" h 5

WATCH FOBS

A watch fob is a useful and decorative
item attached to a man's pocket watch by a
strap. It assists him in removing the watch
from his pocket. Fobs became popular during the last quarter of the 19th century.

Most fobs are made of metal and are
struck from a steel die. Enameled fobs are
scarce and sought after by collectors. If a
fob was popular, a company would order
restrikes. As a result, some fobs were
issued for a period of twenty-five years or
more. Watch fobs still are used today in
promoting heavy industrial equipment.

The most popular fobs are those relating to old machinery, either farm, construction, or industrial. Advertising fobs rank
second in popularity.

The back of a fob is helpful in identifying a genuine fob from a reproduction or
restrike. Genuine fobs frequently have
advertising or a union trademark on the
back. Some genuine fobs do have blank
backs but a blank back should be a warning
to be cautious.

Club: International Watch Fob Assoc., Inc.,
601 Patriot Place, Holmen, WI 54636.

Buster Brown Blue Ribbon Shoes, silvered white metal, oval, relief image
   of Mary Jane admiring her new shoes,
   Buster and girlfriend smile at her, Tige
   sits nearby smiling and waving, 5-star
   logo and text "For Boys For Girls
   Buster Brown Blue Ribbon Shoes"
   and "For Men For Women White
   House Shoes" on reverse, leather
   strap, 3.75" l 150
Bryan, metal, dark silver finish, celluloid
   portrait in center, black leather strap,
   1.375" h 40
Dari-Dan G Men, emb brass, badge
   shape, dairy premium, 1.75" h 20

Indian Motor Cycle, brass, leather strap, $60.

Freymeyer's Harvest Bread, diecut celluloid, bread loaf shape, 1920s 15
Golden Shell Oil, brass with bronze
   luster finish, enameled shell emblem,
   "For Today's Precision-Built Cars...
   So Pure It Lubricates This Watch,"
   1930s, 1.375" h 125
Mickey Mouse, silvered brass, stamped
   image of Mickey with black enamel-
   ing, 1.5" h 40
Teddy Roosevelt, silvered brass, cellu-
   loid portrait in center, emb Capitol,
   eagle, and flag, leather strap, 1.75" h .30

WATT POTTERY

Watt Pottery, located in Crooksville,
Ohio, was founded in 1922. The company
began producing kitchenware in 1935. Most
Watt pottery is easily recognized by its sim-
ple underglaze decoration on a light tan
base. The most commonly found pattern is
the Red Apple pattern, introduced in 1950.
Other patterns include Cherry, Pansy,
Pennsylvania Dutch Tulip, Rooster, and Star
Flower.

Club: Watt Collectors Assoc., P.O. Box 1995,
Iowa City, IA 52244.

Apple, ice bucket, #59 175
Apple, pitcher, #15 110
Apple, platter, #49 200
Apple, spaghetti bowl, #39 150
Autumn Foliage, creamer, #62 285
Autumn Foliage, grease jar 275
Autumn Foliage, ice bucket bottom 50
Autumn Foliage, sugar 175
Basketweave, cookie jar, #101, green . .100
Butterfly, mixing bowl, #6 150
Cross Hatch, cookie jar, #21 160
Cross Hatch, mixing bowl, #5 75
Cross Hatch, pitcher, #16 375
Daisy, pitcher, old style 385

Double Apple, baker, cov, #96 175
Double Leaf, pitcher, #15 100
Double Leaf, pitcher, #16 150
Dutch Tulip, canister, #72 375
Dutch Tulip, cheese crock, #80 500
Dutch Tulip, dinner plate, divided 575
Dutch Tulip, mixing bowl, #5 100
Dutch Tulip, salad bowl, #73 200
Esmond, cookie jar, #34 70
Esmond, lazy susan, round 100
Heirloom, bean pot, #812 65
Loops, casserole, cov, salmon 30
Morning Glory, cookie jar, dome top,
   cream 425
Morning Glory, mixing bowl, yellow, #6 . .75
Nassau, coffee carafe, #115, speckled .150
Open Apple, dip bowl, #120 125
Rooster, bowl, #7 90
Rooster, casserole, French handled, #18 .210
Rooster, creamer, #62 275
Rooster, pitcher, #15 150
Starflower, baker, cov, square, #84 350
Starflower, bowl, #7, 5-petal 45
Starflower, cheese crock, #80 475
Starflower, ice bucket, 4-petal 145
Swirl, pie plate, #9, blue 75
Tear Drop, spaghetti bowl, #39 175
Three Leaf Apple, bean cup, #75 275
Three Leaf Apple, cookie jar, #503 500
Three Leaf Apple, grease jar lid 50
Three Leaf Apple, mug, #121 200
Three Leaf Apple, pitcher, #163 100
Three Leaf Apple, ice lip pitcher, #17 . . .250
Three Leaf Apple, pie plate, #33 175
Tulip, bowl, #65 .75
Tulip, creamer, #62 250

Three Leaf Apple, pitcher, #69, $400. —
Photo courtesy Gene Harris Antique
Auction Center, Inc.

Tulip, ice lip pitcher, #17 250
Tulip, pitcher, #16 165

WELLER POTTERY

Weller's origins date back to 1872 when
Samuel Weller opened a factory in
Fultonham, near Zanesville, Ohio.
Louwelsa, Weller's art pottery line, was
introduced in 1894. Among the famous art
pottery designers employed by Weller are
Charles Babcock Upjohn, Jacques Sicard,
Frederick Rhead, and Gazo Fudji.

Weller survived on production of utilitarian wares, but always managed to produce some art pottery until cheap
Japanese imports captured the market
immediately following World War II.
Operations at Weller ceased in 1948.

Club: American Art Pottery Assoc., P.O. Box
834, Westport, MA 02790.

Centerbowl, Glendale, seagulls and
   nest flower frog, mkd, 15" d bowl . . .425
Console Bowl, Glendale, with flower
   frog, ink stamp mark, 15.25" d 500
Console Set, Hobart, scalloped bowl in
   shaded lavender to teal matte glaze,
   figural female flower frog in matte
   lavender, pair of low scalloped
   candlesticks in matte teal, paper
   label, 15.5" d bowl 160
Console Set, Marvo, flaring centerbowl
   and 2 low candlesticks, 10" d bowl . .160
Console Set, Silvertone, flaring centerbowl, flower frog, and 2 candlesticks,
   12" d bowl 425
Jardiniere, Baneda, green, 4" h, 5.5" d . .400
Lamp Base, Baldin, 10.5" h, 9.75" d 150
Planter, Golbrogreen, 8.5" d 20
Planter, Zona, rect, pink flowers on
   scrolled ground, stamped "Weller,"
   15" l, 6" h 275
Vase, Geode, bulbous, shooting stars
   on midnight blue, incised "Weller
   Pottery, TM," 5.75" h, 5" d 750
Vase, Jap Birdimal, bottle-shaped, Arts
   & Crafts style with band of ducks
   and incised blades of grass, green
   ground, imp "8X--," 7.5" h, 3.75" d . . .350
Wall Pocket, Woodcraft, squirrel at
   base, incised "Weller," 9" h 225

Cookie Jar, Mammy, inscribed "Weller," 11" h, $1,325. —Photo courtesy Collectors Auction Services.

Planter, Zona, square, 4" h, 5.5" sq 125
Planter, Malvern, red, stamped "Weller," 8" h, 6" w 300

WESTERN COLLECTIBLES

Yippy Kiyay partner, let's get a move on and lasso up some Western goodies.

The Western collectible is a style or motif as it relates to the object. The Western theme presents itself in the decorative imagery of the item. The use of Western materials for construction of the item also defines it as a possible Western collectible; i.e. cattlehide carpets and wall hangings, or items constructed from bull horns. The Western motif may also be defined as any item that relates to the Western frontier culture. Native American Indian and Mexican cultures are also part of the Western collectible theme. It is these cultures that contribute so much of the color to the Western heritage.

Clubs: 101 Ranch Collectors, 10701 Timbergrove Ln., Corpus Christi, TX 78410; National Bit, Spur & Saddle Collectors Assoc., P.O. Box 3098, Colorado Springs, CO 80934.

Newsletter: *Cowboy Guide,* P.O. Box 6459, Santa Fe, NM 87502.

Periodical: *American Cowboy,* P.O. Box 6630, Sheridan, WY 82801.

Book, *The Story of the Wild West & Campfire Chats by Buffalo Bill,* 1st edition, illus, 1880 550
Calendar, 1955, cowgirl holding hat, Newman's Red Lodge, Montana 100

Catalog, Al Furstnow Saddlery Co, #36, bucking bronco illus, c1929 175
Cowgirl Outfit, Pendleton Roundup souvenir, vest, fringed skirt, scarf, hat, and boots 135
Cuffs, "Lasso Em Bill," orig box, unused .125
Game, Doc Holliday Wild West Game, Transogram, 1960 25
Hat, Pendleton Roundup souvenir, "Let'er Buck," cowboy riding bronco on crown 250
Magazine, *Buffalo Bill Bids You Good Bye,* "A Farewell Salute, Magazine and Official Review, Price 10¢," story about Cody's horse by Mark Twain, 1910 325
Magazine, *Buffalo Bill Wild West Annual,* #7, Indians attacking stagecoach, 1955 5
Playset, Wild Wild West, orig box, 1960s .5
Postcard, "Buffalo Bill's Bucking Broncos," cowboys on horses 25
Poster, "$50.00 Reward–Wells Fargo & Company Express, will pay a reward of Fifty Dollars for the arrest and detention of James E. Barry," 1911 . .225
Program, Buffalo Bill's Wild West, Buffalo Bill in center oval, buffalo in lower right corner, Indian in lower left, 1888 225
Saddle, child's, Alfred Cornish, Omaha, NE, 11.5" seat 250
Scarf, silk, Will Rogers in center oval, green background, cowboy motif border 175
Sign, "Buffalo Bill's Wild West Rough Riders," litho tin, 12 x 15" 10

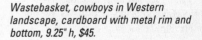

Wastebasket, cowboys in Western landscape, cardboard with metal rim and bottom, 9.25" h, $45.

Spurs, bronze, horse head, 10-point
rowels, North & Judd 375
Tack Bag, canvas, Johnson Harness
Shop of Dillon, MO, W Christensen,
Wisdom, MO 200
Ticket, Buffalo Bill's Wild West Show,
North Platte, NE, 1970s 3

WESTMORELAND GLASS

Westmoreland Glass Company made a
large assortment of glass. Some early
pieces were actually reproductions of earlier patterns and are now collectible in their
own right. Other patterns have been produced for decades.

Expect to pay modest prices. Flea market prices are generally much lower than
contemporary department store prices.

Clubs: National Westmoreland Glass
Collectors Club, P.O. Box 100, Grapeville, PA
15634; Westmoreland Glass Society, 1144 42
Ave., Vero Beach, FL 32960.

Newsletter: The Original Westmoreland
Collectors Newsletter, P.O. Box 143, North
Liberty, IA 52317.

Note: All items are white unless noted otherwise.

Beaded Edge, bread and butter plate,
6" d 4
Beaded Edge, cake stand, sq ft, 9.5" d . .70
Beaded Edge, cup and saucer 8
Beaded Edge, plate, fruit dec, 7.375" d . .12

*English Hobnail, bowl, hexagonal ft, 6" h,
8" d, $30.* —Photo courtesy Ray Morykan
Auctions.

Beaded Edge, tumbler, fruit dec 18
Beaded Edge, wedding bowl, roses and
bows dec 90
English Hobnail, ginger ale tumbler,
square foot, crystal 8
English Hobnail, goblet, round ft, crystal,
6" h 10
English Hobnail, lamp, electric 40
English Hobnail, plate, crystal, 5.5" d 8
English Hobnail, plate, 8" d, amber 10
English Hobnail, puff box, cov, 6" d 20
English Hobnail, sherbet, high, round
foot, crystal 9
Fan & File, child's punch cup, crystal 3
Fan & File, fairy light, 2-part, green mist .75
Hobnail, powder jar, Belgian blue opal-
escent 150
Figurine, owl, dark blue frosted 35
Figurine, pouter pigeon, apricot mist,
2.5" h 35
Figurine, pouter pigeon, crystal, 2.5" h . .25
Old Quilt, candy dish, cov 20
Old Quilt, celery, ftd 40
Old Quilt, cheese dish, cov 55
Old Quilt, shaker, squat, 3.5" h 12
Old Quilt, water goblet 18
Paneled Grape, ashtray, 4" sq 12
Paneled Grape, banana stand 160
Paneled Grape, basket, scalloped foot,
10.5" h 90
Paneled Grape, bowl, lipped, 8.5" d 90
Paneled Grape, bowl, ruffled 25
Paneled Grape, cake salver, pedestal
base, 11" d 50
Paneled Grape, candy dish, cov, roses
and bow dec, 6.25" d 35
Paneled Grape, celery, 6" h 35
Paneled Grape, creamer and sugar 25
Paneled Grape, cup and saucer 20
Paneled Grape, dresser tray, oval, 13" l . .55
Paneled Grape, pitcher, 16 oz 40
Paneled Grape, plate, 8.5" d 18
Paneled Grape, salt and pepper shakers,
pr 25
Paneled Grape, soap dish 125
Paneled Grape, vase, bell-shaped,
11.5" h 45
Paneled Grape, wall pocket 135
Pillow and Sunburst, bowl, amethyst,
8" d 35
Princess Feather, bowl, 4.5" d 16
Princess Feather, plate, 8" d 8
Princess Feather, wine goblet, 1.5 oz . . .18

WHEATON

The Wheaton Glass Company, Millville, New Jersey, manufactured commemorative bottles, decanters, and flasks between 1967 and 1974. Series included Christmas, Great Americans, Movie Stars, Political Campaigns, and Space.

The Wheaton Historical Association continued production of the Christmas and Presidential series from 1975 to 1982. The Millville Art Glass Co. obtained a licensing agreement from the Wheaton Historical Association and added some additional bottles to the series.

The Wheaton Glass Company also manufactured copycat (stylistic copies) of 19th century bottles and flasks between 1971 and 1974. Most were marked "Nuline," "W," or "Wheaton, NJ" on the base. Amber, amethyst, blue, green, milk, and ruby were the colors used.

Club: Classic Wheaton Club, P.O. Box 59, Downingtown, PA 19335.

American Eagle, blue 15
Apollo 14, blue 8
Ben Franklin, aqua 14
Betsy Ross, ruby 14
Calvin Coolidge, amethyst 12
Christmas 1971, green 25
Cornucopia and Eagle, blue 15
Franklin Sailboat, Ocean City, NJ, 1879
　　Centennial 1989, green 15

Spirit of '76, iridescent topaz, $30.

James Madison, ruby, miniature 4
Liberty Bell, topaz 4
Mark Twain, amethyst 15
Mother's Day, clear 14
Robert E Lee, green 14
Robert Kennedy, green 14
Skylab II, frosted 20
Snow Tree, green 20
St Mark, green 20
Uncle Sam Bank, green 40
William McKinley, aqua 8

WHISKEY BOTTLES, COLLECTORS' EDITIONS

The Jim Beam Distillery issued its first novelty bottle for the 1953 Christmas market. By the 1960s the limited edition whiskey bottle craze was full blown. It was dying by the mid 1970s and was buried sometime around 1982 or 1983. Oversaturation by manufacturers and speculation by non-collectors killed the market.

Limited edition whiskey bottle collecting now rests in the hands of serious collectors. Their bible is H. F. Montague's *Montague's Modern Bottle Identification and Price Guide* (published by author, 1980). The book used to be revised frequently. Now five years or more pass between editions. The market is so stable that few prices change from one year to the next.

Before you buy or sell a full limited edition whiskey bottle, check state laws. Most states require a license to sell liquor and impose substantial penalties if you sell without one.

Clubs: International Assoc. of Jim Beam Bottle & Specialties Club, 2015 Burlington Ave., Kewanee, IL 61443; National Ski Country Bottle Club, 1224 Washington Ave., Golden, CO 80401.

Note: bottles are empty unless noted otherwise.

Cyrus Noble, Blacksmith 30
Cyrus Noble, Miner, 1975, miniature 10
Cyrus Noble, Nevada Buffalo Cow and
　　Calf, sealed 35
Cyrus Noble, Nevada Mountain Lion,
　　sealed 35

Lionstone, Woodhawk, Wild West Series, 1969, $20.

Cyrus Noble, USC Trojan 110
Double Springs, 1910 Model Ford
    Convertible 18
Double Springs, Chicago Water Tower,
    1969 10
Double Springs, Owl, 1968 15
Ezra Brooks, Cheyenne Shoot-Out, 1970 .18
Ezra Brooks, Conquistadors Drum and
    Bugle Corps, 1971 20
Ezra Brooks, Elephant, 1973 15
Ezra Brooks, Elk, 1972 15
Ezra Brooks, Horseshoe Club Reno, 1970 .12
Ezra Brooks, Indy Race Car #21, sealed .40
Ezra Brooks, Missouri Mule, 1971 15
Ezra Brooks, South Dakota National
    Guard, 1976 15
Garnier, Eiffel Tower 15
Garnier, Island Girl and Palm Tree 15
Jim Beam, 100th Anniversary of Baseball,
    1869-1969 25
Jim Beam, 100th Anniversary Phi Sigma
    Kappa, 1973 50
Jim Beam, 12th Annual Convention,
    New Orleans, July 17-23, 1982 20
Jim Beam, Boothill & Dodge City, KS,
    1972 12
Jim Beam, Captain and Mate, 1980 20
Jim Beam, Catfish, 1981, sealed 60
Jim Beam, Democrat, donkey on drum . .12
Jim Beam, Ducks Unlimited Canadian
    Goose 130
Jim Beam, King Kamehameha 10
Jim Beam, Muskie, Wisconsin state fish,
    1971, sealed 50
Jim Beam, New Mexico/Taos Pueblo . . .10
Jim Beam, Pearl Harbor Survivors 15
Jim Beam, South Carolina 1670-1970
    Tricentennial 10
Jim Beam, USMC Devil Dog, 1979,
    sealed 100

Lionstone, Photographer, 1976 110
Lionstone, Rhinoceros, 1977, miniature . .20
Lionstone, Sheepherder, 1969 65
Lionstone, Wood Duck, 1980 50
McCormick, Canadian Goose 45
Ski Country, Bobcat and Chipmunk 25
Ski Country, Flycatcher, 1979, miniature .20
Ski Country, Green Wing Teal, miniature .40
Ski Country, Mallard Duck, 1977 25
Ski Country, Peregrine Falcon, 1979,
    miniature 16
Wild Turkey, Flying Wild Turkey #3 25
Wild Turkey, Wild Turkey #4 30
Wild Turkey, Wild Turkey and Fox #7,
    1984, miniature 210

WHISTLES

Webster defines a whistle as an instrument for making a clear, shrill sound. No wonder children love them. Collectors can whistle a happy tune at virtually every flea market. The most desirable whistles are those associated with well-known characters and personalities. They can command prices that are hardly child's play.

Club: Call & Whistle Collectors Assoc., 2839 E. 26th Place, Tulsa, OK 74114.

Buster Brown Shoes, litho tin, double-
    reed, Buster and Tige on brown
    ground, yellow border 20
Hurd Shoes, litho tin, double-reed, red
    logo and inscription on white ground .15
Peters Weatherbird Shoes, litho tin, tube
    siren, 2 Weatherbird heads wearing
    different caps, Germany, 1930s 25
Poll-Parrot Shoes, litho tin, double-reed,
    parrot logo on yellow ground 15

Radio Orphan Annie, Tri-Tone Signaler Badge, litho tin, Ovaltine premium, 2.5" l, $40.

Red Goose Shoes, litho tin, double-reed,
red goose on yellow ground 25
Skyline Scene, litho tin, double-reed,
yellow skyscrapers and biplane on
orange ground, Japan 30
"Whistle For New Members, For the
Reds," celluloid cap on tin disk, white
lettering on red ground, 1930s 8
Yellow Cab, tin, double-reed, yellow
lettering on black ground, "Whistle
for a Yellow Cab or phone CHerry 1-
4900," 1930s-40s 30

WHITE-KNOB WINDUPS

White-Knob Windups are small, plastic
mechanical toys. They arrived on the market in the mid-1970s. Their name is derived
from the small white ridged knob found at
the end of the metal rod that extends from
the body and winds the motor.

Club: White Knob Wind-Up Collectors Club,
61 Garrow St., Auburn, NY 13021.

Alien, from the movie *Alien* 8
Astro, The Jetsons 6
Baby in Walker 6
British Airways Airplane 8
Cabbage Patch Kid, 1983 5
Crawling Baby, Tomy, 1983 6
Devil, 3.5" h 5
Duck, Tomy, 1977 8
Frankenstein 6
Grandfather Clock, Disney 5
Mickey Riding Pluto, Monogram 8
Milissa Screetch, Toonsylvania, MOC 5
Miss Piggy, Swine Trek Flip Flopper,
Tomy, MOC 40
NASA Space Shuttle 4

Triceratops, #7820, $4.

Phil White, Toonsylvania, bunny slippers,
MOC 8
Robot, ©SCL Japan, MOC 10
Shamu the Killer Whale 5
Spider-Man, 1970s, MOC 60
Squidley Diddley, octopus 6
Strolling Bowling, Tomy, 1970s 18
The Thing, Marvel Comics 3
Totoro, plush, gray 16
Wicked Witch, Wizard of Oz 8

WICKER

Wicker and rattan furniture enjoyed its
first American craze during the late
Victorian era. It was found on porches and
summer cottages across America. It realized a second period of popularity in the
1920s and 30s and a third period in the
1950s. In truth, wicker has been available
continuously since the 1870s.

Early wicker has a lighter, airier feel
than its later counterparts. Look for unusual forms, e.g., corner chairs or sewing
stands. Most wicker was sold unpainted.
However, it was common practice to paint it
in order to preserve it, especially if it was
going to be kept outside. Too many layers of
paint decreases the value of a piece.

Armchair, painted white, pink and white
chenille cushion, 30" h, 29" w 210
Chest, painted white, tightly-woven
hinged lid and sides, narrow open-
weave panel near top of front and
back, 16" h, 31" w, 15.5" d 35
Creel, fly fishing, carved fly on wooden
lid, leather strap, 16" w 50
Doll Buggy, natural color with 2 orange
bands woven into sides and good,
wood spoke wheels and hubcaps,
rubber tires, fabric lining, 1920s 60
Doll Cradle, rocker base, painted white,
fabric lining, 10" l 15
Entertainment Center, 2-doors above 2
drawers, 4-shelf int, holes in back for
wiring, 64" h, 33.25" w, 20" d 60
Flask, pewter top, 1870s, 7.75" h 80
Highchair, caned back panel with fan
design, caned seat, painted white,
36.5" h, 16.5" w 75
Picnic Basket, Redman, metal handles,
diamond design woven in sides 20

Purse, box shape, glossy white, plastic
handle, gold tone tab, hinges, and
feet, Koret, 7" w 8
Rocker, ornate openweave design,
circular back panel with tightly-
woven starburst design, pressed
seat, wrapped arms, natural and
dark finish, 40" h, 26" w 150
Rug Beater, open weave head, wrapped
handle, 34" l, 9.75" w 15
Sewing Basket, Princess, pink, sewing
notions decal on wooden lid, 9-dowel
thread rack, 2 pull cords for closing
basket 35
Table, figural elephant shape, removable
serving tray top, 21.5" h, 23" l 50
Wall Mirror, oval mirror plate, shelf,
painted white, 22" h, 12" w, 4.5" d
shelf 20
Wine Bottle, aqua glass bottle, wicker
cov, 15.5" h 12

Coffeepot, Burleigh Ware, Burgess and
Leigh, England, blue, c1930, 8.5" h ...100
Dinner Plate, mkd "Willow, Cauldon
Vitrified Ware, Cauldon Ltd, England,
Furnished by Albert Pick and Company,
Chicago," blue, c1915-27 8
Eggcup, Occupied Japan, blue, 3.75" h,
2.125" d 20
Grill Plate, divided, Charlton & Thompson
Ltd, Burslem Staffordshire, England,
blue, 10" d 16
Plate, Japan, red, 10" d 12
Plate, Losol Ware, blue, 9" d 12
Plate, Royal China, blue, 9" d 10
Sandwich Tray, 2-handled, Royal China,
blue, 11.5" w 15
Serving Bowl, Royal China, pink, 10" d ..15
Tea Set, consisting of teapot, creamer,
and open sugar, Woods Ware, England,
blue, 6.25" h teapot 55
Tidbit, 3-tier, Royal China, blue, 11" h ...20

WILLOW WARE

The traditional Willow pattern, developed by Josiah Spode in 1810, is the most
universally recognized china pattern. A typical piece contains the following elements
in its motif: willow tree, "apple" tree, two
pagodas, fence, two birds, and three figures crossing a bridge.

Willow pattern china was made in
almost every country that produces ceramics. In the 1830s over 200 English companies offered Willow pattern china. Buffalo
China was one of the first American companies to offer the pattern. Japanese production started about 1902, around the
same time Buffalo made its first pieces.

Since the Willow pattern has been in
continuous production, the term reproduction has little meaning. However, the Scio
Pottery, Scio, Ohio, is currently producing
an unmarked set that is being sold in variety
stores. Because it lacks marks, some collectors have purchased it under the mistak-
en belief that it was made much earlier.

Club: International Willow Collectors, 503
Chestnut St., Perkasie, PA 18944.

Newsletter: *The Willow Word*, 1232
Anthony Trace, Waynesville, OH 45068.

WINCHESTER

Mention Winchester and the first thing
that comes to mind is the Wild Wild West
and the firearms used to tame it. Today, the
Winchester name is collectible whether it is
found on tools and cutlery or advertising
and sporting goods.

Club: The Winchester Arms Collectors
Assoc., Inc., P.O. Box 6754, Great Falls, MT
59406.

Ammunition Box, wood, "Winchester
Super Speed," 6.25" h, 15" w, 11.375" d .30

*Clock, Winchester Gun Advisory, c1962,
25.5" w, $165.* —Photo courtesy Collectors
Auction Services.

Baseball Bat, mkd "Winchester Repeating Arms Co, 2825, Winchester, Trademark, Made in U.S.A., New Haven Conn" and "Boys Special" 275

Catalog, Winchester Sporting Arms & Ammunition, 40 pp, 1961, 8.5 x 11" 15

Catalog, Winchester Western Sporting Arms & Ammunition, 1964 12

Fishing Rod, 3-pc, metal rod with wood handle, 30" l 100

Flashlight, mkd "Winchester Trade Mark, Made in U.S.A," oldest patent date Aug 17, 1920, 15.25" l 30

Money Clip, nickel silver, "Winchester 12 GA AA" 12

Pocketknife, "Winchester" on blade, Case XX, orig box 40

Poster, Terri Clark portrait, text at bottom reads "Winchester Super-X Ammunition Presents Mercury Recording Artist Terri Clark, Celebrating 75 Years as the World's Most Reliable and Dependable Ammunition!," 22 x 16" . .15

Poster, Winchester Sportsman's Game Guide, shows various shot and shell sizes and choke for shooting different game with Winchester shotguns, 28.375" h, 23" w 8

Screwdriver, wood handle, "Winchester Trademark Made in USA, #7114-5, Pat Applied For" on brass ferule 30

Wood Plane, mkd "Winchester Trademark No. 3094," Stanley, 2.5" h, 7.75" l, 2" w .65

WORLD'S FAIRS

It says a lot about the status of world's fairs when Americans cannot stage a fair in 1993–1994 that is even half as good as the 1893 Columbian Exposition in Chicago. Was the last great world's fair held in New York in 1964? Judging from recent fairs, the answer is an unqualified yes. Although it is important to stress three-dimensional objects for display purposes, do not overlook the wealth of paper that was given away to promote fairs and their participants.

Clubs: 1904 World's Fair Society, 12934 Windy Hill Dr., St. Louis, MO 63128; World's Fair Collectors' Society, P.O. Box 20806, Sarasota, FL 34276.

1893 Columbian Exposition, paperweight, Gillinder, $125.

1893 Columbian Exposition, book, *Century World's Fair Book For Boys and Girls,* hardcover, pub by Century Co, NY, 248 pp, ©1893, 7.5 x 9.5 12

1893 Columbian Exposition, commemorative coin, silvered metal, "Columbian Half Dollar,"Christopher Columbus profile on obverse, ship, 2 world globes, and "World's Columbian Exposition Chicago 1893" on reverse 8

1898 Trans-Mississippi and International Exposition, pinback button, celluloid, horticultural building, sepiatone photo .40

1904 St Louis Exposition, key chain tag, aluminum disk with diecut openings around points of central star centered by inscription "St. Louis Expo. 1904," owner's name on rim, blank reverse . .10

1909 Hudson-Fulton Celebration, pinback button, color portraits of explorers on pale blue ground, black lettering 20

1933 Century of Progress, cuff bracelet, silvered metal, official symbol, "A Century Of Progress 1933,"and buildings and attractions, .75" h 15

1933 Century of Progress, playing cards, Avenue of Flags design on backs, each face with a different black and white photo of various exhibit buildings and attractions, linen finish, orig box mkd "World's Fair Souvenir Playing Cards, 53 Views Of The Fair" 45

1933 Century of Progress, souvenir plate, white, purpletone transfer and "Fort Dearborn, A Century of Progress, Chicago 1833-1933," emb floral and magic lamp border, Pickard, 8.25" d . .20

1933 Century of Progress, stereoscope and 16 view cards, black metal stereoscope, cards #1 to #6 and #26 to #35, orig box 150

1939 New York World's Fair, Poster Stamps, unopened, $25.

1939 New York World's Fair, clothing buttons, 6 white plastic replica buildings, threaded on orig card with "World's Fairest" above Trylon and Perisphere 20
1939 New York World's Fair, glass disk, dome top, Trylon and Perisphere recessed and hp on back 20
1939 New York World's Fair, miniature views case, dark brown composition book with hinged silvered brass cov, paper fold-out strip with 8 color views of exhibit buildings, emb Trylon and Perisphere on cov 35
1939 New York World's Fair, "Official Souvenir Book," hard cover, Exposition Publications, Inc, 144 pp, 1939, 10.5 x 14" 85
1939 New York World's Fair, trinket box, metal, domed lid with emb Trylon and Perisphere, blue enamel highlights, 2.5 x 3.25" 45
1962 Seattle World's Fair, tumbler, clear glass, blue symbol and inscription "Century 21 Exposition," 4.625" h 15
1964-65 New York World's Fair, ashtray, black plastic, silver plastic figural Unisphere mounted in center, white incription "New York World's Fair, Unisphere" on base, 5" d 18
1964-65 New York World's Fair, inflatable Unisphere, vinyl, 9" d 20
1964-65 New York World's Fair, patch, white flannel, oranged-stitched Unisphere, blue orbit rings, blue lettered "New York World's Fair" 10
1967 Montreal Exposition, ring, silvered metal, adjustable, black-accented Expo symbol and "Expo 67 Montreal" .8

WRESTLING MEMORABILIA

Collecting wrestling memorabilia can be a very frustrating activity. There are no price guides, and most sellers I have encountered profess to having little or no knowledge of any aspect of professional wrestling. In recent years, wrestling has continued to lose the respect it had decades ago. From the 1800s to the 1950s, the results of important wrestling matches could be found in your local newspaper on page one of the sports section. Not anymore. Today, many fans and collectors do not like to admit to following the sport or collecting memorabilia pertaining to this wonderful slice of Americana.

Prices for wrestling memorabilia can vary tremendously. Sellers usually have no idea what to charge when they come across odd wrestling pieces. Pay only what the item is worth to you.

Advisor: John Pantozzi, 1000 Polk Ave., Franklin Square, NY 11010, (516) 488-7728.

Action Figure, Jakks Blue Blazer 15
Action Figure, WCW Hak 15
Biography, Bruno Sammartino 20
Bobbing Head, Hulk Hogan 5
Book, *Pictorial History of Wrestling,* 1985 5
Book, *Wrestling and Jiu-Jitsu,* by E Leiderman 20
Bust, Maurice Tillet, 1950s 80
Camera, digital, WWF 20
Championship Belt, exact replica 125
Child's Mask, Rey Mysterio 20
Doll, Jake the Snake Wrestling Buddy .35
Drinking Glass, Lou Thesz 30

Doll, Jushin Liger, stuffed cloth, Japan, $50.

Necktie, Mankind, WWF 10
Stand-up, cardboard, Hulk Hogan
   Suburban Commando 18
Throw Blanket, Bill Goldberg 15
Trading Cards, O-Pee-Chee, wrestling,
   1985 15
T-Shirt, Blue World Order 25
T-Shirt, The Rock 12

WRISTWATCHES

   The pocket watch generations have been replaced by the wristwatch generations. This category became hot in the late 1980s and still is going strong. There is a great deal of speculation occurring, especially in the area of character and personality watches.

   Since the category is relatively new as a collectible, no one is certain exactly how many watches have survived. I have almost a dozen that were handed down from my parents. If I am typical, the potential market supply is far greater than anyone realizes.

Clubs: National Assoc. of Watch & Clock Collectors, Inc., 514 Poplar St., Columbia, PA 17512; The Swatch Collectors Club, P.O. Box 7400, Melville, NY 11747.

Newsletter: *The Premium Watch Watch,* 24 San Rafael Dr., Rochester, NY 14618.

Periodical: *International Wrist Watch,* P.O. Box 110204 Stamford, CT 06911.

Note: Watches are in working order unless noted otherwise.

Big Jim, image of Big Jim wearing red
   shorts and armbands on dial, brown
   vinyl bands 50
Buster Brown, Buster and smiling Tige
   and small inset of Buster playing
   tug-of-war with Tige on dial, red cloth
   band, 1975 40
Captain Midnight, digital, "Captain
   Midnight, SQ" and rocket on face,
   blue vinyl bands with yellow plastic
   buckle, Ovaltine premium, orig mailing
   envelope, 1988 40
Charlie Tuna, Charlie and "Sorry Charlie"
   note hanging from fishhook on dial,
   black leather sports strap, orig mailing envelope, 1971 45

Mickey Mouse, leather straps with Mickey charms, Ingersoll, 1930s, $350.

Eurodisney First Anniversary, employee's,
   castle on dial, 3 fairies from Sleeping
   Beauty on second hand disk, black
   leather straps, purple leather case . . .75
Evel Knievel, Evel popping wheelie on
   dial, chromed metal expansion band,
   Bradley, ©1975 50
Joe Carioca, Joe on dial, brown leather
   straps, US Time, 1948, not running . . .40
Popeye, images of Popeye, Olive, Swee'
   Pea, and Wimpy on dial, early 1950s .100
Star Wars, C-3PO and R2-D2 on starry
   dial, blue vinyl strap, Bradley, ©1977 .65
Underdog, standing Underdog on dial,
   dark blue vinyl band, Lafayette Watch
   Co, ©1973 125

YARD-LONG PRINTS

   Yard-long prints cover a wide variety of subject matter. Desirability rests not so much with subject as with illustrator. The more recognized the name, the higher the price.

86th Convention of International Typo-
   graphical Union and Golden Jubilee,
   Union Printers Home, Colorado Springs,
   CO, photo, dated Sep 12, 1942, framed,
   8 x 41" 30
Absence Cannot Hearts Divide, framed,
   26.75 x 7.75" .125
American Beauty Roses, Paul de
   Longpre 45
American Poets, portraits of Whittier,
   Emerson, Longfellow, Lowell, Holmes,
   and Bryant, framed, 11 x 31" 110
Beauty Gained Is Love Retained,
   Pompeian adv, Gene Pressler, framed,
   27.5 x 7.5 40

A Yard of Baby's Breath and Roses, $200.
—Photo courtesy Gene Harris Antique
Auction Center, Inc.

Budweiser Girl, wearing red dress,
  holding bottle and rose, vertical,
  1970s, framed, 28 x 14" 15
Camp Wolters, TX, photograph, 1945,
  wood frame, 42.75 x 11.75 160
Honeymooning In the Alps, Pompeian
  adv, Gene Pressler, 1924, framed,
  27 x 9" 130
Indian Maiden, Schlitz Extract, 1909,
  framed, 23.5 x 7" 325
Our White House Queen of 1912 , framed,
  29 x 15" 135
Pabst Blue Ribbon Champion Horses,
  horse-drawn wagon with dog running
  alongside, Wilbur Stock Food adv on
  front and company history on back,
  1904, 14.75 x 31.5" 70
Pompeian Beauty Mary Pickford,
  Pompeian adv, 1923, 27.5 x 7.5 45
Study of Pansies, Grace Barton Allen,
  framed, 33 x 7.5" 15
The Ball, Pompeian adv, Gene Pressler,
  1926, framed 125
Victorian Lady, wearing long pink dress
  and feathery tiara, Pabst Brewing
  adv, framed, 38 x 11" 225

ZEISEL, EVA

The 1990s saw a tremendous growth in
collector interest in products associated
with specific industrial designers. This
trend continues unabated into the first
decade of the 21st century.

From her arrival in the United States in
1938, Eva Zeisel has been involved in
designing dinnerware and accessory lines
for a host of American ceramic companies,
e.g., Castleton China Company, Hall China
Company, Red Wing Pottery, and the
Riverside Ceramic Company. In 1964 Hyalan
produced her "Z" dinnerware line.

In the early 1980s an Eva Retrospective
traveled throughout America as part of the
Smithsonian Institution Traveling Exhibition
series and abroad.

Club: Eva Zeisel Collectors Club, 22781
Flamingo St., Woodland Hills, CA 91364.

Berry Bowl, Fantasy, Hallcraft 20
Bowl, Holiday, Hallcraft, 12" l 15
Bowl, Town & Country, rust glaze, Red
  Wing, 6" l 24
Chop Plate, Fantasy, Hallcraft, 11" 15
Cup and Saucer, Fantasy, Hallcraft 8
Dessert Plate, Bouquet, Hallcraft 3
Dinner Plate, Bouquet, Hallcraft 14
Dinner Plate, Fern, Hallcraft Century 18
Drinking Glasses, Primrose, Federal
  Glass Co, 1954, 2.75" h, set of 4 36
Gravy Boat, white, Hallcraft, 5" d 25
Luncheon Plate, Bouquet, Hallcraft 5
Pie Baker, Town & Country, green, Red
  Wing, 11" d 30
Place Setting, Bouquet, Hallcraft, 5 pcs .35
Platter, Fantasy, Hallcraft, 17.25" l 40
Salad Bowl, Town & Country, Red Wing,
  8.5" l 50
Salad Plate, Fantasy, Hallcraft, 8" d 12
Salad Plate, Fern, Hallcraft Century,
  6" d 15
Salt and Pepper Shakers, pr, figural
  Schmoos, Town & Country, char-
  treuse, Red Wing 80
Serving Bowl, Caprice, Hallcraft, 15" 35
Soup Bowl, Town & Country, peach
  glaze, Red Wing 18
Teapot, Harlequin, Hallcraft 85
Vegetable Bowl, Bouquet, Hallcraft,
  12" l, 8.75" w 5
Vegetable Bowl, Fantasy, Hallcraft 40

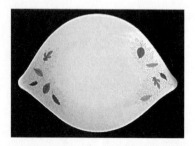

Serving Bowl, Fern, Hallcraft Century, $20.

Part Three

REFERENCE SOURCES

FLEA MARKETEER'S ANNOTATED REFERENCE LIBRARY

A typical flea market contains hundreds of thousands of objects. You cannot be expected to identify and know the correct price for everything off the top of your head. You need a good, basic reference library.

As a flea marketeer, there are two questions about every object that you want to know: "What is it?" and "How much is it worth?" A book that answers only the first question has little use in the field. Titles in the "Books About Objects" list contain both types of information.

This basic reference library consists of fifty titles. I admit the number is arbitrary. However, some limit was necessary. Acquiring all the titles on the list will not be cheap. Expect to pay somewhere between $1,250 and $1,500. You can occasionally find some of these books at clearance prices—25% to 75% off—from the publishers or at discount book sellers.

The list contains a few books that are out-of-print. You will have to pursue their purchase through various used-book sources.

Many antiques and collectibles book dealers conduct book searches and maintain "wants" lists. It is common to find one or more of these specialized dealers set up at a flea market. Most advertise in the trade papers, especially **The Antique Trader Weekly** (700 E. State St., Iola, WI 54945) and "Books For Sale" in the classified section of **AntiqueWeek** (PO Box 90, Knightstown, IN 46148). One dealer that I have found particularly helpful in locating out-of-print books is Joslin Hall Rare Books, PO Box 516, Concord, MA 01742. Also check these web sites: www.Bibliofind.com and www.abooks.com.

Many reference books are revised every year or every other year. The editions listed are those as of Fall 2000. When you buy them, make certain that you get the most recent edition.

One final factor that I used in preparing this list was a desire to introduce you to the major publishers and imprints in the antiques and collectibles field. It is important that you become familiar with Antique Publications (Glass Press), The Charlton Press, Collector Books, House of Collectibles, Krause Publications and its various imprints, L-W Book Sales, and Schiffer Publishing.

General Price Guides

Rinker, Harry L., **The Official Rinker Price Guide to Collectibles, Post-1920s Memorabilia, Fourth Edition**. (New York: House of Collectibles: 2000). This listing is totally self-serving. I firmly believe I author the best price guide to post-1920 collectibles and that you should own it. This guide is truly comprehensive, containing dozens of collecting categories not found in other "collectibles" price guides.

The introduction to each category contains a brief history, list of reference books, names and addresses of periodicals and collectors' clubs, and information about reproductions. It is the perfect companion to **The Official Guide to Flea Market Prices.**

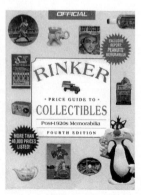

Does a flea marketeer need a general antiques and collectibles price guide? The realistic answer is no. As each year passes, antiques play a smaller and smaller role in the flea market environment. General antiques and collectibles price guides tend to be heavily weighted toward the antiques portion of the market. Most flea marketeers, whether buyers or sellers, deal primarily in 20th century collectibles.

Yet, I believe every flea marketeer should maintain a multiple year run of one general antiques and collectibles price guide for the purposes of tracking market trends and researching and pricing objects that fall outside their knowledge level. The worst mistake a flea marketeer can make is to buy a different general antiques and collectibles price guide from one year to the next. Find the guide that best serves your need and stick to it.

The following price guides are listed in the order of frequency that I see them being used in the field. The order is not by my personal preference. However, I am putting aside personal feelings and reporting facts.

Huxford, Sharon and Bob, eds., *Schroeder's Antiques Price Guide, 19th ed*. (Paducah, KY: Collector Books: 2000).

Kovel, Ralph and Terry, eds., *Kovels' Antiques & Collectibles Price List, 33rd ed*. (New York: Three Rivers Press: 2000).

Husfloen, Kyle, ed., *Antique Trader Books Antiques and Collectibles Price Guide,* (Iola, WI: Antique Trader Books/Krause Publications: 2000).

Rinker Enterprises, Inc., *The Official Price Guide to Antiques and Collectibles, 18th ed*. (New York: House of Collectibles: 2000).

Identification of Reproductions and Fakes

Hammond, Dorothy, *Confusing Collectibles: A Guide to the Identification of Contemporary Objects*. This book provides information about reproductions, copycats, fantasy items, fakes, and contemporary crafts from the late 1950s through the 1960s. Much of this material appears regularly in today's flea markets. Some is collectible in its own right. The best defense against being taken is to know what was produced.

Hammond, Dorothy, *More Confusing Collectibles, Vol. II*. (Wichita, KS: C.B.P. Publishing Company: 1973). Out-of-print. *Confusing Collectibles* took a broad approach to the market. *More Confusing Collectibles* focuses primarily on glass. It contains all new information, so you really do need both volumes.

Lee, Ruth Webb, *Antiques Fakes and Reproductions* (published by author: 1938, 1950). Out-of-print. Note: This book went through eight editions. The later editions contain more information. A good rule is to buy only the fourth through eighth editions. Dorothy Hammond followed in Ruth Webb Lee's footsteps. Lee's book chronicles the reproductions, copycats, fantasy items, and fakes manufactured between 1920 and 1950. While heavily oriented toward glass, it contains an excellent chapter on metals, discussing and picturing in detail the products of Virginia Metalcrafters.

Antique & Collectors Reproduction News. This is not a book, yet it belongs on this list. This monthly publication tracks the latest reproductions, copycats, fantasy items, and fakes. An annual subscription costs $32, an amount you are certain to save several times over during the course of a year. Consider acquiring a full set of back issues. Write *Antique & Collectors Reproduction News*, PO Box 12130, Des Moines, IA 50312.

Books About Objects

Austin, Richard J., *The Official Price Guide to Military Collectibles, 6th ed.* (New York: House of Collectibles: 1998). This book covers military collectibles from medieval to modern times. The book is organized topically, e.g., uniforms and footwear, helmets and headgear, etc. It also includes chapters on military images, military paper, military art, and homefront collectibles. It provides one-volume coverage of the material found in Ron Manion's three-volume set *American Military Collectibles Price* (1995), *Japanese & Other Foreign Military Collectibles* (1996), and *German Military Collectibles* (1995), all published by Antique Trader Books.

Bagdade, Susan and Al, *Warman's American Pottery and Porcelain, 2nd ed.* (Iola, WI: Krause Publications, 2000). Recommended because of its wide range of coverage. The category introductions provide a wealth of good information, including a large number of drawings of marks. Pricing that is auction based is clearly indicated. Use to cross-check information in Duke's *The Official Price Guide to Pottery and Porcelain.*

The Bagdades also authored *Warman's English & Continental Pottery & Porcelain, 3rd ed.* (Iola, WI: Krause Publications, 1998). While most ceramics found at American flea markets are American in origin, European pieces do slip into the mix. If you encounter English and Continental ceramics on a regular basis, consider adding this second Bagdade book to your library.

Baker, Mark, *Auto Racing Memorabilia and Price Guide* (Iola, WI: Krause Publications: 1997). Auto racing collectibles replaced baseball collectibles as the hot sport collecting category of the 1990s. Collecting auto racing memorabilia, from dirt track to Indy cars, has shed its regional cloak and become national in scope. Baker's book is the first off the starting line.

Barlow, Ronald S., *The Antique Tool Collector's Guide to Value* (Gas City, IN: L-W Book Sales: 1991, 1999 value update). This is the book for tools. Barlow has compiled auction and market prices from across the United States. Since this book is organized by tool type, you need to identify the type of tool that you have before you can look it up. There are plenty of illustrations to help. Treat the pricing with some caution.

Bunis, Marty and Sue, *Collector's Guide to Antique Radios, 4th ed.* (Paducah, KY: Collector Books: 1997). There is a wealth of radio books in the market. This one is tuned in to a wide band of radios. Organization is by manufacturer and model number. Although heavily illustrated, the book does not picture the majority of the models listed. The book also covers radio parts and accessories.

Collectors' Information Bureau's Collectibles Market Guide & Price Index, 18th ed. (Barrington, IL: Collectors' Information Bureau: 2000). The best thing about this book is that it covers a wide range of limited edition types, from bells to steins. It serves as a collector's checklist. The worst thing is that it is industry-driven. Important negatives and warnings about the limited edition market are minimized. When the issue value and secondary value are identical or within a few dollars assume the real secondary market value is between 20% and 40% of the issue price.

Cornwell, Sue, and Mike Kott, *House of Collectibles Price Guide to Star Trek Collectibles, 4th ed.* (New York: House of Collectibles: 1996). There is no question that *Star Trek* collectibles will "live long and prosper." This price guide covers over 5,000 items licensed for the initial *Star Trek* television program, the movies, and television spin-off series, *Star Trek: The Next Generation, Star Trek: Voyager, and Deep Space 9.* Includes some foreign licensed materials. Unfortunately, a chapter on convention souvenirs is nowhere to be found.

Cornwell, Sue and Mike Kott, **House of Collectibles Price Guide to Star Wars Collectibles, 4th ed.** (New York: House of Collectibles: 1997). *Star Wars* won the galactic battle over *Star Trek* for universal dominance in the field of space collectibles with Lucas' 1997 re-release of the *Star Wars* trilogy. When the first of the prequels premiered in May 1999, the world went *Star Wars* mad. Many, myself among them, predicted a major pricing jump in older *Star Wars* material. This book documents values prior to their jump to light speed. As an alternate reference source, see *The Galaxy's Greatest Star Wars Collectibles Price Guide, 1999 Edition* by Stuart W. Wells III (Dubuque, IA: Antique Trader Books, 1998).

Cunningham, Jo, **The Collector's Encyclopedia of American Dinnerware** (Paducah, KY: Collector Books: 1982, 1998 price update). This is a profusely illustrated guide to identifying 20th century American dinnerware. In spite of the fact that many new companies and patterns have been discovered since Cunningham prepared her book, it remains a valuable identification tool, especially since its pricing is updated periodically.

Dale, Jean, **The Charlton Standard Catalogue of Royal Doulton Beswick Figurines, 7th ed.** (Toronto, Canada: The Charlton Press: 2000). This is one in a series of four books edited by Dale covering the products of Royal Doulton Beswick. The others are: **The Charlton Standard Catalogue of Royal Doulton Animals, 2nd Ed.** (1998); **Charlton Standard Catalogue Royal Doulton Jugs, 6th ed.** (2001); and **Charlton Standard Catalogue of Royal Doulton Beswick Storybook Figurines, 6th ed.** (2000). A feature of each of these books is that pricing information is provided in English pounds, Canadian dollars, and American dollars. Americans should pay more attention to books published by The Charlton Press. The title list also includes books on chintz and hockey trading cards.

Duke, Harvey, **The Official Identification and Price Guide to Pottery and Porcelain, 8th ed.** (New York: House of Collectibles: 1995). This book is dinnerware, kitchenware, and accessory oriented. As such it is the perfect companion to Cunningham. Duke covers many of the companies and lines of which Cunningham was unaware when she first published her book in the early 1980s. Illustrations are minimal, making it necessary to know the name of your pattern before looking anything up. The book is well-balanced regionally. Many West Coast pottery manufacturers finally receive their due. Its major drawback is the lack of an index.

Florence, Gene, **The Collector's Encyclopedia of Depression Glass, 14th ed.** (Paducah, KY: Collector Books: 2000). This is the Depression glass collector's bible. Among its important features are a full listing of pieces found in each pattern and an extensive section on reproductions, copycats, and fakes. One difficulty is that there are hundreds of glass patterns manufactured between 1920 and 1940 that are not found in this book because they do not have the Depression Glass label. Supplement the book with Gene Florence's **Kitchen Glassware of the Depression Years** and **Collectible Glassware from the 40s, 50s, 60s...,** both published by Collector Books, **Mauzy's Depression Glass** (Schiffer Publishing, 1999) by Barbara and Jim Mauzy, and **Warman's Depression Glass: A Value & Identification Guide, 2nd ed.** (Krause Publications, 2000) by Ellen Schroy.

Foulke, Jan, **14th Blue Book Dolls and Values** (Grantsville, MD: Hobby House Press: 1999). Foulke is the first place doll collectors turn for information. The book is high-end, turning its back on many of the post–World War II and contemporary dolls. Within the doll field, it sets prices more than it reports them. Cross-check Foulke's prices in Dawn Herlocher's **200 Years of Dolls: Identification and Price Guide** (Antique Trader Books, 1996).

Franklin, Linda Campbell, *300 Years of Housekeeping Collectibles* (Books Americana, now an imprint of Krause Publications, Iola, WI: 1993). Books Americana split the second edition of *300 Years of Kitchen Collectibles* into two separate volumes, albeit retaining the edition number for one of the spin-offs. Now, instead of paying $10.95 for a handy-to-use single source, you have to pay $47.90 for two volumes. Hopefully a publisher will see an opportunity and once again put this information in a single volume. Until such time, it makes sense to buy the two Franklin volumes.

Franklin, Linda Campbell, *300 Years of Kitchen Collectibles, 4th ed.* (Iola, WI: Krause Publications: 1997). The fourth edition's format is a considerable improvement over that of the third edition. The book is much easier to use. The wealth of secondary material may be great for researchers and specialized collectors, but it is a pain to wade through when you just want to look up something quickly. This focus is primarily in 19th and early 20th century material. It is not the source to use if your kitchen item dates from the post-1945 era.

Gibbs, P. J., *Black Collectibles Sold in America* (Paducah, KY: Collector Books: 1987, 1996 value update). Black collectibles have gone through a number of collecting cycles in the past fifteen years. Popular among both white and black collectors, Black memorabilia is likely to cycle several more times in the years ahead. Because of this, prices in any Black collectibles book have to be taken with a grain of salt.

Hagan, Tere, *Silverplated Flatware, revised 4th ed.* (Paducah, KY: Collector Books: 1990, 1998 value update). You do not see a great deal of sterling silver at flea markets because most dealers sell it for weight. Silver-plated items are in abundance. This book concentrates only on flatware, the most commonly found form. While you can research silver-plated hollowware in Jeri Schwartz's *The Official Identification and Price Guide to Silver and Silverplate, 6th ed.* (House of Collectibles, 1989, out-of-print), disregard the prices. The market has changed significantly.

Hake, Ted, *Hake's Guide to ...* series (Radnor, PA: Wallace-Homestead). In the first half of the 1990s, Ted Hake authored a five-book priced picture-book series focusing on material sold in Hake's Americana & Collectibles Mail Auction. Each collecting category is introduced with a brief history, often containing information not readily available to the collector. The series consists of: *Hake's Guide to Advertising Collectibles: 100 Years of Advertising From 100 Famous Companies* (1992); *Hake's Guide to Comic Character Collectibles: An Illustrated Price Guide to 100 Years of Comic Strip Characters* (1993); *Hake's Guide to Cowboy Character Collectibles: An Illustrated Price Guide Covering 50 Years of Movie and TV Cowboy Heroes* (1994); *Hake's Guide to Presidential Campaign Collectibles: An Illustrated Price Guide to Artifacts from 1789–1988* (1992); and, *Hake's Guide to TV Collectibles: An Illustrated Price Guide* (1990). Several titles are out-of-print. Some are still available from Krause Publications. Allowing this series to die was one in a long list of mistakes made by Chilton Books in the company's final years as publisher of Wallace-Homestead and Warman titles.

Hake, Ted, *Hake's Price Guide to Character Toys, 3rd ed.* (Timonium, MD: Gemstone Publishing, 2000). Hake is the king of collectibles. If anyone knows, he does. This title covers 360 categories and 200 different types of items. Its 10,000 listings range from common to one-of-a-kind premiums. The category introductions provide historical data not available elsewhere. Also be sure to read the front matter. It provides insights into the latest market trends.

Herlocher, Dawn, *200 Years of Dolls: Identification and Price Guide* (Dubuque, IA: Antique Trader Books: 1996). Doll identification and pricing information presented in a fresh, new, and extremely usable format. Covering 125 doll manufacturers, the book features a mix of antique and collectibles dolls. Use to cross-check the information and pricing in Foulke's *Blue Book of Doll Values.* See also *Doll Makers & Marks: A Guide to Identification* (Dubuque, IA: Antique Trader Books, 1999) by Dawn Herlocher.

Huxford, Bob, *Huxford's Old Book Value Guide, 12th ed.* (Paducah, KY: Collector Books: 2000). There are always piles of old books at any flea market. Most are valued at less than 50 cents. However, there are almost always sleepers in every pile. This book is a beginning. If you think that you have a really expensive tome, check it out in the most recent edition of *American Book Prices Current,* published by Bancroft-Parkman.

Huxford, Sharon and Bob (eds.), *Shroeder's Collectible Toys: Antique to Modern Price Guide, 4th ed.* (Paducah, KY: Collector Books, 1998). See also [O'Brien's] *Collecting Toys: Identification & Value Guide, 9th ed.* edited by Elizabeth Stephan (Iola, WI: Krause Publications, 1999) and *2001 Toys & Prices, 8th ed.* edited by Sharon Korbeck and Elizabeth Stephan (Iola, WI: Krause Publications, 2000).

Malloy, Alex G., *American Games: Comprehensive Collector's Guide* (Iola, WI: Antique Trader Books/Krause Publications, 2000). There are a number of guides to games. Malloy's provides the most comprehensive listing. The descriptions are minimal. Always check a game's instructions for information on what playing pieces are needed to make the game complete. Harry L. Rinker's *Antique Trader's Guide to Games & Puzzles* (Antique Trader Books, 1997) offers a second opinion and expands the coverage to puzzles.

Martinus, Norman E., and Harry L. Rinker, *Warman's Paper* (Radnor, PA: Wallace-Homestead: 1994, out-of-print).The paper market is hot and getting hotter. Paper is available and affordable. The market already has dozens of specialized shows. *Warman's Paper* is organized into seventy-five collecting topics and over two hundred subject topics. Of all the books with which I have been involved, this title ranks number three on my "most proud" list, right behind *The Official Rinker Price Guide to Collectibles, Post-1920s Memorabilia* and *Warman's Furniture* (out-of-print).

Melillo, Marcie, *The Ultimate Barbie Doll Book* (Iola, WI: Krause Publications: 1997). Barbie—the vinyl goddess, the billion dollar baby—has become so important she deserves a separate listing. There are dozens of Barbie price guides available. This is my favorite full coverage guide. When I want information on contemporary Barbies, my choice is the new edition of Jane Sarasohn-Kahn's *Contemporary Barbie: Barbie Dolls 1980 and Beyond* (Antique Trader Books, 1998). Also consider adding a Barbie price guide that includes information on costumes and accessories, two hot Barbie subcollecting categories in the late 1990s.

Morykan, Dana G., *The Official Price Guide to Country Antiques and Collectibles, 4th ed.*, (New York: House of Collectibles: 1999). This is the bible for Country collectibles. Published previously as part of the Warman series, it has found a new home in New York. For those who still feel the need for a picture-oriented guide, check out Don and Carol Raycraft's *Wallace-Homestead Price Guide to American Country Antiques, 16th ed.,* (Krause Publications, 1999).

Osborne, Jerry, **The Official Price Guide to Records, 14th ed.** (New York: House of Collectibles: 2000). This is the book to which everyone refers. It lists every charted hit single and album from the 1950s through 1990. Alas, it provides minimal coverage for pre–1940 records. Today, record collecting is highly specialized. There are dozens of specialized price guides to records, many published by Krause Publications. See also **Goldmine Standard Catalog of American Records: 1950-1975, 2nd ed.** by Tim Neely (Iola, WI: Krause Publications, 2000).

Overstreet, Robert M., **The Overstreet Comic Book Price Guide, 30th ed.** (Timonium, MD: Gemstone Publishing: 2000). Long live the king. Although focused too heavily on the Golden and Silver Age of American comics and not heavily enough on contemporary American comics, foreign issues, and underground comics, Overstreet is clearly the price guide of choice among adult collectors. This book sets the market more than it reports it.

Petretti, Allan, **Petretti's Soda Pop Collectibles Price Guide: The Encyclopedia of Soda Pop Collectibles** (Dubuque, IA: Antique Trader Books: 1997). This is the latest offering from the king of Coca–Cola collectibles. This priced picture guide is organized first by object type and then alphabetically by soda company. Do not overlook Allan Petretti's **Petretti's Coca-Cola Collectibles Price Guide, 10th ed.** (Antique Trader Books, 1997). It introduces the Petretti numbering system, an easy method to describe Coca-Cola collectibles.

Rinker, Harry L., **Dinnerware of the Twentieth Century: Top 500 Patterns** (New York: House of Collectibles: 1997). This book provides detailed information on the 500 most popular dinnerware patterns sought by replacement buyers. Each pattern has an illustration of the plate from the set and a comprehensive checklist of the forms available. There are two other titles in this series: **Stemware of the Twentieth Century: Top 200 Patterns** covers the 200 most popular stemware patterns and **Silverware of the Twentieth Century: Top 250 Patterns** includes the 250 most popular sterling, silver plated, and stainless flatware patterns. Buy all three.

Romero, Christie, ***Warman's Jewelry, 2nd ed.*** (Iola, WI: Krause Publications: 1998). The best general price guide to jewelry available. It utilizes a time period approach, is well illustrated, and features highly detailed listing descriptions. The book is loaded with historical information, hallmarks, manufacturer's marks, reference source referrals, and a time line chronicling the history of jewelry. Appendices include a listing of American costume jewelry manufacturers (with dates of operation) and a glossary.

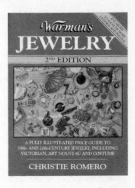

Schroy, Ellen, ***Warman's Glass, 3rd ed.*** (Iola, WI: Krause Publications: 1999). A comprehensive guide to the traditional glass market. While heavily American focused, it does include information on major English and European glass collecting categories. It has a balanced approach, covering everything from the finest art glass to household utilitarian glass. Check out Mark Pickvett's ***The Official Price Guide to Glassware, 3rd ed.*** (New York: House of Collectibles, 2000), a challenger to ***Warman's Glass*** that gets better and better with each new edition.

Shugart, Cooksey, Tom Engle and Richard E. Gilbert, ***Complete Price Guide to Watches, No. 20*** (Cleveland, TN: Cooksey Shugart Publications: 2000). Although this book has been distributed by four different publishers during the past ten years, it has never failed to maintain its high quality. It is the best book available on pocket and wrist watches.

Sports Collectors Digest, ***Baseball Card Price Guide, 14th ed.*** (Iola, WI: Krause Publications: 2000). This book has become a superstar. It is more comprehensive and accurate than its competition. Supplement it with the ***Sports Collectors Digest 2001 Standard Catalog of Baseball Cards, 10th Edition*** (Krause Publications, 2000). The one-two hitting combination of these two books relegate James Beckett's ***Baseball Card Price Guide*** to benchwarmer status.

Swedberg, Robert W. and Harriett, ***Collector's Encyclopedia of American Furniture:*** three volumes: ***Volume 1—The Dark Woods of the Nineteenth Century: Cherry, Mahogany, Rosewood, and Walnut*** (1991, 1998 value update); ***Volume 2—Furniture of the Twentieth Century*** (1992, 1999 value update); and ***Volume 3—Country Furniture of the Eighteenth and Nineteenth Centuries*** (1994, 1998 value update). This series is published by Collector Books in Paducah, KY. The Swedbergs write about furniture. While their most recent work is done for Collector Books, Krause Publications still keeps their Wallace-Homestead series on oak furniture in print. It is worth a referral from time to time. Also do not ignore the ***Swedbergs' Furniture of the Depression Era: Furniture & Accessories of the 1920's, 1930's & 1940's*** (Collector Books, 1987, 1999 value update). All books utilize a priced-picture approach. Text information, including descriptions for individual pieces, is minimal. Sources are heavily Midwest. The plus factor is that the books feature pieces for sale in the field, not museum examples.

Wells, Stuart W., III and Jim Main, ***The Official Price Guide to Action Figures, 2nd ed.*** (New York: House of Collectibles, 1999). Finally, we have a price guide to action figures, and it is excellent. It provides background information and detailed listings for twenty-four major action figure groups such as the A-Team, Masters of the Universe, Marvel Superheroes, Spawn, Teenage Mutant Ninja Turtles, and X-Men. It even includes *Star Trek* and *Star Wars* figures. Its index is top of the line.

Mark Books

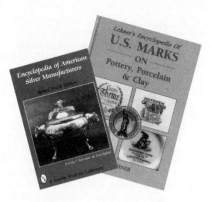

Lehner, Lois, **Lehner's Encyclopedia of U.S. Marks on Pottery, Porcelain, and Clay** (Paducah, KY: Collector Books: 1988). This is the best reference book for identifying the marks of United States pottery and porcelain manufacturers. It contains detailed company histories and all known marks and trade names used. Whenever possible, marks and trade names are dated.

Rainwater, Dorothy T., **Encyclopedia of American Silver Manufacturers, Fourth ed.** (Atglen, PA: Schiffer Publishing: 1998). This book focuses on hand-crafted and mass-produced factory–manufactured silver and silver plate from the mid-nineteenth century to the present. It is organized alphabetically by company. Each detailed company history is accompanied by carefully drawn and dated marks. A glossary of trademarks is another welcome feature.

Business References

Hyman, Dr. Tony, **Trash or Treasure: How to Find The Best Buyers of Antiques, Collectibles and Other Undiscovered Treasures** (Pismo Beach, CA: Treasure Hunt Publications, 2000). Tony Hyman is one of the most magnetic radio personalities that I have ever heard. He writes and compiles. Most importantly, he hustles what he has done. This is a list of people who buy things. One good contact pays for the cost of the book. It is also a great place to get your collecting interests listed.

Johnson, Don, and Elizabeth Borland, **Selling Antiques & Collectibles: 50 Ways To Improve Your Business** (Radnor, PA: Wallace-Homestead: 1993). Out-of-print. In a flea market era when there is a proliferation of dealers and fierce competition for customers, this book gives you the competitive edge. It shows you how to stand out from the crowd, increase clientele, and keep customers coming back. The advice is practical and budget conscious.

Maloney, David, Jr,. **Maloney's Antiques and Collectibles Resource Directory, 5th ed.** (Dubuque, IA: Antique Trader Books: 1999). This is the one reference book to buy if you are only going to buy one. It is a comprehensive directory to the antiques and collectibles market containing approximately 18,000 entries (names, addresses, telephone numbers, and a wealth of other information) in approximately 3,100 categories. It is fully cross-referenced. It covers buyers, sellers, appraisers, restorers, collectors' clubs, periodicals, museums and galleries, show promoters, shops and malls, and many other specialists.

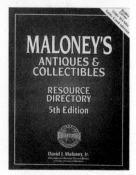

Wanted to Buy, 7th ed. (Paducah, KY: Collector Books: 1999). This is another book listing individuals who want to buy things. If you are a serious collector, write to Collector Books and see if your name and interests can be included in subsequent editions. The book differs from **Trash or Treasure** because it contains several dozen listings and prices for most categories.

Internet Buying & Selling

Boileau, Ray, *The ABCs of Collecting Online, 3rd ed.* (Grantsville, MD: Hobby House Press, 2000).

Hix, Nancy L., *Collector's Guide to Buying, Selling and Trading on the Internet, 2nd ed.* (Paducah, KY: Collector Books, 2000).

Heim, Judy and Gloria Hansen, *Free Stuff for Collectors on the Internet* (Lafayette, CA: C&T Publishing, 2000).

Books on buying and selling on the Internet are appearing as fast as publishers can publish them. Given the rapid changing nature of the Internet, they are outdated by the time they hit the bookstore shelves. Instead of using these books as "how-to" books, use them to hone the skills acquired by your own seat-of-the-pants experiences.

The problem with many "how-to" books is that they make it sound so simple. Buying and selling on the Internet is simple and time consuming. Few individuals factor in the cost of their time, equipment, and other expenses when determining how much they paid or made. After hauling the fiftieth box to the post office, selling or buying at an antiques mall or show is an attractive alternate way to do business.

General References

Long, Jane S. and Richard W. Long, *Caring for Your Family Treasures* (New York, NY: Harry N. Abrams, 2000). You have a responsibility to care for the antiques, collectibles, and desirables in your possession. This book provides practical care tips. Many are nothing more than common sense, approaches that should be natural but not always are. My advice is to read the book once a year. Even if you do not learn something new, you have a chance to re-evaluate your care procedures to see if changes are warranted.

Rinker, Harry L., *Rinker on Collectibles* (Radnor, PA: Wallace–Homestead: 1988). Out-of-print. This book is a compilation of the first sixty text columns from my column, "Rinker on Collectibles." Many are now classics. The book allows you to delve into the mind-set of the collector. It deserves textbook status. I bought the remaining warehouse stock. If you would like a copy, send $10 to: Harry L. Rinker, 5093 Vera Cruz Road, Emmaus, PA 18049. I will even autograph it for you.

Werner, Kitty, ed., *The Official Directory to U.S. Flea Markets, 7th ed.* (New York: House of Collectibles: 2000). My opinion of this book is clearly stated in Chapter 2. Take my suggestion and buy a copy.

Just for the Fun of It

Gash, Jonathan, *The Sleepers of Erin* (New York: Viking Penguin: 1983). If you are unfamiliar with Lovejoy the antiques dealer, it is time you make his acquaintance. You will not regret it. I had a hard time picking a favorite. I could have just as easily chosen *The Judas Pair, Gold by Gemini, The Grail Tree, Spend Game, The Vatican Rip, and The Gondola Scam,* all in paperback from Viking Penguin. I do not like the more recent Lovejoy novels, e.g., *The Tartan Sell, Moonspender, and Pearlhanger*. They do not read well.

Rinker, Harry L. *The Joy of Collecting with Craven Moore* (Radnor, PA: Wallace-Homestead: 1985). Out-of-print. Try never to become so serious about your collecting or dealing that you forget to laugh and have fun. Find out if you are Craven Moore, Anita Moore, Howie Bys or Constance Lee Bys. Trust me, you are in *The Joy of Collecting with Craven Moore.* I guarantee it. Although out-of-print, I still have a few copies around. I will sell you one for $6. Send a check or money order to: Harry L. Rinker, 5093 Vera Cruz Road, Emmaus, PA 18049.

ANTIQUES & COLLECTIBLES TRADE NEWSPAPERS

Rinker Enterprises receives the following general and regional periodicals. Periodicals covering a specific collecting category are listed in the introductory material for that category.

NATIONAL MAGAZINES

Antique Trader's Collector Magazine & Price Guide
Krause Publications
700 E. State St.
Iola, WI 54990
(715) 445-2214
fax: (800) 531-0880
www.collect.com/collector mag
e-mail: traderpubs@Krause.com

Antiques & Collecting Magazine
1006 S. Michigan Ave.
Chicago, IL 60605
(800) 762-7576
fax: (312) 939-0053
e-mail: LightnerPb@aol.com

Collectors' Eye
6 Woodside Ave., Ste. 300
Northport, NY 11768
(631) 261-4100
fax: (631) 261-9684
e-mail: CollectorsEye@aol.com

Collectors' Showcase
7134 S. Yale Ave., Ste. 720
Tulsa, OK 74136
(800) 310-7047
e-mail: sirtm@msn.com

Country Accents Collectibles, Flea Market Finds
Goodman Media Group
419 Park Ave. South
New York, NY 10016
(800) 955-3870

Warman's Today's Collector
Krause Publications
700 E. State St.
Iola, WI 54990
(800) 258-0929
fax: (715) 445-4087
www.todayscollector.com
e-mail:
    todays_collector@krause.com

NATIONAL NEWSPAPERS

The Antique Trader Weekly
Krause Publications
700 E. State St.
Iola, WI 54945
(800) 334-7165
fax: (800) 531-0880
www.collect.com
e-mail: collect@Krause.com

Antique Week (Central and Eastern Editions)
27 N. Jefferson St.
P.O. Box 90
Knightstown, IN 46148
(800) 876-5133
fax: (800) 695-8153
www.antiqueweek.com
e-mail: antiquewk@aol.com

Antiques and the Arts Weekly
The Bee Publishing Co.
P.O. Box 5503
Newtown, CT 06470
(203) 426-8036
fax: (203) 426-1394
www.thebee.com
e-mail: info@thebee.com

Collectors News
506 Second St.
P.O. Box 306
Grundy Center, IA 50638
(800) 352-8039
fax: (319) 824-3414
www.collectors-news.com
e-mail:
    collectors@collectorsnews.com

Maine Antique Digest
911 Main St.
P.O. Box 1429
Waldoboro, ME 04572
(800) 752-8521
fax: (207) 832-7341
www.maineantiquedigest.com
e-mail: mad@maine.com

REGIONAL NEWSPAPERS

New England

Cape Cod Antiques Monthly
P.O. Box 546
Farmington, NH 03835
(603) 755-4568

The Fine Arts Trader
P.O. Box 1273
Randolph, MA 02368
(800) 332-5055
fax: (781) 961-9044
www.fineartstrader.com

The Journal of Antiques and Collectibles
P.O. Box 950
Sturbridge, MA 01566

MassBay Antiques
254 Second Ave.
Needham, MA 02494
(800) 982-4023
e-mail: mbantiques@cnc.com

New England Antiques Journal
4 Church St.
P.O. Box 120
Ware, MA 01082
(800) 432-3505
fax: (413) 967-6009
www.antiquesjournal.com
e-mail: visit@antiquesjournal.com

New Hampshire Antiques Monthly
P.O. Box 546
Farmington, NH 03835
(603) 755-4568
fax: (603) 755-3990

Treasure Chest
564 Eddy St.
Providence, RI 02903
(800) 557-9662
fax: (401) 272-9422

UnRavel the Gavel
14 Hurricane Rd., #1
Belmont, NH 03220
(603) 524-4281
fax: (603) 528-3565
www.thegavel.net
e-mail: gavel96@worldpath.net

The Vermont Antique Times
2434 Depot St.
P.O. Box 1880
Manchester Center, VT 05255
(800) 542-4224
e-mail: antique@vermontel.net

Middle Atlantic States

Antiques & Auction News
Rte. 230 West, P.O. Box 500
Mount Joy, PA 17552
(717) 653-1833
fax: (717) 653-6165

*Antiques Guide of NJ, So.
NY, NYC & Eastern PA*
173 Morris St.
P.O. Box 1715
Morristown, NJ 07962
(973) 605-1877
fax: (973) 605-1883
e-mail: antiquesgd@aol.com

Antiques Tattler (Adamstown)
P.O. Box 938T
Adamstown, PA 19501
www.antiquescapital.com

*The New York Antique
Almanac*
P.O. Box 2400
New York, NY 10021
(212) 988-2700
fax: (212) 988-5255

*New York City's Antique
News*
110 W. 25th St. #1004
P.O. Box 2054
New York, NY 10159
(212) 675-8006
fax: (212) 675-8007
www.nycan.com
e-mail: info@nycan.com

*New York–Pennsylvania
Collector*
73 Buffalo St.
Canandaigua, NY 14424
(800) 836-1868
fax: (716) 394-7725
e-mail:
    collector@MPNewspapers.com

*Northeast Journal of
Antiques & Art*
364 Warren St.
P.O. Box 37
Hudson, NY 12534
(800) 836-4069
fax: (518) 828-3870
www.northeastjournal.com
e-mail: nejourl@mhonline.net

Renninger's Antique Guide
2 Cypress Place
P.O. Box 495
Lafayette Hill, PA 19444
(610) 828-4614
fax: (610) 834-1599

South

Antique Gazette
Krause Publications
700 E. State St.
Iola, WI 54990
(888) 457-2873
www.krause.com

The Antique Shoppe
P.O. Box 2175
Keystone Heights, FL 32656
(352) 475-1679
fax: (352) 475-5326
www.antiquenet.com/
    antiqueshoppe
e-mail: EDSOPER@aol.com

*The Antique Shoppe of the
Carolinas*
P.O. Box 640
Lancaster, SC 29721
(800) 210-7253
fax: (803) 283-8969
e-mail: lanenewsadv@infave.net

Carolina Antique News
P.O. Box 241114
Charlotte, NC 28224
(704) 553-2865
fax: (704) 643-3960
www.carolinaantiques.com
e-mail: publishr@concentric.net

*Cotton & Quail Antique
Trail*
205 East Washington St.
P.O. Box 326
Monticello, FL 32345
(800) 757-7755
fax: (850) 997-3090
e-mail: cottonq@worldnet.att.net

*MidAtlantic Antiques
Magazine*
500 W. Jefferson St.
P.O.Box 5040
Monroe, NC 28111
(704) 289-1541
fax: (704) 289-2929
www.maantiques@theej.com

*The Old News Is Good
News Antiques Gazette*
41429 W. I-55 Service Rd.
P.O. Box 305
Hammond, LA 70404
(504) 429-0575
fax: (504) 429-0576
www.theantiquesgazette.com
e-mail: gazette@i–55.com

*Southeastern Antiquing and
Collecting Magazine*
P.O. Box 510
Acworth, GA 30101
(888) 388-7827
www.go-star.com
e-mail: antiquing@go-star.com

Southern Antiques
P.O. Drawer 1107
Decatur, GA 30031
(404) 289-0054
fax: (404) 286-9727
www.kaleden.com
e-mail:
    southernantiques@msn.com

The Vintage Times
P.O. Box 7567
Macon, GA 31209
(888) 757-4755
www.mylink.met\~antiques
e-mail: antiques@mylink.net

Midwest

*The American Antiquities
Journal*
126 East High St.
Springfield, OH 45502
(800) 557-6281
fax: (937) 322-0294
www.americanantiquites.com
e-mail:
    mail@americanantiquities.com

*The Antique Collector and
Auction Guide*
Weekly Section of *Farm and
Dairy*
185-205 E. State St.
Salem, OH 44460
(330) 337-3419
fax: (330) 337-9550
www.farmanddairy.com

Antique Review
12 E. Stafford St.
P.O. Box 538
Worthington, OH 43085
(800) 992-9757
fax: (614) 885-9762
www.antiquereview.net
e-mail: editor@antiquereview.net

Auction Action Antique News
1404½ E. Green Bay St.
Shawano, WI 54166
(715) 524-3076
fax: (800) 580-4568
www.auctionactionnews.com
e-mail:
  auction@auctionactionnews.com

The Auction Exchange
292 Industrial Pkwy.
P.O. Box 57
Plainwell, MI 49080
(616) 685-1343
fax: (616) 685-8840

Auction World
101 12th St. South
Box 227
Benson, MN 56215
(800) 750-0166
fax: (320) 843-3246
www.infolink.morris.mn.us/~jfield
e-mail:
  jfield@infolink.morris.mn.us

The Collector
204 S. Walnut St.
P.O. Box 148
Heyworth, IL 61745
(309) 473-2466
fax: (309) 473-3610
e-mail: collinc@davesworld.net

Collectors Journal
1800 West D St.
P.O. Box 601
Vinton, IA 52349
(800) 472-4006
fax: (319) 472-3117
www.collectorsjournal.com
e-mail: antiquescj@aol.com

Discover Mid-America
400 Grand, Ste. B
Kansas City, MO 64106
(800) 899-9730
fax: (816) 474-1427
www.discoverypub.com
e-mail: discopub@aol.com

Great Lakes Trader
132 S. Putnam
Williamstown, MI 48895
(800) 785-6367
fax: (517) 655-5380

*Indiana Antique Buyer's
News, Inc.*
P.O. Box 213
Silver Lake, IN 46982
(888) 834-2263
fax: (219) 893-4251
www.indianaantique.com
e-mail: iabn@hoosierlink.net

Ohio Collectors' Magazine
P.O. Box 1522
Piqua, OH 45356
(937) 773-6063
fax: (937) 773-6063

The Old Times
63 Birch Ave. South
P.O. Box 340
Maple Lake, MN 55358
(800) 539-1810
fax: (320) 963-6499
www.theoldtimes.com
e-mail: oldtimes@lkdllink.net

Yesteryear
P.O. Box 2
Princeton, WI 54968
(920) 787-4808
fax: (920) 787-7381
e-mail: yesteryear@vbe.com

Southwest

*The Antique Register &
Country Register, Inc.*
P.O. Bix 84345
Phoenix, AZ 85071
(602) 942-8950
fax: (602) 866-3136
www.countryregister.com

The Antique Traveler
109 E. Broad St.
P.O. Box 656
Mineola, TX 75773
(800) 446-3588
www.antiquetraveler.com
e-mail: antiq@flash.net

Antiquing Texas
P.O. Box 7754
The Woodlands, TX 77387

Arizona Antique News
P.O. Box 26536
Phoenix, AZ 85068
(602) 943-9137

West Coast

Antique & Collectables
500 Fensler, Ste. 201
P.O. Box 12589
El Cajon, CA 92022
(619) 593-2925
fax: (619) 447-7187
www.collect.com

*Antique Journal for
California and Nevada*
2329 Santa Clara Ave., #207
Alameda, CA 94501
(800) 791-8592
fax: (510) 523-5262
www.collect.com
e-mail: antiquesjrl@aol.com

*Antique Journal for the
Northwest*
2329 Santa Clara Ave., #207
Alameda, CA 94501
(800) 791-8592
fax: (510) 523-5262
www.collect.com
e-mail: antiquesjrl@aol.com

Antiques Plus
P.O. Box 5467
Salem, OR 97304
(503) 391-7618
fax: (503) 391-2695
www.AntiquesPlus.com
e-mail: editor@antiquesplus.com

Collector
436 W. 4th St., Ste. 222
Pomona, CA 91766
(909) 620-9014
fax: (909) 622-8152
www.collectorsconference .com
e-mail: Icollect@aol.com

Mountain States Collector
P.O. Box 2525
Evergreen, CO 80439
(303) 987-3994
fax: (303) 674-1253

Old Stuff
VBM Printers, Inc.
P.O. Box 449
McMinnville, OR 97128
(503) 434-5386
fax: (503) 435-0990
www.oldstuffnews.com
e-mail: oldstuff@onlinemac.com

The Oregon Vintage Times
856 Lincoln #2
Eugene, OR 97401
(541) 484-0049
www.efn.org/~venus/antique/
antique.html
e-mail: venus@efn.org

West Coast Peddler
P.O. Box 5134
Whittier, CA 90607
(562) 698-1718
fax: (562) 698-1500
www.WestCoastPeddler.com
e-mail:
antiques@WestCoastPeddler@
earthlink.net

INTERNATIONAL
NEWSPAPERS

Australia

Carter's Antiques &
Collectables
Carter's Promotions Pty. Ltd.
Locked Bag 3
Terrey Hills, NSW 2084
Australia
(02) 9450 0011
fax: (02) 9450 2532
www.carters.com.au
e-mail: info@carters.com.au

Canada

Antique and Collectibles
Trader
P.O. Box 38095
550 Eglinton Ave. West
Toronto, Ontario
Canada M5N 3A8
(416) 410-7620
fax: (416) 784-9796

Antique Showcase
Trajan Publishing Corp.
103 Lakeshore Rd., Ste. 202
St. Catherines, Ontario
Canada L2N 2T6
(800) 408-0352
fax: (905) 646-0995
www.trajan.com

Thompsons' Antiques
Gazette
#50-39026 Range Rd. 275
Red Deer County, Alberta
Canada T4S 2A9
(403) 346-8791
fax: (403) 343-0242
www.antiquesalberta.com/
thompsonantiques
e-mail: mthompson@agt.net

The Upper Canadian
30 D Chambers St.
Box 653
Smiths Falls, Ontario
Canada K7A 4T6
(613) 283-1168
fax: (613) 283-1345
www.uppercanadian.com
e-mail:
uppercanadian@recorder.ca

England

Antiques Trade Gazette
Circulation Dept.
115 Shaftesbury Ave.
London WC2H 8AD U.K.
020 7420 6600
www.atg-online.com
e-mail: subscriptions@
antiquestradegazette.com

Antiques & Art Independent
P.O. Box 1945
Comely Bank
Edinburgh, EH4 1AB U.K.
07000 765 263
fax: 0131 332 4481
www.antiques-UK.co.UK/
independent
e-mail:
antiquesnews@hotmail.com

Finland

Keräilyn Maailma
Vuorikatu 22 B 65
00100 Helsinki
(09) 170090

France

France Antiquités
Château de Boisrigaud
63490 Usson
(04) 73 71 00 04
e-mail:
France.Antiquites@wanadoo.fr

La Vie du Collectionneur
B. P. 77
77302 Fontainbleau Cedex
(01) 60 71 55 55

Germany

Antiquitäten Zeitung
Nymphenburger Str. 84
D-80636 München
(089) 12 69 90-0

Sammler Journal
Journal-Verlag Schwend
GmbH
Schmollerstrasse 31
D-74523 Schwäbisch Hall
(0791) 404-500
e-mail: info.sj@t-online.de

Sammler Markt
Der Heisse Draht
Verlagsgesellschaft mbH
& Co.
Drostestr. 14-16
D-30161 Hannover
(0511) 390 91-0
www.dhd.de/sammlermarkt/

Spielzeug Antik
Verlag Christian Gärtner
Ubierring 4
D-50678 Köln
(0221) 9322266

Tin Toy Magazin
Verlag, Redaktion,
Anzeigen, Vertrieb
Mannheimer Str. 5
D-68309 Mannheim
(0621) 739687

Trödler & Sammeln
Gemi Verlags GmbH
Pfaffenhofener Strasse 3
D-85293 Reichertshausen
(08441) 4022-0
www.vpm.de/troedler

PHOTO CREDITS

The following auctioneers, auction companies, and antiques and collectibles dealers generously supply Rinker Enterprises, Inc., with copies of their auction/sales lists, press releases, catalogs and illustrations, and prices realized. Those in bold typeface also provide numerous photographs and illustrations for use in this and other Rinker Enterprises titles.

If you are an auctioneer, auction company, or antiques and collectibles dealer and would like your name and address to appear on this list in subsequent editions, please send copies of your auction lists, dealer sales lists, press releases, catalogs and illustrations, prices realized, and/or photographs or digital images to: **Rinker Enterprises, Inc., 5093 Vera Cruz Road, Emmaus, PA 18049.**

Auction Houses & Auctioneers

Alderfer Auction Company
501 Fairgrounds Rd.
Hatfield, PA 19440
(215) 393-3000
fax: (215) 368-9055
www.alderfercompany.com
e-mail: info@alderferauction.com

Arthur Auctioneering
563 Reed Rd.
Hughesville, PA 17737
(570) 584-3697
(800) ARTHUR-3

Auction Team Köln
Breker – The Specialists
Postfach 50 11 19
D-50971 Köln, Germany
Tel: -/49/221/38 70 49
fax: -/49/221/37 48 78
www.breker.com
e-mail: auction@breker.com
Jane Herz, USA
   Representative
(941) 925-0385
fax: (941) 925-0487

Aumann Auctions, Inc.
20114 Illinois Rte. 16
Nokomis, IL 62075-1782
(217) 563-2523
(888) AUCTN-4U
fax: (217) 563-2111
www.aumannauctions.com
e-mail:
   info@aumannauctions.com

Butterfields
220 San Bruno Ave.
San Francisco, CA 94103
(415) 861-7500
fax: (415) 861-8951
www.butterfields.com
e-mail: info@butterfields.com

Butterfields
441 W. Huron St.
Chicago, IL 60610
(312) 377-7500
fax: (312) 377-7501
www.butterfields.com
e-mail: info@butterfields.com

Cerebro
P.O. Box 327
East Prospect, PA 17317
(717) 252-2400
(800) 69-LABEL
fax: (717) 252-3685
www.cerebro.com
e-mail: cerebro@cerebro.com

Christie's East
219 E. 67th St.
New York, NY 10021
(212) 606-0400
fax: (212) 452-2063
www.christies.com
e-mail: info@christies.com

Christie's Inc.
20 Rockefeller Plaza
New York, NY 10020
(212) 636-2000
fax: (212) 636-2399
www.christies.com
e-mail: info@christies.com

Christie's South Kensington
85 Old Brompton Rd.
London SW7 3LD England
011 (44 20) 7581-7611
fax: 011 (44 20) 7321-3321

Christmas Morning
1806 Royal Lane
Dallas, TX 75229-3126
(972) 506-8362
fax: (972) 506-7821

Collectors Auction Services
RR 2, Box 431 Oakwood Rd.
Oil City, PA 16301
(814) 677-6070
fax: (814) 677-6166
www.caswel.com
e-mail: director@caswel.com

Collector's Sales and Services
P.O. Box 6
Pomfret Center, CT 06259
(860) 974-7008
fax: (860) 974-7010
www.antiqueglass.com
e-mail: collectors.sales@snet.net

Robert Coup
P.O. Box 348
Leola, PA 17540
(717) 656-7780
fax: (717) 656-8233
e-mail: polbandwgn@aol.com

Craftsman Auctions –Pittsfield
1485 W. Housatonic
Pittsfield, MA 01201
(413) 448-8922
fax: (413) 442-1550
www.craftsmanauctions.com
e-mail: fontaine@taconic.net

Dawson's
128 American Rd.
Morris Plains, NJ 07950
(973) 984-6900
fax: (973) 984-6956
www.dawsonsauction.com
e-mail: info@dawsons.org

William Doyle Galleries
175 E. 87th St.
New York, NY 10128
(212) 427-2730
fax: (212) 369-0892
www.doylenewyork.com
e-mail: info@doylenewyork.com

Early American History
   Auctions, Inc.
P.O. Box 3341
La Jolla, CA 92038
(858) 459-4159
fax: (858) 459-4373
www.earlyamerican.com
e-mail:
   auctions@earlyamerican.com

Robert Edward Auctions
P.O. Box 7256
Watchung, NJ 07069
(908) 226-9900
fax: (908) 226-9920
www.robertedwardauctions .com
e-mail: reaauct@aol.com

Ken Farmer Auctions
105 Harrison St.
Radford, VA 24141
(540) 639-0939
fax: (540) 639-1759
www.kfauctions.com
e-mail: auction@usit.net

Fink's Off The Wall Auctions
108 E. 7th St.
Lansdale, PA 19446-2622
(215) 855-9732
fax: (215) 855-6325
www.finksauctions.com
e-mail:
   lansbeer@finksauctions.com

Flomaton Antique Auction
P.O. Box 1017
320 Palafox Street
Flomaton, AL 36441
(334) 296-3059
e-mail:
   flomatonantiqueauction@
   magbele.com

Garth's Auctions
2690 Stratford Rd.
PO Box 369
Delaware, OH 43015
(740) 362-4771
fax: (740) 363-0164
www.garths.com
e-mail: info@garths.com

**Lynn Geyer's Advertising
   Auctions**
300 Trail Ridge
Silver City, NM 88061
(505) 538-2341
fax: (505) 388-9000

Glass Works Auctions
P.O. Box 180
East Greenville, PA 18041
(215) 679-5849
fax: (215) 679-3068
www.glswrk–auction.com
e-mail: glswrk@enter.net

Greenberg Auctions
1393 Progress Way, Ste. 907
Eldersburg, MD 21784
(410) 795-7448
fax: (410) 549-2553
e-mail: bwimperis@greenberg
   shows.com

Hake's Americana &
   Collectibles
P.O. Box 1444
York, PA 17405-1444
(717) 848-1333
fax: (717) 852-0344
www.hakes.com
e-mail: hake@hakes.com

**Gene Harris Antique
   Auction Center**
203 S. 18th Ave.
P.O. Box 476
Marshalltown, IA 50158
(641) 752-0600
(800) 862-6674
fax: (641) 753-0226
www.geneharrisauctions.com
e-mail: ghaac@marshallnet.com

Horst Auction Center
50 Durlach Rd.
Ephrata, PA 17522
(717) 859-1331
fax: (717) 738-2132

**Michael Ivankovich
   Antiques, Inc.**
P.O. Box 1536
Doylestown, PA 18901
www.wnutting.com
e-mail: mike@wnutting.com

**Jackson's Auctioneers &
   Appraisers**
2229 Lincoln St.
Cedar Falls, IA 50613
(319) 277-2256
fax: (319) 277-1252
www.jacksonsauction.com

S. H. Jemik
P.O. Box 753
Bowie, MD 20718-6753
(301) 262-1864
fax: (410) 721-6494
e-mail: shjemik@aol.com

James D. Julia, Inc.
P.O. Box 830
Rte. 201, Skowhegan Rd.
Fairfield, ME 04937
(207) 453-7125
fax: (207) 453-2502
www.juliaauctions.com
e-mail: jjulia@juliaauctions.com

Charles E. Kirtley
P.O. Box 2273
Elizabeth City, NC 27906
(252) 335-1262
fax: (252) 335-4441
e-mail: ckirtley@coastalnet.com

Kruse International
P.O. Box 190
5540 County Road 11A
Auburn, IN 46706
(219) 925-5600
(800) 968-4444
fax: (219) 925-5467
www.kruseinternational.com
e-mail:
   info@kruseinternational.com

**Lang's Sporting
   Collectables, Inc.**
14 Fishermans Ln.
Raymond, ME 04071
(207) 655-4265
fax: (207) 655-4265

Manions International
Auction House, Inc.
P.O. Box 12214
Kansas City, KS 66112
(913) 299-6692
fax: (913) 299-6792
www.manions.com
e-mail: collecting@manions.com

Mastro Fine Sports Auctions
1515 W. 22nd St., Ste. 125
Oak Brook, IL 60523
(630) 472-1200
fax: (630) 472-1201
www.mastronet.com

Mastro West Auctions
PMB #278
16200 SW Pacific Hwy.
Suite H
Tigard, OR 97224
(503) 579-9477
fax: (503) 579-0887
www.mastronet.com

Ted Maurer Auctioneer
1003 Brookwood Dr.
Pottstown, PA 19464
(610) 367-5024
www.maurerail.com
e-mail: ted@maurerail.com

Mechantiques
75 Prospect Ave.
Eureka Springs, AR 72632
(501) 253-0405
(800) 671-6333
fax: (501) 253-0406
www.mechantiques.com
e-mail: mroenigk@aol.com

**Gary Metz's Muddy River
Trading Co.**
P.O. Box 1430
251 Wildwood Rd.
Salem, VA 24153
(540) 387-5070
fax: (540) 387-3233

Wm Morford
RD #2, Cobb Hill Rd.
Cazenovia, NY 13035
(315) 662-7625
fax: (315) 662-3570
www.morfauction.com
e-mail: morf2bid@aol.com

Ray Morykan Auctions
1368 Spring Valley Rd.
Bethlehem, PA 18015
(610) 838-6634

North Country Antiques and
Ephemera
Joe and Laureen Millard
P.O. Box 404
Northport, MI 49670
(231) 386-5351

Norton Auctioneers
50 W. Pearl St.
Coldwater, MI 49036-1967
(517) 279-9063
fax: (517) 279-9191
www.nortonauctioneers.com
e-mail: nortonsold@cbpu.com

Nostalgia Publications
21 S. Lake Dr.
Hackensack, NJ 07601
(201) 488-4536

Ingrid O'Neil
P.O. Box 872048
Vancouver, WA 98687
(360) 260-8284
fax: (360) 260-8370
www.ioneil.com
e-mail: ingrid@ioneil.com

Ron Oser Enterprises
P.O. Box 101
2600 Philmont Ave., Ste. 307
Huntingdon Valley, PA 19006
(215) 947-6575
fax: (215) 938-7348
www.mastronet.com
e-mail: RonOserEnt@aol.com

Past Tyme Pleasures
PMB #204
2491 San Ramon Valley
Blvd. #1
San Ramon, CA 94583-1601
(925) 484-6442
fax: (925) 484-2551
www.pasttyme.com
e-mail: pasttyme@excite.com

Postcards International
60-C Skiff St., Ste. 116
Hamden, CT 06517
(203) 248-6621
fax: (203) 281-0387
www.vintagepostcards.com
e-mail:
    quality@vintagepostcards.com

Poster Mail Auction Co.
1015 King St.
Alexandria, VA 22314
(703) 684-3656
fax: (703) 684-4535

Provenance
P.O. Box 3487
Wallington, NJ 07057
(973) 779-8785
fax: (212) 741-8756

David Rago Auctions, Inc.
333 N. Main St.
Lambertville, NJ 08530
(609) 397-9374
fax: (609) 397-9377
www.ragoarts.com
e-mail: info@ragoarts.com

Red Baron's Antiques
6450 Roswell Rd.
Atlanta, GA 30328
(404) 252-3770
fax: (404) 257-0268
www.redbaronsantiques.com

L. H. Selman Ltd.
123 Locust St.
Santa Cruz, CA 95060
(800) 538-0766
(831) 427-1177
fax: (831) 427-0111
www.pwauction.com
e-mail: lselman@got.net

Skinner, Inc.
Bolton Gallery
357 Main St.
Bolton, MA 01740
(978) 779-6241
(978) 779-5144
www.skinnerinc.com

Skinner, Inc.
Boston Gallery
The Heritage On The Garden
63 Park Plaza
Boston, MA 02116
(617) 350-5400
fax: (617) 350-5429
www.skinnerinc.com

**Sloan's Washington DC
Gallery**
4920 Wyaconda Rd.
N. Bethesda, MD 20852
(301) 468-4911
fax: (301) 468-9182
www.sloansauction.com

Smith & Jones, Inc. Auctions
12 Clark Ln.
Sudbury, MA 01776
(978) 443-5517
fax: (978) 443-2796
www.smithandjonesauctions.com
e-mail: smthjnes@gis.net

R. M. Smythe & Co., Inc.
26 Broadway, Ste. 271
New York, NY 10004-1701
(800) 622-1880
(212) 943-1880
fax: (212) 908-4047
www.smytheonline.com
e-mail: info@rm-smythe.com

SoldUSA, Inc.
6415 Idlewild Rd., Ste. 207
Charlotte, NC 28212
(877) SoldUSA
fax: (704) 364-2322
www.soldusa.com

Sotheby's London
34-35 New Bond St.
London W1A 2AA England
011-44 (20) 7293-5000
fax: 011-44 (20) 7293-6255
www.sothebys.com

Sotheby's New York
1334 York Ave.
New York, NY 10021
(212) 606-7000
(212) 606-7107
www.sothebys.com

Steffen's Historical Militaria
P.O. Box 280
Newport, KY 41072
(606) 431-4499
fax: (606) 431-3113

Strawser Auctions
200 N. Main St.
P.O. Box 332
Wolcottville, IN 46795-0332
(219) 854-2864
fax: (219) 854-3979
www.majolicaauctions.com
e-mail:
    michael@strawserauctions.com

Swann Galleries, Inc.
104 E. 25th St.
New York, NY 10010-2977
(212) 254-4710
fax: (212) 979-1017
www.swanngalleries.com
e-mail:
    swann@swanngalleries.com

Tool Shop Auctions
Tony Murland
78 High St.
Needham Market
Suffolk, 1P6 8AW England
Tel: 011-44 (14) 4972-2992
fax: 011-44 (14) 4972-2683
www.antiquetools.co.uk
e-mail:
    tony@toolshop.demon.co.uk

John Toomey Gallery
818 North Blvd.
Oak Park, IL 60301
(708) 383-5234
fax: (708) 383-4828
e-mail: toomey@interaccess.com

Tradewinds Antiques
P.O. Box 249
24 Magnolia Ave.
Manchester-by-the-Sea, MA
    01944-0249
(978) 768-3327
fax: (978) 526-3088
www.tradewindsantiques.com
e-mail: taron@tradewinds
    antiques.com

Treadway Gallery
2029 Madison Rd.
Cincinnati, OH 45208
(513) 321-6742
fax: (513) 871-7722
e-mail: treadway2029@
    earthlink.net

Victorian Images, Inc.
P.O. Box 284
Marlton, NJ 08053
(856) 354-2154
fax: (856) 354-9699
www.tradecards.com/vi
e-mail: rmascieri@aol.com

York Town Auction Inc.
1625 Haviland Rd.
York, PA 17404
(717) 751-0211
fax: (717) 767-7729
www.yorktownauction.com
e-mail:
    info@yorktownauction.com

Antiques & Collectibles Catalog Sales

Robert F. Batchelder
P.O. Box 1779
West Chester, PA 19380
(484) 356-0484
fax: (484) 356-0485

Wayland Bunnell
199 Tarrytown Rd.
Manchester, NH 03103
(603) 668-5466
e-mail: wtarrytown@aol.com

J.M. Cohen, Rare Books
2 Karin Court
New Paltz, NY 12561
(845) 883-9720
fax: (845) 883-9142
www.jmcohenrarebooks.com
e-mail:
    judy@jmcohenrarebooks.com

Ephemera Catalog
Harold R. Nestler
13 Pennington Ave.
Waldwick, NJ 07463
(201) 444-7413

Miscellaneous Man
Box 1776
New Freedom, PA
    17349-0191
(717) 235-4766
fax: (717) 235-2853

The Old Paperphiles
P.O. Box 135
Tiverton, RI 02878-0135
(401) 624-9420
fax: (401) 624-4204
e-mail:
    old_paperphiles@edgenet.net

Kenneth E. Schneringer
271 Sabrina Court
Woodstock, GA 30188
(770) 926-9383
www.old-paper.com
e-mail: trademan68@aol.com

Toy Soldiers Etcetera
732 Aspen Ln.
Lebanon, PA 17042-9073
(717) 228-2361
fax: (717) 228-2362

INDEX